Women's Studies Thinking Women

Women's Studies Thinking Women

Jodi Wetzel

Margo Linn Espenlaub

Monys A. Hagen

Annette Bennington McElhiney

Carmen Braun Williams

Metropolitan State College of Denver

KENDALL/HUNT PUBLISHING COMPANY
4050 Westmark Drive Dubuque, Iowa 52002

Cover Design by Rhona Lloyd

Copyright © 1993 by Kendall/Hunt Publishing Company

ISBN 0-7872-0559-1

Library of Congress Catalog Card Number: 92-82798

Printed in the United States of America
10 9 8 7 6 5 4

TO

Barbara Blansett, Irene Blea, Sandra Doe, Eleanor Green,
Megan McClard, Shirley Sims, Gwendolyn Thomas, and the women
of Metropolitan State College of Denver who have shared their vision

AND TO

Marcia Willcoxon
and the members of the Colorado Women's Studies Association

ACKNOWLEDGMENTS

While the collaborative effort that has created *Women's Studies: Thinking Women* is apparent in its five editors and fourteen contributors of previously unpublished work, the names on the cover and in the table of contents are less than half of those who really made this textbook happen. First, the fiscal support of Metropolitan State College of Denver (MSCD) is notable. Larry S. Johnson, founding dean of the School of Letters, Arts, and Sciences, and David W. Williams, provost and vice president for academic affairs, contributed significant resources. The students of ART 440, Advanced Advertising Design, working with their professor, Joye Devine, and Susan Josepher, chair of the MSCD Department of Art, created twenty-five designs from which we selected Rhona Lloyd's cover. Orlando Archibeque, women's studies librarian, along with Nikki Dilgarde, Marilyn Grotzky, and the reference and interlibrary loan staff of the Auraria Campus Library significantly eased our research, as did Arlene Grier, women's studies librarian at the University of Northern Colorado.

Eleanor Green, director of Adult Learning Services at MSCD, and Jan Delasara, Elsie Haley, Megan McClard, Gwendolyn A. Thomas, and Barbara Wright of the MSCD English faculty assisted as did Frank Nation and Laura McCall of the history faculty, and Andrea Edwards of the Speech/Theater faculty. Mitzi Cline, who teaches with us as well as practicing feminist therapy, inspired our title. Barbara Storcamp of the University of Kansas faculty also helped with research and resources. Carla Pacheco, Minority Student Affairs, offered technical computer expertise, and Kristin Lucas, secretary for the Institute for Women's Studies and Services, most willingly rearranged her other priorities to meet our needs. The staff of the office of Colorado's First Congressional District and Delores M. Bischof, Women's Bureau, United States Department of Labor, Region VIII, did the same.

Students, some on work-study, others interns or volunteers, also assisted: Jody Andrade, Louise Bundock, Kathleen Corbett, Cheryl Gallagher, Kathleen Kitzman, Barbara Luna, Xeturah Woodley, and Claire Wright.

Charles Dobbs, professor of history and assistant to the president; Joan Foster, interim dean of Letters, Arts, and Sciences; and Elizabeth Friot, professor of teacher education and president of the MSCD Faculty Senate, were always available for advice and counsel, and to help with problem solving.

Then, there were our partners, families, colleagues, and friends, those who sustained us: Dana Bryson, Linda M. Cote, Cathlin Donnell, Nancy Ehrenreich, Jeanne Elliot, Alan Espenlaub, Cara Johnson, Julie Lees, John McElhiney, Sandra J. Pfaff, Robin Rissler, Julia Willis, David Wetzel, and Lorraine Jones. Alice Reich, in particular, thanks the many women of spirit who have shaped her thinking, and all of us thank the students in our classrooms.

Last, there is one person in particular whom we thank for the fact that this text is in your hands—Geraldine R. Madrid, who, in addition to being a contributor, served as staff assistant to the project and was a moral as well as a practical guide.

CONTENTS

CONTENTS

CONTENTS

Readings

PREFACE

Background

We have written this beginning women's studies textbook in response to two needs. First, faculty who teach the interdisciplinary introductory women's studies survey not only have diverse life experience, but their training cuts across all the academic disciplines. Second, and more importantly, students who take the course are increasingly diverse and have a variety of both academic and personal reasons for being in women's studies classrooms. Students on our own campus, for example, are largely older, probably work full-time in the paid labor force, often have children, frequently are of the first generation in their family of origin to attend college, and are more likely to be of color than are students on most traditional campuses that have dormitories, sororities and fraternities, and football teams.

Many of the editors and contributors to this volume have taught the women's studies introductory survey for years, some at two or more institutions, and we have watched the course materials evolve from the early days when appropriate textbooks did not even exist to the present where we now have a number of excellent choices. Our problem has been that none of those choices has met all of our faculty's needs let alone the even more diverse needs of our students.

Thus, we have created *Women's Studies: Thinking Women*. It is designed specifically with the interests of large, urban, non-residential, public campuses in mind. Its content not only crosses disciplines but uses materials and methods in interdisciplinary ways. Its perspective is multi-cultural, and it uses poetry, short fiction, public historical documents, biography, and art as interpretive tools to clarify the kaleidoscopic nature of women's experience. It also reprints several of the classic essays in the field, giving students a sense of important feminist scholarship. The references at the end of each chapter point to further opportunities for exploration and research. Together all these features combine to address the needs of students whether they take the course as beginning majors/minors in the field; to fulfill a general studies requirement; as a corollary to the major/minor in other disciplines; or out of personal interest.

Purpose

Women's Studies: Thinking Women does four things. It

- delivers information;
- introduces widely diverse ideas and responses;
- provokes thought, discussion, and critical thinking in the classroom; and
- suggests avenues for further exploration of the issues.

In addition, *Women's Studies: Thinking Women* includes essays, literature, photographs, and personal narratives written by women from different racial or ethnic backgrounds, economic classes, disciplines, and sexual identities. Because the classroom composition ideally includes students from these backgrounds, the works should provoke a variety of response in both thought and discussion.

Scope and Organization

Precisely because the book is designed for use in the introductory course, we limit the scope of *Women's Studies: Thinking Women* to women in the United States, understanding that U.S. students may relate first to the social institutions within which women construct their lives and define their experience. Still, each chapter discusses women from varied backgrounds and includes writers who are American but whose roots may be in different cultures: African, Asian, Latina, or Native. The chapter reference lists suggest further resources on diverse cultures as well.

The arrangement of *Women's Studies: Thinking Women* reflects our collective experience in teaching women's studies at an institution where the norm in the classroom is diversity but where a lack of awareness about women's studies, about the lives of women in general, and about women whom students may see as "other" still exists. The Introduction, "Women's Studies and The Transformation of Higher Education," by Jodi Wetzel, provides students with an outline of what women's studies is, what it does, and a brief history of how it has sought to fundamentally change higher education.

Part One, "The Shaping of Gender," gives students information on the psychology of women and on the ways social institutions in the United States have shaped definitions of gender. Chapter I, "The Psychology of Women," by Carmen Braun Williams, critically analyzes the male-centered depiction of female development and presents feminist theories of female development, uniquely emphasizing the distinctions between the psychology of women of color and white women. Chapter II, "Understanding Gender Shaping Institutions," a collaborative effort by Alette Hill, Joan Van Becelaere, and Annette Bennington McElhiney, emphasizes how language, education, and religion have devalued women in the past and how feminists are reevaluating these institutions.

Part Two, "Women's Well Being," looks at the questions: What promotes women's well being and what hinders it? Chapter III, "Redefining Women's Health," also by McElhiney, a registered nurse before becoming an academic, discusses women's health during adolescence, the young adult years, and the mature years, exploring how feminists can redefine the prescribed patriarchal health care practices of the past. Chapter IV, "Women's Relationships: Families, Kin, Partners, and Friends," by Margo Linn Espenlaub and Williams, discusses not only the traditional definition of the family but current realities of chosen families, contemporary partnership arrangements, biological kin, and extended kinship networks, dispelling cultural myths by examining the positive aspects of these arrangements. Chapter V, "Violence against Women," also by McElhiney, traces the epidemic occurrence of psychological and emotional abuse, incest, rape, domestic abuse, and femicide back to their roots in the patriarchal beliefs in: 1) the dominance of men and the submissiveness of women, and 2) women as property.

Part Three, "Within Patriarchal Institutions," documents women's past and present status economically, politically, and legally. In Chapter VI, "Women and Economics," Monys Hagen explains women's participation historically in the workplace, their challenges in combining family work and work outside the home, types of gender discrimination in the workplace, the government's anti-discrimination efforts, and the feminization of poverty. In Chapter VII, "Equality and Liberation: U.S. Feminism and Women's Rights in the

Nineteenth and Twentieth Centuries," Hagen covers the history, challenges, tensions, and successes of the women's movement in general, starting from the eighteenth century and moving to the present, and outlines the philosophies of the varied efforts within the larger movement.

In Chapter VIII, "Women and Politics," Patricia Schroeder—Colorado's First District Representative in Congress—discusses the history of women's participation in politics; their advances; the Congressional Caucus for Women's Issues, including legislation, for example, the Economic Equity Act; and the Women's Health Equity Act. In Chapter IX, "Women and the Law," Jacqueline St. Joan—Denver County judge specializing in domestic violence—discusses the role of the law in women's lives, the history of laws specifically related to women, equity laws, protective legislation, sexual harassment, and feminist jurisprudence.

Part Four, "Imagination, Creation, and Expression," emphasizes the positive action women have taken and are taking to recreate themselves and share those selves with others through their spirituality, their rituals, and their artistic expression. Chapter X, "Women's Spirituality," by Alice Reich, defines spirituality as different from traditional religion and discusses its history, the spiritual traditions of women from various racial and ethnic backgrounds, the practice of spirituality through symbol and ritual, the history of goddess worship, and the concept of the divine as inside oneself rather than as external. Chapter XI, "Women in the Arts: Perspectives on Gender and Creativity," also by Espenlaub, presents a history of the exclusion of women artists from the patriarchal art world except for "notable exceptions" (notable according to male criteria); the history of women creating

"usable" art; the exclusionary politics of patriarchal art criticism; the inclusive politics of feminist-defined artistic criteria; and the consideration of whether women artists create different artistic forms than do men.

The last section stands alone, not only as a conclusion but really as a beginning, outlining the work feminists need to do. "The Future of Feminism: The Struggle to Work Together," by Tara Tull, focuses on the imperative that *all women* embrace coalition politics over identity politics and work toward global alliances. It suggests what students, instructors, and other feminists, need to do in order to analyze and change the negative environment which was—and still is—the world in which women live, love, and work.

Unique Contributions

We, the writers, editors and contributors, believe *Women's Studies: Thinking Women* uniquely integrates a variety of materials so that students and instructors from various disciplines will have their interests sparked. For those who want historical documentation, the text includes primary materials in the form of public documents. For those who require a theoretical approach, it includes essays written from the perspectives of anthropologists, historians, creative writers, psychologists, economists, sociologists, health care workers, and philosophers. Likewise, if students or instructors respond to art, literature, or personal narratives, most chapters include examples.

Even more important, students and instructors from all racial and ethnic backgrounds; from all sexual identities; from ages eighteen through seventy or older; from economic classes other than the middle; and from all educational backgrounds

should find information they can relate to
in each chapter. What we offer seeks to
encourage pluralism and the appreciation
of the unique differences in each of us.

Annette Bennington McElhiney

INTRODUCTION

Women's Studies and the Transformation of Higher Education

Jodi Wetzel

Initially, the framework for women's studies is built upon the answers to several questions. First, *what is women's studies?* Second, how does women's studies fit into the higher education curriculum? Implicit in this second question is the nature of academic disciplines themselves and of interdisciplinary courses of study. Third, why should students, both women and men, study women? Fourth, what is the relationship between women's studies and the contemporary women's movement?

While women's studies is obviously the study of women, it is more complex than such an answer to the first question might seem. It is more complex because, while women share many similarities, much of women's experience is different—the difference resulting from each woman's race, age, economic class, education, sexual identity, nationality, and differing abilities. As a result, women's studies is both *multicultural,* as it looks at United States women's diverse experience, and *cross-cultural,* as it examines how United States women are similar to and different from women in other countries. Women's studies, then, is the study *of* women, *by* women, and *for* women. It is the study of more than half of human knowledge and experience; it represents the disciplined search to find women and to know women on their own terms, to give women their own voice.

In the traditional higher education curriculum, women are often omitted, overlooked, or invisible. If they are included, their inclusion is incidental, stereotyped, exceptional, or limited to those who are attached to powerful men. Such inclusion represents unexamined and uncritical assumptions about who and what women are, controlling what is known about women, which in turn controls women themselves, limiting their imagination, their creativity, their very ability to discover who they are and who they will become. The unexamined assumptions of the uncritical tradition represent how patriarchal, "gender defining institutions" (Sapiro 1990) have seen—and still see—women and women's place in society. That tradition asserts a male prerogative to mediate and interpret women's experience to women themselves. In doing so, that tradition ensures women's conformity to a male hegemonic world view. Further—and even more uncritically—that tradition asserts that its own world view constitutes reality.

In women's studies, students and faculty together employ critical thinking skills and examine assumptions, discovering the "anomalies" of that hegemonic world view (Kuhn 1970); deciding for themselves *what* knowledge has value; and asserting new interpretations of knowledge. In doing so, they name the biased world view of male privilege political, and they deny the validity of its claim to mediate knowledge because that mediation is not in women's own interest.

Doing so is important because in the past, formal education has been limited to the study *of* men, *by* men, and *for* men—an education in men's interest. Further, that education has been limited, for the most part, to the interests of white, Western, mostly elite men of privilege who lead notable public lives. Indeed, history illuminates a continuing struggle to transform such an education, to broaden the context of what is known and how it is known, to make legitimate *all* of human knowledge, and to ensure access to that knowledge beyond that small, and growing smaller, group with such privilege. Put another way, one question is often raised in the context of women's studies. That query asserts a need for what it calls "men's studies." Yet, "men's studies" by a more familiar name is the higher education curriculum itself.

The higher education curriculum then, and the academic disciplines which constitute it, is not actually a comfortable place for women's studies to seek a home. The fit is imperfect at best. Yet, women's studies belongs in higher education because as a social institution higher education's primary roles are the creation and transmittal of knowledge. Those functions find their expression through academic disciplines such as history, the arts, mathematics, the physical and biological sciences, languages and literature, and the social sciences. On campuses the disciplines are organized into administrative units—the academic departments. The way in which women's studies fits within both the academic profession of the disciplines and the administrative structure of the departments is imperfect for a number of reasons, but

primarily because of its subject matter, its pedagogy, and its interdisciplinary nature. Its subject matter creates discomfort for members of the academy because it questions everything: 1) what constitutes knowledge? 2) how should that knowledge be taught and to whom? and 3) do disciplinary boundaries confine and limit that knowledge? Women's studies refuses to accept as given what the academy is; indeed, it questions the very identity of higher education itself. It does so through generation of new knowledge which flies in the face of what academicians may see as the truth about human nature (Jagger 1983); it does so through questioning the veracity of the concept of scientific objectivity (Harding 1986). It does so through the pedagogy of feminist education and through insistence that higher education be open and accessible to *all* women and to men of color. Mere openness and accessibility, however, are not enough. The academy's "climate" (Hall 1982) both within and outside of the classroom must be hospitable to these learners, which means the institution must create a safe environment and must provide appropriate student services.

Of the utmost importance, the curriculum offered must speak to the experience of all students not merely to the experience of white privilege/male privilege (McIntosh 1988). Such a curriculum does this in two ways. First, it includes programs of study which offer degrees in both women's studies and multicultural studies. In addition, women's studies *must* be multicultural, that is, it must speak to the experience of *all* women, not just to that of white, privileged women; and multicultural studies must speak to the experience of women of color, not just to the experience of men of color. The second way such a curriculum speaks to the experience of all students is that across the curriculum, in *all* academic disciplines, courses offered are inclusive of *all* students' experience, not centered upon the experience of privileged white Western males.

Finally, women's studies refuses to be bound by the limits that the disciplines impose on themselves and each other. It is, instead, interdisciplinary; it thinks holistically, freeing student learning from compartmentalization not only within the discrete subjects they may study but from compartmentalization of their learning from their lives. Thus, women's studies uses both methods and materials from a variety of disciplines, pushing beyond the limits those disciplines might allow. Such a construct as women's biology, for example, is investigated from a number of perspectives at once, weaving together the insights of the new scholarship on women not only in biology itself, but perhaps in chemistry, theology, philosophy, psychology, history, autobiography, literature, and the arts.

Women's studies, then, through its use of gender, race, class, and other critical categories of analysis, seeks not only to understand all women and their experience, but to know each woman and her experience, to learn both what women hold in common and what factors account—and how they account—for women's difference. Beyond that, it holds educational institutions accountable for precisely that awareness and for the inclusion within its curriculum of the experience of us all—women and men with all our differing abilities; people of color and "colorless people" (as one women's studies student put it); non-Western as well as Western; those of us who lack economic privilege as well as those of us who have it; and those of us who either embrace or deny what Charlotte Bunch (1975) has called "heterosexual privilege."

How this framework came to demand its place within the academy is illustrative. Women's exclusion from formal education and their resistance to that exclusion has a long history, one which includes their being denied the right to literacy and the access to resources. Their status as property, as some*thing*, not quite some*one*, has meant historically that men have had rights in women that women have not had in men (Rubin 1974; Lerner 1986).

Examples of that exclusion are legion, but two types will suffice. First, women were traditionally excluded from learning on the grounds that they were incapable of it because their brains were somehow inadequate. Further, though such thinking denied the already accepted laws of gravity, women's brains were said to "drain" energy from their wombs, thus jeopardizing women's natural and most important function. So much, as well, for the rules of logic. Secondly, the denial of resources would assure that women remained "natural." While they were admitted to the world of human creativity as the "muse," the inspiration, for the exercise of the highest human achievements in art, literature, and music, for example (or as the model, visually often the nude), their sensibilities were thought not appropriate for the creation of art—or of science, for that matter. They were excluded from the library, the studio, and the laboratory. As they resisted that exclusion, and the limits of their role as "object" rather than "subject," they were often robbed of what they did create. Maintaining the fiction of their inadequacies would have been difficult had their accomplishments become known. Thus, women's lives were restricted through enforced ignorance, control of their sexuality, control of their mobility, enforced economic dependence, control of their spirituality, and indeed, through control of their very being.

But women's resistance to this colonization somehow could not be controlled after all. In these United States this resistance has expressed itself both individually and collectively, most recently growing from women's participation in the civil rights movement, the new left, and the anti-war movement (Evans 1979). Finding that even social change movements had male worldviews which restricted, or attempted to restrict, women's autonomy, women asserted an analysis which countered male ideology and saw their own equality and freedom as something both personal *and* political (Millett 1970). That analysis held the two inextricable rather than dualistically opposed. That analysis also argued the concrete context of human experience rather than only the individualistic abstraction of human freedom. The response was largely one of ridicule bolstered by the argument that women's analysis was not only politically incorrect, it threatened the outcome of social change itself. What it really threatened was male power and hegemony. Yet, women persisted, even as they confronted each other with similar charges of privilege based on race, class, and heterosexuality (Rich, 1980; Hull, Scott, and Smith 1982).

Early on, Jo Freeman (1975) analyzed this women's movement noting two basic components: the first consisting of older, more traditionally organized women's groups, and the other, younger women— many of them intellectuals—relatively unorganized but politically active in the post-World War II social change movements. This second group, the grassroots feminists, using their own experience as a guide, developed an in-depth and thorough sociopolitical/psychological/economic critique of United States culture. Their ac-

tivism and their developing theory, both part of who they were, became part of what many of them brought to the academy, first as graduate students and later as faculty and administrators. Though trained in male-centered disciplines, their own marginal and tentative status within the academy gave them a certain awareness which challenged both the form and the content of higher education. By the late 1960s these women were demanding institutional change for both themselves and their students.

For themselves, that change advocated centrality to the academic enterprise: increased hiring of and more tenured faculty positions for women; more women in administrative positions; a larger role in institutional governance; and respect for the professionalism of clerical staff, which almost by definition meant women. For their students, they advocated support services designed specifically to meet women's needs, for example, day care and gynecology services, and they advocated the centrality of women and women's experience to the curriculum: both more women studying in predominantly male disciplines and more content focusing on women's lives.

The arrival of these women on campus coincided with the somewhat belated awareness that the number of women students, many of them older, was rapidly increasing. Almost ten years earlier through a phenomenon called "continuing education for women" the student body of this country's higher education system had begun to change. Though these women were not taken seriously and were demeaned through the application of the label "rusty ladies" (Schletzer et al. 1967), they represented an increasingly demanding women's presence on campus. Soon, also, the concept of *in loco parentis*, which had traditionally governed higher education's approach to student residential life on campus, came under fire; and, with the increasing permissiveness of social life in general, it was discarded in favor of student autonomy and responsibility. Discarded with it was the one administrative position to which women had been allowed to aspire in coeducational institutions, that of the dean of women (Brooks 1988). As the presence of women on campus became more visible and their needs more varied, due to the greater span of their ages, some continuing education for women's programs or offices of the dean of women evolved into women's centers (Brooks 1988). Students themselves founded campus-based feminist political action groups and petitioned institutions for financial support of their own women's programs (Wetzel 1988).

At the same time, students and faculty joined together in advocating courses on women for credit. By the end of the 1960s women's studies had a name, and throughout the 1970s program growth was phenomenal. Finally, in 1977 feminist academics were becoming organized nationally and an interdisciplinary professional group, the National Women's Studies Association (NWSA), was founded. Unlike other academic professional associations, NWSA's structure was designed not only to support the development and growth of women's studies programs but to be responsive to the needs of grass roots feminist organizers through a governance system including caucuses and task forces and a directly representative democratically elected body, the delegate assembly, which participated annually in policy making decisions and in charting the association's priorities and direction. Women's studies was now the "academic arm" of the contemporary feminist movement.

With its roots clearly in social change movements, women's studies saw itself differently than traditional academic disciplines. That different vision led to a comparative analysis of what type of activity was proper and appropriate for the classroom. From the New Left student movement, which found much of traditional higher education irrelevant, women's studies developed its own critique, not only of course content but also of the methodology and the pedagogy used to teach that content. Adapting an aphorism from architecture, women's studies sought not just to integrate content and pedagogy, but to fuse it—form did not simply follow function, form *was* function.

Paramount in this approach was a feminist perspective which first valued women's experience and knowledge on women's own terms. That perspective informed selection of course material and the analysis and interpretation of that material and determined *how* that material was both taught and learned. First, teaching and learning from a feminist perspective constituted a conscious resocialization process for both instructors and students (Wetzel 1978). Whereas traditional forms of teaching and learning were tacit—socializing both learners and teachers through a process of increasing mystification designed to perpetuate elitism and exclusion—feminist forms were based on concrete articulation and intentional socialization designed to increase access and inclusion. Whereas traditional models depended on student passivity in the classroom, the feminist model thrived upon students assuming active responsibility for their own learning—indeed, the process required that of students. Openness and flexibility in the classroom were additional important characteristics of the feminist mode. Course syllabi, for example, became "working" documents, open to revision and clarification as courses unfolded. Proponents of traditional modes often found such features threatening and subversive.

Traditional modes held competitiveness as a prime virtue in students—and students, recognizing that, learned to hoard knowledge from one another. They were socialized, too, in the present/attack method of developing ideas. The feminist perspective, on the other hand, held cooperation among members of a learning community to be of primary value as students reciprocally built on others' ideas, enriching their own. Critical thinking, documentation, and refinement of those ideas were rigorous, but the process of critique was developmental rather than judgmental. Imagination, creativity, and consistently thorough questioning were characteristic of feminist pedagogy. It recognized that students may learn more from ideas which they find they cannot work through than from those which are more easily, and often more superficially, developed. Using such a model, students frequently became teachers, critically examining course materials, expanding them, heightening their impact through analysis and application of their own experience, and constantly testing data and their conceptual frameworks against the reality of that experience. Traditional modes, instead, employed the accepted standard of objectivity, stressing value free inquiry and the disinterestedness of academic pursuits. As feminist academics grounded their analysis in the explication of women's lives as women lived them, they progressively illuminated the previously invisible context of values embedded in traditional academic inquiry. With their students, they uncovered and exposed an inherent androcentric bias and its unexamined imposition on learning itself. Recognizing that bias as a major element in the process of mystification, they stressed instead the importance of the recognition that values and privilege are significant factors in the creation of human knowledge. They held as primary the importance of value articulation and the awareness of bias in privileged value systems. Particularly, their concern focused on the danger inherent in dominant value systems as they had power to impose certain conceptual frameworks of reality on others, not acknowledging their own perception as biased. Another danger of traditional education and its invisible hegemony is that it isolates learning from living while compartmentalizing, fragmenting, and reifying it. The feminist model integrates, indeed fuses, the experiential and the theoretical, seeking wholeness for both the learner and the teacher.

Ultimately, the traditional ideal, that of the "self-sufficient, self-reliant, autonomous individual" (Noble 1965)—in this case, the learner—grows out of the perpetuation of traditional characteristics not only in the classroom but throughout the whole learning process. The feminist model seeks, instead, to develop leadership qualities in students and rigorous critical thinking skills within the context of the collective learning experience. Ultimately, feminist pedagogy's very consciousness of the process itself points to the illusive excellence sought by the academy (Wetzel 1979).

To say that the characteristics of feminist pedagogy differ from the characteristics of traditional education is not to say that feminist educational techniques are necessarily unique. The question is rather whether they are singular or merely one expression of the attempt to humanize the educational process. Other pedagogical models, while they may seek to humanize a process perceived as dehumanizing, lack the particular focus

6

characteristic of feminist education: education which is by, for, about, and in the interest of women.

Such a pro-woman standpoint is thought by definition to be anti-male—the accusation comes from traditionalist and liberal humanist educators alike. Limited by dualistic oppositional thought, one of their unexamined assumptions is that if males are not at the center of inquiry they may cease to exist. Their second unexamined assumption is that feminist inquiry will mimic androcentric inquiry with its premise that what has been of value to human knowledge is that which has been thought, felt, and created by men. The effect of these two unexamined assumptions is that these educators name only their own fear and project only their own behavior by labeling women's studies as "male bashing."

In articulating the difference between feminist education and other liberal humanist or radical pedagogies a useful conceptual framework is that outlined by feminist therapist Anne Wilson Schaef in her book *Women's Reality* (1981). Growing from her practice, Wilson Schaef's work is important, first, because it exposes the myths of patriarchal hegemony and in doing so demystifies its ideological bases, and second because it posits a number of concrete differences in the ways male and female systems function. Feminist pedagogy may be viewed as growing from a female system with its attendant perception of what constitutes reality, or, one might say, "realities." Though originally developed as a way of working with women in therapy, Wilson Schaef's conceptualization is one practical tool for the articulation of feminist pedagogy. In exposing the myths of patriarchy, Wilson Schaef articulates the characteristics of its mythological order and makes apparent the inconsistency of its logic. Charac-

teristically, patriarchy first claims it knows reality, a premise grounded in its hegemonic worldview. Secondly, it views that reality as innately superior. The implication of the use of the superlative contradicts the first premise thus revealing that premise to be illogical. Third, in claiming to know all and understand everything in its articulation of reality, it positions itself in the place of its own deity, an arrogant and prideful assumption at the very least. Finally, even as it contradicts its own internal logic, it asserts the primacy of the logical and the rational, aggressively expressing the power of its position in labeling dissenters from such a world view "sick, bad, crazy, stupid, ugly and incompetent" (Wilson Schaef 1981, p. 8).

Adrienne Rich in her essay "Toward a Woman-Centered University" (1975), aptly illustrates how this mythology functions to maintain a particular kind of power and authority within an educational institution. A feminist perspective, particularly given a visible focus in women's studies programs, can act as a powerful antidote to that labeling, asserting that the mythological structure of that worldview is contradictory, irrational and, above all, self-serving.

Women's studies also, having rejected the controlling power of the labeling myth, posits an alternative worldview based on characteristics Wilson Schaef outlines in what she calls the "female system." That worldview, she asserts, conceptualizes time procedurally. That is to say time, rather than being simply one dimensionally linear, is a process, one which is characterized also by depth. It is not a precise measurement of reality. Hence, feminist pedagogy is concerned with the process of change which occurs as students and faculty work together to clarify the elements of feminist education.

This process is characterized by "response-ability," what Wilson Schaef sees as the ability to respond, the ability to be responsive, rather than characterized by accountability (Wilson Schaef 1981). Thus, feminist education seeks to respond to the needs expressed within the community of learners as they approach, react to, and interact with the materials—indeed, "the text"—of their education. It seeks to blend the personal, the experiential, with the public, the political, with the process itself. Until they come to a feminist classroom, few learners ever see their own experience within the context of what is called "education" as actually a part of human knowledge.

Characterized also by what Wilson Schaef calls "multivarient thinking" (1981), rather than one-dimensional linear thinking, or dualistic oppositional thinking, feminist pedagogy helps students explore the diverse nature, the richness, and the complexity of all women's experience simultaneously with their own. It does so within a context which seeks to define women in relation to themselves— to other women—rather than defining women in relation to men (Rich 1975). The intimacy of this at once intellectual and personal exploration/identification finds expression in the systematic examination of women's culture, a microcosm precisely of which is the feminist classroom. Finding expression through feminist research, scholarship, and pedagogy, this search for knowledge—indeed for self—consciously articulates, evaluates, and restructures the educational process, seeing the content as its expression, moving experientially through it in a continually heightened state of awareness.

As expressed in feminist pedagogical techniques, this new worldview advocates self-definition, actively building its community of learners out of the raw materials of all women's lives. It does not limit its definition to characterizing people by their sexuality; it refuses to simplify at the cost of wholeness. While patriarchy single-mindedly holds self and work at the center of things, only moving beyond that narrow base when it can redefine a given focus as "work," a woman-centered worldview also sees the self within the complexity of relationships, and sees that contextual web at the center. Developing a vision of that complexity—reweaving that web, highlighting its filaments simultaneously—within the classroom is the test of the adequacy of feminist pedagogy. Finally, patriarchy operates in a one-up/one-down fashion which holds that influence, power, and success are commodities existing in only limited quantity. Men must compete with other men to attain them. Inevitably, given such a world view, some must fail. Thus, to paraphrase the poet William Butler Yeats (1921) the center, the self, cannot hold. It disintegrates and things fall apart. A feminist worldview, with human context in space, time, and place at its center, sees "ex"-change and "inter"-change as the processes which create and configure power for us all. Such power is crucial for the center to hold. Thus, feminist pedagogy encourages women to see power in new and different ways, to acknowledge and grant themselves power through the feminist educational experience.

Patriarchy as expressed through traditional modes of education emphasizes agency, the exertion of power. Its exaggerated autonomy and individualism separates and isolates learners from teachers; teachers from learners; learners from other learners; and teachers from other teachers. It assumes achievement only at others' expense. The feminist world view—drawing strength from both the similarity of the bonds of womanhood (Cott 1977) and from the diversity of "US" women signifying both "us" and U. S. (Cole 1986)—is communal, characterized by sharing resources, giving freely, and articulating a reality which actually values women's lives.

It is not by accident that feminist pedagogy has therapeutic elements. In fact, feminism *as* therapy is one way of looking at what may happen in a women's studies classroom. The pedagogy itself models the concept. Just as traditional therapies restrict and control women—holding individual women's unhappiness to be self-imposed (blaming the victim, as it were); damaging women's self-esteem through indiscriminate labeling; hindering their identity formation, intellectual development, aspirations, and emotional well being through adjustment theories designed to make them malleable to the patriarchal world view, so has traditional education done the same. Just as feminist therapy frees women to recapture their self-esteem and power; to redirect their rage; to find a "safe" place for their first attempts to assert themselves; to gain the support of other women in that process; and to find "counsel" in the best sense of that word, so, too, does feminist pedagogy guide women to explore, to claim their power. It frees them to be, to act, and to become—for the rest of their lives.

Within that context, women's studies students, actively involved in and taking responsibility for their own education, are able to identify a number of their own responses to the study of women—the study, for a change, of themselves. Researchers at the same time began to document those responses and to note the diversity of experience with women's issues they reflected (Guzell 1977). The importance of recognizing that diversity cannot be overstated. It is a very real presence in a women's studies classroom:

re-entry students, who bring the rich life experience of their age, are likely to see the material through a lens of expanded awareness, while many eighteen-year-olds may believe the "woman problem" has been solved and, indeed, at times may wonder that such courses are even offered. Women of color are often less sanguine than white women, even when they are younger. Students' socioeconomic class also colors their reactions differently, as perceptions may reflect more the attitude of the dominant culture, depending upon the degree of privilege conferred through the particular men to whom they may be attached. More marginal women, women who are blind, or deaf, or who use wheelchairs, for example, may identify less with that attitude. Men in women's studies classes bring yet other perspectives.

Early on, Judith Palmer (1979) classified some of these differences in awareness: curiosity; identification; anger; consolidation; and personal power. Other researchers, both before and since noted similar phenomena and created different schemas and scales reflecting what they observed (Meda, Hefner, and Oleshansky 1976; Downing and Roush 1984; Hyde and Bargad 1991). Palmer's stages of awareness, however, may be usefully applied in discussing differences among students in women's studies courses primarily because of her initial focus on intellectual curiosity. Students motivated by curiosity are likely to constitute the majority in the introductory classroom. Many will firmly maintain they have not suffered the stigma of their gender. They may see feminists as middle-aged and older women who are bitter and angry. Some are reluctant to relinquish what they see as the privilege of being feminine. They may question the authority of even the most basic facts of women's inequality—

the issue of equal pay, for example (Culley, 1985). Yet, they have opened the door, as Palmer (1979) aptly puts it, just by registering for a women's studies class. Other students, some of them even of traditional age, may already identify with women and thus may be critical of men generally and of male institutions. These students, perhaps also social activists with a more heightened awareness, may be zealous in their assertion of the need for change (Palmer 1979).

Still others bring to the classroom their anger, indeed even their rage, and these strong feelings may play out in almost diametrically opposed fashion. Some angry students may not only find men in general and male institutions to be oppressive, but in addition may fault the men in their own lives. Frustrated, they may come to see the problem as overwhelming, finding misogyny and gynophobia in all directions (Palmer 1979). Others, perhaps expressing their own fear and anxiety as anger, may see things quite differently and indeed may view other students and, perhaps, the professor, too, as hating men and thus come to view the entire course as biased and negative. Killing the messenger, they often label the class dynamic as male-bashing (Guzell 1977; Culley 1985). Projecting self-hatred (Culley 1985) through their resistance to the material, they are likely to focus on exceptions, assert contradictory anecdotal examples, and continue to raise issues prefaced by "But what about the men?" Student anger, thus, may be divisive. Such a classroom, however, may also offer real opportunity for growth, development, and the application of critical thinking skills.

Palmer's last two classifications, consolidation and personal power, provide a way of looking at two different perspectives for approaching the issues of women's lives. Consolidation (Palmer also calls it "sisterhood") provides focus as students bring energy to directed collective action and develop, through community activism in women's organizations, a sense of the possibility of a brighter future for themselves and other women. Personal power, a decision to assume individual responsibility rather than focusing one's energy on collective action for social change, seeks the end of individual effectiveness using power, traditionally defined, as the major tool. Such personal power is characterized by competition (Palmer 1979).

The former perspective, consolidation, reflects the view that social institutions and arrangements, far from being natural, are rather historical creations and therefore amenable to change (Lerner 1986). Such a view holds those institutions responsible for women's lack of equality; holds them and the men who control them accountable for change. The latter, personal power, rather than making "gender defining" institutions (Sapiro 1990) accountable for women's position in society, holds women as individuals to be responsible themselves for the social roles they play and how they play them. Without the former, there is clear danger in the latter. The element of competition may be reduced merely to competitiveness between and among women, particularly when resources are scarce. Without collective action, women cannot compete effectively because our social structure limits women's individual effectiveness. This is not to say that women's power of another sort—power *with*, power *for*, and power *to*—is not effective. Power *over* is the danger, power as it is structurally defined in our culture. One or the other of these last two classifications is not sufficient. Together, they have the potential to redefine and redistribute power, making it a tool for both social and individual realization. Such is the goal of women's studies education.

Yet, the difference students may experience in women's studies courses is not, in and of itself, sufficient to challenge alone the institution of higher education to better meet the needs of *all* women. Growing out of women's studies and from an analysis of the status of *all* women in higher education, two broad concurrent social change theories simultaneously confront the traditional academic environment, also enumerating its failure to take into account the experience, indeed the very existence, of students whose ancestry is not white and European. Over ten years ago, Ruth B. Cowan noted one historic demographic revolution confronting higher education: women then constituted for the first time, a *majority* of college students (1980). And that majority has persisted, even grown larger. By the year 2000 another historic demographic shift will place white males of European descent in a decided minority. Though the diversity of women students—by age, race, ethnicity, class, sexual identity, and other variables—has necessitated change in both pedagogical approaches and student services, such change has been marginal, underfunded, and often given only patronizing lip service. The business of higher education has remained relatively unchanged: it still operates narrowly, through a lens clouded by its own arrogance, believing yet that patriarchal reality is *the* reality; that other world views are the fantasies of deviance. Thus, it continues to offer an education that predominately serves only privileged white Western males.

These concurrent social change theories are, and not just metaphorically, environmental. The first clearly places itself within such a framework, using the word "climate" prominently and pronouncing the academic climate "chilly" for women— *all* women: students (undergraduate and graduate), staff, and faculty. Additionally, the climate is chilly both in and outside the classroom (Hall 1982; Hall and Sandler, 1984; Sandler, 1986). Sexual harassment, lesbian bashing, campus safety, date/acquaintance rape, affordable child care, adequate financial aid, for example, are all campus climate issues, and the climate itself is generally more or less hostile depending on a woman's color, class, age, ableness, and sexual identity. Nor is the climate necessarily any more hospitable in the classroom.

The second of these theories, feminist phase theory, has been articulated, developed, and applied by many women's studies scholars (Westkott 1979; McIntosh 1981; McIntosh and Minnich, 1984; Schuster and Van Dyne 1985; Schmitz 1985; McIntosh, 1986; and Tetreault, 1986; for example). Its application is intended for implementation across the curriculum. Designed actually to be used primarily in disciplines other than women's studies, indeed in *all* other disciplines throughout higher education, its usefulness goes beyond the conduct of research and scholarship alone to reflect actual content and focus, to effect change in the curriculum. In the readings which follow, Tetreault's outline of the phases, or levels, of this theory illuminates the intent of the second environmental social change strategy: to have women and men come to see *all* women within the context of a holistic multicultural perspective of human knowledge and human action. Once implemented, feminist phase theory allows women's experience to be learned as it is lived, expanding human knowledge exponentially.

The two essays immediately following also expand upon the ideas outlined in this introduction. They illustrate concretely what women's studies is, what it does, and why it is important. They show clearly how a women's studies perspective sees beyond the limits of traditional teaching and research. The authors challenge preconceptions, expand awareness, and raise new and different questions. Inherently, an understanding of the questions necessitates careful reading and critical analysis. Things may never again be quite so simple as may have been thought.

References

Anzaldúa, Gloria. 1987. *Borderlands/La frontera: The new mestiza.* San Francisco: Spinsters/Aunt Lute.

Association of American Colleges. 1982. *Recommendations from the Wingspread Conference: Liberal education and the new scholarship on women: Issues and constraints in institutional change.* Washington, D.C.: Project on the Status and Education of Women.

Association of American Colleges. 1988. *Evaluating courses for inclusion of the new scholarship on women.* Washington, D.C.: Project on the Status and Education of Women.

Bale, Sylvia. 1990. *Transformations: The New Jersey Project journal.* Wayne, N.J.: William Paterson College.

Berger, Peter L., and Thomas Luckmann. 1966. *The social construction of reality: A treatise in the sociology of knowledge.* Garden City, N.Y.: Doubleday.

Brooks, Kathryn H. 1988. The women's center: The new dean of women? *Initiatives* 51(2–3):17–21.

Bunch, Charlotte. 1975. Not for lesbians only. *Quest: A Feminist Quarterly* 2 (Fall):50–57.

Cole, Johnnetta B., ed. 1986. *All-American women: Lines that divide, ties that bind.* New York: Free Press.

Collins, Patricia Hill. 1989. The social construction of black feminist thought. *Signs: Journal of Women in Culture and Society* 14(4):745–73.

Cott, Nancy F. 1977. *The bonds of womanhood: "Woman's sphere" in New England, 1780–1835.* New Haven: Yale University Press.

Cowan, Ruth B. 1980. Higher education has obligations to a new majority. *The Chronicle of Higher Education* 20 (23 June):48.

Cross, W. E. 1971. Negro to black conversion experience: Toward a psychology of black liberation. *Black World* 20:13–27.

———. 1978. The Thomas and Cross models of psychological nigrescence: A review. *Journal of Black Psychology* 5:13–31.

Culley, Margo. 1985. Anger and authority in the introductory women's studies classroom. In *Gendered subjects: The dynamics of feminist teaching*, eds. Margo Culley and Catherine Portuges, 209–17. Boston: Routledge and Kegan Paul.

Downing, Nancy E., and Kristin L. Roush. 1984. Passive acceptance to active commitment: A model of feminist identity development for women. *Counseling Psychologist* 13:695–709.

Evans, Sara. 1979. *Personal politics: The roots of the women's liberation movement in the civil rights movement and the New Left.* New York: Alfred A. Knopf.

Freeman, Jo. 1975. *The politics of women's liberation.* New York: David McKay.

Gunn Allen, Paula. 1986. *The sacred hoop: Recovering the feminine in American Indian traditions.* Boston: Beacon Press.

Guzell, Marie Celeste. 1977. Problems of personal change in women's studies courses. In *Psychotherapy for women: Treatment toward equality.* Edited by Edna I. Rawlings and Dianne K. Carter, 310–27. Springfield, Ill.: Charles C. Thomas.

Hall, Roberta M., with assistance from Bernice R. Sandler. 1982. *The classroom climate: A chilly one for women?* Washington, D.C.: Association of American Colleges, Project on the Status and Education of Women.

Hall, Roberta M., and Bernice R. Sandler. 1984. *Out of the classroom: A chilly campus climate for women?* Washington, D.C.: Association of American Colleges, Project on the Status and Education of Women.

Harding, Sandra. 1986. *The science question in feminism.* Ithaca, N.Y.: Cornell University Press.

hooks, bell. 1984. *Feminist theory: From margin to center.* Boston: South End Press.

Hull, Gloria T., Patricia Bell Scott, and Barbara Smith, eds. 1982. *All the women are white, all the blacks are men, but some of us are brave: Black women's studies.* Old Westbury, N.Y.: Feminist Press.

Hyde, Janet Shibley, and Adena Bargad. 1991. Women's studies: A study of feminist identity development in women. *Psychology of Women Quarterly* 15(2):181–201.

Jagger, Alison, M. 1983. *Feminist politics and human nature.* Brighton, Sussex: Harvester Press.

Jaggar, Alison M., and Paula S. Rothenberg, eds. 1984. *Feminist frameworks: Alternative theoretical accounts of the relations between women and men.* 2nd ed. New York: McGraw Hill.

Johnson, Liz, with assistance from Roberta M. Hall. 1984. *Selected activities using "The classroom climate: A chilly one for women?"* Washington, D.C.: Association of American Colleges, Project on the Status and Education of Women.

Kuhn, Thomas S. 1970. *The structure of scientific revolutions.* 2nd ed. Chicago: University of Chicago Press.

Lerner, Gerda. 1986. *The creation of patriarchy.* New York: Oxford University Press.

Marshall, James P. 1988. Practicing critical thinking through the scholarship on women. Paper presented at the 30th annual conference of the Western Social Science Association, Denver, Colorado.

McIntosh, Margaret. 1981. Women's studies in the 1980s. Keynote address, Colorado Women's Studies Association, 1–2 May, University of Denver, Denver, Colorado.

———. 1986. Women in the curriculum. *Comment* 15 (February):3–4.

———. 1988. White privilege and male privilege: A personal account of coming to see correspondences through work in women's studies. Wellesley, Mass.: Wellesley College, Center for Research on Women, Working Paper #189.

McIntosh, Margaret, and Elizabeth Kamarck Minnich. 1984. Varieties of women's studies. *Women's Studies International Forum* 7(3):139–48.

Meda, Rebecca, Robert Hefner, and Barbara Oleshansky. 1976. A model of sex-role transcendence. *Journal of Social Issues* 32:197–206.

Millett, Kate. 1970. *Sexual politics.* Garden City, N.Y.: Doubleday.

Minnich, Elizabeth K. 1982. A feminist critique of the liberal arts. Recommendations from the Wingspread Conference: *Liberal education and the new scholarship on women: Issues and constraints in institutional change.* Washington, D.C.: Association of American Colleges.

National Women's Studies Association. 1991. *Liberal learning and the women's studies major: A report to the profession.* Washington, D.C.: Association of American Colleges.

Noble, David W. 1965. *Historians against history: The frontier thesis and the national covenant in American historical writing since 1830.* Minneapolis: University of Minnesota Press.

Palmer, Judith A. 1979. Stages of women's awareness: The process of consiousness raising. *Social Change: Ideas and Applications* 9(1): 1–4.

Rich, Adrienne. 1979. Toward a woman-centered university. In *On lies, secrets, and silence.* New York: W. W. Norton and Co.

———. 1979. Claiming an education. In *On lies, secrets, and silence.* New York: W. W. Norton and Co.

———. 1979. Taking women students seriously. In *On Lies, secrets, and silence.* New York: W. W. Norton and Co.

———. 1980. Compulsory heterosexuality and lesbian existence. *Signs: Journal of Women in Culture and Society* 5(4):631–60.

Rothenberg, Paula S., ed. 1988. *Racism and sexism: An integrated study*. New York: St. Martin's Press.

Rubin, Gayle. 1974. The traffic in women: Notes on the political economy of sex. In *Toward an anthropology of women*. Edited by Rayna Reiter, 157–210. New York: Monthly Review Press.

Sandler, Bernice R., with assistance from Roberta M. Hall. 1986. *The campus climate revisited: Chilly for women faculty, administrators, and graduate students*. Washington, D.C.: Association of American Colleges, Project on the Status and Education of Women.

Sapiro, Virginia. 1990. *Women in American society*. 2nd ed. Mountain View, Calif.: Mayfield Publishing Company.

Schletzer, Vera M., Elizabeth L. Cless, Cornelia W. McCune, Barbara K. Mantini, and Dorothy L. Loeffler. 1967. *A five-year report, 1960–1965, of the Minnesota Plan for the Continuing Education of Women*. Minneapolis: University of Minnesota.

Schmitz, Betty. 1985. *Integrating women's studies into the curriculum: A guide and bibliography*. Old Westbury, N.Y.: The Feminist Press.

Schuster, Marilyn, and Susan K. Van Dyne. 1985. *Women's place in the academy: Transforming the liberal arts curriculum*. Totowa, N.J.: Rowman and Allenheld.

Tetreault, Mary Kay Thompson. 1986. Women in the curriculum. *Comment* 15 (February):1–2.

Thomas, C. 1970. Different strokes for different folks. *Psychology Today* 4:48–53, 78–80.

Tuan, Yi-Fu. 1977. *Space and place: The perspective of experience*. Minneapolis: University of Minnesota Press.

Twombly, Susan B. 1991. New directions for studying women in higher education. *Initiatives* 54(1):9–17.

Westkott, Marcia. 1979. Feminist criticism of the social sciences. *Harvard Educational Review* 49(4):422–30.

Wetzel, Jodi. 1978. The introductory women's studies sequence: A resocialization process. Paper presented at Rethinking Research and Teaching about Women at the University of Minnesota: First Annual Conference on Women's Studies at the University of Minnesota, 28–29 April, Spring Hill Conference Center, Long Lake, Minnesota.

———. 1979. Defining feminist pedagogy: A female systems model. Paper presented at Common Differences: Second Annual Conference on Women's Studies at the University of Minnesota, 22–23 April, Spring Hill Conference Center, Long Lake, Minnesota.

———. 1988. Women's centers: The frameworks. *Initiatives* 51(2–3):11–16.

Wilson Schaef, Ann. 1981. *Women's reality: An emerging system in the white male society*. Minneapolis: Winston Press.

Woolf, Virginia. 1929. *A room of one's own*. New York: Harcourt Brace Jovanovich.

Yeats, William Butler. 1931. The second coming. From *Collected poems*. New York: Macmillan.

Toward a Woman-Centered University

Adrienne Rich

There are two ways in which a woman's integrity is likely to be undermined by the process of university education. This education is, of course, yet another stage in the process of her entire education, from her earliest glimpses of television at home to the tracking and acculturating toward "femininity" that become emphatic in high school. But when a woman is admitted to higher education—particularly graduate school—it is often made to sound as if she enters a sexually neutral world of "disinterested" and "universal" perspectives. It is assumed that coeducation means the equal education, side by side, of women and men. Nothing could be further from the truth; and nothing could more effectively seal a woman's sense of her secondary value in a man-centered world than her experience as a "privileged" woman in the university—if she knows how to interpret what she lives daily.

In terms of the content of her education, there is no discipline that does not obscure or devalue the history and experience of women as a group. What Otto Rank said of psychology has to be said of every other discipline, including the "neutral" sciences: it is "not only man-made . . . but masculine in its mentality." Will it seem, in forty years, astonishing that a book should have been written in 1946 with the title *Woman as Force in History*? Mary Beard's title does not seem bizarre to us now. Outside of women's studies, though liberal male professors may introduce material about women into their courses, we live with textbooks, research studies, scholarly sources, and lectures that treat women as a subspecies, mentioned only as peripheral to the history of men. In every discipline where we *are* considered, women are perceived as the objects rather than the originators of inquiry, thus primarily through male eyes, thus as a special category.

That the true business of civilization has been in the hands of men is the lesson absorbed by every student of the traditional sources. How this came to be, and the process that kept it so, may well be the most important question for the self-understanding and survival of the human species; but the extent to which civilization has been built on the bodies and services of women—unacknowledged, unpaid, and unprotested in the main—is a subject apparently unfit for scholarly decency. The witch persecutions of the fourteenth through seventeenth centuries, for example, involved one of the great historic struggles—a class struggle and a struggle for knowledge—between the illiterate but practiced female healer and the beginnings of an aristocratic nouveau science, between the powerful patriarchal Church and enormous numbers of peasant women, between the pragmatic experience of the wise woman and the superstitious practices of the early male medicine.

Rich, Adrienne. 1975. "Toward a Woman-Centered University." As it appeared in *The Chronicle of Higher Education*. Reprinted with permission of the author and W. W. Norton.

INTRODUCTION

The phenomena of woman-fear and woman-hatred illuminated by these centuries of gynocide are with us still; certainly a history of psychology or history of science that was not hopelessly one-sided would have to confront and examine this period and its consequences. Like the history of slave revolts, the history of women's resistance to domination awaits discovery by the offspring of the dominated. The chronicles, systems, and investigations of the humanities and the sciences are in fact a collection of half-truths and lacunae that have worked enormous damage to the ability of the sexes to understand themselves and one another.

If this is changing within the rubric of women's studies, it is doing so in the face of prejudice, contempt, and outright obstruction. If it is true that the culture recognized and transmitted by the university has been predominantly white Western culture, it is also true that within black and Third World studies the emphasis is still predominantly masculine, and the female perspective needs to be fought for and defended there as in the academy at large.

I have been talking about the content of the university curriculum, that is, the mainstream of the curriculum. Women in colleges where a women's studies program already exists, or where feminist courses are beginning to be taught, still are often made to feel that the "real" curriculum is the male-centered one; that women's studies are (like Third World studies) a "fad"; that feminist teachers are "unscholarly," "unprofessional," or "dykes." But the content of courses and programs is only the more concrete form of undermining experienced by the woman student. More invisible, less amenable to change by committee proposal or fiat, are the hierarchical image, the structure of relationships, even the style of discourse, including assumptions about theory and practice, ends and means, process and goal.

The university is above all a hierarchy. At the top is a small cluster of highly paid and prestigious persons, chiefly men, whose careers entail the services of a very large base of ill-paid or unpaid persons, chiefly women: wives, research assistants, secretaries, teaching assistants, cleaning women, waitresses in the faculty club, lower-echelon administrators, and women students who can be used in various ways to gratify the ego. Each of these groups of women sees itself as distinct from the others, as having different interests and a different destiny. The student may become a research assistant, mistress, or even wife; the wife may act as secretary or personal typist for her husband, or take a job as lecturer or minor administrator; the graduate student may, if she demonstrates unusual brilliance and carefully follows the rules, rise higher into the pyramid, where she loses her identification with teaching fellows, as the wife forgets her identification with the student or secretary she may once have been.

The waitress or cleaning woman has no such mobility, and it is rare for other women in the university, beyond a few socially aware or feminist students, to support her if she is on strike or unjustly fired. Each woman in the university is defined by her relationship to the men in power instead of her relationship to other women up and down the scale.

Now, this fragmentation among women is merely a replication of the fragmentation from each other that women undergo in the society outside; in accepting the premise that advancement and security—even the chance to do one's best work—lie in propitiating and identifying with men who have some power, we have always found ourselves in competition with each other and blinded to our common struggles. This fragmentation and the invisible demoralization it generates work constantly against the intellectual and emotional energies of the woman student.

The hidden assumptions on which the university is built comprise more than simply a class system. In a curious and insidious way the "work" of a few men—especially in the more scholarly and prestigious institutions—becomes a sacred value in whose name emotional and economic exploitation of women is taken for granted. The distinguished professor may understandably like comfort and even luxury and his ego require not merely a wife and secretary but an *au pair* girl, teaching assistant, programmer, and student mistress; but the justification for all this service is the almost religious concept of "his work." (Those few women who rise to the top of their professions seem in general to get along with less, to get their work done along with the cooking, personal laundry, and mending without the support of a retinue.)

In other words, the structure of the man-centered university constantly reaffirms *the use of women as means* to the end of male "work"—meaning male careers and professional success. Professors of Kantian ethics or Marxist criticism are no more exempt from this exploitation of women than are professors of military science or behavioral psychology. In its very structure, then, the university encourages women to continue perceiving themselves as means and not as ends—as indeed their whole socialization has done.

It is sometimes pointed out that because the majority of women working in the university are in lower-status positions, the woman student has few if any "role models" she can identify with in the form of women professors or even high-ranking administrators. She therefore can conceive of her own future only in terms of limited ambitions. But it should be one of the goals of a woman-centered university to do away with the pyramid itself, insofar as it is based on sex, age, color, class, and other irrelevant distinctions.

I have been trying to think of a celebrated literary utopia written by a woman. The few contenders would be contemporary: Monique Wittig's *Les Guerillères*—but that is really a vision of epic struggle—or Elizabeth Gould Davis's early chapters in *The First Sex*—but those are largely based on Bachofen. Shulamith Firestone noted the absence of a female utopia in *The Dialectic of Sex* and proceeded, in the last chapter, to invent her own. These thoughts occur because any vision of things-other-than-as-they-are tends to meet with the charge of "utopianism," so much power has the way-things-are to denude and impoverish the imagination. Even minds practiced in criticism of the status quo resist a vision so apparently unnerving as that which foresees an end to male privilege and a changed relationship between the sexes.

The university I have been trying to imagine does not seem to me utopian, though the problems and contradictions to be faced in its actual transformation are, of course, real and severe. For a long time, academic feminists, like all feminists, are going to have to take personal risks—of confronting their own realities, of speaking their minds, of being fired or ignored when they do so, of becoming stereotyped as "man-haters" when they evince a primary loyalty to women. They will also encounter opposition from successful women who have been the token "exceptions." This opposition—this female misogyny—is a leftover of a very ancient competitiveness and self-hatred forced on women by patriarchal culture. What is now required of the fortunate exceptional women are the modesty and courage to see why and how they have been fortunate at the expense of other women, and to begin to acknowledge their community with them. As Susan Sontag has written:

The first responsibility of a "liberated" woman is to lead the fullest, freest, and most imaginative life she can. The second responsibility is her solidarity with other women. She may live and work and make love with men. But she has no right to represent her situation as simpler, or less suspect, or less full of compromises than it really is. Her good relations with men must not be bought at the price of betraying her sisters.

To this I would add that from a truly feminist point of view these two responsibilities are inseparable.

I am curious to see what corresponding risks and self-confrontations men of intelligence and goodwill will be ready to undergo on behalf of women. It is one thing to have a single "exceptional" woman as your wife, daughter, friend, or protégé, or to long for a humanization of society by women; another to face each feminist issue—academic, social, personal—as it appears and to evade none. Many women who are not "man-haters" have felt publicly betrayed time and again by men on whose good faith and comradeship they had been relying on account of private conversations. I know that academic men are now hard-pressed for jobs and must fear the competition of women entering the university in greater numbers and with greater self-confidence. But masculine resistance to women's claims for full humanity is far more ancient, deeply rooted, and irrational than this year's job market. Misogyny should itself become a central subject of inquiry rather than continue as a desperate clinging to old, destructive fears and privileges. It will be interesting to see how many men are prepared to give more than rhetorical support today to the sex from which they have, for centuries, demanded and accepted so much.

If a truly universal and excellent network of child care can begin to develop, if women in sufficient numbers pervade the university at all levels—from community programs through college and professional schools to all ranks of teaching and administration—if the older, more established faculty women begin to get in touch with their (always, I am convinced) latent feminism, if even a few men come forward willing to think through and support feminist issues beyond their own immediate self-interest, there is a strong chance that in our own time we would begin to see some true "universality" of values emerging from the inadequate and distorted corpus of patriarchal knowledge. This will mean not a renaissance but a *nascence*, partaking of some inheritances from the past but working imaginatively far beyond them.

It is likely that in the immediate future various alternatives will be explored. Women's studies programs, where they are staffed by feminists, will serve as a focus for feminist values even in a patriarchal context. Even where staffed largely by tokenists, their very existence will make possible some rising consciousness in students. Already, alternate feminist institutes are arising to challenge the curriculum of established institutions. Feminists may use the man-centered university as a base and resource while doing research and writing books and articles whose influence will be felt far beyond the academy. Consciously woman-centered universities—in which women shape the philosophy and the decision making though men may choose to study and teach there—may evolve from existing institutions. Whatever the forms it may take, the process of women's repossession of ourselves is irreversible. Within and without academe, the rise in women's expectations has gone far beyond the middle class and has released an incalculable new energy—not merely for changing institutions but for human redefinition; not merely for equal rights but for a new kind of being.

Rationale for Developing A Contract Major in Women's Studies

Geraldine R. Madrid

When I began classes at Metropolitan State College of Denver in the fall of 1987, I had every intention of completing a degree in social welfare and going back to La Junta, Colorado to work for the county social services division as a social worker. Yet, unbeknownst to me, all that would change in my first semester at Metro with an introductory course in anthropology. In that semester, with that class, it seemed like the whole world was available to me. Within weeks, I dove head first into the field, sure that I would be the next Margaret Mead. Yet, again, in the spring of 1988, my journey took me elsewhere. In that semester, I began a course in women's studies, and I have continued my feminist education ever since. It is startling to consider how much that first course, WMS 101, Women in Transition, changed my life.

While I had always done well in school and was well skilled in the technique of rote memorization and repeating what the instructor had said, I was completely disengaged from my learning, and except for anthropology, not at all excited about learning. But women's studies classes were like no other courses I had ever taken. They forced me to think independently, thoughtfully, and with rigor. Not surprisingly, my first women's studies classes were uncomfortable to say the least. *The courses challenged everything I knew, everything I had learned, everything I believed in.* At times I feared I would never understand the material, and at other times I feared that my understanding was so complete that it would destroy me. Consequently, there have been many times when I considered leaving the discipline and attempting to forget everything I knew to be true—but each time I thought I might give up, I continued.

Deciding to undertake a contract degree in women's studies was a long and difficult process. Initially, I considered a minor in women's studies and a major in anthropology. My reasoning was not my own, but rather based on well-meant, but ill-conceived, advice that a degree in women's studies would not be "marketable." I was told, both outright and subtly, not by one but by many professors that "A smart girl like you should concentrate her energies in a *real* science, a *real* discipline." Initially I bought into these patriarchal assumptions, which were often cloaked in academic rhetoric and "my best interests." Fortunately, as my training progressed, I realized how wrong those assumptions were, and how they have maliciously kept women from discovering all that women's studies has to offer. What I realize now is that women's studies, and ethnic

Madrid, Geraldine R. 1992. "Rationale for developing a contract major in women's studies." Printed by permission of the author.

studies as well, have been the most relevant of disciplines in all of my college course work. Through these disciplines I have learned about political science, the law, art, literature, sociology, psychology, science, different cultures, different peoples, and the world.

Because of the interdisciplinary nature of women's studies, my contract degree has allowed me to incorporate many disciplines, which, had I studied in a traditional field or developed a traditional degree, I would not have been allowed to incorporate. My interests and goals guided my choices in courses. My concentration was on research methods, feminist theory, and women of color. Initially, when drafting my contract degree, I considered the courses I developed into my degree to be a more inclusive, general studies curriculum. Yet, as I added more advanced course work, I realized it had become much more than that. While working to fulfill my contract, I sometimes wondered if what I had chosen was enough. I worried that I hadn't taken enough classes within the given disciplines to have a solid understanding of the frameworks of each. What became clear to me was that because of the interdisciplinary approach of women's studies, I was often able to make connections that other students who weren't majors couldn't discern.

In terms of research methods, I chose courses in statistics and research in social sciences, including sociology, psychology, history, and women's and urban studies. To develop my theoretical frameworks and analytical skills, I chose a course in feminist theory, and the women's studies Senior Seminar, as well as completing two undergraduate teaching assistantships. The majority of my course work was concentrated on gaining more information about women of color, specifically African American women and Latinas. Finally, the remainder of my courses include the general women's studies curriculum—women in art and literature, women and work, women and violence, and women and the law. I also completed a cooperative education internship, which allowed me to apply much of what I had learned.

A degree in women's studies has given me a solid foundation upon which to build the rest of my future. From here, I am certain that I want to continue my education with an emphasis in women's studies. At the present time I have not found the "perfect" program for me, or chosen which discipline I want to concentrate on, but I am exploring all the possibilities, and thankfully I have time to decide. I chose, after eighteen straight years of school, to take at least a year off to adequately prepare myself for the challenges of graduate school. In addition to working, I contemplate the GRE, and attempt to catch up on all the reading I didn't do as an undergraduate. Once I have finished my Ph.D., I would like to teach and administrate on the college level. My capstone goal is to become a college president, and while it may be too soon to plan, it's not too soon to dream.

Levels of Feminist Phase Theory

Mary Kay Thompson Tetreault

Characteristics of Phases

Male Scholarship

The absence of women is not noted. There is no consciousness that the male experience is a "particular knowledge" selected from a wider universe of possible knowledge and experience. It is valued, emphasized and viewed as the knowledge most worth having.

Compensatory Scholarship

The absence of women is noted. There is a search for missing women according to a male norm of greatness, excellence or humanness. Women are considered as exceptional, deviant or "other."

Women are added into the traditional structure of the discipline but the structure and methodology are not challenged.

Bifocal Scholarship

Human experience is conceptualized primarily in dualist categories: male and female; private and public; agency and communion. Emphasis is on a "complementary but equal" conceptualization of men's and women's spheres and personal qualities.

There is a focus on women's oppression and misogyny. Women's efforts to overcome that oppression are presented.

Efforts to include women lead to the insight that the traditional content, structure, and methodology of the disciplines are more appropriate to male experience.

Feminist Scholarship

Scholarly inquiry pursues new questions, new categories and new notions of significance which illuminate women's traditions, history, culture, values, visions, and perspectives.

A pluralistic conception of women emerges which acknowledges diversity and recognizes that other variables besides gender shape women's lives, for example, race, ethnicity, and social class.

Tetreault, Mary Kay. 1985. "Levels of Feminist Phase Theory." Printed by permission of the author.

Women's experience is allowed to speak for itself. Feminist criticism is rooted in the personal and the specific; it builds from that to the general.

The public and private are seen as a continuum in women's experiences.

Women's experience is analyzed within social, cultural, historical, political, and economic contexts.

Efforts are made to reconceptualize knowledge to encompass the female experience. The conceptualization of knowledge is not characterized by disciplinary thinking but becomes multidisciplinary.

Disciplinary standards of excellence are questioned. Excellence begins to be defined as more than superior models of artistic creation judged by the criteria of formal genre.

Works are evaluated according to their insight into any aspect of human experience rather than according to how they measure up to a predetermined canon derived from the experience of a privileged few.

Multifocal, Relational Scholarship

A multifocal, gender-balanced perspective is sought which weaves together women's and men's experiences into multilayered composites of human experience. At this stage, scholars are conscious of positionality. Positionality represents the insight that all women and men must be located in historical contexts, contexts defined in terms of race, class, culture, and age as well as gender, and that they gain their knowledge and their power from the specifics of their situation.

Scholars must begin to define what binds together and what separates the various segments of humanity.

Scholars have a deepened understanding of how the private as well as the public form a continuum in individual experience. They search for the nodal points where comparative treatment of men's and women's experience is possible.

Efforts are made to reconceptualize knowledge to reflect this multilayered composite of women's and men's experience. The conceptualization of knowledge is not characterized by disciplinary thinking but becomes multidisciplinary.

Questions Commonly Asked about Women

In History

- What is the knower's specific position in this historical context?
- How is gender asymmetry linked to economic systems, family organization, marriage, ritual, and political systems?
- How can we compare women and men in all aspects of their lives to reveal gender as a crucial historical determinant?
- Are the private, as well as the public, aspects of history presented as a continuum in women's and men's experiences?
- How is gender a social construction? What does the particular construction of gender in a society tell us about the society that so constructed gender?
- What is the intricate relation between the construction of gender and the structure of power?

- How can we expand our conceptualization of historical time to a pluralistic one which conceives of three levels of history: structures, trends, and events?
- How can we unify approaches and types of knowledge of all social sciences and history as a means of investigating specific problems in relational history?

In Literature

- How does the author's specific position, as defined by gender, race, and class effect this literary work?
- How can we validate the full range of human expression by selecting literature according to its insight into any aspect of human experience rather than according to how it measures up to a predetermined canon?
- Is the private as well as the public sphere presented as a continuum in women's and men's experiences?
- How do the variables of race, ethnicity, social class, marital status, and sexual orientation affect the experience of female and male literary characters?
- How can we rethink the concept of periodicity to accentuate the continuity of life and to contain the multitude of previously ignored literary works, for example, instead of Puritanism, the contexts for and consequences of sexuality?
- How can we deconstruct the opposition between masculinity and femininity?

In Science

- What explicit questions need to be raised about male-female relations in animals? How do variables such as age, species, and individual variation challenge current theories?
- What are the limits to generalizing beyond in data collected on limited samples to other genders, species, and conditions not sampled in the experimental protocol?
- How have sex differences been used to assign men and women to particular roles in the social hierarchy?
- How have differences between the male and female body been used to justify a social agenda that privileges men economically, socially, and politically?

Introduction: Women's Studies and the Transformation of Higher Education
Study Questions

1. What is the importance of women's studies?

2. Explain the importance of critical thinking, using examples of what constitutes reality in patriarchal society versus the reality of women as presented in higher education. Connect these concepts to your own life using five examples.

3. Why does women's studies belong in higher education? Is there also a need for men's studies? Why or why not?

4. What needs to be done to make higher education responsive to women? List some examples from your own experience when you have felt alienated from the educational system.

5. In a historical context, how have the politics of exclusion affected women?

6. Does pro-woman education mean anti-male? Explain your answer.

7. From Ann Wilson Schaef's viewpoint, discuss how "multivarient" thinking differs from patriarchal "linear" thinking.

8. Briefly outline the two social change theories that confront higher education's effect on women.

9. What are the key pedagogical techniques of women's studies? How do they differ from the traditional classroom as you have experienced it? What are the advantages of feminist pedagogy? Are they only of benefit to women students? Why or why not?

10. From Adrienne Rich's essay, define *hierarchy*. Within that definition, discuss how women lose their identification with each other within the hierarchical system.

11. From the same article, define Susan Sontag's two responsibilities of "liberated" women. Do you agree with Sontag fully, partially, at all? Explain your opinion.

12. In small groups, use the reading by Geraldine Madrid, "Rationale for Developing a Contract Major in Women's Studies," to compare your feelings to hers concerning choosing to take a women's studies course. What were your preconceived notions about the discipline? Have your ideas changed even in the short time you have been in class? Why or why not?

PART ONE

THE SHAPING OF GENDER

THE PSYCHOLOGY OF WOMEN

Carmen Braun Williams

Over one hundred years of psychological theory and research have preceded the study of women from a female perspective. Masculine concepts have shaped women's sense of self since the beginning of psychological study, casting women's development as inferior to men's and relegating women to an unalterably deficient status. New theory and research, ushered in by a heightened women's consciousness over the past two decades, have begun to deconstruct traditional, male-centered depictions of women's development. This chapter will examine from a feminist perspective these traditional, "phallocentric" psychological theories as well as the patriarchal context in which these theories thrive. New theories of female psychology that offer a positive, strength-based model of women's experience will then be explored.

This chapter will address the following questions:

- How does patriarchal culture affect women's development?
- What is meant by masculine models of women's psychology?
- What is the connection between men's fears of women and masculine psychology's devaluation of women?
- What are the major differences between traditional models of the "psychology of femininity" and feminist models of the "psychology of women"?
- What "mental disorders" are associated with women?
- How does feminist psychological theory reinterpret "women's pathology"?
- What is the key difference between the psychology of women of color and that of white women?
- What distinction do ethnic researchers make between behavior and identity in women of color?
- What are some of the feminist psychological interpretations of "penis envy"?
- Why is depression such a salient emotional experience for women?
- What are the risk factors leading to depression in women of color?
- What paradox do feminist researchers cite related to the issue of women's dependency?
- How is anger typically experienced by women; i.e., what modes of expression of anger are culturally permissible?
- What is "cultural schizophrenia"? Why is it associated primarily with women of color?
- What is the significance of a strength-based paradigm for the understanding of women's psychology?

- What are the key features of feminist psychotherapy?

The Sociocultural Context

The psychology of women cannot be fully understood without addressing the context in which women's experience occurs. The construction of self is inextricably tied to the sociocultural milieu that surrounds the lives of women and men. The values, expectations, and norms associated with gender in our society powerfully affect women's self-perception and behavior. Indeed, as cultural conditions shift, so too does behavior associated with gender. For example, prior to American industrialization in the 1800s, white women—typically part of an extended social network of female kin and friends—engaged in crucial tasks that were centered in the home: nursing, food preservation, textile production, candle-making, and soap-making, and passed these skills down through the generations (Davis 1981; Herman and Lewis 1986). When the home ceased to be the center of production, women's tasks were curtailed and their status was diminished. "An ideological consequence of industrial capitalism was the shaping of a more rigorous notion of female inferiority" (Davis 1981, 32). The "cult of true womanhood," with its prescriptions for women's domesticity, submissiveness, piety, and purity, sought to solidify the white woman's isolation in the home and severely limit her sphere of influence to caretaking of men and children. Of course, the cult ideology had no applicability to black women, who at that time labored both in the home and in the slave masters' fields (Giddings 1984).

Though nineteenth-century industrialization ushered in new roles and images for women as private and public domains became rigidly demarcated, the concept of a patriarchy was certainly not new. Anthropological studies are generally in agreement that patriarchy has existed for many thousands of years and characterizes virtually all human societies. Though variation exists regarding the extent and kinds of power women may hold in various cultures, male domination and female subordination is a universal aspect of human experience (Ortner 1974; Rosaldo 1974).

Under male domination, women and men are socialized to uphold and perpetuate a system that grants white men entitlement to special privileges and to power over others, and that reduces all women to second-class citizenship. "The social requirements of patriarchy surround a girl from the moment of her birth," write Luise Eichenbaum and Susie Orbach (1983a), who recognize the profound effects upon women's psyche of the deep developmental conditioning to the rules of the masculine order.

The notion of gendered characteristics furthers the dichotomization of male and female and reinforces women's inferior status. Certain human traits receive the label "feminine" and others "masculine," the latter being those valued by our culture and granted exclusive ownership by men. Generally, the masculine traits are those of autonomy, self-determination, and rationality, while the traits assigned to women are those on the relational/emotional end of the spectrum. According to Eichenbaum and Orbach (1983a), rules women must adhere to are deference to others, connection to others, and nurturance of others. The other-directedness imposed upon woman prohibits her from taking decisive action on her own behalf. The rigidity of this delineation of male and female traits also proscribes woman's displaying "masculine" behavior without severe penalties. Yet, the feminine qualities to which she is relegated are devalued. Hence,

> The woman is put in a precarious double bind: if she is feminine, she embodies a collection of traits which are negatively valued. If she is masculine, she violates the behavioral norms for her sex and becomes subject to all the sanctions imposed upon deviants. (Williams 1987, 458)

Because of this double bind, it becomes common for the oppressed—women—to begin to act in ways consistent with the dominant group's view of them (Miller 1976). This exquisite bind in which women are deftly placed, and the concomitant self-constructions that women must engineer to negotiate their precarious position, are the cornerstones of much of the psychological suffering experienced by women in our culture.

Male domination enforces strict allegiance to patriarchal constructs of femininity and masculinity. Many studies of racial-ethnic populations in the United States parallel the patriarchal social order of white Americans. Lee (1982) describes Chinese American women as subordinates under an "unequal power distribution in Chinese families" (538). Comas-Diaz (1988) and Zavala-Martinez (1988) describe traditional Latino cultures as having a rigid division of sex roles typified by the socialized subservience of women. Cade (1970) and Lorde (1984) examine sexism in African American culture, and Dasgupta (1986) describes rigid Asian Indian gender divisions that assign women to the home while affording men engagement with the world.

Ethnic researchers on women's identity issues, however, caution that apparent similarities in patterns of subordination between women of color and white women may mask underlying disparities.

In fact, it is the belief of many of these scholars that the Anglo bias of most social science research fails to capture the complexities of the roles of racial-ethnic women. Maxine Baca Zinn (1980), for example, posits the importance of distinguishing between sex role behavior and internalized identity, suggesting that for some Latinas, multiple sources of identity (such as work roles, social roles, and family roles) mitigate against a one-dimensional view of women as submissive. Michelene Malson (1980), in her study of sex role norms for African American women, addresses the reality for these women of a self-concept that is a synthesis of traditional and nontraditional (i.e., "feminine" and "masculine") traits, owing largely to black women's unique history of labor force participation. Thus, it appears that conditions of racial oppression for women of color combine with sexist oppression to translate into ethnic role-multiplicity, signaling key differences in self-concept between women of color and white women.

Many ethnic researchers also point to sources of power available to women of color in circumscribed spheres, usually in the role of mother in the family (Lee 1982; Comas-Diaz 1988), to the functionality of traditional roles for women, and to the skillful use of manipulation and other covert strategies for survival as characteristics uniquely defining racial-ethnic women (Zavala-Martinez 1988). Yet, indirect avenues of power are available to and utilized by white women as well. Power in limited roles and covert maneuvers to acquire power are hallmarks of *all* women's oppression. Because research on psychological issues of women of color is in the nascent stages, insufficient data exist that would afford a more finely tuned elucidation of differences that may indeed exist between white women and women of color in spheres of power and the uses of covert survival strategies under patriarchy.

It is within this sociocultural context of patriarchy that traditional theories about women's psychology have been formulated. Without explicit recognition of the male bias infused in these theories, women have received a double dose of disempowerment, first from a culture which limits women's influence and then devalues those spheres they inhabit, and then from phallocentric psychological theory which furthers women's devaluation by measuring them against the yardstick of male models of psychological health and development. In both culture and traditional psychology, women are second class.

Phallocentric Psychological Theory

Prior to the birth of a feminist psychology of women, phallocentric, or male-centered, theories about women's development dominated the psychological literature. These theories, steeped in patriarchal bias, make maleness the standard for psychological health; thus, the behavior socialized in men becomes the normative behavior against which women's emotional health and stability are evaluated, always to women's discredit. Judith Jordan and Janet Surrey (1986), two feminist psychological theorists, state that a fundamental problem in phallocentric theory is that "women's development is viewed as the mirror image of male development" (81), so that women's difference becomes "deviance" when seen in the mirror of male norms. Virginia Woolf's metaphor of women "as looking glasses . . . reflecting the figure of man at twice its natural size" (Woolf 1929, 35) echoes the ideas of Jordan and Surrey. A diminished image of woman—

the *sine qua non* of this looking-glass vision—is essential for the affirmation of man's power. Woman's reality, effectively silenced in traditional theory, upholds the myth of man's superiority. "[I]f she begins to tell the truth, the figure in the looking glass shrinks . . ." (Woolf 1929, 36). Phallocentric psychology's suppression of women's "truth" thus supports the false equations of male as normal and female as deviant.

Offering a similar perspective, Karen Horney, perhaps the first feminist critic of traditional psychological theory, wrote that male-centered theories of female psychology amount to men's infantile fantasies about women (Horney 1967). In other words, far from revealing the truth about women's experience, masculine psychology simply elevates to the status of theory men's distorted ideas about what makes women different. Unfortunately, because these infantile fantasies are promulgated as truth, real knowledge about women's reality has been obscured for a very long time, and has only recently begun to be resurrected from the sediment of men's erroneous assumptions.

In a discipline such as psychology, which purports to be value-free in its examination of human behavior, how does such flagrant distortion of half the human experience occur? Juanita Williams (1987) traces phallocentric psychological theory's origin to traditional Western philosophy, which, with its inherent misogyny, cultivated the masculine bias that has informed Freudian views on women. Sherry Ortner (1974), a cultural anthropologist, goes a step further in her analysis and offers an explanation as to how such a philosophical bias was conceived. For millennia, culture has been seen in the Western ethos as superior to nature. Ortner argues that women, because they are viewed in the nature/culture dichotomy as being closer to nature—men being associated with culture—are consequently devalued. But why should women be associated with nature? It is, Ortner explains, women's bodily and reproductive functions—bloody, mysterious, awesome, sometimes painful and dangerous—which connect them to nature (Ortner 1974). The subsequent devaluation of women rests upon the splitting off of nature from culture, hence feminine qualities from masculine, and ascribing to women what has been called the "grubby" aspects of the social order: birth, death, feeding, cleaning, disposing of feces, reinforcing their association with nature and disorder (Rosaldo 1974), i.e., with natural, often unpredictable events and functions. These notions of women's inherent inferiority underlined the philosophy out of which, in the late 1800s, an emergent discipline of psychology grew (Williams 1987). Thus, when Freud began to record his psychoanalytic formulations, the stage had already been set for another variation on the theme of women's denigration.

Freud's work, based largely on his psychoanalytic sessions with patients, makes central to women's development the concept of a missing penis, which, according to Freud, girls once possessed but lost through castration, branding them as inferior to men and forever desirous of the lost genitalia (Horney 1967). Because he presented a theory of biologically determined inferiority and ignored the influence of patriarchal socialization on women, Freud and psychoanalytic approaches have been roundly criticized by feminist scholars (Horney 1967; Eichenbaum and Orbach 1983a; Lerner 1988).

Given the deeply masculine foundation of Freudian theory, feminist scholars have argued that it is fear and awe of women's biological power that is the unconscious underpinning of Freud's views about women. Specifically, these theorists argue that male envy of women's reproductive-related organs and functions lies at the heart of phallocentric interpretations of women's inadequacy. "Devaluation of an envied object is a typical defense maneuver . . ." (Lerner 1988, 8) And the envied object? The breast. Eichenbaum and Orbach (1983a) comment:

> Had Freud written at a different time, he might have developed a theory according to which the main focus in the psychological development of both boys and girls was on the mother's breasts, the hopes that [if] a girl would have that she would then grow up to have a mother's body, and the boy's feelings of inadequacy because he did not possess those marvelous breasts. After all, babies have far more contact with breasts than with penises. (29)

Similarly, Horney (1967) suggests the possibility that, if psychological theory were free of masculine bias, "the other great biological difference" (59) between women and men, namely reproduction—women's indisputable physiological superiority over men—would shape psychology. Horney sees masculine psychology's depreciation of women as connected to a deep envy of women's biological abilities ("womb envy") and dread of women's power. In addition to depreciation, man masks his dread of women, according to Horney, by objectification and glorification. All three—depreciation, objectification, and glorification—are symptoms of male fear of female power, a subject unaddressed in masculine psychology where, instead, penis envy—never shown to have objective reality—is sanctified (Williams 1987).

The control and subjugation of women, then, is rooted in envy of women's special power. Adrienne Rich (1976), in her fascinating study of the institution and experience of motherhood, lends further credence to the feminist view of men's unconscious reversal of their fear of women's procreational power:

> The ancient, continuing envy, awe, and dread of the male for the female capacity to create life has repeatedly taken the form of hatred for every other female aspect of creativity. (40)

In light of feminist psychological theorists' contentions about the unconscious motivations for males' subordination of females, it follows that alternative interpretations of penis envy have been offered. Most of these feminist reinterpretations rest on a metaphorical rendering of the Freudian construct. For example, Miller (1976) offers that what women actually envy is men's sense of security which women believe, falsely, that they do not have. Similarly, Eichenbaum and Orbach (1983a) translate penis envy into women's missing not male genitalia, but a sense of wholeness due to their conditioning away from self-identity.

Perhaps the most unique rendition of penis envy is that offered by Harriet Goldhor Lerner (1988). In an insightful essay on the mislabeling of women's genitals, she discusses how, because girls are typically told only that they have a vagina, a part of their genitalia that is not visible to them, they are deprived of the validation of their external genitals (e.g., labia, clitoris) and, more significantly, of the experience of themselves as sexual beings. Lerner connects the shame women often feel about sexuality to this lack of validation:

> [T]his miseducation may be one contributing factor to penis envy in women, and I would speculate that penis envy is not simply the wish for a penis (i.e., the wish to have what boys have), but rather may reflect the wish to . . . have "permission" for female sexual organs, including the sensitive external genitals. I would suggest that at a deeper level penis envy is a symptom that may, in certain women, express an unfulfilled wish to have permission from mother to be a sexually responsive female. (24)

One hundred years or more of phallocentric bias in psychology has produced a sort of male madness about women that is deeply rooted in Western culture. Women did not write early psychological theory. Men did. The study of women has consequently suffered greatly due to men's apparent inability to contextualize women's development, that is, to recognize the profound effects on women's psyche of socialization to a patriarchal worldview. Certainly the study of women has been enormously affected by the powerful influence of phallocentric psychology, but even more critical is the suffering and pain experienced by women as they have struggled to fit themselves into male models of health, to mold themselves to a masculine reality, and to establish a self, however tenuous, against tremendous cultural resistance. It is to the emotional fallout of the pathology of women's socialization that we now turn our attention.

The Pathology of Sex Role Socialization

Discrepancies between masculine psychology's articulation of "human" development and the actual experience of women have resulted in pronouncements, made throughout traditional psychological literature, of women's deficiency. Rather than recognizing their failure to report the realities of women, these theories have placed the source of pathology *in* women (Gilligan 1982). Feminist theorists have pointed out that the emphasis in developmental theory on separation and individuation (i.e., establishing one's identity through strivings toward autonomy) casts women's development, based not on separation but on emotional attachment to others, in a pejorative light (Chodorow 1978; Gilligan 1982). Recognizing this denial of the very substance of women's identity is crucial to an understanding of what has been labeled in traditional psychological literature as "women's pathology."

Alice Miller (1981) tells us that our only true weapon against mental illness is knowing ourselves—discovering our uniqueness, finding our own individual truth. Failure to do so, she says, manifests in the development of an "as if" persona, a false identity, that shapes itself to the expectations of the surrounding environment. The tragedy of this false persona is that the individual systematically cuts off from consciousness parts of her self that are deemed too dangerous to exhibit, furthering the death of her true identity—the source of mental health. Women's truth has been shrouded under the heavy mantle of prescriptive femininity, which is both idealized and denigrated. The effects of this are seen in the prototypically female "mental illnesses": depression, dependency, and suppression of anger. For women of color, add "cultural schizophrenia" (Comas-Diaz 1988) to the list and what we see is a range of emotional maladies women experience as a result of their struggle to arbitrate between the needs of their individual selves and the requirements of social constructs of appropriate female behavior.

What the culture demands, first and foremost, of women is that they take care of other people. The very definition of womanhood revolves around this "nurturing imperative" (Westkott 1986). As women direct their attention to the needs of others, a consuming task, self-nurturance becomes a luxury. Yet, without self-nurturance—without attending to and responding to one's own needs—women are subject to emotional distress and "disease." Sex role socialization not only demands that women take care of others' needs—a task at which women are quite competent—but, at the same time, it extracts any satisfaction women might derive from a job well done by relegating caretaking to secondary status. Thus, we have a required role for women without the attendant valuing that accompanies, for instance, men's prescribed roles. Women develop an "altruistic self" that tends to others' needs, annihilating their "real self" and suffering greatly as a consequence (Westkott 1986). There is tremendous cultural pressure on women to conform to the nurturing imperative. To the extent that they do, they ensure their own emotional demise, not because attachment and responsiveness to others are inherently damaging (to the contrary), but because the rules allow no room for women to act on their own behalf. Lerner (1989) calls this "de-selfing" and attributes many of the difficulties women experience, particularly in relationships, to their having had their needs denied for so long that assertive action for themselves becomes a very difficult step to take.

Given the cultural requirement to deny self, or "de-self," in the service of cultural standards of femininity, it is little wonder that women exhibit higher rates of certain kinds of mental illness. Phyllis Chesler (1972) suggests that the generally higher rates of mental illness for women reflect both overconforming and underconforming to sex role stereotypes (i.e., being either too feminine or not feminine enough), placing women in the double bind noted earlier.

Other researchers cite the possibility that the greater incidence of mental illness in women (i.e., more women than men are treated for mental illness) is explained by women's greater willingness to express symptoms (Kaplan 1983). That is, greater cultural permission is granted to women than to men to talk about their emotional distress. Though this is no doubt true, the explanation competes with arguments that a masculine bias exists in the manner in which psychological health is codified. For example, there are several mental disorders that mimic socialized female behavior: Histrionic Personality Disorder, Dependent Personality Disorder, Passive-Aggressive Personality Disorder, for example (American Psychiatric Association 1987). Consider, then, Kaplan's claim, in "A Woman's View of DSM-III,"* that female dependency is pathologized while male dependency is accepted:

> . . . DSM-III does not mention the dependency of individuals—usually men—who rely on others to maintain their houses and take care of their children [**] . . . DSM-III does not mention the dependency of individuals—usually men—who, when widowed, seek a new spouse to take care of them [**] . . . DSM-III does not mention the dependency of individuals—usually men—whose mental illness rates are higher when they are alone than when they are married [**] (women's rates are higher when they are married than when they are alone [Gove, 1972]). In short, men's dependency, like women's, exists and is supported and

sanctioned by society; but men's dependency is not labeled as such, and men's dependency is not considered sick, whereas women's dependency is. (789–790)

The suggestion of a double standard that pathologizes women's behavior while normalizing men's lends support to the argument that current psychiatric practices are sources of women's victimization. Lending further support are data indicating that black women are more likely than white women to be diagnosed as schizophrenic (Smith 1985). The sexist and racist biases embedded in the psychiatric diagnostic system fuel popular notions about women's "craziness." However, diagnostic biases notwithstanding, women's suffering due to their devaluation is real.

Depression

When women are denied full access to their power as individuals and are obliged instead to shape themselves to cultural standards of femininity, a vital part of women's self is stifled. This is a setup for chronic depression. The seeming ubiquitousness of depression among women is widely documented (Bernardez-Bonesatti 1978; Scarf 1980). Reports indicate that the incidence of depression in the female population is roughly twice that of males (McGrath et al. 1990). This higher rate seems to hold for white women as well as women of color (Roberts and Roberts 1982; Zavala-Martinez 1988). Several explanations for the consistent appearance of depression across groups of women have been proffered.

Scarf (1980), in an in-depth study of depression in women, explains that "[I]t is the female's inherently interpersonal, interdependent, affiliative nature—her affectionateness and her orientation

---

*DSM-III is the previous edition of the *Diagnostic and Statistical Manual of Mental Disorders,* replaced in 1987 by the revised DSM III-R, codified by the American Psychiatric Association, and used by mental health practitioners to diagnose "patients."

**Neither does DSM III-R.

toward other people that underlies her greater vulnerability" (527). Indeed, Scarf found in the course of her research that at every developmental phase from adolescence on, women are far more vulnerable to depression than men. Underscoring her ideas about women's inherent other-directedness, Scarf reports data about infant girls' behavior: that female babies are more responsive to other people, smile more, are more responsive to the cries of other babies, and are more fascinated than male babies with photographs of people. "Women are so powerfully invested in their affectional relationships—and derive such a sense of self from these vital emotional connections . . ." (529), says Scarf, that loss, conflict, or disruption become potential harbingers of depression.

Other theorists agree that, since women's identity is based on attachment, women become threatened by separation whereas men, because their identity is based on separation, tend to become threatened by intimacy (Gilligan 1982). Because woman's self is so heavily invested in her intimate relationships, she will often strike an emotional bargain, stifling feelings that risk the continuation of the relationship in order to preserve the attachment. The suppression and internalization of anger, one of the most heavily sanctioned emotions in women, commonly translates into chronic depression. "Becoming depressed," writes Scarf, "is a way of discharging those awful, negative feelings, and yet having the needed emotional bond intact" (Scarf 1980, 535). Lerner (1988) refers to this as women's sacrificing self to preserve a relationship.

It might appear from these explanations that the problem of women's depression lies in their being too oriented to relationships; that if women, like men, were less other-oriented, they would be healthier. This, however, is not the case. This would amount to blaming women for a problem that lies in a system of socialization that limits women to deriving their sense of self from relationships without, at the same time, permitting women's strivings toward self-realization. Relationships are a primary source of identity for both women and men. It is in the context of our intimate, interpersonal connections that our greatest potential for emotional growth exists. However, whereas men are rewarded for deriving their sense of self from creative endeavors independent of their relationships, a woman's creativity is virtually unrewarded, often leaving her grasping to maintain an intimate connection in order to feel a sense of wholeness that has virtually no other context in which to form. Thus, when the relationship is threatened, women often feel helpless, lost, and depressed.

The other major explanation for the high incidence of depression in women points, in addition to the socialization factors discussed above, to biopsychosocial risk factors; that is, to the interaction of biological, psychological, and environmental elements. A group of women researchers, under the auspices of the American Psychological Association, conducted an extensive study of factors that increase the likelihood of a woman's experiencing one or more episodes of depression in her lifetime (McGrath et al. 1990). The factors they found that place women at high risk for depression include a passive cognitive style; current or past physical and/or sexual abuse; being a young mother, especially of more than one child; and poverty. This research does not negate the influence of socialization; in fact, emotional conditions socialized in women, such as low self-esteem, dependency, and less perceived life control, are also cited as important contributors to women's depressed psychological state.

This study is one of the few that reports on depression in women of color. Scant data exist on the interaction of race, ethnicity, and culture with sex-role socialization and depression, and these researchers caution against drawing firm conclusions. It appears, however, that cultures that especially reinforce female subservience and passivity (for example, some Asian American and Native American groups) may have women who have particular difficulties with power and are more prone to depression. What is certain is that racial-ethnic women are more likely than Anglo women to live in circumstances heavily laden with the socioeconomic risk factors identified in the study: discrimination, lower educational levels, low status/high stress jobs, poor health, large families, marital dissolution, and single parenthood (McGrath et al. 1990). Underscoring this is an alarming statistic reported recently: the leading cause of death for black women aged 15–34 is homicide, a factor contributing to a life expectancy for black women of 70 years as compared to 79 years for white women (Bolden 1990).

Depression has been found to be the most frequently cited problem by black women seeking mental health treatment (Gray and Jones 1987). Related phenomena including alcoholism and suicide also have high rates of occurrence among black females (Smith 1985; Battle 1990). Racism and poverty are cited as the leading socioeconomic conditions leading to depression in women of color (Fulani 1988; McGrath et al. 1990). Along with pathogenic environmental conditions, depression is especially likely when women of color become alienated from their reactions to oppressive external conditions and attribute society's failure to them-

selves (Fulani 1988). Self-blame and its attendant low self-esteem are problems for Latinas and Asian American women as well, among whom a high incidence of depression is found (Loo and Ong 1982; Hernandez 1986). Chinese American women frequently report depression upon admission to mental health clinics, commonly citing causes such as desertion by husbands (Lee 1982; Loo and Ong 1982).

Native American women, according to the American Psychological Association study, are among the least researched group. Citing data from the U.S. Department of Health and Human Services (1988) and other research, this study found that high rates of depression in Native American women are linked in large measure to the level of violence, especially rape, incest, and other assault, perpetrated against them in their communities and to high levels of alcohol use. Deaths of Native American women from alcoholism are six times higher than for other American women. Suicide occurs in Native American women at twice the rate of the general American population. This group of researchers, however, calls attention to the fact that much of what we know about Native American women, because it comes from government agencies whose perspectives in examining Native populations are questionable, if not insensitive, must be evaluated cautiously (McGrath et al. 1990).

Dependency

Dependency in women, called the "hallmark of femininity," is a consequence of gender socialization that directs women to be more competent at taking care of other people and to derive more of their sense of worth from doing so than from taking care of themselves (Lerner 1988). The threat that an intimate other may leave becomes tantamount to the dissolution of a woman's identity. Lerner (1988) writes about the paradox in women's lives in which, despite strong cultural pressures toward dependency, "[w]omen are rarely as dependent as they learn to appear" (160). When faced with the choice of de-selfing to maintain a relationship or "strengthening self at the risk of losing the relationship, women often choose the former" (181). They learn to underfunction in order to maintain equilibrium in a relationship at the expense of claiming their own needs.

Eichenbaum and Orbach (1983a) also recognize dependency as at the core of women's psychology. They, like Lerner (1988), discuss the paradox whereby women are labeled the dependent gender but actually are the ones depended upon. Women learn to act passively and helplessly in heterosexual relationships because they keenly understand that this is the behavior required to maintain the emotional connection. In lesbian relationships, dependency needs may surface, since this is so much a part of women's development and because dependency is, after all, a basic human need. But lesbian relationships, unlike heterosexual, are characterized more by egalitarianism and mutuality (Gartrell 1984).

Dependency has come to be seen as a weakness in our culture when, in fact, dependency is essential for human growth and development. We can feel autonomous only when our dependency needs are met (Eichenbaum and Orbach 1983b). "The more one feels one can count on others and be heard, understood, and validated, the more one feels worthy, and the more solid is one's sense of oneself" (Stiver 1984, 10). However, thanks in part to cultural devaluation of qualities associated with women and in part to a psychoanalytic tradition that equates de-

pendency with regression and immaturity, our culture has come to attach a negative connotation to this fundamentally human characteristic:

> We discover that a women's inner feelings of inadequacy relate to the psychology of femininity, a psychology that had denied her adequate satisfaction of the very basic need to be dependent. (Eichenbaum and Orbach 1983b, 41)

By "psychology of femininity" these authors refer to the psychoanalytic model, which utilized the term "femininity" in its analyses of female development as inadequate. Newer, feminist theories replace this traditional label with references to "women's" psychology and development.

Along with the tendency for women to act dependently to maintain relationships, dependency may also be an expression of negative feelings about themselves. "To put others first carries the message that one is unworthy" (Stiver 1984, 7). Thus, underlying women's tendency to attune themselves to others is, according to Westkott (1986), a feeling of self-contempt. Westkott describes dependency as seeking external affirmation of one's worth, exhibiting altruistic behavior, garnering the approval of others, and an inability to be alone. Needing others to confirm that one has a self is a symptom of self-contempt based upon idealization of the oppressor and the femininity that he demands (Westkott 1986). This begins early, according to Westkott, in parents' relationships with children in which the narcissistic needs of the parents rather than the child's, especially the girl child's, are met. A vital part of women's identity—their feelings and needs—is thus denied from a very early age, resulting in the very "painful feelings of deprivation" that women live with chronically and for which they try to find fulfillment in intimate, interpersonal relationships (Eichenbaum and Orbach 1983b, 50).

Research on African American women points to a somewhat different picture due to differences in socialization that afford black women a less stereotypically feminine view of themselves. Owing largely to a long tradition for black women that combines the role of worker with that of nurturer—thus making available to young black females role models that embody both "feminine" and "masculine" characteristics—socialization of females in black families emphasizes self-reliance (Jeffries 1976). Therefore, the dependency patterns described above find alternative expression in black heterosexual relationships, reflected in greater egalitarianism and role-flexibility between partners (Hines and Boyd-Franklin 1982).

Suppression of Anger

Another characteristically female emotional pattern is the suppression of anger, which is inextricably connected to dependency and depression. Women, whose open expression of anger is not culturally sanctioned, direct their rage internally, against themselves, where it turns into self-blame, feelings of worthlessness, and ultimately, depression (Westkott 1986). Teresa Bernardez-Bonesatti, a feminist researcher who has done significant work on women's difficulties with anger, writes,

> Anger and the attempts to eradicate it are responsible for most of the symptoms and dysfunctional behaviors that women present nowadays: from depression to inhibition of action and creativity, from apathy to disturbances in sexual behavior. . . self betrayal, self-depreciation, self-destructiveness, and

a chronic, bitter resentment that some women are unable to transcend. (Bernardez-Bonesatti 1978, 217)

Indirect, passive-aggressive expressions of anger or, on the other hand, angry outbursts of pent-up rage, characterize, according to Bernardez-Bonesatti, women's ways of being angry in a culture where women's anger is taboo. Bernardez-Bonesatti argues that both men and women collude to suppress women's anger due to their fear of its destructive power. The origin of this belief is in infantile myths of the destructive power of the mother, inverted into a "stereotype of femininity as totally devoid of aggressiveness," thus keeping women's anger in tight check (Bernardez-Bonesatti 1978, 215).

Women not only have an unconscious fear that their anger has the power to destroy, but also, more consciously, suppress their anger out of the fear that its expression may cause the disruption or loss of a valued relationship (Kaplan 1984). The fear that they will be alone keeps many women from being openly angry. And, despite there being some reality to the fear that her anger may be intolerable to those with whom she is intimately involved, the greater loss is that the woman herself has, again, struck a psychological bargain at a tremendous cost to her own authenticity. Recalling the words of Alice Miller, she has lost her most enduring weapon against mental illness—knowing herself.

Cultural Schizophrenia

Women of color, unlike white women, must live in two racial-ethnic worlds: their culture of origin and the dominant, white culture. Lillian Comas-Diaz (1988) discusses the strong impact Latino cultural values have on Latinas. Those able to synthesize Latino values and white American values successfully are "culturally amphibious." Others not so adept at negotiating two worlds are, according to Comas-Diaz, prone to "cultural schizophrenia"—psychological confusion due to conflicting cultural values. The stresses inherent in traversing two, often competing, sets of cultural requirements are experienced to at least some extent by most women of color. Add to this the stress accruing from attempting to construct a viable self-concept in a context of racial as well as sexist oppression, and we get a glimpse of the tenuous, annihilating world in which women of color live.

Bicultural stress becomes more pronounced the farther one travels into white culture, affecting women of color who work in academic and professional spheres perhaps even more than others (Turner 1987). Many women of color in these settings speak of the conflict they experience in wanting to achieve professional success, which carries with it the risk of becoming distant from their culture of origin and racial group. Women's culture is characterized by emotional relatedness; racism increases this sense of connectedness to others because of the shared experience of oppression. This makes the connection women of color feel to their race, family, and community a significant part of their sense of self (Turner 1987). To lose this is to lose a vital part of one's being as a woman of color.

Finally, women of color experience a unique situation in that their role is to socialize young people of color to a society that is racist—i.e., to a violently oppressive environment. This societal role stands in contradiction to the historical role of women of color, which is to develop racial consciousness in young people and to build in them a strong sense of racial solidarity and community. The contradiction in roles is a setup for women of color to experience failure (Fulani 1988).

Racism is a pathological cultural condition that profoundly affects the identities of women of color, a form of oppression to which white women in the United States have not been subjected. This double oppression of women of color, i.e., the experience of both sexism and racism, constitutes one of the key differences in the psychologies of white women and women of color.

Feminist Psychological Theory

Beginning with the work of Karen Horney in the 1920s, feminist, or female-centered, psychological theory seeks to deconstruct phallocentric biases about the psychology of women and to develop strength-based models that capture women's reality. Horney's key contribution was her recasting of biologically derived explanations about women's inferiority into a model that examines the role of women's environment—family and culture—in socializing women to their inferior position (Westkott 1986). Prior to Horney's work, the prevailing, long-held belief was that women, by nature, are defective.

Horney's work paved the way for the development of a feminist consciousness in psychology, but it would take the women's movement with its increasing numbers of women entering the discipline of psychology to shake up the old order and challenge male biases in theory and research. Early studies in the new psychology of women examined issues such as women's roles, gender differences, sex-role socialization, and sociopolitical factors (poverty and abuse, for example) and their effect on women. In the past decade, more complex questions and issues about women's development have been explored, and the interdisciplinary nature of women's psychology has been recognized (Matlin 1987). In the late 1980s, a shift in the sex ratio of those with doctoral degrees in psychology occurred: for the first time, over half of those entering the field of psychology were women. The implications for future theory, research, and psychology curricula centering on women's psychological issues from the perspective of women are exciting indeed (Ostertag and McNamara 1991).

Until relatively recently, because neither the theorists, the researchers, nor the subjects in psychology were women, the focus of study was on masculine attributes:

> Thus, we have learned a great deal about the development of autonomy and independence, abstract critical thought, and the unfolding of a morality of rights and justice in both men and women. We have learned less about the development of interdependence, intimacy, nurturance, and contextual thought. (Belenky et al. 1986, 6–7)

All this has changed. Today, "[w]omen have begun to reflect upon themselves and their lives, to formulate their own questions, to study women, and to tell what they know" (Williams 1987, 20). The result has been nothing short of a total reversal of traditional, deficiency based views of women.

New, female-centered psychological theory posits the centrality in women's development of relational qualities: interdependence, mutuality, and emotional connection. According to self-in-relation theory (constructed and elaborated by a group of women researchers at the Stone Center for Developmental Services and Studies at Wellesley College and based on their clinical work), women's basic sense of self is constructed in the early context of connection to other people, most notably mothers. Their theory derives in part from the work of Nancy Chodorow (1978), who, based on her studies of mother-infant interaction, argues that, because women (as opposed to men) mother, the relational capacities and self-views of girls and boys are profoundly different. Specifically, because mothers are women, boys must, as infants, separate emotionally in order to establish a masculine gender identity, and therefore must deny and repress their emotional connection to a female other. Girls' identification, on the other hand, remains embedded in an ongoing connection with mothers, establishing their female gender identity through attachment, not separation. Girls, therefore, have empathy and relatedness as cornerstones of their identity (Chodorow 1978).

Self-in-relation theory, in placing interdependence as a positive, healthy foundation of women's psychology, contradicts traditional developmental theory's placement of separation and individuation at the core of human psychology. Empathy and mutuality are "consistently found to be more developed in women" and the basis for this empathy is the mother-daughter relationship (Surrey 1985, 2). "Without empathy, there is no intimacy . . ." (Jordan 1984, 2). Emotional connection and interdependence are not only essential for intimacy but are key sources of self-information, self-awareness, and empowerment (Miller 1984). A word about empowerment: cultural definitions of power do not recognize or value ways in which women manifest power. Because cultural definitions of power are based on domination and control, women's power—"the capacity to produce a change"—is unrewarded. Self-in-relation theory recognizes and values women's power to transform, a power manifested consistently in their intimate ties with others (Miller 1976).

Feminist research on cognitive and moral development reflects the self-in-relation model. Clinchy and Zimmerman (1985) examined cognitive, intellectual styles in men and women and found that "separate knowers," often men, take an impersonal stance to intellectual tasks while "connected knowers," often women, adopt an empathic stance, attempting to glean the other's frame of reference. By the same token, Gilligan's work on moral development finds that women's morality rests on interdependence—a "contextual mode of judgment"—while men's focuses heavily on individual rights and non-interference (Gilligan 1982, 22). The self-in-relation model has also been shown to have applicability to women of color; namely, the racial solidarity and connectedness typically experienced by women of color find validation in self-in-relation theory (Turner 1987).

Feminist models of women's psychology take the qualities phallocentric theories pathologize and turn them around, celebrating their healthiness. Women's relational self is not the problem. These models elucidate, instead, the unhealthiness of a culture that casts women's development as deviant. The illness, therefore, resides in the cultural imperative that women take care of others while remaining "self-less" and in the culture's depreciation of these very qualities demanded of women. Feminist psychological theory has asserted the right ". . . to define a female consciousness which is political, aesthetic, and erotic, and which refuses to be included or contained in the culture of passivity" (Rich 1976, 18). Feminist psychological theory has resurrected women's power and given women a voice of their own.

Feminist Models of Psychotherapy

Psychotherapy, the treatment of emotional and behavioral disturbances, has reflected cultural biases regarding gender. Exposing these biases and their deleterious impact on women in treatment was the initial task of feminist efforts in constructing models of psychotherapy that empower women (Frieze et al. 1978). In an oft-cited early exploration of sex-role biases among mental health practitioners, clinicians were asked to describe characteristics of a healthy adult, a healthy male, and a healthy female. Results revealed a high level of agreement among clinicians that a healthy adult and a healthy male had similar characteristics. A healthy female, however, differed significantly from the definition of a healthy adult, reflecting the internalization by clinicians, both male and female, of the culture's sex-role stereotypy (Broverman et al. 1970). Emotional maturity—adulthood—is identified with male characteristics of autonomy and independence rather than with interdependence (Gilligan 1982).

Feminist psychotherapy's central tenet is knowledge about the culture of male domination; as such it seeks a commitment on the part of the therapist to assist women clients to understand the extent to which the culture is responsible for the disturbance they experience (Schaef 1985). This is especially critical in working with women of color and lesbians, for these groups are singled out for additional doses of victimization. Understanding the culture of homophobia that surrounds us is a basic requirement for clinicians working with lesbians, as well as is clinicians' recognition of their own internalized homophobia (Gartrell 1984). Similarly, without a thorough understanding of the interactive effects of racism and sexism in the lives of women of color, clinicians working with these groups will have limited effectiveness. "Women of color have a profoundly conflicted relationship to the institution of therapy" (Fulani 1988, 113). Therapists must address oppressive societal conditions that lead to an internalized sense of failure in women of color so that these women are not further victimized.

Working toward change in the oppressive conditions that surround women's lives is another responsibility of the feminist therapist (Hyde 1985). Other aspects of feminist therapy include an egalitarian relationship between therapist and client so as not to reinforce a woman's feeling of powerlessness. Validation of women's experience and guidance toward an increasing ability on the client's part for self-empathy are important features as well (Jordan and Surrey 1986). Groups, especially leaderless groups, are often the format used in feminist approaches for their intrinsic egalitarian climate as well as for the opportunity for women to establish a network of interdependence and support while sharing life experiences (Hyde 1985).

Feminist models of psychotherapy undo the cultural injunctions against women's self-awareness. In Adrienne Rich's words,

> The most notable fact that culture imprints on women is the sense of our limits. The most important thing one woman can do for another is to illuminate and expand her sense of actual possibilities. (Rich 1976, 246)

This is the goal of feminist psychotherapy.

Women's Changing Vision

Women's sense of self has borne the heavy weight of a long and painful history of cultural misogyny. Woman's essential nature has been manipulated and distorted through socialization that has left her depressed, enraged, helpless, and confused. Feminist visions of women's identity create models for reclaiming the powerful, creative, and caring beings that women are and have always been.

Feminist visions seek to dispel the dualism between masculine and feminine, recognizing that these are arbitrarily defined social constructs that oppress both women and men. In their stead is a vision of an ideal where both women and men are socialized to know themselves, rather than to conform to what is expected of them. Power, self-determination, nurturance, and interdependence are the birthright of women and men. As Jean Baker Miller (1976) suggests, one must take the risk to begin the journey toward authenticity, constantly expanding and enlarging one's capacity for self-truth and awareness. Current gendered social practices impede this vision.

A feminist consciousness—a revisioning of old ways of understanding the world, ways that no longer work—can empower us all, offering us the hope for a psychology of women that liberates rather than limits personal truth.

References

American Psychiatric Association. 1987. *Diagnostic and statistical manual of mental disorders* (DSM III-R). Washington, D.C.: American Psychiatric Association.

Battle, Shiela. 1990. Moving targets: Alcohol, crack, and black women. In *The black woman's health book*. Edited by Evelyn C. White. Seattle, Wash.: Seal Press.

Belenky, Mary F., Blythe M. Clinchy, Nancy R. Goldberger, and Jill M. Turule. 1986. *Women's ways of knowing*. New York: Basic Books.

Bernardez-Bonesatti, Teresa. 1978. Women and anger: Conflicts with aggression in contemporary women. *JAMWA* 33(5):215–19.

Bolden, Tanya. 1990. The facts of the matter. *Essence Magazine,* May.

Broverman, Inge K., Donald M. Broverman, and Frank E. Carlson. 1970. Sex-role stereotypes and clinical judgments of mental health. *Journal of Consulting and Clinical Psychology* 34(1):1–7.

Cade, Toni, ed. 1970. On the issue of roles. In *The black woman.* New York: Signet.

Chan, Connie S. 1988. Asian American women: Psychological responses to sexual exploitation and cultural stereotypes. In *The psychopathology of everyday racism and sexism.* Edited by Lenora Fulani. New York: Harrington Park Press.

Chesler, Phyllis. 1972. *Women and madness.* New York: Avon Books.

Chodorow, Nancy. 1978. *The reproduction of mothering.* Berkeley, Calif.: University of California Press.

Clinchy, Blythe, and Claire Zimmerman. 1985. *Growing up intellectually: Issues for college women.* Wellesley, Mass.: Stone Center for Developmental Services and Studies.

Comas-Diaz, Lillian. 1988. Feminist therapy with Hispanic/Latina women: Myth or reality? In *The psychopathology of everyday racism and sexism.* Edited by Lenora Fulani. New York: Harrington Park Press.

Dasgupta, Shamita Das. 1986. Marching to a different drummer? Sex roles of Asian Indian women in the United States. *Women and Therapy* 5(2/3):297–311.

Davis, Angela. 1981. *Women, race and class.* New York: Random House.

Eichenbaum, Luise, and Susie Orbach. 1983a. *Understanding women.* New York: Basic Books.

———. 1983b. *What do women want?* New York: Coward-McCann, Inc.

Frieze, Irene H., Jacqueline E. Parsons, Paula B. Johnson, Diane N. Ruble, and Gail L. Zellman. 1978. *Women and sex-roles.* New York: W. W. Norton and Co.

Fulani, Lenora, ed. 1988. Poor women of color do great therapy. In *The psychopathology of everyday racism and sexism.* New York: Harrington Park Press.

Gartrell, Nanette. 1984. *Issues in psychotherapy with lesbian women.* Wellesley, Mass.: Stone Center for Developmental Services and Studies.

Giddings, Paula. 1984. *When and where I enter: The impact of black women on race and sex in America.* New York: William Morrow and Company, Inc.

Gilligan, Carol. 1982. *In a different voice.* Cambridge, Mass.: Harvard University Press.

Gove, W. R. 1972. The relationship between sex-roles, mental illness, and marital status. As cited in Marcie Kaplan, A woman's view of DSM-III. *American Psychologist* 38 (1983):789–90.

Gray, B. A., and B. E. Jones. 1987. Psychotherapy and black women: A survey. *Journal of the National Medical Association* 79: 177–81.

Herman, Judith L., and Helen B. Lewis. 1986. Anger in the mother-daughter relationship. In *The psychology of today's woman.* Edited by Toni Bernay and Dorothy W. Cantor. New Jersey: The Analytic Press.

Hernandez, M. 1986. Depression among Mexican American women: A transgenerational perspective. Paper presented at the biannual meeting of the national Coalition of Hispanic Health and Human Services Organization, New York. As cited in Ellen McGrath, Gwendolyn P. Keita, Bonnie R. Strickland, and Nancy F. Russo, eds. 1990. *Women and depression: Risk factors and treatment issues.* Washington, D.C.: America Psychological Association.

Hines, Paulette Moore, and Nancy Boyd-Franklin. 1982. Black families. In *Ethnicity and family therapy.* Edited by Monica McGoldrick, John K. Pearce, and Joseph Giordano. New York: The Guilford Press.

Horney, Karen. 1967. *Feminine psychology.* New York: W. W. Norton and Co.

Hyde, Janet S. 1985. *Half the human experience.* Mass.: D. C. Heath & Company.

Jeffries, Doris. 1976. Counseling for the strengths of the black woman. *Counseling Psychologist* 6:20–22.

Jordan, Judith V. 1984. *Empathy and self boundaries.* Wellesley, Mass.: Stone Center for Developmental Services and Studies.

Jordan, Judith V., and Janet L. Surrey. 1986. The self-in relation: Empathy and the mother-daughter relationship. In *The psychology of today's woman.* Edited by Toni Bernay and Dorothy W. Cantor. New Jersey: The Analytic Press.

Kaplan, Alexandra. 1984. *The self-in-relation: Implications for depression.* Wellesley, Mass.: Stone Center for Developmental Services and Studies.

Kaplan, Marcie. 1983. A woman's view of DSM-III. *American Psychologist* 38:786–92.

Lee, Evelyn. 1982. A social systems approach to assessment and treatment for Chinese American families. In *Ethnicity and family therapy.* Edited by Monica McGoldrick, John K. Pearce, and Joseph Giordano. New York: The Guilford Press.

Lerner, Harriet Goldhor. 1988. *Women in therapy.* New York: Harper and Row.

———. 1989. *The dance of intimacy.* New York: Harper and Row.

Loo, C., and P. Ong. 1982. Slaying demons with a sewing needle: Feminist issues for Chinatown's women. *Berkeley Journal of Sociology* 17:77–88, as cited in *Women and depression: Risk factors and treatment issues.* Edited by Ellen McGrath, Gwendolyn P. Keita, Bonnie R. Strickland, and Nancy F. Russo. Washington, D.C.: American Psychological Association.

Lorde, Audre. 1984. *Sister outsider.* New York: The Crossing Press.

Malson, Michelene R. 1981. *Black women's sex-role integration and behavior.* Wellesley, Mass.: Wellesley College Center for Research on Women.

Matlin, Margaret W. 1987. *The psychology of women.* New York: Holt, Rinehart and Winston, Inc.

McGrath, Ellen, Gwendolyn P. Keita, Bonnie R. Strickland, and Nancy F. Russo. 1990. *Women and depression: Risk factors and treatment issues.* Washington, D.C.: American Psychological Association.

Miller, Alice. 1981. *The drama of the gifted child.* New York: Basic Books.

Miller, Jean Baker. 1976. *Toward a new psychology of women.* Boston: Beacon Press.

———. 1984. *The development of women's sense of self.* Wellesley, Mass.: Stone Center for Developmental Services and Studies.

———. 1988. Women and power. In *Women, power, and therapy.* Edited by Marjorie Braude. New York: Harrington Park Press.

Ortner, Sherry. 1974. Is female to male as nature is to culture? In *Women, culture, and society.* Edited by Michelle Zimbalist Rosaldo and Louise Lamphere. Stanford, Calif.: Stanford University Press.

Ostertag, Patricia A., and J. Regis McNamara. 1991. The "feminization" of psychology. *Psychology of Women Quarterly* 15:349–69.

Rich, Adrienne. 1976. *Of woman born.* New York: W. W. Norton and Co.

Roberts, Robert E., and Catherine R. Roberts. 1982. Marriage, work, and depressive symptoms among Mexican Americans. *Hispanic Journal of Behavioral Sciences* 4(2):199–221.

Rosaldo, Michelle Z. 1974. Women, culture, and society: A theoretical overview. In *Women, culture, and society.* Edited by Michelle Zimbalist Rosaldo and Louise Lamphere. Stanford, Calif.: Stanford University Press.

Scarf, Maggie. 1980. *Unfinished business: Pressure points in the lives of women.* New York: Doubleday.

Schaef, Anne W. 1985. *Women's reality.* San Francisco: Harper and Row.

Smith, Elsie M.J. 1985. Counseling black women. In *Handbook of cross-cultural counseling and therapy.* Edited by Paul Pedersen. Connecticut: Greenwood Press.

Stiver, Irene P. 1984. *The meanings of "dependency" in female-male relationships.* Wellesley, Mass.: Stone Center for Developmental Services and Studies.

Surrey, Janet L. 1985. *Self-in-relation: A theory of women's development.* Wellesley, Mass.: Stone Center for Developmental Services and Studies.

Turner, Clevonne. 1987. *Clinical applications of the Stone Center to minority women.* Wellesley, Mass.: Stone Center for Developmental Services and Studies.

United States Department of Health and Human Services. 1988. *Indian Health Service Chart Series Book.* Washington, D.C.: U.S. Government Printing Office. As cited in Ellen McGrath, Gwendolyn P. Keita, Bonnie R. Strickland, and Nancy F. Russo, eds. 1990. *Women and depression: Risk factors and treatment issues.* Washington, D.C.: American Psychological Association.

Westkott, Marcia. 1986. *The feminist legacy of Karen Horney.* New Haven, Conn.: Yale University Press.

Williams, Juanita H. 1987. *Psychology of women.* New York: W. W. Norton and Co.

Woolf, Virginia. 1929. *A room of one's own.* New York: Harcourt Brace Jovanovich.

Zavala-Martinez, Iris. 1988. En la lucha: The economic and socioemotional struggles of Puerto Rican women. In *The psychopathology of everyday racism and sexism.* Edited by Lenora Fulani. New York: Harrington Park Press.

Zinn, Maxine Baca. 1980. Gender and ethnic identity among Chicanos. *Frontiers: A Journal of Women's Studies* 5:2.

Heartbeat

Joy Harjo

Noni Daylight is afraid.
She was curled inside her mother's belly
for too long. The pervasive rhythm
of her mother's heartbeat is a ghostly track
that follows her.
       Goes with her to her apartment, to her sons'
room, to the bars, everywhere; there is no escape.
She covers her ears but the sound drums
within her. It pounds her elastic body.
Friday night Noni cut acid into tiny squares
and let them melt on her tongue.
       She wanted something
to keep her awake so the heartbeat
wouldn't lull her back.
       She wanted a way to see the stars
complete patterns in her hands, a way to hear
her heart, her own heart.
These nights she wants out.
And when Noni is at the edge of skin she slips
out the back door. She goes for the hunt, tracks the
heart sound on the streets
       of Albuquerque.
She steers her car with the hands her mother gave her.
The four doors she leaves unlocked and the radio
sings softly
       plays softly and Noni takes the hand of the moon
that she knows is in control overhead.
Noni Daylight is afraid.
She waits through traffic lights at intersections
that at four A.M. are desolate oceans of concrete.
She toys with the trigger; the heartbeat
is a constant noise. She talks softly
       softly

to the voice on the radio. All night she drives.
And she waits
        for the moment she has hungered for,
for the hand that will open the door.
It is not the moon, or the pistol in her lap
but a fierce anger
        that will free her.

Talking Back

bell hooks

In the world of the southern black community I grew up in, "back talk" and "talking back" meant speaking as an equal to an authority figure. It meant daring to disagree and sometimes it just meant having an opinion. In the "old school," children were meant to be seen and not heard. My great-grandparents, grandparents, and parents were all from the old school. To make yourself heard if you were a child was to invite punishment, the back-hand lick, the slap across the face that would catch you unaware, or the feel of switches stinging your arms and legs.

To speak then when one was not spoken to was a courageous act—an act of risk and daring. And yet it was hard not to speak in warm rooms where heated discussions began at the crack of dawn, women's voices filling the air, giving orders, making threats, fussing. Black men may have excelled in the art of poetic preaching in the male-dominated church, but in the church of the home, where the everyday rules of how to live and how to act were established, it was black women who preached. There, black women spoke in a language so rich, so poetic, that it felt to me like being shut off from life, smothered to death if one were not allowed to participate.

It was in that world of woman talk (the men were often silent, often absent) that was born in me the craving to speak, to have a voice, and not just any voice but one that could be identified as belonging to me. To make my voice, I had to speak, to hear myself talk—and talk I did—darting in and out of grown folks' conversations and dialogues, answering questions that were not directed at me, endlessly asking questions, making speeches. Needless to say, the punishments for these acts of speech seemed endless. They were intended to silence me—the child—and more particularly the girl child. Had I been a boy, they might have encouraged me to speak believing that I might someday be called to preach. There was no "calling" for talking girls, no legitimized rewarded speech. The punishments I received for "talking back" were intended to suppress all possibility that I would create my own speech. That speech was to be suppressed so that the "right speech of womanhood" would emerge.

Within feminist circles, silence is often seen as the sexist "right speech of womanhood"—the sign of woman's submission to patriarchal authority. This emphasis on woman's silence may be an accurate remembering of what has taken place in the households of women from WASP backgrounds in the United States, but in black communities (and diverse ethnic communities), women have not been silent. Their voices can be heard. Certainly for black women, our struggle has not been to emerge from silence into speech but to change the nature and direction of our speech, to make a speech that compels listeners, one that is heard.

Our speech, "the right speech of womanhood," was often the soliloquy, the talking into thin air, the talking to ears that do not hear you—the talk that is simply not listened

hooks, bell. 1989. "Talking back." In *Talking back: Thinking feminist, thinking black.* Reprinted by permission of the publisher, South End Press.

to. Unlike the black male preacher whose speech was to be heard, who was to be listened to, whose words were to be remembered, the voices of black women—giving orders, making threats, fussing—could be tuned out, could become a kind of background music, audible but not acknowledged as significant speech. Dialogue—the sharing of speech and recognition—took place not between mother and child or mother and male authority figure but among black women. I can remember watching fascinated as our mother talked with her mother, sisters, and women friends. The intimacy and intensity of their speech—the satisfaction they received from talking to one another, the pleasure, the joy. It was in this world of woman speech, loud talk, angry words, women with tongues quick and sharp, tender sweet tongues, touching our world with their words, that I made speech my birthright—and the right to voice, to authorship, a privilege I would not be denied. It was in that world and because of it that I came to dream of writing, to write.

Writing was a way to capture speech, to hold onto it, keep it close. And so I wrote down bits and pieces of conversations, confessing in cheap diaries that soon fell apart from too much handling, expressing the intensity of my sorrow, the anguish of speech—for I was always saying the wrong thing, asking the wrong questions. I could not confine my speech to the necessary corners and concerns of life. I hid these writings under my bed, in pillow stuffings, among faded underwear. When my sisters found and read them, they ridiculed and mocked me—poking fun. I felt violated, ashamed, as if the secret parts of my self had been exposed, brought into the open, and hung like newly clean laundry, out in the air for everyone to see. The fear of exposure, the fear that one's deepest emotions and innermost thoughts will be dismissed as mere nonsense, felt by so many young girls keeping diaries, holding and hiding speech, seems to me now one of the barriers that women have always needed and still need to destroy so that we are no longer pushed into secrecy or silence.

Despite my feelings of violation, of exposure, I continued to speak and write, choosing my hiding places well, learning to destroy work when no safe place could be found. I was never taught absolute silence, I was taught that it was important to speak but to talk a talk that was in itself a silence. Taught to speak and yet beware of the betrayal of too much heard speech, I experienced intense confusion and deep anxiety in my efforts to speak and write. Reciting poems at Sunday afternoon church service might be rewarded. Writing a poem (when one's time could be "better" spent sweeping, ironing, learning to cook) was luxurious activity, indulged in at the expense of others. Questioning authority, raising issues that were not deemed appropriate subjects brought pain, punishments—like telling mama I wanted to die before her because I could not live without her—that was crazy talk, crazy speech, the kind that would lead you to end up in a mental institution. "Little girl," I would be told, "if you don't stop all this crazy talk and crazy acting you are going to end up right out there at Western State."

Madness, not just physical abuse, was the punishment for too much talk if you were female. Yet even as this fear of madness haunted me, hanging over my writing like a monstrous shadow, I could not stop the words, making thought, writing speech. For this terrible madness which I feared, which I was sure was the destiny of daring women born to intense speech (after all, the authorities emphasized this point daily), was not as threatening as imposed silence, as suppressed speech.

Safety and sanity were to be sacrificed it I was to experience defiant speech. Though I risked them both, deep-seated fears and anxieties characterized my childhood days. I would speak but I would not ride a bike, play hardball, or hold the gray kitten. Writing about the ways we are traumatized in our growing-up years, psychoanalyst Alice Miller makes the point in *For Your Own Good* that it is not clear why childhood wounds become for some folk an opportunity to grow, to move forward rather than backward in the process of self-realization. Certainly, when I reflect on the trials of my growing-up years, the many punishments, I can see now that in resistance I learned to be vigilant in the nourishment of my spirit, to be tough, to courageously protect that spirit from forces that would break it.

While punishing me, my parents often spoke about the necessity of breaking my spirit. Now when I ponder the silences, the voices that are not heard, the voices of those wounded and/or oppressed individuals who do not speak or write, I contemplate the acts of persecution, torture—the terrorism that breaks spirits, that makes creativity impossible. I write these words to bear witness to the primacy of resistance struggle in any situation of domination (even within family life); to the strength and power that emerges from sustained resistance and the profound conviction that these forces can be healing, can protect us from dehumanization and despair.

These early trials, wherein I learned to stand my ground, to keep my spirit intact, came vividly to mind after I published *Ain't I A Woman* and the book was sharply and harshly criticized. While I had expected a climate of critical dialogue, I was not expecting a critical avalanche that had the power in its intensity to crush the spirit, to push one into silence. Since that time, I have heard stories about black women, about women of color, who write and publish (even when the work is quite successful) having nervous breakdowns, being made mad because they cannot bear the harsh responses of family, friends, and unknown critics, or becoming silent, unproductive. Surely, the absence of a humane critical response has tremendous impact on the writer from any oppressed, colonized group who endeavors to speak. For us, true speaking is not solely an expression of creative power; it is an act of resistance, a political gesture that challenges politics of domination that would render us nameless and voiceless. As such, it is a courageous act—as such, it represents a threat. To those who wield oppressive power, that which is threatening must necessarily be wiped out, annihilated, silenced.

Recently, efforts by black women writers to call attention to our work serve to highlight both our presence and absence. Whenever I peruse women's bookstores, I am struck not by the rapidly growing body of feminist writing by black women, but by the paucity of available published material. Those of us who write and are published remain few in number. The context of silence is varied and multi-dimensional. Most obvious are the ways racism, sexism, and class exploitation act to suppress and silence. Less obvious are the inner struggles, the efforts made to gain the necessary confidence to write, to re-write, to fully develop craft and skill—and the extent to which such efforts fail.

Although I have wanted writing to be my life-work since childhood, it has been difficult for me to claim "writer" as part of that which identifies and shapes my everyday reality. Even after publishing books, I would often speak of wanting to be a writer as though these works did not exist. And though I would be told, "you are a writer," I was not yet ready to fully affirm this truth. Part of myself was still held captive by domineering forces of history, of familial life that had charted a map of silence, of right speech. I had not completely let go of the fear of saying the wrong thing, of being punished.

Somewhere in the deep recesses of my mind, I believed I could avoid both responsibility and punishment if I did not declare myself a writer.

One of the many reasons I chose to write using the pseudonym bell hooks, a family name (mother to Sarah Oldham, grandmother to Rosa Bell Oldham, great-grandmother to me), was to construct a writer-identity that would challenge and subdue all impulses leading me away from speech into silence. I was a young girl buying bubble gum at the corner store when I first really heard the full name bell hooks. I had just "talked back" to a grown person. Even now I can recall the surprised look, the mocking tones that informed me I must be kin to bell hooks—a sharp-tongued woman, a woman who spoke her mind, a woman who was not afraid to talk back. I claimed this legacy of defiance, of will, of courage, affirming my link to female ancestors who were bold and daring in their speech. Unlike my bold and daring mother and grandmother, who were not supportive of talking back, even though they were assertive and powerful in their speech, bell hooks as I discovered, claimed, and invented her was my ally, my support.

That initial act of talking back outside the home was empowering. It was the first of many acts of defiant speech that would make it possible for me to emerge as an independent thinker and writer. In retrospect, "talking back" became for me a rite of initiation, testing my courage, strengthening my commitment, preparing me for the days ahead—the days when writing, rejection notices, periods of silence, publication, ongoing development seem impossible but necessary.

Moving from silence into speech is for the oppressed, the colonized, the exploited, and those who stand and struggle side by side a gesture of defiance that heals, that makes new life and new growth possible. It is that act of speech, of "talking back," that is no mere gesture of empty words, that is the expression of our movement from object to subject—the liberated voice.

The Bridge Poem

Kate Rushin

I've had enough
I'm sick of seeing and touching
Both sides of things
Sick of being the damn bridge for everybody

Nobody
Can talk to anybody
Without me
Right?

I explain my mother to my father my father to my little sister
My little sister to my brother my brother to the white feminists
The white feminists to the Black church folks the Black church folks
To the ex-hippies the ex-hippies to the Black separatists the
Black separatists to the artists the artists to my friends' parents . . .

Then
I've got to explain myself
To everybody

I do more translating
Than the Gawdamn U.N.

Forget it
I'm sick of it

I'm sick of filling in your gaps

Sick of being your insurance against
The isolation of your self-imposed limitations
Sick of being the crazy at your holiday dinners
Sick of being the odd one at your Sunday Brunches
Sick of being the sole Black friend to 34 individual white people

Find another connection to the rest of the world
Find something else to make you legitimate
Find some other way to be political and hip

I will not be the bridge to your womanhood
Your manhood
Your human-ness

I'm sick of reminding you not to
Close off too tight for too long

I'm sick of mediating with your worst self
On behalf of your better selves

I am sick
Of having to remind you
To breathe
Before you suffocate
Your own fool self

Forget it
Stretch or drown
Evolve or die

The bridge I must be
Is the bridge to my own power
I must translate
My own fears
Mediate
My own weaknesses

I must be the bridge to nowhere
But my true self
And then
I will be useful

Uses of the Erotic: The Erotic as Power

Audre Lorde

There are many kinds of power, used and unused, acknowledged or otherwise. The erotic is a resource within each of us that lies in a deeply female and spiritual plane, firmly rooted in the power of our unexpressed or unrecognized feeling. In order to perpetuate itself, every oppression must corrupt or distort those various sources of power within the culture of the oppressed that can provide energy for change. For women, this has meant a suppression of the erotic as a considered source of power and information within our lives.

We have been taught to suspect this resource, vilified, abused, and devalued within western society. On the one hand, the superficially erotic has been encouraged as a sign of female inferiority; on the other hand, women have been made to suffer and to feel both contemptible and suspect by virtue of its existence.

It is a short step from there to the false belief that only by the suppression of the erotic within our lives and consciousness can women be truly strong. But that strength is illusory, for it is fashioned within the context of male models of power.

As women, we have come to distrust that power which rises from our deepest and nonrational knowledge. We have been warned against it all our lives by the male world, which values this depth of feeling enough to keep women around in order to exercise it in the service of men, but which fears this same depth too much to examine the possibilities of it within themselves. So women are maintained at a distant/inferior position to be psychically milked, much the same way ants maintain colonies of aphids to provide a life-giving substance for their masters.

But the erotic offers a well of replenishing and provocative force to the woman who does not fear its revelation, nor succumb to the belief that sensation is enough.

The erotic has often been misnamed by men and used against women. It has been made into the confused, the trivial, the psychotic, the plasticized sensation. For this reason, we have often turned away from the exploration and consideration of the erotic as a source of power and information, confusing it with its opposite, the pornographic. But pornography is a direct denial of the power of the erotic, for it represents the suppression of true feeling. Pornography emphasizes sensation without feeling.

The erotic is a measure between the beginnings of our sense of self and the chaos of our strongest feelings. It is an internal sense of satisfaction to which, once we have experienced it, we know we can aspire. For having experienced the fullness of this depth of feeling and recognizing its power, in honor and self-respect we can require no less of ourselves.

It is never easy to demand the most from ourselves, from our lives, from our work. To encourage excellence is to go beyond the encouraged mediocrity of our society is to encourage excellence. But giving in to the fear of feeling and working to capacity is a luxury only the unintentional can afford, and the unintentional are those who do not wish to guide their own destinies.

This internal requirement toward excellence which we learn from the erotic must not be misconstrued as demanding the impossible from ourselves nor from others. Such a demand incapacitates everyone in the process. For the erotic is not a question only of what we do; it is a question of how acutely and fully we can feel in the doing. Once we know the extent to which we are capable of feeling that sense of satisfaction and completion, we can then observe which of our various life endeavors bring us closest to that fullness.

The aim of each thing which we do is to make our lives and the lives of our children richer and more possible. Within the celebration of the erotic in all our endeavors, my work becomes a conscious decision—a longed-for bed which I enter gratefully and from which I rise up empowered.

Of course, women so empowered are dangerous. So we are taught to separate the erotic demand from most vital areas of our lives other than sex. And the lack of concern for the erotic root and satisfactions of our work is felt in our disaffection from so much of what we do. For instance, how often do we truly love our work even at its most difficult?

The principal horror of any system which defines the good in terms of profit rather than in terms of human need, or which defines human need to the exclusion of the psychic and emotional components of that need—the principal horror of such a system is that it robs our work of its erotic value, its erotic power and life appeal and fulfillment. Such a system reduces work to a travesty of necessities, a duty by which we earn bread or oblivion for ourselves and those we love. But this is tantamount to blinding a painter and then telling her to improve her work, and to enjoy the act of painting. It is not only next to impossible, it is also profoundly cruel.

As women, we need to examine the ways in which our world can be truly different. I am speaking here of the necessity for reassessing the quality of all the aspects of our lives and of our work, and of how we move toward and through them.

The very word *erotic* comes from the Greek word *eros*, the personification of love in all its aspects—born of Chaos, and personifying creative power and harmony. When I speak of the erotic, then, I speak of it as an assertion of the life force of women; of that creative energy empowered, the knowledge and use of which we are now reclaiming in our language, our history, our dancing, our loving, our work, our lives.

There are frequent attempts to equate pornography and eroticism, two diametrically opposed uses of the sexual. Because of these attempts, it has become fashionable to separate the spiritual (psychic and emotional) from the political, to see them as contradictory or antithetical. "What do you mean, a poetic revolutionary, a meditating gunrunner?" In the same way, we have attempted to separate the spiritual and the erotic, thereby reducing the spiritual to a world of flattened affect, a world of the ascetic who aspires to feel nothing. But nothing is farther from the truth. For the ascetic position is one of the highest fear, the gravest immobility. The severe abstinence of the ascetic becomes the ruling obsession. And it is one not of self-discipline but of self-abnegation.

The dichotomy between the spiritual and the political is also false, resulting from an incomplete attention to our erotic knowledge. For the bridge which connects them is formed by the erotic—the sensual—those physical, emotional, and psychic expressions of what is deepest and strongest and richest within each of us, being shared: the passions of love, in its deepest meanings.

Beyond the superficial, the considered phrase, "It feels right to me," acknowledges the strength of the erotic into a true knowledge, for what that means is the first and most powerful guiding light toward any understanding. And understanding is a handmaiden which can only wait upon, or clarify, that knowledge, deeply born. The erotic is the nurturer or nursemaid of all our deepest knowledge.

The erotic functions for me in several ways, and the first is in providing the power which comes from sharing deeply any pursuit with another person. The sharing of joy, whether physical, emotional, psychic, or intellectual, forms a bridge between the sharers which can be the basis for understanding much of what is not shared between them, and lessens the threat of their difference.

Another important way in which the erotic connection functions is the open and fearless underlining of my capacity for joy. In the way my body stretches to music and opens into response, hearkening to its deepest rhythms, so every level upon which I sense also opens to the erotically satisfying experience, whether it is dancing, building a bookcase, writing a poem, examining an idea.

That self-connection shared is a measure of the joy which I know myself to be capable of feeling, a reminder of my capacity for feeling. And that deep and irreplaceable knowledge of my capacity for joy comes to demand from all of my life that it be lived within the knowledge that such satisfaction is possible, and does not have to be called *marriage*, nor *god*, nor *an afterlife*.

This is one reason why the erotic is so feared, and so often relegated to the bedroom alone, when it is recognized at all. For once we begin to feel deeply all the aspects of our lives, we begin to demand from ourselves and from our life-pursuits that they feel in accordance with that joy which we know ourselves to be capable of. Our erotic knowledge empowers us, becomes a lens through which we scrutinize all aspects of our existence, forcing us to evaluate those aspects honestly in terms of their relative meaning within our lives. And this is a grave responsibility, projected from within each of us, not to settle for the convenient, the shoddy, the conventionally expected, nor the merely safe.

During World War II, we bought sealed plastic packets of white, uncolored margarine, with a tiny, intense pellet of yellow coloring perched like a topaz just inside the clear skin of the bag. We would leave the margarine out for a while to soften, and then we would pinch the little pellet to break it inside the bag, releasing the rich yellowness into the soft pale mass of margarine. Then taking it carefully between our fingers, we would knead it gently back and forth, over and over, until the color had spread throughout the whole pound bag of margarine, thoroughly coloring it.

I find the erotic such a kernel within myself. When released from its intense and constrained pellet, it flows through and colors my life with a kind of energy that heightens and sensitizes and strengthens all my experience.

We have been raised to fear the *yes* within ourselves, our deepest cravings. But, once recognized, those which do not enhance our future lose their power and can be altered. The fear of our desires keeps them suspect and indiscriminately powerful, for to suppress any truth is to give it strength beyond endurance. The fear that we cannot grow beyond whatever distortions we may find within ourselves keeps us docile and loyal and obedient, externally defined, and leads us to accept many facets of our oppression as women.

When we live outside ourselves, and by that I mean on external directives only rather than from our internal knowledge and needs, when we live away from those erotic guides from within ourselves, then our lives are limited by external and alien forms, and we conform to the needs of a structure that is not based on human need, let alone an individual's. But when we begin to live from within outward, in touch with the power of the erotic within ourselves, and allowing that power to inform and illuminate our actions upon the world around us, then we begin to be responsible to ourselves in the deepest sense. For as we begin to recognize our deepest feelings, we begin to give up, of necessity, being satisfied with suffering and self-negation, and with the numbness which so often seems like their only alternative in our society. Our acts against oppression become integral with self, motivated and empowered from within.

In touch with the erotic, I become less willing to accept powerlessenss, or those other supplied states of being which are not native to me, such as resignation, despair, self-effacement, depression, self-denial.

And yes, there is a hierarchy. There is a difference between painting a back fence and writing a poem, but only one of quantity. And there is, for me, no difference between writing a good poem and moving into sunlight against the body of a woman I love.

This brings me to the last consideration of the erotic. To share the power of each other's feelings is different from using another's feelings as we would use a kleenex. When we look the other way from our experience, erotic or otherwise, we use rather than share the feelings of those others who participate in the experience with us. And use without consent of the used is abuse.

In order to be utilized, our erotic feelings must be recognized. The need for sharing deep feeling is a human need. But within the european-american tradition, this need is satisfied by certain proscribed erotic comings-together. These occasions are almost always characterized by a simultaneous looking away, a pretense of calling them something else, whether a religion, a fit, mob violence, or even playing doctor. And this misnaming of the need and the deed give rise to that distortion which results in pornography and obscenity—the abuse of feeling.

When we look away from the importance of the erotic in the development and sustenance of our power, or when we look away from ourselves as we satisfy our erotic needs in concert with others, we use each other as objects of satisfaction rather than share our joy in the satisfying, rather than make connection with our similarities and our differences. To refuse to be conscious of what we are feeling at any time, however comfortable that might seem, is to deny a large part of the experience, and to allow ourselves to be reduced to the pornographic, the abused, and the absurd.

The erotic cannot be felt secondhand. As a Black lesbian feminist, I have a particular feeling, knowledge, and understanding for those sisters with whom I have danced hard, played, or even fought. This deep participation has often been the forerunner for joint concerted actions not possible before.

But this erotic charge is not easily shared by women who continue to operate under an exclusively european-american male tradition. I know it was not available to me when I was trying to adapt my consciousness to this mode of living and sensation.

Only now, I find more and more women-identified women brave enough to risk sharing the erotic's electrical charge without having to look away, and without distorting the enormously powerful and creative nature of that exchange. Recognizing the power of the erotic within our lives can give us the energy to pursue genuine change within our world, rather than merely settling for a shift of characters in the same weary drama.

For not only do we touch our most profoundly creative source, but we do that which is female and self-affirming in the face of a racist, patriarchal, and anti-erotic society.

Part One—The Shaping of Gender
Chapter 1—The Psychology of Women
Study Questions

1. What is meant by the phrase the "cult of true womanhood"? How did this concept affect white women? Women of color?

2. What does *dichotomization of gendered characteristics* mean? What is its impact on women? Give examples other than those listed in the book. What is the consequence of gender stratification? What societal institutions perpetuate this notion, and why?

3. According to feminist psychological theory, what is the cornerstone of women's psychological suffering? What have been the consequences in your own life? Your mother's? Give specific examples from the viewpoint of your ethnicity.

4. How does individual ethnicity affect female roles?

5. Define *misogyny*. What is its impact on traditional psychological theory?

6. Does Horney's theory of "womb envy" tip the balance of power toward women? Why?

7. What are the symptoms of male fear of female power as described in feminist psychology? Give examples of each from your own personal experience.

8. What is the emotional fallout of the pathology of women's socialization? Can you identify with its consequences? If so, how? If not, why not?

9. In Miller's analysis, what creates an "as if" persona in women?

10. What would be the result for women if gender stratification were eliminated? Relate this result to your own life, i.e. mental health, sense of personal power, acquired characteristics and other elements of modeling and choice.

11. Depression is often referred to as anger turned inward. Do women have difficulty expressing anger? What factors put women at high risk for depression? Are the factors the same for women of color? Why or why not, based on the limited research available.

12. What underlying conditions, as stated in this chapter, are present that make lesbian relationships more egalitarian and mutual. Do you agree? Why or why not?

13. What is the "irony of dependency"?

14. Can the feminist approach to psychology help men, as well as women? Why or why not?

15. In Joy Harjo's poem, what does the heartbeat represent? Discuss your answer in the context of female socialization within the family. Transfer these ideas to other societal institutions that shape women's lives.

16. Bell hooks writes: "I was taught that it was important to speak but to talk a talk that was in itself a silence." How does her resistance serve as a model of feminist thinking? What barriers did she have to overcome? What benefits did she realize? Discuss applicable issues of race that differentiate her experience.

17. In the context of Kate Rushin's "The Bridge Poem," discuss the idea of being an "expert." Does this enhance or detract from bridging difference? Why or why not? What is the best way to gain an understanding of difference?

18. Using Audre Lorde's article, demystify the erotic as seen in patriarchal society. Discuss erotica versus pornography.

19. In small groups, explore the concept of madness—feelings gone wild, insight, intuition, power—using Lorde's definition of the erotic and honoring ourselves. Is it madness? Relate an experience in your own life that is unexplainable. Does this reinforce Lorde's theory?

UNDERSTANDING GENDER-SHAPING INSTITUTIONS

Alette Hill
Annette Bennington McElhiney
Joan Van Becelaere

The title of Simone de Beauvoir's book *The Second Sex* aptly describes how women are still perceived by many people—both women and men—in the United States today. In our culture, *being number one* seems to be of primary importance. Corporate executive officers and presidents, national, religious, and political leaders, and people of great wealth, most of whom are white men, receive an over-abundance of recognition for being *number one* in their fields. They have demonstrated their proficiency in wielding power, garnering resources, attracting followers, and making money. In sports and entertainment, number one status is readily accessible for men of color from backgrounds other than European American, but they, too, are frequently barred from being number one in other areas. Supposedly, then, men—at least some men—excel in their chosen fields because of their intelligence, rationality, decisiveness, objectivity, political astuteness, and superior strength—qualities which are highly valued in American society. In general, women receive number one status only because of their sexual appeal, beauty, or, as in Mother Teresa's case, love and nurturing of others—all qualities which are of *secondary* importance in European American society.

In contrast, as Paula Gunn Allen reveals in *The Sacred Hoop: Recovering the Feminine in American Indian Traditions* (1986), many Native American peoples have a different value system, based on beauty, unity, egalitarianism, nature, and cooperativeness rather than power or money. Contemporary American society did not draw its dominant value system from Native American culture, but from Indo-European culture where patriarchy and hierarchy were paramount. From these Indo-European roots emerge past and present perceptions of gender differences and the resulting gender inequality.

Perceptions about gender are carefully nurtured by the ideology of a culture to maintain social control by a powerful ruling faction of one or more groups. Beliefs in the natural, physical, and intellectual superiority of men over women; the separation of worlds into male/public and female/private; the value of so-called "male work" over "female work"; and the emphasis on money and power instead of relationships and caring are structured and perpetrated by the society's sanctioned institutions in order to keep men *the first sex* and women *the second sex*. And what better vehicles for transmission of these beliefs are there than language, the educational system, traditional religion, and the media.

This chapter will suggest how all of these social strategies (except media which is treated in a separate essay immediately following this chapter) have shaped contemporary American concepts about gender so effectively that even many women have come to see themselves as being members of *the second sex*. At the same time, this summary and the pieces that follow it may provoke readers to ask themselves the following questions:

- In what specific ways does our written and spoken language discriminate against women?
- Does emphasis on a female v. male style of communicating affect the perpetuation of inequality? If so how?
- Should a male style of communicating be the norm? Why or why not?
- How important to the future of equality for women is the inequality inherent in the structure of American English?
- How, both in the past and in the present, does access to education promote gender inequality?
- How important is the percentage of female teachers/professors in *all* disciplines, including science and math, to establishing gender equality?
- Is coeducation beneficial or harmful to mitigating/eradicating gender inequality?
- Do women in the late twentieth century receive the same education as males? If so, why? If not, why not?
- How powerful was the impact of religion on women's perceptions of themselves in the past? Has that impact

changed? If so, what evidence supports that change? What denies it?
- Have religious institutions changed as a result of the various women's movements?
- Is it possible to embrace both traditional religion and feminism?
- In what specific ways are Christianity, Judaism, and Islam racist? Sexist?
- What specific evidence do you see in the visual and print media that suggests an agenda concerning gender inequality? Gender equality?
- In what respects has the media's portrayal of gender roles affected women harmfully?

Language and Women's Power

There are at least two significant ways to pursue the subject of language and women: language of any kind as spoken by females ("women's language") and derogatory language as spoken to and about females ("sexist language"). Much earlier evidence exists for "women's language" than for "sexist language" since the word "sexist" was not coined until the late 1960s.

In 1922, the Danish linguist Otto Jespersen published perhaps the first analysis of "women's language," or at least of women's style of speech in *Language: Its Nature, Development and Origin*. He found the speech of women to be superficial, unimaginative, frivolous, illogical, euphemistic, ornamental, conservative, and paratactic (parataxis describes language in which the clauses of a sentence are connected with coordinating conjunctions, e.g., "and"). Jespersen does not directly compare women to children here, but language in which the elements are connected by coordinating conjunctions does bring to mind the language of children. An example is "I went to school and then

I came home and I had a piece of cake and I went out to play." In contrast, men's utterances are characterized according to Jespersen, by hypotaxis, featuring subordination, thus marking more sophisticated, more logically complex structures.

In vocabulary, women have contributions to make, ones valued in the 1920s, but perhaps not in the 1990s. Jespersen suggests:

> There can be no doubt that women exercise a great and universal influence on linguistic development through their instinctive shrinking from coarse and gross expressions and their preference for refined and (in certain spheres) veiled and indirect expressions (1964, 246).

In addition to women's "natural" gentility, Jespersen says that women do not make puns nor do they understand them. Women never swear or curse, nor do they invent new words. They seem rather to perform the function of social censor with respect to language. "Men," writes Jespersen, "will certainly with great justice object that there is a danger of the language becoming languid and insipid if we are always to content ourselves with women's expressions, and that vigour and vividness count for something" (1964, 247).

Jespersen's assertions about the way women speak remained unchallenged until 1975 when the remarkable book by Robin Lakoff, *Language and Women's Place*, appeared. In a way Lakoff agreed with Jespersen that women do speak in a polite, unassertive, even childish manner; but, unlike Jespersen, she judged this style of conversation a disaster for those who would be more than "ladies," whom she designated nonplayers in the important games of life—games played successfully by men.

What Lakoff was proposing to those women who were willing to listen was that they should carefully unlearn all those affectations of "ladies." For example, they should not ask questions in answer to questions. If asked her name, a woman should not reply "Mary Smith?" with rising intonation, implying that she is not quite sure of the answer. Instead, she should let her voice fall, projecting an assertive answer.

At about the same time as the publication of *Language and Woman's Place*, the first assertiveness training classes were advertised, promising much the same focus as Lakoff's book. If women were to be taken seriously, they would have to drop their tentativeness, their apologetic demeanor—in short, their disinclination to use language in a powerful way. Reviewers of Lakoff's provocative little book attacked either her methodology (which was not empirical or quantitative but unashamedly intuitive and introspective) or her conclusions: women should purge their "feminine" style of speech. This advice bothered feminists since a major way in which women behave was judged inadequate and inappropriate. Many feminists then, as now, believed that women's behavior should be analyzed for its excellence; just because women do something differently from men is no reason to abandon it. Indeed, one of the nine features used by Lakoff to characterize women's speech was tact. If women do practice this diplomatic form of verbal art, it can certainly be argued that they should not only retain it, but glory in it. What Lakoff saw as a situation in which women are damned if they do, damned if they don't, has been reframed in the light of subsequent analyses by other linguists.

In her book *Man Made Language* (1985), Dale Spender classified Lakoff as a Jespersenian: Whereas Jespersen pointed to the use of intensives (for example *vastly*) as a trait of women's speech that made it less precise than men's speech, Lakoff does the same thing with the assertion that women use "so" more often than do men. Neither statement has a shred of believable evidence.

Spender explains the very different impressions that people have of the ways in which men and women speak as indicative of a double standard at work—one that rewards men and punishes women. "When men use hyperbole it is frequently classified as slang and designated as a male realm. When women use it, it is an intensifier and it is therefore a lesser form" (Spender 1985, 36). If a woman says "It's such a nice party," that statement is perceived as imprecise, whereas if a man says, "Damned good party," it is a sign of male forcefulness (Spender 1985, 36). *Such*, the "imprecise" word in the first remark, is pointed out by another linguist—the anthropologist Mary Ritchie Key in *Male/Female Language* (1975)—as a typical "feminine" speech choice.

Spender labels both Key and Lakoff "sexists" in the mold of Jespersen: They are too quick, she states, to perceive women's speech habits as inadequate and inferior to the habits of men.

> These studies, because of their inherent sexism, simply do not substantiate the hypothesis that the language of women is a lesser form. Perhaps the only contribution they make is to provide evidence that women and their language have been devalued. In many cases, all that has been measured is the extent to which the patriarchal order imposes its values upon research (Spender 1985, 36).

Spender's agenda for dealing with language questions is to assume (1) that there is nothing wrong with the way women speak and (2) "that any sex differences in language could—or even should—be interpreted in favor of females at least 50 per cent of the time. This would be a very different bias and would give rise to some very different results!" (Spender 1985, 36).

Another researcher, Deborah Tannen, concurs with Spender that women's way of communicating is different and good, but she is far more serene. In her best-seller, *You Just Don't Understand: Women and Men in Conversation* (1990), Tannen describes men's and women's ways of talking as separate but equal and, in fact, complementary. Men perceive talking as a way of imparting information or of solving problems, whereas women use conversation to build or maintain relationships. Men resort to abstract logic to prove a point; women resort to personal observation. Men consider much of what passes for conversation between women as gossip; women find men's reluctance to touch upon personal details boring and colorless.

The reasons for these very different uses for conversation is to be found in the socialization of boys and girls. Boys are taught early on that anything they say or do will put them "one-up" or "one-down" on the social or political scale just like the team sports in which they are expected to engage. By contrast, girls play jacks and hopscotch; they skip rope; they have not traditionally taken part in team sports. Just so, their conversation is designed to mitigate the rough and tumble, the cruel, the violent aspects of life. Tannen's theories of language usage patterns of men and women mirror the relational psychology based on the different moral codes for men and women proposed by psychologist Carol Gilligan in her book *In a Different Voice* (1982).

Suzette Haden Elgin, a linguist of remarkable range and power, cautions against the notion that women speak a language different from men or even a separate dialect. To assert such a claim would be a strategic error, for when women wish to pursue politics or science or any other traditionally male career, they can be rejected on the grounds that they don't even speak the same language! (Elgin 1991) Elgin also warns against the notion that women and men have different communication goals—a rejection of Tannen's "Report-talk" vs. "Rapport-talk," though she does not mention Tannen. Indeed, Elgin does not prove Tannen wrong; she merely labels the two-communication-styles theory bad tactics.

Elgin believes in the Sapir-Whorf hypothesis to some extent. Edward Sapir and his pupil Benjamin Lee Whorf are credited with a view of language that controls its speakers' perceptions of the world. Elgin believes in what she terms a "weak form" of Sapir-Whorf: Language may not control our perceptions of reality, but it certainly structures and constrains them. Her faith in the power of language leads her to propose a halt to any social or political feminist agenda in favor of attempting to eradicate the inherent sexism and denigration of women at the heart of the English language (Elgin 1991). She does not prove that a reform of English would be any easier to accomplish than the passage, say, of an Equal Rights Amendment, yet Elgin believes that a reform of the language would be cost beneficial in both time and money. Whether her "Unifying Agenda" of feminist language change wins acceptance or not, her argument is worth listening to.

Perhaps the most radical exponent of the Sapir-Whorf hypothesis is Julia Penelope, a sociolinguist who has spent twenty years studying sexism in English.

In *Speaking Freely: Unlearning the Lies of the Father's Tongues* (1990), she declares war on the English language, which she labels "The Patriarchal Universe of Discourse" (PUD, for short). Her view of the role of language in our lives is that

> the issue, simply stated, is one of power: who has it and who doesn't. Men do the things they do to protect their territory. The boundaries are sometimes shifting and fuzzy, but men will defend to the death every square inch of what they believe they "own." In this conflict, control of language is the crucial weapon white men must keep from their enemies because it is the first and most important method for internalizing oppression in the minds of those they oppress. Language is an intangible, almost invisible weapon. Its messages are implanted in our minds when we are babies and left there to maintain our allegiance to men and their institutions (Penelope 1990, xx-xxi).

Both the structure of English and its vocabulary have been fashioned by men who have not granted the power of naming to anyone but themselves. Therefore women learn from birth to perceive the world through the eyes of males. The consensus reality is male reality, brokered for us by our language. Penelope's book is a scathing analysis of how English devalues women and exalts men—through, for example, the so-called use of the "get-passive" as in "She got herself raped." In this language construct, the responsibility for the rape is placed upon the victim.

Penelope has unearthed many other such syntactic sneak attacks that deserve attention. She is particularly suspicious of passive verbs that lack agents: "Woman *is intended* for reproduction; she has *been appointed* to take an active part in the reproduction of the race by pregnancy and childbirth" (Penelope 1990, 150; emphasis in original).

> The suppressed agency . . . urges us to accept the idea that a supernatural power has absolute control over our lives . . . the author . . . used agentless passives, *is intended* and *been appointed,* to deny his investment in restricting the scope of women's lives and to pretend that he was merely passing along the "revelation," in which the implied agency of god's [sic] will and biological determinism simultaneously justify his misogyny (Penelope 1990, 150–51).

In effect, Penelope has given us the tools to analyze the destructive effects of everyday English expressions on our lives. We need not wait to see if Elgin's "Unifying Agenda" is adopted. With the help of *Speaking Freely,* we can refuse to use such language or to be manipulated by it.

Education and Women

In Eurocentric America, up until the nineteenth century, most Americans obtained their education informally either through apprenticeship; modeling by parents or other family members; or, in the case of very wealthy men, formally through private schools. While men generally received education directed at preparation for the public world (initially for the ministry), women were instructed in preparation for their roles as wives and mothers. Although some women acted as religious teachers, their communities prohibited them from teaching anything other than what male religious leaders or their husbands allowed. Anne Hutchinson, for example, was banished from the Massachusetts Bay Colony for teaching women of all ages to interpret the Bible for themselves.

Just as in other areas, Colonial America derived its ideas about women's education from European educational theorists like Jean-Jacques Rousseau (1712–78) who believed men should be formally educated to do the work of the world and women should be informally instructed to be obedient mothers and wives. In the 1780s, the American theorist Benjamin Rush supported Rousseau's ideas. However, early European feminist liberals like Mary Wollstonecraft in *A Vindication of the Rights of Women* (1792) said women should receive liberal educations if they were to develop the ability to reason and therefore properly raise a new generation. In America, Judith Sargent Murray (1751–1820) supported Wollstonecraft's ideas and in her essay "On the Equality of the Sexes" offers a similar argument for educating women. Despite these women's early efforts, American women gained little access to formal education until the mid-nineteenth century.

During the 1830s, public education at the elementary level became available for most white children including middle class white females, particularly in the northeastern states. However, even as late as 1850 in the South Atlantic states 22.7 percent of white females could neither read nor write. The southcentral states had an even higher rate of illiteracy: 25.7 percent amongst white females (Foner and Pacheco 1984). Most white educators in the north and south opposed both public and private education for black children. Even though such white women teachers as Prudence Crandall in Connecticut, Myrtilla Miner in Washington, D. C., and Margaret Douglass in Virginia championed education for both black girls and boys, their efforts to establish schools for blacks met with extreme opposition (Foner and Pecheco 1984). Not until after the Civil War was public school education at the elementary level accessible for black children. In 1904 Mary McCloud Bethune, a black woman in Florida, started one of the first small schools for black children; this school later became Bethune Cookman College.

In 1821 Emma Willard established Troy Female Seminary and made higher education available for white women. Later, in 1830, Oberlin College in Ohio admitted students of both genders and races; still later such women's colleges as Mount Holyoke (1837), Vassar (1861), Wellesley (1870), Smith (1871), Radcliffe (1879), Bryn Mawr (1880), and Barnard (1889) made higher education readily available for upper middle class white women. By the end of the nineteenth century, significant numbers of colleges were coeducational, but few were integrated. Even though both black colleges Fisk (1867) and Hampton Normal and Agricultural Institute (1868) were coeducational, black women did not achieve access to the majority of coeducational colleges until the civil rights movement.

Despite laws against discrimination, even in the last decade of the twentieth century, *all* women encounter bias in the methods used to determine admission to prestigious institutions. Frequently, young women graduate from secondary schools with higher grade point averages than male students. Yet because certain colleges also require high scores on the SATs and ACTs, white women and people of color, who earn lower scores only on math because of the sexual and racial bias in the SAT and ACT tests, often do not gain admission.

Women's studies, using "feminist phase theory" or various models for including information about women in the curriculum, has in some institutions dismantled the inequality inherent in the traditional curriculum, particularly in the books selected and in the range and scope of courses taught. Also, an early section of this chapter suggests how the English language creates a linguistic bias in the materials used in the classroom and in academic verbal exchanges.

Yet another aspect of inequality in education includes the climate of the classroom. Many feminists do not find it conducive to women's learning; instead, they find the classroom climate from elementary school through college inhospitable to women. Some of the research conducted on elementary school children suggests that schoolteachers of both genders treat boys in the classroom differently than girls (Sadker and Sadker 1982). Boys receive more attention, get both more discouragement and reprimands which force them to rethink their answers, and are offered more opportunities to learn by trial and error than are girls. Although classroom interactions at the college level do not exactly repeat these patterns, they often reflect the expectations and patterns of responses elicited in the earlier experiences of both students and instructors.

Another contributing factor to the inhospitable climate of the college classroom is the problem of sexual harassment of female students by both professors and peers. This harassment takes the form not necessarily of propositions in exchange for grades, but of the creation of a climate in which women feel intimidated, a climate in which women's comments receive hostile responses or inattention while men's comments receive approval or respect from both the teacher and other students.

Most educational researchers and government statistics show that the majority (between 85 to 98 percent) of kindergarten and elementary teachers and approximately 50 percent of secondary school teachers are female. Yet most also suggest that the majority of kindergarten, elementary school, and secondary school administrators are men. These percentages indicate that just as historically women received education in order to educate their own children, today they are viewed as more suited to classroom teaching than to directing programs or managing schools.

The same pattern of women holding positions clustered at the bottom of the hierarchical structure or in instructors' positions holds true in higher education. For example, Mary Frank Fox suggests that as of 1986 across all institutions (two-year through doctoral-level institutions), women comprise by rank at the professor level only 12.3 percent; at the associate level 24.6 percent; at the assistant level 38.4 percent; and at the instructor level 53.3 percent (Fox 1989). Obviously, these figures illustrate that the same perceptions about women being *second* to men in intellectual rigor still exist. With fewer women in positions of leadership as full professors, deans, vice presidents, or college presidents, gender shaping ideas persist and female students have few leaders on which to model themselves.

Most research also indicates that students evaluate female professors differently than male professors. Women are expected to be nurturing. If they are not, they are penalized in student evaluations. Men, on the other hand, do not face this double requirement; they only need be competent. In addition, students expect women professors to be more available out of class than they do male professors. This expectation simply reflects our society's expectations that women be available to others out of class as well as meet their intellectual needs in class.

Finally, both female students and academicians face considerable bias in the ways in which research in the various disciplines has been defined, selected, conducted, perceived, and funded. The Project on the Status and Education of Women at the Association of American Colleges documented *how* and *why* insufficient research may have been conducted on such topics as housework and sex discrimination in the United States (Project on the Status of Women 1980). Yet even if feminists undertake such research on subjects of extreme importance to women, it frequently is not considered as appropriate for academic study as research which covers a topic of interest to males. In addition, particularly since the early 1980s, government funding for feminist research has decreased to its present low status. Obviously when funding is unavailable, fewer scholars can actively pursue questions about women's lives.

Traditional Religion

Those of us born in western society were raised within the boundaries of a particular worldview which has been heavily influenced by the religious stories, myths, and traditions inherited by our culture. An integrated package of psychological and social concepts, that worldview helps us to interpret the raw data of life and place individual experience into a socially meaningful context.

The three world religions of the west— Judaism, Christianity, and Islam—sometimes called the Faith Family of Abraham in recognition of their common theological, philosophical, and historical roots, share a particular religious worldview. Not only do these three share common roots, but they also share a common traditional view of the role of women in religion. In the history of the Faith Family of Abraham, women have found themselves forced to deny their own experience and interpretation of religious meaning in favor of interpretations provided by some "higher authority"—that is, God, Scripture, or religious tradition as developed and interpreted by male leadership within the religious tradition (Collins 1974, 36).

Through the ages, women in western religions have been informed, by male leadership, of a variety of "divine" laws that forbid them to study the Scriptures, pray certain prayers, talk in church, speak to men on the street, appear in public without a veil, or have any thing to do with, according to Martin Luther, "divine service, the priestly offices, or God's word." The church, the synagogue, and the mosque have repeatedly told women that they are inferior to men, or at best secondary, and they are certainly not worthy to be ordained to the Jewish rabbinate, Catholic and Orthodox priesthood, Islamic clergy, or Protestant ministry or allowed to assume any other form of leadership in a large number of modern denominations and sects.

Women in western society have inherited a world in which a leading clergyman in the *San Francisco Chronicle* could oppose the ordination of women and be taken seriously by a large body of his colleagues:

> In his statement opposed to the ordination of women, Bishop C. L. Meyers said the Episcopalian priesthood is a "masculine conception." "A priest is a 'God symbol' whether he likes it or not. In the imagery of both the Old and New Testament God is represented in masculine imagery," he said in a statement that was circulated among some 760 delegates at Grace Cathedral for the 2 1/2 day convention. "Christ is the source of Priesthood. The Sexuality of Christ is no accident nor is his masculinity inciden-

tal. This is the divine choice," the statement said (Stone 1976).

The religious tradition of western society as it applies to women has had a greater influence than any other on the development of American society to date. American women may deny this inherited religious worldview; we may consciously critique it; but it is the basic structure from which people in our society build the concept of the social self and define our identity in the world.

Debates rage as to why world religions that had their birth in the Middle East adopted a constrained view of women's religious role. This development is even more puzzling when we realize that the first concepts of divinity among early humans were centered upon the powerful symbols associated with the act of giving birth and mothering. Archeological evidence, statues, and shrines from as far back as 25,000 BCE (Before the Common Era) show that ancient humans worshipped many forms of the Great Mother. By the time agricultural civilizations developed in the ancient Middle East, between 9,000 BCE and 7,000 BCE, the concept of divinity as female was widespread in the Middle East, North Africa, and most of Europe.

The Middle Eastern worldview began to change, however, around 2,400 BCE, with increasing waves of northern invaders who brought with them a concept of divinity as male—the divine patriarch who resides on the tops of high mountains and is often symbolized by fire or the fury of volcanic eruptions (Stone 1976). The religion of ancient Israel grew in the midst of these two influences: the older, agricultural goddess-oriented world and the patriarchal, nomadic worldview brought by northern peoples. The oldest traditions, poems, and folktales of the

Bible reflect the early agricultural period as well as the clash of the two cultures. Later editing by the priests connected with the temple in Jerusalem gave the stories their current form and framework (Bright 1974; Child 1979).

Although the narrative of how the various stories, legends, poems, and myths came to be gathered into the Bible over a period of approximately 2,000 years is fascinating, our present concern is with the influence scripture has had on current worldviews and concepts of how life in the world should be ordered if it is to be in accord with the divine will.

Phyllis Bird's article, "Images of Women in the Old Testament," (1974) presents not only the negative images of women that became part of the Bible, but also explores the powerful and positive images of women that are seldom preached from the pulpit and rarely explored outside of theological seminaries. She explores the picture of women found in the laws and proverbs as well as the historical books of the Old Testament and the accounts of creation.

It is important to hear, perhaps for the first time, about the strong and positive leadership women assumed in the Bible. What is important about such women, according to religious analyst Sheila Collins:

> is that they provide an antidote to the traditional assumptions about women's nature and place in the cosmic scheme of things. Through their writings and what is recorded of their actions, we have a spotty, but nevertheless substantial, body of information on the experiences of women who defied authority to assert a different reality for themselves and their sisters (Collins 1974, 37).

In times of social dislocation, as in the time of the Book of Judges, Bird (1974) shows us that women of power did rise to social prominence when courageous leadership was demanded by the community. First, there are the ancient traditions and stories found in Exodus and Numbers. These books provide accounts of the Hebrew midwives who cleverly tricked the Egyptian pharaoh and thwarted his attempt to kill the male Hebrew children at birth. Miriam, a prophetess and leader, is initially known for ecstatic dancing, singing, and prophecy. She is only secondarily known as the sister of Moses in the scripture. It was later male theologians and teachers who stressed Miriam's relation to Moses, thus attempting to anchor her obviously important leadership to a "legitimate' male source (Van Becelaere 1980).

Perhaps most noteworthy is Deborah (Judges 4:1 to 5:31). She is depicted as an accepted resolver of community conflicts during peacetime and as a military leader when her community is under attack. She commands warriors such as the general Barak. Her song of victory in Judges 5 is an extremely ancient piece of literature, one of the oldest separate works included in the Bible, which was set into its current narrative framework by later editors. In the folktales of I Samuel, another strong woman, Hannah, the mother of the prophet Samuel, achieves her goal of bearing a child no matter what the personal cost.

Despite these positive images of women presented in the historical legends and tales, the more common image of women in the Old Testament is shown in the myths or stories of reversal in which the status of women was made inferior to that of men by the conscious usurpation of socially important tasks and roles formerly belonging to women (Daly 1973). A prime example of this reversal occurs in the story of the creation of Eve in Genesis 2:20-25 and its biologically 'absurd' or reversed story of Eve's birth from the side of Adam. The story's reversal is made ironic when we find Adam stating in Genesis 3:20 that the woman shall be called Eve which means life or to live, because she is the "mother of all living beings."

The name Eve is common in the ancient Middle East and is one of the common Middle-Eastern names of the ancient mother goddess. To the Hittites, the goddess was Hawwah—Life. Persians called her Hvov—the earth. To Arameans, she was Hawah—Mother of All living. In Asia Minor, the goddess was called Hebat or Hepat, and Hebe in Greece—Virgin Mother Earth.

Another story of reversal is found among the Exodus traditions in Numbers 12:1–15. In this story, Miriam and Aaron, the sister and brother of Moses, known as leaders in their own right, question the right of Moses to claim sole leadership of the Hebrew people. Miriam, as noted above, has a strong independent claim to prophetic status. She is called a prophetess in Exodus 15:20 and in Micah 6:4. In Numbers 12 she is called both prophet and leader. And her prophetic vocation is not questioned by the story; it simply asserts that Moses' status is higher. Miriam is said to *hear* God in dreams and visions, yet Moses *speaks* to God.

Yahweh hears Miriam's complaint that Moses is claiming false superiority and immediately punishes Miriam, and only Miriam, with leprosy. Yahweh forces her outside the desert camp of the wandering Hebrew people where she is later cured after she accepts Moses' leadership. But the Bible also specifically notes that the people refused to move from the campsite or continue their desert journey without her (Van Becelaere 1980).

In summation, Bird explains that ancient Israel's positive images of women recognize women as a spiritual and social equal with man with equal responsibility to God and creation. "That Israel rarely lived up to this vision is all too apparent," Bird writes, "but the vision should not be denied" (1974, 79).

In early Christianity, as in the times of social dislocation in ancient Israel described above, women served in leadership roles and held influential positions in the early church. The authentic letters of Paul are the earliest church writings of which we have knowledge. They were written long before the gospels, from 50 to 150 years earlier. These authentic letters, as opposed to later letters written by others under the name of Paul, make specific mention of women church leaders and workers. Paul's letters speak of Priscilla the preacher as well as a number of women who are said to have fostered the local churches in their homes, led prayers, and performed a number of other good works (Romans 16:1–6).

Constance Parvey's article, "The Theology and Leadership of Women in the New Testament," describes both the promise and the problems of women's leadership in the early church. She notes that Paul's own ambivalence toward women's place in the church, as displayed in I Corinthians 11:2–16 and Galatians 3:27–28, led later Epistle writers to use Paul's name to justify complete subordination of women in church and society. While Paul's first letter to the Corinthians contained a discussion of why he felt it was more seemly for women to cover their heads when they prayed and prophesied in worship services, later writers forbade women to pray, teach, or even speak aloud in church with or without a veil.

The gospels, particularly Luke, also present a picture of the early church in which women played a prominent role. The pedagogical structure of the parables and stories in Luke display a concern with educating both women and men. The companion book to Luke, the book of Acts, gives stories of the four unmarried daughters of Philip who were called prophets, the woman 'disciple' Tabitha (also known as Dorcas), and Lydia of Tyre who supported a congregation in her home.

The later church inherited two widely different messages: the first was the theological conviction that all women and men are equal in Christ; the second was the social subordination of women as a major element of both Jewish and Roman cultural practice. These two streams joined in the church and gave rise to complex theological arguments in the Middle Ages, the sum of which, according to Parvey, "is that men belong to this world and do the work of the church, while women belong to the next world and act in the church only as hidden helpers and servants to men" (1974, 146).

After the second and third generations of Christians had established themselves as part of the Roman world, the place of women in the church came to mimic the subordinate status of women throughout the Roman world. The church fathers debated over such weighty issues as whether women had souls or not. Writers influenced by Aristotle addressed women as misbegotten males. Tertullian, an influential church father, wrote:

> And do you not know that you are an Eve? The sentence of God on this sex of yours lives in this age; the guilt must of necessity live too. You are the devil's gateway . . . the first deserter of the divine law; you are she who persuaded him whom the devil was not valiant enough to attack. You destroyed so easily God's image, man. On account of your desert—that is, death, even the Son of God had to die (Bullough 112).

Thus women became the favorite spiritual scapegoat of a number of early church fathers. Despite their low state, they were offered hope of salvation only if they gave up their sensuous, physical ways and adopted the rigors of asceticism. The early ascetic Jerome was particularly influential in the spread of this doctrine and considered it his spiritual duty to convince women from wealthy families to give up bathing, good food, clean clothes, and beds for the sake of their souls. After the fall of Rome, Jerome's concept of desert asceticism became the justification for the birth of great convents and abbeys throughout medieval Europe.

These new Christian convents for women borrowed Jerome's ascetic arguments for justification, but often evolved from ancient pagan centers of learning established originally by priestesses of the Great Mother Goddess. In seventh century Gaul, Queen Bathild of the western Franks founded a convent in Chelles despite the fact that she was still a pagan. Bathild was later murdered by Christian bishops, although the people of the area and the women of the convent continued to call her a saint. Culture and learning for women were emphasized in these convents and the writings of ancient women poets like Sappho were kept alive in their libraries.

In the seventh, eighth, and ninth centuries, convents were often centers for wealthy and powerful women who wished to keep their own property. These developed into mini-queendoms. For example, a pagan princess founded a convent in Chester in England in the seventh century for noblewomen who refused to give up their property to husbands as demanded by Roman law. The Saxon convent of Gandersheim in the ninth century held overlordship directly from the king.

The abbess conducted her own courts of law, kept her own seat in the imperial parliament, and maintained her own standing army. Other abbesses had the right to license bishops and priests, to nominate ecclesiastical judges, and to hear criminal cases among their subjects. Abbesses heard confessions in their role of Spiritual Mother.

In the twelfth and thirteenth centuries, as the church consolidated its control over the whole of Western Europe, it began to repress these highly independent groups of monastic women. Slowly, women's ecclesiastical orders were placed under male rule. Even groups like the Cistercian nuns, famous as a medieval teaching order for women, were commanded by the Council of Trent not to found any more teaching convents. Women were threatened with excommunication and prosecution during the height of the Inquisition (thirteenth to fifteenth centuries) to accept strict seclusion and male control.

The Council of Vienne in 1312 deprived the teaching nuns called Beguines of their lands and houses and forbade them to teach or discuss theological matters. Their properties were used to support the Inquisition. The abbess of Jouarre and her nuns were commanded by Pope Innocent III to subject themselves to the authority of the bishop of Meaux. The abbess asked for time to prove her long standing right to independence, at which point she and all her community were excommunicated. The later decrees of the Council of Trent formalized universal church law to assert that women's clerical orders must be taken over and supervised by men's orders.

But worldviews take a long time to change. As late as 1629, an Englishwoman named Mary Ward tried to found an order of teaching nuns to provide education for girls. These English Ladies, as they were called, were accused of heresy and Mary Ward was arrested. Charges read against her claimed that she and her nuns "carried out works by no means suiting the weakness of their sex, womanly modesty, and virginal purity"—that is, teaching! The English Ladies were suppressed for doing what women were not supposed to be able to do.

The Jewish and Christian traditions present paradoxical views of women. As noted above, Israel's positive image of woman as a spiritual and social equal with man was rarely lived in practice. Christianity inherited the theological conviction that all women and men are equal in Christ and that an orderly society required the subordination of women. These contradictory streams fed the Reformation and remain an integral part of Protestant Christianity as well as modern Judaism, Roman Catholicism, and Eastern Orthodoxy. Elaine Huber's article, "A Woman Must Not Speak: Quaker Women in the English Left Wing," chronicles how Christianity's paradoxical view of women manifested itself in the radical Protestant reformation. The Quakers opted to emphasize the theological equality of women and put this belief into practice. This stance served to place the paradox of Christian tradition into high relief. In later years of the twentieth century, other Protestant denominations have tried to restore the theology of equality with varying degrees of commitment and success (1979).

Islam is not to be forgotten in this summary of western religious traditions. Islam grew from the same monotheistic Middle Eastern roots as did Judaism and Christianity. Many of the elements of the Jewish and Christian worldviews can be found in the Islam interpretation of reality. In addition, Islam is one of the world's largest religions and, in the late twentieth century, one of the fastest growing religious bodies in the United States.

Islam had its beginnings in the seventh century with the teaching of Mohammed that there is only one God and Mohammed is His prophet. Mohammed's teachings, summed up in the Koran, did provide some good news for Arabian women. The Koran eased some of the social restrictions on women imposed by the heavily patriarchal Arabic social structure. Women were allowed to inherit property and obtained some limited recourse to divorce in extreme circumstances. The Koran does speak about the value of women to society and their spiritual worth, which was a step forward compared to prior Arabic tribal concepts of women as expendable property.

Essentially, however, Islam incorporated the Middle Eastern worldview of the seventh century, with women viewed as subtly evil and somehow exuding a sinful sexuality that had to be covered with veils to protect the innocence of men. Modern Islam has not evolved to any great extent over the years in terms of the status of women. For example, it is still a scandal in Saudi Arabia for a woman to drive a car or show her bare arms. At the same time, the Islamic traditional concept of heaven places women in a very strange position. In heaven, men are waited upon by hordes of buxom celestial beauties (*houris*) as well as their earthly wives. This one-sided concept of paradise is only one step removed from the medieval theologians who felt certain that since women had no souls, they would never be found in heaven.

Although many American and European Protestant denominations now have at least a token number of women in positions of authority in the ministry and church administration, there are still a great number of religious bodies that refuse to accept the spiritual contributions of women in anything other than traditionally approved roles.

Although theologians of many different traditions have been producing scholarly reports affirming the equal status of women in spiritual matters, many conservative religious organizations still try to perpetuate worldviews inherited from centuries ago. A number of American fundamentalist groups combine an opposition to women in the ministry with an opposition to birth control, abortion, and reproductive rights. The hierarchy of the Roman Catholic church in the United States is facing growing opposition from its congregations to its negative stand on the ordination of women and injunctions against the active participation of women in worship services. Catholic women and nuns have organized to present theologically valid arguments for the ordination of women as priests; an example of this activity is the emergence of the Alliance of Saint Joan. Theologically liberal branches of Judaism accept a few women as rabbis, but the majority of American Jewish congregations do not recognize women rabbis. The rise of Islamic fundamentalism in the Middle East and North Africa currently threatens the recent progress that women have made in the moslem world in asserting their legal rights.

As Shelia Collins says in *A Different Heaven and Earth,* "Theologies rise out of a cultural context; they are promulgated by means of culture; and they change because of changes in the cultural experience. . . . Experience is the crucible out of which theologies rise" (1974, 33–34). Therefore, attitudes toward women and their roles in religion will change only as the existing culture changes.

Conclusion

The unrelenting impact of these gender shaping institutions has been great upon both women and men. Even in women's studies, students often say, "We have made progress in becoming equal, but have a long way to go." This phraseology demonstrates the effectiveness of the internalization of thinking of women as the *second sex* and men as the *first sex*. The use of the phrase *becoming equal* suggests that women do not accept their inherent equality but, instead, have "bought in" to the perceptions that Eurocentric United States society has built on and perpetuated.

The word *feminism* is defined in Merriam Webster (1989) as "the theory of the political, economic, and social equality of the sexes." The underlying assumption is that all women should have these rights because they are inherently created equal. Yet, as feminists proclaim, unless people actively engage in questioning **how** and **why** certain institutions promote gender inequality, no change will occur. The same perceptions about who is *number one* and who is *number two* will continue. On the other hand, as more people insist on rethinking our language, our school curriculum (from preschool through graduate school), and our religious institutions, ideas about gender will change accordingly. Then, a hierarchal relationship between the genders will disappear; in its place will emerge *two different, but entirely equal, sexes.*

References

Allen, Paula Gunn. 1986. *The sacred hoop: Recovering the feminine in American Indian traditions.* Boston: Beacon Press.

Bird, Phyllis. 1974. Images of women in the Old Testament. *Religion and sexism.* Edited by Rosemary Radford Ruether. New York: Simon and Schuster.

Brenzel, Barbara M. 1983. *History of nineteenth-century women's education: A plea for inclusion of class, race, and ethnicity.* Wellesley, Mass.: Wellesley College Center for Research on Women.

Bright, John. 1974. *A history of Israel.* Philadelphia: Westminster Press.

Bullough, Vern L. 1973. *The subordinate sex.* Chicago: University of Illinois Press.

Child, Brevard S. 1979. *Introduction to the Old Testament as scripture.* Philadelphia: Fortress Press.

Collins, Sheila. 1974. *A different heaven and earth.* Valley Forge, Pa.: Judson Press.

Daly, Mary. 1973. *Beyond god the father.* Boston: Beacon Press.

De Beauvoir, Simone. 1952. *The second sex.* New York: Alfred A. Knopf, Inc.

Elgin, Suzette Haden. 1991. *Women, language, and empowerment: A unifying agenda.* Huntsville, Ark.: Ozark Center for Language Studies (audiocassette).

Foner, Philip S., and Josephine F. Pacheco. 1984. *Three who dared: Prudence Crandall, Margaret Douglass, Myrtilla Mine: Champions of antebellum black education.* Westport, Conn.: Greenwood Press.

Fox, Mary Frank. 1989. Women and higher education: Gender differences in the status of students and scholars. *Women: A feminist perspective.* Edited by Jo Freeman. 4th ed. Mountain View, Calif.: Mayfield Publishing Company.

Gabriel, Susan L., and Isaiah Smithson, eds. 1990. *Gender in the classroom.* Urbana, Ill.: University of Illinois Press.

Gilligan, Carol. 1982. *In a different voice: Psychological theory and women's development.* Cambridge, Mass.: Harvard University Press.

Hall, Roberta M., and Bernice R. Sandler. 1982. *The classroom climate: A chilly one for women?* Washington, D.C.: The Association of American Colleges Project on the Status and Education of Women.

Huber, Elaine C. 1979. A woman must not speak: Quaker women in the English left wing. *Women of spirit: Female leadership in the Jewish and Christian traditions.* Edited by Rosemary Radford Ruether. New York: Simon and Schuster.

Hughes, Jean O., and Bernice R. Sandler. 1986. *In case of sexual harassment: A guide for women students.* Washington, D.C.: The Association of American Colleges Project on the Status and Education of Women.

Jespersen, Otto. [1922] 1964. *Language: Its nature, development and origin.* New York: W. W. Norton and Co.

Klein, Susan S., ed. 1985. *Handbook for achieving sex equity through education.* Baltimore: Johns Hopkins University Press.

Key, Mary Ritchie. 1975. *Male/female language.* Metuchen, N.J.: Scarecrow Press.

Lakoff, Robin. 1975. *Language and women's place.* New York: Harper and Row.

Parvey, Constance F. 1974. The theology and leadership of women in the Old Testament. *Religion and sexism.* Edited by Rosemary Radford Ruether. New York: Simon and Schuster.

Penelope, Julia. 1990. *Speaking freely: Unlearning the lies of the fathers' tongues.* New York: Pergamon Press.

Project on the Status and Education of Women. 1980. *Sexist bias and sociological research: Problems and issues.* Washington, D.C.: The Association of American Colleges.

Sadker, Myra Pollack, and David Miller Sadker. 1982. *Sex equity handbook for schools.* New York: Longman, Inc.

Spender, Dale. 1985. *Man-made language.* 2nd ed. London: Kegan Paul.

Stone, Merlin, 1976. *When God was a woman.* New York: Harcourt Brace Jovanovich.

Tannen, Deborah. 1990. *You just don't understand: Women and men in conversation.* New York: William Morrow.

Van Becelaere, Joan. 1980. Miriam, the prophetess: Exegesis of Numbers 12: 1–15. Unpublished paper. St. Louis, Mo.: Eden Theological Seminary.

Walker, Barbara G. 1983. *The women's encyclopedia of myths and secrets.* San Francisco: Harper and Row.

Wollstonecraft, Mary. [1792] 1975. *A vindication of the rights of women.* Boston: Penguin.

The Overvoice: Images of Women in the Media

Sharon Silvas with Barbara Jenkins and Polly Grant

This humanity is male and man defines woman not in herself but as relative to him; she is not regarded as an autonomous being. . . . She is defined and differentiated with reference to man and not he with reference to her; she is the incidental, the inessential as opposed to the essential. He is the Subject, he is the Absolute—she is the Other. (De Beauvoir 1972, xviii–xix)

She stands bewildered in the middle of the kitchen floor in front of a bucket of suds, mop in hand, upper body thrust forward and off balance by the high heels on her feet, totally straight-jacketed by the tight skirt wrapped around her legs. Modern woman fighting off the scourge of the earth—dirt! Flash of lightning, sound of thunder. She starts as Mr. Clean bounds into the room. The deep voice assures her that with the aid of his magic liquid, she can find salvation. Similar deep voices, too, tell her, and us, which toilet tissue is the softest, which fruit juice is best for her children, with which medication "Dr. Mom" can best save her family from the common cold, which soap powder to buy and where to buy it. And the voices assure her that by wearing the essence of the latest trendy perfume she can bring home the bacon as well as fry it up for her man.

Watching television and glancing through daily newspapers, magazines, advertisements, and brochures, one quickly notes that as the voice of God is male, so is the voice of the media in its many forms. And like religion, its liturgy has come to us through white male eyes. From where do these male voices of authority resident in our heads come? The misogyny of our civilization is so rampant, so insidious, so very engineered, that even these innermost voices in our heads, these voices of authority, are male.

The popular culture of the various forms of media is a primary example of one of the "gender defining" institutions (Sapiro 1990) Jodi Wetzel addresses in the introduction to this book. And it is by no mere coincidence that the media are male and authoritarian. The media, in all their forms—advertising, radio, television, music, magazines, newspapers, and film—are merely a microcosm of our political, economic, and religious institutions that are white male dominated. It is a challenge to know and understand the perspective from which media messages are derived and designed.

Literacy as Political Control

How important are the media? Are they merely entertainment? Insignificant? Think back to the typical movie rendition of a small county undergoing a military coup. What is the aggressor's first move? Taking over control of the newspapers, the television, and

Silvas, Sharon with Barbara Jenkins and Polly Grant. 1992. "The Overvoice: The Image of Women in the Media." Printed by permission of the authors.

the radio so that they can broadcast the news of the junta, get into the homes, the minds, and the hearts of the people with their propaganda and assert their new authority.

Before the twentieth century, in the United States and throughout the world, women, children, and the common folk (also indentured servants, slaves, and others deemed incompetent) had no access to media. The elite male rulers of the town, state, country, and church also had the only access to education. Not only were women not allowed, in some cases, to pray, but they were not even allowed to learn to read the prayers. Literacy also has always been a function of class, and until recently only the upper classes were able to obtain the skills with which to read and write.

While mass education is available in the United States today, it is estimated that 20 percent of the women in this country are still functionally illiterate. This handicap keeps them from economic self-sufficiency and forces them to remain in the welfare system or working in minimum-wage, female-intensive occupations (*Colorado Woman News*, May 1992).

The power of the media in the United States is no different from that of other male power-based military-run countries throughout the world. A glimpse at the wide range of media—film, television, radio, newspapers, magazines and advertising, and the entertainment industry—indicates that women are as a rule either possessed or possessions. Even after many years of outrage by feminist activists who have talked directly to local stations, national networks, and local and national print media, these institutions are still overwhelmingly owned and operated by white males. We continue to see our society reflected back at us from the mirror of both news and entertainment through the perceptions of white males. From industry to industry, this control has remained static.

"All the News That's Fit to Print," by Those Fit to Print it

The 1970s were the days when women sat in the balcony, not only in the balcony at church or synagogue—so as not to contaminate or disrupt the men—but in the all-male National Press Club. Nan Robertson, a Pulitzer Prize-winning former reporter with *The New York Times* has vividly described what life was like for the women who worked at that paper in her book *The Girls in the Balcony* (1992). She covers the biographies of early women reporters, but she also leads us through the awakening and maturation of the women's civil rights movement at *The New York Times*, a newspaper thought to be the most liberal of presses.

Robertson outlines how the women employees of *The New York Times* gave management (100 percent male) a five-page letter signed by fifty women on the news staff setting out in dramatic detail the sorry lot of women workers at a newspaper whose public image—whose image of itself—was that of a liberal and benevolent institution. The letter pointed out that there was not one woman executive on the paper's masthead. There was not one woman among the vice presidents, nor any in a position to aspire to a vice presidency. Two of the three women in top editorial positions, the editor and deputy editor of the family/style department, were in jobs traditionally held by women with a staff overwhelmingly made up of women. Only the third woman, the head of the foreign news desk, was in a position traditionally held by men. The statistics were outrageous. There were forty women reporters to 385 men reporters, and eleven of those women were in the family/style department. Of twenty-two national correspondents, not one was a woman. Of thirty-three foreign correspondents, only three were women. There was only one woman bureau chief. In the Washington bureau, with thirty-five reporters, only three were women; the number had not gone up in nine years, although the staff had nearly doubled in that time (Robertson 1992).

It was not just the written word, but the images, too, that men controlled. There were no women photographers. Men even had control of the entertainment section. Of thirty-one critics in culture news, only four were women. Reviewers of drama, music, movies, television, and books were all male. In sports there was one woman and twenty-three men. There were no women on the eleven member editorial board. There were no women columnists. Of the seventy-five copy editors, four were women. And most telling, almost all the lower-paying, lower-ranking jobs at *The New York Times* were confined to women. A breakdown of salaries showed compellingly that across the entire range of jobs at the paper, women with comparable education, ability, and years of service were paid less than men for doing the same work (Robertson 1992).

A Time for Change: Citizen Activism in Radio and Television

The situation of the women at *The New York Times* in 1972 is but one that has been all too frequent at most newspapers, magazines, and television and radio stations throughout the country. The 1970s also showed a good deal of citizen push for changes in the visual stereotypes of women and minorities in the media. Those in this battle knew that until the management changed, nothing in print or on the TV or over the radio would change.

In Colorado in 1977, the National Organization for Women (NOW) and a number of community activist groups representing African Americans, Latinos, and Native Americans were part of a national citizen campaign to improve the image of white women and people of color in the media. Their statewide study (Silvas 1977) found that at fifty-two radio and television stations in Colorado at that time over 95 percent of all management positions were held by white males. Filing the required documentation, an informal objection to deny the license renewal of forty-eight of the fifty Colorado stations, with the Federal Communications Commission (FCC), that body which regulates the electronic media, the group charged race and sex discrimination by forty-eight of the fifty stations, documenting the equal employment records of each station. Unlike newspapers, which anyone can print and distribute, airwaves are limited in number and are controlled by the FCC, which demands that owners leasing individual stations be responsive and responsible to the communities which they serve.

The Colorado stations' own reports showed that the majority of people in management positions—those who decide the who, what, when, where, and how that gets covered in the nightly news, in addition to public affairs and the local feature programs—were white males. They also showed the ghettoization of white women and people of color. White women were mainly employed in clerical positions; people of color in custodial jobs.

The Federal Communications Commission upheld eighteen of the objections made by this community activist coalition (Silvas 1977). What this action and others like it around the country meant was that stations had to seek out white women and people of color to fill sales and management positions. Doing so was critical. Management rarely comes from the faces we see on the screen—for example, the newscasters, who are considered the talent. Management in the electronic and print media industries is derived from the business side—beginning in sales. And management is where the decision-making begins, the process of creating what will eventually be printed, shown on the screen or heard over the air.

Each of these forms of the media, in turn, has had its worst days. Some are showing progress towards more inclusion of women and a broader representation of women of color, size, age, and physical ability. Some are not. Awareness of the underlying influences which seem to normalize these industries is critical to understanding the far-reaching impact they have on our culture.

Film: Madonnas, Whores, Bimbos, Psychotics, and Bitches

According to statistics printed in the April 2, 1992, issue of the *San Diego Women's Times,* many inequities exist for women in the movie business.

- Percentage of Screen Actors Guild *earnings* that goes to women: 32.5
- Of *actors with top billing,* percentage that were women in 1920—57; in 1990—18.
- Percentage of *female screenwriters* at major studios in 1982—17; in 1987—15.5
- *Amount they made* for every male writer's dollar in 1982—73¢; in 1987—63¢.
- *Average annual salary of female directors* today is $40,000; male directors is $85,000.
- *Percentage of feature-film roles* that went to men: 71.
- *Studio with the most female executives:* Columbia (38 percent); the least (tie) Disney and Tristar (23 percent).
- *Age after which actors begin making more than actresses:* age 10 (29)

For the most part, the short history of film has offered a limited range of women characters. These portrayals have mostly been little more than a stereotypic reflection of the times. With nearly a century of movie making to review, we can trace women's roles from days in which there were strong characterizations of independent, bright, useful, and honest women, to other days of dumb blondes, dizzy redheads, and dangerous, destructive brunettes.

We can also trace their evolution from the 1930s when they were tough, savvy women to the 1990s women in jeopardy films where they are victims of demented villains. Crime and violence play a major part in all the entertainment in our country. With few exceptions, when women have been the instigators of crimes, and when they have committed the crimes themselves, they have been shown to be the absolute devil incarnate. In fact, if a woman is strong enough to defend herself, her family, or her values, or weak enough to commit a crime as men do, it is most often not enough that she has done it in self-defense, or that she is guilty. She has no redeeming value.

Most recently, films are showing both this traditional view, as in *Fatal Attraction* (1990), in which an inherently evil woman seduces her prey, and the totally new twist of bravada and macha in *Thelma and Louise* (1990). Of *Thelma and Louise, Time* magazine said: "Women cheer the movie because it finally turns the tables on Hollywood which has been too busy making movies about bimbos, prostitutes, vipers, and bitches and glamorizing the misogynists who kill them to make a movie like *Thelma and Louise*" (Schickel 1991, 54).

Men have, for the main, been the writers, producers, directors, and distributors of film. What we see is their view of women. Because men and women may view the world, no less the world of film and entertainment, differently, it is only recently as women's roles in the industry have expanded somewhat, that we have begun to see some change.

The number of women directors in Hollywood is increasing. *Ms.* magazine reports that women directed only fourteen feature films between 1940 and 1980 but twenty-three out of the 405 features made in 1990. Ally Acker, a filmmaker, lecturer, and author of *Reel Women: Pioneers of the Cinema, 1896 to the Present,* notes "an interesting trend in recent women's films—male protagonists" (Acker 1992, 65). She points out that in the three years previous to 1992, nine films made by eight women directors centered around a male character. These include *Prince of Tides* by Barbra Streisand, *The Doctor* by Randa Haines, *Big* and *Awakenings* by Penny Marshall, *Staying Together* by Lee Grant, *Dogfight* by Nancy Savoca, *Rambling Rose* by Martha Coolidge, *Little Man Tate* by Jodie Foster, and *A Dry White Season* by Euzhan Palcy. Acker explains, "One reason [for the glut of male protagonists] may be that if a woman director can prove herself marketable in a world where most scripts are about men and targeted to a young male audience, she may have a wider array of choices later" (1992, 65).

Whatever the sex of the director, typical women's roles, such as the "mother" are most often maligned. According to an article in *The New York Times* entitled "Saint to Sinner: Movie Moms Are a Tough Act," by Jim Koch, movie mothers fall into certain stereotypic categories starting with Paragon Mothers—movie mothers at their most idealized, full of love and wise counsel, who hold the family together through good times and (more often) bad. These have been played by Irene Dunne in *I Remember Mama* (1948); Katharine Hepburn in *On Golden Pond* (1981); Sally Field in *Places in the Heart* (1984); and Brenda Fricker in *My Left Foot* (1989).

Then there have been the Bad Mothers—those who have made their children's lives miserable. These mothers' sins include domination, coldness, excessive closeness, abandonment, mania, ambition, and abuse. In many cases, mothers are the cause of psychological problems. Prime examples are Mrs. Bates in *Psycho* (1960), Faye Dunaway's portrayal of Joan Crawford in *Mommy Dearest*, Anne Ramsey in *Throw Momma From the Train* (1987), and most recently, Kate Nelligan in *The Prince of Tides* (1991). Torn mothers who deal with the choice between motherhood and career are Meryl Streep in *Kramer vs. Kramer* (1979), Shirley MacLaine in *Postcards from the Edge* (1990), and Julie Kavner in *This Is My Life* (1992). Other stereotypes of mothers include Mobster Mothers, Sacrificing Mothers, Mothers-in-law, and Mother-Daughter Triangles (*The New York Times,* May 10, 1992).

Though women as producers and directors are being welcomed by some viewers, the film industry itself does not deal comfortably with anyone who attempts to alter time-honored stereotypes. Stephen Spielberg found accolades lacking for his film production of Alice Walker's book *The Color Purple,* and while Barbra Streisand's *The Prince of Tides* took Oscar honors, Streisand herself was overtly ignored.

Even with good material, Hollywood usually comes up lacking when the film is left to interpretation and direction by men. In spy or detective thrillers, for example, Kathleen Turner's portrayal of the Chicago private detective, *V.I. Warshawski* (1991), we get yet another somewhat bimboish, stereotypically attractive blonde. The only difference is that she is punched out on the screen just as the men in that kind of role are punched out.

Advertising: The Exploitation of Women

"Suppose an archaeologist of the future dug up women's magazines and used them to judge American women. What would they think of us—and what can we do about it?" (Steinem 1990) Steinem's feminist manifesto outlines just how well controlled by men advertising is. In addition, it is controlling not only of the lives of women in our culture but of the major media designed for women. Appropriately, her critique appears in an article in the first issue of the newly formatted, sans advertising, *Ms.* magazine (1990). In this article, Steinem, the founder and former publisher of *Ms.*, describes the longstanding illicit affair between the advertising industry and mainstream women's media. While advertising agencies and product manufacturers think twice before interfering with the integrity of the separation of editorial and advertising departments in the male-oriented newspaper and magazine industry, this interference has been common in women's magazines such as *Redbook, McCalls, Ladies Home Journal, Vogue,* and *Cosmopolitan.* In this industry, this unhealthy relationship is called "selling editorial." Promising to cover, editorially, advertisers' products taints the story content, sometimes adding to it, oftentimes editing out offensive perspectives. It leaves the control of editorial copy in the hands of the advertisers.

In example after example, Steinem points out the insidiousness of this industry-accepted fact of life and notes how it sucked the lifeblood from the original *Ms.* magazine when its management tried to make changes. She says:

> If *Time* and *Newsweek* had to lavish praise on cars in general and credit General Motors in particular to get GM ads, there would be a scandal—maybe a criminal investigation. When women's magazines from *Seventeen* to *Lear's* praise beauty products in general and credit Revlon in particular to get ads, it's just business as usual. (Steinem 1990).

The negative image of women in the media has ranged from merely showing "body parts"—legs for stockings, lips or eyes for makeup, derrières for jeans—to using women and sex to sell everything from cars to washing machines to tools.

Most ads tend to unjustly portray women as little more than objects of desire, says Jean Kilbourne, an authority on advertising and the media. "These images are wounding us," says the Wellesley College scholar in the article, "Sex Sells in Advertising, but Conveys Wrong Images," by Gary Rhodes (*Rocky Mountain News,* April 12, 1992). Even though critics have lobbied for years to erase female stereotypes from TV commercials, Kilbourne says the problem remains. "Nowhere is sex more trivialized than on TV." Her examples include a Pantene shampoo ad that notes that "If your hair isn't beautiful, the rest hardly matters." She also discusses a piece for Braemar sweaters featuring a young woman wearing a checked sweater vest with the accompanying headline: "Phoebe chose to work, not because she had to, but because it gave her a place to wear her Braemar sweaters." Kilbourne points out how ludicrous this headline is in a society where two incomes are most often a necessity if a family is to maintain a middle-class standard of living.

Advertising also promotes youth and sets up negative images of women aging. Models gracing the covers of most women's magazines are not even twenty years old. Fashion advertising has set up a religious fervor for thinness—having perhaps a major impact on the severe health problems of bulimia and anorexia nervosa.

While the majority of mass communications advertising continues to view women as sex objects, pieces of furniture, and fembots (female robots), a few pioneering advertising campaigns have, at least, begun to confront real social issues. McDonald's has used seniors on its employee lines in advertising. Sportswear manufacturer Benetton and beer manufacturer Anheuser Busch have both taken on campaigns targeting political concerns. Benetton has used controversial topics such as abortion rights in its ads campaigns. Anheuser Busch has shown people with disabilities in its advertising campaign (Gibbs 1992).

Music and MTV: The Most Explicit Sex Sell

"Metaphors describe the penis as a gun, a knife, a sword, a steel rod, a pipe; the vagina is a cake to be cut, or butter to be sliced; ejaculation is the act of shooting the gun; and semen consists of bullets." [Stuessy, telephone interview] Gore 1987, 88)

In the 1970s, the rock group The Rolling Stones outraged feminists with the a Hollywood billboard promoting its album *Black and Blue* showing a woman chained and bruised all over. They have not changed, going on to make record albums title *Stupid Girl* and *Under My Thumb*.

A casual glance through the album covers at any record store shows that sex sells records, and not merely suggestive sex or intriguing or alluring sex, but nasty sex, mutilating sex, bloody sex, pornographic images not related to an X-rated adult store, but easily accessible to youth. Rap music, according to some, is perhaps the worst example.

Tipper Gore notes how such rock musicians as Sting, singer Smokey Robinson, and others point out the movement in popular music toward explicit sexual themes. She says "This 'auditory pornography,' as Smokey Robinson calls it, has become a tempting appetizer on the abundant menu of pornography offered in the United States—one that is being fed to younger and younger audiences" (Gore 1987, 82). Many popular music idols of the young now sing not only about ordinary heterosexual intercourse, but about masturbation, rape, incest, bondage, and sexual violence.

Promoting this music, for the most part, are male singers and groups, but some women have joined them, perpetuating violent and lewd images of and towards women. Gore quotes Michael Goldberg's description in *Rolling Stones* magazine of the image Madonna presents in concert:

"Madonna was a sweaty pinup girl come to life. She wiggled her tummy and shook her ass. She smiled lasciviously and stuck out her tongue. She rolled around on the stage and got down on her knees in front of a guitarist. And when she raised her arms, her scanty see-through blouse also rose, revealing her purple brassiere. . . . What Madonna is really about is sex, and there was plenty of that." (Gore 1987, 84–85)

Madonna is merely cashing in, literally, on what has become the major theme of television music videos, MTV. *Dancing in the Dark: Youth, Popular Culture, and the Electronic Media* (1991) refers to a paper presented by Barry L. Sherman and Joseph R. Dominick entitled "Guns, Sex, and Rock and Roll: A Content Analysis of Music Television" (1984). About videos they say: "The sexual emphasis is pervasive: a study done several years ago indicated that over three-quarters of rock videos depicted sexual intimacy, and over half of all women in videos were dressed provocatively" (Schultze et al. 1991, 195). Feeding the hunger of some young men and women, Madonna and her imitators flaunt sex, sex, sex. While there is some thought to Madonna's business savvy, her independence, and the obviously self-possessed persona in her music, she, too, promotes the image of woman as sex object.

Some women, however, are changing the image of women in music. Beginning in the lesbian community, Olivia Records and other small, woman-owned companies have promoted such singers as Meg Christian, Cris Williamson, and Holly Near. Heralded at women's music festivals and promoted at women's conferences, these often politically radical and talented musicians have sometimes crossed over into mainstream music. These women are transcending typical male stereotypes and bringing an entirely new vision of women to music.

While these changes in music are encouraging, the downside of this new and growing industry is that like most women-owned ventures, it is greatly undercapitalized and finds difficulty in competing with mainstream music for a competitive share of the entertainment dollar.

Comedy: Feminists Have No Sense of Humor

The majority of stand-up comics are young men who poke fun at racism and sexism as well as at homophobia and the plights of people with disabilities. Any night at a local comedy club will bring forth revelry from the audience, too, as they laugh at one joke after another about the prowess of male anatomy. The more virulent and misogynistic the comedian, the more powerful and famous he may become, like the popular comedian Andrew Dice Clay.

Female comedians now appear in comedy clubs but have been more widely seen in television situation comedy. Comic female characters have ranged from Lucille Ball in *I Love Lucy* and Jean Stapleton in *All in the Family* to the female comedians in *Designing Women* and Candice Bergen in *Murphy Brown*. Through scripts for these shows, we have begun to get a glimpse of the female comedian making strong political statements in the tradition that men have for a long time.

With Roseanne Arnold, who has gone from riding the circuit of backwater town bars and comedy clubs to her prime time television sit-com, *Roseanne,* we catch the flavor of what women's humor is all about. *Roseanne,* more than anyone, has caught the average working woman in the funnybone, the way Linda Lavin did years ago with her diner-waitress routine in *Alice*. There is an empathy, a sympathy for women in these shows. They are reflective of the little bit of change that has come about as a result of more women in broadcasting, both at the creative and at the corporate management levels. As Barbara Ehrenreich states, referring to the fact that Roseanne works in a factory and acts as an independent wife, "Roseanne gave working class feminism a force" (Gibbs 1992, 53).

Cartoons

Let us not forget the world of the pen and ink fantasy, the everyday comics that do more to attack our sense of what's right with the world than actually make us laugh. The misogyny of the comic strip is readily apparent. Even a superficial perusal of the Sunday comics can be illustrative. The butt of most jokes is the dumb woman, wife, sister, girl-friend, or that woman who seems to take it all—the mother-in-law.

The common stereotype of the cartoon is the image of the dumb woman standing in the doorway of her home surrounded by new purchases. Off scene we have the bubble of her husband yelling, "I suppose the checkbook is overdrawn again!" Or, the husband, dressed in black-tie, is pacing up and down waiting for the little woman, who is still primping, late again. Of course she has overdrawn her checkbook. Women still earn 79 cents for every dollar men make. Of course she is late. Before she could get ready, she had to give the kids dinner and baths, pick up the babysitter, and settle everyone else for the evening. Her time isn't her own; it belongs to everyone else—her husband, her children, and her boss.

Among the new and refreshing cartoons is "Sylvia," created by Nicole Hollander. With commentary on everything from fashion disaster to sexual harassment to child care to abortion rights, Hollander and a few good women are giving vent to our political and life frustrations.

SYLVIA   Release Friday   by Nicole Hollander

"Sylvia." © 1991 by Nicole Hollander. All rights Reserved. Reprinted with permission of Nicole Hollander.

Pornography: The Eight Billion Dollar Question

Sex is simultaneously potentially liberating and potentially oppressive (Bell 1987, 150).

Contemporary pornography both reinforces and draws strength from the patriarchal ideology which fosters women's domination, and as the most blatant example of sexism in media, pornography is an industry worth over eight billion American dollars, with more outlets than McDonalds (Bell 1987, 162).

In her essay, "Pornography: What Do We Want," Susan Cole asserts that

[Pornographers] are making sexuality look pretty much one-dimensional, the definition of male fused with dominance and the definition of female fused with submission. They are making inequality sexy. (Bell 1987, 160)

Like Susan Cole, many feminists assert that pictorial pornography not only perpetuates the objectification of women but it makes that objectified relationship between men and women desirable. Through the lens of a camera, individual women are turned into sexual parts: long legs, huge breasts, and black tangles of hair covering sexual organs.

These parts are made into images which then are bought and sold to be used at the whim of the male consumer. Once a woman is no longer human but instead a collection of sexual parts which only exist in images, she loses equal footing. Once the norm for a sexy (and sexual) woman becomes a dismantled woman, dehumanization and suppression of women in real life gain a stronghold.

Mass production of images of women as simply a collection of parts reinforces the idea that women are commodities which can be dismembered, bought, owned, used, and sold, and further undermines the individuality and humanity of each woman. Not only is pornography a graphic illustration of the way women have traditionally been treated by patriarchy, pornography perpetuates the belief that dismantling and objectifying women is socially acceptable.

Women's sexuality, seen only through parts, becomes something to be owned and coveted in the same way a desired possession would be. As a mere collection of parts, woman-images in pornography become easy to abuse. These images may be beaten, drugged, shipped, chained, raped, cut, and actually killed. Through these images, the dehumanization of women is complete, for male consumers may assume the image itself has little to do with a real woman.

However, in order to obtain complete satisfaction, the male consumer must believe, at least in part, that the woman-image finds sexual fulfillment in violence. Hence, the popular pornographic images show women bound, gagged, and chained, and yet smiling with a sexually inviting look through submissively lowered eyelashes. Male consumers can believe that their ownership and abuse are actually a response to a genuine desire from the root of female sexuality, that at the heart of female sexuality is the need to be raped and controlled, no matter what female minds or mouths say.

In *Pornography: Men Possessing Women* (1989), Andrea Dworkin says that the sexually degrading use of the female allows the male consumer to experience violent violation as pleasure because women beg for it, and cannot become truly sexually fulfilled without it (1989). Forced sex, then, is really *not* forced because the inner sexual nature of women desires violent sex. This interpretation illustrates the powerful virgin/whore dichotomy: women say no, but really mean yes; they profess that they do not like violent sex, but, in reality, they need it to become fulfilled sexual beings. This, too, is the heart of the control men hold over women in a patriarchally structured society. Men know what women want better than women do. Therefore, women have a need to be controlled, and men have the right to control women as possessions, to decide what is best for them, and to act upon their decisions freely without female consent. Or as Mariana Valverda says, "If you exchange sex for money, then you are saying something about the value of sex" (Bell 1987, 154) and the value of women.

Conclusion

Susan Faludi, in her best-seller, *Backlash: The Undeclared War against American Women* (1991), treats in depth the media's fear and loathing of women. Pointing out the scare tactics based upon little or no accurate research on such wide subjects as the "man shortage," "biological clocks ticking away," and "Mommy tracks" for working women, Faludi's book is an excellent primer.

The backlash is overt in Faludi's examples. She piles them one upon the other in chapter after chapter until the impact of the whole is overwhelming. Misogyny and gynophobia are abundant. Covertly, the noose is tightened as well by those who control the media. What is *not* covered in news, features, and entertainment is just as much a statement of the white patriarchal ideology as what is covered. For instance, how often do we see examples of older women? Of lesbians? Of women of color? Of women with disabilities? Or of women who fail, overcome the odds, and rise to positions of self-sufficiency? Where are our role models? Where are the stories of the women who have championed our civil rights over the past thirty years? Or of those who championed them in the seventeenth, eighteenth, and nineteenth centuries?

Awareness of the media and its money being used by, for, and in the interest of patriarchal institutions is a key element in the struggle for social change. Critical thinking skills are crucial to an analysis of the media which leads to action; to the re-valuing of people currently without power; to re-creating authentic, not stereotypical, news, entertainment, and advertising; and, perhaps, even to re-creation of erotica which is in the interest of women.

References

Acker, Ally. 1992. Women behind the camera. *Ms.* 2(5):64–67.

Bell, Laurie, ed. 1987. *Good girls, bad girls.* Seattle, Wash.: Seal Press.

De Beauvoir, Simone. 1972. *The Second Sex.* Translated by H. M. Parshley. New York: Alfred A. Knopf.

Dworkin, Andrea. 1989. *Pornography: Men possessing women.* New York: E. P. Dutton.

Faludi, Susan. 1991. *Backlash: The undeclared war against American women.* New York: Crown Publishers, Inc.

Gibbs, Nancy. 1992. The war against women. *Time,* March 9.

Gore, Tipper. 1987. *Raising PG kids in an X-rated society.* Nashville: Abingdon Press.

Kamen, Paula. 1991. *Feminist fatale.* New York: Donald I. Fine, Inc.

Penley, Constance. 1989. *The future of an illusion.* Minneapolis: Regents of the University of Minnesota.

Robertson, Nan. 1992. *The girls in the balcony: Women, men, and the new Times.* New York: Random House.

Schickel, Richard. 1991. Gender bender. *Time,* June 24.

Schultze, Quentin J., Roy M. Anker, James D. Bratt, William D. Romanowski, John W. Worst, and Lambert Zuidervaart. 1991. *Dancing in the dark: Youth, popular culture, and the electronic media.* Grand Rapids, Mich.: William B. Eerdmans Publishing Company.

Sapiro, Virginia. 1990. *Women in American society.* 2nd ed. Mountain View, Calif.: Mayfield Publishing Company.

Silvas, Sharon. 1977. *Informal objection to the Federal Communications Commission.*

Steinem, Gloria. 1990. Sex, lies, and advertising. *Ms.* (July/August):18–28.

Just Two Kinds of People in the World[1]

Julia Penelope

As resistant as some readers may be to the idea that our perceptions and descriptions of the world are specifically MALE perceptions and descriptions, consider what we know of history and which sex has been the most vocal and visible when it comes to *naming the world*. Patriarchal religions routinely claim that god gave *men* the "right" to name the world they perceived around them. Like Suzette-Haden Elgin,[2] I think the perceptions and descriptions of the world made possible by English would be vastly different if, in fact, women controlled the naming process. The world, too, would look quite different to us.

Men control naming, an important aspect of any language. What men notice and, therefore, name, is "real." First, men name whatever it is that they think needs labeling. The names, once chosen, set the boundaries on what will make sense to members of a culture. Once they've established the limits of what counts as legitimate commentary and what doesn't, various distinctions must follow as they protect the internal coherence of their discourse against evidence that contradicts their descriptions. Once men have brought something under their control by naming it, recategorizing it or renaming it becomes a difficult task, since most people seem willing to accede to the "what is" (and "is not") of patriarchal reality.

Sitting in a Denny's restaurant, I chanced to overhear the following exchange:

First waitress: " 'Cream and sugar.' Why do we say that? Why not 'sugar and cream?' "
Second waitress (to a third): "We say it because that's the way **they** named it!"

What caught my attention was the second waitress's absolute conviction that what the first waitress had asked was a NON-question; she clearly thought the first was stupid to

1. This section draws on the semantic analysis in my article, "Heteropatriarchal Semantics: 'Just Two Kinds of People in the World,' " in *Lesbian Ethics* Fall 1986: 58–80.

2. In *The Lonesome Node* January/February 1982: 3–4, Suzette Haden Elgin commented, after reading a series of papers by Stanley R. Witkowski, Cecil H. Brown, and Paul K. Chase on how things get named (lexicalization), that she believed that the vocabulary would be very different if women had done the naming. Granting that they are "exceptionally fine articles on what things get named in human languages and why they are named as they are," she said:

> After reading them several times, I realized that they offer the most extraordinarily MALE view of the lexicalization process! Not that I think they are wrong—on the contrary, given the dominance of males in language development, they are probably absolutely right. But I was fascinated by the fact that there is a quite different way of looking at their data.

question something so patently "obvious." Her voice was full of disdain as she affirmed the linguistic *status quo,* even though she might have realized, after a moment's reflection, that we **do** say "sugar and cream." Daring to question what "they" accept as "established" exposes the questioner to ridicule.

Nevertheless, we must challenge the descriptions of men's naming. The vocabulary of a culture, in this case anglo-american society, reflects just those ideas that the speakers believe are "real" and those distinctions that a majority consider to be "meaningful." In order for an utterance to make sense, to be heard as "English," the words and the relations among them must follow the PUD map of the world which most speakers believe to be true. One of the most crucial dichotomies that makes "sense" in English is that between "female" and "male." This allegedly biological (therefore valid) distinction is the defining feature that structures the semantics of English nouns that refer to human beings, and extends into the class of adjectives with several antonymous pairs, *womanly/manly, feminine/masculine, womanish/mannish.* This dichotomy makes sense to most speakers of English, and without it familiar portions of PUD would be exposed as meaningless.

Some adjectives seem to exist only because this society believes that biological sex is a conceptually "useful," that is, "meaningful," way to talk about human beings. Terms like *feminine/masculine, womanish/mannish,* are semantically symmetrical (paired), but conceptually asymmetrical. Socially, being "feminine" means something very different from being "masculine," and dictionary definitions of such terms reflect this asymmetry. To be "feminine" is to behave in "womanly" ways, while being "masculine" is to be a paragon of "manly" virtue (brave, honest, courageous). These paired terms exist only to define the limits of how women may act, while specific adjectives and their derivative adverbs further delimit "acceptable" female behaviors, for example, *appropriate, fitting, proper.* Whenever we hear or read one of these words, it warms us that the judgment it modifies derives it validity from heteropatriarchal values.

Adjectives like *femininity and masculinity* set limits on what is "permissible" appearance and behavior for women and men. Their **meaning** maintains male dominance. Patriarchal semantics equates femininity with femaleness and masculinity with maleness, assuming that biological sex determines behaviors and personality traits. On the basis of that equation, PUD stipulates that only feminine women and masculine men are "valuable." This is not, however, a "separate but equal" dichotomy. It serves an idealized hierarchy in which anything conceived to be male, and, therefore, masculine, is more highly valued than whatever is assigned to femininity/femaleness. The most abstract, highest level in this hierarchy is called *humanness,* but its qualities aren't generic; the qualities attributed to maleness, and described as *masculinity,* are also understood to be the standard by which one's "humanness" is judged.

These two cultural spheres determine how individuals and our behaviors are valued. What is labeled "masculinity" is the ideal of what it means to be **human;** the female who embraces the femininity forced on her by the patriarchal construct is, by definition, **subhuman.** Femininity is made to seem attractive to women because the only other known alternative is to act "like a man," which is to place oneself in the category deviant, and, therefore, "bad." The patriarchal feature hierarchy, with its resulting valuations, places women in a classic "double bind"[3]: women who act "like women," who display "feminine" behaviors, are devalued and trivialized; women who refuse to learn such behaviors are perceived as "like men," and ridiculed because they aren't "real women." Women who try to live out PUD values don't qualify for "personhood," and those who behave as they wish are non-women. Either way, men stigmatize us.

The misogyny that stipulates femininity as inherent in being female simultaneously devalues it as a "human" attribute; masculinity is the human norm, but, because femininity is normal for women, we're "abnormal" if we show behaviors attributed to maleness. If we act human, we're deviant. Positively valuing attributes explicitly devalued and described as inferior keeps women bouncing back and forth within the extremes of the dichotomy. There's no way for a female to live by the patriarchal rules and be considered "good." The words *masculine* and *feminine* exist because they provide descriptions essential to the maintenance of patriarchal reality. But the existence and continual use of these words doesn't mean that they denote real or actual things. In order to understand how such terms function, we need to examine the semantic relations among the terms that make them seem "meaningful."

Diagram 1 presents the basic semantic dichotomy of the patriarchal world of English and its logical structure. It represents an important piece of the semantic system called "consensus reality," a way of visualizing how this portion of semantic space functions in our long-term memory, a picture of the grid patriarchy imposes on our experiences. (Note: I use words rather than abstract semantic features at each level.)

Speaking Freely			
LEVEL	CATEGORY	FEATURE	
		+ MALE	− MALE
I	BIOLOGICAL	MALE	FEMALE
II	FUNCTIONAL (Breeders)	MAN FATHER	WOMAN MOTHER
III	BEHAVIORAL	REAL MAN MASCULINE MANLY	REAL WOMAN FEMININE WOMANLY
		WOMANISH	MANISH

DIAGRAM 1. Patriarchal Semantics

---

3. Gregory Bateson was the first to describe "the double bind" in "A Theory of Play and Fantasy," where he identified a message, 'This is play,' as "a negative statement containing an implicit negative metastatement," comparable to Epimenides' paradox, "This statement is untrue." He interpreted the sentence 'This is play' to mean something like, 'These actions in which we now engage do not denote what those actions *for which they stand* would denote" (1972, 180) [His emphasis]. In "Epidemiology of a Schizophrenia" (1972, 194–200), he linked such messages to a case of schizophrenia in which the patients' mother habitually reclassified messages: "An endless taking of the other person's message and replying to it as if it were either a statement of weakness on the part of the speaker or an attack on her which should be turned into a weakness on the part of the speaker; . . ." (199). In "Toward a Theory of Schizophrenia," co-authored with Don D. Jackson, Jay Haley, and John H. Weakland, this moebius-like communication process was called the "double bind" (1972, 120–27).

Diagram 1 reflects what being born a woman or man means in PUD. These terms are the cultural filter through which we learn to perceive ourselves and others as we move and act in the world. The essential dichotomy that gives this grid its meaning is the much-touted sexual dimorphism of *homo sapiens* [sic!]. That is, the species is described as having two sexes, which differ from each other in primary and secondary sexual characteristics.

Sexual dimorphism is the foundation of patriarchal semantics, politics, and personality. Biological sex dictates personality, according to this universe of discourse. Biology determines behavior, mannerisms, appearance, emotional style, what one wears, and how one thinks. This is a monocausal ideology. Sexual dimorphism is the reproductive strategy for numerous species, but it's neither necessary, inevitable, nor biologically superior to other reproductive methods, as many believe. Species in addition to our own reproduce parthenogenetically (lizards, fish, seagulls, and some plants). Only men seem to be obsessed with their reproductive capacity, as though they'd invented and perfected it. Contrary to popular thinking, it's not at all obvious that biological sex or reproductive potential is the basis of personality. One might just as well posit the position of constellations with respect to the earth at the time of one's birth as the source of personality, as patriarchal astrology does.

Heterosexuality doesn't appear in Diagram 1 because it's assumed in PUD. An individual is assumed to be heterosexual unless proven otherwise; the assumption of heterosexuality is so strong that it overrides all contradictory evidence, no matter how vehemently asserted. The logic of patriarchy assumes that heterosexuality **necessarily** follows from sexual dimorphism. The possession of genitalia of a specific kind is believed to necessitate its use in a specific way. In common terms, this assumption is expressed as the "Stick-in-the-Hole Theory of Behavior," or "Function Follows Form": (1) Men have penises, women have vaginas; (2) penises exist to be stuck in vaginas. This primitive explanation, that form dictates function, and its corollary, that use follows from potential, are essential to the illusion of coherence in PUD. That which is assumed, primary, and implicit is difficult to contradict. Heterosexuality and its "naturalness" aren't supposed to be questioned. If you doubt this, put a bumper sticker on your car, bike, or skateboard that says, "If Abortion is a crime, Fucking Should be a Felony." A female's right to terminate a pregnancy is open to question; the necessity of heterosexual coitus (fucking) isn't.

The leftmost, vertical portion of Diagram 1 divides patriarchal semantic space into three discrete levels: BIOLOGICAL, FUNCTIONAL, and BEHAVIORAL. The internal logic of PUD posits an **entailment** relation between each level: Given that one is born either MALE or FEMALE, it follows that one is either MAN or WOMAN in FUNCTION (*father* or *mother*). From this functional description, it follows that one's BEHAVIOR will necessarily be "appropriate" to one's FUNCTION and BIOLOGY, *masculine* or *feminine*. If one happens to be born female, as a majority are, then one is also necessarily a woman and, being a woman in this patriarchal culture, one is also **necessarily** "feminine" and "womanly." This entailment relation makes *female* and *feminine* synonymous in English; "being feminine" is used as though it meant "being a woman." The meaning of being a female in the u.s. **is** being *feminine*. A female who is not feminine is an unacceptable contradiction in male terms.

At the BEHAVIORAL Level (III), I've placed the most commonly used adjectives that describe the behaviors attributed to each sex. The significance of the +male/–male dichotomy and the rigidity with which PUD maintains it is explicit in two ways. First, I've included "real men" and "real women," which both presuppose the existence of "unreal men" and "unreal women," that is, "queers." In usage, these phrases assume the accuracy of the entailments among Levels I, II, and III. If one is female, then one must be a heterosexual and a breeder, and behavior in appropriate, "feminine" ways. If she doesn't, if she fails to symbolically enact (and validate) the entailments of Level II or III in some way, she isn't a "real woman." She's "something else" because she contradicts the logic of the patriarchal semantic system.

Second, the importance attached to these semantic features is exposed by the final pair of adjectives, *womanish/mannish*. In PUD, both words signal a feature negation (or "violation") within the system. A man described as "womanish" is behaving in some way thought to be *like a woman*, "unmanly." He may cry when he's angry, frustrated, confused, or grieving; he may cross his legs at the knee; he may bend from the waist to pick something up off the ground. Whatever he's done, he has acted inappropriately according to the patriarchal semantics. Likewise, a woman described as "mannish" has negated the feature dichotomy by "crossing the line." She may be aggressive or withdrawn; she may wear her hair "too" short; she may be "too" tall, or weigh "too much"; she may take large steps instead of small ones; she may not smile at men. Whatever the specific behavior interpreted as a violation of her category, the attribute of *mannish* is intended to be both an insult and a warning: Don't go "too far," or you're "out." Semantic violation becomes semantic exclusion; semantic exclusion becomes social exclusion.

Patriarchal semantic space is so well maintained that the attempts of some Feminists to introduce "androgyny" or "gynandry" were bound to fail. First, both terms validate the MASCULINE/FEMININE dichotomy they're intended to replace. If two distinct kinds of behavior didn't exist, one reserved for men, the other for women, there would be nothing to combine. Without the preexisting distinction, no fusion would seem possible. Second, gynandry (or androgyny), as proposed by such Feminists, operates only at Level III, the BEHAVIORAL. They were concentrating on personality traits, habits of behavior, as described by patriarchal conceptual structure. But substituting a combined idea, 'androgyny', did not disturb or challenge the entailment conditions between the levels, and it certainly didn't affect the perceptual foundation, sexual dimorphism. Finally, promoting change within the system would work only if one started at Level I, and infiltrated Level III by establishing different entailment conditions between the levels. But this strategy, too, is blocked by the adjective pair, *womanish/mannish*. The derogation of those terms interrupts attempts to blur the distinction carried by *feminine/masculine*.

Words exist and are created because they serve the values and attitudes central to a culture. Dictionaries record cultural meanings. Definitions of *womanly, mannish,* and *manly, feminine* and *masculine* from the *Random House Dictionary*[4] reveal the cultural values modifiers denote and perpetuate. As long as women use these words as though they describe something real or explain observable phenomena, we lend credence to the idea that people can and should be characterized by the dichotomy they represent. As one could predict, the "real meaning" of each word is revealed in the definition of its opposite.

---

4. Although it was first published in 1960, I chose to use the definitions provided by the *Random House Dictionary* because, where other dictionaries rely on our experience and knowledge of social mores to infer which behaviors are "appropriate," "fitting," and "proper" for women and men, *RHD* is explicit.

womanly—like or befitting a woman; feminine; not masculine or girlish. *Womanly* implies resemblance in appropriate, fitting ways; *womanly decorum, modesty.*

manly—having the qualities usually considered desirable in a man; strong, brave; honorable; resolute; virile. *Manly* implies possession of the most valuable or desirable qualities a man can have, as dignity, honesty, directness, etc., in opposition to servility, insincerity, underhandedness, etc. It also connotes strength, courage, and fortitude.

feminine—pertaining to a woman or girl: *feminine beauty, feminine dress.* Like a woman; weak; gentle.

masculine—having the qualities or characteristics of a man; manly; virile; strong; bold; a deep, *masculine voice.* Pertaining to or characteristic of a man or men; *masculine attire.*

mannish—applies to that which resembles man: . . . Applied to a woman, the term is derogatory, suggesting the **aberrant possession of masculine characteristics.** [My emphasis]

The qualities listed under *manly* and *masculine* are the "good" things an individual might wish to be: strong, brave, determined, honest, and dignified. Not a single one of the negative qualities commonly attributed to maleness are listed here: aggressive, violent, narrow-minded, self-centered, defensive, easily threatened, domineering, penis-obsessed, intrusive, predatory, immature, dependent, energy-sucking, or territorial, egotistical, and war-mongering. In contrast, the adjectives *womanly* and *feminine* are not really defined. Look closely at the long list of characteristics in the definition for *manly* compared to the circularity of the pseudo-definition for *womanly*, "like or befitting a woman." That's not a definition; it assumes that we already know the behaviors that "befit" a woman. The real definitions for *womanly* are **implied** as "oppositions" to "manly qualities": "servility, insincerity, and underhandedness." Under *feminine*, we find two more adjectives, *weak* and *gentle*, but that's it. Positive attributes commonly associated with females, nurturing, kind, and loving, have been omitted, exactly the "feminine" traits that some women want to "reclaim." But those didn't make it into the *RHD* descriptions.

Most speakers of English accept as "fact" the descriptions forced by this semantic structure. They assume that the descriptive limits of English are, in fact, the limits of reality. One is or is not a man. This assumption was expressed in a television advertisement for a magazine, **Savvy,** aimed at a female audience: "You don't have to be *like a man* to succeed in business. You can allow yourself *to be a woman."* The opposition of *woman* and *man* in the ad accepts the idea that members of both sexes are utterly different, assumes as givens the descriptive adjectives for both sexes omitted from the *RHD* definitions, and implies that being "like a man" is an undesirable thing for a woman, even if she wants to "succeed in business" (a "man's world").

But PUD dictates that "being a woman" cannot be a "good thing." What isn't apparent in Diagram 1 is the equation of "feminine" and "childish" behaviors described by Otto Jespersen. This equation turns up in other places where it isn't as obvious. Consider, for example, paired phrases like "jock itch"/"feminine itch," "adult supporter" (jock strap)/"feminine apparel" (underwear), or the euphemistic "adult movies," "adult bookstore," both of which refer to **male** pornography. Such examples reflect the equation of

[+male] with 'adulthood', and the corollary notion that women, because [–male], are non-adult ("childish").

When we consider the definition for *mannish*, "the aberrant possession of masculine characteristics," the idea of a woman who is honest, strong, dignified, forthright, and brave is revealed as negative. Men have reserved the positive attributes for themselves. Women are implicitly defined as "appropriately" weak, gentle, insincere, servile, and underhanded, and any woman who is honest, forthright, dignified, brave, or resolute is "aberrant," that is, *mannish*. PUD dictates that those born female who reject the dichotomy, who refuse to behave in feminine, "appropriate" ways, will be labeled "masculine" by semantic default. This semantic trick makes it seem as though the adjectives describe behavior accurately, but their existence maintains patriarchal consensus reality at the cost of the individual's integrity. These words will become obsolete just as soon as speakers, especially women, realize such words name culturally valued behaviors, not inherent, biological attributes, and stop using them. Our continued use validates these descriptions.

Unlearning to Not Speak

Marge Piercy

Blizzards of paper
in slow motion
sift through her.
In nightmares she suddenly recalls
a class she signed up for
but forgot to attend.
Now it is too late.
Now it is time for finals:
losers will be shot.
Phrases of men who lectured her
drift and rustle in piles:
Why don't you speak up?
Why are you shouting?
You have the wrong answer,
wrong line, wrong face.
They tell her she is womb-man,
babymachine, mirror image, toy,
earth mother and penis-poor,
a dish of synthetic strawberry icecream
She grunts to a halt.
She must learn again to speak
starting with *I*
starting with *We*
starting as the infant does
with her own true hunger
and pleasure
and rage.

Piercy, Marge. 1968. "Unlearning to Not Speak." In *Circles on the Water*. New York: Random House. Reprinted by permission of Random House.

The Classroom Climate for Women

Bernice R. Sandler

The obvious barriers that for so many years stood between women and equal educational opportunity are largely gone. Today, female students can enter academic institutions and fields of study of which their mothers and grandmothers could only dream. Yet, like society as a whole, the academic world is still infected with attitudes that can militate against achievements by women. Thus, although women may now attend most of the same colleges and universities that men do, and be taught in the same class by the same faculty, the female student's classroom experiences are likely to be less positive than her male peer's.

The problem is that although most faculty want—and, indeed, try—to be fair, faculty of both sexes tend to treat female students quite differently from male students. In a variety of subtle ways (often so subtle that neither the professor nor the student notices that anything untoward has occurred), faculty behavior can convey to every student in the room the implication that women are not as worthwhile as men and that they are not expected to participate as fully as men in class, in college, or in life.

These findings were reported in 1982, when the first comprehensive report on the classroom climate for women students was published by the Project on the Status and Education of Women (PSEW) at the Association of American Colleges. Based on a review of the literature, as well as campus and individual reports, the paper, entitled *The Classroom Climate: A Chilly One for women?* by Roberta Hall and the present author, identified over 30 ways in which faculty treated female students differently from male students. Following the publication of the report, some campuses began to pay attention to this issue by disseminating the paper to their faculty, conducting seminars and workshops, and undertaking related research. Nevertheless, both formal and informal information relayed to PSEW indicate that this remains a major problem across the country.

Some of the behaviors observed in the study are so small that they might be considered trivial. They do not happen in every class, nor do they happen all the time, and as isolated incidents, they may have little effect. But when they occur repeatedly, their cumulative effect can damage women's self-confidence, inhibit their learning and classroom participation, and lower their academic and career aspirations. (See, for example, El-Khawas, 1980.)

The behaviors fall into two categories: ways in which female students are singled out and treated differently, and ways in which they are ignored. Some examples:

- Professors tend to make more eye contact with men than with women, so that male students are more likely to feel recognized and encouraged to participate in class.

Sandler, Bernice R. 1987. "The Classroom Climate for Women." In *The American Woman 1987–88: A Report in Depth.* edited by Sare E. Rix for the Women's Research and Education Institute. New York: W. W. Norton & Company. Reprinted by permission of the Women's Research and Education Institute and W. W. Norton.

- Professors are more likely to nod and gesture, and, in general, to pay attention when male students are talking. When women talk, faculty are less likely to be attentive; they may shuffle papers or look at their watches.
- Professors interrupt female students more than male students, thus communicating, at least in part, that what women have to say is less important than what men have to say. Moreover, when a male student is interrupted, the purpose is generally to expand on what the student is saying. Faculty interruptions of a female student, however, often consist of remarks unrelated to what the student has been saying—such as comments on her appearance—that have the effect of bringing her discussion to a halt.
- Female students are not called upon as frequently as male students, even when the women are clearly eager to participate in classroom discussion, again suggesting that what men have to say is more important than what women have to say.
- Male students are called by name more often than female students, as if men had more individual identity than women.
- Women are more likely to be asked questions that require factual answers (e.g., "*When* did the revolution occur?"), while man are more likely to be asked higher-order questions (e.g., "*Why* did the revolution occur?"). Such behavior may subtly communicate a presumption that women are less capable of independent analysis than men.
- Male students are "coached" more than female students by faculty probing for a more elaborate answer (such as, "What do you mean by that?"). This gives male students an advantage, since probing not only encourages students to speak and develop their ideas, but also implies that they know the answer if they will just explain it more fully.
- Faculty are more likely to respond extensively to men's comments than to women's comments. Women's comments are more likely to be ignored or to receive an ambiguous "uh-huh." Often, when a point made by a female student elicits no response, the same point made subsequently by a male student elicits a positive response from the professor, who gives the male student approval and credit for the point as if it had not been raised previously. Thus, men receive much more reinforcement than women for intellectual participation.

Why should these behaviors occur? Many certainly have their origins in patterns and attitudes established long before students and faculty reach the college classroom. A major underlying reason is that throughout our society, what women do tends to be seen as less valuable than what men do.

Numerous experiments have demonstrated that devaluation of women occurs. (See, for example, Paludi and Bauer, 1983; Paludi and Strayer, 1985.) A typical experiment involves two groups of people. Each group is presented with several items, such as articles, works of art or résumés, and asked to evaluate them. The items shown to each group are identical, but those items ascribed to women for one group are ascribed to men for the other. The results of these experiments are remarkably consistent: if people believe a woman was the creator, they will rank the item lower than if they believe it was created by a man. Both men and women devalue those items ascribed to females. Studies of how people view success shows a similar pattern: both men and women tend to attribute males' success to talent, females' successes to luck. (See, for example, Erkut, 1979.)

Thus, female students can be just as well prepared, just as articulate, and just as willing to participate in discussion as their male peers, and still receive considerably less attention and less reinforcement from faculty than do male students. No wonder women students generally participate less in class than men!

The subtle behaviors described above are by no means the only factors that chill the classroom climate for women. Faculty remarks that overtly disparage women are still surprisingly prevalent. PSEW staff continually receive reports of such remarks. So is sexual harassment, which is experienced by 20 to 30 percent of all female students. The campus surveys in PSEW's files confirm these figures. The relatively small percentage of women on most faculties means that female students typically have fewer role models, less opportunity to benefit from mentoring, and less opportunity for informal talk with faculty (male faculty are more likely to engage in those conversations with male students). And there is a widespread lack of structural support for women's concerns: on many campuses there is no women's center at all; on many others the centers are inadequately funded. There are too few programs for reentry students (among whom women substantially predominate); there are still too few women's studies courses, and those that exist too often receive only limited support, if not denigration. All of these factors communicate to female students that although they have been allowed inside the gates, women are still outsiders in the academic world.

How Cruel Is the Story of Eve

Stevie Smith

How cruel is the story of Eve
What responsibility
It has in history
For cruelty.

Touch, where the feeling is most vulnerable,
Unblameworthy—ah reckless—desiring children,
Touch there with a touch of pain?
Abominable.

Ah what cruelty,
In history
What misery.

Put up to barter
The tender feelings
Buy her a husband to rule her
Fool her to marry a master
She must or rue it
The Lord said it.

And man, poor man,
Is he fit to rule,
Pushed to it?
How can he carry it, the governance,
And not suffer for it
Insuffisance? °
He must make woman lower then

So he can be higher then.
Of what cruelty,
In history what misery.

Soon woman grows cunning
Masks her wisdom,
How otherwise will he
Bring food and shelter, kill enemies?
If he did not feel superior
It would be worse for her

And for the tender children
Worse for them.

Of what cruelty,
In history what misery
Of falsity.

It is only a legend
You say? But what
Is the meaning of the legend
If not
To give blame to women most
And most punishment?

This is the meaning of a legend that colors
All human thought; it is not found among animals.

How cruel is the story of Eve,
What responsibility it has
In history
For misery.

Yet there is this to be said still:
Life would be over long ago
If men and women had not loved each other
Naturally, naturally,
Forgetting their mythology
They would have died of it else
Long ago, long ago,
And all would be emptiness now
And silence.

Oh dread Nature, for your purpose,
To have made them love so.

Chapter 2—Understanding Gender-Shaping Institutions
Study Questions

1. "Language constructs reality." What does this mean and what is its effect on women? Why is it an important factor in upholding the patriarchy? Discuss the issue of the double bind for women in reference to Penelope's "Just Two Kinds of People in the World." How does it perpetuate the devaluation of women?

2. What are some of the underlying factors that make women's education unequal to men's?

3. Historically, there have been barriers to research by women and about women. What is the patriarchal viewpoint that has perpetuated these barriers? What is the impact on women?

4. Do you agree that women are the better researchers of women? Why?

5. How did Bishop C. L. Meyers justify his stand against women as Episcopalian priests? What social and political factors in women's lives reinforce his viewpoint?

6. Sheila Collins states, "Theologies rise out of a cultural context." What does this mean? How has this emergence through culture affected women's status?

7. Silvas, Jenkins, and Grant see media as the "overvoice" of sexism. In their article they state that "pictorial pornography not only perpetuates the objectification of women but makes that objectified relationship between men and women desirable." Define *objectification of women*. Do you agree that pornography is an underlying cause of violence against women? Why or why not?

8. In the same essay, the authors state, "Men know what women want better than women do." In what context is this statement made? What does it say about our society as a "rape culture"?

9. Talk about the politics of exclusion within mainstream media. What purpose does it serve? What are the reasons for its perpetuation? Discuss the availability of role models in the media based on race and class issues.

10. Penelope states that: "Sexual dimorphism is the foundation of patriarchal semantics, politics, and personality." Discuss the inflexibility of this phenomenon and the idea of gender roles as socially constructed. Focus on "your own" versus "patriarchal" reality.

11. Compare and contrast bell hook's "Talking Back" with Marge Piercy's "Unlearning to Not Speak."

12. In the context of Sandler's "The Classroom Climate for Women," discuss in depth, in small groups followed by large group, examples of:

    a) the ways women are singled out and treated differently;
    b) the ways women are ignored.

    Observe and note examples you and others have experienced in the classroom. Use your critical thinking skills to uncover the subtle (perhaps unintentional) ways women are devalued. (Note: Sexist classroom treatment is the norm and your teachers are used to behaving that way. As Sandler points out, both male and female instructors use these tactics.)

13. What are some of the other factors that contribute to women's feelings of being on the outside in academe?

14. Using "How Cruel Is the Story of Eve," discuss religion as a patriarchal institution in which language constructs reality. Also, does myth become reality? Have many women been responsible for perpetuating these myths? If so, how? If not, why not?

PART TWO

WOMEN'S WELL BEING

3

REDEFINING WOMEN'S HEALTH

Annette Bennington McElhiney

The preceding essays demonstrate how language, education, religion, and the media shape concepts of gender. In a similar way, patriarchal attitudes have defined women negatively in terms of their bodies and reproductive functions. As early as the fourth century B.C., Aristotle in *On the Generation of Animals* described women as "being as it were a deformity, though one which occurs in the ordinary course of nature" (4.6.461). Centuries later, Freud expanded on women's less than normal status when he proposed his theory of penis envy. Cartoons in the nineteenth century often portrayed women as "walking uteruses." And even in twentieth-century studies of mental health professionals, only a few of them described a healthy individual in feminine terms. This chapter will suggest briefly how women's physiological processes and health issues have come to be defined and controlled by men and how, in the present and future, *thinking* women can redefine and control their own health throughout their life cycles.

This chapter and the following essays, documents, short stories, and poems will also suggest certain questions:

- What factors shape definitions of *whether* or *when* a woman is healthy or unhealthy during adolescence?

- Why do feminists believe women's control of their own bodies is such a fundamental issue?
- What issues or concerns about health have separated white women from women of color? wealthy women from poor women? lesbians from heterosexual women?
- How does *feminist-defined health* differ from *women's health* as defined by the dominant culture?
- How has technology improved women's health? or hindered women's health? How could the use of technology be more responsive to women's health needs?
- Are women controlling their own health any more effectively now than they did in the past?
- Has increased knowledge about women's physiological systems assisted women in being healthier today than they were in the past?
- How does personal experience, race, class, status, ethnicity, religion, educational level, sexual identity, politics, and physical make-up affect women's health?
- What specific characteristics of the U.S. health delivery system contribute to women's health or detract from it?

Genetic Similarities and Differences

Traditionally, men and their bodily processes have been seen as normal, women's bodies and their processes as deviant from men's. Yet genetically the opposite phenomenon occurs. Both male and female embryos start out with the same internal embryonic cells or the gonads, the progenitors later of eggs or sperm. Only the presence of either a y chromosome for males or another x chromosome for females determines whether the embryo remains female and develops ovaries, a uterus, and a clitoris or whether it becomes male and develops testes and a penis. Any time prior to birth, even if a y chromosome is present, should the necessary hormones imprinted on the y chromosome not be released, an embryo may not develop either the internal or external organs of a male even though it is genetically male (Sloan 1985). Hence, theoretically, both males and females start out female and only the differentiation from genetic instructions on the y chromosome results in the formation of a male. Yet ironically, our patriarchal culture defines male physiology as normal and female physiology as abnormal; herein lies many of the problems concerning attitudes and issues in women's health throughout their life cycle: adolescence, young adulthood, and the mature years.

Adolescence: Menstruation

At puberty when young women experience menarche, their first menstrual period, often their feelings about themselves undergo a marked change. Most women remember where they were and how old they were when they had their first menstrual periods. Even though this event may have been greeted as a sign of "growing up," often friends and family heralded it as "the curse" or something which doomed young women to impaired lives. In contrast, to males—especially Jewish males, who celebrate coming of age with religious ceremonies such as a bar mitzvah—few young women and their families celebrate their coming of age. Instead of celebrating publicly, often families shroud menstruation in secrecy and shame causing young women themselves to consider menstruation something that should not be discussed. In contrast, the Navajo, a native American culture, have always celebrated menarche with a ceremony, the kinaalda, designed to ensure the holiness and effectiveness of sexual relations that will be possible as a result of the menarche thus insuring the continuance of the tribe (Delaney, Lupton, and Toth 1988). In Navajo culture, unlike mainstream American culture, menarche represents a joyous occasion worthy of public celebration.

However, the idea that women are "unclean" during menstruation has occurred worldwide and throughout time (Hays 1964; Delaney, Lupton, and Toth 1988). Often in tribal cultures, women were isolated during this period and not allowed to participate in the everyday activities of their villages. In so-called more civilized cultures, like the Hebrew, customs forbade women from having physical contact with others because of their unclean state. This ban was justified in Biblical edicts such as those in Leviticus 15:19–21

> And if a woman have an issue, and her issue in her flesh be blood, she shall be put apart seven days; and whosoever toucheth her shall be unclean until the evening.

> And every thing that she lieth upon in her separation shall be unclean: every thing also that she sitteth upon shall be unclean.

And whosoever toucheth her bed shall wash his clothes, and bathe himself in water, and be unclean until the even.

In pre-twentieth-century England, folktales suggested that menstruating women would sour the milk if they continued their milk maid duties. Even though twentieth-century America considers itself more enlightened, the media uses the "menstruating woman as dirty" concept when it advertises douches and various products to combat that "smell" which emanates from the normal physiological processes of a woman's body.

At the end of the twentieth century, partly as a result of women health educators, many women understand menstruation not as unclean, but as a cleansing process itself—that is the sloughing off of endometrial tissue (lining of the uterus) that occurs when an egg is not fertilized. They recognize that no *one* description can describe their own menstrual cycles as each varies from another, yet may be entirely normal for a given individual. They also recognize that certain emotional and physical changes may occur as a result of hormonal changes in the levels of estrogen and progesterone during each menstrual cycle. Nonetheless, women often feel extreme embarrassment if they are prone to heavy menstrual bleeding and blood stains their outer garments.

Premenstrual Syndrome (PMS)

Throughout time, myths have existed suggesting a tie between women's physiological cycles and their behavior. For example, particularly in the nineteenth century, the concept of the "psychology of the ovaries" suggested that a woman's mood, sexual behavior, and general demeanor were governed by the presence and function of her ovaries.

Myths about the psychological impact of premenstrual syndrome (PMS) reflect the supernatural power of this earlier ideology. A 1984 conference called Ethical Issues for Research on Biological Factors Affecting the Capacity for Responsible Behavior generated a book entitled *Premenstrual Syndrome: Ethical and Legal Implications in the Biomedical Perspective*. Essays in this book suggest some of the questions that acknowledging PMS may raise (Ginsburg and Carter 1987). For example, if some women actually do experience judgment which *could* be considered impaired immediately preceding their periods, should they be held legally responsible for their behavior? Or should they be excused from inappropriate or criminal behavior because they have PMS? The logical trap is that even though a few *rare* women may indeed be impaired, the majority are not. But excusing women for their behavior premenstrually may reenforce the false belief that women should not be in powerful positions because once a month their judgment will be rendered unreliable. Therefore, women must understand the double bind they may find themselves in if they attribute changes in their behavior to PMS. They may recognize that some women do experience certain conditions like water retention, acne, nausea, headache, depression, swollen breasts, and mood fluctuations premenstrually, but should not be trapped into attributing their level of performance to such physiological changes in their bodies.

Dysmenorrhea

Another negative stereotype about women's health concerns pain during menstruation (dysmenorrhea). Sometimes health practitioners oversimplify and tell women that their pain is psychosomatic and culturally induced as a result of messages women get from other women and their culture in general (Boston Women's Health Collective 1984; Sloan 1985; Gannon 1985). Researchers still disagree about why some women experience pain, but they recognize that causes may be categorized as spasmodic or congestive and alleviated accordingly.

Prescribed Feminine Physical Images

In adolescence, and even before, females face considerable pressure to conform to a specific image dictated by the media and other cultural institutions. That image emphasizes being *thin*. Consequently fat becomes an evil, and many young women begin a vicious cycle of dieting to avoid it. Anorexia nervosa or the "starvation disease" primarily affects young women aged 15–30. This disorder begins as an obsessive fear of fatness, but may end in death, as it did with the death of pop music star Karen Carpenter in 1983.

In another eating disorder similar to anorexia nervosa, bulimia or bulimarexia, a person binge eats and then purges with either laxatives or vomiting. Those who have this disorder may be thin, of average weight, or heavy. The long term effects of this disorder range from minor problems like tooth decay, a constant sore throat, and dehydration to more serious problems like digestive disorders, esophageal disorders, and changes in potassium levels which may eventually affect both the kidneys and the heart.

Once again, definitions of women's health and beauty are being made by people other than themselves. If women let cultural prescriptions and the media dictate how thin they should be instead of assessing when excessive fat becomes unhealthy, they are allowing themselves to be evaluated according to a norm which is prescribed by a culture's definition of what is beautiful (being thin) rather than defining themselves as healthy women and beautiful according to their own standards.

Birth Control

The time in a woman's life cycle when society most attempts to control her health occurs during her adult years, especially if she is heterosexual. Lesbian women do not have the ever present fear of pregnancy as a result of their primary intimate relationships, but they do have the same fear as a result of rape or incest.

Cultural mores have always affected women's reproductive choices. For example, during the first century of the Roman Empire, a falling birth rate amongst upper-class couples dictated reproductive policies. For upper-class women, child bearing was part of their civic duty, and under the decrees of Augustus, a system of rewards and penalties was instituted to encourage women to have at least three children. Institution of this policy indicated that the state was well aware that women were in charge of both birth control and abortion through magical, chemical, surgical and mechanical means (Petchesky 1990). Prior to the twentieth century, in the United States, women attempted to control their reproduction through whatever means they could, none of which was completely reliable or safe. Their options included abstinence, pessaries (objects placed in the vagina to block the flow of sperm), cervical caps (the forerunner of the diaphragm), and douches. The condom, originally designed for protection against venereal diseases rather than as a contraceptive, consisted in the sixteenth century of a sheath made from linen. Later condoms were made from sheep's intestines. Not until the manufacture of rubber in the late nineteenth century were they widely available (Gordon 1976; Petchesky 1990).

In early twentieth-century America, birth control activists such as Emma Goldman and Margaret Sanger advocated women's right to use or not use birth control. They tried to educate women, particularly immigrant women, about forms of birth control and to convince them of the extreme importance of preserving their right to control the reproductive functions of their own bodies through whatever means necessary. Sanger's efforts did not extend to black women and, for this reason, some feminists like Angela Davis label her efforts at population control amongst people other than Indo-European immigrants as representative of both classism and racism.

In fact, access to both information about and products for birth control has been quite different for women of color and particularly African American women throughout U. S. history. During slavery African American women were often condemned to a lifetime of child bearing, frequently as a result of rape by the white master, in order to perpetuate the system of slavery. The price paid for female slaves in the slave market, the kind of work they did on the plantation, the kind of treatment they received, and the amount of food allotted to them were often determined by their ability to reproduce. Consequently, sterility for them meant something quite different than it did for white women or even immigrant women. Even as late as the 1950s, long after institutionalized slavery had ceased, some people actively sought to restrict the education of African American women about their own bodies so that those in power could control their reproductive lives. For example, if doctors or institutions thought certain individuals,

predominantly poor women and women of color, should not reproduce, they permanently sterilized them through removal of the ovaries (oophorectomies) or removal of the uterus (hysterectomies). In southern states like North Carolina and South Carolina, where women were frequently kept unaware of what tubal ligation or other gynecological surgical procedures meant, black women were sterilized without their permission (Davis 1981). As a result of this unique historical experience, black feminists view the right to bear children as equally important to the right not to bear children. Even though physicians also sterilized Native American women without their permission, they were reluctant to practice such procedures on white women. White feminists must remember this difference in historical experience and address both issues when fighting for women's reproductive rights.

Not only have availability of products and information about birth control been issues, but so has the issue of its legality. Prior to the twentieth century, controlling the size of one's family was left in the hands of women and was not considered illegal. In fact, to demonstrate the effectiveness of birth control amongst white women, between 1800 and 1900, the fertility rate decreased by half, falling from 7.04 to 3.56 children per woman (Petchetsky 1990). To combat this effectiveness socially an ideology much lauded by middle-class and upper-class white society in the nineteenth century promoted motherhood as sacrosanct (Petchetsky 1990).

In addition, as the practice of medicine became increasingly a male profession, formal and legal attempts were made to wrench control of reproduction from women and put it in the hands of male physicians and/or the state. After the

Civil War, the American Medical Association (AMA), an organization that did not admit a woman member until 1952, led the campaign to criminalize abortion and remove control of reproduction from women, especially midwives (Scully 1980; Corea 1985; Petchetsky 1990). In 1873 Anthony Comstock, president of the New York Society for the Suppression of Vice, proposed, promoted, and orchestrated the passage by the United States Congress of the Comstock laws (Gordon 1976; Corea 1985). These laws made the distribution of information about and the sales or purchase of birth control illegal. Not until the *Griswold v. Connecticut* case in 1965 were states prohibited from passing laws that interfered with a married person's right to privacy or to buying contraceptives. The *Eisenstadt v. Baird* case in 1972 prohibited states from interfering with a single person's rights to the same privacy.

Even the birth control available and the lack of earlier research to ensure women's safety reflect the control of reproduction by others than women themselves. Although the condom has always been available, and in the last decade of the twentieth century provides some protection against sexually transmitted diseases, the majority of birth control methods developed have been for use by women, not men: spermicide, diaphragms, cervical caps, sponges, intrauterine devices (IUDs), the pill, and the hormonal implant. In contrast, even though some research has been done on temporary methods of birth control for men—such as a sperm suppressing pill, self-immunization against sperm, bionyx controls (valves in the sperm duct that can be switched off and on), and a thermal method for temporary male sterilization (TMS)—few of these methods have been widely tested or promoted. Consequently, few men have suffered the ill effects of

insufficient, long-term research on birth control methods on themselves.

In contrast, contraceptives for women have often been promoted prematurely. While the diaphragm and most cervical caps and sponges seem quite safe and effective, some methods, in particular certain kinds of IUDs like the Dalkon Shield and earlier forms of oral contraceptives, were not safe. Some of the suggested ill effects of the early estrogen-only oral contraceptives were headaches, weight gain, sterility, uterine cancer, strokes, breast cancer, blood clots, and heart attacks (Boston Women's Health Collective 1984; Corea 1985; Petchesky 1990). Perhaps the most frightening aspect of birth control since the 1960s when it became readily available for most white, middle-class women is that various methods were often prescribed without knowing the long-term effects. Recent research indicates that while taking oral contraceptives in the past does not increase the risk of cardiovascular disease, "current use of oral contraceptive agents increases the risk of myocardial infarctions [heart attacks] especially among older women and cigarette smokers" (Stampfer et al. 1988, 1313). As for their effect on the incidence of breast cancer, the results are, at present, inconclusive.

Even though the dangerous effects of insufficient long-term research on oral contraceptives has affected predominantly heterosexual women, some lesbian women have had oral contraceptives prescribed for them for various reasons other than birth control, for example for heavy bleeding, dysmenorrhea, or endometriosis. Consequently, just as the issues of the right to bear as well as not to bear children should not be used to separate black feminists from white feminists, the issue of the importance of women controlling the safety of, and their access to, oral contraceptives should not be an issue that separates heterosexual feminists from lesbian feminists. And as long as the control of women's health during their adult years is in the hands of men who control the medical profession, drug companies, and patriarchal health-care institutions, none of these issues will be addressed as readily and thoroughly as they will if *all* feminists work together.

Abortion

The greatest controversy over women's control of their reproductive choices centers on abortion. Throughout history, women have aborted their pregnancies either with herbs which induced abortion or by mechanical means. Anthropological studies have shown that abortion was practiced by both the Greeks and the Romans and was considered legal. Later the Christian church questioned the practice, but did not interfere directly. However as the birth rate amongst white women declined in the late 1800s, both church and state became concerned. Even as early as 1828 in New York, statutes were enacted banning abortions after quickening (when movement of the fetus first occurs, somewhere between 16–20 weeks). By the late 1860s many states had such statutes, and by the 1880s, most abortions, except for those necessary to save a woman's life, were illegal throughout the United States. (Gordon 1977; Petchesky 1990). Out of necessity, women sought illegal abortions, often performed under unsanitary conditions that resulted in infection and sometimes death.

After the 1960s and the rise of the women's movement, pressure to abandon these laws increased. Finally in 1973, *Roe v. Wade* prohibited states from making laws that restricted abortion prior to the third trimester (before the twenty-fourth week). By 1989 public polls suggested that the majority of people in the U.S. thought that if a woman's health was in jeopardy, she should have access to legal abortion. Yet beginning in the late 1970s and continuing into the 1990s some groups and individuals still question the constitutionality of *Roe v. Wade,* possibly because of the resurgence of religious fundamentalism or the decline in child bearing by middle-class white women. However, if, as some political experts suggest, the U.S. Supreme Court allows individual states to make the decision regarding the legality of abortion and to dictate under what conditions, then poor women (often women of color or immigrants) in states that disallow abortion will be more vulnerable than middle-class women who may travel to states where they can get legal abortions. Therefore, as a last resort, poor woman may again be forced to seek illegal and unsafe abortions.

Pregnancy

Women should choose *when, if, how, where,* and *under what conditions* they will give birth. In nineteenth-century America, women gave birth at home where midwives or older women in the community presided and the mother delivered the baby. The method of payment was often informal or through traded services. However, as medicine became a more formal profession, men entered it in large numbers, and it became a lucrative business. When the process of child bearing was considered a potential market for medical practice, the field of gynecology and obstetrics developed and male physicians ran midwives out of business (Ehrenreich and English 1973; Gordon 1977; Scully 1980; Rothman 1980; Corea 1985; Petchesky 1990).

Childbirth, once removed from the expertise of midwives, was treated as a disease which needed to be controlled. The place of birth moved out of the home and into the hospital where a physician, generally male, presided. Instead of allowing the mother's body to set the pace, physicians defined the mother as an object upon which to practice certain obstetric procedures. The process of letting the three stages of labor and delivery evolve naturally was replaced by the options of induced labor, the use of forceps, and sometimes cesarean section. In addition, during delivery practitioners placed women in lithotomy positions (back flat, knees drawn up and spread apart by stirrups) and often gave them both painkillers and anesthetics. Sometimes the position was hazardous to the baby's oxygen supply and retarded the intensity of the woman's contractions. Also, frequently the overuse of drugs sedated the baby as well as the mother, and it needed help breathing after it was born. Often episiotomies (a surgical incision to the side of the back of the vagina to keep the tissue from tearing) were performed. However, some researchers suggest that this procedure was made necessary by the strain the lithotomy position put on the tissue and the inhibiting effect of the anesthetic on a woman's ability to push (Corea 1985).

In the 1970s, recognizing the increasing emphasis on childbirth being defined by and managed for the financial gain and convenience of doctors and hospitals, feminist health educators advocated a return to the earlier natural model of labor and delivery. Women's health centers catering specifically to women opened. Often these centers attached themselves to hospitals so that if additional resources unavailable at the center were needed during labor and delivery, women had access to them. Labor and delivery in these centers were less formal than in a hospital: the labor proceeded naturally and at its own pace through the three stages; the family was present; the woman often walked and remained active until the time of delivery unless conditions required otherwise; the woman was given few drugs and no anesthetics unless absolutely necessary, but was coached through the birthing process by a person of her choice; she gave birth not in the lithotomy position but in bed; and the baby remained in her room. In other words, the birthing process revolved around the comfort and needs of the mother and child rather than the control and convenience of health professionals and the hospital (Lichtman 1980; Michaelson and Alvin 1980; Eakins 1986).

As a result of the pressure placed on the obstetric and gynecological community by feminists, physicians have begun to question some of their earlier practices. For example, in 1987 in an article in the *New England Journal of Medicine,* a group of researchers compared the cesarean rates in nineteen different countries and determined that even though most industrialized countries have had increased incidence of this procedure, the United States had the highest rate. Per 100 hospital deliveries in 1981, the U.S. had a high of eighteen as compared to Czechoslovakia with a low of five (Notzon et al. 1987).

Yet another study reported in the *New England Journal of Medicine* in 1989 yielded interesting data about the socioeconomic differences in the rate of cesarean sections performed. As reported there, women with incomes of $30,000 had a cesarean-section rate of 22.9 percent as compared with a rate of 13.2 percent amongst women with incomes under $11,000. In addition, this study revealed that dominant culture whites had a rate of 20.6 percent primary cesarean sections; Asian Americans a 19.2 percent rate; African Americans a 18.9 percent rate, and Mexican Americans a 13.9 percent rate. Consequently, the researchers concluded that the rates of primary cesarean sections varied greatly in proportion to the income level of various groups and could not be accounted for by differences in maternal age, parity, birth weight, ethnic group, race or any complications of pregnancy or childbirth (Gould et al. 1989). This study suggests that perhaps the decision of performing a cesarean section may be determined more by the individual's ability to pay, either personally or through insurance, than by any medical reasons.

The medical profession has also begun to understand the importance of birth centers. In a study of eighty-four free standing birth centers in the United States, researchers found out of 11,811 women admitted for labor and delivery, 70.7 percent had minor complications or none and only 7.9 percent had serious emergency complications during labor and delivery or soon after. Only 4.4 percent of the women had cesarean sections. The researchers concluded that birth centers offer a safe and acceptable alternative to hospital deliveries as long as the women have low risk for complications and have already had children. They also concluded that such care led to fewer cesarean sections (Rooks et al. 1989).

Two situations occurring simultaneously complicate the reproductive choices of women at the end of the twentieth century. First, infertility is on the rise because of various factors, the use of certain early oral contraceptives, the delay in pregnancy until after age thirty-five, the negative results of illegal abortions, harmful environmental factors, and the after effects of certain sexually transmitted diseases. Second, tremendous technological advances in reproductive technology have made women's choices more complex legally and ethically than they have been previously.

Reproductive technologies such as the use of amniocentesis, a procedure used to determine the health of the fetus in utero; artificial insemination (AI), when a woman is artificially inseminated with a chosen person's sperm or donor sperm; and *in vitro* fertilization (IVF), when the egg is fertilized outside the woman's body are now available to those who can afford them. In addition, improved reproductive technology has made surrogate motherhood and *in utero* protection of the fetus controversial issues. However, with these improvements come increased challenges to women to rethink their options (Woliver 1989).

For example, because amniocentesis allows women the option of knowing the health of their babies prior to labor and delivery, they can choose either to continue or to terminate their pregnancies. In some ways, this knowledge presents extremely useful information, but it also makes the decision more complex (Rothman 1988; Rapp 1988; Woliver 1989). Should one refuse to give birth to a Down's Syndrome baby or to one who will be otherwise handicapped? And if so, what will be the emotional consequences of her decision? In addition, because amniocentesis determines the sex of the baby, parents can now decide whether or not to bear a boy or girl. Particularly in countries like China, where there is a limit of one child and men are valued far higher than women, procedures such as amniocentesis may increase the rate of abortion of female fetuses. While Americans think they have progressed beyond this sexist attitude, some people still prefer male children and, therefore, the same practice may occur.

115

A woman who cannot conceive by traditional methods may, with *in vitro* fertilization, have her egg removed from the ovary, placed in a dish, fertilized by either donor sperm or the sperm of someone of her choice, and returned to her uterus or in the case of surrogate motherhood to another woman's uterus, where it is implanted and brought to term. Because male practitioners usually control the process rather than the woman herself, the woman may begin to consider her body only a vessel or an incubator. In addition, because this procedure today costs approximately $4,000 per ovulation treatment, only those individuals with money will be able to reproduce by these methods (Boston Women's Health Collective 1984). Thus this procedure calls into question the issue of eugenics or controlling which women can or cannot have children. For example, poor women, many of whom are women of color, will not be able to afford this procedure.

At present, most *in vitro* fertilization has been done on or for heterosexual women or couples. Even artificial insemination (AI) or donor insemination (DI) is often not readily available for single women or lesbian women (Boston Women's Health Collective 1984). The issue again is that *all women* should have the right to control their reproductive lives, not just white, middle-class, heterosexual women. Perhaps our society fears lesbian women having access to AI, DI, and *in vitro* fertilization because becoming pregnant by these methods leaves men (except for the donation of sperm) out of the process.

Surrogate motherhood poses a problem for most women and particularly for feminists. One woman agrees to hire out her body for the sole purpose of carrying a baby for another. Not only does this practice reenforce the stereotype of a woman as a walking uterus, but it leaves the potential for real exploitation of some women by others, as portrayed in Margaret Atwood's futuristic novel and film *The Handmaid's Tale*. In this novel, women are categorized according to either their sterility or fertility; those who are fertile become the handmaidens or child bearers for the ruling class.

In addition, as in the celebrated case of "Baby M," for both the host mother and the client/mother, a plethora of questions may arise: What if one or both of the women later change their minds? What if the mother/client changes her mind and decides she doesn't want a baby? What if the baby has birth defects? (Boston Women's Health Collective 1984). For the child of a surrogate mother, additional questions may arise later such as which mother is the "real" mother: the surrogate mother or the genetic mother? So while these advances in reproductive technologies have brought opportunities to have children to women who could not have children by traditional means, they have also brought multiple questions personally, ethically, socially, and financially.

Fetal Rights versus Mother Rights during Pregnancy

Just as American society has become increasingly concerned with fetal rights versus the pregnant woman's rights in abortion, it has also become concerned with the rights of the fetus during pregnancy. The ethics committee of the American College of Obstetricians and Gynecologists has been exploring where the mother's rights end and the fetus's rights begin (Nelson and Milliken 1990). For example, if drinking alcohol, smoking cigarettes, and taking drugs negatively affect the health of the fetus, should a woman be legally prevented from doing them? Would it be ethical to jail an alcoholic pregnant woman until after she has given birth? Or should women who consume such substances while pregnant be charged with child abuse?

In a recent *New England Journal of Medicine* study, researchers reported that many states already have instituted laws protecting the fetus against illicit drug or alcohol use by mothers. Illinois and California have passed child abuse reporting laws that require a hospital to report to authorities any newborn who has a positive result for the presence of drugs. In 1989 Minnesota passed a law requiring health agencies to report any pregnant woman whose urine tests positive for drugs. Florida requires any woman with a history of drug or alcohol abuse to report her pregnancy to health authorities. Most studies have been done on patients using public rather than private facilities. Yet the Florida study, using women from both private and public facilities, revealed the use of alcohol and drugs as similar in both groups (Chasnoff 1990). Researchers in this study also suggested that private physicians seem more reluctant to report drug and alcohol abuse amongst paying patients than amongst welfare patients. Therefore, the potential for poor pregnant women, single women, and women of color being penalized more forcefully than white married women must be considered.

Other questions these studies raise are: If women have access to an abortion and choose pregnancy instead, should they be held legally responsible for taking drugs, smoking, and drinking alcohol? If, on the other hand, they do not have access to abortion, should they be held liable? Feminists suggest that if poor women are both denied access to public funded abortions and charged with child abuse because of their drug and alcohol habits the

question of choice is nonexistent. The ramifications of such are extremely misogynist. All women who are fertile could be subjected to these laws as often women with irregular periods do not even know if or when they are pregnant. And if fertile women always live in this state of potential pregnancy, the next step could be legally prohibiting all fertile women from smoking, drinking alcohol, or taking drugs because they either might be, or might become, pregnant at any time.

Pregnancy in the Workplace

Another reproductive issue facing women is how pregnancy affects their access to or treatment in the workplace. Since early in the twentieth century, states and the federal government have instituted labor laws supposedly to protect women in the workplace. In *Muller v. Oregon* (1907) sex was used as a reason for protective legislation and women were barred from working overtime because doing so might be harmful to their reproductive function. While harmful work or conditions should be avoided by pregnant women, one should question whether women should be barred from such work. In the case of many earlier labor laws, the very work that was deemed harmful for women was also the most highly paid work. Consequently, pregnancy or the potential for being pregnant was definitely a handicap for women in competing with men for certain, often high-paying, jobs. In the early 1990s, this same battle was fought between women working for Milwaukee-based Johnson Controls Inc., a company that makes auto batteries, and the courts. Some women suggest that if work presents unsafe conditions for fertile women, it does the same for men.

Other Health Issues Facing Women

Almost every woman at some time in her life will have one or another of the vaginal infections such as simple vaginitis, a monilial or yeast infection, or trichomoniasis. The normal discharge from the vagina is either clear or slightly creamy and somewhat slippery in consistency. This discharge should vary somewhat according to the menstrual cycle. In this somewhat acid environment, some bacteria normally grow. Yet if, for a variety of reasons, this environment is out of balance, a proliferation of organisms such as yeast and fungi may occur and the vaginal walls may become extremely irritated (Boston Women's Health Collective 1984; Sloan 1985).

Factors such as stress, use of oral contraceptives, irritation from intercourse or even pantyhose, too much douching, or use of feminine hygiene sprays may precipitate such an infection. To avoid vaginal infections, women should, despite advertisers' admonitions otherwise, be extremely careful of the products they use in their genital areas, avoid tight pants, wear cotton underwear, and use only water-soluble jelly for lubrication during intercourse.

Another common ailment that plagues women throughout their life cycle is cystitis or a urinary tract infection (UTI). Symptoms include frequent urination, burning, and sometimes both temperature elevation and back pain. Often a vaginal infection may lead to cystitis as a woman's very short urinary tract allows any bacteria to travel quickly up to and reside in the bladder. When a women gets such an infection, she should take *all* of the physician-prescribed medication because if an insufficient amount is taken, the infection may begin again or lay dormant and infect the kidneys or the ureters (tubes leading to the kidneys). Some women seem to be more prone to bladder infections than other women (Boston Women's Health Collective 1984; Sloan 1985). Often the same methods women use to avoid a vaginal infection will help avoid cystitis.

Sexually Transmitted Disease (STD)

Since the advent of oral contraceptives in the 1960s, increasing numbers of men and women have become sexually active. Fewer people use condoms, people have more sex partners, and the incidence of sexually transmitted disease has increased, particularly amongst heterosexual women with many sex partners. A virus, *herpes genitalis,* that attacks the mucous membranes of the genitalia has become more prevalent. Another disease transmitted by sexual contact is genital warts caused by the human *papillomavirus* or HPV which is similar to the virus causing common skin warts. This viral infection some researchers believe may lead to cervical cancer (Boston Women's Health Collective 1984; Sloan 1985). Yet, another kind of STD—chlamydial infection—may result in pelvic inflammatory disease (PID). All of these disease have slightly different symptoms and outcomes, but all seem to be on the rise (Boston Women's Health Collective 1984; Sloan 1985; Rinear 1986).

The important point for women to remember is that often these diseases affect their health in more profound ways than they affect the health of men. The after effects of such diseases as PID may include sterility. The continued presence of certain viral infections may predispose one to other more serious diseases. In addition, certain STDs may be passed on to newborns at the time of birth.

AIDS

Today women are being affected by autoimmune deficiency syndrome (AIDS) in increasing numbers. Although this disease started off as a disease of predominately gay males, that population accounts for only slightly over half the cases of AIDS today. Many heterosexual women contract the disease through either their unprotected sexual contact with HIV positive males or through exposure to contaminated blood through intravenous drug use. AIDS is contracted in lesbian women primarily through exposure to contaminated blood or needles rather than through direct sexual contact.

As in other sexually transmitted diseases, AIDS tends to affect all women more devastatingly because of several factors. First, often heterosexual women are unsuspecting about the possibility that their sexual partners have the disease. Consequently, if women do not require men to use condoms, they are risking exposure to the virus. Second, if women contract AIDS, statistics show that because they make less money than men, they are often unable to purchase the drugs that will prolong their survival. And finally, women can pass this deadly disease on to their babies.

Endometriosis

Endometriosis is a condition in which the tissue (endometrial) which normally grows inside the uterus grows outside the uterus on the ovaries, fallopian tubes, ligaments suspending the uterus, the exterior of the uterus, the bladder, and, rarely, on other parts of the body such as the lung. As this tissue builds, it bleeds whenever a woman has her menstrual period and often causes severe pain either during the period, ovulation, or sexual intercourse (Boston Women's Health Collec-

tive 1984; Sloan 1985). If a woman has no break in her menstrual periods, endometrial tissue may proliferate. In the 1950s and 1960s pregnancy was frequently recommended as a temporary solution. However, physicians no longer rely solely on such a temporary but drastic solution. Instead, they treat the condition medically, surgically, or naturally depending on the woman's preferences and her particular situation (The Boston Women's Health Collective 84). Lesbian women who chose not to have children may be at higher risk, but certainly have access to a variety of methods to control the condition.

The Mature Years

Both sexes go through a period in their life cycle called the climacteric (sometime between 45 and 55) when their bodies begin the accelerated process of aging. In women, ovarian production declines and eventually menstruation ceases. This cession of menstruation constitutes menopause. Menopause is not considered complete until a woman has not had a menstrual period for one to two years. For some women menopause occurs abruptly; they have menstrual periods one month and then have no more. For others, the process extends over a period of time varying from four to five years. Some women may begin the process before age forty and others not until after age fifty-five (The Boston Women's Health Collective 1984; Sloan 1985; Gannon 1985).

Myths and Realities about Menopause

Prior to the 1960s, before feminists began to study and redefine the various phases of women's lives, myths about menopause predominated. The idea that women's hormones controlled them gave vent to the stereotype of the "out of control" woman who was the victim of the violent fluctuations in her hormones. She was often portrayed as red-faced, stooped, shriveled up, and unattractive. This myth is linked to the same "psychology of the ovaries" myth mentioned earlier and the American culture's definition of beauty and sexual attractiveness as being young, slim, soft, tight-muscled, and vivacious.

For most women the only physical manifestations of menopause are: changes in the menstrual flow, vaginal changes, and hot flashes or sweating. First, as the hormonal levels of estrogen and progesterone shift, women begin to have fewer, shorter, heavier, or lighter menstrual periods. The nature of these changes varies just as the characteristics of different women's periods vary throughout their life cycles (Boston Women's Health Collective 1984; Sloan 1985; Gannon 1985). Between 1950 and 1978, physicians frequently told women, particularly insured women, that after menopause their uteruses were no longer useful; therefore they advocated hysterectomies to remove them and avoid later problems (Corea 1988). However, partly as the result of studies that found the rate of hysterectomies in the U.S. much higher than the rate in other countries, this practice has changed. Insurance companies now require a second opinion validating a serious reason for performing a hysterectomy before paying for such a procedure.

The second characteristic of menopause caused by fluctuations in the hormones estrogen and progesterone is the change in the vaginal walls which become thinner, less flexible, and less well lubricated; consequently, sexual intercourse may be uncomfortable. As a result of these vaginal changes, a woman may also be more prone to vaginal infections

(Sloan 1985; Gannon 1985; Dorris and Sirgil 1987).

Perhaps the most annoying physical characteristics of menopause are the hot flashes and night sweats which may accompany it. When these occur, the blood vessels near the surface of the skin dilate and constrict erratically. The actual body temperature changes little, but the capillaries close to the skin's surface change so that a flush appears on the skin of the upper body, generally the face and chest. This flush may be followed by a drenching sweat, particularly at night. Hot flashes may be triggered by a ringing phone or by no particular culprit, as when a woman is sleeping. The flashes may last only a few seconds or several minutes. Some women have these flashes for only a short period, others for years, and still others not at all. Often physicians, treating menopause as a disease, prescribe estrogen replacement therapy (ERT) which regulates the hormonal balance in the body. As a result, the vagina becomes lubricated again and the hot flashes stop (Sloan [1980] 1985; Gannon 1985; Dorris and Sirgil 1987). However, often as soon as a woman stops taking estrogen, the vaginal changes revert and the hot flashes begin again.

Researchers disagree on the long term effects of ERT for all women. In an editorial in *The New England Journal of Medicine*, Elizabeth Barrett-Conners, M.D. reports that a Swedish study showed a fourfold increase in the incidence of breast cancer in women after more than four years' use of estrogen plus a progestin, a recent additive to ERT. However, she also reports that other studies suggest that an estrogen-progestin regimen reduces the risk of breast cancer. She explains that the combination is necessary to prevent uterine cancer and has only been widely used in the U.S. in postmenopausal women since the l980s. She concludes that more research needs to be done on the relative benefits and risks of ERT, especially the estrogen-progestin regime, over a long period of time (Barrett-Connor 1989).

Other changes that may occur as a result of the drop in production of estrogen accompanying menopause are osteoporosis and insomnia. Women lose bone mass at this time. For that reason, many health providers suggest a diet high in calcium, exercise that helps strengthen bone mass, and possibly a calcium supplement. Also, just as some women may experience insomnia premenstrually, as a result of the fluctuation in hormones, some may experience insomnia with menopause. While not life threatening, this insomnia may lead to the irritability often stereotypically linked to this period in a woman.

Other Health Considerations for Mature Women

As women age, they face additional problems with high cholesterol, high blood pressure, heart disease, arthritis, and other problems commonly associated with aging. One of the particular considerations women face is that most of the research done on various diseases and their treatment has been done on men. Therefore, physicians do not always know how women's symptoms may differ or how they may respond to drugs or treatment. Before this situation will change, women must question their personal health-care practitioners carefully about their awareness of this problem and pressure their legislators to allot more money to research on women's diseases specifically and on how *any* disease, for example heart disease, may affect women.

Conclusion

All thinking women should take some responsibility for their own health and well-being across their life cycles. That means availing themselves of as much up-to-date information as possible about the body's physiological processes and seeking health care from professionals who recognize what redefining women's health means. That also means realizing that the health issues of *all women*—poor women, heterosexual women, lesbian women, and women of all colors—must be addressed. Active participation is necessary before women can be healthy by defining and controlling their own health throughout their life cycles.

References

Aristotle. 1943. *On the generation of animals.* Translated by A. L. Peck. London: Heineman

Atwood, Margaret. 1986. *The handmaid's tale.* Boston: Houghton Mifflin.

Barrett-Conner, Elizabeth, M.D. 1989. Postmenopausal estrogen replacement and breast cancer. *New England Journal of Medicine* 321(5):319–20.

Bergkvist, Leif, M.D., Ph.D, Hans-Olov Adami, M.D., Ph.D., Ingemare Persson, M.D., Ph.D., Robert Hoover, M.D., Sc.D., and Catherine Schairer, M.S. 1989. The risk of breast cancer after estrogen and estrogen-progestin replacement. *New England Journal of Medicine* 321(5):293–97.

Boston Women's Health Book Collective. 1976. *Our bodies, ourselves.* Boston: Simon and Schuster Inc.

———. 1984. *The new our bodies, ourselves.* Boston: Simon and Schuster Inc.

Chasnoff, Ira. J., M.D., Harvey Landress, A.C.S.W., and Marc E. Barrett, Ph.D. 1990. The prevalence of illicit drug or alcohol use during pregnancy and discrepancies in mandatory reporting in Pinellas County, Florida. *New England Journal of Medicine* 322(17):1202–6.

Cochran, Susan D., and Vickie M. Mays. 1989. Women and AIDS-related concerns: Roles for psychologists in helping the worried well. *American Psychologist* 44(3):529–35.

Corea, Gene. 1985. *The hidden malpractice*. 2nd ed. New York: Harper and Row.

Davis, Angela Y. 1981. Racism, birth control, and reproductive rights. In *Women, race and class*. New York: Random House.

Davis, Lisa. 1990. The myths of menopause. *Hippocrates* (May/June):52–59.

Delaney, Janice, Mary Jane Lupton, and Emily Toth. 1988. *The curse: A cultural history of menstruation*. 2nd ed. Urbana: University of Illinois Press.

Dorris, Paula Brown, and Diane Laskin Sirgal. 1987. *Ourselves getting older*. Boston: Simon and Schuster Inc.

Eakins, Pamela. Out-of-hospital births. 1986. In *The American way of birth*. Edited by P. Eakins. Philadelphia: Temple University Press.

Ehrenreich, Barbara, and Deirdre English. 1973. *Witches, midwives, and nurses: A history of women healers*. New York: The Feminist Press.

———. 1981. The sexual politics of sickness. In *The sociology of health and illness*. Edited by Peter Conrad and Rochelle Kern. 2nd ed. New York: St. Martin's Press.

Gannon, Linda R. 1985. *Menstrual disorders and menopause*. New York: Praeger Publishers.

Ginsburg, B., and B. Carter. 1987. *Premenstrual syndrome: Ethical and legal implications in a biomedical perspective*. New York: Plenum Press.

Goldsmith, Marsha F. 1990. Target: Sexually transmitted diseases. *Journal of American Medical Association* 264(17):2179–80.

Gordon, Linda. 1976. *Women's body, woman's right*. New York: Grossman Publishers.

Gould, Jeffrey, M.D., M.P.H., Becky Davey, M.S., and Randall S. Stafford, M.H.S., M.S. 1989. Socioeconomic differences in rates of cesarean section. *New England Journal of Medicine* 321(4):233–39.

Hays, Hoffman Reynolds. 1964. *The dangerous sex*. New York: Putnam and Sons.

Lieberman, Ellice, M.D., and Kenneth J. Ryan, M.D. 1988. Birth-day choices. *The New England Journal of Medicine*. 321(26):1825–26.

Lichtman, R. 1988. Medical models and midwifery: The cultural experience of birth. In *Childbirth in America: Anthropological perspectives*. Edited by Karen Michaelson. Massachusetts: Bergin and Garvey Publishers, Inc.

MacDonald, Nonie., M.D., F.R.C.P.C., George A. Wells, Ph.D., William A. Fisher, Ph.D., Wendy K. Warren, Ed.D, Matthew A. King, Jo-Anne A. Doherty, and William R. Bowie, M.D., F.R.C.P.C. 1990. High-risk STD/HIV behavior among college students. *Journal of the American Medical Association* 263(23):3155-59.

Michaelson, Karen, and Barbara Alvin. 1988. Technology and the context of childbirth: A comparison of two hospital settings. In *Childbirth in America: Anthropological perspectives*. Edited by Karen L. Michaelson. Massachusetts: Bergin and Garvey Publishers, Inc.

Mitchell, James, and Elke D. Eckert. 1987. Scope and significance of eating disorders. *Journal of Consulting and Clinical Psychology* 55(5):628–34.

Nelson, Lawrence J., Ph.D., J.D., and Nancy Milliken, M.D. 1988. Compelled medical treatment of pregnant women. *Law and Medicine*. Reprinted from the *Journal of the American Medical Association* 259(7):1060–66.

Notzon, Francis C., M.S., Paul J. Placek, Ph.D., and Selma M. Taffel, B.A. 1987. Comparisons of national caesarean-section rates. *The New England Journal of Medicine* 316(7):386–89.

Petchesky, Rosalind P. 1990. *Abortion and woman's choice: The state, sexuality, and reproductive freedom*. 2nd ed. Boston: Northeastern University Press.

Rapp, Rayna. 1988. The power of "positive" diagnosis: Medical and maternal discourses on amniocentesis. In *Childbirth in America: Anthropological perspectives*. Edited by Karen L. Michaelson. Massachusetts: Bergin and Garvey Publishers, Inc.

Rinear, Charles. 1986. *The sexually transmitted diseases*. North Carolina: McFarland and Company Publishers, Inc.

Rooks, Judith P. C.N.M., M.A., M.P.H., Norman L. Weatherby, Ph.D., Eurice K. M. Ernst, C.N.M., M.P.H, Susan Stapleton, C.N.M., M.S.N., David Rosen, M.P.H., M.P.A., and Allan Rosenfield, M.D. 1989. Outcomes of care in birth centers: The national birth center study. *New England Journal of Medicine* 321(26):1804–11.

Rothman, Barbara Katz. 1988. The decision to have or not to have amniocentesis for prenatal diagnosis. In *Childbirth in America: Anthropological perspectives*. Edited by Karen L. Michaelson. Massachusetts: Bergin and Garvey Publishers, Inc.

Seaman, Barbara, and G. Seaman. 1978. *Women and the crisis in sex hormones*. New York: Bantam Books.

Scully, Diane. 1980. *Men who control women's health: The miseducation of obstetrician-gynecologists*. Boston: Houghton Mifflin Company.

Sloan, Elaine. 1980. *Biology of women*. 2nd ed. New York: John Wiley and Sons.

Stampfer, Meir J., M.D., Walter C. Willett, M.D., Graham A. Colditz, M.B., B.S., Frank E. Speizer, M.D., and Charles H. Hennekens, M.D. 1988. A prospective study of past use of oral contraceptive agents and risk of cardiovascular diseases. *The New England Journal of Medicine* 319(20):1313–17.

Stroup-Benham, Christine A., M.A., and Fernando M. Trevino, Ph.D., M.P.H. 1991. Reproductive characteristics of Mexican-American, mainland Puerto Rican, and Cuban-American women: Data from the Hispanic health and nutrition survey. *Journal of the American Medical Association* 265(2):222–26.

St. Peter, Christine. 1989. Feminist discourse, infertility, and reproductive technologies. *NWSA Journal* 1(3):353–67.

Vogel, Lise. 1990. Debating difference: Feminism, pregnancy, and the workplace. *Feminist Studies* 16(1):9–32.

Wall, David, M.D., and Maureen P. Roos, M.D. 1990. Update on combination oral contraceptives. *American Family Physician* 42(4):1037–48.

Woods, Nancy Fugate, F.A.A.N., Ph.D., Ellen Olshansky, R.N.C., D.N.Sc, and Mary Ann Draye, M.P.H., A.R.N.P. 1991. Infertility: Women's experiences. *Health Care for Women International* 12:179–90.

Wolliver, Laura. 1989. The deflective power of reproductive technologies: The impact on women. *Women and Politics* 9(3):17–47.

Reproductive Rights
A Brief Chronology

National Organization for Women

Introduction	This chronology provides an historical perspective on women's struggle to gain their reproductive rights. It shows the changing theological, social, political, and legal attitudes toward birth control and abortion.
2600 B.C.	First recorded recipe for abortion-producing drug.
1850 B.C.	Three recipes for contraceptive pessaries recorded in the *Egyptian Petrie Papyrus:* one has a base of crocodile dung; another is a mixture of honey and natural sodium carbonate; the third is a kind of gum.
150 A.D.	Clement of Alexandria teaches that procreation is not merely good but sacred, and that therefore, procreation is the sole lawful reason for conjugal intercourse.
4th century A.D.	St. Augustine maintains that a male embryo becomes a human being forty days after conception, a female eighty days after conception. He expresses the mainstream position of Catholic theologians that although abortion is a sin it is not murder.
13th century	St. Thomas Aquinas teaches that, since body and soul unite to make a human being, there cannot be a human soul in a less than full human body. Therefore, early abortion is not homicide. He continues to uphold Church opposition to contraception as a sin against marriage, however.
1564	Italian anatomist Fallopius, for whom Fallopian tubes are named, publicizes the condom as an anti-venereal disease device.
1588	Pope Sixtus V issues a papal document stating that abortion and contraception are homicide at any stage of pregnancy. The prescribed penance is excommunication, with absolution available only from the Holy See.
1591	Finding this stance too harsh, and in conflict with previous practices and views, Gregory XIV recommends that "where no homicide or no animated fetus is involved, not to punish more strictly than sacred canons or civil legislation does."

"Reproductive rights: A brief chronology." In *Reproductive Rights Resource Kit.* 1981. National Organization for Women. Reprinted by permission of the National Organization for Women.

1798	British philosopher Malthus expounds theories of overpopulation and capitalist economics, holding that the numbers of people will grow geometrically while the resources to feed them grow only arithmetically.
1803	Great Britain makes all abortion a criminal act (a capital felony if induced by poison after quickening).
1821	Connecticut passes a law making it a crime for anyone to administer poison to a pregnant woman after quickening in an attempt to induce abortion. Early abortion remains legal.
1860s	States pass comprehensive, restrictive, criminal abortion laws, many of which remain in effect until 1973.
1869	Pope Pius IX states that all abortion is homicide and requires excommunication.
1873	Federal Comstock laws enacted prohibiting the mailing or distribution of information or devices for birth control and abortion.
1879	Margaret Higgins Sanger, the leader of the movement for birth control in the United States, is born.
1882	First "modern" birth control clinic in the world opens in Holland, sponsored by trade unions.
1913	Margaret Sanger arrested for violation of Comstock laws because she publishes birth control information in her magazine *The Woman Rebel*.
1916	Margaret Sanger and her sister Ethel Byrne jailed for dispensing contraceptive information at first birth control clinic in the United States.
1924	First scientific confirmation of women's ovulation and fertility cycle.
1930	Pope Pius XI calls any use of contraception "an offense against the law of God and of nature" which carries the guilt of grave sin. Intentional abortion of the fetus to save the life of the mother is not allowed.
1937	Federal Appeals Court rules Comstock Act unconstitutional in challenge brought by Dr. Hannah Stone and Margaret Sanger.
1942	Margaret Sanger's Birth Control Federation of America becomes Planned Parenthood Federation of America.
1956	Dr. John Rock and others develop birth control pill. Their research is funded by two women, Mrs. Stanley McCormack and an anonymous woman.
1962	Thousands of women found to be carrying severely malformed fetuses caused by the drug thalidomide, administered during the first trimester of pregnancy. One of these women, Sheri Finkbine, gains widespread sympathetic publicity in her search for an abortion, which she finally obtains in Sweden.

1965	Connecticut law against sale of contraceptives is declared unconstitutional by the Supreme Court in *Griswold* v. *Connecticut*, which finds that access to birth control for married couples is guaranteed by the constitutional right to privacy.
1967	Colorado becomes first state to liberalize harsh anti-abortion statutes enacted a century earlier.
	National Organization for Women makes repeal of criminal abortion laws a priority.
1968	Pope Paul VI issues encyclical *Humanae Vitae* restating traditional condemnation of artificial contraception and teaching that "every conjugal act had to be open to the transmission of life." Over 600 Catholic theologians issue challenge to the Pope.
1970	First major United States government involvement in the provision of birth control with the passage of the Family Planning and Population Research Act, administered in the Department of Health, Education and Welfare.
	Hawaii, Alaska and New York repeal criminal abortion laws and adopt substantially liberalized laws allowing abortion during the first trimester.
1971	National NOW Board condemns Vice President Spiro Agnew's statements that virtually recommend forced sterilization for welfare mothers and states that NOW "opposes governmental interference in the personal decision to bear or not to bear a child."
1972	Equal Employment Opportunity Commission issues guidelines prohibiting employment discrimination on the basis of pregnancy.
January 22, 1973	Supreme Court overturns all criminal abortion laws in the United States, and declares that the constitutional right to privacy protects the choice of abortion from government interference during the first trimester and severely restricts government interference during the second and third trimesters of pregnancy.
1973	On January 30 the first Human Life Amendment is introduced in Congress. The purpose of the proposed HLA is to overturn the Supreme Court decision, to make abortion and some forms of birth control illegal, and to declare fertilized eggs as persons entitled to full constitutional rights.
	Indiana passes first call for a constitutional convention to amend the U.S. Constitution to ban abortion. (By summer, 1981 nineteen states of the thirty-four required pass calls for a constitutional convention.)

National Right to Life Committee, an arm of the Family Life Division of the U.S. Catholic Conference, incorporates as a separate organization.

Series of NOW demonstrations in support of TV show *Maude* which features her deciding to have an abortion.

January 22, 1974	Estimated 20,000 attend first annual March for Life in Washington, D.C. to oppose abortion rights.
March–October 1974	Senate Subcommittee on Constitutional Amendments holds hearings on the Human Life Amendments (HLAs). Subcommittee votes not to endorse. No further action taken.
December 1974	Anti-abortion amendment to HEW/Labor appropriations defeated. The Hyde amendment, cutting off Medicaid funding for most abortions, passes in 1976; is enjoined by Judge Dooling; passes again in 1977, '78, '79, '80, and '81.
February 1975	Dr. Kenneth Edelin convicted of manslaughter in death of fetus in twenty-four week abortion. Conviction overturned on appeal.
April 1975	Roman Catholic Bishop Leo Maner of San Diego issues an order denying communion to Catholics who are "members of pro-abortion groups such as the National Organization for Women." NOW is singled out in his pastoral letter for its "shameless agitation."
May 4, 1975	NOW organizes the Mother's Day of Outrage, which brings 4,000 demonstrators to the Vatican Embassy in Washington, D.C., to publicize the money being spent by the Church to support compulsory pregnancy and childbirth.
November 1975	National Conference of Catholic Bishops issues Pastoral Plan for Pro-Life Activities aimed at organizing a political committee in every parish to work against reproductive rights.
February–March 1976	House Subcommittee on Civil and Constitutional Rights chaired by Don Edwards (D-CA) holds hearings on the proposed constitutional amendments on abortion. No further action taken and discharge move fails.
March 1976	NOW President Karen DeCrow demands IRS investigation of political activities of the Roman Catholic Church against abortion. IRS responds that it will collect data.
June 1976	"How to Disrupt an Abortion Clinic" is well attended workshop at the National Right to Life Convention.
July 1976	Supreme Court rules that a state may not require her husband's consent for a women to obtain an abortion. (*Planned Parenthood* v. *Danforth*)

Ellen McCormack, Democratic candidate for President, takes her single-issue anti-abortion campaign, which has received

	federal matching funds, to the National Democratic Convention.
August 1976	National Republican Convention endorses the so-called Human Life Amendment in its national platform.
October 1976	National NOW action urging taxpayers to protest Roman Catholic Church activity against abortion.
December 1976	Supreme Court overturns EEOC guideline prohibiting discrimination on the basis of pregnancy and allows exclusion of pregnancy from illness and accident disability plans.
April 1977	Letter from the NOW Task Force on Women and Religion to every Roman Catholic bishop urging, among other things, the recognition of reproductive rights of women.
June 1977	Supreme Court upholds state Medicaid regulations prohibiting funds for elective abortions. (*Beal* v. *Doe*)
November 1977	International Women's Year Conference becomes scene of first major collaboration between anti-abortion and right-wing political forces.
February 1978	Akron, Ohio passes comprehensive anti-abortion law designed to severely restrict access to abortion. Law is model for similar attempts in many other localities and states, and becomes known as the "Akron ordinance."
March 1978	Wave of vandalism and harassment of abortion clinics reported. Within last year six clinics forced to close or move because of fire, firebombs or chemical bombs.
Summer 1978	Marla Pitchford prosecuted in Kentucky for self-induced abortion and manslaughter. She is acquitted on grounds of temporary insanity for the first modern prosecution for self-abortion.
	Catholic Church and anti-abortion groups launch major offensive against Planned Parenthood participation in United Way campaigns.
September 1978	Thea Rossi Barron, chief lobbyist for National Right to Life Committee, resigns to protest growing right-wing, anti-abortion collaboration.
October 1978	Pregnancy Discrimination Act requires pregnancy related medical care to be covered on the same basis as other medical conditions under employee comprehensive insurance plans but permits employers to limit coverage of abortion. Complications resulting from an abortion must be covered, even if the abortion was performed for reasons other than to save the woman's life.

January 1979	NOW calls for summit meeting of anti-abortion and reproductive rights groups to explore areas of consensus. After two meetings, one of which is disrupted by an anti-abortion group, no meaningful consensus is reached.
June 1979	Supreme Court rules requirement of parental consent for abortion for minors unconstitutional. (*Baird* v. *Bellotti*, no. 2)
May 1980	National Conference of Catholic Bishops orders end to all sterilizations in Catholic hospitals except where there is danger the hospital may be closed down for not performing a sterilization.
June 1980	Akron-style ordinance defeated in Toledo, Ohio primary election by a two-to-one margin after massive advertising campaign and get-out-the-vote drive by abortion rights supporters.
	Supreme Court in the five-to-four *Harris* v. *McRae* decision upholds the constitutionality of the Hyde amendment on Medicaid coverage for indigent women. Referring abortion rights supporters to the legislatures to effect "this sensitive issue," the Court upholds the power of Congress to deny funds for medically necessary abortions for indigent women.
July 1980	Republican Convention reaffirms its 1976 party platform plank endorsing a Human Life Amendment (HLA) and calls for federal judicial appointments based on the candidate's support for "innocent human life."
August 1980	Democratic National Convention, in a roll call vote, endorses by a two-to-one margin Medicaid funding for abortion. The Medicaid provision is added to a strong reproductive rights plank in the platform. The plank includes opposition to a constitutional amendment to ban abortion and opposition to forced sterilization.
September 1980	Hyde amendment cutting off over 99 percent of the federal Medicaid funds for abortion for indigent women goes into effect after petition for rehearing of *McRae* is denied by Supreme Court.
October 1980	Ballot issue to ban all abortions in several Alaska counties fails.
November 1980	A number of liberal and progressive federal legislators are defeated giving the Republicans a majority in the Senate and making the climate in the Congress more hostile to reproductive rights.
	Ronald Reagan, who supports the HLA, is elected President of the United States.
January 1981	New Republican majority in the Senate passes leadership of the Judiciary Committee to Strom Thurmond (R-SC) and Orrin

Hatch (R-UT), a fervent supporter of HLA, takes over as chair of the Subcommittee on Constitution. Major activity around the proposed constitutional amendments (HLAs) and federal legislation (HLBs), as well as legislation attempting to restrict the jurisdiction of federal courts on abortion related issues, is certain.

Representatives from the annual March for Life are received at the White House. Recently appointed Health and Human Services Secretary Richard S. Schweiker reassures the anti-abortion group that they have "a friend" at HHS. He promises to implement a "pro-life" policy in his department.

February 1981	In a six-to-one decision, Massachusetts Supreme Court rules that medically necessary abortions must be funded under the state Medicaid program.
March 1981	President Reagan announces the appointment of two anti-abortion leaders to positions affecting future reproductive health care and policy formation. Dr. C. Everett Koop, a board member of the National Right to Life Committee and Americans United for Life, is named deputy assistant secretary of the Department of Health and Human Services. Marjory Mecklenburg, president of American Citizens Concerned for Life, takes over the Office of Adolescent Pregnancy Programs.
April 1981	Senate Judiciary Subcommittee on Separation of Powers, chaired by John East (R-NC), holds hearings on the Human Life Bill (HLB). Widespread opposition to HLB erupts from all quarters: chief legal counsel for National Conference of Catholic Bishops, prominent legal and constitutional scholars, and six former Attorneys General. National Academy of Sciences and Board of Trustees of the American Medical Association, among others, adopt resolutions in opposition to HLB. Disagreements over HLB v. HLA strategy further divide anti-abortion groups.
May 1981	On May 14, Dr. Edward Brandt, Jr is sworn in as assistant secretary for health in the Department of Health and Human Services. Two weeks later, Dr. Brandt says that abortion should be outlawed under all circumstances except when the life of the women is in danger. He further endorses a constitutional amendment as the "most appropriate" legal route toward outlawing abortion.
	Medicaid funding for abortion in cases of rape and incest eliminated by Congress.
May–July 1981	Further hearings are held on HLB in Subcommittee on Separation of Powers. On July 9, subcommittee votes three-to-two to report out HLB favorably to the Senate Judiciary Committee with the stipulation that further consideration be

	delayed until hearings on the HLA are held by the Subcommittee on Constitution.
Fall 1981	Hatch (R-UT) holds hearings on HLA in Subcommittee on Constitution and proposes "states' rights" version of HLA. Reagan nominates Dr. C. Everett Koop as Surgeon General of the United States.
	Anti-abortion movement leaders oppose Sandra O'Connor as first woman justice of the Supreme Court.

Celebrating Nelly

Judith Arcana

Nelly cleared her throat, walked up to the counter, and handed the box of sanitary napkins to the boy at the cash register. As he turned it over to see the price, she looked at his plastic name tag; it said, "Walgreens/William." He slid the pale green box into a plastic bag, stapling on the receipt as Nelly paid.

Like a movie editor, Nelly ran this scene over and over in her mind. The boy and the store might be different when the day came, along with the weather and the time and her clothes. But her actions—what she would do and say—would be just as she rehearsed. When she really did begin to menstruate, Nelly wanted to be ready.

Her mother had told her about how, when *she'd* been a girl, she was always embarrassed to buy sanitary napkins, or even to carry them home, unless they were wrapped up and hidden. Nelly was glad May didn't feel that way about her period anymore. She was sure that if her own mother was still embarrassed, it would be a lot harder for *her* to do and feel all the things she was on the edge of doing and feeling, right now.

Nelly had known what menstruation was long before her group at school began their sexuality class. When she was only three or four years old and found the open box on the bathroom shelf, she would ask May to give her a tampon. Nelly liked to fill a glass with water and, holding the tampon by its string, dip it slowly. Like a magician's trick, the cotton would fill and swell. And she'd seen the process in her mother—the cotton candle going tight and clean into May's vagina, and then coming out three times its original size, full of blood. She'd known her mother's periods: the times when May was in a bad mood and yelled at her, or was tired and sad, with no energy for Nelly, at all. May had explained that these moods came mostly when she'd been unhealthy eating more hot dogs and doughnuts than anybody needed—if anybody actually did need hot dogs and doughnuts—or just not getting enough sleep and exercise. So Nelly understood that she could take care of herself when the hard parts came. She even knew how to do the yoga positions May learned in class at the Y—the fish, the plow, and the cross-legged shoulder stand—all good for cramps.

Still, Nelly hadn't really begun to associate her mother's monthly periods with her own body until just after her eleventh birthday, when she thought her breasts might be growing, because sometimes they felt sort of different. Actually, what it was was that they felt *something*, and she couldn't remember having noticed them much at all before. And hair was growing under her arms, and on the mound above her vulva. And really—really—she just felt different lately. Sometimes she was very tired, and even sad, when nothing had happened to make her sad or get her tired. And sometimes, for no reason, she was real excited, "Something must be going to happen to me," she thought, and she wanted to be ready.

Around Thanksgiving of that year, Stella and Eileen—one of the mothers and one of the teachers in her school—began to teach the sexuality class. Nelly, at nearly twelve, was one of the oldest girls in her group, but none of them had had her first period yet. You could pass out and die in there, waiting to get back to the good parts, while younger kids asked questions about stuff the older ones already knew. Once, early on, one of the smaller boys asked, "Are babies *made* of this blood? Is that why it doesn't come out when a lady is pregnant?" Stella said, "Well, not exactly. But that's close, and kind of a good symbol for what really *does* happen." Then she'd had to spend a lot of time explaining what "symbol" meant, and they nearly ran out of time before she got back to the important stuff. The older girls—like Nell and her friend Daisy—wanted to have their own private class with Stella and Eileen.

Even some older girls thought that blood was all that came out when you had your period. Like Monica, Nelly's upstairs neighbor. "It looks like blood to me, Nellybelly," said Monica. "Don't tell *me* it's lotsa other stuff. You don't even *get* your period yet; wadda *you* know?" But Nelly stuck to her argument, having learned from Eileen that menstrual flow contains many things, including water, mucus, and even cells from the uterus walls. She knew that the blood stained everything else deep red, and made it all appear to be blood. Nelly even knew that the name for the lining of the uterus is *endometrium*, but Monica would just call her a bighead show-off if she mentioned that.

The teachers talked about all the different ways women had chosen to take care of themselves during their periods. Eileen used tampons in cardboard tubes; each tube was wrapped in a small sleeve of tissue paper with a zipthread to open it, like a Band-Aid. Stella used Florida sea sponges, which she bought at hardware stores or pottery suppliers. She'd buy a big sponge, boil it, and then cut it into three or four smaller ones, using the larger pieces for the first few days of her period, when there was the most blood. She'd rinse out the used sponges and dry them on the bathroom windowsill in the sunlight.

Nelly and the other girls felt that maybe they'd be more comfortable using pads worn outside the vagina, attached to their underpants or fastened to a small elastic belt. These pads were the sanitary napkins in Nelly's mind movie. They looked like cotton wrapped in spun gauze, and they caught the menstrual fluid just as it came out, because they were held in place right against the vulva, between the outer thighs. Some of the girls said—or thought privately—that they didn't want to have to put something up inside of them. There was a certain amount of shifty-eyed giggling at that point in the conversation.

They talked about the ways their mothers and grandmothers had felt about menstruation. Stella's mother, Gerty, had grown up when tampons and sanitary napkins hadn't even been invented. She was 60 years older than Nelly and Daisy. When she was a girl, Gerty and her sisters had folded up used newspapers and wrapped them in strips of rags, which they arranged inside their underpants. Each night they threw away the newspapers and rinsed the rags in cold water.

Even though Gerty's early menstrual experience had been different from what Nelly's might be, it turned out to be the same in one way. Like Eileen and Stella, and like May, Gerty had felt bad about her period, worried, nervous, and embarrassed. Like Nelly's mother, Stella's mother hadn't wanted anyone to know when she had her period, and had thought there was something sort of dirty about menstruating. They'd all been ashamed of their vaginas, and tried to keep those parts of their bodies secret and hidden, even from other girls and women.

133

Nelly, going over her movie, rehearsing for her own first period, knew that she had some bad feelings about menstruation too. That's why she needed practice buying sanitary napkins from the boy at the Walgreen's. What she couldn't figure out was *why* they all should feel like that. She'd learned that women's bodies are designed to make people, and that menstruation is part of the design. Having vaginas and periods was obviously the regular way to be, the natural way for all human females. "For all mammal females, actually. Dogs and bears, whales and seals, all of us." Nelly thought, "we all menstruate, and we can all grow babies inside of our bodies if we want to. When I thing about that, I feel pretty good; what makes the bad feelings come?"

One day a memory came into her mind. She was on the park swings with Monica—seven and eight years old they were—swinging high, madly pumping their legs, screeching, panting, and laughing at their race. Then, just as they both reached that point where they might actually go over the top, some boys dashed up to the swing poles. One yelled, "Hey, watch these girls go over the top—you can look right up their skirts!" She and Monica jolted and swung wild, stopped pumping and came down fast. They sat on the stopped swings, still a bit breathless, and looked at each other. A bad feeling came into Nelly's body; she jumped from the swing and ran. Without even looking, she knew Monica was running right beside her. "I hated those boys. They made me feel bad." Nelly stopped walking as she realized, "They made me feel ashamed of what they would see; I felt ashamed to be a girl. They made me get ashamed of my own self!"

With this memory, Nelly knew she'd made an important discovery. "Women feel ashamed of just *having* vaginas, of just *being* women and girls—even though we didn't do anything wrong."

A few weeks after her discovery, Nelly walked to the bus stop in the morning thinking, "Chicago smells almost like the beach today; the air is full of warm water." So when she met Monica at the corner after school, without even saying they were going to do it, the girls headed straight for the Rainbow Ladies' Juice Bar on Clark Street, and each ordered an extra large fresh squeezed orange juice. This was an incredible lot of money, but if the warm weather held on, they could rollerskate in the park on Saturday and Sunday—and that was free. The snow had been gone for weeks now.

When Nelly got home, she decided not to do her homework just then. She left her books on the kitchen table and stopped in the bathroom on the way to the sofa in the front room. She sat down on the toilet, pulling down her jeans and underpants with one hand while she picked up a magazine with the other. A few minutes later, about to get up, she glanced down at her knotted shoelaces and saw black shoes, blue socks, blue jeans and pale yellow underpants with a small smudge of bright red blood in them. She looked closer, and sniffed at the blood. Then she tore off a piece of tissue and touched it to her vulva. It came away stained pink. She sat there for another minute or two. "This is it. I've got my period. It's happening just like they said—I've got my period!"

She wasn't sure what to do—she just sat there for a minute with the toilet paper in her hand. She folded a strip of it into a soft pad, arranged it in her underpants and pulled them back up with her jeans.

She called her mother at the store. May answered—"Gardens; may I help you?" She was shocked to find that as her mother spoke, tear came into Nell's eyes, and her own voice sounded strange. "Mom, it's me, Nelly. Mom, I got it. I got my period. I'm bleeding."

May's voice got strange. "Oh, Nell—um, maybe I can get off early—do you feel okay? Is there a lot of blood? Are you alone?"

"I'm alone but, Mom, don't come home early. But don't come home late, okay?"

Nelly walked slowly—she felt very slow—to the living room sofa, where the late afternoon sun was dazzling, casting the leaves of all the plants into sharp outlines on the floor and walls. She lay down with the sun full on her face and body, and closed her eyes. She put her hands lightly on her breasts, her belly, her thighs. She imagined she could feel with her hands the soft throbbing—slight and muted, just enough to know that something was happening inside of her. She lay there with her eyes closed, and pictured her uterus shedding its lining, imagined it squeezing and emptying itself. She saw the blood moving out, pooling in her vagina, so that when she stood up it would slide out into the toilet paper in her underpants.

Nelly slept off and on through the next hour or so, dreaming herself a woman. She was a flier. She built her own glider and rode the highest wind. She was an explorer of caves deep inside the earth, shining her lantern on glistening columns of ice. She was a witch, living in the desert among the birds of the rocks. She herded cattle by the side of the sea, huge cows and great bulls with sympathetic eyes. She talked with jungle serpents who twisted around her body, whispering ancient secrets.

Nelly woke from her dreams and found that the bright sunlight was gone; the sky was dusk. Her mother sat at the end of the sofa. May put her hands on Nelly's cheeks, and held her face.

"I've collected some things for you, Nelly, from the women at the shop." On the windowsill, beside a small heartshaped red candle, was one dark rose, just opening—"Like you, Nell," her mother said. "Now, let's see what you think about all this." May gestured toward a pile of packages on the bed. There were sanitary napkins and five "junior" tampons. A cellophane wrapper held a big sponge, and a little brown bag was filled with herbal tea—'To relax you if you ever get cramps, honey." There was even a tiny dish of moss from the potting table at the shop, because May read that many women of the American nations had used moss to catch their blood.

Nelly said, "It's like my birthday, Mom." "Yes, and we're going to have a party, too. We're going to celebrate you. Too bad your Grandma is so far away—but we'll have the women's group, and whichever close friends you'd like—Monica, Daisy? Your cousin Frankie?" They set the party date for the next Saturday afternoon and May made all the calls. "I'm throwing the party in your honor, after all."

In the meantime, Nelly menstruated. At first, only a little blood came and she felt slow and sleepy all the time. On the second day she had a chance to use the tea and practice some yoga, because she got cramps. "Is this what it feels like to have a baby, Mom?" "Sort of, but it's just a hint, really. Cramps are related to labor contractions the way shadows are to bodies, if you see what I mean." Nelly was doing the shoulder stand, which had always been her favorite—easy for her to go in and out of. "Don't eat much— or don't eat at all—while you have cramps, Nelly. Keep the lower part of your body empty for a few hours, let it concentrate on your uterus." The cramps stopped soon, and Nelly said, "Do you think it would be okay for me to go to the movies, Mom? I really feel fine."

"Of course you feel fine—but I wish you wouldn't just sit in a dark room for two hours. Go skating. It's a lovely warm day."

When Nelly got back from the park, she told May that Monica had said she couldn't take a bath when she had her period because the blood would make the water "dirty." "Monica's wrong, Nell. The flow stops when you put your body in the water; the idea is not to let yourself get chilled. But, shower or bath, you better get in there, because you sure are one dirty kid."

On Monday morning, despite the fact that this was "day four" and Nelly had been wearing sanitary napkins each day, she got nervous. "Can you see this pad when I bend over? Does It bulge out?"

"Okay. Let's see here. Don't wear those tight pants today—wear some baggy ones; in fact, those pants are way too tight anyway. Give 'em here and we'll put them in the box for Frankie's neighbor. Tell Eileen you've gotten your period, and ask her if she'll keep your extra pads in the teacher's room, next to the bathroom. And let me give you a massage to help you calm down a little."

Nelly's period ended on Wednesday, with Nelly counting ahead on the kitchen calendar to see when the next one would begin. Though she'd been told that lots of women are not "regular," and that the first months or even years can include skipped periods, long cycles, and periods of different lengths, she wanted to get an idea of when it might come again. And then she had two more days before the party.

The morning of her period party, after Nelly showered and washed her hair, she walked up and down the hall, in and out of her room. She looked out the windows, at the floorboards, at her fingers. Just before noon a mail carrier brought a package. Inside was a note and a small box. "Three years ago," the note read, "when your mama let you get your ears pierced, I thought you were too young. But now you're a real lady. Love, Grandma." The earrings were delicate and tiny—two gold hearts. Nelly took off her hoops and put the golden hearts in her ears.

May had brought flowers home from the store: tall irises, standing in clear glass containers; fat pots of red and purple tulips; straw baskets of pink and blue hyacinths, whose fragrance drew Nelly from her tasks all morning. The house was so full of spring that even if it rained all day—which didn't seem likely—the front room would feel like the yard. At around three o'clock, the women and girls started to arrive. They came in smiling, carrying wrapped plates, covered bowls, casseroles, loaves of bread in big brown bags, wooden bowls with wet lettuce sticking out the edges—and gifts for Nelly.

She saw bags with yellow and violet tissue, white paper with red ribbon, boxes with stickers and drawings, and one long tube done up in a batik cloth. The women all kissed Nelly, stroked her hair or touched her face, their own faces wistful and proud. The girls seemed shy, quieter than usual. Even on her birthday, Nelly had never felt so important.

There was a rush of activity in the kitchen, and then May took two big old blankets up in her arms and called, "Bring the presents, everybody, and let's go outside." They trooped down the back stairs to the newly green grass, spread out the quilts and sat in a circle.

May began, "I give you greetings from my mother, who could not join us, and welcome you to this celebration of my daughter, Nelly. She had begun to be a woman." Nelly was surprised to hear how formal her mother sounded, and looked to see how the others responded. All the women and girls smiled at her. Suddenly, Nelly felt terribly embarrassed and unworthy. She thought, "How could they all be doing this for me—and just because I started my period?" May was still speaking. ". . . and those of us who no longer menstruate, or haven't begun yet, might want to talk about how it was to end the bleeding, or to look forward to beginning—or whatever," she laughed, breaking into her talking voice.

After a minute of everybody looking at everybody, Frankie said, "I'd like to start, okay?" Everyone turned to her. "I've had my period for a year; I'm sixteen now. Lots of my friends at school started before me, and I felt real bad. I thought there might be something wrong with me. One girl used to ask me all the time if I got it yet, and that made me feel worse. Here, Nelly, this is my gift." She handed Nelly a thin packet of white paper, scattered with tiny specks of glitter. Inside there was an envelope of hand-cut paper butterflies from China; each in a fold of tissue, which Nelly held up to the sun.

Nelly thanked Frankie and they all turned to Rosa, the next woman in the circle. "When I first got my period, the blood wasn't red; it was just a dark trickle, like the color of a scab, and I thought that I was sick. I never told my mother, just sort of stuffed those dirty old underpants way down in the laundry hamper and hoped she wouldn't notice. She never said a word. My mother was just as tense and nervous as I was, poor lady, and didn't know any more about it than I did. The second time the blood came red, lots of it—and I told my gym teacher. She explained everything, and I got the stuff on my way home from school. Never did tell my mother." Rosa handed her the long batik tube Nelly had noticed earlier. The wrapper was a long slim scarf, dark red, and the tube was a calendar, marked with all the phases of the moon, women's holidays, and the birthdates of famous women. As Nelly thanked her, she passed the calendar around the circle.

Then Carmen began. "My mother and her mother always told me what they felt in their bodies with their periods and with having babies and nursing babies. I never saw the blood—they were modest. I always knew it was normal. When I got my period, I told them both, and they got out the belt and napkins they had been keeping for me. I felt very good about it all—even proud." She handed Nelly a white card which said: "One Massage for Nelly from Carmen," with a drawing of a big red poppy.

Clare, one of May's closest friends, watched Carmen lean toward Frankie through the lens of her camera. She snapped the photograph, put down the camera, and said, "I don't have my period anymore. It stopped thirteen years ago. I had it more than 40 years. I was kind of sad to see it go, but now that I'm older, I guess I need *all* my blood." Everyone laughed. Clare continued, "Honey, I was there waiting for you when you were born—you came right to my arms. I actually put down my camera for you, baby. When I get to develop these pictures I'm taking, I'll have a whole set for you."

Daisy said, "I didn't know that periods stopped. I thought we'd all just have them until we die. My cousin gets real bad cramps and once she fainted. Until a few months ago, when we got this special sex—uh, sexuality—class at our school, I always hoped that I'd *never* get mine, because I was afraid I'd be like her. Here, Nelly." Daisy's gift was a stuffed owl, with a miniature pair of glasses sewed onto its beak. "It's the wise old owl, Nelly, get it?"

The next woman in the circle was Jane. "I always wear red on the first day of my period. I like to show it off. I read about the history of menstruation, and I learned that women's blood used to be sacred. That was a long time ago, a *real* long time ago." She passed a box around the circle to Nelly. Inside the wrappings, Nelly found three pairs of bright red cotton underpants. "So you can flaunt it too, Nelly."

Deborah spoke then. "My mother told me the facts of life, as we used to say, and did a pretty good job, too. I wasn't afraid when my period came. But what she hadn't prepared me for was this: when I told her I'd gotten my period, she stood up, came over to me, and slapped me across the face, real hard. Then she explained that this was a "tradition." Some tradition! I like the one Jane told me about, where women smear blood on their faces as a sign of their power, to scare men away. Now *that's* a tradition I can get behind!"

With that, Deborah leaned across and gave Nelly a red book with gold-edged pages. But all the pages were blank, for Nelly to write on. "Tell the story of this day, Nelly, or keep a journal of your dreams. Whatever you want to write in there, Nell, whatever you want to say."

Every woman and girl in the circle told and gave something that taught Nelly what her blood was—the mark of being female, a sign of womanhood, a symbol of life.

The last woman to speak was Moira. "My period was always a problem. I had terrible cramps, and got depressed every month. The clinic gave me pills for the pain, and pills for the depression. But listen to this—ever since I've been doing yoga with May at the Y, and exercising three times a week, me and my period are getting along just fine. I know I sound like I'm on a commercial, but it's true. Nelly, when I worked down in Mexico last year, I found these; I hope you like them as much as I do." She handed Nelly a bag, from which she took seven tiny packages. Opening them, Nelly passed around the circle seven sea shells, each one a different shape, each one a different color.

The shells in the circle came around to May. "I got my period when I was ten, and have had it for 29 years. At first, I was ashamed of the pads, embarrassed by the blood, nervous about the smell—the whole thing, you know? But in the last several years, I've learned a lot about my body—about women's bodies, really—and understand menstruation in another way. I'm learning our history and studying our lives, and now I see the whole menstrual cycle as a bond among us. Even though we're all different in almost every other way, our blood links all women everywhere, going back through time and all across the world. Menstruation is something all women have; the blood of life flows through our bodies. Because we live now in a time when our beauty and power are not recognized, it's hard to feel good about being a woman. I've only understood this for a short time, really. My gift to you, Nelly, is this celebration which is about what I've been able to learn so far, and what I want us to remember."

She paused, "Could we all hold hands around the circle? Let's send some energy, some magic, some vibes to Nelly." They stood in a ring, with Nell in the center. As she turned, slowly looking at the circle of women and girls holding hands, some with eyes closed, she felt like Little Sally Saucer. "That's the last time I was inside a circle," she thought, "when I was in nursery school." She stood still and closed her own eyes. She felt sort of modest, because of being the center of attention. But she liked it. And she really did feel something—like heat, or a kind of pushing, coming into her from all around. She felt bigger, and when she finally opened her eyes she felt so big she expected to look directly into May's face. But she didn't; the top of her head remained at the level of her mother's shoulders but the tall feeling stayed.

The women and girls raised clasped hands into the air, and, with a sort of sigh, dropped their arms. Then as everyone kissed Nelly, Monica called, "Can we eat now? I'm *really* hungry." "Sure we can, Monica," said May, and she led the way back upstairs to dinner.

"Silent Epidemic" of "Social Disease" Makes STD Experts Raise Their Voices

Marsha F. Goldsmith

Immunological virgins seem to be almost the only kind one finds among adolescents anymore, and that fact may in part account for the tremendous increase in sexually transmitted diseases (STDs) in the United States.

At a symposium in New York City on "The 'Other' STDs: A Silent Epidemic," sponsored by the American Medical Association and the Centers for Disease Control (CDC), Atlanta, Ga, authorities who have worked on stopping STD spread for years said the situation is now nearly out of control.

("Other" recognizes that acquired immunodeficiency syndrome [AIDS] has become the overwhelming concern, leaving different STDs in the shade. The meeting was supported by a grant from Burroughs Wellcome Company.)

A major reason for STD increase is that young people are being exposed to infection, and acquisition is often rapid and asymptomatic. A great many of the more than 70% of people who are sexually active by age 19 years may have an initial exposure to an STD, become infected, and pass the infection on without ever feeling ill or knowing they've been infected.

Only years later—when gonorrhea and/or *Chlamydia* have left scarred fallopian tubes that may mean an ectopic pregnancy, or human papillomavirus (HPV) or hepatitis B virus has led to cancer, or genital herpes or syphilis has resulted in a damaged infant— may the cost of careless sex become apparent.

And that's exactly what is going on, state the experts. "We have to think seriously about this or we're going to have an entire infertile cohort," says Mary-Ann Shafer, MD, assistant director, Division of Adolescent Medicine, at the University of California, San Francisco, School of Medicine. "Just saying no" isn't working, she points out, and those who could help people have *careful* sex, specifically public officials, religious authorities, television executives, teachers, and, indeed, physicians—who Shafer says ought to be spreading the word that always using condoms makes for safer sex—won't say yes.

Condoms cut STD rates, Shafer said. (So does being Asian-American and having a strong family structure, but that's another story.) In the 1970s, for example, both Sweden and the United States had a gonorrhea incidence rate of more than 470/100,000.

A vigorous public health campaign in Sweden—with discussion in schools, radio and TV time, and ads on trains and buses—effected a 15-fold decrease in the disease; the rate is now 31/100,000. In the United States, the rate is 300/100,000.

According to John LaMontagne, PhD, director of the Microbiology and Infectious Diseases Program at the National Institute of Allergy and Infectious Diseases (NIAID), Bethesda, Md, these are the best estimates of what else is happening: Each year in the United States, there occur 1 to 2 million new cases of gonorrhea, 4 million new cases of chlamydial infection, and 500,000 to 1 million new cases of pelvic inflammatory disease. There are 12 million cases of genital warts (caused by HPV), with 750,000 new ones per year, and 20 to 30 million cases of symptomatic genital herpes infection (herpes simplex virus type 1 or 2 [HSV-1 or 2]), with 500,000 new ones per year.

Yvonne Bryson, MD, associate professor of pediatrics, University of California, Los Angeles, School of Medicine, says new studies show there are many more cases of asymptomatic genital herpes infection. "I don't think most obstetricians are aware of this yet," she says, citing some startling figures.

In Atlanta, Los Angeles, and Seattle, Wash, says Bryson, as many as 65% of pregnant women may have "silent" HSV-2 infection. While women known to have genital herpes are well managed, "the problem is the women, and their doctors, who don't know." Bryson says, "There should be a push for development of screening tests. We may have to change our thinking about general screening during pregnancy."

Syphilis accounts for about 100,000 new STD cases annually—including congenital cases, which rose fourfold in the 3 years 1985 through 1987 and continue to go up. This disease, which had declined steadily in incidence for many years, is still going down in white men and is fairly stable in white women. However, for the 3 consecutive years since 1986, reported cases of syphilis have risen sharply among blacks.

According to King K. Holmes, MD, PhD, professor and vice-chair, Department of Medicine, University of Washington School of Medicine, Seattle, syphilis is up twofold among black men and up threefold among black women. Gonorrhea is 20 times higher in blacks than in whites. Specific figures were unavailable on Hispanics, but it's known that STDs occur disproportionately among lower socioeconomic groups, primarily among blacks and Hispanics.

That's true even after correcting for reporting bias, which occurs because of how data are gathered, says Willard Cates, MD, MPH, director, Division of Sexually Transmitted Diseases, at the Centers for Disease Control. That agency collects its data from the states, and Cates says physicians underreport. Up to 80% of reports come from public STD clinics and fewer than 20% come from private physicians. In reality, he says, the occurrence of these diseases among public and private patients is probably equal. But many more poor people have turned to public clinics for STD treatment, and clinics report scrupulously.

Now that's changing, said Holmes. Public health clinics can no longer afford to handle the overwhelming caseload. They close earlier, waiting time is longer, and people who most require their services don't have access to care.

Holmes said he thinks the most practical strategy for coping with the STD epidemic in populations at high risk is to establish high school-based sex education programs that include treatment clinics. "We don't know what behavioral interventions work, and the crack-using population [who exchange sex for drugs] isn't very well studied, but we've got to treat this epidemic," he says.

According to Shafer, the *Chlamydia* epidemic is even worse. She said that in many parts of the country, "infection is extremely common and entirely undetected." *Chlamydia* is the most prevalent STD in young women, affecting 15% to 20% (three to five times the rate for gonorrhea), and is mostly asymptomatic. And 8% to 11% of young men have asymptomatic infection, she says.

It's time to reevaluate STD prevention programs, traditionally geared to females, said Shafer, adding, "It's easy to screen males using a leukocyte esterase test that can be done on a urine specimen for 20 cents a stick." She believes "we should be treating all sexually active men. But we also need a better treatment for *Chlamydia*. We have to tell patients, 'Take this medicine for 7 days and you'll feel nauseated.' How can we get teenagers to do that when they don't even realize they're ill?"

Shafer doesn't believe more research will solve all the problems, because "we're dealing with the interaction of biology and behavior. No matter how much money we pour into studies, we'll never completely control STDs medically because there'll always be a new one. The bottom line is changing behavior."

The same thing is said about AIDS, of course. Now, much more federal funding is directed toward AIDS research than toward the "other STDs." This year the NIH has almost $604 million for AIDS. All other STDs combined are allotted $60 million. (Next year, the AIDS figure is more than $750 million and for other STDs, about $65 million.) The NIAID gets about $40 million of the NIH's annual "other STD" budget, and spends about one third of the amount on herpes virus research. (Gonorrhea is second and *Chlamydia* third.) Several other institutes share the total, notably the National Cancer Institute, which studies the many varieties of HPV, three types of which are believed to be the principal cause of genital cancers. LaMontagne said, "Despite the need, the NIH money spent on STDs has not greatly increased. The pattern of support is unchanged over the last decade."

The NIAID has made substantial accomplishments in studying STDs. It has supported research to improve diagnosis of chlamydial infection using hybridization techniques, and investigators at its Rocky Mountain Laboratory have made progress toward developing chlamydial vaccines. With the National Institute of Child Health and Human Development, it has begun a study on vaginal infections and prematurity.

The institute has pioneered in developing model systems to propagate HPV, supported research that led to using the polymerase chain reaction for diagnosing HPV infections, and established the value of interferon for treating them. This is of particular interest to Thomas Becker, MD, PhD, assistant professor of medicine at the University of New Mexico School of Medicine in Albuquerque. Although genital HPV infection is extremely common, Becker said, and more than 60 types of the virus have been identified, scientists still have more questions than answers about these viruses.

Known risk factors for acquiring HPV include having multiple sexual partners, using oral contraceptive pills, being immunocompromised, and smoking cigarettes. Becker says, "Treatment for the lesions has been suboptimal, which is frustrating for the physician and the patient." Add to this worry about the cancer connection and, Becker says, "HPV infection will be of growing concern in the next 3 years."

Another viral disease ought to be of increasing concern now, thinks Miriam Alter, PhD, Chief of Surveillance Activity, Hepatitis Branch, in the CDC's Division of Viral Diseases. A recent study showed that only 10% of physicians recognize heterosexual activity as a risk factor for hepatitis B, she says. But each year, 78,000 cases occur that way, of which 6,000 will result in chronic disease and 1,600 in death. Alter is angry because all this illness is preventable.

Two safe vaccines are available in the United States, she said, "all health care workers know about them," and only about 30% of health professionals have been vaccinated. Her agency's goal is to increase prevention among this group—and also to set up an immunization program for all 12-year-olds. Congress has asked the CDC to put together a strategy for eliminating hepatitis B, and Alter believes it can—and should—be done.

Wendy Wertheimer, deputy executive director of the American Social Health Association, began her presentation with the telephone number of its national STD hotline (1–800–227–8922). Knowing it is probably a good idea because, Wertheimer said, considering the size of the problem in relation to the money being spent to find a solution, "We're trying to contain a 4-alarm fire with a few buckets of water."

She said the association is calling for a "dramatic increase" in federal and state funding, and decried the fact that the issue "has become so politicized, reflecting a national fear of sex." Moreover, said Wertheimer, medical schools have an "abysmal record" in training their students to deal with STDs, and the present lack of funds for training resident physicians will make providing needed care even more difficult.

In summation, the CDC's Cates said,"STDs are an epidemic in a politically disenfranchised, voiceless population." He said it's important to give people messages that will reinforce healthy, safe sexual behavior, and at the same time "motivate tolerance that will eliminate discrimination against those who need the treatment that is available."

According to a recent unpublished study, said Cates, only 10% of primary care clinicians even ask their patients questions that might reveal their risk for STDs. "If we're going to make progress," he proclaimed, "that ought to be 100%!"

Woman-Hole

Carmen Tafolla

Some say there is a
  vacuum—a black hole—
    in the center of womanhood
     that swallows countless
      secrets and has strange
       powers

Yo no sé de'sas cosas
  solo sé que the
    black echo is music
     is sister of sunlight
      and from it
       crece
        vida.

"Woman-Hole," by Carmen Tafolla, reprinted with permission of the publisher from *Woman of Her Word: Hispanic Women Write*, ed. by Evangelina Vigil (Houston: Arte Publico Press of the University of Houston, 1987.)

AIDS: In Living Color

Beth Richie

As the most serious health crisis to affect black women in recent history, AIDS is a vivid symbol of the havoc that has been wreaked on women's quality of life in contemporary American society. In addition to presenting major life-threatening conditions, the AIDS epidemic represents a widespread social, political and cultural backlash. With racism and sexism on the rise in our society, AIDS has given leeway for individuals and social institutions to ignore or further exploit black women.

Once thought to be a disease that only affects white gay men, in recent years the epidemiology of the AIDS epidemic has dramatically shifted. According to the Centers for Disease Control in Atlanta, Georgia, today twenty-five percent of all people with AIDS are black. Fifty-two percent of all women with AIDS-related illnesses or positive HIV status are black. And fifty-nine to eighty percent of all children afflicted with the virus are black. AIDS has become the leading cause of death for black women between the ages of twenty-four and thirty-six. Moreover, black women who contract AIDS do not live as long or die as well as their white or male counterparts.

The problems commonly associated with AIDS, such as poor nutrition, drug use, incarceration, lack of preventative health services and inadequate housing are not new problems for the black community. Nor is denial of the existence of a black gay and bisexual community or competition with other oppressed groups for scarce resources. Premature death is not a new trend among African-Americans. AIDS, in many ways, is like every other health, social and economic crisis that black people have faced for generations. What is alarmingly different about AIDS is the severity of the infection and the particularly repressive political timing of the emergence of the disease. The combined effect of all these elements leaves the black community in an extremely vulnerable position. AIDS has the potential to cripple black people in a way that few other health or social forces have since slavery.

One of the most significant tolls that AIDS has had on our society is to seriously overtax the already strained health care system. Federal, state and local reductions in health care budgets, lack of health planning and punitive health policies have resulted in a dangerously poor quality of health care in most metropolitan areas. In particular, the staffing shortages among nurses and health technicians have become a critical factor contributing to the health service crisis.

Black women comprise a large percentage of the low-level nursing population that provides most of the daily care for people with AIDS. Black female nurses aides, home attendants and medical technicians have been caught in the middle of an inadequate health system, irresponsible government policies and a tremendous increase in patients who require intensive care, usually as they die. Although extensive research has proven

Richie, Beth. 1990. "AIDS: In Living Color." In *The Black Women's Health Book.* ed. Evelyn White, 182–186. Seattle: Seal Press. Reprinted by permission of Seal Press.

that health care workers do not constitute a high risk category for contracting the HIV virus, it is reasonable to assume that there are mental health consequences from working under the stressful conditions that the AIDS epidemic has created. This is especially true for black women in the health care industry who are routinely underpaid, required to work long hours without adequate compensation or support, not given equal access to the necessary training or supervision, and who are otherwise exploited by the health organizations that employ them. This problem is exacerbated by the multitudes of health agencies that hire undocumented black women and do not provide basic health insurance or job protection for them. Such agencies further abuse immigrant black women (primarily from the Caribbean) by threatening deportation to ensure compliance. In the AIDS crisis, the health system is exploiting black women workers just as other industries have done for more than a century.

The culturally dictated gender role of most women in black families requires that they be responsible for the health and well-being of their children, husband or sexual partner. This means when family members become sick, black women care for them, usually alone. The nature of AIDS-related illnesses creates a high level of fear, and requires constant health surveillance, repeated medical appointments and hospitalizations. It is exhausting and expensive, and black women usually carry the burden by themselves.

While the white gay male community has banded together to share resources in the AIDS crisis, the extended family support system which is characteristic of most black communities has been drained. The pattern of the illness is such that many black women are simultaneously caring for children, sex partners and friends dying of AIDS-related illnesses. And of course, many black women are themselves sick.

Institutionalized racism is another critical factor that compounds the situation for black families. Black men are often absent from their families because of poor job opportunities in urban areas, biased criminal justice systems that lead to higher incarceration rates for black men, or the internalization of despair that can result in drug or alcohol abuse. Again, black women are left to devise systems of survival for themselves.

Statistics indicate that the most frequent mode of transmission of the HIV virus to black women is through sexual contact with black men who are intravenous drug users and/or gay/bisexual. This means that to fully understand the impact of AIDS on black women, attention must be given to the politically charged issue of sexuality.

There have always been gay men and women in the black community. However, because of homophobia, their identities and activities have rarely been acknowledged. The AIDS epidemic has forced the black community to address the religious and cultural intolerance that has prompted many black men to live dual existences in both the heterosexual and homosexual worlds.

The prevailing societal view of black women's sexuality is that they are promiscuous, irresponsible and involved in illicit sexual activity such as prostitution. This misrepresentation has serious consequences in that it contributes to sexual harassment, rape and a general lack of sensitivity to the range of sexual expressions black women choose. In the face of these damning images of black women's sexuality, the community has become defensive and hesitant to openly discuss any issue related to sexuality. This silence has, in turn, left black women particularly vulnerable to HIV infection because of a lack of opportunities to discuss sexual behavior or AIDS risks.

This problem is manifested most seriously in the health education campaigns designed for women about condom use and other safe sex practices. These advertisements are not generally culturally sensitive. The result is that the black community (usually the male leadership) rejects the safe sex efforts because they are viewed as either sexually suggestive or culturally inappropriate.

Safe sex campaigns designed for women also must be examined from another angle. On the one hand, all women need information and strategies to protect themselves and their unborn children. On the other hand, many of the safe sex campaigns aimed at women reinforce the premise that women must be responsible for men. The result, unfortunately, is that women are blamed if they become pregnant, contract the HIV virus or another sexually transmitted disease from an infected male partner. For black women, this situation is complicated by the racial stereotypes of black heterosexual couples: the man being highly irresponsible (and consequently excused for his behavior in intimate relationships) and the woman being dominant and controlling.

As previously mentioned, black women are enormously overrepresented in the population of people with AIDS. The lack of AIDS prevention programs in communities of color, the lack of primary health care and the virtual absence of social and emotional support for black women with AIDS have exacerbated the problem. A black woman's health needs are likely to be considered secondary to the needs of her children, her partner, her community or the convenience of the health care system. That is, she is treated as a risk to others rather than in need of assistance herself.

The threat of sterilization abuse has re-emerged as a risky complication of AIDS. When black women are infected by the HIV virus, they may be overtly or covertly pressured to delay pregnancy or to undergo a sterilization operation or abortion. This risk has raised the politically volatile issue of genocide for black people, especially those who are poor, drug-users or sick. Given the repressive social climate and the increase in racial intolerance, it is expected that this risk will become even more profound in the near future.

For black women who are HIV-positive and pregnant, the situation becomes considerably more complicated. There are few prenatal care providers who are trained or willing to help pregnant women who may have contracted AIDS through the use of intravenous drugs, and those that do usually require drug detoxification as a condition of service. Because of a waning commitment to human services during the Reagan-Bush era, most drug detoxification programs have long waiting lists. This means that a growing number of drug-addicted pregnant women who are HIV-positive are completely underserved, and if current trends continue, they may be criminally penalized for giving birth, even though there are few service systems to protect or assist them.

For sure, black women with AIDS who give birth are extremely vulnerable within the child welfare system. There is a great risk that their children will be taken away should their health status be revealed.

The well-being of black women is seriously threatened by the AIDS epidemic and the complexity of its related problems. Yet black women have historically endured in the face of overwhelming odds. Lots of people have wanted us dead before now and thought they had us dying long ago. The challenge we face as individuals and community activists is to develop creative strategies for survival—one more time. As we've done since slavery, we must define issues for ourselves and establish strong and empowering sources of support to combat AIDS. Organizations such as the National Black Women's

Health Project, the California Prostitutes Education Project and Kitchen Table: Women of Color Press are in the forefront of this effort. Reassessing our roles as health care workers, family and community caretakers and sexual beings will also bring insight for solutions. Certainly the AIDS epidemic calls for us to challenge the system to reverse trends that oppress groups based on their race, gender, sexuality and economic status.

After a long silence, black people are beginning to realize just how serious this epidemic is and to address the emergency it has created for our community. As AIDS sufferers and strategists, black women have a lot to gain by battling this new menace with the tenacity with which we have always confronted the obstacles put in our path.

If Men Could Menstruate

Gloria Steinem

A white minority of the world has spent centuries conning us into thinking that a white skin makes people superior—even though the only thing it really does is make them more subject to ultraviolet rays and to wrinkles. Male human beings have built whole cultures around the idea that penis-envy is "natural" to women—though having such an unprotected organ might be said to make men vulnerable, and the power to give birth makes womb-envy at least as logical.

In short, the characteristics of the powerful, whatever they may be, are thought to be better than the characteristics of the powerless—and logic has nothing to do with it.

What would happen, for instance, if suddenly, magically, men could menstruate and women could not?

The answer is clear—menstruation would become an enviable, boastworthy, masculine event:

Men would brag about how long and how much.

Boys would mark the onset of menses, that longed-for proof of manhood, with religious ritual and stag parties.

Congress would fund a National Institute of Dysmenorrhea to help stamp out monthly discomforts.

Sanitary supplies would be federally funded and free. (Of course, some men would still pay for the prestige of commercial brands such as John Wayne Tampons, Muhammad Ali's Rope-a-dope Pads, Joe Namath Jock Shields—"For Those Light Bachelor Days," and Robert "Barretta" Blake Maxi-Pads.)

Military men, right-wing politicians, and religious fundamentalists would cite menstruation ("*men*-struation") as proof that only men could serve in the Army ("you have to give blood to take blood"), occupy political office ("can women be aggressive without that steadfast cycle governed by the planet Mars?"), be priests and ministers ("how could a woman give her blood for our sins?"), or rabbis ("without the monthly loss of impurities, women remain unclean").

Male radicals, left-wing politicians, and mystics, however, would insist that women are equal, just different; and that any women could enter their ranks if only she were willing to self-inflict a major wound every month ("you *must* give blood for the revolution"), recognize the preeminence of menstrual issues, or subordinate her selfness to all men in their Cycle of Enlightenment.

Street guys would brag ("I'm a three-pad man") or answer praise from a buddy ("Man, you lookin' *good!*") by giving fives and saying, "Yeah, man, I'm on the rag!"

TV shows would treat the subject at length. ("Happy Days": Richie and Potsie try to convince Fonzie that he is still "The Fonz," though he has missed two periods in a row.)

Steinem, Gloria. 1978. "If men could menstruate." *Ms. Magazine*, October, 101. Reprinted by permission of the author.

So would newspapers. (SHARK SCARE THREATENS MENSTRUATING MEN. JUDGE CITES MONTHLY STRESS IN PARDONING RAPIST.) And movies. (Newman and Redford in "Blood Brothers"!)

Men would convince women that intercourse was *more* pleasurable at "that time of the month." Lesbians would be said to fear blood and therefore life itself—though probably only because they needed a good menstruating man.

Of course, male intellectuals would offer the most moral and logical arguments. How could a woman master any discipline that demanded a sense of time, space, mathematics, or measurement, for instance, without that in-built gift for measuring the cycles of the moon and planets—and thus for measuring anything at all? In the rarefied fields of philosophy and religion, could women compensate for missing the rhythm of the universe? Or for their lack of symbolic death-and-resurrection every month?

Liberal males in every field would try to be kind: the fact that "these people" have no gift for measuring life or connecting to the universe, the liberals would explain, should be punishment enough.

And how would women be trained to react? One can imagine traditional women agreeing to all these arguments with a staunch and smiling masochism. ("The ERA would force housewives to wound themselves every month": Phyllis Schlafly. "Your husband's blood is as sacred as that of Jesus—and so sexy, too!": Marabel Morgan.) Reformers and Queen Bees would try to imitate men, and *pretend* to have a monthly cycle. All feminists would explain endlessly that men, too, needed to be liberated from the false idea of Martian aggressiveness, just as women needed to escape the bonds of menses-envy. Radical feminists would add that the oppression of the nonmenstrual was the pattern for all other oppressions. ("Vampires were our first freedom fighters!") Cultural feminists would develop a bloodless imagery in art and literature. Socialist feminists would insist that only under capitalism would men be able to monopolize menstrual blood. . . .

In fact, if men could menstruate, the power justifications could probably go on forever. If we let them.

Aqua Prieta—1968

Patricia McVey-Ritsick

This personal narrative begins in 1968 in upper-middle-class suburban southern California. My best friend, Susan, a senior English major, despite using the pill, was pregnant, single, and not ready to marry. She felt that her parents, who were upper income professionals, would not understand her plight and would disown her if they knew of her pregnancy. Because of this, she decided to get an abortion. The only problem was that abortions were illegal in the United States in 1968.

Somehow, through underground connections, Susan learned of a medical clinic in Mexico that performed "legal" abortions for $500. She made the appointment and asked me to accompany her to Aqua Prieta, Mexico. She was afraid to go alone, having heard too many horror stories about botched abortions, and her boyfriend refused to go with her. I agreed to go because I, too, was concerned for her safety and knew I would want a female friend to accompany me. We made flight reservations to Tucson and bus reservations to Douglas, Arizona; we began our trip three days later. We told our parents we had several days off from school and were driving up the coast to visit friends. Instead, we boarded a flight from Los Angeles to Tucson. Both of us were apprehensive, yet Susan was convinced that a full-term pregnancy was a fate worse than any Mexican abortion.

In Tucson, we felt a sense of foreboding and alienation as we looked at the water-starved Southwest. We boarded an old, rundown bus, obviously not meant for the more expensive runs, and traveled four hours southward to Douglas, Arizona. The interior of the bus showed its age even more than the outside; the seats, cracked and worn from the countless bodies filling them through the years, exuded a smell of humanity. That odor, blending with the acrid stench from the indoor toilet, overpowered us. The sun, reaching its height, turned the bus into a foul oven.

Douglas, Arizona, was equally ugly. It was slightly larger than the other towns that we had passed through, but its roads were unpaved and the swirling dust stirred by the bus settled in a grey pall over all it touched. The Douglas Hotel, built in the late 1800s, was once a grand hotel; its interior, rising to a full four stories, encompassed an atrium covered by magnificent antique stained-glass. Grand oak balconies surrounded the lobby on four sides, and the interior furnishings were fine period pieces. Our entry into the lobby made the trip seem more surreal. We felt as out of place as the hotel in this shabby town. We settled in our rooms, took a nap, and walked across the street to have dinner in the only cafe in town.

After dinner, we scurried back to the hotel reception desk and requested a taxi for eight o'clock the next morning. To our surprise, the receptionist asked us if we were going to the "medical" clinic in Aqua Prieta for abortions! At that point, we realized that our trip was a familiar scene repeated almost daily in this border town. We wondered how many women had traveled the same journey seeking abortions the only way they

McVey-Ritsick, Patricia. 1992. "Aqua Prieta—1968." Reprinted by permission of the author.

could in 1968. These quick visitors had created a "cottage industry" for Douglas's economy and everyone in town knew it. We retreated to the safety of our room and slept fitfully through the night.

The next morning the cab driver arrived on time for our fifteen-minute drive to the Medica Clinica in Aqua Prieta. Even though the driver knew little English, he seemed to know exactly where to take us for our appointment. As we crossed the border, we felt the safety we had known in Douglas disappear; we had entered a foreign country to engage in an illegal act. We hadn't even considered whether or not abortion was legal in Mexico—and, when that thought entered our minds, we questioned whether or not we would ever return home to Los Angeles.

As we neared Aqua Prieta, we noticed a definite change in surroundings. What had seemed like desolation and barrenness in Douglas now became a forsaken wasteland. Everything was in total disrepair, soiled and stained by garbage and human waste. The squalid and sordid town was the closest thing to a human cesspool we had ever seen. Dogs roamed everywhere, picking up the refuse that inhabitants had discarded. Children and adults, dressed in rags, stared vacantly at us. We arrived at the clinic, a dirt-washed abandoned-looking building with no sign indicating it was a medical clinic. We questioned the driver as to whether or not this really was the location of the clinic, and he assured us in broken English that it was. I turned to Susan in desperation and begged her not to go through with the abortion. Again she insisted she had no choice. She abruptly got out of the cab, paid the driver, and gave him additional money to wait for us until after the abortion to take us back to Douglas.

We entered the clinic. What should have been the reception room of a doctor's office was a room devoid of all furnishings except a dead palm tree in the corner and decades worth of dirt and grime. We refrained from touching anything and huddled together in the center of the room. Again I begged Susan to return to the United States, but again she refused. The consequences of going through the pregnancy and telling her parents would be worse than the abortion itself. We waited until a man in a filthy white T-shirt, jeans, and tennis shoes came into the room and demanded $500 in cash. Susan gave him the money, he disappeared, and we waited, wondering if he had skipped out the back door with our money. Finally the same man returned and told Susan to come with him. She demanded that I be allowed to go with her and watch, as she did not want to be alone. The man argued that this was not part of the package, while I inwardly panicked at the thought of watching an abortion. I knew nothing about how an abortion should be performed, felt uncomfortable watching my best friend have one, and would not know what to do if the doctor botched it anyhow. I did not want to go with her. At the same time, I did not want to wait in the reception room worrying about whether she was surviving. The man finally agreed to allow me into the "surgical suite."

The operating room, equipped with post-World War II medical equipment, was as filthy as everything else. The "doctor" and his assistant, the man who had escorted us in, were both dressed in dirty white outfits smeared with dried blood and fetal tissue. The "doctor" ordered Susan to take off her shoes, slacks, and panties; to get on the table; and to put her feet in the stirrups. I was horrified. Obviously neither of the men were doctors; yet Susan was not only undressing before them, but climbing on an examination table for a life-threatening procedure. I stayed by her side and held her hand while I tried to control my own horror.

Susan sobbed uncontrollably, but continuously repeated to herself the necessity for her actions. Then, without washing his hands, gloving himself, or giving Susan any type of anesthetic, the "doctor" inserted a long metal "S"-shaped instrument into her vagina and through her cervix into her uterus. With this he then tried to scrape out the fetus and tissue. Susan was in excruciating pain, sobbing and clutching my hands. When the "doctor" removed the instrument, he placed a filthy bucket under her buttocks and told her to sit up so that the fetal material would slide out into the bucket. Susan asked me to look and make sure the fetus had come out. I looked, but saw only large masses of bloody tissue. After about five minutes, the "doctor" inserted a giant tampon, about two inches wide by approximately four inches long, into her vagina and told her to leave it in for twenty-four hours. He told her to dress and leave.

We left the clinic and rode back to Douglas, happy to be back in the United States, in a familiar place, with a familiar language, and some semblance of safety. After several hours, we took the next bus to Tucson and flew home. Throughout our return trip, Susan suffered extreme cramping. When we got back into Los Angeles, I dropped her off at her boyfriend's house because he had agreed to take care of her after the abortion. I drove home, collapsed in bed, and slept soundly through the night.

The next morning, the doorbell awakened me. Susan's boyfriend came to tell me he had taken her to the hospital during the night because of massive hemorrhaging. She had been rushed into surgery to stop the bleeding and to have a dilatation and curettage (D&C), a method of scraping the uterus. The doctors told her she was miscarrying and they had to do the D&C to avoid any possibility of infection from remaining fetal tissue. They were not aware that the "miscarriage" was the result of a botched Mexican abortion. In fact, I found out later that the procedure done by the Mexican abortionist was an incomplete D&C, and the tampon he had inserted had "plugged" her vagina to keep the miscarriage from occurring in Mexico. Susan ended up with a serious septic infection that the U.S. doctors could not account for, but which they cleared up by giving her massive doses of antibiotics.

Susan was one of the lucky ones during that era of illegal abortions. She came away with her life, survived a massive infection introduced into her system during her Mexican abortion, and later had children of her own. Many women suffered a far different fate.

In remembering this experience and talking with many women who have never known the horrors of illegal abortions, I realize I must speak out. Our choices in the 1960s were unacceptable. Yet, if people do not want to experience again this type of medical nightmare, they need to become active in seeing that women continue to have choices as to when and where to bear children. The silent majority of us need to act on our beliefs now or we may again be forced to return to Aqua Prieta, Mexico, for unsafe abortions.

Part Two: Women's Well Being
Chapter 3—Redefining Women's Health
Study Questions

1. Look back to your first menstrual cycle. Did you know what was happening? Was your family open about this life-changing event, and did they honor it? Why or why not?

2. Why is the use of PMS to excuse behavior a double bind for women? Explain. Do you feel this has affected the treatment of PMS? Why or why not?

3. Why could anorexia nervosa and bulimia be considered cultural diseases?

4. What are the economic, social, and political effects on women if they are not allowed to control their own fertility?

5. Women could be seen as guinea pigs for birth control. Why? Are men subjected to the same experimentation? Why or why not?

6. Discuss birth control as a class/race issue.

7. Historically, what condition in the United States led to the illegalization of abortion? Today, if states are given the right to uphold or ban abortion, what will be the result? Could this be considered classist and/or racist? Why or why not?

8. What precipitated the decline of midwives? How has this affected women's medical treatment? Has this treatment changed within the last two decades? Why or why not?

9. What are the ethical questions surrounding amniocentesis? What is your opinion concerning these issues?

10. Draw some parallels between the view of the onset of menarche, PMS, and menopause. How does the way they are viewed affect women culturally? Personally?

11. Why is it important to take charge of your health?

12. In "The Silent Epidemic . . . ," what does Goldsmith consider the practical strategy for stemming the STD epidemic for populations at high risk? What are some of the barriers to implementing this plan? What is the most effective way to control STDs?

13. What is the most common STD among young women? Why does it go virtually undetected? What percentage of young women contract it? Young men?

14. What are the known risk factors for acquiring human papillomavirus (HPV)? According to Wendy Wertheimer, what does the politicization of the STD crisis reflect? Are other issues of young women's health affected in the same way? Why?

15. Referencing "AIDS: In Living Color," name ways in which black women bear the major burden of the AIDS epidemic in their community.

16. How have cultural and racial stereotypes affected the campaign encouraging women, especially black women, to practice safe sex?

17. The politics of reproductive rights has become an issue of dichotomous thinking and semantics. After reading McElhiney's piece on fetal rights versus mother's rights and "Aqua Prieta-1968," explore your views on this issue.

18. In her spoof on menstruation, Steinem states: "The characteristics of the powerful . . . are thought to be better than the characteristics of the powerless." In small groups, list ten positive characteristics of men that when applied to women are seen as negative. List ten positive characteristics of women that are seen as negative when applied to men. In the large group, discuss these lists and whether one list was more difficult to compile than the other.

WOMEN'S RELATIONSHIPS: FAMILIES, KIN, PARTNERS, AND FRIENDS

Margo Linn Espenlaub and Carmen Braun Williams

Introduction

As human involvements that affect the very core of women's well-being, interpersonal relationships are essential for emotional and psychological growth and development. The composition of women's relationships is based on a multitude of factors: biology, shared interests and tasks, physical proximity, racial and ethnic identity, and chance. And, as lifestyles change, choices once heavily sanctioned become viable possibilities. Women in contemporary society face complex issues and multiple options when they decide to remain single, marry, form committed partnerships, remain child-free, create biological or chosen families, and establish friendships with other women or men. Choices often appear to be based upon individual and informed decision-making, but in fact many women do not *choose* to remain in oppressive partner relationships, endure economic struggles and discrimination as parents and sole providers, or exist without friendships and supportive female networks. Relationship decisions are seldom straightforward actions with predictable outcomes. Yet women continue to be charged, unlike men, with the responsibility of either making their relationships "work" better or accepting cultural and economic consequences as the price of change and personal growth.

The family, as an ever-changing dynamic, can provide self-identification, rewarding interpersonal relationships, and security to its female members; yet it can also be the location in which neglect, repression, control, or violence can occur. This latter reality stands in marked contrast to the ideal of family as a place of refuge from an uncompassionate and hostile world. Within kinship and extended family networks, female members often support one another. Such arrangements can serve as spheres of women's empowerment, as in African American kinship networks, or, under negative conditions, may perpetuate subordinate and stereotypical female roles.

Women also develop friendships outside the structure and location of family and kin relations. Friendships with other women or men often become lifelong bonds, frequently challenged by heterosexist assumptions and ideologies. Barriers to these bonds between women of color and white women and between lesbians and heterosexual women may occur due to the impact of these same cultural proscriptions. Similarly, committed partnerships formed with other women or men may not appear to be "natural" if they are lesbian, non-married, or child-free.

Perspectives on sex and gender systems and stereotypes associated with prescribed female roles are key to an understanding of women's lives. Families, friendships, and partnerships offer the potential for individual growth and identity, just as they continue to mirror dominant values and assumptions accepted as cultural norms. Indeed, *thinking women* can advocate redefinition of interpersonal relationships addressed by the following questions:

- What is meant by a "traditional" family?
- How does the definition of "traditional" differ across women's racial groups?
- How do family members fill prescribed sex and gender roles?
- What are the key aspects of black women's socialization in the family?
- How has unequal power in relationships oppressed women?
- What have been traditional sources of power within families and kinship networks for racial-ethnic women?
- How are chosen family or partnership arrangements a viable alternative to the nuclear family?
- Can mutually collaborative relationships be "equal" between partners?
- What are the barriers to friendships between white women and women of color?
- What are the obstacles to friendships between lesbian and heterosexual women?

Family Structure

During the industrial period of the late eighteenth and early nineteenth centuries,

modern nuclear family structure emerged in the United States (Luepnitz 1988a; Stacey 1990; Zinn and Eitzen 1990). Families of this period, largely composed of white middle- and working-class men and women, were increasingly segregated by gendered definitions of work. Paid labor in the public sector became the location of men's work promoting "institutionalized subordination" of women within the domestic sphere (Stacey 1990, 8).

Women, children, and extended kin in privatized middle-class families of the nineteenth century participated in unpaid domestic labor in households "whose buying power was determined by the husband's income" (Gerstel and Gross 1989, 95). Changes in household structure brought about with industrial capitalism affected working-class families as well. For example, European immigrant populations "practiced some aspects of the family- and gender-role patterns found in the middle class" even though women's familial support work necessitated participation in both domestic and paid labor (Gerstel and Gross 1989, 96).

Hierarchically ordered with father as head, the white middle-class family as a cultural norm persisted as such well into the twentieth century. Indeed, in the closing decade of the 1990s, this norm continues to be enforced by patriarchal systems of authority even though this family type is now a smaller minority. Still, the idealized "family is one of the primary mechanisms for perpetuating social inequality" (Zinn and Eitzen 1990, xiv.) Insistence upon this traditionalist model perpetuates a familial unit that maintains control of husband over wife, an adherence to male and female sex roles, and transfer to children of culturally or religiously based moral values that support heterosexist and racist ideologies. As sociologist Judith Stacey states, "this is precisely the form of family life that many mistake for an ancient, essential, and now-endangered institution" (Stacey 1990, 5). In fact, American families of this century, and in previous centuries as well, reflect a range of diversity and difference shaped by factors of race, ethnicity, geography, and economics (Zinn and Eitzen 1990). Underscoring this is research by anthropologist Johnnetta Cole who notes that a "multiplicity of family forms have always existed in the United States" (Cole 1986, 109) and that the idealized nuclear family represents "no more than 7% of all families in the United States" (Cole 1986, 11).

Yet, biases based on the traditional white middle-class family structure persist and skew research on groups outside this framework. As Monica McGoldrick notes, when blacks and other people of color are studied, "positive aspects of ethnicity— traditions, coping skills, belief systems—are ignored" (McGoldrick et al. 1982, 8). This damaging oversight has perpetuated pejorative views of black family systems, systems in which women's traditional roles are models of power. An understanding of the centrality of black women within these systems requires an appreciation for both the resilience of familial patterns that derive from black Americans' West African origins and the resourcefulness of black families in response to white patriarchal oppression. Both of these major influences have shaped roles that reflect African American women's value as significant contributors to the economy and health of families. Examination of these roles and relationships using a feminist framework contradicts earlier, negative portrayals presented by scholars holding a traditional bias and reveals, instead, a complex picture of adversity, vulnerability, and strength. The power inherent in African American women's traditional roles and relationships stands in marked contrast to that of white women.

The traditional white family is believed to be an intact and well-balanced unit, ideally structured with husband as primary wage earner and an economically dependent wife essentially responsible for all domestic duties, including the care of children. Problematic in this idealized structure is the unequal positions of power among its members, each of whom must adhere to prescribed sex roles based on patriarchal assumptions and gender stereotypes (Zinn and Eitzen 1990). The role of wife and mother has no fixed schedule, implying that her support to family members is always available and accessible. Reflected in the primary management of household duties and care giving, women's work "contributes much to both the husband's economic success and the wife's economic dependence" (Gerstel and Gross 1989, 103). Also problematic is an economic imperative that unrealistically implies that a single income can support the traditional family model along with all necessary material needs of its members (Stacey 1990).

Assumed to be an autonomous unit, the family has been expected to function in isolation from larger society and solve its problems and conflicts internally. Espoused as the American norm during the post World War II 1950s, television programs glorified "the male breadwinner nuclear household and modern family ideology [in] *Father Knows Best, Leave it to Beaver*, and *Ozzie and Harriet*" (Stacey 1990, 10). Yet, standard portrayals of idealized family life fail to present the realities of families of color, further reinforcing the marginalization of family models that diverge from this narrow standard.

Significant cultural value has been placed on families in which children are raised in one household by both biological parents. This family profile, however, is not the cultural norm in the 1990s, nor is it a reality for the future (Zinn and Eitzen 1990). Children often live with a single parent, non-biological parents, extended family, or within kin networks; "divorce and the formation of new households now result in families extending across two or more households as children retain ties with both parents" (Zinn and Eitzen 1990, 15). Feminist scholars have also noted that while contemporary families may be "father-absent" (Luepnitz 1988, 17), other forms of patriarchal authority are exercised through the legal system, government agencies, and health care services (Ferguson 1983; Luepnitz 1988). These conditions signal "the patriarchal state [to be] more powerful than any single father" (Luepnitz 1988b, 17). Additionally shaped by cultural, ethnic, racial, religious, and heterosexual or homosexual identities, diverse living arrangements more realistically represent the contemporary American family (Zinn and Eitzen 1990).

Economic factors also affect family composition. For example, as socioeconomic conditions worsened in the 1980s for segments of the black community (especially those living in the inner cities), the challenges facing African American families in those settings multiplied, forcing alternative family arrangements. Poor women who manage families as single parents are increasing among blacks and whites and represent a population especially vulnerable in the face of diminishing economic opportunity. Single-parent families constitute the fastest growing family type, and because they diverge from the two-parent cultural ideal, are often subject to negative labels that impute instability. "Single parenthood does *not* necessarily make a family dysfunctional" (Boyd-Franklin 1989, 191); how-

ever, because poor women who head families are increasingly faced with adverse social conditions, their ability to maintain a healthy family system may be severely strained.

Poor black families constitute approximately one third of all black families; 70 percent of poor black families are headed by women (Collins 1991). Because black women are typically socialized to pursue an education, to work, and to be economically self-reliant, many are able to function at least adequately if not always optimally. Certainly those who maintain extended kinship ties have access to child care and financial assistance to augment their individual resources (Stack 1974). However, as certain jobs in which working-class black men have been concentrated become scarcer, such as manufacturing, dual-income families become less an option for low-income-earning black women (Collins 1991). Indeed, even middle-class heterosexual black women may find—due to a variety of factors including their greater representation than black men in professional and managerial positions and their lesser likelihood than white women to remarry—that they too face the prospect of single parenthood in greater numbers than in the past (Collins 1991). Of course, it should be added that there are and always have been black women for whom single parenthood is a deliberate choice and who live volitionally in black communities among women-centered networks and extended kin.

Carolyn Attneave, a psychologist who has worked extensively with Native American groups, describes a bleaker picture. Whereas in traditional Native American societies each gender's contribution within a stable extended network was equally valued, the situation has shifted for single, urban Native American women who head families. With economic changes, such female-headed households have become more numerous and often operate in the absence of kinship support. "In general, Indians have not formed ties with others to the extent that the Black community has in making up a similar deficit" (Attneave 1982, 79). This "deficit"—the lack of connection to an extended network of kin and non-kin—significantly affects the well-being and functioning of single-parent urban women.

Poor families headed by women, due to their severely limited financial resources, face in growing numbers the possibility of becoming part of the population of homeless people. The numbers of homeless women sharply increased in the 1980s (Caton 1990; Thorman 1988). Leading the list of causes are poverty, family dissolution (in some cases directly precipitated by domestic violence), and housing that is inaccessible because it is unaffordable to poor women (Sullivan and Damrosch 1989). No-fault divorce laws, while enabling women to leave bad marriages, have also played a part in women's homelessness in that domiciles customarily granted women in divorce settlements may be sold, leaving women without sufficient resources to secure housing independently.

Women with families are among the fastest growing segment of the homeless (Bassuk 1992). These women face severe difficulties, including inadequate health care (Sullivan and Damrosch 1989) and social isolation (Caton 1990). "A homeless woman is more of a social outcast than a homeless man because she violates the stricter prescriptions of the proper role for women" (Merves 1991, 229). Female heads of homeless families also face obstacles to regaining economic independence due to lack of work and unavailability of child care (McChesney 1992).

Contemporary white, middle-class, nuclear families are assumed to be "natural," implying that other family arrangements are not normal, desirable, or healthy. Black families headed by women have been especially vulnerable to these pejorative labels. Early studies on the black family labeled black women "matriarchal" and denounced them as responsible for the disorganization of black families and the failure of black men in mainstream American society (Moynihan 1965). What was labeled "disorganization" in black families, as clarified in subsequent studies (Hill 1972) was, in fact, a departure from the nuclear structure of traditional white families. What was criticized as "matriarchal" reflected a difference in women's roles, that is, a mislabeling of black women's traditional positions of shared power and decision-making. These differences represent, in fact, healthy alternative familial arrangements.

Negative stereotypes are also applied to familial relationships where Latina women are assumed to accept passively subordinate roles as wives and mothers. Latino households, dislocated and displaced by changing economic and population dynamics in the United States, have developed unified networks of immediate and extended families. "Familism" (Zinn and Eitzen 1990, 124) represents the necessary emotional and economic support structures that extend across generations of Latino families. Racial and ethnic oppression and discrimination by the dominant white culture with its imposed norms create conditions under which family members must rely upon each other for health and child care, maintenance of domestic responsibilities, and essential material needs (Zinn and Eitzen 1990; Sánchez-Ayéndez 1986).

In a study on elderly Puerto Rican women living in Boston, Melba Sánchez-Ayéndez assesses the "dual standard of conduct for men and women" within family and kin networks (173). Women maintain family unity by avoiding confrontation with male family members who, as providers and protectors, often stand in "a dominant position in relation to females" (Sánchez-Ayéndez 1986, 173). Within domestic arrangements women's authority and responsibility is perceived by family members as essential to the well-being of children and kin alike. It is here that motherhood identifies women's primary role, one which "is viewed as leading her toward more commitment to and a better understanding of her children than is shown by the father" (Sánchez-Ayéndez 1986, 174). This "undercover power" of Latina women due to their centrality as mothers in the family network mitigates against the submissiveness often ascribed to them by researchers and other observers. For many Latinas, this purported submissiveness is a "social fiction" that obscures the wide variation in marital roles in Latino families from patriarchal to egalitarian (Falicov 1982, 139).

The covert power of many Asian American women is similarly described. Asian American mothers, although traditionally embedded in a hierarchical role structure wherein women's position is subordinate to men's, form very strong emotional bonds with their children, often interceding on their behalf with the father, the authority figure. Furthermore, the mother's power may be strengthened later in life after the death of the father. Although at that point explicit authority is placed with the eldest son, the mother, because of the strength of her emotional bond with the son, may actually exercise covert authority (Shon and Ja 1982). These sources of power available to racial-ethnic women, while subsumed within male-dominated family structures, contradict

simplistic interpretations of female passivity.

Patricia Hill Collins (1991) presents information about the centrality and transformative power of women's positions in the black family network. Power is different from domination (i.e., power-over), which is how earlier theorists characterized black women's influence. The power to transform—women's power—does not take away from, does not oppress, indeed *contributes* to another's sense of self (Miller 1976; French 1985).

Strong bonds between women, especially mothers and daughters, carry forward throughout a lifetime as sources of empowerment. Researchers in the area of black mother-daughter relationships are often critical of white feminist work on the mother-daughter dyad. Its narrow focus, failing to account for the broader familial context—the extended family—and to adequately address the implications of oppressive cultural factors on women's socialization, does not reflect the realities of black families (Joseph and Lewis 1981). Gloria Joseph, a black feminist researcher who has studied mother-daughter relationships in black family systems, identifies a theme of collaboration in the relationship between black mothers and daughters. Daughters are taught by mothers, often through the mothers' direct sharing of personal experience, to cope with racist oppression in its many forms and disguises and to deal with sexist oppression perpetrated by both white and black men. Black daughters' socialization in the black family thus focuses heavily on teaching self-reliance and survival skills (Joseph 1984).

Over the last two decades, feminists of color have challenged the inequity and oppressiveness of traditional roles for women in both public and private realms. Chicana feminism, developing early in the

1970s, parallels the development of black feminist and white feminist movements of this period (Garcia 1989). Facing attack from their respective social movements for identifying male hegemony and sexism, Latina and Asian American feminists have been charged with dividing the core issues of racism and classism (Garcia 1989; Chow 1987). Similarly, black feminists face criticism and hostility from elements in the black community that perceive feminist struggle as a betrayal—that is, as siphoning energy and resources from the struggle against racial oppression (Terrelonge 1975; hooks 1989). Black feminists maintain that the two—sexism and racism—are intersecting aspects of patriarchal domination (Collins 1991).

Originating in grassroots organizations, broad-based activism of Latina women has addressed political issues affecting both family and community concerns. Mary Pardo has noted that frequently these "women speak of their communities and their activism as extensions of their family and household responsibilities" (1990, 1). For example, the "Mothers of East Los Angeles" (MELA), a diverse group of women experienced as community activists, challenged state and local governments' attempts to impose undesirable and hazardous conditions for residents in urban neighborhoods. As a result of its collective efforts, MELA has "transformed social identity—ethnic identity, class identity, and gender identity—into an impetus as well as a basis for activism" (Pardo 1990, 2).

Black mothers' and "othermothers'" long tradition of involvement beyond the privatized domestic sphere out into the black community reflects the transformation of black women's roles as well. Motherhood, a role afforded much status and respect in the black community, is one that is not limited to biological mothers but extends to "othermothers" (Collins's term for women who may or may not be related biologically to the children for whom care is provided and who are not even necessarily biological mothers). That is, African American women's influence as mothers and othermothers extends beyond child care to community activism where their personal power helps to transform black institutions (e.g., religious, educational) into places of greater responsiveness to the needs of the children and others in the community (Collins 1991). In their many roles as mother, daughter, grandmother, aunt, sister, cousin, and othermother, black women, whose sense of self is firmly grounded in community and responsibility (Brown-Collins and Sussewell 1986), have lent stability and strength to black families. Women-centered networks have thus played a significant part in the politicization of the black and Latina family and community.

Kin

Largely responsible for providing support services within their immediate domestic settings as well as to extended family networks, women influence and activate decisions regarding the welfare of all kin members (Di Leonardo 1987). Black extended family networks, including biological kin and non-biological "fictive kin" (Stack 1974), comprise a cultural pattern whose legacy has African roots and that has provided backbone to a system of survival under oppression. This kinship system provides "a coherent network of mutual emotional and economic support" (Boyd-Franklin 1989, 43). Women have been important figures in these extended kinship groups.

Anthropologist Louise Lamphere has identified the importance of women's roles within Native American kinship networks. In studies conducted among Navajo populations in Arizona and New Mexico, Lamphere (1974) noted that such networks are female-centered when egalitarian relationships exist between women and men. This dynamic values and supports authoritative decision-making and community leadership from women, strong ties between female kin, and mother-daughter bonds that sustain women throughout their lives.

Exploring the diversity in Native American women's roles, particularly among Plains Indians, anthropologist Beatrice Medicine describes the position of "warrior women" as being a "healthy and self-actualized role" (Medicine 1983, 267). Such roles, sanctioned and expressed in a variety of ways within Native American communities, challenge white, patriarchal definitions of female as daughter, mother, and wife. Empowered to act decisively, the "manly-hearted woman," for example, "excelled in every important aspect of tribal life—property ownership, ceremonialism, and domestic affairs" (Medicine 1983, 270). Positions of female authority within kin and community networks offer, according to Medicine, "an anomaly in the customary view of Plains Indian women as submissive and oppressed" (271). Also important in shaping the roles of daughter, wife, mother, and sister was birth order and its accompanying responsibilities for female kin. Medicine notes further that the "range of socially accepted roles for women in Plains Indian societies permits us to understand the role of warrior women as one aspect of this variation" (173).

Women of diverse ethnic, racial, and class backgrounds participate in similar functions within their respective kin groups. Anthropologist Micaela di Leonardo, in research conducted on female kin networks among Italian-Americans living in northern California, has identified maintenance tasks associated with kinship networks as "women's work" (1987, 443), since men generally do not undertake these activities. Duties associated with kinswomen's work would be difficult, if not impossible, to replace with paid, outside support services (Di Leonardo 1987). Indeed, such responsibilities comprise a complex, interpersonal integration of tasks on which all kin members rely. The Puerto Rican woman relies on these women-centered networks to assist in child care and domestic tasks. "Without the help of the extended family, she may experience those tasks as unbearable" (Garcia-Preto 1982, 173).

Close kinship ties are reinforced by Latina women who have frequent contact with immediate and extended family members. Maintaining a "caring attitude" signifies a woman's contribution to family identity and unity across households and generations of kin (Sánchez-Ayéndez 175). Ill and aging relatives, often cared for by adult children, receive different types of support from daughters than from sons. Emotional support is generally expected of female kin, especially daughters, who "are perceived as being inherently better able to understand their mothers due to their shared status and qualities as women" (178).

Kin networks are often structured across households to include family members who may not live in close proximity to one another. "Kinswomen" (Di Leonardo 1987, 443), responsible for maintaining continuation of family identity and unity, initiate occasions of recognition for birthdays, anniversaries, and traditional or religious holidays" as in the differing emphases on Friday or Sunday family dinners among Jews and Christians" (447).

In many black extended kin groups as women become elderly they often serve as the culture-bearers, passing along family and cultural history and practices to younger generations. Connie Young Yu, a Chinese American historian and writer, describes a similar function for Chinese American grandmothers. In searching for information about the achievements of the women immigrants in her family, Yu found the grandmothers to be the "historical links," filling in the gaps and bridging the generations with their oral history (Yu, 1989, 35). Author Amy Tan, in her novel *The Joy Luck Club*, has described such intergenerational connections between Chinese-born and American-born Asian women in which cultural definitions of female identity and position in kinship groups converge. Following the death of her mother, it is the "aunties" who reveal to their American-born niece the legacy of her mother's secret—that of two daughters residing in China. Entrusted with new knowledge of extended family, the female initiate thus enters her kin community as a future bearer of its cultural history (Tan 1989).

Aging women frequently offer essential support, particularly child care, to younger members of their extended families. Given the dual responsibilities of work and child care faced by most black women, a grandmother is sometimes "'the only prop' in a child's life" (Wade-Gayles 1984). Indeed, as Nancy Boyd-Franklin discusses in her research on psychotherapy with black families, the death of the grandmother—so potentially great a loss due to the centrality of her position in many families—may well be the factor that motivates a single-parent black woman to seek therapy, particularly if other, more traditional supports are unavailable to her (1989).

Interestingly, with the increase in teenage pregnancies, many black women are finding themselves to be young grandmothers in their thirties. One implication of this developing phenomenon that has been observed is that the traditional role of the grandmother is shifting to one that is less available, due to the many demands in these grandmothers' own lives, to meet the needs of the grandchild (Ladner and Gourdine 1984). Given the very young age of these mothers (signaling a potentially diminished capacity to offer the child the necessary resources for healthy emotional development), the consequences for a portion of the future generation of black children may be deleterious.

Women frequently have difficulty balancing paid labor outside the home with unpaid domestic kinship work. Kinswomen, particularly, must alter their household schedules in order to maintain the immediate or long-term needs of family members. Women can experience considerable guilt when faced with fears of not doing enough for family members. Similarly, decisions regarding the raising of children, maintenance of home, and communication with extended family can become topics of debate and mitigation among female kin. Thus, the work of kinswomen "takes place in an arena characterized simultaneously by cooperation and competition, by guilt and gratification" (Di Leonardo 1987, 446).

Collins (1991) identifies these paradoxes in black kinship groups by describing the black family as a "contradictory location," that is, one in which women experience both confinement and self-empowerment. This contradictory aspect is reflected in ways in which daughters sometimes feel overprotected by mothers who seek to shield them from racism's injurious impact while, at the same time,

163

actively inculcating them with the "toughness" needed to cope and survive (Joseph and Lewis 1981). Daughters are taught to balance the pejorative cultural valuations associated with the low-status occupations in which they as black women are overly represented, against *self* valuations of dignity and worth. The appearance of acquiescence in the face of injustice, acquiescence that may mask silent rebellion, is yet another example of the pattern of contradiction endemic to the black female experience (Collins 1991).

Partners

Lifestyles and family arrangements that present alternative patterns to the narrowly conceived cultural ideal of the two-parent, heterosexual union bound by legal contract have always existed. "What is new is a greater recognition and tolerance of persons who choose to live in some kinds of nontraditional ways" (Zinn and Eitzen 1990, 391). Ideally, mutual respect, collaboration, caring, and commitment are elements of partner relations whether these are heterosexual, homosexual, married, or nonmarried. Partnerships may include children or extended family members in arrangements based upon economic necessity. Children of divorced parents, biological children, and chosen children might share living arrangements with partners who parent them full time or co-parent them part time.

African American women's partnerships include informal and common-law marriages*: relationships with black men where there is a commitment without

legal marriage. Common-law marriages among blacks are not unusual. "In Black communities, there have always existed legal and non-legal 'marriages' in which the couple is treated within their community as if they were married" (Boyd-Franklin 1989). This pattern of extralegal marriage dates back to slavery, when blacks, for reasons including the prohibition by law of marriages between slaves and the frequent selling of partners by slaveholders, often perceived their attachments as tenuous (Davis 1981; Giddings 1984). "The threat of disruption was perhaps the most direct and pervasive cultural assault on families that slaves encountered" (Dill 1992, 220). External exigencies continue to impede the formation of long-term heterosexual relationships. For example, in Carol Stack's study (1974) of poor urban black families in the 1970s, a number of factors "that appear to mitigate against the formation of long term relationships" (120) are identified, one of the most salient of which is unemployment. Stack predicted in the 1970s that, without major changes in job opportunities, "it is unlikely that urban low income Blacks will form lasting conjugal units" (123). Indeed, we are witnessing in the 1990s the accuracy of her prediction with the rise in the number of single black female heads of households among the urban lower class.

Although economic factors may influence a couple's choice to become partners outside of marriage, other factors, especially the desire to create a space and structure that allows for greater autonomy for women in relationships, are also significant in many women's choice of alternative couple arrangements. "Some women interpret cohabitation as a source of intimate relationship without the confinement of traditional gender roles that

___

*The criteria for common-law marriages vary across states. Some states designate a time period (e.g., seven years) after which a couple living together is considered married. Other states recognize as married a couple who present themselves as husband and wife.

marriages tend to promote" (Zinn and Eitzen 1990, 406).

The need to form partnership patterns that reflect equal valuing of women's and men's participation and contribution is a priority for many women. For example, many women and men, regardless of marital status, choose to live in egalitarian partnerships sharing economic concerns, domestic tasks, and child care. Establishing personal boundaries is an important aspect of egalitarian relations between adults, and between children and adults, the maintenance of which may be difficult given society's pervasive patriarchal conditioning. Those holding more power in a relationship can violate another's autonomy when, for example, "men presume the right to invade, rather than respect, a less powerful person's boundaries" (Kasl 1989, 259–60). The addition of children usually upsets an equal sharing of domestic work, imposing stress upon partnerships (Zinn and Eitzen 1990). Women are charged with the burden of child care and domestic responsibilities, therefore limiting and disrupting their access to outside employment. "Women's lower average earnings mean that wives still rely more than husbands do on their spouses for financial support, and that unmarried mothers often face poverty" (Gerstel and Gross 1989, 105).

In a ground-breaking study, sociologist Jessie Bernard (1972) found that marriage as an institution is generally more beneficial to men than it is to women, and that wives become less psychologically healthy within marriage than do husbands. Identified in the 1960s as "the problem that has no name," feminist Betty Friedan (1963, 11) exposed the pervasive tyranny experienced by white, middle-class, married women; traditional marriage, as a hegemonic institution, presumes wives' subordination and defer-

ence to husbands' authority. Given this dynamic, it is not surprising, affirms psychologist Deborah Luepnitz, "that women who stay in the house and are financially dependent on their husbands are more likely to develop anxiety disorders, phobias, and depressions" (Luepnitz 1988b, 10). Indeed, as sociologist Shelley Coverman (1989) has pointed out, women often experience physical and psychological burdens "from simultaneously fulfilling too many roles (e.g., parent, spouse, paid worker, homemaker)" (365). For women of color, on the other hand, multiple roles have been associated with psychological strength and self-empowerment (Malson 1981; Zinn 1980).

Idealized as self-sacrificing caregivers endlessly seeing to others' needs, women frequently find themselves powerless within partnership and familial arrangements. Luepnitz (1988b) identifies this unequal gendered dynamic within "normal" families consisting "of a husband and children who are functioning adequately and a wife who is not" (11). Ironically, women as mothers are also blamed when partnership or family problems arise. Luepnitz adds that sexist attitudes perpetuating male-defined female roles, frequently occurring in therapy sessions with women, encourage single mothers to be more accessible to men—that they are somehow incomplete as women and mothers without a male partner (1988b). As lesbian feminist poet Adrienne Rich has stated, "only when women recognize and name as force and bondage what has been misnamed love or partnership, can we begin to love and nurture out of strength and purpose" (1979, 216–17).

A departure from this model of female powerlessness is reflected in traditional black marital partnership patterns. Because the African American woman has historically combined the role of nurturer (i.e., primary supplier of child care) with that of economic provider, she had shared with the black man a characteristically egalitarian relationship. Though there certainly exist variations in this partnership pattern, egalitarianism is identified by many scholars as normative and a major strength in African American families (Hill 1972; Hines and Boyd-Franklin 1982; Pinderhughes 1982). Due to the egalitarian norm of black parental relationships, children learn flexibility in family roles and observe reciprocity and shared decision-making between family members (McAdoo, 1986), especially in caring for children and others in need of assistance (e.g., the ill and elderly) and in providing monetary support (Boyd-Franklin 1989).

However, many black scholars note the increasing expression of sexist norms in contemporary black couple relationships (Wallace 1982; hooks 1989; Collins 1991) and the concomitant loss of the egalitarian tradition, a pattern that contributes to a divorce rate for black couples that is twice that for whites (Ladner and Gourdine 1984). Egalitarian partnerships, sought by women of all races, struggle against powerful patriarchal forces that continue to perpetrate male domination and control over women's lives and exertion of male rights to ownership of women as property. These deeply embedded cultural patterns have been and continue to be challenged by white women and women of color who refuse to acquiesce to cultural demands for female subordination. Much work is needed on the part of women and men to create heterosexual partnerships that foster mutual growth and empowerment.

Alternative partnership arrangements for women are heavily constricted by what Adrienne Rich ([1980], 1986) has termed "compulsory heterosexuality" (23). Heterosexism, "the belief in the inherent superiority of one pattern of loving and thereby its right to dominance" (Lorde 1984, 45), maintains that women must seek men as sexual and marital partners, that women's primary role is reproductive, and that other sexual identities and relationships are suspect as morally wrong and unnatural. "The crushing of this sexual component by male authorities," according to Bettina Aptheker, historian and feminist scholar, "is not an act of moral purification but an enforcement of patriarchal privileges and powers" (1989, 88). Oppression, when enacted from a position of ownership, is precisely what disallows women full equality within relationships. These arrangements, in which men feel threatened by women's emerging self-identity, paid work outside the home, or attainment of educational goals, foster deference and submission from female partners.

Heterosexism is racist in that it posits white heterosexual couples as the norm. From their feminist perspectives, lesbians of color have articulated ways in which sexuality is constructed by white patriarchal institutions and internalized by people of color. White privilege enacts upon women a necessary loyalty to these arrangements. Therefore, women of color who are lesbian-identified represent a group multiply oppressed by sex, race, and class (Moraga and Anzaldúa [1981] 1983; Lorde 1984; Aptheker 1989).

Heterosexism and homophobia, "the fear of feelings of love for members of one's own sex and therefore the hatred of those feelings in others" (Lorde 1984, 45), are closely connected. The homophobia of mainstream white culture has, according to many black feminists, filtered into the consciousness of black communities, often making them inhospitable places for the expression of lesbian lifestyles (Clarke 1983; Joseph 1984). Interestingly, there exists in many black communities greater tolerance for gay males than for lesbians, whose choice is erroneously viewed as an abdication of what is considered to be women's innate mothering imperative (hooks 1989). Though they have played integral roles in black families and communities throughout history, black lesbians often suffer from the lack of open acceptance and seek networks of lesbians in other, often white, communities (Cornwell 1983; hooks 1989).

Being "woman-identified" is to recognize women as central to relationships (Faderman 1981). This has great importance for lesbian couples who value women's lives and experience, just as it is important for lesbian feminists who have identified masculine authority and violence in male-female partner relationships (Rich 1979; Faderman 1981; Aptheker 1989). It is from this perspective that lesbian feminists articulate lesbian identity as "a political act, a refusal to fulfill the male image of womanhood or to bow to male supremacy" (Faderman 1981, 413).

Lesbianism among Native American women is expressed as spiritual power integrated with material experiences of female identity. This construct, profoundly different from Western ideologies of religious power and authority, holds expanded concepts of women's roles in family and community (Medicine 1983; Allen 1984). Paula Gunn Allen, a poet and professor of Native American literature, has articulated the strength of "women known as Beloved Women who were warriors, leaders, and influential council members" (1984, 84). Because "the concept of woman" is distinctly different than that found in white Anglo-European cultures, Native American female roles and relationships

to family, kin, and other females must be "understood in a tribal matrix" (85). In this matrix all species of the earth are held to be part of a "spirit world" where personal and familial relationships are guided and directed by powerful forces that are "more closely linked than blood-related persons" (86). Allen conjectures that many tribal systems "did not use sexual constraint as a means of social control" thus allowing the possibility "that lesbianism was practiced rather commonly" (87).

Deeply connected to powers in nature, women's capacity to menstruate and give birth has signified her value, even her deification as goddess, in other cultures. Here, the concept of women was valued, not in relation to men as a sexual being to be owned and controlled, but rather for her unique life experiences of womanhood. According to Allen, even the term "lesbian" holds different meaning and significance for "traditional Indian culture" (90) in which female sexuality was not considered deviant but rather part of a woman's chosen destiny "nurtured by nonhuman [spirit] entities, and . . . therefore acceptable and respectable" (91). In light of needed research in this area, Allen's term "medicine-lesbian" (94) coincides well with a particular form of female power expressed in diverse traditions within Native American communities. Such women-centered traditions, unfortunately, have been eclipsed by masculinist ethnographic and historical biases (Albers and Medicine 1983; Allen 1984).

For Latina women, "in a political climate that already viewed feminist ideology with suspicion, lesbianism as a sexual lifestyle and political ideology came under even more attack" (Garcia 1989, 226). Indeed, rejection of lesbians is common in Latino cultures, according to Oliva Espín (1992), a Latina scholar. She notes further the added stress of keeping one's lesbianism closeted in a culture that is characterized by "strong interdependence among family members, even in adulthood"; that is, being open about one's lesbianism risks the maintenance of highly valued family ties (Espín 1992, 145).

For women who are lesbian and Asian American, struggle for self-identity conflicts with cultural mores that define sex as "shameful" (Pamela H. 1989, 284). From this perspective "homosexuality is seen as a Western concept, a product of losing touch with one's Asian heritage, of becoming too assimilated" (284). Prevailing cultural assumptions hold that the female child must become a wife or she might "reflect negatively on the woman's family" (287). The attribution of lesbianism as an American cultural sickness is voiced in Latino cultures as well, even among otherwise radical thinkers, a sentiment that adds to the oppression of the Latina lesbian (Espín 1992).

Women as partners must also face decisions regarding the raising of biological or chosen children. The idea that children are raised to recapitulate misogynist societal values has been the concern of many feminists. Audre Lorde, a black lesbian feminist mother, writes poignantly of her struggle to raise her son in a manner that encourages him to experience his full humanity rather than conform to prescribed gender roles (Lorde 1984). "It [the knowledge that we are not omnipotent] is an important step for a boy, whose societal destruction begins when he is forced to believe that he can only be strong if he doesn't feel, or if he wins" (76). In confronting heterosexism and homophobia, lesbian partners, as in all aspects of their public lives, must endure discrimination for choosing to parent children. Homophobic attitudes place limitations on les-

bian couples' participation in life choices primarily available to white heterosexual partners. For example, no states recognize marriages among lesbians, allow lesbians to adopt children, acknowledge lesbian partners in health insurance claims,* grant custody in divorce cases to lesbian mothers, or award next-of-kin inheritance to surviving lesbian partners without a will (Zinn and Eitzen 1990). Heterosexual partnerships continue to be viewed as the only legitimate arrangement.

In both heterosexual and lesbian partnerships, giving up one's identity as inferior to the other's is a result of patriarchal/heterosexist beliefs in power over one's partner. While it may be true in most instances that lesbian women, having shared in the reality of sexual oppression (Sang 1984), relate more consciously to one another's needs, power issues between partners still apply. For example, the assignment of domestic tasks according to a partner's available time and individual skill requires valuing both partners' abilities and efforts. Creation of personal space and time for oneself is another consideration in partner relations, particularly for lesbian couples.

---

*Two exceptions arise here: (1) The city of Minneapolis' Domestic Partner Act, passed in 1991, legally extends benefits to registered partners (heterosexual and homosexual) that include "immediate-family status, . . . visitation rights should their partners become ill, and the ability for a city employee to take sick or bereavement leave should one partner became ill or die" (Southgate 1992, 1). Within one year of this legislation, lesbian couples comprise 49 percent of registered partnerships (Southgate 1992). See also the text of the Minneapolis domestic Partner Act in the document section of this chapter. (2) Regarding lesbian partner health care: after nearly ten years of litigation, Karen Thompson won legal guardianship of her disabled lesbian partner Sharon Kowalski in 1991. The Minnesota "court's finding that Thompson and Kowalski were a 'family of affinity' will help not only lesbian and gay families but other types of nontraditional families as well" (*The Disability Rag* 1992, 20).

Conflict may arise when one partner feels she is not investing enough time in, or bringing emotional support to, the relationship. According to psychologist Barbara Sang, "because women have the capacity to give of themselves emotionally, two women frequently expect a lot from each other. In more traditional relationships, women are not as apt to expect as much from men emotionally" (56).

What Adrienne Rich (1986) has phrased a "lesbian continuum" (51) holds that all women share experiences across generations and cultures, and within family/kin communities, partnerships, and friendships. This legacy of "women's choices of women as passionate comrades, life partners, co-workers, lovers, community" (27), silenced and condemned by a heterosexist imperative, remains, nevertheless, central to women's identities. It is through reclaiming a lost history of women's partnerships and networks and the creativity and empowerment of women arising from these vital connections that, according to Rich, liberation for all women can occur.

Interracial partnerships between whites and people of color comprise another arena that has been legally prohibited (that is, until 1967 when miscegenation laws were struck down by the Supreme Court as unconstitutional) and often met with contempt and sometimes violence by whites and people of color. A black woman's choice to form a relationship with a white man is arguably met with the greatest resistance in the black community, due to the still highly charged legacy of frequent, forced, violent rape of black women perpetrated during slavery by white men (Bass 1982). The research that exists in this area suggests that a pattern of secrecy surrounds interracial relationships due to the expectation of non-support from family and friends. In-

deed, Zinn and Eitzen (1990) note that "the likelihood of choosing cohabitation over marriage is especially common among interracial couples" (405). Further findings indicate that radical black female college students are the group of women least likely, for political reasons, to date interracially, and that, not surprisingly, in settings where there is greater interracial interaction, a higher incidence of interracial partnerships is observed (Bass 1982). This last finding has obvious implications for African American professional women as they find themselves moving into work environments located in settings dominated by white men. A similar consequence of loss of proximity to one's cultural group has been noted in reference to young Native Americans who live in urban areas. Tensions and misunderstanding between women and men stemming from women's relative adherence to tribal traditions and men's relative separation from these patterns lead to Native American women's seeking interracial relationships among the alternatives to intra-racial conflict (Attneave 1982).

Friends

Throughout history, women have sought other women for emotional connection and nurturance. In the nineteenth century, female friendships among white, middle-class women provided guidance and support throughout a lifetime (Smith-Rosenberg 1975). Intimate friendships, inscribed within the experience of the private sphere and its imposed standards of "feminine" behavior for white women, became lasting bonds between mothers, daughters, sisters, aunts, cousins, and non-related female companions. Written accounts of these "sisterhoods" were frequently recorded in diaries, journals, and letters where women exchanged mutual love and regard for one another, sharing their private lives and public work (Smith-Rosenberg 1975; Cott 1977; Faderman 1981; Lasser 1988). As historian Nancy Cott notes, "sisterhood expressed in an affective way the gender identification—the consciousness of 'womanhood'" in which females' "reliance on each other to confirm their values embodied a new kind of group consciousness, one which could develop into a political consciousness" (194).

College classmates from the mid-1800s, Lucy Stone and Antoinette Brown corresponded frequently, revealing in letters their feelings of "mutual supportiveness as well as their need to 'agree to disagree.'" Upon graduation from Oberlin in 1847, Stone worked for abolition and women's rights while Brown later "became the first woman ordained into the regular Protestant ministry" (Lasser 1988, 159). Eventually becoming sisters-in-law, Stone and Brown shared in the nineteenth-century experience of opposing ideals for white women—feminism and social advocacy versus "feminine" identity aligned with domestic roles.

African American women's friendships reflect a powerful bond of "shared sisterhood," the strong sense of connectedness and mutuality, that has infused African American women's networks for hundreds of years (Collins 1991). These networks of women continue to exist for moral, spiritual, physical, practical, and financial support. Such sustained interdependence among African American women has been a significant factor in the survival of black families and communities.

The strength of these relationships is envied today by many women. Often isolated from female-centered communities, white women frequently perceive other women with suspicion, distrust, and as competitors in male-controlled systems.

"Because most women in a patriarchal society come to feel less than good about themselves, it is often impossible for mothers to transmit a sense of encouragement and confidence to their daughters" (Eichenbaum and Orbach 1983, 195). The persistent devaluation of women and their relationships to each other perpetuates divisiveness among them. As feminist author Judith Arcana (1979) states, "male culture has separated us from our mothers with its definitions of 'mother' and 'daughter,' in this first of a series of alienations, woman from woman, women from women" (94). This "failure to love" (Lugones 1987) other females becomes a legacy that women frequently perpetuate toward one another, a syndrome informed by heterosexism and racism.

For example, Audre Lorde, in an essay on black women's interpersonal relationships (1984), writes about the importance black women hold for one another due to their shared history and struggle for self-empowerment and describes how black women "rise to each other's defense against outsiders" (168). However, she notes that as with so many aspects of black women's experience, their friendships cannot be reduced to simplistic, positive descriptions of connection-through-struggle, but are complicated by the heavy residue of patriarchal oppression and its internalization. While black women indeed share a history of interdependence and support, the internalization of patriarchy's misogyny, with its distinctive features in application to black women, affects and distorts African American women's attachments to one another. Lorde discusses how the anger that black women feel about both blatant and insidious racism and sexism, while often silenced in order to survive, converts itself into the "mistrust and distance" that gets redirected to other black women.

Regarding this inaction on the part of white women and women of color, philosopher María Lugones (1987) points out the necessity of recognizing "the failure to see oneself in other women who are quite different from oneself" (7). Embracing diversity in race, ethnicity, and class within feminist perspectives promotes, even necessitates, according to Lugones, "traveling" to other "worlds" of experience (3). Confronting one's own racism and privilege can be, then, a form of self-advocacy. Conscious action on the part of white women in opposing racism and heterosexism, notes lesbian poet and essayist Minnie Bruce Pratt (1984), occurs "when we know and *feel* [author's italics] them as part of a positive process of recreating ourselves, of making a self that is not the negative, the oppressor" (41).

Black feminist writers identify white women's privileged position due to their proximity to white men as a major barrier to genuine connections with black women on several levels, from friendship to organizational alliance. "White women's inability to acknowledge their own racism, especially how it privileges them" is a symptom of their participation in patriarchal domination that constructs a wall between African American and white women (Collins 1991). The anger, hostility, and distrust many black women deeply feel toward white women because of the perception on black women's part of white women's collusion in the oppression of people of color has prompted one black feminist scholar to conclude that, for many African American women, "fully human relationships with whites remain out of reach" (Collins 1991, 192). Several others concur that racial privilege, especially when unacknowledged and unexamined, is a primary factor that hinders successful cross-racial connections between women (Walker 1983; Cornwell

1983; hooks 1989). Certainly, friendships between black and white women exist. But, as Lorde (1984) suggests, they may be sustainable only at a "middle depth"; that is, they may in some ways be easier than close friendships with other black women because they are more superficial, less threatening emotionally. Alice Walker (1983) writes of friendship with a Jewish woman, suggesting that white women whose experiences reflect a commonality of understanding of patriarchal hegemony may offer a promise for genuine connection across race.

Women also find it difficult to engage in mutual friendships with other women and men because of the cultural ideology of heterosexism. This view assumes that women are "naturally" and biologically attracted to men and vice versa. Therefore, friendships cannot easily develop between a woman and a man without an implied sexual component. Similarly, same-sex friendships between women, as between men, are suspect for their sexual potential thus diminishing the possibility of strong, supportive relationships developing over time between two individuals.

Collins (1991) identifies an interesting parallel between the barriers to meaningful connections between black lesbians and heterosexual women and those, described above, between black and white women. Black women's exercise of "heterosexual privilege," perhaps the one privilege available to them, has erected walls between them and lesbians. "Especially troubling to Black lesbians has been the reluctance on the part of Black heterosexual women to examine their own homophobia" (193). The pervasiveness throughout black communities of the message to black women to "support the black man" (Walker 1983), with its attendant widespread denial by many black women of black male sexism, is particularly frustrating for black lesbians (Cornwell 1983). The optimistic note is that, as feminist scholars continue to enlighten women (and men) about the damaging effects that patriarchal oppression has had on intra-racial and interracial alliances, the walls that separate black lesbians and black heterosexual women, black women and white, will begin, piece by painful piece, to be torn down.

Conclusion

The range of relationships entered into by women offers a spectrum of diversity and difference shaped by many cultural, economic, and political factors. Patriarchal norms defining limited spheres of female roles and behavior continue to be challenged by feminists of color and white feminists as those that deny personal and collective authority, identity,

and power to women. Women's efforts to define and develop alternative patterns to traditional, circumscribed definitions of relationship include egalitarian partnerships with men, lesbian partnerships, single parenthood, extended female-centered kin networks, and friendships with other women and with men that embrace non-hierarchical values. These efforts go against heterosexist and patriarchal strictures; but women, urged by the women's movement and their ineluctable need for genuine and mutual caring and support, continue to seek connections that create space for personal empowerment through relationship. The legacy of feminist scholarship in all areas of women's relationships with family, friends, partners, and kin bears truth to the continued centrality of women's worth and action in all communities and cultures.

References

Albers, Patricia, and Beatrice Medicine. 1983. *The hidden half: Studies of Plains Indian women.* Latham, N.Y.: University Press of America.

Allen, Paula Gunn. 1984. Beloved women: The lesbian in American Indian culture. In *Women-identified women.* Edited by Trudy Darty and Sandee Potter. Palo Alto, Calif.: Mayfield Publishing Company.

Aptheker, Bettina. 1989. *Tapestries of life: Women's work, women's consciousness, and the meaning of daily experience.* Amherst: University of Massachusetts Press.

Arcana, Judith. 1979. *Our mothers' daughters.* Berkeley, Calif.: Shameless Hussy Press.

Attneave, Carolyn. 1982. American Indians and Alaska native families: Emigrants in their own homeland. In *Ethnicity and family therapy.* Edited by Monica McGoldrick, John K. Pearce, and Joseph Giordano. New York: Guilford Press.

Bass, Barbara Ann. 1982. Interracial dating and marital relationships: A lecture. In *The Afro-American family.* Edited by Barbara Ann Bass, Gail Elizabeth Wyatt, and Gloria Johnson Powell. New York: Grune and Stratton.

Bassuk, Ellen L. 1992. Women and children without shelter: The characteristics of homeless families. In *Homeless: A national perspective.* Edited by Marjorie J. Robertson and Milton Greenblatt. New York: Plenum Press.

Bernal, Guillermo. 1982. Cuban families. In *Ethnicity and family therapy.* Edited by Monica McGoldrick, John K. Pearce, and Joseph Giordano. New York: Guilford Press.

Bernard, Jessie. 1972. *The future of marriage.* New York: World Publishing.

Boyd-Franklin, Nancy. 1989. *Black families in therapy.* New York: Guilford Press.

Brown-Collins, Alice, and Deborah Ridley Sussewell. 1986. The Afro-American woman's emerging selves. *Journal of Black Psychology* 13(1):1–11.

Cade, Toni. 1970. On the issue of roles. In *The black woman*. New York: Signet.

Caton, Carol L. M. 1990. *Homeless in America*. New York: Oxford University Press.

Chafetz, Janet Saltzman. 1989. Marital intimacy and conflict: The irony of spousal equality. In *Women: A feminist perspective*. 4th ed. Edited by Jo Freeman. Mountain View, Calif.: Mayfield Publishing Company.

Chow, Esther Ngan-Ling. 1987. The development of feminist consciousness among Asian American women. *Gender and Society* 1(3): 284–99.

Clarke, Cheryl. 1983. Homophobia in the black community. In *Home girls*. ed. Barbara Smith. New York: Kitchen Table: Women of Color Press.

Cole, Johnnetta, ed. 1986. *All American women: Lines that divide, ties that bind*. New York: Free Press.

Collins, Patricia Hill. 1987. The meaning of motherhood in black culture and black mother/daughter relationships. *SAGE: A Scholarly Journal on Black Women* 4(2):3–10.

————. 1991. *Black feminist thought*. New York: Routledge, Chapman, and Hall.

Cornwell, Anita. 1983. *Black lesbian in white America*. Florida: Naiad Press.

Cott, Nancy. 1977. *The bonds of womanhood: "Woman's sphere" in New England, 1780-1835*. New Haven: Yale University Press.

Cott, Nancy F., and Elizabeth H. Pleck, eds. 1979. *A heritage of her own*. New York: Simon and Schuster.

Coverman, Shelley. 1989. Women's work is never done: The division of domestic labor. *Women: A feminist perspective*. 4th ed. Edited by Jo Freeman. Mountain View, Calif.: Mayfield Publishing Company.

Darty, Trudy, and Sandee Potter. 1984. *Women-identified women*. Palo Alto, Calif.: Mayfield Publishing Company.

Davis, Angela. 1981. *Women, race and class*. New York: Random House.

DiCanio, Margaret. 1989. *The encyclopedia of marriage, divorce, and the family*. New York: Facts on File, Inc.

Di Leonardo, Micaela. 1987. The female world of cards and holidays: Women, families, and the work of kinship. *Signs: Journal of Women in Culture and Society* 12(3):440–53.

Dill, Bonnie Thornton. 1983. Race, class, and gender: Prospects for an all-inclusive sisterhood. *Feminist Studies* 9:131–50.

————. 1992. Our mother's grief: Racial ethnic women and the maintenance of families. In *Race, class, and gender*. Edited by Margaret L. Andersen and Patricia Hill Collins. Belmont, Calif.: Wadsworth Publishing Company.

Disability Rag. March/April 1992. Advocado Press, Inc. Indexed in Alternative Press Index, Box 33190, Baltimore, Md., 21218-0401.

Ehrenreich, Barbara, and Deirdre English. 1978. *For her own good: 150 years of the experts' advice to women*. New York: Anchor Books.

Eichenbaum, Luise, and Susie Orbach. 1983. *What do women want?: Exploding the myth of dependency*. New York: Coward-McCann.

Espín, Oliva M. 1992. Cultural and historical influences on sexuality in Hispanic/Latin women: Implications for psychotherapy. In *Race, class, and gender*. Edited by Margaret L. Anderson and Patricia Hill Collins. Belmont, Calif.: Wadsworth Publishing Company.

Faderman, Lillian. 1981. *Surpassing the love of men: Romantic friendship and love between women from the Renaissance to the present*. New York: William Morrow.

Falicov, Celia Jaes. 1982. Mexican families. In *Ethnicity and family therapy*. Edited by Monica McGoldrick, John K. Pearce, and Joseph Giordano. New York: Guilford Press.

Ferguson, Ann. 1983. On conceiving motherhood and sexuality: A feminist materialist approach. In *Mothering: Essays in feminist theory*. Edited by J. Trebilcot. Totowa, N.J.: Rowman and Littlefield.

French, Marilyn. 1985. *Beyond power*. New York: Summit Books.

Friedan, Betty. 1963. *The feminine mystique*. New York: Dell Publishing Company.

Garcia, Alma M. 1989. The development of Chicana feminist discourse. *Gender and Society* 3(2):217–38.

Garcia-Preto, Nydia. 1982. Puerto Rican families. In *Ethnicity and family therapy*. Edited by Monica McGoldrick, John K. Pearce, and Joseph Giordano. New York: Guilford Press.

Gerstel, Naomi, and Harriet Engle Gross. 1989. Women and the American family: Continuity and change. In *Women: A feminist perspective*. 4th ed. Edited by Jo freeman. Mountain View, Calif.: Mayfield Publishing Company.

Giddings, Paula. 1984. *When and where I enter: The impact of black women on race and sex in America*. New York: William Morrow.

H., Pamela. 1989. Asian American lesbians: An emerging voice in the Asian American community. In *Making waves: An anthology of writings by and about Asian American women*. Edited by Asian Women United of California. Boston: Beacon Press.

Hartmann, Heidi I. 1981. The family as the locus of gender, class, and political struggle: The example of housework. *Signs: Journal of Women in Culture and Society*. 6(3):366–94.

Hill, Robert. 1972. *The strengths of black families*. New York: Emerson Hall.

Hines, Paulette Moore, and Nancy Boyd-Franklin. 1982. Black families. In *Ethnicity and family therapy*. Edited by Monica McGoldrick, John K. Pearce, and Joseph Giordano. New York: Guilford Press.

hooks, bell. 1981. The myth of the black matriarchy. In *Ain't I a woman: Black women and feminism*. Boston: Beacon Press.

———. 1984. Revolutionary parenting. In *Feminist theory: From margin to center*. Boston: South End Press.

———. 1989. *Talking back*. Boston: South End Press.

Joseph, Gloria. 1984. Black mothers and daughters: Traditional and new populations. *SAGE: A Scholarly Journal on Black Women* 1(2):17–21.

Joseph, Gloria I., and Jill Lewis. 1981. *Common differences: Conflicts in black and white feminist perspectives*. Boston: South End Press.

Kasl, Charlotte, 1989. How did I get this way?: Culture, family and the grace of god. In *Women, sex, and addiction*. New York: Ticknor and Fields.

Kaye/Kantrowitz, Melanie, and Irena Klepfisz. 1986. *The tribe of Dina: A Jewish women's anthology*. Boston: Beacon Press.

Koppelman, Susan, ed. 1985. *Between mothers and daughters: Stories across generations*. New York: The Feminist Press.

Ladner, Joyce A., and Ruby Morton Gourdine. 1984. Intergenerational teenage motherhood: Some preliminary findings. *SAGE: A Scholarly Journal on Black Women* 1(2):22–24.

Lamphere, Louise. 1974. Strategies, cooperation, and conflict among women in domestic groups. In *Women, culture, and society*. Edited by Michelle Zimbalist Rosaldo and Louise Lamphere. Stanford: Stanford University Press.

Lasser, Carol. 1988. "Let us be sisters forever": The sororal model of nineteenth-century female friendship. *Signs: Journal of Women in Culture and Society* 14(1):158-81.

Lee, Evelyn. 1982. A social systems approach to assessment and treatment for Chinese American families. In *Ethnicity and family therapy*. Edited by Monica McGoldrick, John K. Pearce, and Joseph Giordano. New York: Guilford Press.

Lorde, Audre. 1984. *Sister outsider*. New York: The Crossing Press.

Luepnitz, Deborah Anna. 1988a. The family in history: Gender and structure in five types of families from antiquity to the present. In *The family interpreted*. New York: Basic Books.

————. 1988b. Re-membering the family. In *The family interpreted*. New York: Basic Books.

Lugones, María. 1987. Playfulness, 'World'-travelling, and loving perception. *Hypatia* 2(2):3–19.

Malson, Michelene R. 1981. *Black women's sex-role integration and behavior*. Wellesley, Mass.: Wellesley College Center for Research on Women.

Marshall, Paule. 1959. *Brown girl, brownstones*. New York: The Feminist Press.

Mass, Penelope L., and Judy H. Hall. 1988. *Homeless children and their families: A preliminary study*. Washington, D.C.: Child Welfare League of America.

McAdoo, Harriette P. 1986. Societal stress: The black family. In *All American women*. Edited by Johnnetta Cole. New York: Free Press.

McChesney, Kay Young. 1992. Homeless families: Four patterns of poverty. In *Homelessness: A national perspective*. Edited by Marjorie J. Robertson and Milton Greenblatt. New York: Plenum Press.

McGoldrick, Monica. 1982. Ethnicity and family therapy: An overview. In *Ethnicity and family therapy*. Edited by Monica McGoldrick, John K. Pearce, and Joseph Giordano. New York: Guilford Press.

Medicine, Beatrice. 1983. "Warrior women": Sex role alternatives for Plains Indian women. In *The hidden half: Studies of Plains Indian women*. Edited by Patricia Albers and Beatrice Medicine. Lanham, N.Y.: University Press of America.

Merves, Esther S. 1992. Homeless women: Beyond the bag lady myth. In *Homelessness: A national perspective*. Edited by Marjorie J. Robertson and Milton Greenblatt. New York: Plenum Press.

Miller, Jean Baker. 1976. *Toward a new psychology of women*. Boston: Beacon Press.

Moraga, Cherrie, and Gloria Anzaldúa. eds. 1983. *This bridge called my back: Writings by radical women of color*. Latham, N.Y.: Kitchen Table: Women of Color Press.

Moynihan, Daniel Patrick. 1965. *The Negro family: The case for national action*. Washington, D.C.: Office of Policy Planning and Research, United States Department of Labor.

Pardo, Mary. 1990. Mexican American women grassroots community activists: Mothers of east Los Angeles. *Frontiers* 11(1):1–7.

Payne, Karen, ed. 1983. *Between ourselves: Letters between mothers and daughters, 1750–1982*. Boston: Houghton Mifflin.

Peplau, Letitia Anne, and Susan Miller Campbell. 1989. The balance of power in dating and marriage. In *Women: A feminist perspective*. 4th ed. Edited by Jo Freeman. Mountain View, Calif.: Mayfield Publishing Company.

Pinderhughes, Elaine. 1982. Afro-American families and the victim system. In *Ethnicity and family therapy*. Edited by Monica McGoldrick, John K. Pearce, and Joseph Giordano. New York: Guilford Press.

Pratt, Minnie Bruce. 1984. Identity: Skin blood heart. In *Yours in struggle: Three feminist perspectives on anti-Semitism and racism*. Edited by Elly Bulkin, Minnie Bruce Pratt, and Barbara Smith. Ithaca, N.Y.: Firebrand Books.

Rich, Adrienne. 1976, 1986. *Of woman born: Motherhood as experience and institution*. New York: W. W. Norton and Co.

————. 1979. *On lies, secrets, and silence: Selected prose 1966–1978*. New York: W. W. Norton and Co.

————. 1986. Compulsory heterosexuality and lesbian existence. In *Blood, bread, and poetry: Selected prose, 1979–1985*. New York: W. W. Norton and Co.

Sánchez-Ayéndez, Melba. 1986. Puerto Rican elderly women: Shared meanings and informal supportive networks. In *All American women: Lines that divide, ties that bind*. Edited by Johnnetta B. Cole. New York: The Free Press.

Sang, Barbara. 1984. Lesbian relationships: A struggle toward partner equality. In *Women-identified women*. Edited by Trudy Darty and Sandee Potter. Palo Alto, Calif.: Mayfield Publishing Company.

Shon, Steven P., and Davis Y. Ja. 1982. Asian families. In *Ethnicity and family therapy*. Edited by Monica McGoldrick, John K. Pearce, and Joseph Giordano. New York: Guilford Press.

Smith, Althea. 1989. Women's interracial friendships. *Woman of Power* (Spring):34-35.

Smith-Rosenberg, Carroll. 1975. The female world of love and ritual: Relations between women in nineteenth-century America. *Signs: Journal of Women in Culture and Society* 1(1):1–29.

Southgate, David. 1992. One year later, 179 couples have registered as domestic partners. *Equal Time* (Minnesota) 259 (13–27 March).

Stacey, Judith. 1990. *Brave new families: Stories of domestic upheaval in late twentieth-century America*. New York: Basic Books.

Stack, Carol. 1974. Sex roles and survival strategies in an urban black community. In *Women, culture, and society*. Edited by Michelle Zimbalist Rosaldo and Louise Lamphere. Stanford: Stanford University Press.

Sullivan, Patricia A., and Shirley P. Damrosch. 1989. Homeless women and children. In *The homeless of contemporary society*. Edited by Richard D. Bingham, Roy E. Green and Sammis B. White. Newbury Park, Calif.: Sage Publications.

Tan, Amy. 1989. *The Joy Luck Club*. New York: G. P. Putnam's Sons.

Thorman, George. 1988. *Homeless families*. Springfield, Ill.: Charles C. Thomas.

Terrelonge, Pauline. 1975. Feminist consciousness and black women. In *Women: A feminist perspective*. 4th ed. Edited by Jo Freeman. Palo Alto, Calif.: Mayfield Publishing Company.

Wade-Gayles, Gloria. 1984. *No crystal stair*. New York: Pilgrim Press.

———. 1984. The truths of our mothers' lives: Mother-daughter relationships in black women's fiction. *SAGE: A Scholarly Journal on Black Women* 1(2):8–12.

Walker, Alice. 1983. *In search of our mothers' gardens*. New York: Harcourt Brace Jovanovich.

Wallace, Michele. 1982. A black feminist's search for sisterhood. In *All the women are white, all the blacks are men, but some of us are brave*. Edited by Gloria T. Hull, Patricia Bell Scott, and Barbara Smith. New York: The Feminist Press.

Yu, Connie Young. 1989. The world of our grandmothers. In *Making waves: An anthology of writings by and about Asian American women*. Edited by Asian Women United of California. Boston: Beacon Press.

Zinn, Maxine Baca. 1980. Gender and ethnic identity among Chicanos. *Frontiers* 52:18–24.

Zinn, Maxine Baca, and Stanley Eitzen. 1990. *Diversity in families*. 2nd ed. New York: Harper Collins Publishers.

Minneapolis Domestic Partner Act

142.10. **PURPOSE.** The City of Minneapolis recognizes that nationwide debate has advanced an expanded concept of familial relationships beyond traditional marital and blood relationships. This expanded concept recognizes the relationship of two non-married but committed adult partners. Recognizing this the Minneapolis City Council hereby adopts a process to provide persons to declare themselves as Domestic Partners, thus enabling employers to voluntarily provide equal treatment in employment benefits for such partners and their dependents. Reprinted from *Minneapolis Civil Rights Ordinance*. 1991. City of Minneapolis Commission on Civil Rights and Department of Civil Rights. Chapter 142 (142.10), page 67.

The Meaning of Motherhood in Black Culture and Black Mother/Daughter Relationships

Patricia Hill Collins

"What did your mother teach you about men?" is a question I often ask students in my courses on African-American women. "Go to school first and get a good education—don't get too serious too young," "Make sure you look around and that you can take care of yourself before you settle down," and "Don't trust them, want more for yourself than just a man," are typical responses from Black women. My students share stories of how their mothers encouraged them to cultivate satisfying relationships with Black men

Collins, Patricia Hill. (1987). "The Meaning of Motherhood in Black Culture and Black Mother/Daughter Relationships." *SAGE: A Scholarly Journal on Black Women* 4(2):3–10. Reprinted by permission of the author and publisher.

while anticipating disappointments, to desire marriage while planning viable alternatives, to become mothers only when fully prepared to do so. But above all, they stress their mothers' insistence on being self-reliant and resourceful.

These daughters from varying social class backgrounds, ages, family structures and geographic regions had somehow received strikingly similar messages about Black womanhood. Even though their mothers employed diverse teaching strategies, these Black daughters had all been exposed to common themes about the meaning of womanhood in Black culture.[1]

This essay explores the relationship between the meaning of motherhood in African-American culture and Black mother/daughter relationships by addressing three primary questions. First, how have competing perspectives about motherhood intersected to produce a distinctly Afrocentric ideology of motherhood? Second, what are the enduring themes that characterize this Afrocentric ideology of motherhood? Finally, what effect might this Afrocentric ideology of motherhood have on Black mother/daughter relationships?

Competing Perspectives on Motherhood

The Dominant Perspective: Eurocentric Views of White Motherhood

The cult of true womanhood, with its emphasis on motherhood as woman's highest calling, has long held a special place in the gender symbolism of white Americans. From this perspective, women's activities should be confined to the care of children, the nurturing of a husband, and the maintenance of the household. By managing this separate domestic sphere, women gain social influence through their roles as mothers, transmitters of culture and parents for the next generation.[2]

While substantial numbers of white women have benefitted from the protections of white patriarchy provided by the dominant ideology, white women themselves have recently challenged its tenets. On one pole lies a cluster of women, the traditionalists, who aim to retain the centrality of motherhood in women's lives. For traditionalists, differentiating between the experience of motherhood, which for them has been quite satisfying, and motherhood as an institution central in reproducing gender inequality, has proved difficult. The other pole is occupied by women who advocate dismantling motherhood as an institution. They suggest that compulsory motherhood be outlawed and that the experience of motherhood can only be satisfying if women can choose not to be mothers. Arrayed between these dichotomous positions are women who argue for an expanded, but not necessarily different role for women—women can be mothers as long as they are not *just* mothers.[3]

Three themes implicit in white perspectives on motherhood are particularly problematic for Black women and others outside of this debate. First, the assumption that mothering occurs within the confines of a private, nuclear family household where the mother has almost total responsibility for childrearing is less applicable to Black families. While the ideal of the cult of true womanhood has been held up to Black women for emulation, racial oppression has denied Black families sufficient resources to support private, nuclear family households. Second, the assumption of strict sex-role segregation defining male and female spheres of influence within the family has been less applicable to African-American families than to white middle class ones. Finally, the assumption that motherhood and economic dependency on men are linked and that to be a "good" mother, one must stay at home, making motherhood a full-time "occupation," is similarly uncharacteristic of African-American families.[4]

Even though selected groups of white women are challenging the cult of true womanhood and its accompanying definition of motherhood, the dominant ideology remains powerful. As long as these approaches remain prominent in scholarly and popular discourse, Eurocentric views of white motherhood will continue to affect Black women's lives.

Eurocentric Views of Black Motherhood

Eurocentric perspectives on Black motherhood revolve around two interdependent images that together define Black women's roles in white and in African-American families. The first image is that of the Mammy, the faithful, devoted domestic servant. Like one of the family, Mammy conscientiously "mothers" her white children, caring for them and loving them as if they were her own. Mammy is the ideal Black mother for she recognizes her place. She is paid next to nothing and yet cheerfully accepts her inferior status. But when she enters her own home, this same Mammy is transformed into the second image, the too-strong matriarch who raises weak sons and "unnaturally superior" daughters.[5] When she protests, she is labelled aggressive and non-feminine, yet if she remains silent, she is rendered invisible.

The task of debunking Mammy by analyzing Black women's roles as exploited domestic workers and challenging the matriarchy thesis by demonstrating that Black women do not wield disproportionate power in African-American families has long preoccupied African-American scholars.[6] But an equally telling critique concerns uncovering the functions of these images and their role in explaining Black women's subordination in systems of race, class and gender oppression. As Mae King points out, white definitions of Black motherhood foster the dominant group's exploitation of Black women by blaming Black women for their characteristic reactions to their own subordination.[7] For example, while the stay-at-home mother has been held up to all women as the ideal, African-American women have been compelled to work outside the home, typically in a very narrow range of occupations. Even though Black women were forced to become domestic servants and be strong figures in Black households, labelling them Mammys and matriarchs denigrates Black women. Without a countervailing Afrocentric ideology of motherhood, white perspectives on both white and African-American motherhood place Black women in a no-win situation. Adhering to these standards brings the danger of the lowered self-esteem of internalized oppression, one that, if passed on from mother to daughter, provides a powerful mechanism for controlling African-American communities.

African Perspectives on Motherhood

One concept that has been constant throughout the history of African societies is the centrality of motherhood in religions, philosophies, and social institutions. As Barbara Christian points out, "There is no doubt that motherhood is for most African people symbolic of creativity and continuity."[8]

Cross-cultural research on motherhood in African societies appears to support Christian's claim.[9] West African sociologist Christine Oppong suggests that the Western notion of equating household with family be abandoned because it obscures women's family roles in African cultures.[10] While the archetypal white, middle-class nuclear family conceptualizes family life as being divided into two oppositional spheres—the "male" sphere of economic providing and the "female" sphere of affective nurturing—this type of rigid sex role segregation was not part of the West African tradition. Mothering was not a privatized nurturing "occupation" reserved for biological mothers, and the economic support of children was not the exclusive responsibility of men. Instead, for African women, emotional care for children and providing for their physical survival were interwoven as interdependent, complementary dimensions of motherhood.

In spite of variation among societies, a strong case has been made that West African women occupy influential roles in African family networks.[11] First, since they are not dependent on males for economic support and provide for certain key dimensions of their own and their children's economic support, women are structurally central to families.[12] Second, the image of the mother is one that is culturally elaborated and valued across diverse West African societies. Continuing the lineage is essential in West African philosophies, and motherhood is similarly valued.[13] Finally, while the biological mother/child bond is valued, child care was a collective responsibility, a situation fostering cooperative, age stratified, woman-centered "mothering" networks.

Recent research by Africanists suggests that much more of this African heritage was retained among African-Americans than had previously been thought. The retention of West African culture as a culture of resistance offered enslaved Africans and exploited African-Americans alternative ideologies to those advanced by dominant groups. Central to these reinterpretations of African-American institutions and culture is a reconceptualization of Black family life and the role of women in Black family networks.[14] West African perspectives may have been combined with the changing political and economic situations framing African-American communities to produce certain enduring themes characterizing an Afrocentric ideology of motherhood.

Enduring Themes of an Afrocentric Ideology of Motherhood

An Afrocentric ideology of motherhood must reconcile the competing world views of these three conflicting perspectives of motherhood. An ongoing tension exists between efforts to mold the institution of Black motherhood for the benefit of the dominant group and efforts by Black women to define and value their own experiences with motherhood. This tension leads to a continuum of responses. For those women who either aspire to the cult of true womanhood without having the resources to support such a lifestyle or who believe stereotypical analyses of themselves as dominating matriarchs, motherhood can be an oppressive institution. But the experience of motherhood can provide Black women with a base of self-actualization, status in the Black community, and a reason for social activism. These alleged contradictions can exist side by side in African-American communities, families, and even within individual women.

Embedded in these changing relationships are four enduring themes that I contend characterize an Afrocentric ideology of motherhood. Just as the issues facing enslaved African mothers were quite different from those currently facing poor Black women in inner cities for any given historical moment, the actual institutional forms that these themes take depend on the severity of oppression and Black women's resources for resistance.

Bloodmothers, Othermothers, and Women-Centered Networks

In African-American communities, the boundaries distinguishing biological mothers of children from other women who care for children are often fluid and changing. Biological mothers or bloodmothers are expected to care for their children. But African and African-American communities have also recognized that vesting one person with full responsibility for mothering a child may not be wise or possible. As a result, "othermothers," women who assist bloodmothers by sharing mothering responsibilities, traditionally have been central to the institution of Black motherhood.[15]

The centrality of women in African-American extended families is well known.[16] Organized, resilient, women-centered networks of bloodmothers and othermothers are key in understanding this centrality. Grandmothers, sisters, aunts, or cousins acted as othermothers by taking on childcare responsibilities for each other's children. When needed, temporary child care arrangements turned into long-term care or informal adoption.[17]

In African-American communities, these women-centered networks of community-based childcare often extend beyond the boundaries of biologically related extended families to support "fictive kin."[18] Civil rights activist Ella Baker describes how informal adoption by othermothers functioned in the Southern, rural community of her childhood:

> My aunt who had thirteen children of her own raised three more. She had become a midwife, and a child was born who was covered with sores. Nobody was particularly wanting the child, so she took the child and raised him . . . and another mother decided she didn't want to be bothered with two children. So my aunt took one and raised him . . . they were part of the family.[19]

Even when relationships were not between kin or fictive kin, African-American community norms were such that neighbors cared for each other's children. In the following passage, Sara Brooks, a Southern domestic worker, describes the importance of the community-based childcare that a neighbor offered her daughter. In doing so, she also shows how the African-American cultural value placed on cooperative childcare found institutional support in the adverse conditions under which so many Black women mothered:

> She kept Vivian and she didn't charge me nothin either. You see, people used to look after each other, but now it's not that way. I reckon it's because we all was poor, and I guess they put theirself in the place of the person that they was helpin.[20]

Othermothers were key not only in supporting children but also in supporting bloodmothers who, for whatever reason, were ill-prepared or had little desire to care for their children. Given the pressures from the larger political economy, the emphasis placed on community-based childcare and the respect given to othermothers who assume the responsibilities of childcare have served a critical function in African-American communities. Children orphaned by sale or death of their parents under slavery, children conceived through rape, children of young mothers, children born into extreme poverty, or children, who for other reasons have been rejected by their bloodmothers, have all been supported by othermothers who, like Ella Baker's aunt, took in additional children, even when they had enough of their own.

Providing as Part of Mothering

The work done by African-American women in providing the economic resources essential to Black family well-being affects motherhood in a contradictory fashion. On the one hand, African-American women have long integrated their activities as economic providers into their mothering relationships. In contrast to the cult of true womanhood where work is defined as being in opposition to and incompatible with motherhood, work for Black women has been an important and valued dimension of Afrocentric definitions of Black motherhood. On the other hand, African-American women's experiences as mothers under oppression were such that the type and purpose of work Black women were forced to do greatly impacted on the type of mothering relationships bloodmothers and othermothers had with Black children.

While slavery both disrupted West African family patterns and exposed enslaved Africans to the gender ideologies and practices of slaveowners, it simultaneously made it impossible, had they wanted to do so, for enslaved Africans to implement slaveowner's ideologies. Thus, the separate spheres of providing as a male domain and affective nurturing as a female domain did not develop within African-American families.[21] Providing for Black children's physical survival and attending to their affective, emotional needs continued as interdependent dimensions of an Afrocentric ideology of motherhood. However, by changing the conditions under which Black women worked and the purpose of the work itself, slavery introduced the problem of how best to continue traditional Afrocentric values under oppressive conditions. Institutions of community-based childcare, informal adoption, greater reliance on othermothers, all emerge as adaptations to the exigencies of combining exploitative work with nurturing children.

In spite of the change in political status brought on by emancipation, the majority of African-American women remained exploited agricultural workers. However, their placement in Southern political economies allowed them to combine childcare with field labor. Sara Brooks describes how strong the links between providing and caring for others were for her:

> When I was about nine I was nursin my sister Sally—I'm about seven or eight years older than Sally. And when I would put her to sleep, instead of me goin somewhere and sit down and play, I'd get my little old hoe and get out there and work right in the field around the house.[22]

Black women's shift from Southern agriculture to domestic work in Southern and Northern towns and cities represented a change in the type of work done, but not in the meaning of work to women and their families. Whether they wanted to or not, the majority of African-American women had to work and could not afford the luxury of motherhood as a noneconomically productive, female "occupation."

Community Othermothers and Social Activism

Black women's experiences as othermothers have provided a foundation for Black women's social activism. Black women's feelings of responsibility for nurturing the children in their own extended family networks have stimulated a more generalized ethic of care where Black women feel accountable for all the Black community's children.

This notion of Black women as community othermothers for all Black children traditionally allowed Black women to treat biologically unrelated children as if they were members of their own families. For example, sociologist Karen Fields describes how her grandmother, Mamie Garvin Fields, draws on her power as a community othermother when dealing with unfamiliar children.

She will say to a child on the street who looks up to no good, picking out a name at random, "Aren't you Miz Pinckney's boy?" in that same reproving tone. If the reply is, "No, ma'am, my mother is Miz Gadsden," whatever threat there was dissipates.[23]

The use of family language in referring to members of the Black community also illustrates this dimension of Black motherhood. For example, Mamie Garvin Fields describes how she became active in surveying the poor housing conditions of Black people in Charleston.

I was one of the volunteers they got to make a survey of the places where we were paying extortious rents for indescribable property. I said "we," although it wasn't Bob and me. We had our own home, and so did many of the Federated Women. Yet we still felt like it really was "we" living in those terrible places, and it was up to us to do something about them.[24]

To take another example, while describing her increasingly successful efforts to teach a boy who had given other teachers problems, my daughter's kindergarten teacher stated, "You know how it can be—the majority of children in the learning disabled classes are *our children*. I know he didn't belong there, so I volunteered to take him." In these statements, both women invoke the language of family to describe the ties that bind them as Black women to their responsibilities to other members of the Black community as family.

Sociologist Cheryl Gilkes suggests that community othermother relationships are sometimes behind Black women's decisions to become community activists. Gilkes notes that many of the Black women community activists in her study became involved in community organizing in response to the needs of their own children and of those in their communities. The following comment is typical of how many of the Black women in Gilkes' study relate to Black children: "There were a lot of summer programs springing up for kids, but they were exclusive . . . and I found that most of *our kids* (emphasis mine) were excluded."[26] For many women, what began as the daily expression of their obligations as community othermothers, as was the case for the kindergarten teacher, developed into full-fledged roles as community leaders.

Motherhood as a Symbol of Power

Motherhood, whether bloodmother, othermother, or community othermother, can be invoked by Black women as a symbol of power. A substantial portion of Black women's status in African-American communities stems not only from their roles as mothers in their own families but from their contributions as community othermothers to Black community development as well.

The specific contributions Black women make in nurturing Black community development form the basis of community-based power. Community othermothers work on behalf of the Black community by trying, in the words of late nineteenth century Black feminists, to "uplift the race," so that vulnerable members of the community would be able to attain the self-reliance and independence so desperately needed for Black community development under oppressive conditions. This is the type of power many African-Americans have in mind when they describe the "strong, Black women" they see around them in traditional African-American communities.

When older Black women invoke this community othermother status, its results can be quite striking. Karen Fields recounts an incident described to her by her grandmother illustrating how women can exert power as community othermothers:

> One night . . . as Grandmother sat crocheting alone at about two in the morning, a young man walked into the living room carrying the portable TV from upstairs. She said, "Who are you looking for *this* time of night?" As Grandmother (described) the incident to me over the phone, I could hear a tone of voice that I know well. It said, "Nice boys don't do that." So I imagine the burglar heard his own mother or grandmother at that moment. He joined in the familial game just created: "Well, he told me that I could borrow it." "*Who* told you?" "John." "Um um, no *John* lives here. You got the wrong house."[27]

After this dialogue, the teenager turned around, went back upstairs and returned the television.

In local Black communities, specific Black women are widely recognized as powerful figures, primarily because of their contributions to the community's well-being through their roles as community othermothers. Sociologist Charles Johnson describes the behavior of an elderly Black woman at a church service in rural Alabama of the 1930s. Even though she was not on the program, the woman stood up to speak. The master of ceremonies rang for her to sit down but she refused to do so claiming, "I am the mother of this church, and I will say what I please." The master of ceremonies later explained to the congregation—"Brothers, I know you all honor Sister Moore. Course our time is short but she has acted as a mother to me. . . . Any time old folks get up I give way to them."[28]

Implications for Black Mother/Daughter Relationships

In her discussion of the sex-role socialization of Black girls, Pamela Reid identifies two complementary approaches in understanding Black mother/daughter relationships.[29] The first, psychoanalytic theory, examines the role of parents in the establishment of personality and social behavior. This theory argues that the development of feminine behavior results from the girls' identification with adult female role models. This approach emphasizes how an Afrocentric ideology of motherhood is actualized through Black mothers' activities as role models.

The second approach, social learning theory, suggests that the rewards and punishments attached to girls' childhood experiences are central in shaping women's sex-role behavior. The kinds of behaviors that Black mothers reward and punish in their daughters are seen as key in the socialization process. This approach examines specific experiences that Black girls have while growing up that encourage them to absorb an Afrocentric ideology of motherhood.

African-American Mothers as Role Models

Feminist psychoanalytic theorists suggest that the sex-role socialization process is different for boys and girls. While boys learn maleness by rejecting femaleness via separating themselves from their mothers, girls establish feminine identities by embracing the femaleness of their mothers. Girls' identify with their mothers, a sense of connection that is incorporated into the female personality. However, this mother-identification is problematic because, under patriarchy, men are more highly valued than women. Thus, while daughters identify with their mothers, they also reject them because, in patriarchal families, identification with adult women as mothers means identifying with persons deemed inferior.[30]

While Black girls learn by identifying with their mothers, the specification of the female role with which Black girls identify may be quite different than that modeled by middle class white mothers. The presence of working mothers, extended family othermothers, and powerful community othermothers offers a range of role models that challenge the tenets of the cult of true womanhood.

Moreover, since Black mothers have a distinctive relationship to white patriarchy, they may be less likely to socialize their daughters into their proscribed role as subordinates. Rather, a key part of Black girls' socialization involves incorporating the critical posture that allows Black women to cope with contradictions. For example, Black girls have long had to learn how to do domestic work while rejecting definitions of themselves as Mammies. At the same time they've had to take on strong roles in Black extended families without internalizing images of themselves as matriarchs.

In raising their daughters, Black mothers face a troubling dilemma. To ensure their daughters' physical survival, they must teach their daughters to fit into systems of oppression. For example, as a young girl in Mississippi, Black activist Ann Moody questioned why she was paid so little for the domestic work she began at age nine, why Black women domestics were sexually harassed by their white male employers, and why whites had so much more than Blacks. But her mother refused to answer her questions and actually became angry whenever Ann Moody stepped out of her "place."[31] Black daughters are raised to expect to work, to strive for an education so that they can support themselves, and to anticipate carrying heavy responsibilities in their families and communities because these skills are essential for their own survival as well as for the survival of those for whom they will eventually be responsible.[32] And yet mothers know that if daughters fit too well into the limited opportunities offered Black women, they become willing participants in their own subordination. Mothers may have ensured their daughters' physical survival at the high cost of their emotional destruction.

On the other hand, Black daughters who offer serious challenges to oppressive situations may not physically survive. When Ann Moody became involved in civil rights activities, her mother first begged her not to participate and then told her not to come home because she feared the whites in Moody's hometown would kill her. In spite of the dangers, many Black mothers routinely encourage their daughters to develop skills to confront oppressive conditions. Thus, learning that they will work, that education is a vehicle for advancement, can also be seen as ways of preparing Black girls to resist oppression through a variety of mothering roles. The issue is to build emotional strength, but not at the cost of physical survival.

This delicate balance between conformity and resistance is described by historian Elsa Barkley Brown as the "need to socialize me one way and at the same time to give me all the tools I needed to be something else."[33] Black daughters must learn how to survive in interlocking structures of race, class and gender oppression while rejecting and transcending those very same structures. To develop these skills in their daughters, mothers demonstrate varying combinations of behaviors devoted to ensuring their daughters' survival—such as providing them with basic necessities and ensuring their protection in dangerous environments—to helping their daughters go farther than mothers themselves were allowed to go.

The presence of othermothers in Black extended families and the modeling symbolized by community othermothers offer powerful support for the task of teaching girls to resist white perceptions of Black womanhood while appearing to conform to them. In contrast to the isolation of middle class white mother/daughter dyads, Black women-centered extended family networks foster an early identification with a much wider range of models of Black womanhood which can lead to a greater sense of empowerment in young Black girls.

Social Learning Theory and Black Mothering Behavior

Understanding this goal of balancing the needs of physical survival of their daughters with the vision of encouraging them to transcend the boundaries confronting them sheds some light on some of the apparent contradictions in Black mother/daughter relationships. Black mothers are often described as strong disciplinarians and overly protective parents; yet these same women manage to raise daughters who are self-reliant and assertive.[34] Professor Gloria Wade-Gayles offers an explanation for this apparent contradiction by suggesting that Black mothers:

> do not socialize their daughters to be "passive" or "irrational." Quite the contrary, they socialize their daughters to be independent, strong and self-confident. Black mothers are suffocatingly protective and domineering precisely because they are determined to mold their daughters into whole and self-actualizing persons in a society that devalues Black women.[35]

Black mothers emphasize protection either by trying to shield their daughters as long as possible from the penalties attached to their race, class and gender status or by teaching them how to protect themselves in such situations. Black women's autobiographies and fiction can be read as texts revealing the multiple strategies employed by Black mothers in preparing their daughters for the demands of being Black women in oppressive conditions. For example, in discussing the mother/daughter relationship in Paule Marshall's *Brown Girl, Brownstones*, Rosalie Troester catalogues some of these strategies and the impact they may have on relationships themselves:

> Black mothers, particularly those with strong ties to their community, sometimes build high banks around their young daughters, isolating them from the dangers of the larger world until they are old and strong enough to function as autonomous women. Often these dikes are religious, but sometimes they are built with education, family, or the restrictions of a close-knit and homogeneous community . . . this isolation causes the currents between Black mothers and daughters to run deep and

the relationship to be fraught with an emotional intensity often missing from the lives of women with more freedom.[36]

Black women's efforts to provide for their children also may affect the emotional intensity of Black mother/daughter relationships. As Gloria Wade-Gayles points out, "Mothers in Black women's fiction are strong and devoted . . . but . . . they are rarely affectionate."[37] For far too many Black mothers, the demands of providing for children are so demanding that affection often must wait until the basic needs of physical survival are satisfied.

Black daughters raised by mothers grappling with hostile environments have to confront their feelings about the difference between the idealized versions of maternal love extant in popular culture and the strict, assertive mothers so central to their lives.[38] For daughters, growing up means developing a better understanding on the daughter's part that offering physical care and protection is an act of maternal love. Ann Moody describes her growing awareness of the personal cost her mother paid as a single mother of three children employed as a domestic worker. Watching her mother sleep after the birth of another child, Moody remembers:

> For a long time I stood there looking at her. I didn't want to wake her up. I wanted to enjoy and preserve that calm, peaceful look on her face, I wanted to think she would always be that happy. . . . Adline and Junior were too young to feel the things I felt and know the things I knew about Mama. They couldn't remember when she and Daddy separated. They had never heard her cry at night as I had or worked and helped as I had done when we were starving.[39]

Renita Weems' account of coming to grips with maternal desertion provides another example of a daughter's efforts to understand her mother's behavior. In the following passage, Weems struggles with the difference between the stereotypical image of the super strong Black mother and her own alcoholic mother's decision to leave her children:

> My mother loved us. I must believe that. She worked all day in a department store bakery to buy shoes and school tablets, came home to curse out neighbors who wrongly accused her children of any impropriety (which in an apartment complex usually meant stealing), and kept her house cleaner than most sober women.[40]

Weems concludes that her mother loved her because she provided for her to the best of her ability.

Othermothers often play central roles in defusing the emotional intensity of relationships between bloodmothers and their daughters and in helping daughters understand the Afrocentric ideology of motherhood. Weems describes the women teachers, neighbors, friends, and othermothers that she turned to for help in negotiating a difficult mother/daughter relationship. These women, she notes, "did not have the onus of providing for me, and so had the luxury of talking to me."[41]

June Jordan offers one of the most eloquent analyses of a daughter's realization of the high personal cost Black women have paid as bloodmothers and othermothers in working to provide an economic and emotional foundation for Black children. In the following passage, Jordan captures the feelings that my Black women students struggled to put into words:

> As a child I noticed the sadness of my mother as she sat alone in the kitchen at night. . . . Her woman's work never won permanent victories of any kind. It never enlarged the universe of her imagination or her power to influence what happened

beyond the front door of our house. Her woman's work never tickled her to laugh or shout or dance. But she did raise me to respect her way of offering love and to believe that hard work is often the irreducible factor for survival, not something to avoid. Her woman's work produced a reliable home base where I could pursue the privileges of books and music. Her woman's work invented the potential for a completely different kind of work for us, the next generation of Black women: huge, rewarding hard work demanded by the huge, new ambitions that her perfect confidence in us engendered.[42]

Jordan's words not only capture the essence of the Afrocentric ideology of motherhood so central to the well-being of countless numbers of Black women. They simultaneously point the way into the future, one where Black women face the challenge of continuing the mothering traditions painstakingly nurtured by prior generations of African-American women.

Notes

1. The definition of culture used in this essay is taken from Leith Mullings, "Anthropological Perspectives on the Afro-American Family," *American Journal of Social Psychiatry* 6 (1986), pp. 11–16. According to Mullings, culture is composed of "the symbols and values that create the ideological frame of reference through which people attempt to deal with the circumstances in which they find themselves," p. 13.

2. For analyses of the relationship of the cult of true womanhood to Black women, see Leith Mullings, "Uneven Development: Class, Race and Gender in the United States Before 1900," in *Women's Work, Development and the Division of Labor by Gender*, eds. Eleanor Leacock and Helen Safa (South Hadley, MA: Bergin & Garvey, 1986), pp. 41–57; Bonnie Thornton Dill, "Our Mothers' Grief: Racial Ethnic Women and the Maintenance of Families," Research Paper 4, Center for Research on Women (Memphis, TN: Memphis State University, 1986); and Hazel Carby, *Reconstructing Womanhood: The Emergence of the Afro-American Woman Novelist* (New York: Oxford University, 1987), especially chapter two.

3. Contrast, for example, the traditionalist analysis of Selma Fraiberg, *Every Child's Birthright: In Defense of Mothering* (New York: Basic, 1977) to that of Jeffner Allen, "Motherhood: The Annihilation of Women," in *Mothering, Essays in Feminist Theory*, ed. Joyce Trebilcot (Totawa, NJ: Rowan & Allanheld, 1983). See also Adrienne Rich, *Of Woman Born: Motherhood as Experience and Institution* (New York: Norton, 1976). For an overview of how traditionalists and feminists have shaped the public policy debate on abortion, see Kristin Luker, *Abortion and the Politics of Motherhood* (Berkeley, CA: University of California, 1984).

4. Mullings, 1986, note 2 above; Dill, 1986; and Carby, 1987. Feminist scholarship is also challenging Western notions of the family. See Barrie Thorne and Marilyn Yalom, eds., *Rethinking the Family* (New York: Longman, 1982).

5. Since Black women are no longer heavily concentrated in private domestic service, the Mammy image may be fading. In contrast, the matriarch image, popularized in Daniel Patrick Moynihan's, *The Negro Family: The Case for National Action*

(Washington, DC: U.S. Government Printing Office, 1965), is reemerging in public debates about the feminization of poverty and the urban underclass. See Maxine Baca Zinn, "Minority Families in Crisis: The Public Discussion," Research Paper 6, Center for Research on Women (Memphis, TN: Memphis State University, 1987).

6. For an alternative analysis to the Mammy image, see Judith Rollins, *Between Women: Domestics and Their Employers* (Philadelphia: Temple University, 1985). Classic responses to the matriarchy thesis include Robert Hill, *The Strengths of Black Families* (New York: Urban League, 1972); Andrew Billingsley, *Black Families in White America* (Englewood Cliffs, NJ: Prentice-Hall, 1968); and Joyce Ladner, *Tomorrow's Tomorrow* (Garden City, NY: Doubleday, 1971). For a recent analysis, see Linda Burnham, "Has Poverty Been Feminized in Black America?" *Black Scholar* 16 (1985), pp. 15–24.

7. Mae King, "The Politics of Sexual Stereotypes," *Black Scholar* 4 (1973), pp. 12–23.

8. Barbara Christian, "An Angle of Seeing: Motherhood in Buchi Emecheta's *Joys of Motherhood* and Alice Walker's *Meridian*," in *Black Feminist Criticism*, ed. Barbara Christian (New York: Pergamon, 1985), p. 214.

9. See Christine Oppong, ed., *Female and Male in West Africa* (London: Allen & Unwin, 1983); Niara Sudarkasa, "Female Employment and Family Organization in West Africa," in *The Black Woman Cross-Culturally*, ed. Filomina Chiamo Steady (Cambridge, MA: Schenkman, 1981), pp. 49–64; and Nancy Tanner, "Matrifocality in Indonesia and Africa and Among Black Americans," in *Woman, Culture, and Society*, eds. Michelle Rosaldo and Louise Lamphere (Stanford, CA: Stanford University, 1974), pp. 129–156.

10. Christine Oppong, "Family Structure and Women's Reproductive and Productive Roles: Some Conceptual and Methodological Issues," in *Women's Roles and Population Trends in the Third World*, eds. Richard Anker, Myra Buvinic and Nadia Youssef (London: Croom Helm, 1982), pp. 133–150.

11. The key distinction here is that, unlike the matriarchy thesis, women play central roles in families and this centrality is seen as legitimate. In spite of this centrality, it is important not to idealize African women's family roles. For an analysis by a Black African feminist, see Awa Thiam, *Black Sisters, Speak Out: Feminism and Oppression in Black Africa* (London: Pluto, 1978).

12. Sudarkasa, 1981.

13. John Mbiti, *African Religions and Philosophies* (New York: Anchor, 1969).

14. Niara Sudarkasa, "Interpreting the African Heritage in Afro-American Family Organization," in *Black Families*, ed. Harriette Pipes McAdoo (Beverly Hills, CA: Sage, 1981), pp. 37–53; and Deborah Gray White, *Ar'n't I a Woman? Female Slaves in the Plantation South* (New York: W.W. Norton, 1984).

15. The terms used in this section appear in Rosalie Riegle Troester, "Turbulence and Tenderness: Mothers, Daughters, and 'Othermothers' in Paule Marshall's *Brown Girl, Brownstones*," *SAGE: A Scholarly Journal on Black Women* 1 (Fall 1984), pp. 13–16.

16. See Tanner's discussion of matrifocality, 1974; see also Carrie Allen McCray, "The Black Woman and Family Roles," in *The Black Woman*, ed. LaFrances Rogers-Rose

(Beverly Hills, CA: Sage, 1980), pp. 67–78; Elmer Martin and Joanne Mitcheli Martin, *The Black Extended Family* (Chicago: University of Chicago, 1978); Joyce Aschenbrenner, *Lifelines, Black Families in Chicago* (Prospect Heights, IL: Waveland, 1975); and Carol B. Stack, *All Our Kin* (New York: Harper & Row, 1974).

17. Martin and Martin, 1978; Stack, 1974; and Virginia Young, "Family and Childhood in a Southern Negro Community," *American Anthropologist* 72 (1970), pp. 269–288.

18. Stack, 1974.

19. Ellen Cantarow, *Moving the Mountain: Women Working for Social Change* (Old Westbury, NY: Feminist Press, 1980), p. 59.

20. Thordis Simonsen, ed., *You May Plow Here, The Narrative of Sara Brooks* (New York: Touchstone, 1986), p. 181.

21. White, 1985; Dill, 1986; Mullings, 1986; note 2 above.

22. Simonsen, 1986, p. 86.

23. Mamie Garvin Fields and Karen Fields, *Lemon Swamp and Other Places, A Carolina Memoir* (New York: Free Press, 1983), p. xvii.

24. Ibid, p. 195.

25. Cheryl Gilkes, " 'Holding Back the Ocean with a Broom,' Black Women and Community Work," in Rogers-Rose, 1980, pp. 217–231; "Going Up for the Oppressed: The Career Mobility of Black Women Community Workers," *Journal of Social Issues* 39 (1983), pp. 115–139.

26. Gilkes, 1980, p. 219.

27. Fields and Fields, 1983, p. xvi.

28. Charles Johnson, *Shadow of the Plantation* (Chicago: University of Chicago, 1934, 1979), p. 173.

29. Pamela Reid, "Socialization of Black Female Children," in *Women: A Developmental Perspective*, eds. Phyllis Berman and Estelle Ramey (Washington, DC: National Institute of Health, 1983).

30. For works in the feminist psychoanalytic tradition, see Nancy Chodorow, "Family Structure and Feminine Personality," in Rosaldo and Lamphere, 1974; Nancy Chodorow, *The Reproduction of Mothering* (Berkeley, CA: University of California, 1978); and Jane Flax, "The Conflict Between Nurturance and Autonomy in Mother-Daughter Relationships and Within Feminism," *Feminist Studies* 4 (1978), pp. 171–189.

31. Ann Moody, *Coming of Age in Mississippi* (New York: Dell, 1968).

32. Ladner, 1971; Gloria Joseph, "Black Mothers and Daughters: Their Roles and Functions in American Society," in *Common Differences*, ed. Gloria Joseph and Jill Lewis (Garden City, NY: Anchor, 1981), pp. 75–126; Lena Wright Myers, *Black Women, Do They Cope Better?* (Englewood Cliffs, NJ: Prentice-Hall, 1980).

33. Elsa Barkley Brown, "Hearing Our Mothers' Lives," paper presented at Fifteenth Anniversary of African-American and African Studies at Emory College, Atlanta,

1986. This essay will appear in the upcoming Black Women's Studies issue of *SAGE: A Scholarly Journal on Black Women*, Vol. VI, No. 1.

34. Joseph, 1980; Myers, 1980.

35. Gloria Wade-Gayles, "The Truths of Our Mothers' Lives: Mother-Daughter Relationships in Black Women's Fiction," *SAGE: A Scholarly Journal on Black Women* 1 (Fall 1984), p. 12.

36. Troester, 1984, p. 13.

37. Wade-Gayles, 1984. p. 10.

38. Joseph, 1980.

39. Moody, 1968, p. 57.

40. Renita Weems, " 'Hush, Mama's Gotta Go Bye Bye': A Personal Narrative," *SAGE: A Scholarly Journal on Black Women* 1 (Fall 1984), p. 26.

41. Ibid, p. 27.

42. June Jordan, *On Call, Political Essays* (Boston: South End Press, 1985), p. 145.

A Poem for My Daughter

Marjorie Saiser

this is not the poem you asked for
it will not unfurl from the foremost
vessel in great shimmers of satin
to wave a tree,
the white branches folding
and unfolding in a south wind
snapping and springing back as if
to herald a strong young king

it will not carry under its mantle
under the arm
a soft mute animal
holding close, lying hidden,
comforting against the skin

rather it will say *fly*
and the word will be torn away
in the wind from your powerful
wings

and before it can say *hurt*
and lie down on the sand

it will be glad
and say *love*
to a dark speck on the sky

Elena

Pat Mora

My Spanish isn't enough.
I remember how I'd smile
listening to my little ones,
understanding every word they'd say,
their jokes, their songs, their plots.
    Vamos a perdirle dulces a mama.
        Vamos.
But that was in Mexico.
Now my children go to American
    high schools.
They speak English. At night they
    sit around
the kitchen table, laugh with one
    another.
I stand by the stove and feel dumb,
    alone.
I bought a book to learn English.
My husband frowned, drank more
    beer.
My oldest said, "Mama, he doesn't
    want you
to be smarter than he is." I'm forty,
embarrassed at mispronouncing
    words,
embarrassed at the laughter of my
    children,
the grocer, the mailman. Sometimes
    I take
my English book and lock myself
    in the bathroom,
say the thick words softly,
for if I stop trying, I will be deaf
when my children need my help.

Saiser, Marjorie. 1985. "A poem for my daughter." In *Adjoining Rooms*. eds. Elizabeth Banset, et al., p. 125. Lincoln, NE: Pltte Valley Press. Reprinted by permission of the author.

"Elena," by Pat Mora. Reprinted with permission of the publisher from *Chants*, by Pat Mora (Houston: Arte Publico Press of the University of Houston, 1985). p. 50.

A Passion for Female Friends

Connie Griffin

Editor's note: For more than a decade Janice Raymond has dedicated her life and work to feminism. She has contributed a great wealth of knowledge and insight to the development of feminist theory and is one of our foremothers in developing women's studies courses and programs in the university. She has also forged new territory in approaches to feminist research, moving beyond stale, academic, so-called "objectivity" and coming to her work with a passionate commitment to integrating the experiences and perspectives of women.

From her first published writings in the early seventies—in which she analyzes patriarchy from an ethical perspective, critiques cultural concepts such as masculinity and femininity, and exposes male morality for the self-serving system that it is—to her recent tracing of a genealogy of female friendship, relationship and community internationally, Janice has applied feminist research to the rigorous challenge of radical feminist philosophy.

In her recently published book, A Passion for Friends, she draws on a number of methods in uncovering a tradition of relationships among women comparable to the classical society of men which has its roots in the writings of Plato. She ingeniously becomes anthropologist and archaeologist, genealogist and historian, philosopher and visionary. Janice not only celebrates the personal worth of women's relationships to one another, but she stresses the political ramifications and, she notes, "they are powerful indeed!"

In the following interview, Janice shares her philosophy of the power of women's friendship for one another in effecting world change, but, perhaps more importantly, she shares her own experience of friendship with women as a deeply profound source of inner strength enabling us to live creatively and with vision in an imperfect world.

Connie: How did you come to develop a philosophy of female friendship?

Jan: Actually, all of the issues of my whole life's experiences were raised as I began working on female friendship. Sisterhood has been talked about a great deal—communities and collectives of women—and yet many of them have failed to fulfill our expectations. Having felt the loss of unfulfilled expectations, I wanted to reaffirm a vision of female friendship, because the ideal of the spirit of friendship lives on in my self and in other women.

Connie: Many of us are facing those issues right now as we attempt to bridge the ideal and the real in our own lives. I felt affirmed by your concept of female friendship as a way of living in the present while also envisioning what could be, if we only create it together.

Jan: Yes. The book was an attempt on my part to bring together the materialist/idealist tension, which is also the tension between feminist politics and feminist spirituality. I

Griffin, Connie. 1987. "A passion for female friends: An interview with Janice Raymond." *Woman of Power* 7(Summer): 68–71. Reprinted with permission of the author and publisher.

hoped that the book would represent that tension, including the actual existence of women's communities and groups as alive and well, while also acknowledging the many obstacles to their very existence. I especially wanted to identify for feminists the tension created by living out that vision in a larger world that is woman-hating.

Connie: I was struck by the dual tension that you see radical feminists having to live with in the world as insiders/outsiders, as materialists/spiritualists.

Jan: I began to look at the concept of vision itself. Vision, in its literal definition, is seeing with the faculty of ordinary sight, but there is also seeing with other than literal sight. I call these two ways of seeing "two sights-seeing": near-sightedness and far-sightedness. And that has all sorts of ramifications. This dual vision is the *essential tension* of feminism and it is present in every aspect of women's lives. We must learn how to live with this tension or we will be crushed by the contradictions between our vision and the worldly reality. Having dual vision holds us to a sobering recognition of the conditions of women's existence in a man-made world even as it requires imagining a world that women are capable of creating together. The central challenge to feminists is to learn how to implement what our vision presents to us given the real structure within which we must live; we must use the farsighted vision to implement a nearsighted vision.

Connie: You envision female friendship as a means of moving beyond the struggle with male rule, and of beginning relationship out of shared strength and not simply shared struggle.

Jan: I want to put a caveat on that, because it is likely to be misinterpreted; it has been misinterpreted already. I did not mean to say that women ever get to the point, while we are living in a hetero-relational world, of being beyond the world as men have made it. I don't want that point misunderstood. It is another tension that we must recognize that we have to live with. The book is based on the conviction that it is not possible for women to be free, nor to be realistic about the state of women's existence in a man-made world, nor to struggle against those forces that are waged against us all, nor to win, if we do not have a vision of female friendship—if women do not come to realize how profound are the possibilities of being *for* each other, and that recognition usually comes with the realization of how completely men have hidden those possibilities from us.

Feminist theory, feminist resistance, and activism have exposed the ways in which men have oppressed women, but we need to also go beyond that and see what is in feminism for women beyond the communion of resistance. That commonality, that unity cannot sustain us unless there is something else there. And for me that is female friendship; what keeps me going is female friendship. I see women burning out who don't have community beyond that of resistance; they get so despondent about the overwhelming nature of the "state of atrocity," as Mary Daly has aptly called it, that they cannot see anything beyond.

Connie: You take the lens of feminism and turn it toward women in a powerfully woman-identified, self-identified way, bringing feminism to a new level of understanding for me. Everyone assumes that if you're feminist, you're about the work of gaining equality—and that "equality," of course, has to do with relationships with men.

Jan: For me the essence of feminism has never meant the equality of women with men; it has meant the equality of women with women—with our selves—it has meant being equal to those women who have been for women, those who have lived for women's freedom and those who have died for it; those who have fought for women and survived by women's strength; those who have loved women and who have realized that without the consciousness and conviction that women are primary in each others lives, nothing else is in perspective. Hetero-relational feminism, like hetero-relational humanism, obscures the necessity of female friendship as a foundation for and a consequence of feminism. The imperative of female friendship is that women be equal to our vital "womanist"* selves, equal to the task of creating a woman-centered existence.

Certainly feminism is about equality, in a secondary sense, with men, because women have the right to live as unendangered in this world as men do, women have the right to the same kinds of goods and power and prestige that men have. But if that is the primary focus, then women lose sight of ourselves; and that is a very dangerous position to be in.

The tension of keeping a woman-identified vision in focus in a man-centered world is a powerful one, indeed, because the notion that feminism is primarily about our equality with other women defies the world as it has been constructed; everything in this culture, as well as in most cultures, gives out the message that women are *for* men.

There are different ways in which women acknowledge and live out female friendship, and I do not wish to simplify these differences. Gyn/affection—my term for affection among women that is *primary*—expresses a continuum of female friendship, but I would distinguish between that continuum and the choice of Lesbian love. We need to be clear about the choice of being Lesbian as contrasted to Gyn/affection. Many women do not choose to live Lesbian lives, including some Lesbians. They may choose to move in the world of female friendship, and their friendships may be intense and essential in their lives; nonetheless they may choose to relate sexually, and in other ways, with men. To include them in the term Lesbian is a false inclusion. We must acknowledge that some female friends know and live their own truths and have consciously chosen their own paths; to do otherwise is both patronizing and pretentious, and often leads us to assume that we know these women better than they know themselves.

Lesbian feminists have analyzed quite well the institutionalization of heterosexuality, as well as the quantum leap it often requires to even discover the *choice* of Lesbian living in a hetero-relational culture. To live as a Lesbian is a particular choice that involves particular risks, as well as a specific, unique life. And so the *intentionality* of living as a Lesbian is in my opinion very important. More than any other group, Lesbian feminists have shrunk the power of hetero-reality and have expanded the range of what had previously been perceived as a sexual category—lesbian sexuality—far beyond the sexual to encompass a social, spiritual, and political reality.

But Gyn/affection, as a term, is an attempt to be honest and truly inclusive of all women who put each other first in some or in all ways, while avoiding a simplistic and sentimental false inclusiveness. Gyn/affection and female friendship, as realities and as concepts, are meant to affirm the vast range, degrees, and various manifestations of affection among women. They connote the *passion* that women feel for women, and they acknowledge the profound attraction for and the movement of vital women toward other

---

*A term used by Alice Walker to denote a "Black feminist . . . A woman who loves other women, sexually and/or nonsexually. Appreciates and prefers women's culture, women's emotional flexibility . . . and women's strength." (From *In Search of Our Mothers' Gardens* by Alice Walker, Harcourt, Brace, Jovanovich, 1983.)

vital women. Being a woman-identified-woman is far more expansive than simply saying that we live in a hetero-sexist world and are trying to correct the problem; the wider problem is that we live in a hetero-relational world where not only our sexual relations, but all of our relations are determined by the value system, the norm, and the ideological superstructure that woman is *for* man. Once this assumption is defied—and female friendship defies it—there is a powerful, political act. Once women start choosing to be *for* women, the distribution of power is altered in all societies.

Now affection is a very personal word, but it is far more than a mere private attachment, although it is that too. When women *affect* one another it becomes a political as well as a personal experience. What the presence of women to each other means is not only that women are taking women's presence away from men, but also that women are taking *power* from men. Men need women to recognize their power, to give them power, without complicity on the part of women, the structures of hetero-reality crumble; without the gaze of women being fixated on men, and with that gaze being redirected toward women, the power that that gaze endows is redistributed. Women have been the endless spectators of men being with other men, of sports events, of wars, of patriarchal religious and educational rites—always it is women watching men, and that watching is necessary as a reinforcement of male bonding, of male power, of male authority. We must redirect that gaze and begin to recognize our selves, our power and one another as the true sources of that power. And then, men will return to normal size. When I was studying women's communities, all of the explanations that even recognized the existence of those communities of women did so in a typically hetero-relational way—that is, they saw it as negative, and defined their existence together as deprived, because they were living lives that did not include men. As I studied the records, I noted that it was never seen as an enriching choice, and seldom even a conscious choice. Absurd explanations were used. For example, the sex ratio in medieval Europe was cited as explanation for why so many women entered convents; the brutality of the Chinese system of treating women, such as foot binding, female infanticide, and the high rate of female suicide were used as reasons for the formation of communities of Chinese marriage resisters.

Women's history must clarify these false definitions and explanations. Women who were/are *for* other women are much more prolific in most cultures than we think. It just takes someone to go in and excavate the evidence.

Connie: You speak of your methodology in writing the book as one of a genealogical study; therefore, it is important to note that you are not merely describing an ideal, but are tracing what is in fact quite real for many women of the world.

Jan: Yes. I wanted the book to represent a tradition of women's ideas, a tradition of women *affecting* one another, of women whose movement was toward one another. Genealogy traces a line of descent, so in charting a genealogy of female friendship, it was necessary to trace the lines of interaction between various groups of women to show that we have a common ancestry. I wanted to depict the historical and cultural diversity of women's association with one another while also envisioning a future in which friendship will provide the basis for feminist purpose.

I looked at the convents of the Middle Ages which offered women an alternative to obligatory marriage, a place where they could receive an education and a legitimate setting for a strong community of women. I looked at the Beguine movement, which provided economic self-sufficiency and separate living spaces in which women banded together in common purposes throughout Europe. And I examined the marriage resisters in China, communities which thrived in the nineteenth and twentieth centuries, providing longterm cooperative living and security, but also lifelong companionship and social recognition customarily denied unmarried women in China.

We have traditions and ancestries of communities and groups of women and we ignore them at our peril.

Connie: Do you think that we sometimes romanticize friendship between and among women? I mean, creating and maintaining friendship is hard work; it doesn't simply happen, and there can be a great deal of pain in the loss of friendship. Practically speaking, how do you deal with the negative side of friendship between women?

Jan: As soon as I began writing the book, women said to me, "I hope you are going to deal with what prevents female friendship as well as what fosters it," and I said, "yes, that has to be looked at, too." And that is the painful aspect of it all; we have all wanted to chuck our friendships with other women at certain points along the way because the obstacles to their being alive and healthy are enormous. And, as I stated earlier, part of the impetus for wanting to write the book was to put away the grief that comes when for some reason a friendship is lost, betrayed, or made invisible in some way that is beyond one's control. Not all women can befriend other women. An uncritical acceptance of all women as friends derives from a lack of discernment, or a lack of what Alice Walker termed the "rigors of discernment"—discerning who is the real friend and who is not the real friend. If friendship is indeed gyn/affection, and if a friend has the ability to affect and move us, then we're not talking about a superficial relationship; we're talking about a relationship that is posited on some kind of common values that we share. That takes time to discover, and it requires discernment to know whether or not one can be friends with a woman who seemingly has the same values, or who appears to share in what one believes in or what one works for. Discernment is discussed in religious traditions as one of the "gifts of the spirit," but it is rigorous, and to consistently employ it within a friendship is difficult yet rewarding work. Friends have to continually do that for one another. Many women do *not* do that for other women but that is where my focus on *thoughtfulness* comes in.

The feminist maxim, "the personal is political" has become a tenet of the feminist movement; the corollary is "the political is personal." If one lives a thinking life, it has to translate into some kind of thoughtfulness. Women have been socialized to be caring and nurturing, but that's not what I'm talking about; that kind of thoughtfulness is done at the expense of thinking. True thoughtfulness restores thinking to the notion of thoughtfulness, and this is the element of discernment.

Connie: You have a powerful alliterative phrase in your book that I think could serve as a strong tool for us as we try to live out our deep friendships with and love for women. You state, and I paraphrase, that women need women's wisdom, but must use it with worldly integrity. That's the vision and it's a large task. Can you give us some sense of how to go about that practically speaking?

Jan: The difficult task is living in the man-made world without disassociating from it and without assimilating into it, and without allowing it to define or victimize us as women. Now that to me is where we really need some guidance and direction, because as radical feminists we struggle with those tensions every day, just in terms of daily living. And although we may be rooted in gyn/affection, we also have to go out from that affection, in that we live and work in the world, the world that men have dominated. In order to be separatists in the purest sense of that word, women would have to step off the face of the planet. Some real distinctions have to be made about what radical integrity is, versus a negative dissociation from the world, and a downward mobility of mind, appearance, and money. As if women have always had access to money and can simply choose to throw it away!

Again, it's not enlightenment in one fell swoop; it's living a life that is continually walking that dividing line between dissociation on the one hand and assimilation on the other. Mary Daly used the term "living on the boundary," which I believe is better than talking about making compromises, because it's more positive and more visual; it recognizes the fact that being a woman living in a man's world is precarious business, and it recognizes that there is a boundary to be walked in the course of daily living. The phrase "living as a woman among women among men" came out of the recognition of the continual tension created by living on the boundary, of *not* compromising our integrity as radical feminists, of being in the world for our selves and for other women, and from recognizing that that is where our source of strength comes from.

Connie: And how is the vision a part of that process?

Jan: The very *act* of being and living among women keeps the vision a present reality, and it comes from the sharing of that vision, from the mutuality and reciprocity of the reflection—so that what you have is not only a reality check, but a living vision which exists in your life; you know it, you find it, and you coexist with it with women who *give* to, *do* for, and *are for women.*

Some women have said to me, "you're asking the impossible." But it's *not* impossible; to me, it is living in the truest sense, it is existence in the truest sense; it is not the impossible, it is the *essential!*

When I was Growing Up

Nellie Wong

I know now that once I longed to be white.
How? you ask.
Let me tell you the ways.

when I was growing up, people told me
I was dark and I believed my own darkness
in the mirror, in my soul, my own narrow vision

when I was growing up, my sisters
with fair skin got praised
for their beauty, and in the dark
I fell further, crushed between high walls

when I was growing up, I read magazines
and saw movies, blonde movie stars, white skin,
sensuous lips and to be elevated, to become
a woman, a desirable woman, I began to wear
imaginary pale skin

when I was growing up, I was proud
of my English, my grammar, my spelling
fitting into the group of smart children
smart Chinese children, fitting in,
belonging, getting in line

when I was growing up and went to high school,
I discovered the rich white girls, a few yellow girls,
their imported cotton dresses, their cashmere sweaters,
their curly hair and I thought that I too should have
what these lucky girls had

when I was growing up, I hungered
for American food, American styles,
coded: white and even to me, a child
born of Chinese parents, being Chinese
was feeling foreign, was limiting,
was unAmerican

when I was growing up and a white man wanted
to take me out, I thought I was special,
an exotic gardenia, anxious to fit
the stereotype of an oriental chick

when I was growing up, I felt ashamed
of some yellow men, their small bones,
their frail bodies, their spitting
on the streets, their coughing,
their lying in sunless rooms,
shooting themselves in the arms

when I was growing up, people would ask
if I were Filipino, Polynesian, Portuguese.
They named all colors except white, the shell
of my soul, but not my dark, rough skin

when I was growing up, I felt
dirty. I thought that god
made white people clean
and no matter how much I bathed,
I could not change, I could not shed
my skin in the gray water

when I was growing up, I swore
I would run away to purple mountains,
houses by the sea with nothing over
my head, with space to breathe,
uncongested with yellow people in an area
called Chinatown, in an area I later learned
was a ghetto, one of many hearts
of Asian America

I know now that once I longed to be white.
How many more ways? you ask.
Haven't I told you enough?

Chapter 4—Women's Relationships: Families, Kin, Partners, and Friends
Study Questions

1. "Family is one of the primary mechanisms for perpetuating social inequality." Under what institutionalized system? What are the consequences of such a system on individual family members? What healthy avenues are open for women to compensate for the inequality? What unhealthy avenues are often used?

2. Is the "traditional family" the norm today? Discuss the return to "family values" in its political and social context. Is it a return that is needed, or an excuse for what really ails American society? Why or why not?

3. How does being "outside the norm" affect black families, both positively and negatively?

4. What are the causes of homelessness among poor women?

5. Explain power versus the realization of a woman's own power within the black family network. How does this compare to women's perceived role within the patriarchal family? What are the factors that contribute to the support of women's power within "nontraditional" families?

6. What does Collins mean by the black family being a "contradictory location" for women? What contradictions exist?

7. What are the ideals of a healthy partner relationship? What encourages people to form partnerships outside of marriage?

8. Define *heterosexism* and *homophobia*. How do these issues affect choice? In your opinion, what effects do these issues have on lesbian relationships? How are these effects mitigated within different cultures?

9. What are the barriers to lesbian motherhood? Are they realistic? Why or why not?

10. Do power issues between lesbians exist? Why or why not? How does Adrienne Rich relate lesbianism to the realization of power for all women? Do you agree? Why or why not?

11. How do patriarchy, heterosexism, and racism affect women's friendships? How is women's isolation from each other manifested?

12. Think about your most lasting and intimate relationships in the context of oppression. Are they same-sex or with those of the opposite sex? Why? Did your choice of friends change as you grew older? If so, why?

13. How does crossing patriarchically imposed racial, cultural, and class boundaries give women a better sense of their own power? In the feminist analysis, why is it important to do so? What is the primary factor that divides white women and women of color?

14. What is the source of internalized oppression for black mothers? What stereotypes are attributed to black mothers? How do they differ from those attributed to white mothers?

15. What differentiates West African women's roles from those of Western women? How do these differing roles determine influence in the family structure? Is motherhood used as a political tool? At what cost?

16. In small groups, describe in your own words the support networks of black women. Compare and contrast them to the idea of the "cult of true womanhood" to which Collins refers.

17. Part of the backlash against feminism is grounded in the theory that women became more economically independent in the 1970s, wanted more, and abandoned their husbands. Using Collins's article, discuss in the large group ideas for countering this assumption.

18. Describe the delicate balance young women of color must achieve between conformity and resistance. Why is it necessary? Give examples.

19. In "A Passion For Friends," Raymond describes the importance of dual vision. What does this mean? What is its import? What is essential to its realization?

20. Raymond asserts: "Women need women's wisdom, but must use it with worldly integrity." What is the basic tension feminist women face in today's society? What line must they walk, and why?

VIOLENCE AGAINST WOMEN

Annette Bennington McElhiney

Most Americans remember as children hearing or singing such little rhymes as:

Who's afraid of the Big Bad Wolf,
the Big Bad Wolf,
the Big Bad Wolf?

or

Georgie Porgie Pudding and Pie
Kissed the girls and made them cry!

Most of us thought these little nursery rhymes were harmless suggesting the natural tendencies for "wolves" to pursue innocent girls like little Red Riding Hood, or for boys to intimidate and pester girls. In addition, many young women remember being called "Daddy's little girl" or "Granddad's little girl," a label that denotes possession of young girls by older male relatives. Today, feminists question the innocence of these childhood ditties and labels. We ask what attitudes they engender and reenforce. In fact, Katha Pollit in a special issue of *Time* entitled "Women: The Road Ahead" (fall 1990) says "Georgie Porgie Is a Bully." Daily stories in the newspapers document the epidemic occurrences of various violent acts perpetrated on women by men.

According to the U.S. Senate Committee on the Judiciary, three out of four women will be the victims of some violent crime in their lifetimes. Since 1980, U.S. rape rates have risen nearly four times as fast as the total crime rate. A woman is raped every six minutes. Every eighteen seconds a woman is beaten for a grand total of three to four million battered women each year. A woman is less likely to be killed in a car accident than to be raped. Every year one million women seek help for some kind of injury as a result of domestic violence. And the crime rate against women in the United States is significantly higher than in other countries: thirteen times the rape rate in England, four times the rate in Germany, and more than twenty times that in Japan (U.S. Senate, Committee on the Judiciary, June 20, 1990). In addition, in another study conducted in 1986, out of a survey of 10,000 children, 15.7 percent were sexually maltreated, 8.3 percent emotionally maltreated, and 21.6 percent maltreated in other ways. Out of all abused children, over half or 52.5 percent were female (Statistical Abstract of the United States 1990).

Not compiled, but equally significant are the numbers of women whose sense of self-esteem is destroyed in the classroom by teachers and in the office by bosses; who are forced to give birth to babies they do not want; who are treated disrespectfully the older they get; and who are forced to live alone, often unsupported emotionally by family and friends, in their senior years.

In fact, from birth until death, women must actively ward off a variety of violations perpetrated against them both by the society they live in and by individuals, some violations as mild as the silly nursery rhymes and labels quoted above and others not so mild and silly. These violations range from the verbal to the physical, from the mildest to the harshest, and from those committed by strangers to those committed by loved ones. They also include criminal physical violations and, more difficult to define, unethical emotional violations condoned by our institutions. Yet all of the violations have two things in common: They spring, first, from America's habit of sanctioning male dominance and female submissiveness and, second, from women being seen as the property of men. Whether the violation is verbal and emotional abuse, an unhealthy environment resulting from our culture's negative attitudes toward women, sexual harassment, incest, rape, domestic abuse, or femicide, each springs from the belief that men are the superior sex and therefore are entitled to exercise the necessary power to subordinate or possess women.

This chapter will not only give factual information about the extent of all of the above forms of abuse, but it will suggest why and how this abuse has come to be sanctioned by most men and even some women in the United States today. In addition, it will suggest how attitudes about men and women must change before such rampant abuse will cease. This chapter will raise the following questions:

- What specific role does male dominance play in each form of violence against women?
- How does the concept of women as the property of men affect sexual violence against women?
- What constitutes verbal/emotional abuse?
- What constitutes sexual harassment and why is it considered abuse?
- What is incest and what are its effects on its survivors?
- How do feminists explain incest differently from many social psychologists?
- What are the myths and realities about rape?
- Why does our society seemingly accept domestic abuse as a private family matter rather than as a crime against women and society?
- Why do women stay in abusive situations?
- What is femicide, how prevalent is it, and who commits it?
- What can men and women in our culture do to reverse attitudes about male dominance and female submissiveness and about women as the property of men?

Emotional and Verbal Abuse

Our system of language and such institutions as the educational establishment, traditional religion, and the media shape attitudes about gender, and all contribute to the emotional and verbal abuse which many women face throughout their lives.

Ideology, the dominant ideas characterizing a culture, always reenforces the beliefs and behavior, both public and private, of people in a particular culture. Because most Americans accept the idea of men as dominant and women as subordinate, both verbal and nonverbal communication used every day publicly bombards women with messages about their own inadequacies. These messages may be in the form of sexist jokes in which women are made the targets of negative comments; curriculum in which women's presence as contributors to culture is scarce; hierarchies (political, religious, or military) in which women's absence is notable; or electronic or print media in which women are portrayed as sex objects. Consequently, women internalize the commonly held beliefs of their culture and unconsciously view themselves as less than, rather than equal to, males. This constant devaluing causes emotional damage often impossible to reverse without professional guidance or support of others who understand it.

Likewise in their private lives, many women become targets of extreme verbal abuse or humiliation often leading to emotional problems or depression. According to Richard J. Gelles and Murray A. Straus, one of the most hidden and least researched, but perhaps more damaging, kinds of victimization may be that of emotional abuse by someone the victim loves (Gelles and Straus 1988). They point out the difficulty in specifically defining *what* constitutes emotional abuse in American culture. Overtly abusive verbal behavior by fathers, husbands, boyfriends, brothers, or other male relatives includes patronizing, ignoring, tearing down, harping, criticizing, and taunting (Gelles and Straus 1988). Such comments as "That is just the sort of dumb thing a woman would do" or "Isn't that just like a woman" seem harmless, but actually reenforce a woman's sense of inferiority. More subtle, but equally eroding, comments made by men about women as dependents who keep men from doing what they would prefer if not burdened with a wife and family chip away at women's self image. Yet even more damaging may be nonverbal forms of torment such as deliberately showing affection for, attention to, or respect for another woman while withholding it from the spouse, daughter, or sister, thus creating or foster-ing female competition between relatives and even strangers.

One reason researchers suggest why so little research has been done on this form of abuse is because some believe that what goes on within the home is private or the business only of those living there. Consequently, conducting objective research may infringe upon the rights of a family. This is an excuse that serves the interests of abusers.

Social and Ideological Conditions Influencing the Institutionalization of Violence Against Women

Dorie Klein states that even though crimes against women have varied over time, they are particularly determined by political, economic, and social circumstances related to a specific historical context. In fact, she identifies three specific areas in which women are victimized by institutionalized male control: 1) child-bearing activities, 2) sexual activities, and 3) nurturance (Klein 1982).

In the twentieth century, particularly since the late 1960s and 1970s when birth control became relatively available to women, women have acquired some control over their bodies. Yet in 1991, with the appointment of yet another conservative judge, Clarence Thomas, to the U.S. Supreme Court, the reversal of *Roe v. Wade* seems quite possible. After all, in the conservative backlash now promoting the virtues of motherhood, the distribution of birth control information at federally funded clinics and the lack of either availability or funding of abortions for welfare women have already begun. Therefore, as in the past, heterosexual women may well find their emotions curtailed by fear of pregnancy and resort to depending upon unsafe abortions to avoid delivering babies. Thus the damage to both their physical bodies and their emotions will intensify as the conservative backlash against women controlling their own bodies increases. Women of color and women with lower incomes will suffer the greatest because of their lack of access to information and good medical care provided by private medical facilities.

Later this chapter will discuss abusive behavior such as rape and incest. However, a less obvious form of sexual abuse experienced by women of all ages is the damage wrought by defining women as "sex objects" when they are young and as "invisible" when they are old. Popular magazine and newspaper articles abound with suggestions about the physical, psychological, and emotional damage, such damage as eating disorders and mental depression, incurred by young women who allow themselves to be defined as sex objects and, yet, can not measure up to the culturally prescribed standards.

Less is generally said about what happens to women as they age. As reported by *Washington Post* reporter Don Oldenburg, Carolyn Heilbrun, a sixty-five-year-old academician and novelist, says that she notices that women between the ages of fifty and fifty-five begin to enter what she calls "the circle of invisibility" or a time when appearance becomes less important. Women can either be emotionally devastated by this phenomenon or see it as a challenge (Oldenburg 1991). Those who have been brainwashed with the patriarchal idea of the necessity for women to be sexually attractive often resort to all sorts of artificial attempts to retain the illusion of youth: face lifts, infusions of silicone, liposuction (removal of fat cells), tummy tucks, and other kinds of cosmetic surgery. While these desperate attempts to stave off old age seem trivial to most feminists, the effects on women who pur-

sue them can be emotionally devastating and even physically damaging; note the disaster stories in newspapers about failures in liposuction. Even more prevalent are the FDA warnings about the dangers of silicone implants. The institutionalized culprit creating the damage is the way in which our culture encourages women to define themselves primarily by their sexual attractiveness as prescribed by others.

Finally, our culture's expectation of women of all ages to nurture children, men, other women, and seniors creates a "triple burden" on mothers, wives, and workers (Klein 1982). Harriet B. Braiker talks about women as being particularly susceptible to acquiring a Type E personality, wanting to be everything to everyone (Braiker 1986). Is it any surprise that so many women today are treated either through therapy or drugs for mild or clinical depression?

Also the Older Woman's League says a woman can expect to spend seventeen years caring for her children and approximately eighteen years helping elderly parents. Furthermore, women average 11.5 years out of the paid labor force whereas men average only 1.3 years (Costa 1989). Yet ironically even though women throughout their lives nurture others, they themselves often must live alone: 40.9 percent of women age 65 and over; 33.5 percent aged 65–74; 50.5 percent aged 75–84; and 54 percent aged 85 years and over (*Current Population Reports* 1990). Often they live on fixed incomes and receive little time, respect, or attention from either society or their loved ones. Obviously, this lack of attention is not necessarily the fault of individuals—usually daughters or daughter-in-laws since sons or sons-in-law are rarely charged with this task—but rather of a society that has few programs supportive of dependent care.

Sexual Harassment as Emotional Abuse

In the fall of 1991, the U.S. congressional hearings to confirm Clarence Thomas for the Supreme Court presented a graphic picture of the emotional pain of Anita Hill as she gave her testimony before the Senate confirmation committee. Few victims of sexual harassment ever experience such public exposure, yet many feel the painful effects of such abuse throughout their lives.

Catherine MacKinnon wrote about this problem in the 1970s. She reported that in a pioneering survey of the Working Women United Institute, using a sample of 155 women workers, 40 percent had been harassed by bosses or supervisors; 22 percent by a colleague or co-worker; 29 percent by a client or customer; and 8 percent by "other." This form of abuse affects women from all races, classes, ages, and professions regardless of their sexual orientation, pay range, physical appearance, and marital status. However, MacKinnon also sees that race is an important variable in sexual harassment as harassment of black women by white men seems an extension of white male behavior during slavery. In fact, she suggests that sexual harassment can serve as a "sexist way to express racism and a racist way to express sexism" (MacKinnon 1979, 358). At any rate, sexual harassment is not about sex itself, but about power, who has it and who intends to keep it.

All too frequently, women put up with sexual harassment on campuses and in the workplace in order to earn their degrees and maintain their jobs and what little potential they have for advancement. Often, even those women who sue for damages in such cases settle out of court; a condition of their settlement frequently is that they will not reveal the amount of money they win. Even in 1988, out of a sample of 100,000 women in the workplace in several states, in California alone, only twenty-four Title VII cases were filed. In Texas, in 1988, only 2.2 cases were filed (Morgenson 1989). Consequently, because information about the prevalence of, and settlement of, lawsuits on sexual harassment has been kept so quiet, many women do not know what their legal rights are.

While the chapter on law covers this subject in greater depth in terms of defining sexual harassment and its legal aspects, this chapter, in contrast, focuses on the damage such emotional violence does to women. Professional self-esteem accrues through a sense of doing a job well or through the rewards one receives for performance. Obviously, if a woman is made to feel that she is retained or has been promoted as an employee because she does not complain when she is either verbally or physically harassed, her sense of her own value is tremendously diminished. In addition, if she frequently feels intimidated, uncomfortable, or afraid of what will happen in her place of employment, she must spend excessive energy coping with a difficult situation which men less frequently have to face. Often a feeling of powerlessness or inability to control the course of her life ensues. It may affect her work performance; her frustration, for example, may manifest itself in physical symptoms such as high blood pressure, eating disorders, headaches, or recurring illnesses or in emotional symptoms such as extremely high levels of stress or depression. Although this form of abuse may seem trivial to those not targeted by it, such is not the case. The damage shows up not as a bruise or a broken arm, but often as a broken spirit.

In addition, all of the above cases of verbal and emotional abuse of women become instrumental in creating a cultural environment receptive to the more violent forms of abuse against women. In fact, as Christine Dinsmore suggests, throughout women's lives their culture teaches them that if they "get out of line" they will risk physical harm; yet even when they "tow the line" they risk physical harm. She shares a story about Dr. Judith Herman's presentations on sexual violence. In these sessions, Herman often asks audiences of women to raise their hands if they have ever experienced: a harassing phone call, an encounter with an exhibitionist, or an encounter with a toucher. The hands go up and laughter begins. Herman then explains that even though women laugh about these experiences now, these so called "minor" encounters effectively teach women how to know their place. Furthermore, these "minor abuses" serve as ominous warnings of the rape and murder that can occur if women do not tolerate the lesser offenses (Herman 1984; Dinsmore 1991, 3). In other words, these brief encounters establish men as dominant and women as subordinate and reenforce women's belief in themselves as potential victims. Therefore, they condition women to tolerate later abuses like domestic violence, incest, date rape, and marital rape.

Incest

Sandra Butler in an article entitled "Incest: Whose Reality, Whose Theory?" (Butler 1982) looks at what incest is, to whom it happens, and what the causes and the effects on survivors *really* are as opposed to what some theorists propose as the causes and effects of incest. A feminist perspective on *why* incest occurs and *how* it damages women is paramount.

A number of feminist researchers have collected information on incest from the victims and survivors themselves (Butler [1978] 1985; Herman 1981; Russell 1986; and Dinsmore 1991). One of the most influential studies was Russell's (1986) which used a random survey of 930 adult female residents of San Francisco. In this study, incest is defined as either attempted or completed exploitive sexual contact occurring between a relative, regardless of the distance in relationship, and victim under the age of eighteen. Russell found that 16 percent of the women were incest survivors. Twenty-five percent of the perpetrators were uncles; 24 percent were fathers (including biological, foster, and step-); 16 percent were first cousins; 13 percent were brothers; 8 percent were other male relatives; 6 percent were grandfathers; 4 percent were brothers-in-law; 2 percent were female first cousins; 2 percent were other female relatives; and 1 percent were biological mothers. In this same study, she found that fathers were more likely to have had vaginal intercourse and to use violence or force on their daughters. The average age of fathers when they committed incest was 39.6 years. The demographics also showed that the rate of incest amongst races was similar except for Asians where it was lower. Women coming from Jewish religious upbringing were also less likely to be incestuously abused (Russell 1986; Lundberg-Love 1990).

Historically, incest has always existed: Religion, folk tales, and psychology have, in some respects, recognized it, but often attributed it to the fault of the woman. Judith Herman shows how the "Seductive Daughter" is a part of both religious and literary tradition. She illustrates by retelling the biblical story of Lot who impregnates both daughters but manages to maintain his innocence. As the story is told in Genesis 19:30–36, Lot's daughters, in order to preserve their father's seed, get him drunk on wine and then lie down with him. As Herman says:

> Lot's nameless daughters at least have the dignity of a serious motive. In extraordinary circumstances, the Bible story makes clear, the higher good of preserving the father's seed takes precedence over the incest taboo. Thus, even though the daughters are portrayed as entirely responsible for the incest, their actions are to some extent excused. No such charity applies to the Seductive Daughters in secular literature. Their motives are assumed to be entirely perverse. (1981, 37).

To illustrate, Herman talks about the more contemporary character Lolita in Vladimir Nabokov's novel by the same name; she suggests that *Lolita* is the "brilliant apologia for an incestuous father" and becomes the "model for countless nymphets who appear, unredeemed by Nabokov's elegant prose, in the literature of male sexual fantasy" (1981, 37–38).

In addition, Sigmund Freud listened to his patients tell about their own childhood sexual abuse by male family members. Initially, he believed their stories. However, bowing to the negative comments of his colleagues, he changes his story. As Dinsmore suggests:

> In essence he was saying that he had been naive when he had believed his clients' reports of childhood sexual abuse and that he now realized that these women had been reporting merely their fantasies, their desire for sexual involvement with adults—primarily, he believed with their fathers. Thus Freud, who had an opportunity to intervene on behalf of his women clients, instead began the long history of the denial of women's reality (Dinsmore 1991, 12).

Consequently, modern society has continued to deny the existence of incest and silenced those who reported it.

Even though the women's movement ended the silence surrounding sexual violence against women, initial efforts to explain it were as misogynist as Freud's earlier attempts. One explanation for the occurrence of incest was based on studies (Groth 1979) done in the late 1970s in prison with men convicted for sex crimes. These studies suggested that incest is committed primarily by pedophiles who are either regressed in their sexual development or fixated on having sex with children. One objection feminists like Russell and Dinsmore raise to this theory is that these studies were done on only a prison population. (Dinsmore 1991, 14).

Another theory frequently proposed was that incest resulted from dysfunctional or bad families, families that had somehow gone wrong. Terms which Dinsmore says often emerged with this theory were "the complicitous mother; the distant, detached wife; the absent, disabled mother; and the frustrated father" (Dinsmore 1991, 15). The major problem with this theory is that if a family goes wrong, somehow each member in it has a part to play; hence again the victim is blamed as is the mother. The violation turns out to be the woman's fault.

The more logical, and certainly credible, theory according to Christine Dinsmore and others (Armstrong 1982; Herman 1984) is that incest is the direct result of the exaggerated male norms in our society. That does not mean that all men sexually abuse children, but it does mean that our society has and does encourage men to be "aggressive, dominant, victorious, sexual, and powerful and to see sexual involvement as an entitlement" (Dinsmore 1991, 17). Incest is another example of men being dominant whether incest relates to sexual pursuit, harassment, or assault.

The result of male feelings of entitlement is the victimization of women. Paula K. Lundberg-Love refers to Russell's 1986 study which suggests the following long-term consequences for survivors of incest: increased negative feelings, attitudes, or beliefs about men; increased negative feelings, attitudes, or beliefs about the specific perpetrator; increased negativity towards self, including self-hatred, shame, guilt, and a negative body image as well as lowered self-esteem; feelings such as fear, anxiety, depression, and mistrust; deleterious effects on sexuality; worry about the safety of others; negative effects on other relationships; a change in ability to show physical affection; and a tendency to avoid certain relatives (Russell 1986; Lundborg-Love 1990).

Perhaps one of the most frightening facts about our culture's attitude toward incest is the existence of a pro-incest lobby called the Rene Guyon Society which purports that incest is not only *not* harmful, but may also be beneficial. Members of this organization believe that consensual sex between a child and an adult can be a beautiful, loving experience and can serve as a vehicle through which the child learns about sex from a parent (Armstrong 1982; Dinsmore 1991). However, one should certainly ask how such a power differential between a parent and a child could allow for the child making any kind of a consensual agreement.

To combat such collective misogynist efforts, individual therapists and supportive organizations like WINGS (Women Incested Needing Group Support) a non-profit organization have dedicated themselves to reducing the trauma and giving support to survivors of incest. In addition, various schools and health groups work together to educate young children on what is appropriate behavior and what is not and in speaking out about sexual abuse. In refusing to deny the abuse, women are setting examples for other women and for children to follow in coming forward and speaking about the unspeakable. Perhaps as a result, change will eventually occur.

Rape

Susan Griffin, in her classic *Rape: The All-American Crime* says:

> I have never been free of the fear of rape. From a very early age I, like most women, have thought of rape as a part of my natural environment—something to be feared and prayed against like fire or lightening. I never asked why men raped; I simply thought it one of the many mysteries of human nature (224).

Most women feel the same way as they have been cautioned since they were little girls to fear rape and to protect themselves against it by not going too far from home, not going with strangers, or not "provoking" men. Ironically, these precautions do not necessarily protect women as they are often raped in their homes, by people they know, and often by people they love.

In fact, Mary P. Koss and Barry R. Burkhart say that recent studies suggest that 15 to 22 percent of women have been raped at some point in their lives and many by acquaintances. Surveys also show that approximately 31 to 48 percent of rape victims eventually, years after the rape, seek some kind of professional psychotherapy (Koss and Burkhart 1989). Although the high incidence of rape is well known, few people ask why rape occurs.

Traditionally, explanations about rape have centered around two causes: 1) biological reasons related to male needs or

2) social learning supported by our culture. Obviously, the biological explanation accounts for women seeing rape as a part of the natural environment and as the source of comments like "boys will be boys." To understand how resistant many researchers are to critiques of the biological explanation, note Craig Palmer's article: "Twelve Reasons Why Rape is not Sexually Motivated: A Skeptical Examination" (1988). In it, he disputes the arguments of many theorists like Susan Brownmiller in her book *Against Our Will* (1975) and Nicholas Groth in his book *Men Who Rape* (1979) who say rape is not caused by biological reasons or by sex. A summary of some of the arguments used by theorists disbelieving in the biological explanation include: 1) the act of sex, especially in rape, is not always associated with romantic feelings, affection, or love; 2) most rapists are not deprived of sex, but have stable sexual partners; 3) rapes are often premeditated, not spontaneous, as often biologically motivated sex is; 4) rapes occurring during war are motivated by hostility, not sex; 5) rape is a form of "social control" because it is used as punishment in some societies; 6) some interviewed rapists have said they rape out of a need for power and control, not out of sexual desire; 7) a number of rapists have sexual dysfunctions suggesting the unimportance of sexual desire in rape; 8) castrated rapists find other ways to violate women; 9) many rape victims report being held or physically abused during the act, suggesting the need of the rapist to overpower, not merely to complete the sex act; and 10) rape victims are not only the young, beautiful and sexy, but sometimes the aged and infirm. Despite the overwhelming logic of these arguments, Palmer says they use vague semantics and one can never know whether for the rapist sex is the "means" or the "end"

(Palmer 1988, 515). However, feminists remain skeptical and see more reasons why rape is not sexually motivated than they do in this critique by Palmer.

Many feminists see rape as the result of a form of social learning, not biology. One study by Baron and Straus suggests that rape increases as a result of four aspects of a cultural climate: 1) gender inequality, 2) circulation of pornography, 3) culturally legitimate violence, and 4) social disorganization. Throughout this text appear countless examples of the gender inequality in U.S. culture. This chapter emphasizes the prevalence of violence. Interesting, but ambivalent evidence, suggests pornography may influence how individuals perceive rape. Some studies suggest violent pornography creates behavioral models which men then follow. Other studies dispute the causal relationship between pornography and rape, citing in particular the Attorney General's 1986 Commission on Pornography findings (Baron and Straus 1987). However, a study of people who were asked to determine the sentences for rape found that after being exposed to massive amounts of pornography, subjects gave shorter sentences to rapists than did the controls who had not viewed pornography. This study suggests that exposure to pornography can certainly alter perceptions of the seriousness of rape as a crime (Kanin and Jackson 1987).

The legal definition of rape generally includes the absence of consent on the part of the victim; the use of, or threat of, force on the part of the perpetrator; and sexual penetration. Prior to the late 1970s, the laws of many states implied that it was not possible for a husband to rape his wife. Since then, some states have established laws prohibiting rape of a spouse. Yet, marital rape is still a serious problem in the U.S. and cuts across demographic and socioeconomic lines. According to some researchers, it is often found in combination with other forms of family violence (Bidwell and White 1986). Once again issues related to dominance are at the heart of marital rape and reflect the more general patriarchal concept of a husband's entitlement of access to his wife. But married women can be as damaged by rape by a husband as, or more so than, by a stranger. The same physical abuse, emotional abuse, humiliation, and feeling of helplessness accompany both.

Another form of rape that has not always been seen as fitting the traditional or legal definition is date or acquaintance rape. According to some research, one of the problems is that a woman's behavior still remains a determinant in the social definition of rape. In other words, the nature of "the victim-assailant relationship" remains an issue for both police and others, including jurors. Questions that often arise about date rape are: 1) How long has the woman known or dated the man? 2) How well has she known him? 3) Did she struggle or let him know she did not want sex? 4) Was she on drugs or alcohol? 5) Was she dressed provocatively or did she entice him? 6) Had she had sex with the man before? 7) Had this ever happened to her before? and, of course, 9) What kind of sex life has she had in the past? (Larrabee and McGeorge 1989).

In a study by the *Ms.* Magazine Project on Campus Sexual Assault, a questionnaire was sent to 6,159 U.S. women college students (Koss et. al 1987). Out of that total sample, 53.7 percent of college women reported they had been victimized; however, 15 percent called it rape; 12.1 percent called it attempted rape; 11.9 percent called it sexual coercion; and 14.4 percent called it forced sexual contact. (Koss and Berkhart 1989; Larrabee and McGeorge 1989).

Yet, men and women seem to view the issue of consensual agreement concerning sex differently. In a recent article in *The Chronicle of Higher Education* entitled "'A Sure-Fire Winner Is to Tell Her You Love Her: Women Fall for It All the Time': Men Talk Frankly with Counselor to Assess Harassment and Acquaintance Rape," a counselor says that most men have "sex by deception" or lie to women and lead them to drink too much in order to get them to bed. He says the men are not rapists, but "have admitted to certain behaviors" obviously interpreted by many women, and some men, as date rape (Collison 1991). The need for behavioral or values education on this issue seems obvious.

Yet another article in *Newsweek* tells an even more devastating effect of rape: "A Frightening Aftermath: Concern about AIDS Adds to the Trauma of Rape." This article points out the ongoing controversy over the defendant's right to privacy against the victim's need to know if her attacker tests positive for the HIV virus. As the author states, "Defense attorneys have always forced rape victims to prove they weren't asking for it. AIDS has upped the ante" (Salholz and Sprigen 1990, 53). Thus the survivors of rape may eventually be the victims of AIDS as well as of rape because their rights are overlooked in favor of the rights of the rapists.

Perhaps even more frustrating is information about how rape victims are treated in the courts. If women decide to prosecute their rapists, their personal lives and reputation often come under scrutiny. Even though feminists have made great strides in establishing and staffing rape crisis centers, providing advocates for the court proceedings, and provoking changes in the rape law, considerable bias still exists. If no corroborating witnesses come forward, a woman's word stands against the word of the rapist and the presumption of innocence. And in a society where men are valued more highly than women, their credibility is often greater. Therefore, even successful prosecution exacts its toll on the victim's emotional and physical health. Even if the rapist is convicted, frequently he is back on the streets in a short time and may continue to threaten the survivor or even rape her again.

Domestic Violence

Perhaps in domestic abuse more than in any other form of violence, the deeply rooted ideas about women as the possession of men impinge upon current attitudes. Wife beating has been a serious problem throughout history, but only in the last thirty years, since the emergence of the women's movement, has it received the attention it should have had earlier. Beatrice Whiting, an anthropologist, observed that among societies she had studied, those which lived in communal residences had no violence; yet when separate walls went up "the hitting started" (Gelles and Straus 1988). In other words, when private property became an issue for families and they moved into individual family units within which property could be passed down, therefore controlled, even women and children became part of that property.

Because European culture has so influenced our own, its public values concerning attitudes towards women within marriage did likewise. As early as the eighteenth century, English Common law shaped attitudes about women as the property of men. Therefore, it was perfectly acceptable legally, and otherwise, for husbands to discipline their wives if necessary as long as they did not use a stick larger than the width of their thumbs, hence the phrase "rule of thumb." As Del Martin in her study of the social variables and their impact on wife battering suggests, multiple institutions operate effectively to perpetuate this belief. Obviously, the Christian church sanctioned women's subjection to their husbands "in everything" (Ephesians 6:22–24). Therefore, clergy often advised women to be submissive and to endure (Martin 1978).

Despite changes in the church and in many laws, social attitudes endure that allow domestic abuse to flourish. One such attitude is the right of the nuclear family to privacy. As families have become more mobile, moving from state to state searching for employment, they have left their extended families and communities and isolated themselves within urban areas. According to some researchers, the family has therefore become off limits for social controls. The attitude is that what goes on behind the front door is acceptable as long as it does not impinge on the rights of others outside the door. Therefore, if one family member, generally male, wishes to impose his dominance over another member, he may do so with little fear that outsiders will intervene.

According to the U.S. Senate Committee on the Judiciary, each year more than 1,000,000 women seek medical help for injuries caused by battering (U.S. Senate 1990). In a 1987 study on 290 pregnant women living in a large city, 8 percent reported some battering during their pregnancy. Out of those abused women, 29 percent reported that battering increased during pregnancy. The abuse resulted in babies with lower birth weights than those whose mothers had not been abused (McFarlane 1989).

Yet often those not affected directly by domestic abuse ask why women stay in the abusive environment. The economic reasons are often great. Even in the 1990s, women earn only 64 to 70 percent of what men earn. This factor in combination with years spent out of the paid labor force or in part-time positions and an economy which is downsizing rather than hiring is reason enough.

In addition, because abused women undergo years of erosion of their self-esteem through emotional and psychological abuse, they develop learned helplessness. They simply do not know where to turn or from whom to seek support. Often their immediate support systems, their churches, or families encourage them to stay in the situation for the sake of the children, especially if the batterer is a good financial provider, a "community pillar," or does not abuse the children.

Also, some women stay in abusive relationships because they blame themselves. Dale T. Miller and Carol A. Porter (1983) suggest that everyone has a need to feel she has some control over her life; therefore, if one accepts blame for what happens, one has the illusion of control. They point out that one difference between victims of domestic abuse and those of stranger rape is that the former are *intimately* involved and generally over a long period of time with their attackers. In other words, often the survivors of domestic abuse still have feelings for their attackers which may include: love; a wish to save their attackers from their own obsessions, whether those obsessions are drugs or alcohol; a feeling of connection with their abusers because together they have conceived children; and a sense of gratitude for the attention of the abuser, however negative the attention may be.

Also, as Lenore E. Walker proposes in her book *The Battered Woman* (1979), many women are not constantly battered or are battered in a random pattern. In fact, Walker describes a distinct cycle of abuse characterized by three stages: the tension building stage, the acute battering stage, and the kindness and contrite loving stage. And because many abusers during this final stage are charming, affable, and loving partners, the women who love them stay with them just to experience this loving period.

Perhaps an even more significant reason why women do not leave abusive relationships is because they know help from outside may not be immediately forthcoming and that leaving an abusive relationship is when most women are killed. According to an article in *The Rocky Mountain News*, in 1991 alone ten women died in Denver, Colorado as a result of their attempts to leave their abusive husbands (Massaro and McCullan 1992).

Femicide

Homicide has been a familiar term in U.S. culture; it aptly illustrates the androcentric (male-defined) tendency to define murder of both men and women with generic terms. Femicide, on the other hand, refers strictly to the murder of women. According to *Violent Crime in the United States,* (March 1991), 28 percent of all female murder victims were killed by husbands or boyfriends. According to one study, the risk of being killed by a spouse is 1.3 in 100,000; in 1989, approximately 6.5 percent of all murders were committed by spouses killing spouses. While between 500 to 1,000 husbands are murdered by their wives each year, the number doubles for husbands killing wives: 1,000 to 1,300. Those deemed most at risk were black women at 7.1 per 100,000; white women were murdered at a lesser rate of 1.3 per 100,000. The age at which black women were murdered peaked between 15 and 24 and then dropped sharply; for white women, the murder rate peaked between 15 and 24 but only dropped gradually after that. Firearms were used most frequently (71.5 percent) in most spouse murders between 1976 and 1985 (Mercy and Saltzman 1989). These statistics seem frightening when most people believe that they are safest at home with those they love and whom they believe love them.

Jane Caputi and Diana E. H. Russell in "Femicide: Speaking the Unspeakable" report a conversation between Margaret Atwood, a Canadian novelist, and her male friend. When Ms. Atwood asked her friend what threatened men most about women, she was told the fear of being laughed at. When she asked a group of women what threatened them most about men, they replied they were afraid of being killed. That fear, the article asserts, is not unfounded. On December 6, 1989, a twenty-five year old man rushed the school of engineering at the University of Montreal, separated male students from female students, shot and killed fourteen young women, wounded nine women, and then killed himself. During this massacre he shouted "You're all fucking feminists." These women students, given their non-traditional career choice, would have been unlikely to see themselves as feminists. A suicide note found later blamed all of his failures on women (Caputi and Russell 1990).

If women are at the mercy of both those whom they love and those whom they do not even know, then the fear of being killed by men is *real*. As Caputi and Russell state, femicide is simply the "ultimate end of the continuum of terror that includes rape, torture, mutilation, sexual slavery," incest, and many other atrocities perpetrated upon women (Caputi and Russell 1990, 35).

Conclusion

While this chapter started with light and seemingly frivolous nursery rhymes and labels suggesting men's and boy's dominance over women and little girls, it ends with startling and horrifying statistics about incest, rape, domestic abuse, and femicide. Such rhymes and labels create a climate in which dominance over and possession of women is taught and accepted. Since violence is the ultimate enforcer of dominance, some men and women end up the subjects of police files.

However, knowledge can be powerful, especially when it provokes action. In their paper "A Social Change Approach to the Prevention of Sexual Violence toward Women," Caroline H. Sparks and Bat-Ami Bar On suggest that violence must be "deinstitutionalized." Their premise is, instead, to "institutionalize the principle of respect for persons" (1985, 1) a principle obviously incompatible with sexual violence. In an attempt to do this, they suggest the mobilizing of support to effect change in the ways institutions operate.

Their suggestions fall in two areas: legal action and social action. First, they suggest that feminists should take *legal action* by identifying current laws and policies supporting violence and then creating new laws and policies that value women as people. Second, they suggest that feminists take *social action* by identifying the current norms that support violence against women. (Sparks and Bar On 1985).

This chapter, the essays, and the personal narratives that follow try to do both. However, identification is not sufficient; rather women, and men, must create new norms which will reflect respect for women as individuals, not as subordinates or possessions of men. That goal can be reached through women's studies classes;

women's groups; families that seek to communicate about these issues; the media; churches; support groups; and other institutions: education, medicine, and the paid labor force; but only if all are committed to eradicating violence against women.

Then, children will not simply sing along to simple little rhymes like:

> Who's afraid of the Big Bad Wolf?
> the Big Bad Wolf,
> the Big Bad Wolf?

> or

> Georgie Porgie Pudding and Pie
> Kissed the girls and made them cry!

or respond to being called "Daddy's little girl." Instead, all of society will question what these rhymes and labels mean. Should a woman need to be afraid of a man? Should Georgie Porgie's kisses elicit pleasure or cries of embarrassment or pain? Is a girl child ever really the possession of daddy or should she be? When these questions are raised, the potential for change discussed, and new, more humane answers given, then the restructuring of our culture will have begun. Slowly, over time, the violence against women in terms of emotional and psychological abuse, institutionalized violence, incest, rape, domestic abuse, and femicide will cease and women will be somewhat safer than they are today.

References

Age, sex, and race of murder victims. 1989. *Crime in the United States 1989* 10 (August 5, 1990). In Murder victim by age. *Statistical record of women worldwide.* Edited by Linda Schmittroth. Detroit: Gale Research Inc., 1991.

Armstrong, Louise. 1982. The cradle of sexual politics: Incest. In *Women's sexual experience: Exploration of the dark continent.* Edited by M. Kirkpatrick. New York: Plenum Press.

Barron, Larry, and Murray A. Straus. 1987. Four theories of rape: A macro/sociological analysis. *Social Problems* 34(5):467–89.

Bidwell, Lee, and Pricilla White. 1986. The family context of marital rape. *Journal of Family Violence* 1(3):277–87.

Braiker, Harriet B. 1986. *The Type E woman.* New York: Dodd, Mead and Co.

Brownmiller, Susan. 1975. *Against our will: Men, women, and rape.* New York: Simon and Schuster

Butler, Susan. 1985. *The conspiracy of silence: The trauma of incest.* San Francisco: Volcano Press Inc.

Butler, Susan. 1982. Incest: Whose reality, whose theory? In *The criminal justice system and women.* Edited by Barbara Raffel Price and Natalie J. Sokoloff. New York: Clark Boardman Co.

Caputi, Jane, and Diana E. H. Russell. 1990. Femicide: Speaking the unspeakable. *Ms.* (September/October): 34–37.

Child maltreatment cases reported—Summary: 1976–1986. *Statistical abstract of the United States, 1990,* 176. In Child abuse cases reported: 1960–1986. *Statistical record of women worldwide.* Edited by Linda Schmittroth. Detroit: Gale Research Inc., 1991.

Collison, Michelle. 1991. "A sure-fire winner is to tell her you love her: Women fall for it all the time": Men talk frankly with counselor to assess harassment and acquaintance rape. *The Chronicle of Higher Education,* November 13, 1991.

Costa, Maryanne Sugerman. 1989. Women who care are women who need relief. *National Business Women* (Summer):20. In Women as caretakers: An overview. *Statistical record of women worldwide.* Edited by Linda Schmittroth. Detroit: Gale Research Inc., 1991.

Dinsmore, Christine. 1991. *From surviving to thriving: Incest, feminism, and recovery.* Albany: State University of New York Press.

Forcible rape by month: 1985-1989. *Crime in the United States, 1989,* 14–15. In *Statistical record of women worldwide.* Edited by Linda Schmittroth. Detroit: Gale Research Inc., 1991.

Gelles, Richard J., and Murray A. Strauss. 1988. *Intimate violence.* New York: Simon and Schuster.

Griffin, Susan. 1982. Rape: The all-American crime. *The criminal justice system and women: Women offenders/victims/workers.* Edited by Barbara Raffel Price and Natalie J. Sokoloff. New York: Clark Boardman Co.

Groth, Nicholas. 1979. *Men who rape: The psychology of the offender.* New York: Plenum Press.

Herman, Judith. 1981. *Father-daughter incest.* Cambridge, Mass.: Harvard University Press.

Herman, Judith. 1984. *Work in progress.* No. 83–05. Wellesley, Mass.: Wellesley College, Center for research on women.

Kanin, Eugene J., and Eugene C. Jackson. 1987. Personal sexual history and punitive judgment for rape. *Psychological Report* 61:439–42.

Klein, Dorie. 1982. Violence against women: Some considerations regarding its causes and elimination. *The criminal justice system and women: Women offenders/victims/workers.* Edited by Barbara Raffel Price and Natalie J. Sokoloff. New York: Clark Boardman Co.

Koss, Mary, and Barry Burkhart. 1989. A conceptual analysis of rape victimization: Long-term effects and implications for treatment. *Psychology of Women Quarterly* 13:27–40.

Koss, Mary, C. Gidycz, and N. Wisniewski. 1987. The scope of rape: Incidence and prevalence of sexual aggression and victimization in a national sample of higher education students. *Journal of Consulting and Clinical Psychology* 55:162–70.

Larrabee, Marva, and Shelley A. McGeorge. 1989. Date rape: Understanding the acquaintance assault phenomenon. *Counseling and Human Development* 22(2).

Lundberg-Love, Paula K. 1990. Adult survivors of incest. *Treatment of family violence: A sourcebook.* Edited by Robert T. Ammerman and Michel Hersen. New York: John Wiley and Sons.

Mackinnon, Catharine A. 1982. Sexual harassment: The experience. *The criminal justice system and women: Women offenders/victims/workers.* Edited by Barbara Raffel Price and Natalie J. Sokoloff. New York: Clark Boardman Co.

MacFarlane, Judith, R.N. 1989. Battering during pregnancy: Tip of an iceberg revealed. Women and Health, 15(3):69. In *Statistical record of women worldwide.* Edited by Linda Schmittroth. Detroit: Gale Research Inc., 1991.

Marital status and living arrangements: March 1989. *Current Population Reports.* Series P20, No. 445. Living arrangements of the elderly. In *Statistical record of women worldwide.* Edited by Linda Schmittroth. Detroit: Gale Research, Inc., 1991.

Martin, Del. 1981. *Battered Women.* San Francisco: Volcano Press.

Massaro, Gary, and Kevin McCullan. 1992. Domestic violence echoes. *Rocky Mountain News,* January 25, 1992.

Masson, Jeffrey Moussaieff. 1984. *The assault on truth: Freud's suppression of the seduction theory.* New York: Farrar, Straus and Giroux.

Mercy, James, and Linda E. Saltzman. 1989. *American Journal of Public Health.* In Spouse murder. In *Statistical record of women worldwide.* Edited by Linda Schmittroth. Detroit: Gale Research, Inc., 1991.

Miller, Dale T., and Carol A. Porter. 1983. Self-blame in victims of violence. *Journal of Social Issues* 39(2):139–52.

Morgenson, Gretchen. 1989. Watch that leer, stifle that joke. Corporations and activists crusade against sexual harassment, yet we're told the problem's getting worse. Is it really? *Forbes,* May 15, 1989. In Sexual Harassment in the workplace: Selected states. In *Statistical record of women worldwide.* Edited by Linda Schmittroth. Detroit: Gale Research Inc., 1991.

Murder circumstances by relationship. *Crime in the United States, 1989, 12.* (August 5, 1990). In *Statistical record of women worldwide.* Edited by Linda Schmittroth. Detroit: Gale Research, Inc., 1991.

Oldenburg, Don. 1991. Novelist attempts to glorify the middle-aged woman. *Denver Post,* October 28.

Palmer, Craig. 1988. Twelve reasons why rape is not sexually motivated: A skeptical examination. *The Journal of Sex Research:* 25(4):512–30.

Pollitt, Katha. 1990. Georgie Porgie is a bully. *Time.* Special Issue: Women: The Road Ahead, 24.

Russell, Diana. 1986. *The secret trauma: Incest in the lives of girls and women.* New York: Basic Books.

Salholz, Eloise, and Karen Sprigen. 1990. A frightening aftermath: Concern about AIDS adds to the trauma of rape. *Newsweek,* July 23.

Sparks, Caroline H., and Bat-Ami Bar On. 1985. A social change approach to prevention of sexual violence toward women. Wellesley, Mass.: Stone Center for Development Services and Studies.

U.S. Senate, Committee on the Judiciary. 1990. 101st Cong. 2nd sess. Legislation to reduce the growing problem of violent crime against women. June 20, 1990, Part 1, Serial No. J-101–80. 12. In ten facts about violence against women. In *Statistical record of women worldwide.* Edited by Linda Schmittroth. Detroit: Gale Research Inc., 1991.

Violent Crime in the United States. 1991. As cited in female victims of violent crime. In *Statistical record of women worldwide.* Edited by Linda Schmittroth. Detroit: Gale Research, Inc., 1991.

Walker, Lenore. 1979. *The battered woman.* New York: Harper and Row.

Released at Last

Linda Bennington Nolan

I was raised on a modest, working farm by my widowed mother. When I was nine, my father died, so I grew up unfamiliar with masculine ways. I fell in love the first time at thirteen with a sweet, dimpled boy who showed me only joy and kindness, but broke up with him soon after. A self-assured young woman, Pep Club president, and a member of the National Honor Society, I graduated in the top ten of my class in 1972, a time of great changes: Vietnam, Haight-Ashbury, flower power, and the free-love generation. Although I enrolled in college, I attended classes sporadically. My best friend, Becky, and I were anti-establishment, interested primarily in protesting anything or anyone who represented authority and order.

I met HIM on a warm May night in a nearby town where college kids went to drink 3.2 beer and socialize. Becky and I hadn't gone there to drink, but to check out the parade of hippies and rednecks meandering from one to another of three bars on the main drag. I noticed one man in particular because of his long, wavy, bronze hair and trim, yet brawny physique. His dimples fascinated me, just as had those of my first love. I was too immature to recognize his charm as a line.

Later he followed me home. We sat on the hood of his car talking about life in general and our own childhoods. I felt as if I'd met a kindred spirit. Bruce talked about growing up in a large family without any advantages. I decided then that I would be the one to save him and win his love forever. As the sun rose, he left me at my door with a kiss on the forehead. I was instantly in love with my dimpled prince.

Soon Bruce, with no warning or planning, simply at his convenience, began coming to my apartment. Of course, I was more than willing to be with him whenever he chose. College classes became even less important than my newfound love. Within several weeks, we were sleeping together intermittently. Bruce was my first lover, and I believed he would be my soul mate forever. What he didn't bother to tell me was that he was married and had two toddlers. His wife did. It didn't matter to me, however, because HE LOVED ME and nothing in the world mattered except us and our love. He often said he should return to his marriage "for the kids' sake," yet I was surprised when he did.

Over the months, like a ping-pong ball, he'd be first with his wife and then with me. I lived in emotional turmoil, alternately waiting by the phone and spending stolen hours with him. Finally, they divorced; Bruce was free. Consequently, I thought our own relationship would improve. Three months into our affair, he began to verbally abuse me, slap me, and accuse me of infidelities. He convinced me that his mistreatment of me was my fault. He was angry with me for visiting with an old boyfriend from out of town during the time he was alternating between his two households.

By the time the abuse started, I had alienated my family and dropped out of college. My only friend was Becky. In a drunken rage, Bruce wrecked my car and was arrested. I

Nolan, Linda Bennington. 1992. "Released at Last." Printed by permission of the author.

quickly forgave him and searched for a job to support us. The day his divorce was final, we left the area—and my nearby family. We moved to his older sister's home to start anew. I turned twenty-one sleeping on a stranger's living room floor in an unfamiliar town next to my inebriated lover, yet I was ecstatic.

I worked full-time while Bruce drank. I had no friends and suffered repeated abuse. I finally left him to return to my hometown, but he came after me, promising to quit drinking. I forgave him because I believed that if he only didn't drink, we would be happy. I felt it was my *duty* to help him.

In 1975, two years after we had met, Bruce decided we should marry. I overlooked the mental and physical battering, blaming it on his drinking. Yet my life did not improve after our marriage. I gave up all chances for fun, including going out with friends. Even my going to the grocery store set off his anger, especially when I took longer than he expected.

When sober, Bruce was usually loving and sweet. He said he had never wanted to hurt me, but that I had made him do it. He had had several affairs throughout the years resulting in at least three illegitimate children. I was unendingly faithful, but he called me "the slut" and complained I did not understand him. I worked consistently to pay our bills, while he hardly worked at all. When we ran low on money, he blamed me.

Within a year, I became pregnant. He had said that "if only we had a child to prove our love for one another," he would stop drinking and become responsible. I believed him. One sultry summer night at 3:00 a.m., Becky walked me two blocks to the hospital. My labor pains had become unbearable, but I couldn't awaken my passed-out spouse. After the birth of my cherished daughter, Liebe, I had more reason to hold the marriage together. But I was more afraid of him because the drinking and assaults got worse. The colicky baby, tiny apartment, and lack of money provoked him; he became more abusive and I more terrified.

Bruce wasn't always cruel. His behavior was cyclical. After seeing me with black eyes and bruised face, he would stop drinking briefly and try to maintain a job and sobriety. Those fleeting interludes of apparent normalcy were idyllic. He was wonderful with Liebe, playing with her and caring for her after I returned to work. He was never abusive directly to her. I was the sole object of his obsessive love and incurable wrath.

Yet I was as addicted as Bruce to the highs of intense passion and love after the violence. His tenderness and solicitude were worth the pain, until the day before Thanksgiving 1981. I had made an innocent comment about his cousin's boyfriend. Through his alcohol-induced haze, he misinterpreted it and beat me up in front of our five-year-old daughter. This time, I had *somewhere* to go. The local YWCA had recently opened a shelter for battered women, and Liebe and I were two of its first occupants. Although I had failed to protect myself, I wanted to protect my daughter. I was afraid that she would eventually become a target for his irrational anger.

At the shelter, I shared with other abused women the stories of my clothing being ripped and burned, wedding and family pictures shredded, cars wrecked, guns shot off in my home, a waterbed stabbed, household possessions destroyed, and loved ones threatened. I realized I was not alone, I was not a failure, and Bruce's violence was not my fault. Did I leave then? No. How could I, when I still loved him and he needed me so! Since he'd begged for my forgiveness so convincingly and promised that things would be different, I returned to dreams of the fairy tale marriage I'd been reared to expect. It lasted five weeks.

On January 2, 1982, I stayed home from work with the flu. That night, after lying down with Liebe, I'd fallen asleep waiting for my husband to arrive home sober, as he had earlier promised. Later, a powerful arm jolted me out of bed, threw me against the wall, punched me repeatedly, and kicked at my sides. I lay stunned on the floor in a pool of my own blood. Barely conscious, I begged him, "Please stop! I love you. Why are you doing this?" But as I looked into his glazed eyes, I saw nothing of the man I loved, only emptiness and hatred. Suddenly Bruce picked me up and threw me out the front door, down three steps, onto the ice and snow-covered ground. Barefoot, covered in blood and bruises, dressed only in a T-shirt and suffering from shock, I quickly ran to my neighbors' home, crying and pounding on their door for help. Fortunately, they let me in, called the police, and then called my friend Becky. My neighbor, along with the police, rescued my daughter as my husband lay passed out on the couch. The police did not arrest him even though a hardening puddle of blood two feet wide stained the living room carpet. Becky took me to the emergency room for treatment of a fractured nose, three cracked ribs, and a wide assortment of cuts and abrasions.

After nearly eight years of obsession, I finally fled this destructive relationship and filed for a divorce, which became final in March 1982. My ex-husband, a recovering alcoholic after two inpatient confinements, continued to harass me and to profess his undying love for me. I will always feel love for him; after all, he is the father of my only child. However, I know now that Bruce learned to be abusive and manipulative from his own alcoholic father. I, yearning for a father who had died when I was nine, readily gave him the love he sought and accepted the blame for his behavior.

It took years of soul-searching, counseling myself through books, and accepting the support of an excellent network of friends as well as my truly phenomenal family, to attain the happiness I feel today.

Once a prisoner, I am free at last. I have a decent job; I am buying a home, and I am bringing up my teenaged daughter in a safe and healthy environment.

Domestic Violence

Janet Mickish

Domestic Violence Defined

Although commonly thought of as hitting, shoving, kicking, stabbing, and other serious physical attacks, domestic violence may also be sexual or psychological. According to Colorado law, domestic violence is defined as:

> the infliction or threat of infliction of any bodily injury or harmful physical contact or the destruction of property or threat thereof as a method of coercion, control, revenge, or punishment upon a person with whom the actor is involved in an intimate relationship . . . [i.e.,] between spouses, former spouses, past or present unmarried couples or persons who are both the parents of a child regardless of whether the persons have been married or have lived together at any time. (CRS, Sec.1, 18–6-800.3)

Inflicting physical injury is a crime and the resulting harm may be lethal, but threats are emotionally abusive. Left unchecked, the threatening abuser's behavior frequently escalates into physical violence (Walker 1980). Threats made by the perpetrator before, during, and after infliction of violence reinforce the battered woman's belief that he will act on his threats again. She is usually right.

Like threats and physical violence to a person, destruction of property or violence toward pets reinforces the victim's fear of the perpetrator, for these acts symbolize the perpetrator's power to control and destroy. His behavior is domestic terrorism and conveys messages such as: "I am destroying the picture of your parents, or kicking your dog, or smashing a hole in the wall, or poking the eyes out of the picture of the baby. If I don't like what you do, say, look like, cook, etc., I'll be more violent to you or to them." Or, they constitute sexual terrorism: "I'm cutting the crotch out of all your underpants. If I don't like how I feel about you sexually, I'll use these scissors on you." Common targets of violence include the victim's clothes, pictures of her family, wedding gifts, school books, and anything she values. To underscore his propensity for violence, the perpetrator may even damage or destroy things that also have sentimental value to him.

The tactics batterers use to control their partners permeate the whole of the couple's life. Psychological and emotional abuse usually occur simultaneously and the elements are interrelated in a culture that facilitates males' gaining and maintaining power over "their" families. One key factor is economic domination. Frequently, men who abuse attempt to secure the survivor's economic dependence upon them by controlling the household finances or by keeping the survivor from working in the paid labor force. Even women who have their own source of money are often accountable to the batterer for every penny of their earnings. Second, the children become pawns. Batterers may belittle or degrade the children as a means of harassing the survivor. In many cases they

---

Mickish, Janet. 1992. "Behind Closed Doors: Domestic Violence." Printed by permission of the author.

threaten to take the children away from the woman, should she try to leave. Many men are able to do just that (Weitzman 1985; Chesler 1987). Third, intimidation is often used. Abusers may frighten their victim by malevolent looks, actions, gestures or loud voices; by smashing things, or by destroying property. They often act like bullies, asserting what they believe is their entitlement to the woman's services. Verbal degradation, cursing, and name calling are also part of the terrorism and humiliation.

Fourth, in an attempt to gain compliance through fear, abusers may threaten to kidnap or harm the children, kill the victim or commit suicide. They also threaten to kill or harm other members of the family, relatives, friends, co-workers, or pets. Fifth, batterers often exhibit extreme controlling behavior. Many men who abuse seek to control their partners' activities, companions, telephone conversations, and whereabouts. They are suspicious and intrusive, feeling compelled always to know what the woman is thinking, feeling, or doing and are possessive and jealous of her attention to and relationships with others. Sixth, batterers seek to isolate their victims. Abusers consider themselves the center of their partners' universe. As the abuse and subsequent insecurity of both partners grow, they often limit their contact with others, he fearing exposure of his violence and the flawed belief system that spawned it, she fearing further violence if she does not totally focus on him.

Batterers and Victims

There is no typical batterer or victim. We do not know as much about domestic violence in same-sex relationships as we do about its occurrence in heterosexual relationships. Increasing evidence shows that it does exist between same-sex couples and can be as lethal as in heterosexual relationships (Lobel 1986; Boston Lesbian Psychologies Collective 1987; Renzetti 1988; Island and Letellier 1991). We do know that 98 percent of all currently documented domestic assaults are committed by men against women (Federal Bureau of Investigation 1989).

While many men who batter love their partners and do not want to use violence, others do not love their partners, feel comfortable using violence, and do not care whether their partners stay or leave. Likewise, many battered women love the man who is beating them, do not want to see him hurt, and just want him to stop being violent; others hate their batterers and would like them to go away or die. Although we cannot fully describe the batterer/perpetrator or the victim/survivor, the applicable terms used interchangeably enhance our understanding of the complex adaptations of those involved in domestic violence. Batterers do share certain general characteristics. So do survivors.

Not only do perpetrators of domestic violence come from every walk of life, they also vary widely in mental health, from the normal man who uses his male privilege and power to dominate his family, to the psychopathic man who stalks, tortures, and kills his family and others. The *reasons* men batter are a complex mix of psychological and cultural factors.

Frequently perpetrators feel frightened, inadequate, isolated, victimized, empty, abandoned, and worthless. Because males are socialized to believe they should be invulnerable, unemotional, and active in controlling the world and people around them, they act out violently. This violence creates crises that remain more immediate, tangible, real, and compelling than the surrounding "ordinary" stimulation that they perceive as constantly threatening to distract the victim from focusing on them.

Men who batter use power to gain control over those to whom they have assigned responsibility for their lives and feelings. They seek to establish control by using physical, sexual, and psychological violence; lavishing affection and gifts; isolating their partners from social supports; and creating crisis and chaos (Ewing, Lindsey, and Pomerantz 1984).

Most women who are victims of battering leave violent relationships. Fewer and fewer stay. Typically, a battered woman will leave a violent relationship three to five times before she feels safe enough and has established enough resources to make the break permanent (Walker 1980). Because a batterer is most violent when he perceives that his partner is leaving him, battered women must be very cautious in their preparations to leave and in the departure itself.

Many factors combine to keep a victim in a battering relationship: first, fear of injury, death, or violence against herself or others; of losing her children; of being alone; second, lack of perceived alternatives, isolation, and economic and emotional dependence; third, love and emotional investment (Shaw 1991). Additional factors are social expectations including shame at failure in marriage, potential loss of social status and networks, duty (religious training and social pressure to keep the family together), and habituation to abuse or domestic violence—change can be frightening.

These factors make the cost of leaving a battering relationship for most women almost as high as staying. They are created by women's socialization, their experience, and the batterers' violence, and they are perpetrated by a society that excuses battering behavior, blames women who leave their marriages, and fails to protect or support victims of violence.

Recent Trends in Controlling Domestic Violence

Sparked by a fledgling domestic violence movement in England and the second women's movement in the United States, projects to help battered women sprang up in hundreds of rural and urban areas across the country between 1974 and 1980. Declaring "We will not be beaten," women organized in large and small groups to address the problems arising from domestic violence. By 1982 there were more than 300 shelters, 48 state coalitions of service providers, a national domestic violence organization, and a multitude of social and legal reforms.

A fundamental tenet of most domestic violence programs is that the roots of domestic violence lie in our society's perpetuation of sexism, racism, classism, ageism, homophobia, fear of disabilities, and militarism—in short, in oppressive, elitist, and violence-oriented belief systems, attitudes, and behavior.

Within the last ten years, victim services have sprung up in most major cities and many rural locations. Four major factors are behind their creation: first, increased consideration for all victims' rights and needs, in general; second, increased knowledge that over 50 percent of all police calls involve domestic violence; third, an increased number of lawsuits requiring the criminal justice system to take domestic violence seriously; and fourth, an increased number of jurisdictions (either through legislation or policies and procedures) requiring probable cause arrests, prohibiting prosecutors from dropping charges, and making judges accountable to victims through consideration of their rights and more appropriate sentencing of perpetrators.

Perpetrator treatment programs, though founded later, are a result of some societal recognition, finally, that domestic violence is, first, not the victim's fault, and second, that perpetrators must be held responsible for their behavior just as other criminals are.

Because domestic violence is still seen differently than many other crimes, however, the emphasis is not on incarceration. Thus many perpetrator treatment services recognize that coordination and cooperation with battered women's services is essential because "fixing" the perpetrator is not the goal of perpetrator treatment programs. Stopping domestic violence is the goal. This requires more than one-on-one counseling with batterers. It requires a commitment on the part of the batterer to working with the battered women's movement and to changing himself as well as to facilitating change in the attitudes of others and working for institutional change that recognizes the autonomy of women. They are not men's property.

Emerging in perpetrator treatment programs is a recognition that battered women and their children are the primary clients and that perpetrators are the secondary clients. Once acknowledging the primacy of the safety and welfare of the victim or survivor and her children, the critical task for treatment programs is to end the perpetrator's violence. After the violence is under control, the counselor can help the batterer establish a real sense of empowerment and self-esteem. Most perpetrators need long-term treatment, for without it they may learn techniques like anger management to control their behavior but never address underlying causes of their anger or understand the socialization that encourages them to express anger through violence. Without appropriate long-term treatment, many perpetrators will not be able to maintain this internal control and will again lash out at the perceived source of their pain.

Within the last ten years, the battered women's movement has also been able to convince the criminal justice system in many jurisdictions to treat domestic violence as a crime worthy of intervention. Thus, many more domestic violence cases have been added to already overloaded criminal court dockets. This means that perpetrators often come into the system at an earlier stage in the evolution of their violence with the result that sentencing to treatment programs may work to stop their violence.

New information about domestic violence and its impact and the necessity for intervention has increased our awareness that community-wide coordination is essential if domestic violence is to be stopped. Toward this end, many jurisdictions have implemented specialized policies and procedures and enacted laws along with developing special educational programs on domestic violence.

Criminal justice intervention can significantly influence domestic violence offenders and survivors. In the now-famous Minneapolis police experiment, Sherman and Berk (1984) found that where an arrest was made, the batterer was reported to have repeated his physical violence within the next six months in only 10 percent of the cases; in contrast, he was physically violent in 19 percent of the cases in which the police gave a verbal warning and 24 percent of the cases in which the police merely told the suspect to leave the premises.

Similar findings were reported in Ontario (Jaffe et al. 1986). The positive effect of criminal justice intervention increases as each segment of the system (police, prosecutor, courts, corrections) treats domestic violence cases as the serious crimes they are (Mickish and Calhoun-Stuber 1990; Steinman 1991). These studies in conjunction with lawsuits against the police and prosecutors and the work of the battered women's movement have had a dramatic impact on increasing sanctions and controls on batterers. In 1984 only 10 percent of all police departments in cities over 100,000 had probable cause arrest policies for domestic violence offenders. Two years later that number had soared to 46 percent (Cohen and Sherman 1987).

Yet, criminal justice intervention can be effective only with the active participation of the total community. Toward this end, many communities are developing task forces to address domestic violence. For example, since 1988, the Colorado Trust, a charitable foundation, has provided seed money enabling many Colorado communities to establish community-based task forces similar to those recommended by many social policy analysts.

Awareness of the causes and effects of violence against women is growing. Resistance by millions of women, in concert with the battered women's movement, has forced a transformation in the public climate, set a new agenda focused on nonviolence, and changed the minds of many women and men about what should go on behind closed doors.

References

Boston Lesbian Psychologies Collective. 1987. Urbana/Chicago: University of Chicago.

Chesler, Phyllis. 1987. *Mothers on trial*. Seattle: Seal Press.

Cohen, E. G., and L. W. Sherman. 1987. Police policy on domestic violence. Paper presented at annual meeting of the Academy of Criminal Justice Sciences, St. Louis, Missouri.

Colorado Revised Statutes. Sec. 1, 18–6-800.3.

Ewing, Wayne, M. Lindsey, and J. Pomerantz. 1984. *Battering: An AMEND manual for helpers*. Denver: Abusive Men Exploring New Directions.

Federal Bureau of Investigation. 1989. *Uniform crime reporting handbook*. Washington, D.C.: U.S. Government Printing Office.

Island, D., and P. Letellier. 1991. *Men who beat the men who love them: Battered gay men and domestic violence*. Binghamton, N.Y.: Haworth Press.

Jaffe, P., D. Wolf, A. Telford, and G. Austin. 1986. The impact of police charges in incidents of wife abuse. *Journal of Family Violence* 1(1):37–49.

Lobel, Kerry, ed. 1986. *Naming the violence: Speaking out about lesbian battering*. Seattle: Seal Press.

Mickish, Janet, and Susan Calhoun-Stuber. 1990. Effects of criminal justice intervention in domestic violence cases: The next step. Paper presented at the annual meeting of the Academy of Criminal Justice Sciences, St. Louis, Missouri.

Renzetti, C. 1988. Violence in lesbian relationships. *Journal of Interpersonal Violence* 3(4):381–99.

Shaw, Barbara. 1991. Executive director, Project Safeguard, Denver, Colorado. Interview.

Sherman, L. W., and R. Berk. 1984. The Minneapolis Domestic Violence Experiment. *Police Foundation Reports*. New York: Police Foundation.

Steinman, M. 1991. *Woman battering: Policy response*. Cincinnati: Anderson Publishing.

Walker, Lenore. 1980. Battered Woman. In A. Brodsky and R. Hare-Mustin, *Women and psychotherapy*. New York: Guilford Press

Weitzman, Lenore. 1985. *The divorce revolution: The unexpected social and economic consequences for women and children in America*. New York: Free Press.

Sex Without Consent: The Hidden Story of Date Rape

Sandra Herzog

It was a quiet night. After being out, my friends and I decided to go back to the fraternity that a couple of guys in the group belonged to. We just went back to play pool, drink a few beers and listen to music. When one of the pool games was over, I went to get another beer.

In the kitchen stood a guy from the fraternity whom I had seen around campus for about a year and a half. I knew his first name, and my friends knew him—there was no reason not to talk to him when he started up a conversation. It was obvious he had been drinking, and he claimed he had been getting "stoned."

During the conversation, he mentioned he wanted a back rub. I made it clear that if I gave him a back rub, it was all he would get.

As we walked through the fraternity, he stopped in the hallway and opened the door to a storage room. He asked me to follow him in there. I didn't know why he wanted to go in there, but I had no reason to distrust him. As the door shut behind me, however, he turned around and said, "If anybody did this to my sister, I'd kill him."

With that, JoAnne was raped. Although she struggled, he grew extremely forceful. To protect herself and to get it over with, she did what he wanted. Immediately afterward, he climbed out a window, leaving JoAnne bruised and in need of stitches. But even worse, she was left with emotional scars and the feeling that she was to blame.

Whether preceded by the words date, hidden or acquaintance, it's still rape. And despite the fact that acquaintance rape has been a taboo topic for so long, our culture has started to acknowledge it as a serious, widespread epidemic that must be learned about and stopped.

Acquaintance rape, or the instance of a victim being forced to have sex with and by someone the victim knows, is an illicit act of dominance and violence rather than sex.

According to Dr. Helena Yioti, program director of the Northwest Action Against Rape crisis center in Rolling Meadows, Ill., women between the ages of 15 and 25 are most likely to be the victims of acquaintance rape. However, statistics show that such cases occur among women of all ages, irrespective of their marital status and socio-economic background.

Yioti's statistics also conclude that by the age of 18, one out of four women and one out of six men have been raped. In 70 percent of all sexual assault cases, the victim knew the attacker.

Herzog, Sandra. 1990. "Sex without consent: The hidden story of date rape." *Family Safety & Health* Spring: 22–23. Reprinted by permission of the publisher.

Why does it happen?

Pauline Bart, Ph.D., co-author of the book *Stopping Rape: Successful Survival Strategies* (Pergamon Press, 1985) and professor of sociology in psychiatry at the University of Illinois in Chicago, cites a number of studies done in 1980 in the United States and Canada.

Males were asked to respond to the question, How likely would you be to commit the following acts if you were assured that there would be no negative consequences to yourself (i.e., you would not be caught or punished)? The list of acts included rape, petting, intercourse, anal sex, robbery and murder, to name a few. The results varied from study to study but, on average, 40 percent of the respondents didn't rule out the possibility of forcing a woman to have sex if there were no negative consequences.

"Many men do not consider forcible sex as rape," says Bart. Her findings, which coincide with those of others, indicate that society breeds this belief through traditional values, stereotypes and the media.

"I was never against porn until I started doing this research," states Bart, who found that media, R-rated movies and pornography desensitize men to the harm of rape. "In television and movies, how many times have we seen a man force himself on a woman, only to have her struggle and then give in? The false message here is that the victim will ultimately enjoy it."

"Our society uses sex to sell products and ideas," states Polly Poskin, director of the Illinois Coalition Against Sexual Assault in Springfield. Both women believe traditional advice and stereotypes leave women vulnerable and don't work in everyday society.

After interviewing 94 women, of whom 43 had been raped and 51 had avoided an attack, Bart found that women who had avoided the attack had high self-esteem, knew self-defense or fought if provoked, knew what to do in everyday emergency situations, were more responsible and independent and had real-life role models.

Who is the rapist?

The acquaintance rapist is not hiding behind a bush or in a dark alley. This type of rapist is someone the victim trusted, be it an acquaintance, a coworker, a neighbor, a date or a family member. The humiliation, which some psychologists believe to be part of the rapist's motivation, is much greater in acquaintance rape because the victim trusted this man and usually blames herself. The acquaintance rapist knows this. He plays upon the idea that she is partially to blame; he preys upon the victim's insecurities.

According to Poskin's statistics, 50 percent of rape victims do just as the rapist had hoped: They do not report the rape.

The acquaintance rapist can come from any economic background and be attractive, intelligent, nice and respectable. After the attack, the victim is left confused and ashamed and cannot believe that this "nice guy" actually raped her.

According to Poskin, Yioti and Bart, the acquaintance rapist is a male who believes, "If I can get away with this, I'll do it." All three women agree that acquaintance rapists tend to have macho personalities and believe men are superior to women. They view women as sex objects and they have a deep hostility toward, or a lack of respect for, women. They also think women owe them sex for a date or for spending money on them.

Can you avoid it?

No matter how flirtatious or provocatively dressed, no woman is asking to be raped. To misread verbal or nonverbal (body language) communication, to blame the incident on alcohol or drugs, or to assume that a woman wanted it or deserves it is ignorant. The words *sex* and *rape* are not interchangeable.

"Even people trained in rape prevention and counseling have been raped," says Yioti, who offers the following tips:

- Know that it can happen to you.
- Communicate in a clear and confident manner.
- If you feel uncomfortable with someone, avoid being alone with that person.
- Never give personal information to an acquaintance, such as your address or telephone number.
- Avoid drugs or too much alcohol.
- Avoid a person who consumes too much alcohol or uses drugs.

Parents are encouraged to talk with their children—both boys and girls—in an open manner about sex, personal rights and respect for others. Poskin recommends that parents not deny that their children are sexual beings. She also states that it is not a matter of rules but of rights.

"Parents should teach respect toward others and let their children know what is acceptable and what is not," says Poskin. "Yes means yes and no means no."

Bart adds to teach girls self-defense at an early age and encourage them to participate in sports. It's better not to teach girls to be quiet and to act like ladies. "It's important to teach your kids to speak up because the prevention of being hurt is much more important than being polite."

What should you do?

Bart says that if you look like an easy target, you probably will be.

"Women who avoided being raped used anything from yelling to physically fleeing to fighting," says Bart. "The combination of yelling and physical force worked the best." In some cases, women avoided rape because the attacker was frightened away by such things as an alarm suddenly going off or a dog barking.

Studies have concluded that women who were raped focused on not getting mutilated or murdered, says Bart. Women who avoided rape focused on the point that no man had the right to rape them. "Telling the rapist you're a virgin or you have your period does nothing because already it is obvious he doesn't care about you as a person, nor your feelings or your body," concludes Bart.

If you are a victim of acquaintance rape, many crisis hot lines recommend the following:

- Go to a loved one for emotional support and have that person take you to the hospital immediately. If a loved one is not available, call a crisis hot line. Get to a hospital so you can be treated and have important medical information recorded for you. Yioti adds that a woman should never douche, bathe, shower or change her clothes before going.
- Report the rape. Remember, you may prevent it from happening to someone else.

- Seek help from a professional who is trained and knowledgeable in rape counseling.

It is at this time that a victim of acquaintance rape needs someone to turn to. The victim needs medical attention, shelter, an open mind, an attentive ear and a nonjudgmental attitude, no matter what. It is important that you do not let the victim blame herself.

What are the effects?

Bart explains that the victim must recover from physical and psychological effects, both short- and long-term. Short-term effects include nausea, nightmares, intense fear, and feelings of powerlessness, guilt and, sometimes, physical pain. Long-term effects include sleeping problems, depression, lack of trust in oneself and others, and anger.

"Some victims' sexual ability may be inhibited," adds Bart. "Trying to become intimate with someone may take a while."

The trauma of acquaintance rape is real and can last from a few months to a few years. People generally expect the victim to be back to normal in a couple of weeks or months. This is a false belief, and if loved ones find it hard to cope, they should seek counseling as well. Yioti states, "Although there are some serious effects of acquaintance rape, with the help of counseling, the victim can really work through all of her feelings and emerge stronger, plus have a better sense of herself and others."

Rape

Susan Brownmiller

Man's structural capacity to rape and woman's corresponding structural vulnerability are as basic to the physiology of both our sexes as the primal act of sex itself. Had it not been for this accident of biology, an accommodation requiring the locking together of two separate parts, penis and vagina, there would be neither copulation nor rape as we know it. Anatomically one might want to improve on the design of nature, but such speculation appears to my mind as unrealistic. The human sex act accomplishes its historic purpose of generation of the species and it also affords some intimacy and pleasure. I have no basic quarrel with the procedure. But, nevertheless, we cannot work around the fact that in terms of human anatomy the possibility of forcible intercourse incontrovertibly exists. This single factor may have been sufficient to have caused the creation of a male ideology of rape. When men discovered that they could rape, they proceeded to do it. Later, much later, under certain circumstances they even came to consider rape a crime.

In the violent landscape inhabited by primitive woman and man, some woman somewhere had a prescient vision of her right to her own physical integrity, and in my mind's eye I can picture her fighting like hell to preserve it. After a thunderbolt of recognition that this particular incarnation of hairy, two-legged hominid was not the Homo sapiens with whom she would like to freely join parts, it might have been she, and not some man, who picked up the first stone and hurled it. How surprised he must have been, and what an unexpected battle must have taken place. Fleet of foot and spirited, she would have kicked, bitten, pushed and run, *but she could not retaliate in kind.*

The dim perception that had entered prehistoric woman's consciousness must have had an equal but opposite reaction in the mind of her male assailant. For if the first rape was an unexpected battle founded on the first woman's refusal, the second rape was indubitably planned. Indeed, one of the earliest forms of male bonding must have been the gang rape of one woman by a band of marauding men. This accomplished, rape became not only a male prerogative, but man's basic weapon of force against woman, the principal agent of his will and her fear. His forcible entry into her body, despite her physical protestations and struggle, became the vehicle of his victorious conquest over her being, the ultimate test of his superior strength, the triumph of his manhood.

Man's discovery that his genitalia could serve as a weapon to generate fear must rank as one of the most important discoveries of prehistoric times, along with the use of fire and the first crude stone axe. From prehistoric times to the present, I believe, rape has played a critical function. It is nothing more or less than a conscious process of intimidation by which *all men* keep *all women* in a state of fear.

Brownmiller, Susan. 1975. "Rape." In *Against Our Will.* New York: Simon & Schuster. Reprinted by permission of the publisher.

In the Beginning Was the Law

From the humblest beginnings of the social order based on a primitive system of re-taliatory force—the *lex talionis:* an eye for an eye—woman was unequal before the law. By anatomical fiat—the inescapable construction of their genital organs—the human male was a natural predator and the human female served as his natural prey. Not only might the female be subjected at will to a thoroughly detestable physical conquest from which there could be no retaliation in kind—a rape for a rape—but the consequences of such a brutal struggle might be death or injury, not to mention impregnation and the birth of a dependent child.

One possibility, and one possibility alone, was available to woman. Those of her own sex whom she might call to her aid were more often than not smaller and weaker than her male attackers. More critical, they lacked the basic physical wherewithal for punitive vengeance; at best they could maintain only a limited defensive action. But among those creatures who were her predators, some might serve as her chosen protectors. Perhaps it was thus that the risky bargain was struck. Female fear of an open season of rape, and not a natural inclination toward monogamy, motherhood or love, was probably the single causative factor in the original subjugation of woman by man, the most important key to her historic dependence, her domestication by protective mating.

Once the male took title to a specific female body, and surely for him this was a great sexual convenience as well as a testament to his warring stature, he had to assume the burden of fighting off all other potential attackers, or scare them off by the retaliatory threat of raping *their* women. But the price of woman's protection *by some men* against an abuse *by others* was steep. Disappointed and disillusioned by the inherent female incapacity to protect, she became estranged in a very real sense from other females, a problem that haunts the social organization of women to this very day. And those who did assume the historic burden of her protection—later formalized as husband, father, brother, clan—extracted more than a pound of flesh. They reduced her status to that of chattel. The historic price of woman's protection by man against man was the imposition of chastity and monogamy. A crime committed against her body became a crime against the male estate.

The earliest form of permanent, protective conjugal relationship, the accommodation called mating that we now know as marriage, appears to have been institutionalized by the male's forcible abduction and rape of the female. No quaint formality, bride capture, as it came to be known, was a very real struggle: a male took title to a female, staked a claim to her body, as it were, by an act of violence. Forcible seizure was a perfectly acceptable way—to men—of acquiring women, and it existed in England as late as the fifteenth century. Eleanor of Aquitaine, according to a biographer, lived her early life in terror of being "rapt" by a vassal who might through appropriation of her body gain title to her considerable property. Bride capture exists to this day in the rain forests of the Philippines, where the Tasadays were recently discovered to be plying their Stone Age civilization. Remnants of the philosophy of forcible abduction and marriage still influence the social mores of rural Sicily and parts of Africa. A proverb of the exogamous Bantu-speaking Gusiis of southwest Kenya goes "Those whom we marry are those whom we fight."

It seems eminently sensible to hypothesize that man's violent capture and rape of the female led first to the establishment of a rudimentary mate-protectorate and then sometime later to the full-blown male solidification of power, the patriarchy. As the first permanent acquisition of man, his first piece of real property, woman was, in fact, the original building block, the cornerstone, of the "house of the father." Man's forcible extension of his boundaries to his mate and later to their offspring was the beginning of his concept of ownership. Concepts of hierarchy, slavery and private property flowed from, and could only be predicated upon, the initial subjugation of woman.

The Drama of the Long Distance Runners

Jacqueline St. Joan

(Dedicated to workers in the battered women's movement)

I watch you in the court
house coffee shop. Sitting next
to the angry young woman. The one with
a newborn tied to her chest. Fear
and despair criss-cross her back. You

listen to her insults. She storms away. You
chase after her touch her
cold shoulder, her tears on the brink. You
hand her a card your
home number on it. Her
link to hope on
some other day
some other day. Some

other day she calls you
the lawyer and sets a date and later you
rant about her
she didn't show up she
didn't even call. At night you

sip bourbon and seven you
empty your pockets you
search for change you
search for change you
have to know:

is she safe? is she still
alive? On your way home you

check the back seat, look over your
shoulder from your car to your
door. At midnight you
search for keys you
rattle the kitchen lock one
more time before you
climb the stairs weary
to bed.

I watch you
her therapist prepare your

St. Joan, Jacqueline. 1992. "The drama of the long distance runners." Pritned by permission of the author.

testimony your
expert psychological testimony you
review the research you
draft the report with your
clinical observations you
substantiate your opinions
bear witness to corroborate her
reality with your colder, calmer
objectivity. You try to balance her
accounts, reconcile your perceptions with
those of your science and those of the law.

Sometimes you stare at the wall and you
cry. You sit there cradling her fate
so carefully in your learned, aging hands.

I swallow
the Sunday news with my coffee.
Yet another woman killed by her
husbandwhoshothimselftoo. But
this one,

this one might have been mine,
this one,

Had I not been booked up
and had to say no,

this one,

Had she had the money on Thursday
instead of on Monday,

this one. I enter the funeral
home to see her dead body
dressed like a bride in a box

this familiar stranger I
talked to over the phone
once.

this one

whose Monday appointment I
could now scratch from my book. I
sign the book at the funeral home today for

this one

and I walk away.

'A Sure-Fire Winner Is to Tell Her You Love Her; Women Fall for It All the Time'

Men Talk Frankly With Counselor to Assess Harassment and Acquaintance Rape

Michele N-K Collison

Ronald E. Campbell is talking with 20 young men slouched in lounge chairs in a dormitory at George Mason University here.

"What are some of the lines you give women to get them to go to bed with you?" Mr. Campbell asks.

"A sure-fire winner," says one young man, "is to tell a woman that you love her. Women fall for it all the time."

Adds another: "Tell her, 'You can trust me. I wouldn't hurt you.'"

Yet another: "I tell her, 'I never met anyone like you before.'"

The meeting was billed as a no-holds-barred session "for men only"—a frank discussion of the facts of life as publicity surrounding such issues as acquaintance rape and sexual harassment prompt changes in relationships between men and women.

Mr. Campbell looks concerned. "This is part of what I call the intergenerational corruption of men," he tells the students. "We all learn from our brothers, our fathers, and friends—that you have to lie to women to get sex."

The men have come to the session for different reasons. Some saw a flier and were curious. Some were told by their fraternities to attend. Others were drawn because of a sexual assault that had happened on the campus this fall. (Campus officials are still investigating the incident, in which a woman reported that she had been assaulted in her dormitory room.)

A reporter was allowed to sit in on the discussion but agreed not to identify the young men who spoke. Some of the men agreed to talk for attribution in interviews after the discussion was over.

At a time when most colleges and universities have been focusing on helping women understand what constitutes date rape and encouraging them to speak out, Mr. Campbell, George Mason's director of housing, is one of a few administrators who have been talking about the issues with young men.

Collison, Michele N-K. 1991. "'A sure fire winner is to tell her you love her; women fall for it all the time': Men talk frankly to counselors." *The Chronicle of Higher Education* November 13. Reprinted by permission of the publisher.

Mr. Campbell, who has a master's degree in counseling, gives a series of talks at George Mason and a handful of other campuses each year, covering such subjects as date rape, female sexuality, orgasms, and the lies men tell women to seduce them. He says it is important to address those issues because of the increasingly strained relationships between men and women on campuses.

The Specter of Lawsuits

Women are reporting more instances of acquaintance rape and are challenging men's treatment of them. In addition, the specter of lawsuits against colleges over their handling of acquaintance-rape allegations has made some institutions more willing to discipline men who they find have pressured women into sex.

Mr. Campbell tries to get men to understand that they must change their behavior. "If a woman accuses you of rape, a judge will ask you, 'Did you ask her?' " he tells the men at the George Mason workshop. "You can't say, 'Well, Judge, the lights were down low and Barry White was on in the background and, well, one thing led to another.' "

Last year, in between his duties as housing director, Mr. Campbell traveled to seven campuses. Often using the same locker-room language as the young men he meets, Mr. Campbell, dapper in his trademark kente-cloth suspenders, tries to encourage students to ponder long-held stereotypes about sex.

"I want to get across to young men that times are changing," Mr. Campbell says. "Date rape is a crime and they will go to jail. There is a lot of anger and frustration on the part of men. They see the rules are changing, but they don't know how to act anymore. But they know they have to be accountable."

Ignorant About Women

Mr. Campbell says many young men treat women badly because they are ignorant about women's bodies and have learned to think of them as sex objects. "If they think all women are whores, then that's how they will treat them," Mr. Campbell says. "On one campus, the men called all the women 'bitch.' "

Mr. Campbell says he can relate so well to the young men he talks to because he remembers his own experiences all too well.

Says Ellie DiLapi, director of the University of Pennsylvania's Women's Center: "It's easy for men to say acquaintance rape is a women's issue. But men can't blow Ron off so easily, because they know he's talking from personal experience. He knows what goes on in the locker rooms and the fraternity houses, and he calls them on it." Mr. Campbell was assistant director for residential services at the University of Pennsylvania and worked with Ms. DiLapi on acquaintance-rape issues.

In addition to his work on college campuses, Mr. Campbell is a member of two statewide groups that are studying the problem of sexual assault. The Fox Television network broadcast a special on one of his workshops last year.

Mr. Campbell's own attitudes about women and sex began to change 10 years ago, when as a graduate student he attended a workshop on acquaintance rape. "I walked out of there saying, that sounds like me," says Mr. Campbell. "I said, I'm not a rapist. But I did lie to women. I did take them out and give them alcohol. But I figured that I'm not the only one who has a problem. I said, let me start spreading the word that we may have done something that people are now calling rape."

Mr. Campbell says most met have "sex by deception." They lie to women and lead women to drink too much in an effort to get them into bed. "Most men are not rapists," he says. "But they have admitted to certain behaviors."

He says part of the problem is that men are self-centered when it comes to sex. "All most men are thinking about is, 'I'm happy,'" he says. "They're not paying any attention to how their partner feels or to the signals she may be sending out."

Mr. Campbell tries to encourage the young men he meets to communicate more with women. He is adept at persuading students to talk about intimate subjects by encouraging them to laugh at themselves and by relating to them on their own terms.

"How many of you have ever asked permission for sex?" Mr. Campbell asks the students attending the workshop at George Mason. A few men raise their hands.

"How do you ask a woman for sex?" Mr. Campbell asks.

A young man looks around, then replies sheepishly: "Do you want to do the sex thing?"

"I'm sure that gets them every time," Mr. Campbell responds.

"He makes it very comfortable," says Robb Finan, a freshman who attended the discussion. "You don't feel like you have to hold back."

Adds John Ireland, another freshman: "I'm glad it wasn't a male-bashing session."

Others wish more men had attended. "I think many men are ignorant," says Rick Mudd, a freshman. "They are clueless. I don't think a large percentage of men know what normal intercourse is."

Mr. Campbell says that during his sessions, some men have realized they have raped women. "Three men have admitted to me forceable violent behavior when they were drunk," he says. "They came to me and said, 'I'm having problems. I must be guilty. I've done that.'"

'Only a Few Vicious Rapists'

Mr. Campbell refers men who have admitted they have raped women to university counselors.

He challenges men on their attitudes about women. "Only a few of us are vicious rapists, but we're all contributing to the problem," Mr. Campbell tells the group at George Mason. "We still laugh at the same jokes, still tell the same lies, still listen to the same sexual-conquest stories. Why don't we challenge each other?"

One man in the group replies: "Because most of these guys are my friends and I know I have to hang out with them. It's very hard to separate ideals from reality."

Mr. Campbell's goal is not to convict young men of crimes, but to get them to realize that much of their behavior is wrong. "When I talk about acquaintance rape, I can see they are identifying," he says. "They are playing back tapes in their minds to see it was them. Those are the kinds of experiences you want them to have—not necessarily to raise their hands and say, 'I'm a rapist.'"

Chapter 5—Violence Against Women
Study Questions

1. Why, in Western culture, are old women rendered "invisible"? How does our culture perpetuate this notion? How do women react? What are some of the negative stereotypes of old women?

2. How are women affected by the fear of aging? How are old women today often treated within the family system? How does this differ historically? By culture?

3. Go to a card shop and look at birthday cards, ones you might send to women friends. In the large group, discuss what you find and its connection to ageist stereotypes.

4. What are the consequences of sexual harassment in women's lives?

5. The continuum of violence ranges from silence to femicide. How do verbal and emotional abuse contribute to the continuum? From the information presented in the text, what other factors fall along the continuum? In small groups, fill in the continuum and then compare suppositions in a large group discussion.

6. What do some feminist theorists see as the underlying reason for incest? What do earlier theories espouse as causes?

7. How do Barron and Strauss see rape as culturally constructed? What are your views about why rape occurs? Do you agree or disagree with the feminist perspective? Why?

8. Define *acquaintance rape*. Why is it so difficult to prove?

9. What questions arise when police and the legal system confront date rape? How does victim blaming affect women's ability to control their lives in respect to violence?

10. How does conviction of the male rapist exact a toll on the woman's life?

11. Collison describes the importance of educating men about acquaintance rape. Discuss this critically, pointing to issues with which you agree or disagree. Does this apply to domestic abuse?

12. In Bart's study, summarized in "Sex Without Consent . . . ," what are the characteristics of women who avoided rape?

13. From the same essay, explain how society breeds the notion that forcible sex is not rape? What is meant by "the words *sex* and *rape* are not interchangeable"?

14. Discuss in the large group why women stay in abusive relationships. What do you think is the most important thing you can do when a woman reveals her history of abuse? Why?

15. Linda Bennington's poignant story illustrates vividly the cycle of abuse. How does Lenore Walker describe this cycle?

16. What are the roots of the idea of women as property? What institutions perpetuate these notions?

17. Domestic violence, as defined in Mickish's article, is not limited to physical abuse. What other forms of abuse are used? What are the primary needs of the abuser?

18. Historically, what has been the major cultural stumbling block to police intervention in domestic violence calls? How is this changing?

19. What are the tools abusers use to control their victims?

20. What are some ways to help children avoid becoming victims and/or perpetrators?

PART THREE

WITHIN PATRIARCHAL INSTITUTIONS

WOMEN AND ECONOMICS

Monys A. Hagen

Introduction

As early as 1884, Frederick Engels, in *Origins of the Family, Private Property, and the State*, hypothesized an economic explanation for women's subordination, linking it to the creation of private property. Briefly stated, Engels argued that the development of more efficient methods of production created a surplus with an exchange value. Because men produced these goods, they occupied a position of economic power, not only over the surplus and the means of production, but over women and their labor. While many aspects of the Engels thesis do not stand the test of historical scrutiny, this basic tenet holds true. A direct relationship exists between women's status in society, the economic roles they perform, and the value assigned to those contributions.

Concern over this vital connection has continued, and economic issues occupy a central place in contemporary feminist discourse. Scholars try to identify and analyze the complex set of factors that fostered women's entrance into the labor force and simultaneously blocked opportunities for equal participation in the economy. Discussion frequently focuses upon wages, demographic trends, and market forces, issues not divorced from life. Equally important are the ways in which women experience the effects of discrimination, poverty, and economic dependence upon men.

Understanding women's economic position in society is vital, because it provides one of the keys to women's emancipation. Without an equitable distribution of labor in the home and workplace, women will continue to experience the devaluation of their labor. Without equal opportunity and remuneration, women and men will never be equal partners in society or in personal relationships. The following questions form the framework for this chapter on women and economics.

- How has women's role in the household economy changed over time? What aspects have remained constant?
- How have traditional obligations to the home and family shaped women's economic opportunities and affected their labor force participation?
- What are the demographic changes that have taken place in the labor force since World War II?
- How do age, race, sexual identity, and marital status affect women's economic lives?
- What forms of conscious and unconscious discrimination do women workers and women managers face in hiring and promotion decisions?

- What are the major antidiscrimination initiatives implemented by the federal government? Why have they failed to alter appreciably the economic position of women in society?
- What causes the feminization of poverty? What can be done to end it?
- How do affirmative action and comparable worth differ in their approaches to labor force inequality? Why have these strategies for change been surrounded by so much controversy?
- How do sex-based economic inequities affect the relations between the sexes?

Historic Overview

The economic history of American women begins prior to the arrival of Europeans on the shores of North America. The Native American tribes were precapitalist societies, recognizing forms of kinship and tribal ownership other than private property. North America's major economic development was part of the first agricultural revolution, which brought about the domestication of plant life. With the cultivation of plants, societies became more sedentary, population increased, and a more rigid sexual division of labor evolved than had been possible in hunting and gathering societies. Even though indigenous societies were in different stages of the agricultural revolution and exhibited variability in the division of labor, in general women planted and cultivated crops and processed foods while men hunted. In this complementary division of labor, men and women existed in an economic partnership without a valuation or devaluation of the contributions of either (Oswalt 1978; Leacock and

Lurie 1971; Spencer et al. 1977). The Iroquois, a matrilineal and matrilocal society, held the tribal lands in common, but women controlled them. They planted, tended the crops, harvested, and controlled the distribution of all commodities, including those brought back from the hunt. Economic centrality served as a base of power for Iroquois women. They were spiritual leaders and healers, and the senior women of the clans appointed and deposed the men who sat on the tribal councils (Rothenberg 1980; Brown 1975). An early observer said of Iroquois women:

Nothing, however, is more real than this superiority of the women. It is of them that the nation really consists; and it is through them that the nobility of the blood, the genealogical tree and the families are perpetuated. All real authority is vested in them. The land, the fields and their harvest all belong to them. (Brown 1975, 238)

The economic character of North America changed dramatically with the arrival of Europeans in the early 1600s. The southern colonies quickly developed a single cash crop economy, based on the cultivation of tobacco and characterized by plantations and slavery. Dutch traders brought the first blacks to North America in 1619, and by mid-century the institution of slavery, supported by law, was in place (Morgan 1975; Walton and Shepherd 1979). Slave owners initially preferred purchasing males, but they soon realized that the presence of female slaves not only made black males more servile but also provided for the natural increase of the slave population. By the 1800s, plantation owners anticipated a 5- to 6-percent annual profit from the natural increase of their human property. Black women under slavery received no favors because of their sex. They worked side by side with black men from sunup to sundown in the tobacco, cotton, and rice fields of the South. At the end of the day they returned to the slave quarters to care for their families. After a lifetime of exploiting black women for their productive and reproductive labors, because profitability was the bottom line, some masters turned old black women off their plantations to fend for themselves rather than supporting them until death (Jones 1985; White 1985).

The economic system of the North, based on commerce and family farms, evolved differently (Walton and Shepherd 1979; Bailyn 1979). The household was the basic economic unit, and women's contributions were recognized as vital to the family's survival and prosperity. Many tasks performed by women of colonial America—doing the laundry, caring for the sick, processing foods, tending the gardens, and raising children—are familiar responsibilities to women of today. In the pre-industrial society of the 1600s and 1700s, women also engaged in domestic manufacturing, producing goods for home consumption such as soap, candles, and cloth (Ulrich 1982). By the end of the eighteenth century, the American commercial economy expanded and families increasingly purchased items previously manufactured by women in their homes. This development marked the beginning of a shift in women's role from home producers to consumers. The tasks women continued to perform in their homes were not only less visible, but since they had no market value, they were considered less significant than the market-oriented jobs performed by men (Cott 1977).

This trend intensified with the industrial revolution, as machines produced goods more rapidly and efficiently than before. The first expression of the indus-

trial revolution in the United States was the textile industry. Large-scale manufacturing began in the 1820s at Lowell, Massachusetts, with mill owners recruiting young single women from New England farms for their work force. Initially the operatives were treated well: they made relatively high wages, lived in company boardinghouses, and enjoyed the libraries, churches, and lectures provided by the owners for their leisure hours. Conditions of labor began to deteriorate and many mill workers reported ill health caused by long hours, poor ventilation in the factories, and the inhalation of cotton fibers. The operatives protested these conditions in a series of futile strikes. During the 1840s, mill owners replaced America's first industrial work force, the Lowell "mill girls," with immigrant laborers (Dublin 1979).

During the first half of the nineteenth century, in addition to mill work, women found employment as domestic servants and primary school teachers. These jobs were considered appropriate endeavors for women since they were an extension of the traditional tasks performed by women in their homes. Still, they were only appropriate for single women, and were to be abandoned upon marriage, women's true vocation in life. The vast majority of women did not pursue employment; they devoted their lives to caring for their homes, which for the white middle and upper classes had become privatized and considered a refuge from the economic world rather than a part of it (Cott 1977; Katzman 1981).

During the last quarter of the nineteenth century, economic opportunities opened up for women, and they made a steady advance into the labor force. Women workers took jobs in the expanding urban-industrial centers, but opportunities were not equal for all women. Black and immigrant women worked in the lowest paying, least desirable jobs in garment industry sweatshops, in laundries, and as domestic servants in hotels and private homes. White native-born women held more public and prestigious positions as teachers, nurses, office workers, and sales clerks. During this period, called "the era of the working girl" (Weiner 1985), social attitudes still dictated that wage labor was something that a woman only did until marriage. While many married women worked because of economic need, three out of four white women and four out of five black women working in urban areas were single (Katzman 1981; Weiner, L. 1985; Kessler-Harris 1982).

The history of America's working women in the twentieth century is intimately tied to the experiences of war and depression. With the entrance of the United States into World War I, American industry geared up for the demands of wartime production. American women served the cause by working in airplane factories and munitions plants or as volunteers with the Red Cross. This was the first time a significant minority of women moved into traditionally male-dominated occupations. Even though they were not able to hold onto the economic gains made during the war, there was a lasting consequence. The wartime expansion of federal and corporate bureaucracies continued in the postwar years and absorbed increasing numbers of women into clerical positions (Weiner, L. 1985; Kessler-Harris 1982).

The Great Depression of the 1930s was the worst economic catastrophe to befall this country. As the United States slid into depression, production fell dramatically and unemployment rose to unprecedented levels. Public opinion polls indicated that most Americans opposed married women's employment, believing that families did not need women's incomes, that working mothers contributed to juvenile delinquency, and that working women took jobs away from men. State governments and school boards responded by imposing sanctions against employing married women. Public perception did not accurately reflect the economic reality. Women who sought jobs during the depression needed to support themselves and their families and they did not compete for men's jobs. The industries first and most dramatically affected by the depression were construction, heavy industry, and mining which primarily employed men. In contrast, nursing, teaching, and service positions did not experience the same rates of unemployment and did not attract male applicants (Ware 1982; Kessler-Harris 1982).

World War II clearly and decisively ended the economic crisis. The United States geared up for war and the nation again experienced a labor shortage as men entered the armed forces. By late 1942, the labor shortage had become acute, and government and industry began a campaign to recruit women into the work force. Films, posters, and advertisements in magazines urged women to enter the industrial sector. The campaign appealed to women on many levels, citing economics, patriotism, and helping to end the war sooner as reasons to join the labor force. The efforts at mobilization worked: 4.7 million women responded to the call. For most women, this was their first opportunity to move into high paying industrial jobs, and for black women it marked their movement out of domestic service. Surveys taken during the war indicated that approximately 75 percent of women war workers wanted to retain their jobs, but when the war ended, women were once again called upon to show their patriotism, this time by returning to the home (Hartmann 1982; Kessler-Harris 1982; Weiner, L. 1985).

The Demographic Transformation of the Labor Force

The conclusion of World War II ushered in a new era of women's labor force participation. Close to eighteen million women continued to work after the war, indicating that they were not willing to retreat to the home. Historians debate the actual impact that the war had on women's labor force participation (Rupp 1978; Chafe 1972; Hartmann 1982; Kessler-Harris 1982). The inroads women made into the higher paying jobs did not last past reconversion to a peacetime economy as the traditional sex-stratification of the labor force reemerged. In the postwar decades, however, the number and percentage of employed women rose dramatically. In 1940 women were only 25.3 percent of the labor force; by 1950 they were 29 percent; an additional 6 percent increase had occurred by 1965; and as the 1980s ended, women comprised approximately 46 percent of American workers (Kessler-Harris 1982; Goldberg 1990). Lasting changes had taken place. The difference in labor force participation rates for black and white women virtually disappeared and opposition to married women's employment eroded. Whereas before the war the typical employed woman was young and single, after the war, she was older, married, and had children (Hartmann 1982; Kessler-Harris 1982; Weiner, L. 1985).

It had always been acceptable for women to work because of family need. Previously, Americans defined need as putting food on the table, clothes on the children, and a roof over the family's head, but in the postwar decades economic need became closely aligned with elevating the family's standard of living. Purchasing a home, buying a new car, acquiring new household appliances, and saving for the children's college educations became the justifications for women's paid employment. By 1990 over two thirds of all mothers worked outside the home, and there ceased to be a correlation between the husband's level of income and likelihood of the wife's participation in the labor force (Weiner, L. 1985). Other factors contributed to the advance of women into the labor force. Today the likelihood of employment has risen because more women live in urban areas; they have higher levels of education than ever before; the increase in real wages provides a powerful incentive for employment; and the forty-hour work week enables women to balance home responsibilities more effectively with paid employment. Family patterns also influence women's economic choices. The declining birth rate allows more women to seek jobs, while increases in divorce and separation rates make employment imperative. By heightening awareness of the importance of self-fulfillment and by encouraging women to use their talents, the contemporary women's movement prompted women to establish economic identities of their own (Weiner, L. 1985; Kessler-Harris 1982; Goldberg 1990).

Despite the dramatic growth in the numbers of employed women, occupational segregation continues to limit women's advancement and earning potential. Women are clustered in positions that have low status and low pay and provide less security and benefits than jobs held by men. Seventy percent of all full-time employed women hold jobs in female-dominated occupations, known as the "pink collar ghetto." Clerical work absorbs the greatest numbers of women, but nursing, child care work, bookkeeping, and domestic service all employ a work force that is over 90 percent female. With a few exceptions, pink collar work is identified in the labor market as a job, not a career, implying that it is not permanent employment and that there are limited opportunities for upward mobility. These jobs are oriented toward serving the needs of others and supporting the work performed by men (Howe 1977; Goldberg 1990; Barrett 1987; Rhode 1990; Tobias and Megdal 1985; Kanter 1977).

Even where women have entered professions previously dominated by men, new types of occupational segregation emerge. In some instances companies give women different job titles for performing the same work as men. More telling of the resistance to occupational integration is the creation of lower-paid female ghettos within the professions. In corporations, women are clustered in the personnel, human resources, and marketing departments and remain underrepresented in production and plant management, the established routes to the executive level. The legal profession provides another example of employment segregation. Women comprise over 20 percent of the legal profession, but the majority practice in the less lucrative areas of family and estate law. Inroads against labor market segregation have been negligible (Rhode 1990; Barrett 1987; Barrett 1982; Hardesty and Jacobs 1986; and Kanter 1977). According to a 1984 U.S. Commission on Civil Rights report, it will take seventy-five to one hundred years to achieve occupational integration if the rate of change proceeds at its current pace (Rhode 1990).

Another indicator of sex-based economic inequality is the wage gap, the difference in average income between full-time employed women and men. Legislation and public policy has had no effect on closing the wage gap in the last thirty years. In 1955 women's median annual wages were 64 percent of men's; during the 1960s and 1970s, the ratio dropped to 59 percent before again rising to 64 percent in 1986. At the conclusion of the 1980s, women earned only sixty-six cents to every dollar earned by men (Rhode 1990; Goldberg 1990). Pay differentials hit women of color the hardest. While a white female college graduate earns less on average than a white male with a high school diploma, the average black woman with a college degree earns less than a white male high-school dropout (Rhode 1990). Equally disheartening is that the wage gap increases with age. Men's wages continue to rise throughout their careers, but by the age of twenty-five women reach a plateau in their earning potential. Additional years of work experience do not alter the situation because women work in low paying jobs with limited opportunities for advancement (Arendell 1987; Barrett 1987; National Center for Health Services Research 1986).

Some economists and corporate leaders argue that women earn less than men because historical factors shape female employment preferences and that women choose to invest less time and money in education and training, work fewer hours on the job because they believe leisure and family are more important, and avoid jobs that are competitive and demanding (Weiner, J. 1985; Barrett 1987; Rhode 1990; Hennig and Jardim 1977). Studies generally show, however, that variance in education, hours worked, and experience account for less than 50 percent of the income disparity. Furthermore, when these variables are equal, women still do not advance at the same rate or to the same level as men (Barrett 1987; Rhode 1990; Weiner, J. 1985; Hennig and Jardim 1977).

Deborah L. Rhode, director of the Institute for Research on Women and Gender at Stanford University, explained the factors affecting women's employment: "For many individuals, career decisions have been less the product of fully informed and independent preferences than the result of preconceptions about 'women's work' that are shaped by cultural stereotypes, family and peer pressure, and the absence of alternative role models" (1990, 186).

Institutional and attitudinal barriers and discrimination limit women's opportunities for economic equality. Women do not have access to the recruitment networks that lead to influential positions in business, law, politics, medicine, and the other professions. Socially and culturally constructed attitudes prove more insidious. Women are socialized to be feminine and to act passive, nurturing, and emotional. However, businesses and the professions reward confidence, assertiveness, and rationality. When women do not behave in this manner, managers and coworkers consider them lacking in the competitiveness necessary for success; when they demonstrate these characteristics, rather than being applauded as go-getters, they are denounced as pushy, bitchy, difficult, and unfeminine. This behavioral double standard, based upon stereotypes about women's capabilities, promotes unconscious, often unwitting, discrimination that makes it difficult for women to be evaluated fairly in a male work environment (Hardesty and Jacobs 1986; Rhode 1990).

Home and family obligations also limit women's full and equal participation in the labor market. Despite the dramatic advance of married women with children into the labor force, there has not been an appreciable reduction in women's domestic responsibilities. Women continue to perform nearly 70 percent of the housework and child care (Rhode 1990). This combination of paid and unpaid labor places a double burden on working women. The absence of a comprehensive national parental policy, affordable child care facilities, and flexible scheduling in most work places directly impact job performance and evaluation. Time off for maternity and infant care not only fosters a discontinuous work record, seen as detrimental by many employers, but places women in the position of losing benefits at a time when they are needed most. Taking days off to care for sick children and leaving work early for school conferences appears to managers as a lack of commitment to the job or as an inability to leave personal matters at home. Because society defines women as primary caretakers of the home and family, neither public nor private employers feel compelled to offer programs that would ease the burden of being homemaker and economic provider (Weiner, L. 1985; Rhode 1990; Barrett 1987; Pleck 1977).

Women in Business

The 1970s and 1980s heralded the entrance of women into managerial positions in corporate America. From 1972 to 1985 the number of women in managerial and administrative positions rose from 322,000 to 1.3 million, as women entered careers in business at a rate more than twice that of men (Hardesty and Jacobs 1986). A number of factors contributed to this phenomenon. The women's movement exerted pressure on American companies to hire women, and the Civil Rights Act of 1964 mandated nondiscriminatory practices in hiring. In order to comply with affirmative action guidelines, businesses actively recruited qualified women. Magazines like *Ms., Savvy,* and *Working Woman* also promoted the progress of women in management by encouraging women to pursue challenging careers in business, while providing them with information on how to succeed in the corporation (Hardesty and Jacobs 1986).

On the surface it would seem that women and men share an equal partnership in American corporations. Women's experiences, however, belie this impression. A 1985 *Harvard Business Review* study showed that only 33 percent of the women respondents believed women had equal opportunity within their own firms, and a mere 18 percent thought women had equal opportunity in the business world (Van Dyke 1987). Sarah Hardesty and Nehama Jacobs captured women's frustration in their book *Success and Betrayal.* "Like Nora in Ibsen's *A Doll's House,* women managers perceive themselves as trapped in a corporate house of glass walls (and ceilings) through which they can see but which they cannot penetrate" (1986, 20). Women managers believe that antifemale/antifeminist executives, an inability to be accepted into male corporate culture, and exclusion from recruitment and promotion networks all prevent their advancement in the business world (Kanter 1977; Hardesty and Jacobs 1986; Blum and Smith 1988). Perceptions of inequality are supported by statistics. Women hold only 3 percent of the seats on boards of directors of the thousand largest corporations, and only 15 of the country's 6,500 public companies are headed by women (Hardesty and Jacobs 1986). The wage gap is greater in business than in the work force in general, with women managers earning only 61 percent of their male counterparts' salary (Blum and Smith 1988).

Still, the presence of women in American corporations is an achievement for women in the economic arena. Even though they experience discrimination, as personnel and middle-tier managers women increasingly make decisions that affect the working lives of women in their companies. In time corporate policies may recognize the importance of child care facilities and show sensitivity to the double burden shouldered by employed women.

Because female managers have experienced a sense of betrayal in corporate America, are not evaluated on the basis of their own merit, and cannot break through the glass ceiling of middle management, many women find establishing their own businesses an attractive alternative to the corporation. Individual proprietorships enable women to exercise their managerial skills, provide more flexibility, and allow some women to balance career goals with family responsibilities. Between 1973 and 1983, women opened their own businesses at a rate twice that of men, and have continued to outpace men, though at a reduced rate since the mid-1980s. In 1980 women owned 25.9 percent of all small businesses; by 1985 this number had risen to 28.1 percent, and by 1987 it was approximately 30 percent (Blackford 1991; Van Dyke 1987; Hardesty and Jacobs 1986; Ando 1990).

Like sex-typed job titles, women-owned businesses reflect the sex segregation of the labor market. Approximately 74 percent of these enterprises are in the service sector and only 4.7 percent in the more lucrative areas of construction, manufacturing, and transportation. This contributes to the fact that women-owned businesses generate a disproportionately low share of small business revenues, only 10 to 12 percent during the 1980s (Blackford 1991; Van Dyke 1987; Hardesty and Jacobs 1986). Opening a small business is a risky venture under the best circumstances, and women frequently begin operations in a disadvantaged position. They experience greater difficulty than men in obtaining credit from banks and Small Business Administration loans. Consequently many women's businesses are not adequately capitalized. In addition, female entrepreneurs tend to have less managerial experience than their male counterparts, and because of familial responsibilities they devote fewer hours per week to the enterprise. The failure rate of women-owned businesses is greater than that of male-owned, and is highest for women of color, who are less likely to succeed in business proprietorship than either white women or males of their ethnic/racial group (Ando 1990; Blackford 1991; Hardesty and Jacobs 1986).

The outlook for women in business is perhaps more optimistic than in other areas of the economy. While it would appear that women-owned proprietorships are precariously situated in the sex-segregated service and retail trades, this may actually contribute to their success (Van Dyke 1987). The service sector is the fastest growing sector of the American economy. Talented entrepreneurs can benefit from this expansion and find ample opportunities for growth, profit, and innovation.

Public Policy and Antidiscrimination

The federal government first attempted to provide equality in the work place during World War II. The National War Labor Board, in an attempt to allay strike activity and to ensure a high level of industrial output, required employers in defense industries to pay women and men equally for performing the same jobs (Kessler-Harris 1982; Mezey 1992). With reconversion to a peacetime economy, employers in all industries reestablished pre-war discriminatory practices. Discrimination remained an accepted feature

of public and private employment until the 1960s, when the civil rights movement and the women's movement prompted the government to condemn discrimination in the work place.

The catalyst for change was the 1963 report of the President's Commission on the Status of Women, which chronicled glaring inequalities in pay between men and women, discriminatory employment practices, and the disadvantaged position of women in the economy. Under pressure from the Women's Bureau of the Department of Labor, the U.S. Congress passed the 1963 Equal Pay Act (EPA). Congress debated whether the bill should adopt the concept of "equal pay for equal work" or that of "equal pay for comparable work." For the sake of expediency, Congress enacted the less far-reaching principle of equal pay (Hartmann 1989; Mezey 1992; Stetson 1991). The government gave women an important tool for challenging overt wage discrimination, but it failed to grant them a means to rectify the inequities of a sex-segregated labor market.

Title VII of the 1964 Civil Rights Act went beyond equal pay and sought an end to discriminatory practices in private-sector recruiting, hiring, and promotion. Title VII prohibited discrimination on the basis of sex, as well as race, color, religion, and national origin. Women quickly demonstrated the need for a weapon against sex discrimination in the work place. Approximately one fourth of all complaints filed during the first five years were by women charging their employers with sex discrimination (Hartmann 1989; Mezey 1992).

The Civil Rights Act created the Equal Employment Opportunity Commission (EEOC) and charged it with overseeing all complaints of discrimination. Yet congressional compromises virtually stripped the EEOC of any real powers of enforcement, permitting the agency only to review charges and persuade employers to cease discriminatory practices. If these measures failed, the EEOC referred cases to the Justice Department for legal action. Unfortunately, the commission initially showed hostility and indifference to issues of sex discrimination. The Equal Employment Opportunity Act of 1972 resolved the problems with the EEOC's inefficiency in enforcement by granting the commission the power to file lawsuits. The act also included public sector employees and workers in educational institutions and government offices under the protections guaranteed in the 1964 Civil Rights Act. During the 1970s, President Carter appointed Eleanor Holmes Norton to head the EEOC. Under her direction the commission became an effective agency and took an aggressive stand against all forms of discrimination. While not unconcerned with individual cases of discrimination, the EEOC focused primarily upon institutionalized, systemic forms of discrimination and urged victims to join in class-action suits (Hartmann 1989; Mezey 1992; Stetson 1991).

Another form of discrimination that fell during the 1970s was sex-segregated job advertisements. Initially the EEOC maintained that sex-segregated classified ads were not in violation of Title VII, but under pressure from women's groups the commission amended its guidelines and required newspapers to inform readers that qualified applicants, regardless of sex, could apply for any job listed. In 1968 the commission refined its position and determined that Title VII prohibited sex-segregated classified ads. When tested on the grounds of First Amendment guarantees of freedom of commercial speech in *Pittsburgh Press v. Pittsburgh Commission on Human Rights* (1973), the Supreme Court upheld the new EEOC guidelines (Mezey 1992).

The Reagan and Bush administrations seriously threatened the inroads made against sex discrimination during the 1960s and 1970s. Lacking a commitment to eradicating sex discrimination, both presidents dismantled programs and undermined the effectiveness of existing agencies. Under Clarence Thomas, appointed by Reagan to head the EEOC, the commission reversed the course set by Eleanor Holmes Norton. Thomas stood firmly against affirmative action programs aimed at ending institutionalized discrimination and pursued a conservative course of action, showing a marked preference for individual cases of blatant discrimination over the more far-reaching class-action suits. By the end of the 1980s, the EEOC ceased to be an effective weapon in the fight against sex discrimination and increasingly lent a sympathetic ear to cases of reverse discrimination that were brought by white males believing themselves to be the victims of affirmative action legislation (Hartmann 1989; Mezey 1992).

George Bush dealt a serious blow to the cause of antidiscrimination in his veto of the 1990 Civil Rights Act. This bill would have forbidden racial harassment in the work place, would have forced employers to justify business decisions adversely affecting women, and would have enabled women to sue for compensatory and punitive damages in cases of discrimination, a course of action previously only available to minorities. Bush argued that the 1990 Civil Rights Act would force employers to adopt quotas for women and minorities in order to avoid prosecution. Despite overwhelming support, the Senate fell one vote short of overriding the presidential veto (Hartmann 1989; Mezey 1992).

Instead of standing as a landmark bill for the cause of equality in employment, the failure of the 1990 Civil Rights Act marked a stunning defeat for women. The issue of compensatory and punitive damages for women figured prominently in Bush's veto. In defense of the administration's position, a White House representative said, "We fought a Civil War for blacks, we didn't fight a Civil War for women" (Mezey 1992, 71). The veto of the 1990 Civil Rights Act sent the message that public policy no longer stands against discriminatory employment practices and that discrimination against women is not to be taken seriously.

The Feminization of Poverty

One of the most alarming manifestations of economic inequality is the feminization of poverty, also known as the impoverishment of women. The discovery of poverty in a nation of plenty first shocked the nation during the 1960s, and the federal government took prompt action through Lyndon Johnson's Great Society programs. Funding for the War on Poverty dried up because of war in Southeast Asia and subsequent economic recessions. Poverty did not disappear, however, only the public awareness of it did. When the unequal distribution of income and resources came to bear disproportionately upon elderly and divorced women and women of color during the 1970s, there were few effective assistance mechanisms in place.

A number of interrelated economic and demographic factors combine to make gender the primary determinant of low economic status. Occupational segregation and low wages figure prominently. Many full-time employed women maintain a standard of living barely above the poverty line, and as many as three

fourths of working-age women would live in poverty if they were the sole support of themselves and one dependent (Goldberg and Kremen 1990). The overrepresentation of women among temporary, part-time, and minimum-wage workers makes the situation more tenuous because these women lack access to benefit plans considered vital to economic security (Barrett 1987; Goldberg 1990). Seventy percent of part-time employees are not protected by pension plans and 42 percent are not covered by employer-provided health care policies (Goldberg 1990).

The consequences of economic inequality have a cumulative life-long effect, placing women in a disadvantaged position during their working years and devastating them in old age. As stated by Robyn Stone in her study of "The Feminization of Poverty and Older Women," published by the Department of Health and Human Services, "The feminization of poverty is rooted in the pre-retirement work and family history of women which determine, in large part, the economic status of women in old age" (National Center for Health Services Research 1986, 11). Many elderly women today were full-time homemakers during their working years. These women did not accrue retirement benefits and they find themselves solely dependent upon Social Security, based on lifetime contributions and salary at the time of retirement. Social Security reforms adjusted payments to account for inflation and maintain recipients above the poverty threshold. Still, these efforts have proved inadequate, as 15 percent of all elderly women live in poverty. The statistics are higher for women of color who have borne the effects of sexual and racial discrimination throughout their lives. Thirty-six percent of black and 22 percent of Latina women find themselves impoverished in old age

(National Center for Health Services Research 1986). Failing health and impaired mobility accentuate the economic vulnerability of the elderly. Medicare, the major source of medical insurance for the aged, covers only 33 percent of health care expenditures. The result is that elderly women, on average, pay about 16 percent of their household income for medical care and risk plummeting into poverty within a year if confronted with a chronic illness (National Center for Health Services Research 1986).

Changing family patterns are closely linked to the feminization of poverty. Because of the increasing incidence of separation and single motherhood and a divorce rate of approximately 50 percent, the number of female-headed households has risen dramatically since the 1960s. Establishing an independent household, while far preferable to unhappy or abusive marriages, is not without economic risks. Female-headed families are swelling the ranks of the country's poor and homeless. In 1960 female-headed households were less than 25 percent of the families living in poverty; by the mid-1980s, they comprised the majority. As the 1990s began, 60 percent of impoverished Americans were women and their children (Arendell 1987; Goldberg and Kremen 1990).

Divorced women's experiences underscore the ways in which the economy reinforces women's dependence upon men. During marriage, women have a higher standard of living than they would living alone because of their husbands' greater earning potential and employee benefits. Many women who believe in traditional values choose to remain in the home and care for the needs of the family. For those women who work outside the home, their paychecks usually supplement their husbands' incomes, enabling some families to maintain a middle-class lifestyle and raising others out of poverty. Marriage masks sex-based economic inequality, but it becomes painfully evident in divorce as the man's standard of living increases and the woman's declines. The result is that the median income of female-headed families is 56 percent below that of married couples (Arendell 1987; Faludi 1991; Goldberg 1990).

Economic recovery is very difficult for women after divorce. Women who worked during marriage have a better chance of maintaining their families above the poverty line than do women who embraced the traditional role of full-time homemaker. Most women who became housewives thought that their husbands would provide for them "'til death do us part," never suspecting that they had chosen a risky career path. Since the 1960s, divorce has affected couples of all ages and marriages of all durations. Twenty percent of all divorces involve couples married at least fifteen years, and each year approximately a half million women over the age of forty-five find themselves joining the ranks of "displaced homemakers." Women over the age of thirty-five who have been out of the job market for a prolonged period of time have difficulty supporting themselves. Their work experience before marriage is discounted by employers, and the unpaid labor they performed in the home does not translate into marketable skills. Without job training, displaced homemakers face the prospect of low-paying jobs, a wage gap that most dramatically impacts women of their age group, and age discrimination in hiring (Arendell 1987; Barrett 1987; Bergmann 1981).

Even though the rates of impoverishment are greatest for white, single mothers, women of color and their children disproportionately bear the effects of the feminization of poverty (Goldberg 1990).

Black and Latina female-headed households are 50 percent more likely to live in poverty than are their white counterparts. Divorce contributes to poverty among women of all races and ethnic groups, but for Latina and especially black women teen pregnancy and the formation of families outside of marriage has become more critical. The rise from poverty is particularly difficult for women of color and their dependents. They are the most likely group of workers to be underemployed, unemployed, and involuntarily working part-time. Since the cycle of poverty is difficult to break and pre-retirement experiences determine economic status in old age, the future prospects are grave, especially for teen mothers without an education or marketable skills (Goldberg 1990; Barrett 1987).

There are few mechanisms available to help women and their dependents escape from poverty. In the case of divorce, child support payments make a negligible impact. Only about 60 percent of divorced mothers are awarded child support by the courts, and of this number only one half receive regular payments. The inadequacies of this form of assistance have been pointed out by Irwin Garfinkel and Sara McLanahan, who have calculated that alimony and child support comprise 10 percent of the income for white, female-headed families and a mere 3.5 percent for black female households (Garfinkel and McLanahan 1988). The presumption of many people is that welfare is the primary means of support for many of these households. They resent people who they believe are abusing the system; and, increasingly from the 1980s, they believe that welfare has been treated as a social tax that is awarded to the undeserving poor. However, a minority of divorced and separated women and single mothers receive benefits, and in no state do payments from Aid to Families with Dependent Children (AFDC) raise recipients out of poverty, even when combined with food stamps. When women on welfare enter the labor market, their standard of living may actually decrease. Their welfare benefits are reduced; they lack access to affordable child care; and they confront an economic system that only awards males a "family wage" (Garfinkel and McLanahan 1988; Goldberg and Kremen 1990; Goldberg 1990; Barrett 1987; Helburn and Morris 1988; Arendell 1987).

Strategies for Change

The movement of women out of the home and into the paid labor force indicates the importance of women's employment to the nation's economic growth and the centrality of women's income to their families' standard of living. Nevertheless, neither the household economy nor employment practices have adjusted to this shift. The disproportionate share of work women perform in the home, the feminization of poverty, the wage gap, and occupational segregation point toward systemic economic inequality that can only be remedied by aggressive action that goes beyond mandates for equal pay and equal opportunity.

Two such strategies are affirmative action and comparable worth, which attack economic inequality from different perspectives. Affirmative action dates to 1965, when President Lyndon Johnson issued Executive Order 11246 requiring all organizations and businesses holding contracts with the federal government to take "affirmative action to ensure that applicants are employed, and employees treated during employment without regard to their race, color, religion, or national origin" (Stetson 1991, 168). In 1968, faced with pressure from women's organizations, Johnson issued Executive Order 11375, which included sex in affirmative action provisions. A 1971 executive order by President Richard Nixon strengthened federal commitment to affirmative action by requiring employers with government contracts to establish timetables or goals for integration of their labor forces (Stetson 1991; Mezey 1992; Goldberg 1990; Crosby and Clayton 1990). The most common affirmative action initiatives are special efforts to recruit female candidates for job vacancies and training programs, preferential treatment for members of underrepresented groups, and quotas or timetables for hiring members of groups that have historically been discriminated against (Barrett 1987; Binion 1987).

Ensuring the representation of women in businesses, educational institutions, and professions appears to be a simple goal that embraces the principles of justice and equality. Still, considerable controversy surrounds affirmative action programs. Critics frequently charge that affirmative action discriminates against white males, that beneficiaries could not have attained their positions on the basis of established standards of merit, and that affirmative action erodes the self-esteem of those it is designed to benefit. These arguments are erroneous and often disguise sexist and racist economic views. Affirmative action initiatives only apply to people who meet the minimum qualifications for the position; temporary exclusion of some white males from job considerations is not comparable to the institutionalized discrimination faced by women; and studies repeatedly show that persons hired under affirmative action experience no negative psychological effects. Nevertheless, the antiaffirmative action stance of the Reagan and Bush administrations has given free reign to

these views with the consequence that affirmative action proponents have been placed on the defensive. They devote considerable attention to answering charges of reverse discrimination and work to maintain existing programs (Binion 1987; Crosby and Clayton 1990; Mezey 1992; Barrett 1987).

Administrative opposition has not dismantled affirmative action. Congressional support remains intact and affirmative action continues as an effective strategy for increasing the numbers of women in educational institutions and nontraditional careers. The benefits of affirmative action are not in the numbers alone. As more women enter positions from which they were previously excluded, their presence challenges sex-based job stereotyping and provides role models for those who follow. Affirmative action represents a commitment to equality and a recognition of the value of diversity in economic considerations. It challenges occupational segregation and the hegemonic position of white males in the American economy (Binion 1987; Barrett 1987; Crosby and Clayton 1990; Rhode 1990). Perhaps even more important, affirmative action lays bare the faulty logic of one of America's most widely held economic myths: those who succeed and those who fail have only themselves to blame.

Another effective strategy for economic change is comparable worth, also known as pay equity. Comparable worth emerged as the foremost feminist economic issue of the 1980s. As the term implies, this strategy advances the principle of "equal pay for comparable worth" that was rejected in the debates over the Equal Pay Act of 1963. In contrast to affirmative action, this policy acknowledges that occupational segregation is an employment characteristic that will not disappear in the near future. Comparable worth seeks to eliminate pay inequities between men and women caused by sex-bias and discrimination rather than the conditions of employment (Taylor 1989; Rhode 1990; Westkott et al. 1988). Actual examples of this type of pay inequity are that members of the female-dominated professions of public school teaching and nursing are paid less than liquor store clerks and tree trimmers, respectively (Rhode 1990).

Comparable worth requires a job evaluation, a standard business practice already used by most employers for assessing employee performance. What distinguishes comparable worth from existing evaluation instruments is that employers apply the same standards consistently across job categories. The evaluation instrument weighs various characteristics associated with job performance such as educational investment, training requirements, skill, responsibility, experience, and conditions of employment. At the conclusion of the evaluation, employers adjust salaries so that jobs with comparable ratings receive comparable remuneration (Rhode 1990; Taylor 1989; Westkott et al. 1988).

Criticisms levied against pay equity frequently center upon a defense of the free market and its ability to act as a fair and impersonal arbiter of the value of labor. According to this view, a balance exists between supply and demand, and because the supply of women workers exceeds the demand in female-dominated jobs, low wages result. One serious flaw of the free market argument is that the invisible hand of market forces long ago yielded to the visible hand of government regulation and managerial manipulations. More fundamental to issues of discrimination is that market forces historically evolved within and continue to reflect cultural attitudes that devalue women

and women's work (Rhode 1990; Taylor 1989; Westkott et al. 1988).

The case for comparable worth is very powerful. It eliminates sex- and race-based pay inequities, provides fairness in employment, and demonstrates an employer's commitment to equity. Comparable worth can be reconciled with even the most conservative business environments because it fosters high morale, low rates of turnover, and job satisfaction (Taylor 1989; Rhode 1990; Westkott et al. 1988). Deborah Rhode presented one of the most compelling cases for comparable worth in *The American Woman, 1990–91*:

> Pay equity initiatives will focus attention on fundamental questions not only of gender equality but of social priorities. . . . Are we comfortable with a society that pays more for jobs such as parking attendant than for those such as child care attendant, whatever their male/female composition? (1990, 198)

Affirmative action and comparable worth are complementary strategies addressing different aspects of labor force inequality. If fully implemented in conjunction with the Equal Pay Act and Title VII, tremendous progress would be made toward ending institutionalized discrimination; however, for women to fully and equally participate in the economic life of the nation, additional measures will be needed. Since one of the greatest problems facing American women today is low wages, the federal government must reassess its minimum wage policy. Historically the justification for paying women low wages has been that women's income is a supplement to men's and that male breadwinners should receive the family wage. The high percentage of women in the labor force and the growth of female-headed households indicate that women no longer spend their lives economically dependent upon men (Kessler-Harris 1990; Goldberg 1990; Arendell 1987; Rhode 1990). The minimum wage should be adjusted so that every full-time employed person receives a living wage, adjusted annually for inflation, that maintains a standard of living above the poverty level.

Vocational training programs also would help to break the cycle of poverty that traps many women. During the 1970s, training provided through the Comprehensive Employment and Training Act (CETA), though aimed primarily at men, demonstrated its effectiveness in increasing economic opportunities for the poor. Vocational programs, accompanied by an effective placement service, would provide women with the skills and means needed to support themselves and their children. The power of any training or educational program is minimized if it reinforces occupational segregation. Safeguards must be built into vocational programs to ensure that women have opportunities to learn drafting and design as well as data entry. Since women experience the effects of occupational segregation at all educational levels and in all professions, reform in higher education is needed. Colleges and universities, working in conjunction with government student loan programs, could earmark monies and establish scholarships as an incentive for talented women to pursue careers in the hard sciences, mathematics, engineering, aviation, and architecture (Rhode 1990; Barrett 1987; Goldberg 1990).

The absence of a national maternity leave program continues to hinder women's career advancement and penalizes them for choosing motherhood. Congresswoman Patricia Schroeder and a bipartisan coalition of representatives championed the issue of parental leave in Congress. The result of their efforts was the Family and Medical Leave Bill, introduced in the Ninety-ninth Congress. This bill proposed that any employee, male or female, had the right to take an unpaid leave of absence of up to eighteen weeks for the care of an infant, a recently adopted child, or an ill dependent. Because of its gender-conscious language, this legislation would not only have eliminated the choice between motherhood and employment, it would have enabled men to take a more active role in parenting or the care of an ill parent. Congress passed the Family and Medical Leave Bill in 1990, and despite resounding support from women's organizations across the nation, President Bush vetoed it (Hartmann 1989; Goldberg 1990).

There is also a need for employer-sponsored initiatives. An important first step is the voluntary implementation of comparable worth and an aggressive affirmative action program. Equally important is the provision of affordable, quality day-care facilities. With close to eighteen million mothers working, the issue of child care can no longer be ignored (Weiner, L. 1985; Barrett 1987; Hardesty and Jacobs 1986). Awareness of the issue has grown in recent years; however, it has not translated into action. Only about 1 percent of U.S. companies, or 3,000, have established day-care facilities for their employees (Faludi 1991). Even though cost and feasibility are cited as the primary deterrents, the demographic composition of the labor force merits an expansion of the traditional employee benefits package to include child care in addition to pensions and insurance. As is the case with other benefits, employer participation is less costly than an across-the-board wage adjustment that would permit workers to pay for services privately. Most large and many medium-sized firms have the resources for limited capacity, on-site facilities, but other alternatives are available. Small companies can collaborate on a cooperative facility, or a day-care program can be established through shared contributions by the federal and state governments, corporations, and parents. Other initiatives that enable women to balance economic need with family responsibilities are job sharing and flexible scheduling. In either instance, by allowing women to work hours other than a regular nine-to-five schedule, employers provide alternatives to low paid, part-time work and offer women the opportunity to pursue meaningful employment (Weiner, L. 1985; Hardesty and Jacobs 1986; Barrett 1987).

While economists, academics, and feminists in business repeatedly emphasize how the aforementioned strategies will improve the position of women in the American economy, perhaps the best strategy of all is making employers realize how discrimination against women is detrimental to business and economic growth. By forcing women to chose between job and motherhood, employers as well as women lose out. Companies experience an exodus of talent and incur costs related to turnover and training new employees. By limiting women's opportunities for advancement, companies limit their own access to human and intellectual resources. Economic equality must be recognized as good business practice.

Conclusion

Throughout the history of this country, women have always worked. Women's experiences and opportunities have existed within, and have been shaped by, prevailing economic forces. During the various stages of American economic development, women have made valuable contributions to the household economy through unpaid labor as well as working in the labor force. Women have supported their families and participated in the economic growth of the nation as agriculturalists, producers, caretakers, and consumers.

The dramatic advance of women into the labor force since the 1950s has not been accompanied by a transformation of the household economy. The dichotomy of the private and public spheres has not been eliminated. Women find themselves caught in an economic double bind; their labor in the home is devalued because it is unpaid; and their contributions in the labor market are considered secondary in importance to their domestic responsibilities. Society expects that women will balance the demands of paid and unpaid labor, an expectation not placed upon men. Many strategies for economic change have surfaced in recent decades such as affirmative action and comparable worth—but any plan for economic equality must challenge the sex-based division of labor in the home as well as in the work place.

References

Ando, Faith H. 1990. Women in business. In *The American woman, 1990–91: A status report.* Edited by Sara E. Rix, 222–30. New York: W. W. Norton and Co.

Arendell, Terry J. 1987. Women and the economics of divorce in the contemporary United States. *Signs: Journal of Women in Culture and Society* 13:121–35.

Bailyn, Bernard. 1979. The New England merchants in the seventeenth century. Cambridge: Harvard University Press.

Barrett, Nancy S. 1982. Obstacles to economic parity for women. *American Economic Review* 72:160–65.

————. 1987. Women and the economy. In *The American woman, 1987–88: A report in depth.* Edited by Sara E. Rix, 100–149. New York: W. W. Norton and Company.

Bergmann, Barbara R. 1981. The Economic risks of being a housewife. *American Economic Review* 71:81–85.

Binion, Gayle. 1987. Affirmative action reconsidered: Justifications, objections, myths and misconceptions. *Women and Politics* 7:43–62.

Blackford, Mansel G. 1991. *A history of small business in America.* New York: Twayne Publishers.

Blum, Linda, and Vicki Smith. 1988. Women's mobility in the corporation: A critique of the politics of optimism. *Signs: Journal of Women in Culture and Society* 13:528–45.

Brenner, Johanna. 1987. Feminization of poverty and comparable worth: Radical versus liberal approaches. *Gender and Society* 1:447–65.

Brown, Judith K. 1975. Iroquois women: An ethnohistoric note. In *Toward an anthropology of women.* Edited by Rayna Reiter, 235–51. New York: Monthly Review Press.

Chafe, William H. 1972. *The American woman: Her changing social, economic, and political roles, 1920–1970.* New York: Oxford University Press.

Cott, Nancy F. 1977. *The bonds of motherhood: "Woman's sphere" in New England, 1780-1835.* New Haven, Conn.: Yale University Press.

Cowan, Ruth Schwartz. 1983. *More work for mother: The ironies of household technology from the open hearth to the microwave.* New York: Basic Books.

Crosby, Faye, and Susan Clayton. 1990. Affirmative action and the issue of expectancies. *Journal of Social Issues* 46:61–79.

Dublin, Thomas. 1979. *Women at work: The transformation of work and community in Lowell, Massachusetts, 1826–1860.* New York: Columbia University Press.

Faludi, Susan. 1991. *Backlash: The undeclared war against American women.* New York: Crown Publishers.

Garfinkel, Irwin, and Sara McLanahan. 1988. The feminization of poverty: Nature, causes, and a partial cure. In *Poverty and social welfare in the United States.* Edited by Donald Tomaskovic-Devey, 27–52. Boulder: Westview Press.

Goldberg, Gertrude Schaffner. 1990. The United States: Feminization of poverty amidst plenty. In *The feminization of poverty, only in America?* Edited by Gertrude Schaffner Goldberg and Eleanor Kremen, 17–58. New York: Greenwood Press.

Goldberg, Gertrude Schaffner, and Eleanor Kremen. 1990. The feminization of poverty: Discovered in America. In *The feminization of poverty, only in America?* Edited by Gertrude Schaffner Goldberg and Eleanor Kremen, 1–15. New York: Greenwood Press.

Groneman, Carol, and Mary Beth Norton. 1987. *"To toil the live-long day": America's women at work.* Ithaca, N.Y.: Cornell University Press.

Hardesty, Sarah, and Nehama Jacobs. 1986. *Success and betrayal: The crisis of women in corporate America.* New York: Touchstone, Simon and Schuster, Inc.

Hartmann, Susan M. 1989. *From margin to mainstream: American women and politics since 1960.* New York: Alfred A. Knopf.

————. 1982. *The home front and beyond: American women in the 1940s.* Boston: Twayne Publishers.

Helburn, Suzanne, and John Morris. 1988. Economic needs of low-income single mothers in Denver: Their cost of living, labor market readiness, and job opportunities. Unpublished paper presented to the Denver Area Women's Research Colloquium, Metropolitan State College of Denver, February 5, 1988.

Hennig, Margaret, and Anne Jardim. 1977. *The managerial woman.* New York: Anchor Press.

Howe, Louise Kapp. 1977. *Pink collar workers: Inside the world of women's work.* New York: G. P. Putnam's Sons.

Jones, Jacqueline. 1985. *Labor of love, labor of sorrow: Black women, work, and the family from slavery to the present.* New York: Basic Books.

Kanter, Rosabeth Moss. 1977. *Women and men of the corporation.* New York: Basic Books.

Katzman, David M. 1981. *Seven days a week: Women and domestic service in industrializing America.* Urbana: University of Illinois Press.

Kennedy, Susan Estabrook. 1979. *If all we did was to weep at home: A history of white working class women in America.* Bloomington: Indiana University Press.

Kessler-Harris, Alice. 1990. *A woman's wage: Historical meanings and social consequences.* Lexington: The University of Kentucky Press.

———. 1982. *Out to work: A history of wage-earning women in the United States.* Oxford: Oxford University Press.

———. 1981. *Women have always worked: A historical overview.* Old Westbury, N.Y.: The Feminist Press.

Leacock, Eleanor Burke, and Nancy Oestreich Lurie. 1971. *North American Indians in historical perspective.* New York: Random House.

Mezey, Susan Gluck. 1992. *In pursuit of equality: Women, public policy, and the federal courts.* New York: St. Martin's Press.

Morgan, Edmund S. 1975. *American slavery, American freedom: The ordeal of colonial Virginia.* New York: W. W. Norton and Company.

Oakley, Ann. 1974. *The sociology of housework.* New York: Pantheon Books.

———. 1974. *Woman's work: The housewife, past and present.* New York: Vintage Books.

Oswalt, Wendell H. 1978. *This land was theirs: A study of North American Indians.* 3rd ed. New York: John Wiley and Sons.

National Center for Health Services Research. 1986. *The feminization of poverty and older women.* Washington, D.C.: U.S. Department of Health and Human Services.

Pleck, Joseph H. 1977. The work-family role system. *Social Problems* 24:417–27.

Rhode, Deborah L. 1990. Gender equality and employment policy. In *The American woman, 1990–91: A status report.* Edited by Sara E. Rix, 170–200. New York: W. W. Norton and Company.

Rothenberg, Diane. 1980. Mothers of the nation: Seneca resistance to Quaker intervention. In *Women and colonization: Anthropological perspectives.* Edited by Mona Etienne and Eleanor Leacock, 63–87. New York: Praeger Publishers.

Rupp, Leila. 1978. *Mobilizing women for war: German and American propaganda, 1939-1945.* Princeton, N.J.: Princeton University Press.

Spencer, Robert F., Jesse D. Jennings et al. 1977. *The Native Americans: Ethnology and backgrounds of the Native American Indians.* New York: Harper and Row.

Strasser, Susan. 1982. *Never done: A history of American housework.* New York: Pantheon Books.

Stetson, Dorothy McBride. 1990. *Women's rights in the U.S.A.: Policy debates and gender roles.* Pacific Grove, Calif.: Brooks/Cole Publishing Company.

Taylor, Susan H. 1989. The case for comparable worth. *Journal of Social Issues* 45:23-37.

Tobias, Sheila, and Sharon Bernstein Megdal. 1985. Rethinking comparable worth: Do all roads lead to equity? *Educational Record* (Fall 1985):27–31.

Ulrich, Laurel Thatcher. 1982. *Good wives: Image and reality in the lives of women in northern New England, 1650–1750.* New York: Alfred A. Knopf.

Van Dyke, Joyce. 1987. Women in business. In *The American woman, 1987–88: A report in depth.* Edited by Sara E. Rix, 197–201. New York: W. W. Norton and Company.

Vertz, Laura L. 1987. Pay inequalities between women and men in state and local government: An examination of the political context of the comparable worth controversy. In *Women and Politics* 7:93–57.

Walton, Gary M., and James F. Shepherd. 1979. *The economic rise of early America.* Cambridge: Cambridge University Press.

Ware, Susan. 1982. *Holding their own: American women in the 1930s.* Boston: Twayne Publishers.

Waring, Marilyn. 1988. *If women counted: A new feminist economics.* San Francisco: Harper and Row.

Weiner, Jon. 1985. Women's history on trial. In *The Nation* (September 1985):176–80.

Weiner, Lynn Y. 1985. *From working girl to working mother: Female labor force in the United States, 1820–1980.* Chapel Hill, N.C.: The University of North Carolina Press.

Westkott, Marcia, Jody Fitzpatrick, Lynda Dickson, and Gay Francis. 1988. Comparable worth versus the free market: A case study. *Frontiers* 10:6–13.

White, Deborah Gray. 1985. *Ain't I a woman? Female slaves in the plantation south.* New York: W. W. Norton and Company.

Zopf, Paul E., Jr. 1989. *American women in poverty.* New York: Greenwood Press.

Peril and Promise: Lesbians' Workplace Participation

Beth Schneider

Lesbians must work. Put most simply, few lesbians will ever have, however briefly, the economic support of another person (man or woman); lesbians are dependent on themselves for subsistence. Thus, a significant portion of the time and energies of most lesbians is devoted to working. Working as a central feature of lesbian existence is, however, rarely acknowledged. As with any significant primary commitment by a woman to job or career, a lesbian's relationship to work is obscured, denied, or trivialized by cultural assumptions concerning heterosexuality.[1]

Moreover, the concept "lesbian" is so identified with sexual behavior and ideas of deviance, particularly in social science literature,[2] that it has been easy to ignore the fact that lesbians spend their time at other than sexual activities; for a lesbian, working is much more likely to be a preoccupation than her sexual or affectional relations. Given the limited research on the sexual behavior of lesbians over the course of their lives, it is no surprise that there is decidedly less known about the working lives and commitments of lesbians.

In asserting the centrality, if not the primacy, of a working life to lesbians, we assume that work provides both a means of economic survival and a source of personal integrity, identity, and strength. While lesbians are certainly not the only women whose identities are at least partially formed by their relationship to work, in a culture defined for women in terms of heterosexual relations and limited control over the conditions of motherhood, most lesbians are likely to have fewer of the commitments and relations considered appropriate and necessary to the prevailing conceptions of women.

On the other hand, work and one's relationship to it is considered a major source of economic and social status, personal validation, and life purpose—certainly for men—in this society.[3] For lesbians then, whose lives will not necessarily provide or include the constraints or the comforts that other women receive ("heterosexual privileges"), working may well take on additional and special meaning. Thus, lesbians' workplace participation is shaped by the possibility of a unique commitment to working, an outside status by dint of sexual identity, and the set of conditions common to all women workers. The conflicting aspects of these forces define the problematic and often paradoxical context within which lesbians work.

Schneider, Beth. 1984. "Peril and Promise: Lesbians' workplace participation." In *Woman-Identified Women*. eds. Trudie Darty and Sandee Potter. Mountain View, CA: Mayfield Publishing Company. Reprinted by permission of the editor, Sandee Potter.

Being a woman worker has many implications for lesbians' material, social, and emotional well-being. Compared to their male counterparts, women employed full-time continue to receive significantly less pay.[4] Most do not have college degrees and enter occupations of traditional female employment where unionization is rare, benefits meager, and prestige lacking.[5] Continued employment in female-dominated occupations maintains women's disadvantage relative to men, since it is associated with lower wages; typically, lower wages keep women dependent on men—their husbands (when they have them) or their bosses.[6] In those situations in which women and men are peers at work, status distinctions remain, reflecting the realities of sexism in the workplace and the society.[7] In general, then, women are on the lower end of job and authority hierarchies. In addition, basic to the economic realities of all working women is the need to appear (through dress and demeanor) sexually attractive to men, who tend to hold the economic position and power to enforce heterosexual standards and desires.[8]

Thus, as one portion of the female labor force, lesbians are in a relatively powerless and devalued position, located in workplaces occupied but not controlled by women. Herein lies one paradox of a great many lesbians' working lives. The world of women's labor—with its entrenched occupational and job segregation—creates a homosocial female environment, a milieu potentially quite comfortable for lesbians.

But lesbians must also manage their sexual identity difference at work.[9] As women whose sexual, political, and social activities are primarily with other women, lesbians are daily confronted with heterosexual assumptions at work. The nature and extent of heterosexual pressures (over and above those experienced by all women) condition the nature of their social relationships. Two markedly different dynamics simultaneously affect lesbians in their daily interactions at work.

Negative attitudes toward homosexuality are still widespread in the society. The statements and activities of New Right leaders and organizations and the research results of a number of studies on less politicized populations indicate that lesbians and male homosexuals must continue to be cautious in their dealings with the heterosexual world and to be wary of being open about their sexual identity in certain occupations—especially teaching.[10]

Directly related to these public attitudes, employment-related issues and articles tend to predominate in the lesbian and gay press. Either legislative and political efforts toward an end to discrimination are detailed and progress assessed, or some person or persons who have lost their jobs or personal credibility when their sexual identity has become known or suspected are written up. For example, recently readers of both the alternative press and mass media have seen accounts of the anticipated disastrous financial consequences of a publicly revealed lesbian relationship on the women's tennis tour, community censure of public officials who spoke in favor of antidiscrimination laws, lesbian feminists fired or not rehired at academic jobs, and a purge of suspected lesbians aboard a Navy missile ship, among others.[11]

Nevertheless, there is little systematic evidence that indicates how particular heterosexuals react to lesbians in concrete situations. It is these daily encounters and interactions with heterosexuals that are of crucial concern to lesbians; at work, the disclosure of one's sexual identity might have serious consequences. In a recent study of job discrimination against lesbians, fully 50 percent anticipated discrimination at work and 22 percent reported losing a job when their sexual identity became known.[12] But in addition, lesbians fear harassment and isolation from interpersonal networks; often they live under pressure or demands to prove they are as good or better workers than their coworkers.[13]

Whether anyone is fired or legislation is won or lost, the world of work is perceived and experienced by lesbians as troublesome, ambiguous, problematic. And while it is generally assumed that lesbians are more tolerated than gay men and therefore safer at work and elsewhere, a climate of ambivalence and disapproval pervades the world within which lesbians work; most are not likely to feel immediately comfortable about their relationships to coworkers.

Despite these significant disadvantages and potential troubles, a number of studies consistently show that lesbians have stable work histories, are higher achievers than comparable heterosexual women,[14] and have a serious commitment to work, giving it priority because they must support themselves.[15] These findings suggest, but do not describe or document, that lesbians' workplace survival results from a complicated calculation of the degree to which a particular work setting allows them freedom to be open and allows for the negotiation and development of a support network.

At work and elsewhere, lesbians want and have friendships and relationships with other women; while some research suggests that lesbians are no different than single heterosexuals in the extent of their friendship networks, other describe much greater social contacts for lesbians since they must negotiate two possibly overlapping worlds (work and social life) and most are free of familial constraints that pull other women away from work relationships.[16] Whatever the extent of their networks, it is these friendships and relationships that are a major source of workplace support—and complication—for lesbians, as well as an important facet of their emotional well-being and job satisfaction.

However, there is virtually no research that systematically explores lesbian work sociability, the creation of a support mechanism there, or the conditions under which lesbians are willing to make their sexual identity known. Most of what is known about these problems is based on findings from research on male homosexuals, and therefore does not take into account the greater importance women as a group, and lesbians specifically, attach to emotional support and relationships.[17] Nevertheless, this research indicates that the more a male is known as a homosexual, the less stressful are his relationships with heterosexuals because he does not anticipate and defend against rejection.[18] But economic success frequently requires denying one's sexual identity: research findings over the last decade are consistent in showing that high-status males are less open than low-status males.[19] A combination of avoidance, information control, and role distance are strategies used by homosexuals to preserve secrecy; the result is often the appearance of being boring, unfriendly, sexless, or heterosexual.[20]

In addition to focusing on men, many of these studies were completed prior to, or at the onset of, the gay liberation movement, which has continued to encourage and emphasize "coming out" for reasons of either political principle and obligation or personal health.[21] Certainly, in the last decade many lesbians have taken extraordinary risks in affirming their sexual identities and defending their political and social communities.[22]

In sum, lesbians' relationship to the world of work is both ordinary and unique. Based on findings from a recent study of 228 lesbian workers, a number of previously unexamined aspects of the conditions of lesbian participation at the workplace are explored here. Following a brief description of the research project from which these data are taken and a discussion of the sample generation and characteristics, four aspects of lesbian existence at work are discussed: (1) making friends, (2) finding a partner, (3) coming out, and (4) being harassed.

Research Methods and Sample

The findings are part of a larger research project on working women (both lesbian and heterosexual) and their perspectives and experiences concerning sociability, sexual relationships, and sexual harassment at the workplace.[23] The project was not explicitly designed to directly examine instances of discrimination against lesbians and cannot adequately address that problem. It was designed to explore some of the more subtle interpersonal terrain that all women are likely to encounter at work, as well as those situations of particular concern to lesbians.

The lesbian sample was gathered with the assistance of twenty-eight contacts who provided me with the names, addresses, and approximate ages of women who they thought were lesbians. The contacts provided 476 names. A self-administered questionnaire with 316 items was mailed to 307 of these contacts during the period between January and March 1980. The letter that accompanied the questionnaire did not assume any knowledge of a particular woman's sexual identity. Eighty-one percent of these women returned the questionnaire, a very high rate of return that seems to reflect significant interest in all the topics covered.

There were 228 women who identified themselves as either lesbian or homosexual or gay in the question asking for current sexual identity. This sample of lesbians ranged in age from 21 to 58 (median = 29.4); 10 percent were women of color (most Afro-American).[24] The sample was unique in that it was not a San Francisco– or New York City–based population; 55 percent were from New England, 33 percent from Middle Atlantic states, and the rest from other locations east of the Mississippi River.

The lesbians in this study were employed in all kinds of workplaces.[25] More than half (57 percent) were in professional or technical occupational categories (in such jobs as teaching and social work), with the remaining distributed as follows: administrative and managerial (10 percent), clerical (11 percent), craft (7 percent), service (7 percent), operative (5 percent), and sales (2 percent). Sixty-nine percent worked full-time, 20 percent part-time, and the rest were unemployed at the time of the survey. Fifty-two percent were employed in predominantly (55 to 100 percent) female workplaces, 25 percent in workplaces with 80 percent or more females; 10 percent worked in units with 80 percent or more males. While the educational attainment of this group of lesbians was very high for a population of adult women (82 percent were at least college graduates), their median income was $8,800 (in 1979). The low income of the total group reflects a combination of its relative youth and the proportion with less than full-time or full-year employment.

Two questions were asked to determine lesbians' openness about themselves at work, a matter of crucial concern to any understanding of daily workplace experiences. The first asked: "How open would you say you are about your lesbianism at your *present* job?" The choices were: "Totally," "Mostly," "Somewhat," "Not at all." The participants varied widely in the extent to which they felt they were open at work: Only 16 percent felt they were totally open, while 55 percent tended to be and 29 percent were closed about who they were at work.

The second question asked the proportion of each woman's coworkers who knew she was a lesbian. Twenty-five percent estimated that *all* their coworkers knew about their sexual identity,[26] half estimated that at least one or "some" knew, and 14 percent stated that "none knew." The remainder simply "didn't know" if anyone knew they were lesbians, a difficult and often anxiety-provoking situation.

Making Friends

Most lesbians sampled believed it desirable to integrate their work and social lives in some ways.[27] Thus the distinction between public and private life is not terribly useful in describing their lives, despite its persistence as ideology throughout the culture.[28] For example, only one-third maintained that they kept their social life completely separate from their work life, and 39 percent tried not to discuss personal matters with persons from work. Alternatively, 43 percent believed that doing things socially with coworkers makes relationships run more smoothly.

There obviously was variability in beliefs. Lesbians who most consistently and strongly held the view that work and social life should be integrated fell into two categories: those who had to—that is, lesbians in professional employment whose jobs required a certain level of sociability and collegiality; and those who had nothing to lose—women in dead-end jobs with no promise of advancement, those with few or no supervisory responsibilities, and those who were already open with persons from work about their sexual identity.

On the other hand, women who could not or did not believe these spheres could be easily or truly integrated were constrained by powerful forces that limited and denied the possibility of such integration: lesbians in male-dominated workplaces and those in worksites with male supervisors and bosses, in which males bond with each other, often to the exclusion and detriment of the females.

The beliefs of the lesbians in the sample were quite consistent with the actual extent of their social contacts with persons from work. Most lesbians (in fact, most women) maintained social ties with at least some persons from work—at the job and outside it. Not surprisingly, 84 percent ate lunch with coworkers, but fewer engaged in social activities outside the work setting. For example, 9 percent visited frequently, 55 percent visited occasionally at each other's homes, 8 percent frequently and 47 percent occasionally went out socially with persons from work.

Two aspects of these findings merit further comment. First, the figures for the lesbians differ by less than 1 percent from those of the heterosexual women workers in the larger research project; if lesbians curtail contact or make certain judgments about coworkers as acquaintances or friends, they may do so for different reasons, but they do so to an extent similar to heterosexual women.

Second, certain conditions determine both lesbians' beliefs about and the extensiveness of their social contacts. Those in professional employment have more social ties with persons from work than lesbians in working-class jobs (which as a rule require less sociability); lesbians who are older, who have come to be familiar with a particular job setting over a length of time, and those who are open about their sexual identity are much more likely to maintain social contacts with coworkers than their younger or more closeted counterparts. In this particular study, there were no differences of any significance between lesbians of color and whites with regard to sociability; in fact, the lesbians of color had, as a group, more contact with coworkers. This is not surprising in that the networking that produced the original sample reached only as far as a particular group of lesbians of color, who were disproportionately employed in feminist workplaces such as women's centers and women's studies programs, locations that facilitate, however imperfectly, such sociability. Those conditions in which a female culture can develop (granted, often within the limits of a male work world) allow lesbians greater possibilities for being open about their sexual identity with at least some coworkers. Familiar and supportive conditions tend to foster friendships and, as will become clear in the next section, provide the basis upon which more intimate relationships may also develop.

When there is a need to be social, lesbians are; professional jobs require sociability, but very many also require some degree of secrecy as well. This is particularly true for work in traditionally male occupations. In addition, and more important given women's location in the occupational structure, working with children (as teachers, nurses, social workers) can be cause for a relatively closeted existence. In this research, working with children did not seem to influence the extent of lesbian sociability, but it did affect how open they were about themselves at their workplaces. Here lies a classic instance of a highly contradictory situation, one common to many persons in human services and educational institutions. An ideology prevails that encourages (often demands) honesty, trust, and congenial nonalienating working relationships, but a lesbian's ability to actively involve herself in the prescribed ways is often limited or contorted. Frye's description of her experience in a women's studies program captures the essence of the difficulties:

> But in my dealings with my heterosexual women's studies colleagues, I do not take my own advice: I have routinely and habitually muffled or stifled myself on the subject of Lesbianism and heterosexualism . . . out of some sort of concern about alienating them. . . . Much more important to me is a smaller number who are my dependable political coworkers in the university, . . . the ones with some commitment to not being homophobic and to trying to be comprehending and supportive of Lesbians and Lesbianism. If I estrange these women, I will lose the only footing I have, politically and personally, in my long-term work-a-day survival in academia. They are important, valuable, and respected allies. I am very careful, over-careful, when I talk about heterosexuality with them.[29]

More traditional workplaces provide even fewer possibilities for support than the one described above.

Finding a Partner

In the last section, brief reference is made to lesbians' sexual relationships at work. The typical story of the office affair seems to have little to do with lesbians. It centers on a boss (the powerful person, the man) and his secretary (the powerless person, the woman); the consequences of this double-edged inequality of occupational status and gender are of prime concern. As the story would have it, the powerful one influences the other's (the woman's) career in such a way that she is highly successful ("She slept her way to the top") or her work and career are permanently ruined. It is rarely acknowledged that relationships at work occur between coworkers or between persons of the same gender, or that the consequences may be close to irrelevant—at least with regard to the job. When acknowledged, it seems that heterosexual affairs are more tolerated than are lesbian or homosexual relations.[30]

But the facts tell another story.[31] Twenty-one percent of the lesbians in this study met their current partners at work; overall, 52 percent of the lesbians had had at least one sexual relationship with a person from work during their working lives. This amazingly high proportion makes sense when it is remembered that the vast majority of women (and lesbians) are employed in female-dominated workplaces. Such a work setting is a good location for a lesbian to find a potential lover. But in addition, there have traditionally been few places—other than bars—for lesbians to meet each other socially; most met, and still meet, through friendship networks (44 percent). While recently the women's and lesbians' communities have provided some alternatives—restaurants, clubs, political activities—employment plays such a significant part in lesbians' lives (and takes such a significant part of their time) that the workplace becomes an important, almost obvious, site for creating and having friendships and more intimate relationships.

Nineteen percent of the currently self-identified lesbians were heterosexual and 9 percent were married at the time of the sexual relationship they reported. This means that 81 percent were lesbians when they entered into at least a somewhat committed (and potentially risky) relationship with a person from work.

The chances that a lesbian will have a relationship with someone at work increase with age. To illustrate, while 79 percent of the sampled lesbians over forty had had a relationship with someone at work sometime in their lifetime, 59 percent in their thirties and 42 percent in their twenties had had such an involvement. In addition, the longer a woman has identified herself as a lesbian (whatever her age), the more likely she is to have an intimate relationship with a person at work. This certainly suggests that some part of the freedom to pursue an involvement in the work setting is an easiness with oneself as a lesbian and a flexibility and wisdom gained from years of managing the complexities of sexual identity difference at work.

Most of the relationships reported were not brief affairs; 60 percent of the lesbians had been or were currently in a relationship of a year or more duration. Having such a relationship can have many effects, many small and predictable, others large and less controllable. Perhaps most obviously, the longer a relationship lasts, the more likely are some people at work (in addition to friends outside work) to know of the involvement. (In contrast to the heterosexuals in the larger study, lesbians tended to be more secretive about the relationship with people from work.)

Since the "office affair" mythology assumes a heterosexual relationship and the dynamic of superior-subordinate, it is useful to examine who in fact the lesbian workers were involved with. Eighteen percent of the lesbians were involved with a man (most, but not all, were heterosexual at the time); the few self-identified lesbians who were nevertheless involved with a man were almost exclusively involved with their boss in relatively brief affairs. Overall, 75 percent were involved with coworkers, 14 percent with boss or supervisor, 6 percent with subordinates, and 5 percent with customers, clients, and the like. With the female boss still very much a rarity, lesbians are less likely to have the option of a relationship with a woman with institutionalized authority over their working lives. This is in contrast to heterosexual women, whose relationships at work tend to be unequal as a result of the mix of gender and status inequality.

There were only a few consistent and predictable patterns in the effects and consequences of these relationships for the lesbians as a group. Seventy-two percent enjoyed their work more than usual. Some involvements improved relationships with other coworkers (25 percent) while others caused problems with coworkers (35 percent) or trouble with a boss or supervisor (20 percent). Much of the difficulty during the course of the relationship seemed to stem from jealousies, irritation at undone work, or inattention on the part of one or both of the parties to others. Also, the involvements often highlighted the lesbians' sexual identity, forcing them to be less closeted. The data suggest that one of the conflicts a lesbian must face in having a relationship at work is a willingness to either engage in massive secrecy and denial of the situation or become more clear about who she is. Many lesbians (30 percent) reported relief at the end of their involvements in part because hostility or gossip was lessened, in part because the pressures of enforced secrecy were removed.

The effects of being and becoming open about one's sexual identity as a consequence of the relationship are mixed and complicated, and often contradictory. For example, 62 percent of the more open lesbians compared to 19 percent of the more closed ones reported significantly greater friction with coworkers and some (22 percent) felt their chances for advancement were diminished. On the other hand, 31 percent of the more open lesbians reported improvement in workplace relations and improved advancement possibilities (10 percent); they enjoyed their work more than the closed lesbians. It is interesting to note that not one lesbian who was closed about her sexual identity at work believed that her chances for promotion were affected one way or the other by her involvement.

Almost everyone reported suffering the usual kinds of emotional problems at the termination of the relationship, obviously the longer the relationship the more so. The work-related consequences of lesbian involvements with women of similar job status are much simpler and less harmful than those with a superior. Thirteen percent of the lesbians resigned or quit because of the breakup; most of the lesbians who resigned were involved with a boss, rather than a coworker, some few of whom were women. A very few lesbians (4 percent) reported losing out on some career-related opportunity, such as a promotion or pay increase; none reported gaining any work benefit. In 15 percent of the instances, the other person left the job at the termination of the relationship; in all these cases, these were female coworkers.

In general, involvements at work are an integral part of a lesbian's emotional commitments to women. This extension of the prescribed limits of relationships beyond friendship is consistent with most other research on lesbians that similarly shows fluid boundaries between friends and lovers and friendship networks of former lovers.[32]

Coming Out

Most lesbians are acutely aware that their openness about their lesbianism is not an all-or-nothing phenomenon at work or elsewhere but that it varies depending at the very least on the context and on the particular individuals involved. The lesbians in this study clearly varied in their own sense of how open they *felt* they were at work. As we already saw, being open allowed lesbians greater contact with coworkers, facilitating network-building and support as well as being a basis for (and a possible result of) having a sexual relationship with someone at work.

This study indicates that lesbians tend to be open about their sexual identity when their workplace has a predominance of women and most of their work friends are women, when they have a female boss or supervisor, when they are employed in small workplaces, when they have few supervisory responsibilities, when they have relatively low incomes, and when they are not dealing with children as either students, clients, or patients.

Two aspects of these findings require special comment. First, as noted earlier, the situation of professionally employed lesbians is terribly contradictory. Since the jobs require socializing and contacts with others either at work or in the business or professional communities, lesbians maintain those social contacts; on the other hand, high-income professional lesbians are likely to be closeted. The result of this predicament is a well-managed, manicured lie delivered to people with whom one is spending a great deal of time.

Second, the influence of gender proportions is crucial. For example, in workplaces that were heavily female-dominated (80 percent or more women as employees), 55 percent of the lesbians were totally or mostly open about their sexual identity. It is worth noting that this still means that 45 percent tended to be somewhat closeted even in these settings. In contrast, in heavily male-dominated workplaces (80 percent or more men as employees) only 10 percent of the lesbians were open.

A workplace with a predominance of women may include other lesbians to whom a lesbian can be open; they may also become friends or lovers. Of the lesbians who met another lesbian at work, almost all (94 percent) did in fact become friends. But even when there are not other lesbians at work, lesbians take certain risks, trusting at least one heterosexual woman not to react negatively to knowledge of her sexual identity. Moreover, most women are not in a structurally powerful position to affect the conditions under which lesbians work. When lesbians do have a female supervisor or boss, they are more often open about their sexual identity than with a male boss. For example, only 21 percent of lesbians with a male boss were open, compared to 47 percent who were open with a female boss. When lesbians were themselves the boss or were self-employed, 88 percent were open about their sexual identity.

How open a lesbian is at her current job is not related to her age or race or the length of time she has been at that position. However, if she has lost a previous job because she is a lesbian, she is less sociable with people from work at her current job and tends to be more cautious about "coming out" at work. In this study 8 percent of the lesbians reported losing a job when their sexual identity became known and another 2 percent believed (bud did not know for certain) they lost a job for this reason. The relatively young age of this sample may account for the lower proportion of job loss than in other studies. Whatever the extent of their openness, 75 percent of all lesbians were concerned that their lesbianism might cause damage to their job or career.

In summary, openness is most likely under conditions that are intimate and safe, free of potentially serious consequences for a lesbian's working life. That is, lesbians are most likely to be open in a small workplace, with a female boss, in a job with relatively little financial or social reward (and possibly few career risks).

The consequences of being open are substantial. Open lesbians have more friends and more social contact at work than closed lesbians; they are more willing to have, and do have, sexual relationships with women from their workplace. In contrast, and almost by definition, lesbians who are closed about the sexual identity at work are more likely to avoid certain situations with coworkers and feel reluctant to talk about their personal life.

While cause and effect is admittedly difficult to disentangle here, open and closed lesbians differ in the extent to which they feel that their sexual identity causes problems in many areas of their life. This research indicates that lesbians who remain closeted at work are obviously more concerned and afraid than open lesbians about losing their jobs. But in addition, closeted lesbians are much more concerned than open ones about losing their friends, harming their relationship with their parents, and where applicable, harming their lovers' careers or child custody situations. Consistent with this is the finding that openness at work is related to a general freedom to be open elsewhere as well: lesbians who are open at work are more likely to be open with parents and with both female and male heterosexual friends.

Not surprisingly, closed and open lesbians have uniquely different feelings about their positions at work. Closeted lesbians suffer from a sense of powerlessness and significant strain and anxiety at work, while open lesbians have greater emotional freedom. Eighty-four percent of the closed lesbians in the study felt they had no choice about being closeted; two-thirds felt uncomfortable about that decision, and 39 percent felt that the anxiety about being found out was "paralyzing." A significant 35 percent devoted time and emotion to maintaining a heterosexual front at work.

On the other hand, 94 percent of the open lesbians felt better since coming out, and while the strength of their feelings varied, most felt they were treated with respect because of their candor. Forty percent reported that their work relationships were a lot better than they were before coming out. Disclosure of one's sexual identity at work allows for the possibility of integrating into the workplace with less anxiety about who one is and how one is perceived. But there are some negative consequences to coming out. Twenty-nine percent of the open lesbians sensed that some coworkers avoided them and 25 percent admitted to working harder to keep the respect they had from their peers. While these consequences seem insignificant in contrast to the benefits of disclosure, it is good to remember that coming out often can be a quite limited communication to a quite limited number of persons; thus, protection is built into the very choice of context and relationship.

Being Harassed

Eighty-two percent of the lesbians studied experienced sexual approaches at work in the year of the study; that is, 33 percent were sexually propositioned, 34 percent were pinched or grabbed, 54 percent were asked for a date, and 67 percent were joked with about their body or appearance by someone at the workplace.[33] These figures are high for one year; they are, however, comparable to those for the heterosexual women in the larger research project who were of similar race and age. Relatively young, unmarried women (this fits the description of most of the lesbians in the study) and those who worked in male-dominated work settings were most often the recipients of these sexual approaches. Ironically enough, the lesbians who tended to be secretive about their sexual identity (therefore presumed to be heterosexual) were more often sexually approached in these particular ways than the more open lesbians. For example, while 32 percent of the more closed lesbians were pinched or grabbed, only 12 percent of the more open were; likewise, 26 percent of the more closed in contrast to 13 percent of the more open were sexually propositioned.

In comments written to the researcher, it became evident that some lesbians were occasionally referring to both women and men in reporting on date requests and jokes, the more prevalent types of interactions. Unfortunately, the data for these experiences did not specify the gender of the initiator, thus making impossible a true profile of all interpersonal dynamics of this sort.

When asked their emotional response to these experiences ("like," "mixed," "dislike"), the great majority (more than 90 percent) reported disliking pinching or grabbing and sexual propositions—whoever initiated them; few lesbians in fact ever reported liking any such incident. The one exception was being asked for a date by a coworker, and even here only 9 percent said they liked this interaction, with 46 percent "mixed." Toleration (mixed feelings) was the main response to jokes and date requests. And in all cases, coworkers were the most tolerated group of initiators; some of these coworkers may well be women. Typically, coworkers do not have the institutionalized authority to affect each other's job or career standing though they may nevertheless make life more difficult in these kinds of ways.

We cannot directly infer from these data the meaning of these experiences to lesbian workers. Unwanted sexual approaches can be seen as harassment explicitly targeted at a lesbian because she is a lesbian or as harassment typically experienced by most working women. These sexual approaches highlight the disadvantages of lesbians in a working environment by emphasizing heterosexual norms of intimacy and behavior and accenting further the outsider position many lesbians feel at work. Research that compares lesbian workers with heterosexual women workers indicates that while lesbians and heterosexuals have a quite similar number of such approaches in their daily lives, these interactions are experienced quite differently. Lesbians are more sensitive to the problem of unwanted sexual approaches and are much more willing than heterosexuals to label behaviors of this type as sexual harassment.[34]

Conclusion

This research was an effort using quantative data to describe the context of daily life at work for lesbians and to understand the sources of lesbian survival at work. It was not a definitive study of the prevalence of lesbian job loss or harassment.

The findings showed fewer difficulties at work than other studies seem to indicate, but like that research, it insufficiently explored the meanings lesbians attach to particular situations. One obvious question that remains is the extent to which a problem or harassment situation at work is attributed specifically to discrimination on the basis of sexual identity rather than understood as a reflection of the general condition of women. In this research (in which all but one of the lesbians indicated that she was a feminist), the interpretation of events is complicated and complex.

Applying a feminist interpretation to certain workplace situations could diminish or exaggerate the extent to which lesbians perceive those instances as resulting from, or in reaction to, their lesbianism. Sexual harassment is a particularly clear case. A lesbian may well wonder why she was hugged by a male coworker: was it a gesture of friendship,

273

harassment specifically directed to her as a lesbian, or harassment similar to that most women encounter at work? If most lesbians considered the variety of harassing experiences at work discrimination against them as lesbians, the proportion reporting workplace problems would surely increase.

While a more complete picture of workplace problems awaits additional research, these findings underscore some important dimensions of lesbians' workplace participation. First, the experience of lesbians is both similar and different from that of heterosexual women workers. It is similar in (1) the creation of a supportive environment of work friends, (2) the experience of unwanted sexual approaches from various parties with whom they interact, and (3) the use of the workplace to meet sexual partners. It is different in (1) the necessity of strategizing in the face of fear of disclosure and possible job loss, and (2) the meanings attached to interactions and events in the workplace.

While the fear of job or career loss or damage is often uppermost in a recitation of workplace problems, most lesbians do not lose their jobs. Two mutually reinforcing aspects of a strategy seem to account for this general lack of this most serious and negative sanction. First, lesbians tend to remain closeted, keeping their sexual identity secret from most persons at work; at the same time, they create an environment that protects them, emotional ties with a few people who contribute to a sense of a less hostile and alienating work world.

Coming out is clearly a process; within any particular institutional context, such as work, an assessment is made as to the degree to which a lesbian can be open about who she is. The extent of disclosure varies, dependent on the particulars of personnel and place; it changes over time. Certainly few are the lesbians and fewer still the workplaces that can manage or tolerate complete disclosure. At the minimum, lesbians come out when they are ready and conditions are good, meaning in some workplaces and with some people. While the exact process is not detailed here, it is clear that coming out occurs when a woman believes that a person is trustworthy, sensitive, or politically aware. This is an assessment over which a lesbian has some control. When a lesbian is known as such at work, a congenial and supportive relationship has typically preceded disclosure.

The ease with which a lesbian is disclosing about her sexual identity reflects historically specific conditions as well. In this sample of highly politicized lesbian women workers in late 1979, 40 percent felt they were totally or most open about being lesbians; 75 percent were concerned that their lesbianism might affect their employment situation. In the current climate of conservatism reflected in recent efforts to defend and preserve the "sanctity of the family,"[35] lesbians are forced constantly to weigh the costs of disclosure. Thus, a combination of forces—personal choice, workplace characteristics, and political concerns—continues to define the options and limitations of the workplace environment.

Finally, female support systems at work—allies and networks—can be seen as an integral part of lesbians' emotional commitments to women. While it is certainly ironic and contradictory to proclaim the virtues of "women's work," with its devalued economic and social worth, those workplaces do provide an easier, more congenial atmosphere than is immediately available in more highly paid, male-segregated locations. Many lesbians know these facts and in decisions regarding work may well take them into account.

While the fear and peril of lesbians' workplace situation cannot be denied or diminished, neither can the challenge. Lesbians' participation and relationship to work is similar to the kind of "double vision" shared by other groups who are outsiders:[36] an acute awareness of the strength and force of an oppressive ideology of heterosexuality and its structural manifestations, coupled with an active accommodation and creation of a livable working environment.

Notes

1. The socioemotional climate of work is based on strong cultural assumptions of heterosexuality. An ideology of heterosexuality includes the following beliefs: (1) All persons are heterosexual. (2) All intimate relationships occur between persons of opposite gender. (3) Heterosexual relationships are better—healthier, more normal—than homosexual relations. With regard to employment, the ideology assumes that every woman is defined by, and in some way is the property of, a man (father, husband, boss); thus a woman's work is secondary, since she is, will be, or ought to be supported by a man. See the following for statements concerning the cultural and structural dimensions of heterosexuality: Charlotte Bunch, "Not for Lesbians Only"; Gayle Rubin, "The Traffic in Women: Notes on the 'Political Economy' of Sex," in Rayna Rapp, ed. *Toward an Anthropology of Women* (New York: Monthly Review Press, 1975), pp. 157–210; Catharine A. MacKinnon, *Sexual Harassment of Working Women: A Case of Sex Discrimination* (New Haven: Yale University Press, 1979); Adrienne Rich, "Compulsory Heterosexuality and Lesbian Existence"; Lisa Leghorn and Katherine Parker, *Woman's Worth: Sexual Economics and the World of Women* (Boston: Routledge & Kegan Paul, 1981).
2. See Anabel Faraday, "Liberating Lesbian Research," and Kenneth Plummer, "Homosexual Categories: Some Research Problems in the Labelling Perspective of Homosexuality," in Kenneth Plummer, ed., *The Making of the Modern Homosexual* (Totowa, N.J.: Barnes & Noble, 1981).
3. For a review of the literature on the relationship of work to individual well-being, see Rosabeth Moss Kanter, *Work and Family in the United States: A Critical Review and Agenda for Research and Policy* (New York: Russell Sage, 1977).
4. U.S. Bureau of Labor Statistics, *Perspectives of Working Women: A Databook*, Bulletin 2080 (Washington, D.C.: U.S. Government Printing Office, 1980).
5. Louise Kapp Howe, *Pink-Collar Workers: Inside the World of Women's Work* (New York: G. P. Putnam, 1977).
6. Heidi Hartman, "Capitalism, Patriarchy, and Job Segregation by Sex," in Zillah Eisenstein, ed., *Capitalist Patriarchy and the Case for Socialist Feminism* (New York: Monthly Review Press, 1979), pp. 206–47.
7. Neal Gross and Anne Trask, *The Sex Factor and Management of Schools* (New York: Wiley, 1976); and Rosabeth Moss Kanter, *Men and Women of the Corporation* (New York: Basic Books, 1977).
8. MacKinnon (see n. 1 above).
9. Throughout this article, sexual identity, rather than sexual orientation or sexual preference, is the term used to describe and distinguish heterosexual and lesbian

women. As a construct, sexual identity most adequately describes the process of creating and maintaining an identity as a sexual being. In contrast to sexual orientation, it does not assume an identity determined by the end of childhood; in contrast to sexual preference, it does not narrow the focus to the gender of one's partner or to particular sexual practices. See Plummer (n. 2 above) for a recent discussion of the issues and problems of homosexual categorization in the social sciences.

10. Amber Hollibaugh, "Sexuality and the State: The Defeat of the Briggs Initiative," *Socialist Review* 45 (May–June 1979): 55–72; Linda Gordon and Alan Hunter, "Sex, Family and the New Right," *Radical America* 11 November 1977–February 1978); George Gallup, "Report on the Summer 1977 Survey of Attitudes Toward Homosexuality," *Boston Globe*, September 10, 1977; Albert Klassen, Jr., and Eugene Levitt, "Public Attitudes Toward Homosexuality," *Journal of Homosexuality* 1 (1974): 29–43.

11. See any issue of *Gay Community News* and any newsletter of the National Gay Task Force for a more complete sampling of these types of stories; also see Judith McDaniel, "We Were Fired: Lesbian Experiences in Academe," *Sinister Wisdom* 20 (Spring 1982): 30–43; and J. R. Roberts, *Black Lesbians* (Tallahassee, Florida: Naiad Press, 1981), pp. 74–76.

12. Martin P. Levine and Robin Leonard, "Discrimination Against Lesbians in the Workforce," paper presented at annual meeting of the American Sociological Association, September 1982.

13. Sasha Gregory Lewis, *Sunday's Women: A Report on Lesbian Life Today* (Boston: Beacon Press, 1979); Laud Humphreys, *Out of the Closets: The Sociology of Homosexual Liberation* (Englewood Cliffs, N.J.: Prentice-Hall, 1972).

14. Jack Hedblom, "The Female Homosexual: Social and Attitudinal Dimensions," in Joseph McCaffrey, ed., *The Homosexual Dialectic* (Englewood Cliffs, N.J.: Prentice-Hall, 1972); William Simon and John Gagnon, "The Lesbians: A Preliminary Overview," in W. Simon and J. Gagnon, eds., *Sexual Deviance* (New York: Harper & Row, 1967), pp. 247–82.

15. Fred A. Minnegerode and Marcy Adelman, "Adaptations of Aging Homosexual Men and Women," paper presented at Convention of the Gerontological Society, October 1976.

16. For an analysis that suggests a similarity of friendship networks between lesbians and single heterosexual women, see Andrea Oberstone and Harriet Sukoneck, "Psychological Adjustment and Lifestyles of Single Lesbians: and Single Heterosexual Women," *Psychology of Women Quarterly* 1 (Winter 1976): 172–88; for one that suggests differences between these two groups, see Alan Bell and Martin Weinberg, *Homosexualities: A Study of Diversity Among Men and Women*.

17. E. M. Ettorre, *Lesbians, Women, and Society* (New York: Methuen, 1980).

18. Martin Weinberg and Colin Williams, *Male Homosexuals: Their Problems and Adaptations* (New York: Oxford University Press, 1975).

19. Joseph Harry, "Costs and Correlates of the Closet," paper presented at annual meeting of the American Sociological Association, September 1982; also, Humphreys (n. 13 above).

20. Kenneth Plummer, *Sexual Stigma: An Interactionist Account* (London: Routledge & Kegan Paul, 1977).

21. Karla Jay and Allen Young, eds., *Out of the Closets: Voices of Gay Liberation* (New York: Pyramid Books, 1972); Karla Jay and Allen Young, eds., *Lavender Culture* (New York: Jove, 1978). See particularly Barbara Grier, "Neither Profit Nor Salvation," in *Lavender Culture*, pp. 412–20.

22. William Paul et al., eds., *Homosexuality: Social, Psychological, and Biological Issues* (Beverly Hills, Calif.: Sage, 1972).

23. For those interested in more detailed statistical and analytical discussion of the findings of this research, see Beth E. Schneider, "Consciousness about Sexual Harassment Among Heterosexual and Lesbian Women Workers," *Journal of Social Issues* 38 (December 1982): 75–97; and Beth E. Schneider, "The Sexualization of the Workplace" (Ph.D. dissertation, University of Massachusetts, 1981).

24. It is difficult to assess the accuracy of the proportion of lesbians of color in this sample since the population is unknown. Moreover, because of racism in the feminist and lesbian communities as well as the varying extent to which sexual identity rather than race or class identity is most salient to lesbians of color, many may not be part of lesbian community networks. Thus, the sampling procedures used here—working through contacts (only two of whom were lesbians of color)—likely proved inadequate to reach them.

25. The only concern of this article is with lesbians in paid employment. Necessarily excluded are volunteer labor in political activities and unpaid labor of household maintenance and child care responsibilities. While there are 17 lesbians who are working for wages in consciously organized feminist workplaces, and they are included in the discussion, no effort is made to talk about the particular challenges of working in such locations.

26. Ninety-four percent of the lesbians who reported that *all* coworkers knew they were lesbians also reported being "totally" or "mostly open" about their sexual identity. They were employed in all occupations, but a disproportionate number were in human service jobs (40 percent), and 27 percent were in explicitly feminist work organizations. Thirty-one percent were self-employed, in a collective, or were the boss or owner of a workplace; of those who worked for someone else, almost all had a woman supervisor.

27. Women workers' beliefs about the integration of their public and private lives were measured using an index composed of four statements. These were: "The best policy to follow is to keep work separate from friendship," "You try to keep your social life completely separate from your work life," "Doing things socially with coworkers makes work relationships run more smoothly," and "You follow the general rule of not discussing personal matters with people from work." The sociability index combined four behaviors to measure the extent of social contact the women had with people at their current jobs. These four were eating lunch together, talking on the phone after work hours, visiting at each other's home, and going out socially.

28. For a discussion of these issues, see Kanter (n. 3 above) and Lydia Sargent, ed., *Women and Revolution: A Discussion of the Unhappy Marriage of Marxism and Feminism* (Boston: South End Press, 1981).

29. Marilyn Frye, "Assignment: NWSA-Bloomington-1980: Lesbian Perspectives on Women's Studies," *Sinister Wisdom* 14 (1980): 3–7, esp. 3.

30. For one effort to discuss this distinction, see Richard Zoglin, "The Homosexual Executive," in Martin P. Levine, ed., *Gay Men: The Sociology of Male Homosexuality* (New York: Harper & Row, 1979), pp. 68–77.

31. The results described here are in response to a series of questions about involvement in a sexual relationship at the workplace. The initial item—"Have you *ever* been involved in an intimate sexual relationship with someone from your workplace?"—was followed by a series of descriptive questions about the relationship.

32. Ettore (n. 17 above); Lewis (n. 13 above); Sidney Abbott and Barbara Love, *Sappho Was a Right-On Woman: A Liberated View of Lesbianism* (New York: Stein & Day, 1972); Del Martin and Phyllis Lyon, *Lesbian/Woman* (San Francisco: Glide, 1972).

33. Sixteen questions measured the frequency of experiences in the last year of requests for dates, jokes about body or appearance, pinches or grabs, and sexual propositions by four initiators (boss, coworker, subordinate, and recipient of service). Sixteen additional questions measured levels of dislike of these experiences. In the larger study, there were also questions concerning the general problem of unwanted sexual approaches at work and those behaviors that women most likely define as sexual harassment.

34. Schneider (n. 23 above).

35. Zillah Eisenstein, "Antifeminism in the Politics and Election of 1980," *Feminist Studies* 7 (Summer 1981): 187–205; Susan Harding, "Family Reform Movements," *Feminist Studies* 7 (Spring 1981): 57–75; Rosalind Pollack Petchesky, "Antiabortion, Antifeminism, and the Rise of the New Right," *Feminist Studies* 7 (Summer 1981): 206–246.

36. See Barry Adam, *The Survival of Domination: Inferiorization and Everyday Life* (New York: Elsevier, 1978); Dorothy E. Smith, "A Sociology for Women," in Julia A. Sherman and Evelyn Torton Beck, eds., *The Prism of Sex: Essays in the Sociology of Knowledge* (Madison: University of Wisconsin Press, 1977); Albert Memmi, *Dominated Man: Notes Toward a Portrait* (Boston: Beacon Press, 1968); Erving Goffman, *Stigma: Notes on the Management of Spoiled Identity* (Englewood Cliffs, N.J.: Prentice-Hall, 1963).

By the Day or Week: Mexicana Domestic Workers in El Paso

Vicki L. Ruiz

In a controversial series, journalists for the *El Paso Herald Post* wrote that even though Mexican women seeking domestic employment in Texas "risk being overworked, swindled, and even sexually abused, they come to El Paso by the thousands, taking off their shoes, rolling up their pants and wading the Rio Grande in the early morning hours."[1] Segmented by class, gender, and ethnicity, Mexican women workers have historically occupied the bottom rung of the economic ladder.[2] Marginalized members of the work force, they have also been marginalized in academic scholarship. Their day-to-day struggles for survival and dignity have gone largely unrecorded in the annals of Chicano history, labor theory, women's history, and border studies. While some scholars decry the paucity of research materials available to document the lives of Mexican women, an important resource is as accessible as the nearest tape recorder. Oral history not only increases the visibility of minority women but fosters understanding and appreciation as well. Oral interviews, housed at the Institute of Oral History, University of Texas at El Paso, form the core of this study.[3]

The situation of Mexicana domestics in El Paso provides one of the more dramatic examples of the impact of economic segmentation among women of color in the United States. In providing an overview of this significant, specifically female, segment of the labor force along the border, this essay examines a number of key issues: the centrality of women to the border economy; the nature of exploitation attendant on what has historically been

---

Ruiz, Vicky L., "By the Day or Week: Mexicana Domestic Workers in El Paso." In *"To Toil the Livelong Day"*: *America's Women at Work, 1780–1980*, edited by Carol Groneman and Mary Beth Norton. Copyright © 1987 by Cornell University. Reprinted by permission of the publisher, Cornell University Press.

I am grateful for the help provided by my research assistants for this project: Sylvia Hernández, Julieta Solis, and Anna Montalvo. ¡Gracias por todo!

1. Michael Quintanilla and Peter Copeland, "Mexican Maids: El Paso's Worst-Kept Secret," in *Special Report: The Border* (El Paso Herald Post, Summer 1983), 83.

2. Denise Segura, "Labor Market Stratification: The Chicana Experience," *Berkeley Journal of Sociology* 29 (1984): 57–91; Mario Barrera, *Race and Class in the Southwest: A Theory of Racial Inequality* (Notre Dame, Ind., 1979), 131, 151; Vicki L. Ruiz, "Working for Wages: Mexican Women in the American Southwest, 1930–1980," Working Paper no. 19, Southwest Institute for Research on Women (Tucson, 1984), 1–4.

3. The Institute of Oral History at the University of Texas, El Paso, has the largest collection of taped interviews (over 700) dealing with the U.S.–Mexico border. A significant number of these interviews focus on the lives of Mexicana and Mexican-American women workers, many of whom were interviewed as part of the institute's Border Labor History Project. From August 1983 to May 1985 I served as director of the Institute of Oral History.

termed "women's work"; and the question of ethnicity and women's employment in a border town.

El Paso is one of the most impoverished cities in the United States. In per capita income, only five other urban areas (of a total of 303) rank lower than this border community. More important, El Paso has the dubious distinction of having the lowest per capita income of any city with a population in excess of 100,000. The city also has a reputation as a minimum-wage town, yet 15 percent of El Paso County households earn less than the minimum wage of $6,968 a year.[4] Unemployment here, furthermore, exceeds both the national and state averages. While unemployment figures hovered around 7.1 to 7.8 percent for the state of Texas and for the nation as a whole during the winter of 1985, El Paso's joblessness rate approached 12 percent.[5]

An ethnic dimension complicates the earnings and employment patterns in a city where 63 percent of the population has been classified as of "Spanish origin." A representative Anglo head of household, for instance, earns $20,400 annually; a Hispanic counterpart's yearly income averages $12,600. Eighty-five percent of El Paso residents whose income dips below the poverty level are Mexican. Conversely, Anglos compose 81 percent of persons earning $50,000 or more per year. Forty percent of Hispanic workers hold blue-collar jobs, while 47 percent of Anglo employees fill high-level professional positions.[6]

The economic situation in Ciudad Juárez, directly across the border, appears even more dismal. Despite the absence of reliable employment figures for El Paso's sister city, a safe estimate places joblessness at between 10 and 15 percent of the area's work force. Salaries for blue-collar operatives are extremely low in comparison with those in the United States. In the "twin plants" (*maquiladoras*),[7] the take-home pay for line personnel averages 523 pesos a day ($3.48 in 1983), a wage set by the Mexican government. With such a low pay scale, it is not surprising that thousands of Juarenses (both men and women) cross the Rio Grande in search of employment. In fact, a typical El Paso domestic worker can earn almost five times the wage garnered by her peers in the *maquiladoras*. Twin-plant employers, however, hold out the promise of business- and government-sponsored social service benefits, the lure of which prove more attractive to workers than the actual pay.[8] As a twenty-year-old Mexicana *maquila* worker remarked, "If I didn't work here, I don't know if I would have a job. Maybe I would be a maid."[9] The choice

---

4. John Rebchook, "El Paso Is a Minimum Wage Town" and "The Poor in El Paso," in *Special Report: The Border* (*El Paso Herald Post*, Summer 1983), 74, 66.

5. "Labor Force Estimates for Texas Counties—Feb. '85," prepared by the Economic Research and Analysis Department, Texas Employment Commission. The El Paso figure is 11.9 percent, or 24,175 unemployed persons actively seeking work.

6. Peter Copeland, "Border Ambiente," and "The Two Cities of El Paso," both in *Special Report: The Border* (*El Paso Herald Post*, Summer 1983), 12, 21.

7. Many multinational corporations have constructed facilities on both sides of the U.S.–Mexico border in order to lower their labor costs. A "twin plant" is thus one that has a twin on the other side of the border. See María Patricia Fernández-Kelly, *For We Are Sold* (Albany, 1983), for an insightful glimpse into life in the *maquiladoras*.

8. Interview with economist Jeffrey T. Brannon, 27 March 1985, conducted by the author; Debra Skodack, "Border Business: Twin Plants Give Boost," *Special Report: The Border* (*El Paso Herald Post*, Summer 1983), 68–69; *El Paso Herald Post*, 8 April 1985. The extent to which these promises of benefits are realized is currently the subject of considerable controversy.

9. Skodack, "Border Business," 69.

for many Juárez women seems clear: employment as *trabajadoras* (workers) in the twin plants or as maids in either Ciudad Juárez or El Paso.[10]

How many women work as domestics in El Paso? There are no reliable estimates. According to the 1980 census, 1,063 El Paso women identified themselves as maids in private homes. This figure is very low, for it does not include Juárez commuters with work permits or the undocumented women who compose the bulk of the city's domestic labor force. Nestor Valencia, director of the City Planning, Research, and Development Department, stated, "If only 10 percent of El Paso's households had maids, that would be more than 13,400 maids and a significant employment sector."[11] Although an accurate measure is impossible, probably more than 10 percent of El Paso homemakers hire domestic help. Perhaps as many as 15,000 to 20,000 women are private household workers.

The salaries of Mexican domestics are sadly deficient in comparison with those earned in other parts of the nation for similar work. In El Paso a daily maid (a women who comes in to clean once a week) earns an average of $15 a day, while a live-in household worker receives from $30 to $60 a week. Some employers, however, offer no more than $80 a month for live-in services. The ready availability of domestic help at bargain-basement prices has led to the commonly heard comment: "The best thing about El Paso is the cheap maids."[12]

Domestic workers are so welded into the city's lifestyle, particularly for middle- and upper-income families, that many homes contain areas identified as "maid's quarters." These accommodations vary from large, light, airy rooms with a separate bath and entrance to a small bed nestled against the washer and dryer. It is very fashionable to have domestic help. As one person observed, "Once you get a microwave, the next status item is a maid." Not only Anglos employ household workers; Mexican-Americans and Mexican nationals who live in El Paso hire them too. In fact, many working-class homes benefit from live-in labor; Mexican-American factory operatives frequently hire domestic help.[13] The ready availability of Mexicana maids is not attributable solely to the recent economic crises in Mexico; Mexican domestic workers have played important roles in El Paso's economy at least since the turn of the century.

According to a sample of 393 families taken from the 1900 census, only twenty-three El Paso homes had live-in maids; of those families, only one had a Spanish surname and was, in fact, the family of the Mexican consul. Many Anglos, however, hired Mexicanas as day servants.[14] Elizabeth Rae Tyson, a native of El Paso, explained: "Every Anglo American family had at least one, sometimes two or three servants: a maid and laundress, and perhaps a nursemaid. . . . The maid came in after breakfast and cleaned up the breakfast dishes, and . . . last night's supper dishes . . . did the routine cleaning, washing,

---

10. Employment in the El Paso apparel trades is considered a step up from domestic work, in both pay and prestige. Most maids seem to view sewing slacks at Farah as a "good" job.

11. Quintanilla and Copeland, "Mexican Maids," 86.

12. Quintanilla and Copeland, "Mexican Maids," 83–84, 86; *El Paso Shopping Guide*, 21 December 1983; *El Paso Herald Post*, 26 March 1985; *El Paso Times*, 9 April 1985; personal observations by the author.

13. Quintanilla and Copeland, "Mexican Maids," 83, 86; interview with Mr. M., 8 June 1983, conducted by the author; personal observations by the author. Real estate brokers frequently mention "maid's quarters" in advertising their listings.

14. Mario T. García, *Desert Immigrants: The Mexicans of El Paso, 1880–1920* (New Haven, Conn., 1981), 254n.

and ironing, after the family dinner . . . washed dishes again, and then went home to perform similar service in her own home."[15] These Mexicanas worked from 7 A.M. to 5 P.M. for $3 to $6 a week.[16]

Domestic labor provided the most common form of employment for Mexican women during the first half of the twentieth century. In 1919 the U.S. Employment Bureau opened an office in El Paso. According to the historian Mario García, bureau personnel expended large amounts of time and energy in placing Mexican domestics in area residences. In November 1919, for example, 1,740 Mexicanas applied to the agency for employment assistance and 1,326 found work. During the 1930s and 1940s, the Rose Gregory Houchen Settlement House, operated by the Methodist church, also found jobs for Mexican women as domestics. Staff members operated an informal bureau that endeavored to locate Christian homes for Christian women. The settlement also provided child care and medical services to the people of El Segundo, a poor, predominantly Hispanic neighborhood.[17]

In 1933, in the midst of the Great Depression, many El Paso housewives were horrified to learn that more than 500 domestics had organized themselves into the Domestic Workers Association—in other words, they had formed a maids' union. These women, led by the political and labor activist Charles Porras, had banded together because they simply could not support their families on the then-average wage of $1.75 a week.[18] Porras recalled: "I organized the Domestic Workers Association—all women, local from *here*. Mind you, $3 a week! I wouldn't let them take a nickel less; and they had to get carfare. . . . You'd be surprised to see the number of women, I mean the upper class women *here* that went to the Immigration outfit and tried to get me deported . . . [or] arrested because I was getting these women to stay away from them."[19]

Although these Mexicanas received financial and organizational support from a few area locals affiliated with the American Federation of Labor, the maids' association appears to have been short-lived.[20] Community hostility to the union, as well as rampant unemployment on both sides of the border, ensured a ready supply of domestic servants for El Paso middle- and upper-income housewives at any wage these homemakers deemed suitable.

In 1953 Anglo housewives formed an organization of their own, the Association for Legalized Domestics, in response to the McCarran-Walters Immigration Act, which placed controls on the flow of Mexican nationals into the United States. The Association for Legalized Domestics sought the assistance of the Immigration and Naturalization

15. Mary Wilson Barton, "Methodism at Work among the Spanish-Speaking People of El Paso, Texas" (master's thesis, Texas Western College, 1950), 15.

16. García, *Desert Immigrants*, 77.

17. García, *Desert Immigrants*, 60; Vicki L. Ruiz, "A History of Friendship Square: Social Service in South El Paso" (manuscript, 1983), 37–38.

18. *El Paso Herald Post*, 23 September 1933; interview with Charles Porras, 18 November 1975, conducted by Oscar Martínez (on file at the Institute of Oral History, University of Texas, El Paso). My thanks to Mario García for providing the news clipping.

19. Charles Porras interview. During this period in other sections of the United States, domestic workers did generally earn $3 a week. See Lois Rita Helmbold, "Class Conflict and Class Cooperation among Women during the Depression," paper presented at the Fifth Berkshire Conference on the History of Women, Poughkeepsie, N.Y., June 1981.

20. *El Paso Herald Post*, 23 September 1933.

Service (INS) in contracting (legally) for the labor of Juárez women. Members of this organization desired the importation of domestic help along the lines employed by Southwest agribusiness to recruit Mexicanos to work as farm labor under the *bracero* program. Maids, classified as "non-immigrants," would be contracted to specific employers with specific conditions.[21] The proposed "bracero maid" contract comprised the following provisions:

1. The non-immigrant must be asked for by name and must be between the ages of 18 and 35.
2. The non-immigrant must supply the prospective employer with an acceptable health certificate. . . .
3. Non-immigrants must supply the prospective employer with a certificate from Mexican authorities stating that they are free of any civil or criminal record. . . .
4. Non-immigrants must have character references. . . .
5. The contractor must pay a minimum salary of $15 a week.
6. The contractor must provide acceptable living quarters and food. . . .
7. The non-immigrant . . . must have at least one and one-half days of rest per week, at which time the non-immigrant is free to leave the premises and return to Mexico.
8. The non-immigrant may visit Mexico within a limited area designated by the Immigration and Naturalization Service. . . .
9. A $10 fee must be paid by the prospective employer to the [INS]. . . .
10. Non-immigrant domestic working visas will cost the prospective employer $41.50. This sum will be paid to the U.S. Consular Service.
11. The contract may be terminated by either employer or employee and employee returned to Mexico at any time. . . .
12. The contract and working period . . . is for a period of one year and may be renewed at that time for a fee of $10 providing the U.S. Labor Department states that no qualified domestics are available in the United States. . . .[22]

Mexican-American household workers vehemently protested the proposal. In a letter to a local advice columnist, one El Paso maid stated that an ample supply of domestic help was available on the Texas side of the border. Local housewives preferred women from Juárez, she asserted, because they would work for lower wages: "We charge $3 a day and most ladies want to pay just $12 or $14 a week." The columnist responded by chiding the woman for not accepting the pay scale offered by El Paso homemakers; she did, however, recognize the magnitude of the household tasks assigned to many domestics. "I think that the amount of work . . . and the hours have a lot to do with the wages," the columnist wrote. "That $14 and $12 a week can be too little when a maid is expected to do everything but breathe for her employer."[23] Reflecting conventional attitudes of the 1950s, she rebuked housewives for their reliance on household workers: "I

---

21. *El Paso Times*, 25 September 1953; *El Paso Herald Post*, 12 October 1953; Rodolfo Acuña, *Occupied America: A History of Chicanos*, 2d ed. (New York, 1981), 144–50. One of the most comprehensive accounts of the bracero program is Ernesto Galarza's *Merchants of Labor: The Mexican Bracero Story* (Charlotte, N.C., 1964).

22. *El Paso Herald Post*, 12 October 1953.

23. *El Paso Herald Post*, 15 and 30 October 1953.

think American women could do more housework than they are doing these days. . . . I believe that a good healthy tiredness from housecleaning and cooking a mighty good meal for their family or digging in the garden would stave off more nervous breakdowns than all this hub-bub and how-dya-do over civic . . . duties. I have heard doctors say so."[24]

As it turned out, the controversy generated by the Association of Legalized Domestics became moot when the Department of Justice refused to consider a bracero-type program for Mexican maids.[25]

This formal organization among El Paso homemakers stands out as an isolated case. Typically, the regulation of household labor takes place on a one-to-one basis between *patrona* and maid within the confines of a private residence. The experiences of the Mexicanas in domestic service have ranged from rewarding, fulfilling employment to sexual abuse. While one woman proudly displays pictures of the Anglo children she helped rear, another recounts how she was sexually harassed and even assaulted by her employers' husbands.[26] Subtle day-to-day humiliation, however, often leaves the deepest scars. As the domestic worker Enriqueta Morales recounted:

> There are those that treat me very well. I feel even as if I were one of the family. And with others, it was very different. They humiliated me. With some, they give something to eat . . . they sit you down at the table and everything. As we sit together, we eat, we talk—it's all the same. And others, well, it's different. They only give you a sandwich and a glass of water. And that's all they put on our plate. [They say] "Look, this is your lunch." In time, you may be given a glass of tea, even a soda. Or sometimes, they didn't give me any lunch. That hurts.[27]

Many domestics provide a variety of services for little pay. One employer, while entertaining friends, instructed his Mexican maid to wash all of the guests' automobiles. The book *Your Maid from Mexico: A Home Training Course for Maids* encourages Mexicanas to "always . . . find new ways to help and please your employers." These little extras range from hairstyling to sewing to shining shoes. The routine duties of most household workers include cleaning, babysitting, cooking, even gardening, for a mere $30 to $60 a week. Little wonder, then, that many El Paso women emphatically declare, "I couldn't live without my maid."[28]

Many *señoras* have little understanding of the everyday realities facing the women they employ. Although written over twenty years ago, the following excerpt from *Your Maid from Mexico* reflects the apparent ignorance and patronizing attitudes characteristic of many contemporary El Paso homemakers:

> You girls who work in homes can soon become more valuable to your employers than girls who work in offices, stores, or factories because our homes . . . are closest

24. *El Paso Herald Post*, 30 October 1953.

25. *El Paso Herald Post*, 9 and 18 November 1953.

26. Michael Quintanilla, "Legal Maid: She Devotes Her Life to Others," *Special Report: The Border* (*El Paso Herald Post*, Summer 1983), 88; interview with Rocío, 29 May 1979, conducted by Oscar Martínez and Mario Galdós (on file at the Institute of Oral History, University of Texas, El Paso).

27. Interview with Enriqueta Morales, 14 June 1979, conducted by Oscar Martínez, Mario Galdós, and Sarah John (on file at the Institute of Oral History, University of Texas, El Paso).

28. Quintanilla and Copeland, "Mexican Maids," 84; Gladys Hawkins, Jean Soper, and Jane Pike Henry, *Your Maid from Mexico: A Home Training Course for Maids in English and Spanish* (San Antonio, 1959), 6, 8; personal observations by the author.

to our hearts. . . . Remember, as you learn new skills day by day, you are not only learning how to become a better wife and mother . . . but you are learning to support yourself and your family in a worthwhile career in case you must be the breadwinner.[29]

In fact, some women believe that they are doing Mexicanas a favor by hiring them. As one poorly phrased classified advertisement stated: "Permanent live-in child carer of 3 in exchange for private room and food."[30] This potential employer obviously did not feel compelled to offer any sort of monetary remuneration. Middle- and upper-income residents, in particular, often have definite opinions concerning domestic workers. Mike Trominski, a deputy director of the INS, succinctly summed up common sentiments: "People think that it is a God-given right in El Paso to have a wet maid that they can pay a few dollars and will do anything they want."[31] Such employers, whether Anglo or Mexican-American, are generally unappreciative of the household services they enjoy. At social functions, some women swap maid stories that begin: "My maid is so stupid that . . ." This denigration of intelligence has not been lost on the domestic worker, even though she often cannot speak the language of her employer. Describing her communication with her Anglo *patrona*, one Mexicana poignantly revealed: "She didn't know any Spanish and I no English. But she has learned much from me. I believe I have learned very little from her because, well, Mexicans, we aren't, well, I'm not so intelligent."[32] The low self-esteem of this woman is undoubtedly the product of years of prejudice and humiliation. INS official James Smith sums it up: "It's human nature—the abuse and the exploitation."[33]

The superior attitudes assumed by many *patronas* can reach preposterous proportions. Some women, perhaps unwittingly or perhaps deliberately, forget to pay their housekeepers at the end of the day or week. When the maids ask for their wages, these employers act offended, as if to convey the message: "Just who do you think you are?" In addition, *patronas* sometimes believe that they are entitled to regulate the private lives of their domestic workers. When one Mexicana who cleans several homes in the Coronado area (a middle- to upper-middle-class, largely Anglo neighborhood) informed her clients that she was pregnant with her second child, she received mixed responses: two of her employers offered maternity leaves with pay, but another callously issued an ultimatum: "Get an abortion or lose your job." In Señora Chavarría's words, "I tell her, I get other work."[34]

Blatant discrimination can even be detected in the classified sections of El Paso's newspapers and shopping guides. Advertisements appearing under "Domestic Help" frequently contain such phrases as "must be clean," "neat appearance," and the ubiquitous

29. Hawkins et al., *Your Maid from Mexico*, 2.

30. *El Paso Herald Post*, 26 March 1985.

31. Peter Copeland, "INS Checks Maids' U.S. Entry," *Special Report: The Border* (*El Paso Herald Post*, Summer 1983), 89; personal observations by the author.

32. Enriqueta Morales interview.

33. Quintanilla and Copeland, "Mexican Maids," 84.

34. Interview with Martina Hernández, 29 November 1983, conducted by Sylvia Hernández (on file at the Institute of Oral History, University of Texas, El Paso); interview with Mónica Santos de Chavarría, 13 December 1983, conducted by the author.

"some English necessary." A few area women refuse to hire Mexicanas. One recent advertisement noted: "Wanted: European housekeeper."[35]

An Anglo businessman offered the following reasons why he and his wife are delaying parenthood:

> The major dilemma would be what to do with the child. We don't really like the idea of leaving the baby at home with a maid . . . for the simple reason if the maid is Mexican, the child may assume that [the] Mexican is its mother. Nothing wrong with Mexicans; they'd just assume that this other person is its mother. There have been all sorts of cases where they [the infants] learned Spanish before they learned English. There've been incidents of the Mexican maid stealing the child and taking it over to Mexico and selling it.[36]

This winding statement reveals the (at best) ambivalent attitudes that many Anglo El Pasoans harbor toward Mexicans and their culture.

However, life may not be any easier for maids employed by Mexican-Americans. Some women assert that Hispanics treat them worse than Anglos do. "Mexican women; they are the worst," one women stated simply. Many prefer to work for newly arrived Anglos. Perhaps newcomers to the area (often first-time *patronas*) feel a bit guilty about hiring Mexicanas at such bargain rates; as a result, they may be more considerate and appreciative of their household workers.[37]

Of course, strong, harmonious relationships can develop between a Mexican domestic worker and her El Paso employer. When one Mexicana's infant became ill with severe diarrhea, for instance, she called her *patrona,* Mrs. C., who escorted the mother and baby to Thomason General Hospital. During the early-morning hours, both Mr. and Mrs. C. waited with the mother until the child was examined and treated, then drove the woman and her infant home. This display of genuine concern may be uncommon, but it does indicate that the relationship between a private household worker and her employer need not be one of humiliation, callousness, or exploitation.[38]

Economic necessity propels Mexican women into domestic labor. Many live-in maids have their own families in Ciudad Juárez; their own children are generally cared for by relatives. Typically they visit their families on weekends. Younger women, some recruited from the interior of Mexico, often stay with a family for months at a time. A youthful Mexicana may enter domestic service in order to earn money for her family or to save for her own marriage. "I go home about once every month," one eighteen-year-old stated. "Sometimes I stay a week. . . . Most of the time I go home for the weekend. I miss my family. . . . Sometimes I miss them too much."[39]

---

35. *El Paso Times,* 20 February 1984; *El Paso Herald Post,* 17 February 1984; *El Paso Shopping Guide,* 21 December 1983, 14 February 1984.

36. Interview with Robert Lyons, 23 July 1984, conducted by Mary Ann White (on file at Institute of Oral History, University of Texas, El Paso).

37. Interview with María Cristina Carlos, 20 June 1979, conducted by Oscar Martínez (on file at Institute of Oral History, University of Texas, El Paso); interview with Mrs. C., 1 June 1983, conducted by the author; personal observations by the author.

38. Mrs. C. interview.

39. Quintanilla and Copeland, "Mexican Maids," 84; personal observations by the author; Michael Quintanilla, "Illegal Maid: She Plays Cat and Mouse with La Migra," *Special Report: The Border (El Paso Herald Post,* Summer 1983), 87.

"Commuter" maids of all ages form the majority of the live-in domestic labor force in El Paso. These women wade across the river early Monday morning, catch a Sun City Area Transit (SCAT) bus, work all week, and then return home for the weekend. While their pay remains low, it is enough to provide food, clothing, and shelter for their families in Ciudad Juárez. In fact, their earnings are comparable to those earned by white-collar Juarenses.[40]

The prize-winning poet Pat Mora has clearly captured the divergent worlds of the Mexicana employee and her Anglo employer in a poem titled "Mexican Maid."

> Would the moon help?
> The sun did,
> changed the *señora's* white skin
> to red, then copper.
> > "I'm going to take a sun
> > bath, Marta, sun bath, *sí?*"
> Marta would smile, nod,
> look at her own dark skin
> > and wish
> that she could lie
> outside at night
> bathed by moonlight,
> lie with her eyes closed
> like the *señora* wake to a new skin
> that would glisten white
> when she stepped off the dusty bus
> at the entrance to her village.[41]

It is important to remember that not all domestics internalize the negative attitudes imposed upon them. Even if they experience psychological and physical abuse, many retain their sense of humor, their pride, their integrity. When María Cristina Carlos left her job in a private home to work in a tortilla factory, her employer refused to pay her for her final two weeks' work. Adding insult to injury, the *patrona* then spread the rumor that her maid had robbed her. With rising indignation, Señora Carlos demanded, "But just who had robbed who?"[42] Another woman recounted how her employer's husband had offered her $20 if she would take off her clothes and dance on the dining room table. Although trembling inside, she managed to reply, "I'm not looking for that kind of work. There are many places where you can see women dance and for less money."[43]

The issue of household labor is not confined to employer–employee relationships; domestic workers make significant contributions to the city's economy. Nestor Valencia, director of the city planning office, remarked, "It's an industry that is part of the fiber of

40. Quintanilla and Copeland, "Mexican Maids," 84–86; Jeffrey Brannon interview.

41. "Mexican Maid," reprinted from *Borders*, by Pat Mora (Houston, 1986), 36.

42. María Carlos interview.

43. Rocío interview.

the community." In fact, the Sun City Area Transit depends on domestic workers for at least half of its riders. One SCAT official even claimed, "If they ever cracked down on domestic help, especially illegals, we would lose our ridership." By midafternoon in this West Texas community, the suburban bus stops are thronged with Mexicanas, some wearing old sweaters in the winter and holding umbrellas in the summer, some sitting on benches, others on hard pavement. The city bus system is so clearly identified with its Mexican clientele that the Border Patrol routinely boards SCAT vehicles to check the citizenship documents of the passengers.[44]

The apprehension of undocumented maids is not a high priority for the INS, however. While the Border Patrol will take women into custody at the river or from city buses, these officials will not search private residences. The rationale for this policy centers on the fact that domestic work is not a lucrative position coveted by U.S. citizens. INS Deputy Director Mike Trominski bluntly pointed out, "It doesn't make sense looking for one illegal maid in Eastwood when we could be removing an alien from a good paying job." Still, commuter maids are routinely picked up near the river and driven back to Juárez. Border Patrol agents apprehend some women so frequently that they call them by name. "Norma, again?" they asked, after detaining one women for the third time in a single day.[45]

Mexicana domestics have developed elaborate strategies for crossing the U.S.–Mexican border. Some will time their routes precisely to arrive at a border bus stop at the same time as the scheduled bus. Rocío remembered that once when she and several other women were crossing the river near a Border Highway bus stop, the driver purposely held his vehicle for them; and after they had boarded, he offered each of them a tissue to wipe their mud-streaked legs.[46]

Others prefer to cross before daybreak and then depend on catching rides to the downtown plaza, where they can board SCAT buses to all parts of the city. However, women dread accepting rides from strangers (often "coyotes," who demand a small *mordida* [bribe] for their services); indeed, they could be and have been sexually assaulted. "Tu cuerpo es tu morida" (Your body is your bribe) may not be an uncommon phrase among coyotes. Because of their dubious status in the United States, these rape victims do not report the incidents. Women also fear crossing the four-laned Border Highway and the six lanes of Interstate 10. The gangs of Mexican and Mexican-American youths who congregate on both sides of the river pose another threat. In view of all the hazards involved, many Mexicanas cross in groups and often with family or friends.[47]

Household workers with some knowledge of English and of El Paso may take a more direct approach: they cross at one of the three bridges and declare their citizenship as "American." One woman who has used this tactic remarked that she

44. Quintanilla and Copeland, "Mexican Maids," 84, 86; personal observations by the author.

45. Quintanilla and Copeland, "Mexican Maids," 83, 85; Copeland, "INS Checks Maids," 89; Quintanilla, "Illegal Maid," 87.

46. Interview with Esperanza Avila, 10 May 1979, conducted by Mario Galdós and Sarah John (on file at Institute of Oral History, University of Texas, El Paso); Rocío interview.

47. Esperanza Avila interview; interview with Irene González, 12 October 1979, conducted by Mario Galdós and Virgilio Sánchez (on file at Institute of Oral History, University of Texas, El Paso); Quintanilla, "Illegal Maid," 87; Mónica Santos de Chavarría interview.

preferred Anglo to Mexican-American immigration officials because the former tend to ask fewer questions.[48]

Another government service agency concerned about the role of domestic workers in the El Paso economy is the local branch of the Social Security Administration. By law, if any person pays another person more than $50 for services over a three-month period, both parties must pay 6.7 percent of the weekly wages in social security taxes. Even if the employee is undocumented, the employer must still pay the tax. The reasoning behind this regulation is simple: after forty to fifty years of service, a domestic worker who has received wages on a cash-only basis throughout her life is often left with nothing in her declining years. Yet even if her *patrona* has paid into the social security system, she still cannot collect benefits unless or until she has legal resident status in the United States. This law is flagrantly violated. Many employers are reluctant to deduct the taxes and to keep the appropriate records. Domestic workers, too, tend to be unwilling to give up any of their meager, hard-earned wages. "I want my money now," one Mexicana stated flatly.[49]

Another piece of legislation ignored by most *patronas* is the minimum-wage law. Few Mexican domestics receive the $3.35 an hour to which they are entitled, regardless of their citizenship or residence. The average daily wage of $15 for a woman who cleans once a week for six to eight hours translates into $1.88 to $2.50 an hour. The hourly wage of a live-in maid earning $30 to $60 a week is considerably less. Interestingly, social security was not extended to private household workers until 1952, and these women were also excluded from minimum-wage legislation until 1974.[50]

As long as high unemployment and a surplus labor pool persist on both sides of the border, El Paso homemakers will continue to employ Mexican household workers at bargain wages. Economic segmentation and sexual exploitation are likely to continue as long as Mexicana household workers face a quadruple whammy—class, gender, ethnicity, and citizenship. Their dubious status in the United States compounds the barriers confronted by working-class women of color. Further research by historians and social scientists is needed before we can comprehend fully the economic contributions and experiences of Mexicana domestics on the U.S.–Mexico border. Though frequently victimized, Mexicana domestics are not victims but women who meet each day with integrity and endurance. As one woman puts it, "I go where I have to go. I do what I have to do."[51]

---

48. Rocío interview.

49. Peter Copeland, "Social Security Head Went on Warpath," *Special Report: The Border* (El Paso Herald Post, Summer 1983), 89; Quintanilla and Copeland, "Mexican Maids," 84; Quintanilla, "Illegal Maid," 87.

50. Copeland, "Social Security," 89; *El Paso Herald Post*, 26 March 1985; *El Paso Times*, 9 April 1985; Alice Kessler-Harris, *Women Have Always Worked: A Historical Overview* (Old Westbury, N.Y., 1981), 84.

51. Personal observations by the author.

The Welder

Cherríe Moraga

I am a welder.
Not an alchemist.
I am interested in the blend
of common elements to make
a common thing.

No magic here.
Only the heat of my desire to fuse
what I already know
exists. Is possible.

We plead to each other,
we all come from the same rock
we all come from the same rock
ignoring the fact that we bend
at different temperatures
that each of us is malleable
up to a point.

Yes, fusion *is* possible
but only if things get hot enough—
all else is temporary adhesion,
patching up.

It is the intimacy of steel melting
into steel, the fire of our individual
passion to take hold of ourselves
that makes sculpture of our lives,
builds buildings.

And I am not talking about skyscrapers,
merely structures that can support us
without fear
of trembling.

For too long a time
the heat of my heavy hands
has been smoldering
in the pockets of other
people's business—
they need oxygen to make fire.

I am now
coming up for air.
Yes, I *am*
picking up the torch.

I am the welder.
I understand the capacity of heat
to change the shape of things.
I am suited to work
within the realm of sparks
out of control.

I am the welder.
I am taking the power
into my own hands.

Part III - Within Patriarchal Institutions
Chapter 6—Women and Economics
Study Questions

1. Does inequality in the public sector affect equality in the private sector? Is the reverse true? Answer why, or why not, to both questions.

2. Define *matrilineal*. In general, what are the effects of such a system? Give examples.

3. Discuss in small groups the specific rewards of women's unpaid labor to a capitalist society. In the large group make a list of the duties performed by women in their homes that are paid under different circumstances.

4. What was the effect of the industrial revolution on the division of labor? Who comprised the majority of paid women workers at that time?

5. What was the result of the devaluation of women's work? How does the issue of race affect women's paid work?

6. How does war affect the status of women's paid work? In general, what occurs after war ends, especially what happened after World War II? Are these consequences affected by race? How?

7. How was women's paid work once justified? How did this change following World War II? Why?

8. What are the indicators of sex-based economic inequality?

9. Name the factors that limit women's full and equal participation in the paid labor market. Why do you think women reach a wage and advancement plateau?

10. Although there has been a threefold increase in women managers in the past two decades, what do these women see as blocks to further advancement?

11. Distinguish between "equal pay for equal work" (enacted in the 1963 Equal Pay Act) and "equal pay for comparable work." Which is most likely to help eliminate a sex-segregated labor market? Why?

12. What is meant by the *feminization of poverty*? What factors make gender the primary determinant of low economic status?

13. What are the stereotypes that surround women on welfare? How do these stereotypes affect women and their families? When women on welfare enter the paid labor market, many experience a lowered standard of living. Why?

14. What are the two strategies seen as having the greatest potential for changing gender inequality in the workplace? Briefly, how does each strategy work? What other initiatives must be implemented to provide women an equal opportunity?

15. What is the economic double bind women face? What other factors affect their employment opportunities?

16. According to Schneider's "Peril and Promise . . . ," how does the assumption of heterosexuality in the workplace affect lesbians? What effects for heterosexual women are the same? Different? Through this example, why is it important for women to bridge their differences in the face of oppression?

17. What are some of the insights gained from Ruiz's article on domestic workers regarding women's work and how women workers view themselves? Compare this to the issues of "women's work" (paid or unpaid) for all women.

EQUALITY AND LIBERATION, FEMINISM AND WOMEN'S RIGHTS IN THE NINETEENTH AND TWENTIETH CENTURIES

Monys A. Hagen

Introduction

Women's history is in part a history of resistance to the various forms of exclusion and subjection that women have faced over time. In many instances, individual women have voiced their discontent and opposed the constraints they personally experienced. At other times, women have articulated a philosophy for social change and equality. Most effective have been the women's rights and feminist movements, when women banded together, acting as women *for* women, to improve their collective position in society.

Women of today are the beneficiaries of two centuries of feminist thought and activism. The historical memory of this in and of itself is important, but the implications are more far-reaching. In order to fully understand our current position in society and to formulate strategies for continued progress toward true equality, awareness of past struggles and successes is imperative. Women's history provides us with models of courage and dedication, a sense of continuity with the past, and an appreciation of how far women have come and of how far we have yet to go before we achieve personal and collective liberation.

In reading the following essays and documents consider these questions:

- How have the contradictions between established political ideals and cultural norms helped foster the emergence of a women's rights movement?
- What is the relationship of the single issues, suffrage and the Equal Rights Amendment, to the broader women's rights movement?
- What have been the advantages of, and problems related to, focusing the women's rights movement on single issues?
- How have the philosophies and tactics of radical and moderate women's rights activists differed? How have the tensions between the two factions contributed to the advancement of a feminist agenda?
- How close have we come to realizing the principles set forth in the 1848 Seneca Falls Declaration of Sentiments?

- How successful has the women's movement been in accommodating the issues of class, race, and sexual orientation, and other demographics of difference?

Republicanism and Women

During the American Revolution, republicanism and the doctrine of natural rights gained ascendancy as the revolutionary generation embraced the political philosophy of the Enlightenment. Political discourse of the time centered upon the definitions of citizenship, civic freedom, and inalienable rights and questioned the nature of society, the proper relationship between government and the governed, and the rights of man. For women, however, central questions remained unaddressed. Did *man* mean all people? Were women considered citizens of the republic?

A careful examination of the principal works of the Enlightenment by Adam Smith, John Locke, and Jean Jacques Rousseau as well as those by American writers and statesmen such as Thomas Paine, Thomas Jefferson, and Benjamin Franklin reveals that the public sector, as defined by the political vocabulary of the time, was a male arena. Women were not considered part of the political community, and their role in the state remained largely unexamined and unacknowledged. A few female thinkers, notably Mary Wollstonecraft and Catharine Macauly, applied the principles of the Enlightenment to women's rights in society, but they made a negligible impact on political thought (Kerber 1980).

American women of the 1770s and 1780s, however, participated in the American Revolution and contributed to the cause of freedom in many ways. Women played an influential role in enforcing the economic sanctions against British goods, and the Daughters of Liberty produced cloth for the nation. Some patriots served as nurses for the Continental Army, others acted as spies for the American cause, and a few, like Deborah Sampson, took up arms and fought for liberty. Nevertheless, women's subordination was deeply entrenched in American political, social, legal, economic, and religious thought; and though few women called for their inalienable rights, it would be naive to assume they were ignorant of the principles and implications of the American Revolution (Kerber 1980; Norton 1980).

Because of education and social standing, women like Abigail Adams, Mercy Otis Warren, and Judith Sargent Murray had the means and opportunity to make their views known and to challenge the attitudes that barred women from access to centers of political power. Abigail Adams is most frequently remembered in history because she was First Lady during John Adams's administration and the mother of America's sixth president, John Quincy Adams. But Abigail Adams was a revolutionary in her own right, and no better feminist application of the principle that governments derive "their just powers from the consent of the governed" exists than her famous March 1776 letter to John Adams (Rossi 1974):

> . . . and by the way in the new Code of Laws which I suppose it will be necessary for you to make I desire you would Remember the Ladies, and be more generous and favorable to them than your ancestors. Do not put such unlimited power into the hands of the Husbands. Remember all Men would be tyrants if they could. If particular care and attention is not paid to the Ladies we are determined to foment a Rebellion, and will not hold ourselves bound by any Laws in which we have

no voice, or Representation (Rossi 1974, 10).

The future president found this appeal amusing and replied that the "Masculine systems" would not be repealed and that the men would not be made politically subject to "Despotism of the Petticoat" (Rossi 1974, 11).

John Adams's response underscored the fact that it would take more than a revolution to abolish the deepseated assumptions about women's inferiority. The daughters of the Revolution's inability to achieve political or social equality does not point toward a resounding failure.* Women like Adams articulated a feminist position based on the principles of republicanism, and their writings pointed out that the American Revolution was incomplete. The philosophical groundwork for women's equality had been laid during the Revolution, and "the sustained tension between natural rights doctrines and assumptions about the nature of woman provided the basic dynamic for a struggle that would last over a hundred years" (Scott and Scott, 1975, 4).

From Abolition to Women's Rights

A movement for social change is born whenever the contradictions between the principles and practices of a society can no longer be contained. In antebellum America (1820–1860), as white male suffrage expanded and new, though limited, economic opportunities opened for women, a current of female discontent surfaced. Individuals like Margaret Fuller began to write about the disadvantaged position of women in society, while others simultaneously worked to improve educational opportunities, admission to the professions, and property rights for married women. But it was the religious-based reform movements, particularly antislavery, that opened the way for the emergence of the first women's rights movement. Participation in reform activities underscored the unequal partnership of women and men in society, and placed women in contact with other women who were experiencing similar injustices in their lives. Once individual isolation had ended, women built upon the friendships and networks formed through years of activism, this time acting on behalf of themselves as women. A women's rights movement materialized, and with it came not only a critique of society but a new philosophical perspective—feminism.

The first to articulate sexism in the abolitionist ranks were Sarah and Angelina Grimké. Because the Grimké sisters had been born into a wealthy slave-holding family from South Carolina, their antislavery message was particularly powerful and intriguing. When they began their speaking tour, they addressed only groups of women, but as their popularity grew, men as well came to hear their message. Because they spoke to mixed audiences, critics charged that the sisters had overstepped the boundaries of appropriate female behavior. As Sarah and Angelina Grimké labored for the cause of abolition, they increasingly had to defend their right to speak and act, and, in the process, began to see parallels between the rights of blacks and of women (Lerner 1967). Angelina Grimké's response to their critics illustrated this:

> The denial of our duty to act in this case is a denial of our right to act; and if we have no right to act, then we may well be termed the 'white slave of the North'; for like our brethren in bonds,

---

*New Jersey, where women voted from 1790 to 1807, was the exception to women's political disfranchisement.

we must seal our lips in silence and despair. (Lerner 1971, 162)

Criticisms from clergymen and others also moved Sarah Grimké to answer the charges levied against the sisters. One of her major achievements was a series of "Letters on the Equality of the Sexes" which articulated a feminist position that went far beyond the rights of free speech and attacked the basic assumptions held about women in American society:

"Her influence is the source of mighty power." This has ever been the flattering language of man since he laid aside the whip as a means to keep woman in subjection. He spares her body; but the war he has waged against her mind, her heart, and her soul has been no less destructive to her as a moral being. (Rossi 1974, 308)

Strong currents in the antislavery forces sought to keep women's rights separate from abolition; consequently, women's rights proved to be a divisive issue in the movement. Two factions formed: one which believed all issues but antislavery should be excluded from the agenda, and the other which embraced a broader human rights perspective. Throughout these trials, the Grimké sisters held firm in the principle expressed by Sarah Grimké:

I ask no favors for my sex. . . . All I ask of our brethren, is that they will take their feet from off our necks, and permit us to stand upright on that ground which God designed us to occupy. (Learner 1967, 192)

Other manifestations of conflict over "the woman question" arose. One of the most famous and most important occurred in 1840 at the World Antislavery Convention in London. Several American societies had sent women delegates, and despite their protests, the convention assembly refused to seat the women. Among those relegated to the galleries were Lucretia Mott and Elizabeth Cady Stanton. As they watched the proceedings, it became increasingly clear that they were not equal participants in the cause; regardless of their dedication to abolition, their labors were blocked at every turn because of their sex (Flexner 1975; Scott and Scott 1975).

The discontent they experienced at the London convention found expression eight years later when Stanton and Mott met in Waterloo, New York. The time for action had arrived, and a call went forth for a women's rights convention. On July 19, 1848, the women's rights movement in America was born at Seneca Falls, New York. From this meeting emerged the Declaration of Sentiments that would guide three generations of women's rights activists and provide the framework for a comprehensive women's rights ideology. The declaration presented a full account of the injustices and contradictions of American society and cited specific legal, professional, political, economic, religious, and social disabilities faced by women.* While some have argued that the Declaration of Sentiments was moderate and reformist in tone, it must be remembered that in 1848, to declare "All men and women are created equal" was a radical pronouncement which called for a revolution in the social relations between the sexes.

Seneca Falls was only the beginning. From 1848 until the outbreak of the Civil War in 1860, a social movement slowly coalesced around a dedicated group of leaders. Most of these women were white, middle-class, educated, and had been friends and coworkers in other social reform activities, such as temperance, prior

---

*Ironically, the suffrage resolution was the only resolution not unanimously passed at the Seneca Falls Convention.

to their commitment to women's rights.* Together they faced the formidable task of tapping into the discontent of nineteenth-century womanhood and mobilizing others for action. Even though no formal association formed, annual national and state conventions became an important means for communicating feminist principles and reaching other women. Through these efforts, support for the women's rights movement grew (Scott and Scott 1975).

The process of building a movement was not easy. The prescriptive domestic ideology of nineteenth-century America was a powerful force, relegating women to the private, domestic sphere and censuring public activity. Before women could be effective agents in their own behalf, they had to defy accepted definitions of appropriate female behavior and develop organizational and speaking skills. A life of feminist activism did not exempt women from the domestic responsibilities of home, husband, and children; and a special courage was needed since they frequently had only each other to rely upon for support. Even Elizabeth Cady Stanton faced hostility from her father, Judge Daniel Cady, and husband, Henry Stanton, a social activist. As she wrote to Susan B. Anthony in 1855,

> I passed through a terrible scourging when last at my father's. . . . I never felt more keenly the degradation of my sex. To think that all in me of which my father would have felt a proper pride had I been a man, is deeply mortifying to him because I am a woman. . . .

Henry sides with my friends, which oppose me in all that is dearest to my heart. They are not willing that I should write even on the woman question. But I will both write and speak. (DuBois 1981, 58–59)

The kind of antagonism Stanton experienced at home was expressed publicly by other men. The presence of such vocal opposition was a formidable obstacle to overcome and underscored a central dilemma faced by the movement: How could women gain access to a political system controlled by men who were hostile to the prospect of relinquishing any power to women?

Disappointment and Division

The Civil War temporarily disrupted the women's rights movement. Over the objections of Susan B. Anthony, the movement's leaders decided to suspend activism and devote their time and energy to the war effort. But with the conclusion of the war and the ratification of the Thirteenth Amendment to the Constitution of the United States, attention could once again be turned to women's rights. Since black male enfranchisement was imminent, the vote presented itself as the foremost issue. On May 10, 1866, at the first postbellum women's rights convention, suffrage activists established the American Equal Rights Association to work for the political inclusion of "both classes [black men and all women] of disfranchised citizens" (Buhle and Buhle 1978, 224).

Initial hopes rested with the Fourteenth Amendment, but when it emerged from Congress and went to the states for ratification, it was not the anticipated black suffrage amendment. Instead of enfranchising women, the Fourteenth Amendment would threaten women's

---

*Among the notable leaders of the antebellum women's rights movement were Susan B. Anthony, Elizabeth Cady Stanton, Lucretia Mott, Lucy Stone, Frances Dana Gage, and Paulina Wright Davis. Sojourner Truth has gone down in history as the most famed black women's rights activist of the time.

rights by inserting the word "male" into the Constitution of the United States. The American Equal Rights Association saw no alternative but to oppose ratification. For their position, the women again faced heated opposition from their former male allies in the abolition movement who believed that the amendment should pass regardless of the consequences for women (Buhle and Buhle 1978; Scott and Scott 1975; Flexner 1975). Anthony answered the critics:

> The question is . . . what are the principles under discussion. As I understand the difference between Abolitionists, some think this is harvest time for the black man, and seed sowing time for woman. Others, with whom I agree, think we have been sowing the seed of individual rights, the foundation idea of a republic for the last century, and that this is the harvest time for all citizens who pay taxes, obey the laws and are loyal to the government. (Buhle and Buhle 1978, 344)

When their efforts to block the Fourteenth Amendment failed, the forces of Stanton and Anthony set their sights toward the forthcoming Fifteenth Amendment. Women's rights activists lobbied congressmen to include sex, as well as race and previous condition of servitude, in the definition of citizens whose right to vote could not be denied (Buhle and Buhle 1978; Scott and Scott 1975; Flexner 1975). When the states ratified the Fifteenth Amendment without enfranchising women, the suffrage forces faced their second major setback.

The inclusion of the three Reconstruction amendments to the Constitution of the United States left unanswered questions regarding women's political status. In 1872 Virginia Minor tested constitutional ambiguity when she attempted to register to vote in the state of Missouri.

Upon being denied the right to register, Minor and her husband, Francis Minor, filed suit against the St. Louis registrar, Reese Happersett. Three years later, the Supreme Court of the United States unanimously upheld an earlier lower court decision against the Minors. The opinion, written by Chief Justice Waite, maintained that while women were citizens of the United States (Flexner 1975), "the Constitution has not added the right of suffrage to the privileges and immunities of citizenship as they existed at the time it was adopted" (Scott and Scott 1975, 85). The decision made clear that women had not been enfranchised by the Fourteenth and Fifteenth amendments, and that citizenship and suffrage were not coextensive under the Constitution. To many suffrage activists, the Minor decision underscored the need for a national woman suffrage amendment.

Unified action toward this end was not possible, however, because the suffrage forces remained divided after the Reconstruction amendment disputes. Two suffrage associations had emerged, the National Woman Suffrage Association (NWSA), led by Stanton and Anthony, and the American Woman Suffrage Association (AWSA), headed by Lucy Stone and her husband, Henry Blackwell. The division was more than in name alone and reflected profound ideological, tactical, and strategic differences. The more moderate AWSA favored a state-by-state approach to woman suffrage while NWSA attacked on many fronts, working for a national amendment to the Constitution, testing state laws in the courts, and forging political alliances with all parties receptive to woman suffrage. More central to the schism was Stone's and Blackwell's unwillingness to challenge social conventions that defined women's lives in relation to motherhood and home. While they feared arousing negative public opinion, Stanton and Anthony continued a controversial attack on the inequalities in marriage, divorce, and education and advocated equal pay for women and women's control over their own sexuality (Flexner 1975; Scott and Scott 1975).

On the surface, it would seem that two suffrage associations, vying for members and competing with one another for resources, impeded progress toward their shared objective. However, the opposite was probably true. The two associations with their divergent approaches to women's rights reached a broader audience than either could have done alone. For those supporters who were not ready to embrace the position held by NWSA, the more conservative AWSA was a comforting alternative. For their part, Stanton and Anthony, through their dramatic actions and candid oratory, kept women's rights in the public eye. Their agitation for a wide variety of issues prevented a narrowing of the focus to a singular issue, the vote, and their continued adherence to the principles of Seneca Falls kept a broad-based feminist agenda alive through the years of division in the movement (Scott and Scott 1975).

Domestic Feminism

While many suffragists challenged the division between the public sphere of men and the private sphere of women, other feminists accepted women's dominion in the home and used it as a base of power for female activism. According to nineteenth-century social norms, women were to guard their homes from corrupting influences, preserve the traditional values of family and God, and exercise their natural piety and morality to influence and redeem the public sector. While some scholars have maintained that this cult of domesticity closely circumscribed women's lives, it can also be argued that this ideology conferred genuine social and political significance to women's traditional roles, opened the way for women to enter the public sphere, and provided a source of sex solidarity based on shared female experiences (Matthews 1987). The reverence accorded feminine qualities granted women the right not only to act in the preservation of the home but also to use their moral influence to change men's behavior.

The Women's Christian Temperance Union (WCTU), the largest women's organization of its time, epitomized nineteenth-century domestic feminism. Alcohol and alcoholism were considered problems of severe proportions, draining family resources, promoting degeneracy, and destroying home life. Under these circumstances, it was not only appropriate but divinely sanctioned for women to work against this evil. Led by the dynamic and charismatic Frances E. Willard, the members of the WCTU identified themselves as "organized mother love" and rallied against alcohol "For God, For home, For native land."

The majority of women who joined the WCTU undoubtedly acted upon a heartfelt sense of responsibility to home and family. Frances Willard, however, unmarried and a professional educator, had committed herself to women's rights prior to the founding of the WCTU. For her, the motivating factor behind participation may have been the feminist potential of the WCTU rather than temperance itself. During her presidency Willard demonstrated a talent for manipulating the cult of domesticity and expanding the central definition of woman's place (Matthews 1987; Evans 1989; Bordin 1980):

Home is woman's climate, her vital breath, her native air. A true woman carries home with her everywhere. Its atmosphere surrounds her. Its mirror is her face. Its music attunes her gentle voice. Its longitude may be reckoned from wherever you happen to find her.

Based on such logic, women's action and activism never exceed the parameters of home.

Without ever abandoning the principles of Gospel Temperance, the WCTU added a number of causes that reflected Willard's "Do Everything Policy": world peace, labor reform, and woman suffrage. Unlike the suffrage associations, Willard did not demand the right to vote; she presented woman suffrage as a necessity for the preservation of the home and public morality and thereby allayed the charges that voting, a public act, would in any way tarnish women's respectability. What began as a fulfillment of women's domestic responsibilities became a powerful political and social force, creating new opportunities for women and helping to make suffrage a respectable issue (Bordin 1980; Evans 1989).

The same type of domestic feminism exhibited in the WCTU also found expression in the Progressive era of the early 1900s. The reform impulse during this period took many forms: school nursing and lunch programs; muckraking, a form of exposé journalism; and improved working conditions for women, a reform particularly important to the National Consumers League.* The most famous example of women's activism was the settlement house movement, which attracted many young, educated, reform-minded women. Settlement houses, located in the

poorest immigrant neighborhoods, sponsored many programs designed to improve the quality of life and health of the local residents. The initial intent may have been to uplift the poor, ignorant immigrant; however, when settlement workers, like Jane Addams of Chicago's Hull House, saw the interrelationship of poverty, inadequate city services, infant mortality, and deplorable conditions of labor, their focus shifted to broad-based municipal reform (Davis 1984; Sklar 1985; Evans 1989).

Addams, perhaps the most famous woman of her time, clearly articulated a domestic feminist critique of municipal problems. Shrewdly referring to the business of the city as "enlarged housekeeping," Addams argued that the American city had failed because "the traditional housekeepers have not been consulted as to its multiform activities" (Norton 1989, 260). The conclusion to be drawn from this was that women would use the vote to improve sanitation, educate children, clean the streets, and provide needed health care programs. The Progressive reform movement played an important role in promoting social change, sanctioning women's efforts at factory, prison, and government reform, and contributing to the legitimization of woman suffrage.

Education and economic privilege enabled hundreds of thousands of white, middle-class women to engage in reform and feminist activism. For black women the situation was different; only one generation from slavery, their activism had to incorporate an analysis of race as well as gender. A significant organizational impulse came from their women's club movement. Originally established as self-improvement groups, they rapidly expanded in focus to include civic improvement and social reform issues. Black women's clubs began to appear in the

---

*The National Consumers League was an association that attempted to use women's power as consumers to influence the labor and manufacturing practices of companies. A white label affixed to a product indicated it was produced and marketed by a firm with sound labor practices.

1890s, and in 1896, the two most influential organizations, the National Association of Afro-American Women and the Colored Women's League of Washington, consolidated to form the National Association of Colored Women (NACW) with Mary Church Terrell as its first president. The agenda of the NACW reflected many traditional female reform interests, providing kindergartens and schools for children, rescuing of prostitutes, establishing homes for orphans and the aged, and arranging adequate nurseries for working mothers. The NACW addressed "not only those things that are of vital importance to us as women, but also the things that are of special interest to us as colored women," and the members consciously "worked with might and main to improve the condition of their colored people" (Norton 1989, 258–59). Because of this dual focus, woman suffrage proved to be a problematic issue for the black women's clubs. The majority of black Americans lived in the South where Jim Crow laws enforced segregation and poll taxes and grandfather clauses had effectively disenfranchised black men.* Under these circumstances, it would have been inappropriate for NACW affiliates to work singularly for woman suffrage. Instead, the black women's clubs of the South initially devoted considerable attention to petitioning state legislatures for the repeal of Jim Crow laws and worked

in anti-lynching campaigns. While black women, like their white counterparts, operated from a position of female solidarity and common sisterhood, for them the issues of race and gender were inextricably intertwined, creating an agenda different from that of white feminists (Lerner 1972; Giddings 1984; Flexner 1975; Lerner 1979).

Suffrage Comes of Age

By 1890 a new generation of feminists entered the scene; having had no role in the earlier conflicts, it pushed for reconciliation and reunion. That year NWSA and AWSA merged to form the National American Woman Suffrage Association (NAWSA). Among the challenges faced by NAWSA was that of articulating its philosophical approach to women's rights, and from there establishing an agenda and devising appropriate strategies. The vote, a symbol of women's social and political powerlessness, emerged as an identifiable and attainable goal around which NAWSA could mobilize support (Scott and Scott 1975).

The period from 1890 to 1915 was one of adjustment, organization, and planning as NAWSA actively recruited and trained new members and experimented with new tactics. These efforts led to the adoption of woman suffrage amendments in a number of states.* Still, NAWSA had one problem to solve—finding a dynamic captain who could lead the movement to victory. Stanton and Anthony were the natural choices, and both women faithfully served terms as president of the association; however, it was time for the

---

*Jim Crow is a term applied to the segregation laws enacted in the South during the late 1800s and early 1900s which legally mandated the separation of the race. Initially applied to passenger trains, Jim Crow laws came to include toilets, drinking fountains, ticket windows, and even facilities such as hospitals and prisons. Southern states implemented poll taxes and grandfather clauses to effectively disfranchise black men. Poll taxes levied $1.00 to $2.00 on each citizen who went to the polls. Grandfather clauses required a literacy test for all voters except those persons and their sons and grandsons who had voted prior to January 1867.

---

*The major advances had been made in the West. By the mid-1890s, Colorado, Utah, Idaho, and Wyoming were woman suffrage states. It would be the 1910s before any new states granted women the vote, when California and Washington enfranchised women and Illinois did so for presidential elections.

younger generation to take the reins of leadership. When Anthony resigned in 1900, the association instated her hand-picked successor, Carrie Chapman Catt. Personal circumstances forced Catt to step down in 1904, but after the 1915 defeat of the woman suffrage amendment in Congress Catt was again called upon to assume the presidency (Scott and Scott 1975).

The selection of Catt was a wise decision. She was an experienced leader and a skilled organizer with a keen political sense. It was a crucial time for Catt to assume NAWSA's presidency. The campaigns, suffrage parades, and years of lobbying had helped to shift public opinion. In 1916, faced with the full force of the suffrage ranks at their national conventions, both political parties endorsed the conservative state-by-state approach to woman suffrage; and the Republican candidate, Charles Evans Hughes, came out in support of a national amendment.

Catt considered this a crisis period in the history of woman suffrage and called an NAWSA "emergency convention." While not discounting the importance of state-based activism, Catt realized that all women would not be enfranchised by relying on states to pass women's right to vote. At this meeting, she stressed the importance of a federal amendment. "In my judgment the women of this land not only have the right to sit on the steps of Congress until it acts but it is their self-respecting duty to insist upon their enfranchisement by that route." Corresponding to this view, Catt's "Winning Plan" called for a coordinated plan of attack on all fronts. In order to ensure success for the massive state and federal efforts, NAWSA authorized a million-dollar budget (Scott and Scott 1975).

NAWSA had become an effective, cohesive organization with two million members, but this did not point to unity within the women's rights movement. Two young suffragists, Alice Paul and Lucy Burns, had received their training in the militant and radical British suffrage movement and, upon their return to the United States, joined forces with NAWSA. Initially their efforts were welcomed, and their daring actions achieved considerable notoriety. Once again significant tactical and philosophical differences made it impossible for moderates and radicals to continue collaborative efforts within the same organization. A permanent break between the two factions occurred in 1913, with Burns and Paul forming the Congressional Union, later known as the National Woman's Party (NWP). Each suffrage association proceeded along its own path toward the common goal. While NAWSA representatives lobbied congress in a ladylike, decorous manner and exerted steady but diplomatic pressure on President Wilson, the Woman's Party engaged in smaller-scale lobbying efforts and picketed the White House. NAWSA adopted a bipartisan approach, courting congressmen from both parties, while the Woman's Party blamed the party in power for inactivity on woman suffrage (Kraditor 1965; Flexner 1975; Scott and Scott 1975).

Another division took place in the suffrage ranks, one that would stand as a blemish in the history of the women's rights movement. By the 1910s, black women had become outspoken supporters of suffrage. Their efforts were based on the belief that

colored women, quite as much as colored men, realize that if there is ever to be equal justice and fair play in the protection in the courts everywhere for all races, then there must be an equal chance for all women as well as men to express their preference through their votes (Lerner 1972, 446).

Black women's suffrage associations and influential regional and national groups like NACW and the Northeastern Federation of Colored Women's Clubs mounted campaigns for the Nineteenth Amendment. NAWSA and the NWP, however, rejected their actions and made every attempt to disavow the work of the black suffragists. NAWSA even went so far as to request that the Northeastern Federation of Colored Women's Clubs withdraw its application for membership, urging that the federation delay such action until after ratification of the Nineteenth Amendment. Ostensibly, the reason for these exclusionary measures was that too close association with blacks would thwart the alliance with white southern women and jeopardize the prospects of ratification in the South. The position held by NAWSA and the NWP was an unfortunate reflection of the racism and fear that permeated American society in the early twentieth century. By catering to the argument that white women's enfranchisement in the South would guarantee white supremacy in that region, NAWSA and the NWP betrayed the human rights, universal suffrage position that had been a cornerstone of nineteenth-century women's rights activism (Kraditor 1965; Terborg-Penn 1983).

When the United States entered World War I, difficult choices had to be made. Because Catt believed that contributing to the war effort would demonstrate the value of women's citizenship and enhance women's political credibility, NAWSA continued its suffrage activities unabated while pledging its support of the war effort. The NWP continued working singularly for suffrage. During the summer of 1917, the NWP became more militant and provocative in its public demonstrations and capitalized upon the themes of World War I by carrying placards and banners with slogans like "Kaiser Wilson" and "Democracy Should Begin at Home." The arrest and jailing of close to one hundred women for the questionable charge of obstructing sidewalk traffic made front-page headlines. The drama heightened when the women, in protest of the arrests and conditions in jail, went on a hunger strike and were subsequently force-fed. The media attention became a political embarrassment for the Wilson administration, and its only choice was to release the suffrage activists, who were by this time requesting the status of political prisoners (Flexner 1975; Kraditor 1965). NAWSA understandably did everything in its power to dissociate itself from the NWP, but, as had been the case in the late nineteenth century with the AWSA and NWSA, the presence of moderates and radicals was important to the advancement of their common cause. As noted by historians Anne Firor Scott and Andrew Scott, "Nervousness about what the radical women might do next encouraged both Congress and the president to make concessions to and to embrace the more conservative suffragists as the lesser evil" (Scott and Scott 1975, 41).

At the conclusion of 1917, it was no longer a question of if, but when, a national suffrage amendment would pass. The 1917 New York suffrage referendum had been a landmark event for the movement and had set a positive tone for the suffrage forces as the Sixty-fifth Congress convened. Hopes ran high as the House of Representatives passed the woman suffrage bill, but despite President Wilson's strong endorsement, the bill was defeated in the Senate. Though disappointed, the suffrage associations maintained their lobbying efforts and worked for the defeat of selected antisuffrage legislators. When the Sixty-sixth Congress convened, the House passed the Woman Suffrage Act by a margin of 215 votes, and on June 4, 1919, the Senate approved the bill. It was now up to the states to ratify the amendment. Thirty-six states were needed, and the well-organized NAWSA was ready for the challenge. On August 19, 1920, with Tennessee's affirmative vote, woman suffrage was attained (Scott and Scott 1975).

The seventy-two-year history of the woman suffrage movement is an important example of how a disfranchised group, on the periphery of the centers of political power, transformed the political system and gained access to it. Many factors contributed to final passage of the Nineteenth Amendment. First and foremost was the dedication of the first feminists. These women devoted much of their time and energy to political equality, and importantly, to a vision of the future that many of them, like Susan B. Anthony and Elizabeth Cady Stanton, would never live to see. The dynamic that existed between the radical and moderate factions served to keep the movement alive, and the reform movements set a tone for social change that helped make woman suffrage a respectable issue. Changes in society had given women increasing control over property, greater levels of education and more opportunities in the labor market, and together they pointed toward new public and political possibilities for American women. Finally, the political principles of natural rights and the consent of the governed upon which this country is based laid the groundwork for the political equality of all citizens.

Feminism after Suffrage

Suffrage had provided a focal point for the women's movement since the 1860s, but the passage and ratification of the Nineteenth Amendment eliminated the foremost symbol of common purpose. Two important historical questions emerged in the post-suffrage years: What happened to feminism after suffrage, and what did suffrage mean for American women? Until recently, historians have variously interpreted the seventy-year drive for suffrage as either culminating in women's freedom and liberation or as ending in failure. These views, respectively, were based upon an erroneous tendency to see the vote as the true measure of political and legal equality and an unrealistic assumption that all women should have or could have, for their own self-interest, constituted themselves into a sex-based voting bloc. Critics of the women's movement further clouded the situation when, failing to see unified action toward a common goal, hastily pronounced that feminism faced its demise in the 1920s (Freedman 1974).

While there ceased to be an identifiable women's movement, feminist activity continued on many fronts. One of the most significant and enduring channels for activism was the peace movement, where women comprised the majority of the rank and file. Reform and former suffrage associations such as the General Federation of Women's Clubs, the NWP, and the National League of Women Voters joined in advocating peace through arms reduction, disarmament, and international law. The most influential organization, however, was the Women's International League for Peace and Freedom (WILPF), which worked for peace on many fronts: investigating danger areas that threatened world peace, circulating petitions domestically, and lobbying political leaders internationally. The WILPF was internationally renowned and its leaders were honored as recipients of the Nobel Peace Prize—Jane Addams in

1931 and Emily Green Balch in 1946 (Brown 1987).

After passage of the Nineteenth Amendment, the powerful NAWSA reorganized as the National League of Women Voters (NLWV). Under the direction of former NAWSA leader Maude Wood Park, the NLWV pursued a pragmatic agenda: mobilizing women voters, educating them on issues and the functioning of the political system, and pressuring the major parties for the inclusion of women's concerns in the party platforms. NAWSA's ideological nemesis, the NWP, continued a radical course during the following decades, campaigning for the introduction and passage of the Equal Rights Amendment (ERA). In Alice Paul's estimation, a national amendment was more than the natural successor to suffrage; it was the only way to eliminate the myriad of local, state, and national laws that blocked women's equality in the legal, political, economic, and educational arenas (Brown 1987; Cott 1987; Cott 1991; Rupp and Taylor 1987).

The ERA was an important issue from 1920 through the 1950s, but it proved to be a divisive force in American feminism.* The NWP came into conflict with reform-minded social feminists who believed that an ERA would undermine decades of progress in protective legislation for women workers. Protective legis-

lation had done much to improve the conditions of employment for women. The problem arose because such laws set women apart as a distinct class in the labor force, according them special treatment with regard to maximum hours, minimum wages, and prohibitions on working night shifts. Fearing that the ERA would mandate that women and men be accorded identical treatment in the work place, the Women's Joint Congressional Committee, dominated by the NLWV, the National Women's Trade Union League, and the National Consumers League, openly fought both the NWP and the amendment (Brown 1987; Cott 1991; Cott 1987; Rupp and Taylor 1987).

Feminist fighting over the merits of the ERA may seem ironic and counterproductive, but the protracted debates were based on divergent conceptions of womanhood and definitions of equality. The social feminists believed that fundamental differences distinguished women from men, with women primarily defined by physiological and reproductive factors, particularly the biological fact of motherhood. In contrast, the NWP rejected biological determinist arguments, crediting differences to social and historical factors that influenced the development of men and women. Following from these opposing views of womanhood, two definitions of equality emerged. Opponents of the ERA embraced a separate but equal position analogous to that advanced in the 1896 *Plessy v. Ferguson* decision. Advocates of the ERA advanced the idea that women should be granted equal access and opportunity and accorded equal treatment in all areas of American life and society (Cott 1991; Cott 1987; Rupp and Taylor 1987).

In many respects, the tide of historical events turned against the social feminists with the enactment of minimum wage

---

*Despite disagreement within feminist ranks and hostility to women's equality, the ERA has had a long history in Congress. It was first introduced into Congress in 1923 and into both houses in 1924, 1925, and 1929. In 1936–37, the ERA received favorable reports from both House and Senate committees but was returned to committee by the full Congress. The year 1946 marked the first postwar time that the ERA was voted on in the Senate, and in 1950 and 1953 the ERA passed the Senate. The closest that the amendment has come to success was in the 1970s, when the ERA passed both houses in 1972 only to fail ratification despite the extension of the deadline from March 23, 1979, to June 30, 1982.

and maximum hour legislation in the 1930s, the admission of women into the military during World War II, and the 1954 Supreme Court decision *Brown v. Board of Education,* which ideologically challenged and overturned the previous separate but equal ruling regarding black Americans. The major flaws in the social feminist analysis were that it uncritically accepted the discriminatory sex-based division of labor in the home and work place and it failed to challenge popular notions that claimed women had physical limitations because of their reproductive functions (Cott 1987; Cott 1991). Proponents of the ERA also erred in placing too much faith in the power of a single amendment. In order to transform women's place in society and eradicate all forms of discrimination, what was needed in addition to the ERA was an alteration of deeply entrenched social attitudes and values that sustained and perpetuated women's subordination.

Women's Liberation

By 1960 the contradictions and inequalities in American society had again created an environment conducive to social change. One of the greatest contradictions was the continued degradation of blacks in a nation of presumed equality. When black Americans refused to accept the injustice any longer, they raised their voices in protest. The resulting civil rights movement became the model and inspiration for other groups in society, who began to call for their rights.

Women also acutely felt the contradictions by the 1950s and 1960s. They had held the vote for forty years but wielded no real political power. They had higher levels of education than ever before in American history, yet had limited opportunities to apply their intellects. Women

were expected to work for pin money in part-time, semi-skilled jobs rather than apply their knowledge and education to high paying and challenging careers. As a consequence of Cold War international and domestic tensions, the United States looked inward and embraced traditional values and institutions. Home and motherhood were once again glorified and presented as women's path to complete fulfillment despite the fact that approximately 40 percent of American women worked outside the home. Those women who tried to live up to the ideal filled their time and lives with PTA meetings, girl scouts, and church activities; yet many felt unfulfilled. The "feminine mystique" and "the problem that has no name," exposed and articulated by Betty Friedan, plagued their lives.

The opportunity for systematic examination of women's position in society began in 1961 when President John F. Kennedy appointed Eleanor Roosevelt to head the President's Commission on the Status of Women. The commission's 1963 report provided a distressing account of systemic and pervasive discrimination, unequal treatment under the law, and unequal remuneration in the labor force. Direct consequences of the commission's findings were passage of the Equal Pay Act of 1963 and the inclusion of sex in Title VII of the 1964 Civil Rights Act. These acts provided women with the legal tools needed to challenge economic discrimination, and the Equal Employment Opportunity Commission (EEOC), established to investigate grievances, was deluged with complaints from women. Unfortunately, without an organizational presence to exert pressure on the legal and political systems, discrimination on the basis of sex was still not taken seriously. The EEOC acted slowly, apathetically, and sometimes with hostility to reports of sex discrimination (Hartmann 1989; Evans 1989).

By 1966 discontent had mounted; and when the Third National Conference of State Committees on the Status of Women refused to allow a resolution demanding enforcement of Title VII, representatives led by Betty Friedan decided to form their own organization, the National Organization for Women (NOW). Moderate in tone and reformist in ideology, NOW has worked within the established institutions of society to achieve equal access to and an equal place for women in "the mainstream of American society" (National Organization for Women 1966). Through lobbying, petitions, lawsuits, and political campaigning, NOW has challenged the inequalities of American society. Despite periods of internal strife, NOW successfully galvanized support for the ERA, women's reproductive rights, and the inclusion of women in affirmative action programs (Hartmann 1989; Evans 1989).

Since its inception, NOW has become a strong national voice for women, and has grown into the largest U.S.-based organization of women today. Through advocacy of political, legal, and economic equality, NOW has clearly articulated the interests of middle-class, educated women whose personal struggles are and will continue to be eased by institutional equality. While NOW addresses many of the major problems faced by professional women, it does not address the fundamental nature and source of women's repression. For that reason, NOW alone has not been able to trigger a broad-based women's movement.

The driving force behind the women's liberation movement was the younger, more radical women whose political training had begun in the civil rights and the New Left movements of the 1960s. They did not believe that liberation for women could be obtained through equal access to and opportunity within inherently oppressive institutions. Consequently, they were not content seeking legal remedies or strict enforcement of EEOC guidelines. These women challenged not only the fundamental principles of NOW, they challenged the fundamental order of society; and among the issues central to their analyses were a cultural critique of femininity, the social relations between the sexes, the relationship of politics to personal life, and the meaning of sisterhood.

In the politically charged atmosphere of the 1960s, many college women joined the campus-based New Left organization Students for a Democratic Society (SDS) and the student branch of the civil rights movement, the Student Nonviolent Coordinating Committee (SNCC). Like their male counterparts in these organizations, they acted upon a belief in equality, democracy, and peace; and they participated in antiwar demonstrations, voter registration drives, community organization projects, freedom schools, and campus protests. Through these activities, they became increasingly politicized; and like the women in the abolitionist movement of the 1800s, they began to apply the activist ideals of equality to their own position in society. To their dismay, the men of the left and the civil rights movements proved to be no more enlightened or egalitarian than other men in society. Women's issues were not given credibility in the male-dominated movements, and attempts to integrate women's issues into the movements met with open hostility or ridicule (Evans 1989; Evans 1978; Hartmann 1989). One of the most famous examples of this hostility occurred in 1964 when SNCC leader Stokely Carmichael stated, "The only position for women in SNCC is prone" (Morgan 1970, 35).

Repeated subtle and overt sexist acts prompted the radical women to create their own movement. They began to apply the skills they had acquired in public speaking and grassroots organizing for their own benefit and built upon the female networks forged as a consequence of campus activism. Their grievances were deeply felt and the issues addressed cut to the heart of woman's subordination: the right of women to control their bodies; the right to walk the streets free from fear; the end to an ideology that defines women as sex symbols; the end to sexual division of labor in the home and paid labor force; and the right of women to develop their full potential as human beings. Unlike the moderates, radical women dared to critique the origins and extent of women's oppression (Evans 1978; Evans 1989).

These demands were repeated in the literature, protests, and manifestoes of the women's liberation movement. What made the movement so dynamic was that, instead of one single organized group, there was a proliferation of groups and organizations embracing many different perspectives and strategies. Collectively, through the use of tactics like Zap action and guerilla theater, the radicals successfully kept feminist issues in the public eye.*

One of the more dramatic and creative groups was the Women's International Terrorist Conspiracy from Hell, commonly known as WITCH. Dressed in hoods and robes, members went down New York's Wall Street placing hexes on bankers who loaned money to corporations that made the instruments of war. Another time WITCH hexed United Fruit Company headquarters for sex discrimination at home and for exploitative labor practices abroad. Perhaps the most famous example of feminist guerilla theater occurred on September 7, 1968, in Atlantic City at the Miss America pageant. In order to illustrate how "beauty" pageants degraded women, feminist protesters held their own coronation crowning a sheep in honor of the event. Organizers of the demonstration also set up freedom trash cans where they deposited the symbols of women's oppression—curlers, make-up, wigs, girdles, and bras. From this event came the famed phrase "bra burners," subsequently used by opponents of feminism to deride and demean feminist activism (Evans 1989; Morgan 1970).

While the sheer drama of such events was important in keeping attention focused on feminist issues, the heart and soul of the women's liberation movement of the 1960s and 1970s was the consciousness raising (CR) group. CR groups were informal meetings where female friends, neighbors, or work associates got together and discussed their life experiences. Sometimes the meetings were free-flowing discussions, and at other times they focused on specific issues like marriage-career conflicts, inequality in intimate heterosexual relationships, or traditional female socialization's role in impeding self-fulfillment. During these discussions women realized the shared experience of oppression, and out of this grew anger which led beyond personal growth to mobilized attempts to change all women's lives. The CR group proved to be an effective organizing tool and provided the point of entry into the movement for many women (Evans 1979; Evans 1989).

The moderates and radicals, though ideological rivals, again complemented

---

*Zap action and guerilla theater were spontaneous and improvisational theatrical demonstrations designed to draw attention to increase public awareness of social inequalities, exploitative practices, and sexism in the media and in cultural attitudes.

the efforts of each other. Pressure on the legal and political systems yielded significant results: Affirmative action was an important stride forward in achieving equal consideration in the labor market; *Griswold v. Connecticut* and *Roe v. Wade* helped guarantee reproductive freedom; the National Women's Political Caucus, created in 1971, worked diligently to increase the number of women in the political arena; and Title IX of the 1972 Higher Education Act protected women from discrimination in educational institutions, programs, and activities.* Still, the feminist movement has faced defeats: The ERA failed ratification in 1982, and the 1989 Supreme Court decision *Webster v. Missouri* has withdrawn much federal protection from abortion by allowing states to pass laws that limit abortion rights (Hartmann 1989; Stetson 1991; Evans 1989). The feminist revolution hoped for by many radicals has not yet come, but in the process of examining society and their experiences, women learned the meaning of Kate Millet's assertion that "the personal is political" and discovered a new sense of themselves and their potential. This awareness produced hundreds of thousands of personal revolutions in individual women's lives, and the course of women's history has been changed.

Feminist Perspectives and Challenges

One of the most exciting developments within the women's liberation movement has been the emergence of many feminist perspectives. Women are members of all

*Title IX of the 1972 Higher Education Act has become most known for the advances it permitted in women's intercollegiate athletics. The threat of lawsuits and the potential withdrawal of federal funding enabled women athletes to challenge discriminatory allocations of money for men's and women's programs.

racial and ethnic groups, are found in all socioeconomic classes, and support all political views; in turn, these divergent experiences inform a variety of gender analyses. Issues and concerns based in socialist, black, Asian, Latina, Native American, Jewish, and lesbian feminism have come forth and helped to expand and redefine feminism.

Women who are members of racial minorities face a double oppression—as women and as members of their racial group. This fact has shaped their feminist perspective and has charted for many of them a different path toward the women's movement than that of their white counterparts. In the civil rights movement, women's central place in the black community and churches enabled them to play a critical role in grassroots organizing, and many women like Pauli Murray, Angela Davis, Shirley Chisholm, and Florence Kennedy became prominent civil rights and feminist activists. Most black women of the 1960s and 1970s identified race as the primary oppression they faced and believed it was imperative to maintain a sense of racial solidarity with black men. Still, within the civil rights movement, and particularly in the male-dominated Black Power groups, women faced a cult of manliness that, in part, blamed black women for the anger, frustration, and economic lack of power faced by black men. Women were expected to play supporting roles, and if they acted too aggressively or in their own behalf, they were charged with attempting to destroy black manhood (Jones 1985; Evans 1989; Giddings 1984). Women in the movement recognized this marginalization of women and their issues, as Sonia Presman pointed out in 1970: "When most people talk about civil rights, they mean the rights of Black people. And when they talk about the rights of Black people, they generally mean the rights of Black men" (Giddings 1984, 319).

Despite the overt sexism in the civil rights movement, few black feminists eagerly rushed to the women's movement. A longstanding history of exclusionary policies preconditioned black women to be suspicious of white feminists, and contemporary insensitivity to race and racism justified their fears of forging an alliance. Much of the problem initially lay within NOW. Often seen as synonymous with the women's movement, NOW demonstrated an early unwillingness to expand its agenda beyond the interests of white, middle-class women. While equality within the mainstream was a valid objective, it was naive to assume that it was a realistic objective for women struggling with basic survival. The feminization of poverty, poor or nonexistent health care, a lack of job training programs for women, and inadequate pre- and post-natal care would have provided an excellent foundation for collaborative efforts since these issues affected poor women of all races. Black women failed to recognize these commonalities as well because of an erroneous tendency to characterize all white feminists as privileged members of the middle class (Jones 1985; Giddings 1984; Evans 1989).

Black feminists of the 1960s and 1970s were literally creating a new perspective that explained the double oppression of sex and race and that addressed the many manifestations of this "double jeopardy." As Toni Morrison said of the black woman involved in this process, she "had nothing to fall back on: not maleness, not whiteness, not ladyhood, not anything. And out of the profound desolation of her reality she may have very well invented herself" (Jones 1985, 315). By the mid-1970s, women like Morrison, Alice Walker, Frances Beal, and Angela Davis had articulated a black feminist perspective that was based on black women's unique sources of oppression and historical strengths. By this time, the women's movement had matured and diversified along class and racial dimensions, making some black feminists feel less estranged.

The black civil rights movement encouraged other minority groups to organize in their own behalf. Two of the most visible and important examples were the American Indian Movement (AIM) and the Chicano movement. The strength of these movements was their foundation in a shared sense of community, culture, and oppression. Women's traditional roles enabled them to play an important part in community organization. This participation pattern was especially true of the farm-worker-based Chicano movement, where Chicana leaders like Jesse Lopez de la Cruz and Dolores Huerta ardently worked to bring women into the United Farm Workers. Issues of gender oppression and sexism emerged, but identification with and ties to family structures, culture, and religion prevented an immediate attempt to create alliances with the feminist movement. The response was to establish autonomous associations for the formulation of a women's agenda based in their own cultural context. In 1970 the North American Indian Women's Association was organized, and in 1971 the first national Chicana conference was held. This type of organized presence not only served to introduce women's issues into AIM and the Chicano movement but challenged white feminists to adopt a more inclusive perspective (Hartmann 1989).

The issue of sexual orientation, and specifically of lesbianism, proved to be a problematic and divisive force in the women's movement. The problem lies in the fact that just as lesbianism cuts across all racial, ethnic, and class boundaries, so does homophobia. Lesbian feminism is peculiarly located between the gay liberation movement and the women's movement, having historical origins in both but belonging to neither. With regard to the women's movement, lesbians occupied a curious and contradictory position, being among the leaders and founders, yet having their concerns identified as threatening to the very movement that they helped to create.

Gays and lesbians long endured police harassment and bar raids. These actions had a particularly demoralizing effect since the gay community, having been forced underground by hatred and discrimination, had created a thriving social and cultural lifestyle where bars provided one of the primary meeting places. On the weekend of June 27–28, 1969, gays and lesbians said "no more" and faced down police at the Stonewall Bar in New York's Greenwich Village. From the ashes of Stonewall, gay liberation was born. Informed by the same radicalizing forces affecting other groups in society, the gay liberation movement from its inception focused less upon specific civil rights issues than upon eradicating the deep-seated homophobia in society that defined homosexuality as an illness, that imposed heterosexuality upon all people, and that condemned to silence all who did not fit the heterosexual model (Adam 1987; Faderman 1991).

Lesbians actively participated in the movement, building coalitions, establishing support groups, and forming gay and lesbian organizations. Women, however, were the minority in the gay liberation movement, and they struggled against both the androcentric bias that took for granted the privileges that men enjoyed in society and the heterosexist as-

sumption that all women existed in relationships with men who could and would support them. Many women became disillusioned with gay men's unwillingness to incorporate such issues into their analysis and realized that lesbian liberation was something different from gay liberation. The natural place for lesbians to turn was the women's movement, where many were already among the leaders and founders of NOW and the campus groups. Those who believed that the women's movement would embrace lesbian issues were sorely mistaken. The most famous example of betrayal occurred in 1970, when lesbian feminists led by Rita Mae Brown confronted NOW for its heterosexist position and exclusion of lesbian issues. Betty Friedan, then president of NOW, responded to the criticism by charging that lesbianism, "the lavender menace," threatened the success of the women's movement by tarnishing its image and undermining its credibility (Adam 1987; Faderman 1991; Evans 1989).

Facing sexism in one movement and homophobia in the other, some women remained loyal to their historical allies, working to establish the legitimacy of lesbian concerns. Others, however, who believed that they could not rely upon heterosexual feminists or gay men to advance lesbian issues, articulated their own idealized perspective. Refusing to accept traditional definitions of femininity, living beyond the dictates of patriarchy, and defining their lives in relationship to women instead of to men, they defied all social norms as they explored the meaning of women's culture, identity, and art. Many came to embrace the view expressed by Ti Grace Atkinson, "feminism the theory, lesbianism the practice." From a position of collective strength, radical lesbians responded to the feminists who sought to purge lesbianism from the movement, charging them with betraying their own cause by perpetuating the attitudes and values they purported to change: "As long as the label 'dyke' can be used to frighten women into a less militant stand, keep her separated from her sisters, keep her from giving primacy to anything other than men and family—then to that extent she is controlled by the male culture" (Evans 1989, 294). Because of insightful statements like this, lesbian feminism challenged the philosophical underpinnings of the women's movement and became a central component of contemporary feminist thought. Together, the perspectives introduced by black, Latina, and lesbian feminists have infused the women's movement with new ideas and ideals; one of the most important tasks faced by today's feminists is the full incorporation of these views in both thought and action.

During the late 1970s and 1980s, a reactionary New Right emerged to challenge the women's movement and women's right to control their sexuality and their own bodies. Marked by an antiliberal ethos that glorified Christianity, home, family, and marriage, the New Right found a symbol for its vision and values in President Ronald Reagan. Reagan held steadfast in his commitment to conservatism, and from 1980 onward, feminists watched the erosion of some hard-won advances of the 1960s and 1970s. The Reagan years brought forth not only a decline in the number of female appointments to the judiciary but a weakening of criteria for compliance with equal opportunity and affirmative action. The mandate for equality in education provided by Title IX was weakened in the 1984 *Grove City College* decision, which ruled that even when colleges discriminated against women in some areas of programming, they could continue to re-

ceive federal funding for those activities in which there was no discrimination. Because of the priorities of the Reagan administration, the unfortunate consequence of budget cutbacks was a devastating reduction in social spending. The burden fell on America's poor, who were disproportionately women and children. The reduction in support for human services not only took its toll in welfare and infant and child care programs, but it left rape crisis centers and shelters for battered women struggling for survival with dwindling resources (Hartmann 1989; Evans 1989; Stetson 1991).

The attempts of the New Right to undermine feminism and return women to the home failed. As explained by historian Sara Evans, "The Reagan revolution was unable to significantly alter the gender shifts that had already taken place: new roles for women in the labor force, the changing demographics of marriage and family size, the reemergence of single women, and greater sexual freedom" (Evans 1989, 307). In addition to holding ground on these fronts, new organizations emerged locally and nationally in response to specific issues and conditions. Increasing numbers of women became elected officials, especially at the local and state levels, and over the objections of the Reagan administration some state and local governments adopted comparable worth policies. In the academies, as well, feminism advanced as women's studies programs grew in size and number, reaching ever-increasing numbers of women.

The feminist movement, since its inception in 1848, faced forces hostile to change, and the 1980s were no exception. But this time, more so than in the past, feminists met their opponents from a position of strength. The shifts noted by Evans had stabilized women's position in society, and the decentralized nature of the movement with its multi-issue agenda protected it from attack, or defeat, on any one front. Though necessity required feminists to confront anti-liberal, anti-feminist threats, it did not prevent them from looking toward a vision of the future.

Conclusion

Two centuries of feminist thought and women's rights activism have permanently altered the position of women in American society. Women have gained access to higher education and the professions; they have guaranteed the right to their own wages and to custody of their children in the event of divorce. Dedicated activists have secured access to the political system and have pressured lawmakers to acquire more equitable treatment for women in the economic, legal, political, and educational arenas of American life. These dramatic achievements should in no way be diminished or dismissed; neither should they be interpreted as evidence of full equality. Women remain underrepresented in the professions, in Congress, and in the judiciary; they remain concentrated in traditional female jobs and, consequently, receive approximately 65 percent of the wages that men earn. Relaxed divorce laws of the 1970s have freed women from oppressive marriages but have simultaneously contributed to the feminization of poverty as women's standard of living drops over 70 percent on average with divorce. Perhaps most illustrative of the continued subordination of women is the pervasive social attitude that condones violence against women in the streets, in the media, in their homes, and on the job.

The advances in women's status and the gains yet to be made underscore both the power of feminism to transform society and the power of patriarchy to limit change. This tension points to the continued need for both moderate and radical feminist thought and action. Institutional protections like affirmative action and Title IX, largely the concerns of moderate feminists, have secured greater influence and provided needed safeguards for women in society. But the present threats to reproductive freedom and the weakening of the EEOC during the Reagan and Bush years serve as examples of the danger involved in focusing inordinate attention on legal change. Legal and political change always exists within a social fabric, and this context must change as well in order to give true meaning and significance to legislative gains and allow them to remain viable despite periods of social conservatism. It is for this reason that a radical perspective is still imperative to challenge patriarchal institutions and attitudes that perpetuate women's dependence and subordination and to eradicate the inequities of the social relations between the sexes.

References

Adam, Barry D. 1987. *The rise of a gay and lesbian movement.* Boston: Twayne Publishers.

Banner, Lois W. 1980. *Elizabeth Cady Stanton: A radical for women's rights.* Boston: Little, Brown.

Bordin, Ruth. 1980. *Women and temperance: The quest for power and liberty, 1873–1900.* Philadelphia: Temple University Press.

Brown, Dorothy M. 1987. *Setting a course: American women in the 1920s.* Boston: Twayne Publishers.

Buhle, Mari Jo, and Paul Buhle. 1978. *The concise history of woman suffrage: Selections from the classic work of Stanton, Anthony, Gage and Harper.* Urbana: University of Illinois Press.

Cott, Nancy F. 1977. *The bonds of womanhood: "Woman's sphere" in New England, 1780–1835.* New Haven: Yale University Press.

———. 1987. *The grounding of modern feminism.* New Haven: Yale University Press.

———. 1991. Equal rights and economic roles: The conflict over the Equal Rights Amendment in the 1920s. In *Women's America: Refocusing the past.* 3rd ed. Edited by Linda Kerber and Jane Sherron De Hart, 356–68. New York: Oxford University Press.

Davis, Allen F. 1984. *Spearheads for reform: The social settlements and the Progressive movement, 1890–1914.* New Brunswick: Rutgers University Press.

De Hart, Jane Sherron. 1991. The new feminism and the dynamics of social change. In *Women's America: Refocusing the past.* 3rd ed. Edited by Linda Kerber and Jane Sherron De Hart, 493–521. New York: Oxford University Press.

DuBois, Ellen Carol. 1978. *Feminism and suffrage: The emergence of an independent women's movement in America, 1848–1869.* Ithaca: Cornell University Press.

DuBois, Ellen Carol, ed. 1981. *Elizabeth Cady Stanton, Susan B. Anthony: Correspondence, writing, speeches.* New York: Schocken Books.

Evans, Sara M. 1979. *Personal politics: The roots of women's liberation in the civil rights movement and the New Left.* New York: Alfred A. Knopf.

———. 1989. *Born for liberty: A history of women in America.* New York: Free Press.

Faderman, Lillian. 1991. *Odd girls and twilight lovers.* New York: Columbia University Press.

Feree, M. M., and Beth B. Hess. 1985. *Controversy and coalition: The new feminist movement.* Boston: Twayne Publishers.

Flexner, Eleanor. 1975. *Century of struggle: The women's rights movement in the United States.* Rev. ed. Cambridge: Harvard University Press.

Freedman, Estelle B. 1974. The new woman: Changing views of women in the 1920s. *Journal of American History* 61:372–93.

Giddings, Paula. 1984. *When and where I enter: The impact of black women on race and sex in America.* New York: Bantam Books.

Hartmann, Susan M. 1989. *From margin to mainstream: American women and politics since 1960.* New York: Alfred A. Knopf.

hooks, bell. 1981. *Ain't I a woman: Black women and feminism.* Boston: South End Press.

Jones, Jacqueline. 1985. *Labor of love, labor of sorrow: Black women, work, and the family from slavery to the present.* New York: Basic Books.

Kerber, Linda K. 1980. *Women of the republic: Intellect and ideology in revolutionary America.* Chapel Hill: University of North Carolina Press.

Kraditor, Aileen S. 1965. *The ideas of the woman suffrage movement, 1890–1920.* New York: W. W. Norton and Co.

Lerner, Gerda. 1971. *The Grimké sisters from South Carolina: Pioneers for women's rights and abolition.* New York: Schocken Books.

———, ed. 1972. *Black women in white America: A documentary history.* New York: Random House, Vintage Books.

———. 1979. *The majority finds its past: Placing women in history.* New York: Oxford University Press.

Matthews, Glenna. 1987. *Just a housewife: The rise and fall of domesticity in America.* New York: Oxford University Press.

Morgan, Robin. 1970. *Sisterhood is powerful: An anthology of writings from the women's liberation movement.* New York: Vintage Books, Random House.

Norton, Mary Beth. 1980. *Liberty's daughters: The revolutionary experience of American women, 1750–1800.* Boston: Little, Brown.

Norton, Mary Beth, ed. 1989. *Major problems in American women's history.* Lexington, Ken.: D. C. Heath and Company.

Rossi, Alice S. 1973. *The feminist papers from Adams to de Beauvoir.* New York: Bantam Books.

Rupp, Leila J., and Verta Taylor. 1987. *Survival in the doldrums: The American women's rights movement, 1945 to the 1960s.* New York: Oxford University Press.

Scharf, Lois, and Joan M. Jensen, eds. 1983. *Decades of discontent: The women's movement, 1920–1940.* Contributions in Women's Studies, no. 28. Westport, Conn.: Greenwood Press, Inc.

Scott, Anne F., and Andrew M. Scott. 1975. *One half the people: The fight for woman suffrage.* Philadelphia: J. B. Lippincott Company.

Sklar, Kathryn Kish. Hull House in the 1890's: A community of woman reformers. *Signs* 10 (1985):657–77.

Stage, Sarah J. 1983. Women. *American Quarterly* 35:169–190.

Stetson, Dorothy McBride. 1991. *Women's rights in the U.S.A.: Policy debates and gender roles.* Pacific Grove, Calif.: Brooks/Cole Publishing Company.

Tanner, Leslie B. 1970. *Voices from women's liberation.* New York: New American Library, Signet Book.

Terborg-Penn, Rosalyn. 1983. Discontented black feminists: Prelude and postscript to the passage of the Nineteenth Amendment. In *Decades of discontent: The women's movement, 1920–1940.* Edited by Lois Scharf and Joan M. Jensen, 261–68. Contributions in Women's Studies, no. 28. Westport, Conn.: Greenwood Press.

Ware, Susan. 1981. *Beyond suffrage: Women in the New Deal.* Cambridge, Mass.: Harvard University Press.

Crisis of Faith

Catherine Wiley

Today doesn't look like the time
To resuscitate
A movement.
You went to jail
Fifteen years back
Just to keep the bars open.
Seeing them now filled with women
Who don't feel the need
(Or scorn it)
For leather, brass knuckles, weighted socks
Makes you afraid.

Having made those women possible
Taking their forgotten fear
Into your eyes, shoulders, stance
Tilted for a fight,
Carelessness weighs hard,
Harder than the metal
Freezing your pockets,
Harder than the leather
That made men itch and shift their eyes
Before they hit.

You say to me now,
Tears filling the creases
Those fifteen years have earned,
There's no space for what I am,
And I respond,
There never was.
Not anywhere a place
For the differently committed,
The outraged and outrageously
Political.

You who would have died
For an abstraction like commitment
Will die someday anyway.
Do anything but disappear
For you know the others wanted/

Wiley, Catherine. 1992. "Crisis of Faith." Printed by permission of the author.

Want you gone.
Do anything
But stop.

News of takebacks
Comes down like a fist
In your face, on your shoulders,
AIDS having given their fear
A shape and a name
Another weapon,
As if they needed any more.

Those safe spaces you made—
Bars, classrooms where you dare
To be you
And let your students love—
Look tenuous now, fragility
Shored up against itself
Cannot withstand such attack.

Cannot
But has to.

Such lack of choice
Is what you choose to live with.
Before you go
Be sure to turn around and look behind you.
Count, and count well
How many of us you've engendered,
How many are waiting yet
To be born.

Declaration of Sentiments

When, in the course of human events, it becomes necessary for one portion of the family of man to assume among the people of the earth a position different from that which they have hitherto occupied, but one to which the laws of nature and of nature's God entitle them, a decent respect to the opinions of mankind requires that they should declare the causes that impel them to such a course.

We hold these truths to be self-evident: that all men and women are created equal; that they are endowed by their Creator with certain inalienable rights; that among these are life, liberty, and the pursuit of happiness; that to secure these rights governments are instituted, deriving their just powers from the consent of the governed. Whenever any form of government becomes destructive of these ends, it is the right of those who suffer from it to refuse allegiance to it, and to insist upon the institution of a new government, laying its foundation on such principles, and organizing its powers in such form, as to them shall seem most likely to effect their safety and happiness. Prudence, indeed, will dictate that governments long established should not be changed for light and transient causes; and accordingly all experience hath shown that mankind are more disposed to suffer, while evils are sufferable, than to right themselves by abolishing the forms to which they were accustomed. But when a long train of abuses and usurpations, pursuing invariably the same object, evinces a design to reduce them under absolute despotism, it is their duty to throw off such government, and to provide new guards for their future security. Such has been the patient sufferance of the women under this government, and such is now the necessity which constrains them to demand the equal station to which they are entitled.

The history of mankind is a history of repeated injuries and usurpations on the part of man toward woman, having in direct object the establishment of an absolute tyranny over her. To prove this, let facts be submitted to a candid world.

He has never permitted her to exercise her inalienable right to the elective franchise.

He has compelled her to submit to laws, in the formation of which she had no voice.

He has withheld from her rights which are given to the most ignorant and degraded men—both natives and foreigners.

Having deprived her of this first right of a citizen, the elective franchise, thereby leaving her without representation in the halls of legislation, he has oppressed her on all sides.

He has made her, if married, in the eye of the law, civilly dead.

He has taken from her all right in property, even to the wages she earns.

He has made her, morally, an irresponsible being, as she can commit many crimes with impunity, provided they be done in the presence of her husband. In the covenant of marriage, she is compelled to promise obedience to her husband, he becoming, to all intents and purposes, her master—the law giving him power to deprive her of her liberty, and to administer chastisement.

†From: Susan B. Anthony et al., *History of Woman Suffrage* (Rochester: Susan B. Anthony, 1887), vol. I, pp. 70–71.

He has so framed the laws of divorce, as to what shall be the proper causes, and in case of separation, to whom the guardianship of the children shall be given, as to be wholly regardless of the happiness of women—the law, in all cases, going upon the false supposition of the supremacy of man, and giving all power into his hands.

After depriving her of all rights as a married woman, if single, and the owner of property, he has taxed her to support a government which recognizes her only when her property can be made profitable to it.

He has monopolized nearly all the profitable employments, and from those she is permitted to follow, she receives but a scanty remuneration. He closes against her all the avenues to wealth and distinction which he considers most honorable to himself. As a teacher of theology, medicine, or law, she is not known.

He has denied her the facilities for obtaining a thorough education, all colleges being closed against her.

He allows her in Church, as well as State, but a subordinate position, claiming Apostolic authority for her exclusion from the ministry, and, with some exceptions, from any public participation in the affairs of the Church.

He has created a false public sentiment by giving to the world a different code of morals for men and women, by which moral delinquencies which exclude women from society, are not only tolerated, but deemed of little account in man.

He has usurped the prerogative of Jehovah himself, claiming it as his right to assign for her a sphere of action, when that belongs to her conscience and to her God.

He has endeavored, in every way that he could, to destroy her confidence in her own powers, to lessen her self-respect, and to make her willing to lead a dependent and abject life.

Now, in view of this entire disfranchisement of one-half the people of this country, their social and religious degradation—in view of the unjust laws above mentioned, and because women do feel themselves aggrieved, oppressed, and fraudulently deprived of their most sacred rights, we insist that they have immediate admission to all the rights and privileges which belong to them as citizens of the United States.

In entering upon the great work before us, we anticipate no small amount of misconception, misrepresentation, and ridicule; but we shall use every instrumentality within our power to effect our object. We shall employ agents, circulate tracts, petition the State and National legislatures, and endeavor to enlist the pulpit and the press in our behalf. We hope this Convention will be followed by a series of Conventions embracing every part of the country.

Resolutions: Whereas, The great precept of nature is conceded to be, that "man shall pursue his own true and substantial happiness." Blackstone in his Commentaries remarks, that this law of Nature being coeval with mankind, and dictated by God himself, is of course superior in obligation to any other. It is binding over all the globe, in all countries and at all times; no human laws are of any validity if contrary to this, and such of them as are valid, derive all their force, and all their validity, and all their authority, mediately and immediately, from this original; therefore,

Resolved, That such laws as conflict, in any way, with the true and substantial happiness of woman, are contrary to the great precept of nature and of no validity, for this is "superior in obligation to any other."

Resolved, That all laws which prevent woman from occupying such a station in society as her conscience shall dictate, or which place her in a position inferior to that of man, are contrary to the great precept of nature, and therefore of no force or authority.

Resolved, That woman is man's equal—was intended to be so by the Creator, and the highest good of the race demands that she should be recognized as such.

Resolved, That the women of this country ought to be enlightened in regard to the laws under which they live, that they may no longer publish their degradation by declaring themselves satisfied with their present position, nor their ignorance, by asserting that they have all the rights they want.

Resolved, That inasmuch as man, while claiming for himself intellectual superiority, does accord to woman moral superiority, it is pre-eminently his duty to encourage her to speak and teach, as she has an opportunity, in all religious assemblies.

Resolved, That the same amount of virtue, delicacy, and refinement of behavior that is required of woman in the social state, should also be required of man, and the same transgressions should be visited with equal severity on both man and woman.

Resolved, That the objection of indelicacy and impropriety, which is so often brought against woman when she addresses a public audience, comes with a very ill-grace from those who encourage, by their attendance, her appearance on the stage, in the concert, or in feats of the circus.

Resolved, That woman has too long rested satisfied in the circumscribed limits which corrupt customs and a perverted application of the Scriptures have marked out for her, and that it is time she should move in the enlarged sphere which her great Creator has assigned her.

Resolved, That it is the duty of the women of this country to secure to themselves their sacred right to the elective franchise.

Resolved, That the equality of human rights results necessarily from the fact of the identity of the race in capabilities and responsibilities.

Resolved, therefore, That, being invested by the Creator with the same capabilities, and the same consciousness of responsibility for their exercise, it is demonstrably the right and duty of woman, equally with man, to promote every righteous cause by every righteous means; and especially in regard to the great subjects of morals and religion, it is self-evidently her right to participate with her brother in teaching them, both in private and in public, by writing and by speaking, by any instrumentalities proper to be used, and in any assemblies proper to be held; and this being a self-evident truth growing out of the divinely implanted principles of human nature, any custom or authority adverse to it, whether modern or wearing the hoary sanction of antiquity, is to be regarded as a self-evident falsehood, and at war with mankind.

Resolved, That the speedy success of our cause depends upon the zealous and untiring efforts of both men and women, for the overthrow of the monopoly of the pulpit, and for the securing to women an equal participation with men in the various trades, professions, and commerce.

Certain Amendments to the United States Constitution

Amendment XIV

[Adopted 1868]

Section 1 All persons born or naturalized in the United States, and subject to the jurisdiction thereof, are citizens of the United States and of the State wherein they reside. No State shall make or enforce any law which shall abridge the privileges or immunities of citizens of the United States; nor shall any State deprive any person of life, liberty, or property, without due process of law; nor deny to any person within its jurisdiction the equal protection of the laws.

Section 2 Representatives shall be apportioned among the several States according to their respective numbers, counting the whole number of persons in each State, excluding Indians not taxed. But when the right to vote at any election for the choice of Electors for President and Vice-President of the United States, Representatives in Congress, the executive and judicial officers of a State, or the members of the legislature thereof, is denied to any of the male inhabitants of such State, being twenty-one years of age and citizens of the United States, or in any way abridged, except for participation in rebellion, or other crime, the basis of representation therein shall be reduced in the proportion which the number of such male citizens shall bear to the whole number of male citizens twenty-one years of age in such State.

Amendment XV

[Adopted 1870]

Section 1 The right of citizens of the United States to vote shall not be denied or abridged by the United States or by any State on account of race, color, or previous condition of servitude.

Section 2 The Congress shall have power to enforce this article by appropriate legislation.

Amendment XIX

[Adopted 1920]

Section 1 The right of citizens of the United States to vote shall not be denied or abridged by the United States or by any State on account of sex.

Section 2 The Congress shall have power to enforce this article by appropriate legislation.

The Development of Chicana Feminist Discourse, 1970–1980

Alma M. Garcia

The years between 1970 and 1980 represented a formative period in the development of Chicana feminist thought in the United States. During this period, Chicana feminists addressed the specific issues affecting Chicanas as women of color in the United States. As a result of their collective efforts in struggling against racial, class, and gender oppression, Chicana feminists developed an ideological discourse that addressed three major issues. These were the relationships between Chicana feminism and the ideology of cultural nationalism, feminist baiting within the Chicano movement, and the relationship between the Chicana feminist movement and the white feminist movement. This article describes the development of Chicana feminism and compares it with Asian American and Black feminism, which faced similar problems.

Between 1970 and 1980, a Chicana feminist movement developed in the United States that addressed the specific issues that affected Chicanas as women of color. The growth of the Chicana feminist movement can be traced in the speeches, essays, letters, and articles published in Chicano and Chicana newspapers, journals, newsletters, and other printed materials.[1]

During the sixties, American society witnessed the development of the Chicano movement, a social movement characterized by a politics of protest (Barrera 1974; Muñoz 1974; Navarro 1974). The Chicano movement focused on a wide range of issues: social justice, equality, educational reforms, and political and economic self-determination for Chicano communities in the United States. Various struggles evolved within this movement: the United Farmworkers unionization efforts (Dunne 1967; Kushner 1975; Matthiesen 1969; Nelson 1966); the New Mexico Land Grant movement (Nabokov 1969); the Colorado-based Crusade for Justice (Castro 1974; Meier and Rivera 1972); the Chicano student movement (Garcia and de la Garza 1977); and the Raza Unida Party (Shockley 1974).

Chicanas participated actively in each of these struggles. By the end of the sixties, Chicanas began to assess the rewards and limits of their participation. The 1970s witnessed the development of Chicana feminists whose activities, organizations, and writings can be analyzed in terms of a feminist movement by women of color in American society. Chicana feminists outlined a cluster of ideas that crystallized into an emergent Chicana feminist debate. In the same way that Chicano males were reinterpreting the historical and contemporary experience of Chicanos in the United States, Chicanas began to investigate the forces shaping their own experiences as women of color.

The Chicana feminist movement emerged primarily as a result of the dynamics within the Chicano movement. In the 1960s and 1970s, the American political scene witnessed far-reaching social protest movements whose political courses often paralleled and at times exerted influence over each other (Freeman 1983; Piven and Cloward 1979). The development of feminist movements has been explained by the participation of women in larger social movements. Macias (1982), for example, links the early development of the Mexican feminist movement to the participation of women in the Mexican Revolution. Similarly, Freeman's (1984) analysis of the white feminist movement points out that many white feminists who were active in the early years of its development had previously been involved in the new left and civil rights movements. It was in these movements that white feminists experienced the constraints of male domination. Black feminists have similarly traced the development of a Black feminist movement during the 1960s and 1970s to their experiences with sexism in the larger Black movement (Davis 1983; Dill 1983; Hooks 1981, 1984; Joseph and Lewis 1981; White 1984). In this way, then, the origins of Chicana feminism parallel those of other feminist movements.

Origins of Chicana Feminism

Rowbotham (1974) argues that women may develop a feminist consciousness as a result of their experiences with sexism in revolutionary struggles or mass social movements. To the extent that such movements are male dominated, women are likely to develop a feminist consciousness. Chicana feminists began the search for a "room of their own" by assessing their participation within the Chicano movement. Their feminist consciousness emerged from a struggle for equality with Chicano men and from a reassessment of the role of the family as a means of resistance to oppressive societal conditions.

Historically, as well as during the 1960s and 1970s, the Chicano family represented a source of cultural and political resistance to the various types of discrimination experienced in American society (Zinn 1975a). At the cultural level, the Chicano movement emphasized the need to safeguard the value of family loyalty. At the political level, the Chicano movement used the family as a strategic organizational tool for protest activities.

Dramatic changes in the structure of Chicano families occurred as they participated in the Chicano movement. Specifically, women began to question their traditional female roles (Zinn 1975a). Thus, a Chicana feminst movement originated from the nationalist Chicano struggle. Rowbotham (1974, p. 206) refers to such a feminist movement as "a colony within a colony." But as the Chicano movement developed during the 1970s, Chicana feminists began to draw their own political agenda and raised a series of questions to assess their role within the Chicano movement. They entered into a dialogue with each other that explicitly reflected their struggles to secure a room of their own within the Chicano movement.

Defining Feminism for Women of Color

A central question of feminist discourse is the definition of feminism. The lack of consensus reflects different political ideologies and divergent social-class bases. In the United States, Chicana feminists shared the task of defining their ideology and movement with white, Black, and Asian American feminists. Like Black and Asian American feminists,

Chicana feminists struggled to gain social equality and end sexist and racist oppression. Like them, Chicana feminists recognized that the nature of social inequality for women of color was multidimensional (Cheng 1984; Chow 1987; Hooks 1981). Like Black and Asian American feminists, Chicana feminists struggled to gain equal status in the male-dominated nationalist movements and also in American society. To them, feminism represented a movement to end sexist oppression within a broader social protest movement. Again, like Black and Asian American feminists, Chicana feminists fought for social equality in the 1970s. They understood that their movement needed to go beyond women's rights and include the men of their group, who also faced racial subordination (Hooks 1981). Chicanas believed that feminism involved more than an analysis of gender because, as women of color, they were affected by both race and class in their everyday lives. Thus, Chicana feminism, as a social movement to improve the position of Chicanas in American society, represented a struggle that was both nationalist and feminist.

Chicana, Black, and Asian American feminists were all confronted with the issue of engaging in a feminist struggle to end sexist oppression within a broader nationalist struggle to end racist oppression. All experienced male domination in their own communities as well as in the larger society. Ngan-Ling Chow (1987) identifies gender stereotypes of Asian American women and the patriarchal family structure as major sources of women's oppression. Cultural, political, and economic constraints have, according to Ngan-Ling Chow (1987), limited the full development of a feminist consciousness and movement among Asian American women. The cross-pressures resulting from the demands of a nationalist and a feminist struggle led some Asian American women to organize feminist organizations that, however, continued to address broader issues affecting the Asian American community.

Black women were also faced with addressing feminist issues within a nationalist movement. According to Thornton Dill (1983), Black women played a major historical role in Black resistance movements and, in addition, brought a feminist component to these movements (Davis 1983; Dill 1983). Black women have struggled with Black men in nationalist movements but have also recognized and fought against the sexism in such political movements in the Black community (Hooks 1984). Although they wrote and spoke as Black feminists, they did not organize separately from Black men.

Among the major ideological questions facing all three groups of feminists were the relationship between feminism and the ideology of cultural nationalism or racial pride, feminism and feminist baiting within the larger movements, and the relationship between their feminist movements and the white feminist movement.

Chicana Feminism and Cultural Nationalism

Throughout the seventies and now, in the eighties, Chicana feminists have been forced to respond to the criticism that cultural nationalism and feminism are irreconcilable. In the first issue of the newspaper, *Hijas de Cuauhtemoc*, Anna Nieto Gomez (1971) stated that a major issue facing Chicanas active in the Chicano movement was the need to organize to improve their status as women within the larger social movement. Francisca Flores (1971b, p. i), another leading Chicana feminist, stated:

[Chicanas] can no longer remain in a subservient role or as auxiliary forces in the [Chicano] movement. They must be included in the front line of communication, leadership and organizational responsibility. . . . The issue of equality, freedom and self-determination of the Chicana—like the right of self-determination, equality, and liberation of the Mexican [Chicano] community—is not negotiable. Anyone opposing the right of women to organize into their own form of organization has no place in the leadership of the movement.

Supporting this position, Bernice Rincon (1971) argued that a Chicana feminist movement that sought equality and justice for Chicanas would strengthen the Chicano movement. Yet in the process, Chicana feminists challenged traditional gender roles because they limited their participation and acceptance within the Chicano movement.

Throughout the seventies, Chicana feminists viewed the struggle against sexism within the Chicano movement and the struggle against racism in the larger society as integral parts of Chicana feminism. As Nieto Gomez (1976, p. 10) said:

Chicana feminism is in various stages of development. However, in general, Chicana feminism is the recognition that women are oppressed as a group and are exploited as part of *la Raza* people. It is a direction to be responsible to identify and act upon the issues and needs of Chicana women. Chicana feminists are involved in understanding the nature of women's oppression.

Cultural nationalism represented a major ideological component of the Chicano movement. Its emphasis on Chicano cultural pride and cultural survival within an Anglo-dominated society gave significant political direction to the Chicano movement. One source of ideological disagreement between Chicana feminism and this cultural nationalist ideology was cultural survival. Many Chicana feminists believed that a focus on cultural survival did not acknowledge the need to alter male-female relations within Chicano communities. For example, Chicana feminists criticized the notion of the "ideal Chicana" that glorified Chicanas as strong, long-suffering women who had endured and kept Chicano culture and the family intact. To Chicana feminists, this concept represented an obstacle to the redefinition of gender roles. Nieto (1975, p. 4) stated:

Some Chicanas are praised as they emulate the sanctified example set by [the Virgin] Mary. The woman *par excellence* is mother and wife. She is to love and support her husband and to nurture and teach her children. Thus, may she gain fulfillment as a woman. For a Chicana bent upon fulfillment of her personhood, this restricted perspective of her role as a woman is not only inadequate but crippling.

Chicana feminists were also skeptical about the cultural nationalist interpretation of machismo. Such an interpretation viewed machismo as an ideological tool used by the dominant Anglo society to justify the inequalities experience by Chicanos. According to this interpretation, the relationship between Chicanos and the larger society was that of an internal colony dominated and exploited by the capitalist economy (Almaguer 1974; Barrera 1979). Machismo, like other cultural traits, was blamed by Anglos for blocking Chicanos from succeeding in American society. In reality, the economic structure and colony-like exploitation were to blame.

Some Chicana feminists agreed with this analysis of machismo, claiming that a mutually reinforcing relationship existed between internal colonialism and the development of the myth of machismo. According to Sosa Riddell (1974, p. 21), machismo was a myth "propagated by subjugators and colonizers, which created damaging stereotypes of Mexican/Chicano males." As a type of social control imposed by the dominant society on Chicanos, the myth of machismo distorted gender relations within Chicano communities, creating stereotypes of Chicanas as passive and docile women. At this level in the feminist discourse, machismo was seen as an Anglo myth that kept both Chicano and Chicanas in a subordinate status. As Nieto (1975, p. 4) concluded:

> Although the term "machismo" is correctly denounced by all because it stereotypes the Latin man . . . it does a great disservice to both men and women. Chicano and Chicana alike must be free to seek their own individual fulfillment.

While some Chicana feminists criticized the myth of machismo used by the dominant society to legitimate racial inequality, others moved beyond this level of analysis to distinguish between the machismo that oppressed both men and women and the sexism in Chicano communities in general, and the Chicano movement in particular, that oppressed Chicana women (Chavez 1971; Cotera 1977; Del Castillo 1974; Marquez and Ramirez 1977; Riddell 1974; Zinn 1975b). According to Vidal (1971, p. 8), the origins of a Chicana feminist consciousness were prompted by the sexist attitudes and behavior of Chicano males, which constituted a "serious obstacle to women anxious to play a role in the struggle for Chicana liberation."

Furthermore, many Chicana feminists disagreed with the cultural nationalist view that machismo could be a positive value within a Chicano cultural value system. They challenged the view that machismo was a source of masculine pride for Chicanos and therefore a defense mechanism against the dominant society's racism. Although Chicana feminists recognized that Chicanos faced discrimination from the dominant society, they adamantly disagreed with those who believed that machismo was a form of cultural resistance to such discrimination. Chicana feminists called for changes in the ideologies responsible for distorting relations between women and men. One such change was to modify the cultural nationalist position that viewed machismo as a source of cultural pride.

Chicana feminists called for a focus on the universal aspects of sexism that shape gender relations in both Anglo and Chicano culture. While they acknowledged the economic exploitation of all Chicanos, Chicana feminists outlined the double exploitation experienced by Chicanas. Sosa Riddell (1974, p. 159) concluded: "It was when Chicanas began to seek work outside of the family groups that sexism became a key factor of oppression along with racism." Francisca Flores (1971a, p. 4) summarized some of the consequences of sexism:

> It is not surprising that more and more Chicanas are forced to go to work in order to supplement the family income. The children are farmed out to a relative to babysit with them, and since these women are employed in the lower income jobs, the extra pressure placed on them can become unbearable.

Thus, while the Chicano movement was addressing the issue of racial oppression facing all Chicanos, Chicana feminists argued that it lacked an analysis of sexism. Similarly, Black and Asian American women stressed the interconnectedness of race and gender oppression. Hooks (1984, p. 52) analyzes racism and sexism in terms of their "intersecting, complementary nature." She also emphasizes that one struggle should not take priority over the other. White (1984) criticizes Black men whose nationalism limited discussions of Black women's experiences with sexist oppression. The writings of other Black feminists criticized a Black cultural nationalist ideology that overlooked the consequences of sexist oppression (Beale 1975; Cade 1970; David 1971; Joseph and Lewis 1981). Many Asian

American women were also critical of the Asian American movement whose focus on racism ignored the impact of sexism on the daily lives of women. The participation of Asian American women in various community struggles increased their encounters with sexism (Chow 1987). As a result, some Asian American women developed a feminist consciousness and organized as women around feminist issues.

Chicana Feminism and Feminist Baiting

The systematic analysis by Chicana feminists of the impact of racism and sexism on Chicanas in American society and, above all, within the Chicano movement was often misunderstood as a threat to the political unity of the Chicano movement. As Marta Cotera (1977, p. 9), a leading voice of Chicana feminism pointed out:

> The aggregate cultural values we [Chicanas] share can also work to our benefit if we choose to scrutinize our cultural traditions, isolate the positive attributes and interpret them for the benefit of women. It's unreal that *Hispanas* have been browbeaten for so long about our so-called conservative (meaning reactionary) culture. It's also unreal that we have let men interpret culture only as those practices and attitudes that determine who does the dishes around the house. We as women also have the right to interpret and define the philosophical and religious traditions beneficial to us within our culture, and which we have inherited as our tradition. To do this, we must become both conversant with our history and philosophical evolution, and analytical about the institutional and behavioral manifestations of the same.

Such Chicana feminists were attacked for developing a "divisive ideology"—a feminist ideology that was frequently viewed as a threat to the Chicano movement as a whole. As Chicana feminists examined their roles as women activists within the Chicano movement, an ideological split developed. One group active in the Chicano movement saw themselves as "loyalists" who believed that the Chicano movement did not have to deal with sexual inequities since Chicano men as well as Chicano women experienced racial oppression. According to Nieto Gomez (1973, p. 35), who was not a loyalist, their view was that if men oppress women, it is not the men's fault but rather that of the system.

Even if such a problem existed, and they did not believe that it did, the loyalists maintained that such a matter would best be resolved internally within the Chicano movement. They denounced the formation of a separate Chicana feminist movement on the grounds that it was a politically dangerous strategy, perhaps Anglo inspired. Such a movement would undermine the unity of the Chicano movement by raising an issue that was not seen as a central one. Loyalists viewed racism as the most important issue within the Chicano movement. Nieto Gomez (1973, p. 35) quotes one such loyalist:

> I am concerned with the direction that the Chicanas are taking in the movement. The words such as liberation, sexism, male chauvinism, etc., were prevalent. The terms mentioned above plus the theme of individualism is a concept of the Anglo society; terms prevalent in the Anglo women's movement. The *familia* has always been our strength in our culture. But it seems evident . . . that you [Chicana feminists] are not concerned with the *familia*, but are influenced by the Anglo woman's movement.

Chicana feminists were also accused of undermining the values associated with Chicano culture. Loyalists saw the Chicana feminist movement as an "anti-family, anti-cultural, anti-man and therefore an anti-Chicano movement" (Gomez 1973, p. 35).

Feminism was, above all, believed to be an individualistic search for identity that detracted from the Chicano movement's "real" issues, such as racism. Nieto Gomez (1973, p. 35) quotes a loyalist as stating:

And since when does a Chicana need identity? If you are a real Chicana then no one regardless of the degrees needs to tell you about it. The only ones who need identity are the *vendidas*, the *falsas*, and the opportunists.

The ideological conflicts between Chicana feminists and loyalists persisted throughout the seventies. Disagreements between these two groups became exacerbated during various Chicana conferences. At times, such confrontations served to increase Chicana feminist activity that challenged the loyalists' attacks, yet these attacks also served to suppress feminist activities.

Chicana feminist lesbians experienced even stronger attacks from those who viewed feminism as a divisive ideology. In a political climate that already viewed feminist ideology with suspicion, lesbianism as a sexual lifestyle and political ideology came under even more attack. Clearly, a cultural nationalist ideology that perpetuated such stereotypical images of Chicanas as "good wives and good mothers" found it difficult to accept a Chicana feminist lesbian movement.

Cherrie Moraga's writings during the 1970s reflect the struggles of Chicana feminist lesbians who, together with other Chicana feminists, were finding the sexism evident within the Chicano movement intolerable. Just as Chicana feminists analyzed their life circumstances as members of an ethnic minority and as women, Chicana feminist lesbians addressed themselves to the oppression they experienced as lesbians. As Moraga (1981, p. 28) stated:

My lesbianism is the avenue through which I have learned the most about silence and oppression. . . . In this country, lesbianism is a poverty—as is being brown, as is being a woman, as is being just plain poor. The danger lies in ranking the oppressions. The danger lies in failing to acknowledge the specificity of the oppression.

Chicana, Black, and Asian American feminists experienced similar cross-pressures of feminist-baiting and lesbian-baiting attacks. As they organized around feminist struggles, these women of color encountered criticism from both male and female cultural nationalists who often viewed feminism as little more than an "anti-male" ideology. Lesbianism was identified as an extreme derivation of feminism. A direct connection was frequently made that viewed feminism and lesbianism as synonymous. Feminists were labeled lesbians, and lesbians as feminists. Attacks against feminists—Chicanas, Blacks, and Asian Americans—derived from the existence of homophobia within each of these communities. As lesbian women of color published their writings, attacks against them increased (Moraga 1983).

Responses to such attacks varied within and between the feminist movements of women of color. Some groups tried one strategy and later adopted another. Some lesbians pursued a separatist strategy within their own racial and ethnic communities (Moraga and Anzaldua 1981; White 1984). Others attempted to form lesbian coalitions across racial and ethnic lines. Both strategies represented a response to the marginalization of lesbians produced by recurrent waves of homophobic sentiments in Chicano, Black, and Asian American communities (Moraga and Anzaldua 1981). A third response consisted of working within the broader nationalist movements in these communities and the feminist movements within them in order to challenge their heterosexual biases and resultant homophobia. As early as 1974, the "Black Feminist Statement" written by a Boston-based feminist group—the Combahee River Collective—stated (1981, p. 213): "We struggle together with Black men against racism, while we also struggle with Black men against sexism." Similarly, Moraga (1981) challenged the white feminist movement to examine its racist tendencies; the Chicano movement, its sexist tendencies; and both, their homophobic tendencies. In this way, Moraga (1981) argued that such movements to end oppression would begin to respect diversity within their own ranks.

Chicana feminists as well as Chicana feminist lesbians continued to be labeled *vendidas* or "sellouts." Chicana loyalists continued to view Chicana feminism as associated, not only with melting into white society, but more seriously, with dividing the Chicano movement. Similarly, many Chicano males were convinced that Chicana feminism was a divisive ideology incompatible with Chicano cultural nationalism. Nieto Gomez (1976, p. 10) said that "[with] respect to [the] Chicana feminist, their credibility is reduced when they are associated with [feminism] and white women." She added that, as a result, Chicana feminists often faced harassment and ostracism within the Chicano movement. Similarly, Cotera (1973, p. 30) stated that Chicanas "are suspected of assimilating into the feminist ideology of an alien [white] culture that actively seeks our cultural domination."

Chicana feminists responded quickly and often vehemently to such charges. Flores (1971a, p. 1) answered these antifeminist attacks in an editorial in which she argued that birth control, abortion, and sex education were not merely "white issues." In response to the accusation that feminists were responsible for the "betrayal of [Chicano] culture and heritage," Flores said, "Our culture hell"—a phrase that became a dramatic slogan of the Chicana feminist movement.

Chicana feminists' defense throughout the 1970s against those claiming that a feminist movement was divisive for the Chicano movement was to reassess their roles within the Chicano movement and to call for an end to male domination. Their challenges of traditional gender roles represented a means to achieve equality (Longeaux y Vasquez 1969a, 1969b). In order to increase the participation of and opportunities for women in the Chicano movement, feminists agreed that both Chicanos and Chicanas had to address the issue of gender inequality (Chapa 1973; Chavez 1971; Del Castillo 1974; Cotera 1977; Moreno 1979). Furthermore, Chicana feminists argued that the resistance that they encountered reflected the existence of sexism on the part of Chicano males and the antifeminist attitudes of the Chicana loyalists. Nieto Gomez (1973, p. 31), reviewing the experiences of Chicana feminists in the Chicano movement, concluded that Chicanas "involved in discussing and applying the women's question have been ostracized, isolated and ignored." She argued that "in organizations where cultural nationalism is extremely strong, Chicana feminists experience intense harassment and ostracism" (1973, p. 38).

Black and Asian American women also faced severe criticism as they pursued feminist issues in their own communities. Indeed, as their participation in collective efforts to end racial oppression increased, so did their confrontations with sexism (Chow 1987; Hooks 1984; White 1984). Ngan-Ling Chow (1987, p. 288) describes the various sources of such criticism directed at Asian American women:

Asian American women are criticized for the possible consequences of their protests: weakening the male ego, dilution of effort and resources in Asian American

331

communities, destruction of working relationships between Asian men and women, setbacks for the Asian American cause, co-optation into the larger society, and eventual loss of ethnic identity for Asian Americans as a whole. In short, affiliation with the feminist movement is perceived as a threat to solidarity within their own community.

Similar criticism was experienced by Black feminist (Hooks 1984; White 1984).

Chicana Feminists and White Feminists

It is difficult to determine the extent to which Chicana feminists sympathized with the white feminist movement. A 1976 study at the University of San Diego that examined the attitudes of Chicanas regarding the white feminist movement found that the majority of Chicanas surveyed believed that the movement had affected their lives. In addition, they identified with such key issues as the right to legal abortions on demand and access to low-cost birth control. Nevertheless, the survey found that "even though the majority of Chicanas . . . could relate to certain issues of the women's movement, for the most part they saw it as being an elitist movement comprised of white middle-class women who [saw] the oppressor as the males of this country" (Orozco 1976, p. 12).

Nevertheless, some Chicana feminists considered the possibility of forming coalitions with white feminists as their attempts to work within the Chicano movement were suppressed. Since white feminists were themselves struggling against sexism, building coalitions with them was seen as an alternative strategy for Chicana feminists (Rincon 1971). Almost immediately, however, Chicana feminists recognized the problems involved in adopting this political strategy. As Longeaux y Vasquez (1971, p. 11) acknowledged, "Some of our own Chicanas may be attracted to the white woman's liberation movement, but we really don't feel comfortable there. We want to be a Chicana *primero* [first]." For other Chicanas, the demands of white women were "irrelevant to the Chicana movement" (Hernandez 1971, p. 9).

Several issues made such coalition building difficult. First, Chicana feminists criticized what they considered to be a cornerstone of white feminist thought, an emphasis on gender oppression to explain the life circumstances of women. Chicana feminists believed that the white feminist movement overlooked the effects of racial oppression experienced by Chicanas and other women of color. Thus, Del Castillo (1974, p. 8) maintained that the Chicana feminist movement was "different primarily because we are [racially] oppressed people." In addition, Chicana feminists criticized white feminists who believed that a general women's movement would be able to overcome racial differences among women. Chicanas interpreted this as a failure by the white feminists movement to deal with the issue of racism. Without the incorporation of an analysis of racial oppression to explain the experiences of Chicanas as well as of other women of color, Chicana feminists believed that a coalition with white feminists would be highly unlikely (Chapa 1973; Cotera 1977; Gomez 1973; Longeaux y Vasquez 1971). As Longeaux y Vasquez (1971, p. 11) concluded: "We must have a clearer vision of our plight and certainly we cannot blame our men for the oppression of the women."

In the 1970s, Chicana feminists reconciled their demands for an end to sexism within the Chicano movement and their rejection of the saliency of gender oppression by separating the two issues. They clearly identified the struggle against sexism in the Chicano movement as a major issue, arguing that sexism prevented their full participation

(Fallis 1974; Gomez 1976). They also argued that sexist behavior and ideology on the part of both Chicano males and Anglos represented the key to understanding women's oppression. However, they remained critical of an analysis of women's experiences that focused exclusively on gender oppression.

Chicana feminists adopted an analysis that began with race as a critical variable in interpreting the experiences of Chicano communities in the United States. They expanded this analysis by identifying gender as a variable interconnected with race in analyzing the specific daily life circumstances of Chicanas as women in Chicano communities. Chicana feminists did not view women's struggles as secondary to the nationalist movement but argued instead for an analysis of race and gender as multiple sources of oppression (Cotera 1977). Thus, Chicana feminism went beyond the limits of an exclusively racial theory of oppression that tended to overlook gender and also went beyond the limits of a theory of oppression based exclusively on gender that tended to overlook race.

A second factor preventing an alliance between Chicana feminists and white feminists was the middle-class orientation of white feminists. While some Chicana feminists recognized the legitimacy of the demands made by white feminists and even admitted sharing some of these demands, they argued that "it is not our business as Chicanas to identify with the white women's liberation movement as a home base for working for our people" (Longeaux y Vasquez 1971, p. 11).

Throughout the 1970s, Chicana feminists viewed the white feminist movement as a middle-class movement (Chapa 1973; Cotera 1980; Longeaux y Vasquez 1970; Martinez 1972; Nieto 1974; Orozco 1976). In contrast, Chicana feminists analyzed the Chicano movement in general as a working-class movement. They repeatedly made reference to such differences, and many Chicana feminists began their writings with a section that disassociated themselves from the "women's liberation movement." Chicana feminists as activists in the broader Chicano movement identified as major struggles the farmworkers movement, welfare rights, undocumented workers, and prison rights. Such issues were seen as far removed from the demands of the white feminist movement, and Chicana feminists could not get white feminist organizations to deal with them (Cotera 1980).

Similar concerns regarding the white feminist movement were raised by Black and Asian American feminists. Black feminists have documented the historical and contemporary schisms between Black feminists and white feminists, emphasizing the socioeconomic and political differences (Davis 1971, 1983; Dill 1983; LaRue 1970). More specifically, Black feminists have been critical of the white feminists who advocate a female solidarity that cuts across racial, ethnic, and social class lines. As Thornton Dill (1983, p. 131) states:

> The cry "Sisterhood is powerful!" has engaged only a few segments of the female population in the United States. Black, Hispanic, Native American, and Asian American women of all classes, as well as many working-class women, have not readily identified themselves as sisters of the white middle-class women who have been in the forefront of the movement.

Like Black feminists, Asian American feminists have also had strong reservations regarding the white feminist movement. For many Asian Americans, white feminism has primarily focused on gender as an analytical category and has thus lacked a systematic analysis of race and class (Chow 1987; Fong 1978; Wong 1980; Woo 1971).

White feminist organizations were also accused of being exclusionary, patronizing, or racist in their dealings with Chicanas and other women of color. Cotera (1980, p. 227) states:

Minority women could fill volumes with examples of put-down, put-ons, and out-and-out racism shown to them by the leadership in the [white feminist] movement. There are three major problem areas in the minority-majority relationship in the movement: (1) paternalism or materialism, (2) extremely limited opportunities for minority women . . . , (3) outright discrimination against minority women in the movement.

Although Chicana feminists continued to be critical of building coalitions with white feminists toward the end of the seventies, they acknowledged the diversity of ideologies within the white feminist movement. Chicana feminists sympathetic to radical socialist feminism because of its anticapitalist framework wrote of working-class oppression that cut across racial and ethnic lines. Their later writings discussed the possibility of joining with white working-class women, but strategies for forming such political coalitions were not made explicit (Cotera 1977; Marquez and Ramirez 1977).

Instead, Del Castillo and other Chicana feminists favored coalitions between Chicanas and other women of color while keeping their respective autonomous organizations. Such coalitions would recognize the inherent racial oppression of capitalism rather than universal gender oppression. When Longeaux y Vasquez (1971) stated that she was "Chicana *primero*," she was stressing the saliency of race over gender in explaining the oppression experienced by Chicanas. The word *Chicana* however, simultaneously expresses a woman's race and gender. Not until later—in the 1980s—would Chicana feminist ideology call for an analysis that stressed the interrelationship of race, class, and gender in explaining the conditions of Chicanas in American society (Cordova et al. 1986; Zinn 1982), just as Black and Asian American feminists have done.

Chicana feminists continued to stress the importance of developing autonomous feminist organizations that would address the struggles of Chicanas as members of an ethnic minority and as women. Rather than attempt to overcome the obstacles to coalition building between Chicana feminists and white feminists, Chicanas called for autonomous feminist organizations for all women of color (Cotera 1977; Gonzalez 1980; Nieto 1975). Chicana feminists believed that sisterhood was indeed powerful but only to the extent that racial and class differences were understood and, above all, respected. As Nieto (1974, p. 4) concludes:

The Chicana must demand that dignity and respect within the women's rights movement which allows her to practice feminism within the context of her own culture. . . . Her approaches to feminism must be drawn from her own world.

Chicana Feminism: An Evolving Future

Chicana feminists, like Black, Asian American, and Native American feminists, experience specific life conditions that are distinct from those of white feminists. Such socioeconomic and cultural differences in Chicano communities directly shaped the development of Chicana feminism and the relationship between Chicana feminists and feminists of other racial and ethnic groups, including white feminists. Future dialogue among all feminists will require a mutual understanding of the existing differences as well as the similarities. Like other women of color, Chicana feminists must address issues that specifically affect them as women of color. In addition, Chicana feminists must address those issues that have particular impact on Chicano communities, such as poverty, limited opportunities for higher education, high school dropouts, health care, bilingual education, immigration reform, prison reform, welfare, and most recently, United States policies in Central America.

At the academic level, an increasing number of Chicana feminists continue to join in a collective effort to carry on the feminist legacy inherited from the 1970s. In June 1982, a group of Chicana academics organized a national feminist organization called Mujeres Activas en Letras y Cambio Social (MALCS) in order to build a support network for Chicana professors, undergraduates, and graduate students. The organization's major goal is to fight against race, class, and gender oppression facing Chicanas in institutions of higher education. In addition, MALCS aims to bridge the gap between academic work and the Chicano community. MALCS has organized three Chicana/Latina summer research institutes at the University of California at Davis and publishes a working paper series.

During the 1982 conference of the National Association for Chicano Studies, a panel organized by Mujeres en Marcha, a feminist group from the University of California at Berkeley, discussed three major issues facing Chicana feminists in higher education in particular and the Chicano movement in general. Panelists outlined the issues as follows (Mujeres en Marcha 1983, pp. 1–2):

1. For a number of years, Chicanas have heard claims that a concern with issues specifically affecting Chicanas is merely a distraction/diversion from the liberation of Chicano people as a whole. What are the issues that arise when women are asked to separate their exploitation as women from the other forms of oppression that we experience?

2. Chicanas are confronted daily by the limitations of being a woman in this patriarchal society; the attempts to assert these issues around sexism are often met with resistance and scorn. What are some of the major difficulties in relations amongst ourselves? How are the relationships between women and men affected? How are the relationships of women to women and men to men affected? How do we overcome the constraints of sexism?

3. It is not uncommon that our interests as feminists are challenged on the basis that we are simply falling prey to the interests of white middle-class women. We challenge the notion that there is no room for a Chicana movement within our own community. We, as women of color, have a unique set of concerns that are separate from white women and from men of color.

While these issues could not be resolved at the conference, the panel succeeded in generating an ongoing discussion within the National Association for Chicano Studies (NACS). Two years later, in 1984, the national conference of NACS, held in Austin, Texas, adopted the theme "Voces de la Mujer" in response to demands from the Chicana Caucus. As a result, for the first time since its founding in 1972, the NACS national conference addressed the issue of women. Compared with past conferences, a large number of Chicanas participated by presenting their research and chairing and moderating panels. A Plenary session addressed the problems of gender inequality in higher education and within NACS. At the national business meeting, the issue of sexism within NACS was again seriously debated as it continues to be one of the "unsettled issues" of concern to Chicana feminists. A significant outcome of this conference was the publication of the NACS 1984 conference proceedings, which marked the first time that the association's anthology was devoted completely to Chicanas and Mexicanas (Cordova et al. 1986).

The decade of the 1980s has witnessed a rephrasing of the critical question concerning the nature of the oppression experienced by Chicanas and other women of color. Chicana feminists, like Black feminists, are asking what are the consequences of the intersection of race, class, and gender in the daily lives of women in American society, emphasizing the simultaneity of these critical variables for women of color (Garcia 1986; Hooks 1984). In their labor-force participation, wages, education, and poverty levels, Chicanas have made few gains in comparison to white men and women and Chicano men (Segura 1986). To analyze these problems, Chicana feminists have investigated the structures of racism, capitalism, and patriarchy, especially as they are experienced by the majority of Chicanas (Ruiz 1987; Segura 1986; Zavella 1987). Clearly, such issues will need to be explicitly addressed by an evolving Chicana feminist movement, analytically and politically.

Note

1. For bibliographies on Chicanas see Balderama (1981); Candelaria (1980); Loeb (1980); Portillo, Rios, and Rodriguez (1976); and Baca Zinn (1982, 1984).

References

Almaguer, Tomas, 1974. "Historical Notes on Chicano Oppression." *Aztlan* 5:27–56.

Balderama, Sylvia. 1981. "A Comprehensive Bibliography on La Chicana." Unpublished paper, University of California, Berkeley.

Barrera, Mario. 1974. "The Study of Politics and the Chicano." *Aztlan* 5:9–26.

———. 1979. *Race and Class in the Southwest.* Notre Dame, IN: University of Notre Dame Press.

Beale, Frances. 1975. "Slave of a Slave No More: Black Women in Struggle." *Black Scholar* 6:2–10.

Cade, Toni. 1970. *The Black Woman.* New York: Signet.

Candelaria, Cordelia. 1980. "Six Reference Works on Mexican American Women: A Review Essay." *Frontiers* 5:75–80.

Castro, Tony. 1974. *Chicano Power.* New York: Saturday Review Press.

Chapa, Evey. 1973. "Report from the National Women's Political Caucus." *Magazin* 1:37–39.

Chavez, Henri. 1971. "The Chicanas." *Regeneracion* 1:14.

Cheng, Lucie. 1984. "Asian American Women and Feminism." *Sojourner* 10:11–12.

Chow, Esther Ngan-Ling. 1987. "The Development of Feminist Consciousness Among Asian American Women." *Gender & Society* 1:284–99.

Combahee River Collective. 1981. "A Black Feminist Statement." Pp. 210–18 in *This Bridge Called My Back: Writings by Radical Women of Color*, edited by Cherrie Morgaga and Gloria Anzaldua. Watertown, MA: Persephone.

Cordova, Teresa et al. 1986. *Chicana Voices: Intersections of Class, Race, and Gender.* Austin, TX: Center for Mexican American Studies.

Cotera, Marta. 1973. "La Mujer Mexicana: Mexicano Feminism." *Magazin* 1:30–32.

————. 1977. *The Chicana Feminist*. Austin, TX: Austin Information Systems Development.

————. 1980. "Feminism: The Chicana and Anglo Versions: An Historical Analysis." Pp. 217–34 in *Twice a Minority: Mexican American Women*, edited by Margarita Melville. St. Louis, MO: C. V. Mosby.

Davis, Angela. 1971. "Reflections on Black Women's Role in the Community of Slaves." *Black Scholar* 3:3–13.

————. 1983. *Women, Race and Class*. New York: Random House.

Del Castillo, Adelaida. 1974. "La Vision Chicana." *La Gente*: 8.

Dill, Bonnie Thornton. 1983. "Race, Class, and Gender: Prospects for an All-Inclusive Sisterhood." *Feminists Studies* 9:131–50.

Dunne, John. 1967. *Delano: The Story of the California Grape Strike*. New York: Strauss.

Fallis, Guadalupe Valdes. 1974. "The Liberated Chicana—A Struggle Against Tradition." *Women: A Journal of Liberation* 3:20.

Flores, Francisca. 1971a. "Conference of Mexican Women: Un Remolino." *Regeneracion* 1(1):1–4.

————. 1971b. "El Mundo Femenil Mexicana." *Regeneracion* 1(10):i.

Fong, Katheryn M. 1978. "Feminism Is Fine, But What's It Done for Asia America?" *Bridge* 6:21–22.

Freeman, Jo. 1983. "On the Origins of Social Movements." Pp. 8–30 in *Social Movements of the Sixties and Seventies*, edited by Jo Freeman. New York: Longman.

————. 1984. "The Women's Liberation Movement: Its Origins, Structure, Activities, and Ideas." Pp. 543–56 in *Women: A Feminist Perspective*, edited by Jo Freeman. Palo Alto, CA: Mayfield.

Garcia, Alma M. 1986. "Studying Chicanas: Bringing Women into the Frame of Chicano Studies." Pp. 19–29 in *Chicana Voices: Intersections of Class, Race, and Gender*, edited by Teresa Cordova et al. Austin, TX: Center for Mexican American Studies.

Garcia, F. Chris and Rudolph O. de la Garza. 1977. *The Chicano Political Experience*. North Scituate, MA: Duxbury.

Gomez, Anna Nieto. 1971. "Chicanas Identify." *Hijas de Cuauhtemoc* (April):9.

————. 1973. "La Femenista." *Encuentro Femenil* 1:34–47.

————. 1976. "Sexism in the Movement." *La Gente* 6(4):10.

Gonzalez, Sylvia. 1980. "Toward a Feminist Pedagogy for Chicana Self-Actualization." *Frontiers* 5:48–51.

Hernandez, Carmen. 1971. "Carmen Speaks Out." *Papel Chicano* 1(June 12):8–9.

Hooks, Bell. 1981. *Ain't I a Woman: Black Women and Feminism*. Boston: South End Press.

————. 1984. *Feminist Theory: From Margin to Center*. Boston: South End Press.

Joseph, Gloria and Jill Lewis. 1981. *Common Differences: Conflicts in Black and White Feminist Perspectives*. Garden City, NY: Doubleday.

Kushner, Sam. 1975. *Long Road to Delano*. New York: International.

LaRue, Linda. 1970. "The Black Movement and Women's Liberation." *Black Scholar* 1:36–42.

Loeb, Catherine. 1980. "La Chicana: A Bibliographic Survey." *Frontiers* 5:59–74.

Longeaux y Vasquez, Enriqueta. 1969a. "The Woman of La Raza." *El Grito del Norte* 2(July):8–9.

————. 1969b. "La Chicana: Let's Build a New Life." *El Grito del Norte* 2(November):11.

————. 1970. "The Mexican-American Woman." Pp. 379–84 in *Sisterhood Is Powerful*, edited by Robin Morgan. New York: Vintage.

————. 1971. "Soy Chicana Primero." *El Grito del Norte* 4(April 26):11.

Macias, Anna. 1982. *Against All Odds*. Westport, CT: Greenwood.

Marquez, Evelina and Margarita Ramirez. 1977. "Women's Task Is to Gain Liberation." Pp. 188–94 in *Essays on La Mujer*, edited by Rosaura Sanchez and Rosa Martinez Cruz. Los Angeles: UCLA Chicano Studies Center.

Martinez, Elizabeth. 1972. "The Chicana." *Ideal* 44:1–3.

Matthiesen, Peter. 1969. *Sal Si Puedes: Cesar Chavez and the New American Revolution*. New York: Random House.

Meier, Matt and Feliciano Rivera. 1972. *The Chicanos*. New York: Hill & Wang.

Moraga, Cherrie. 1981. "La Guera." Pp. 27–34 in *This Bridge Called My Back: Writings by Radical Women of Color*, edited by Cherrie Moraga and Gloria Anzaldua. Watertown, MA: Persephone.

———. 1983. *Loving in the War Years*. Boston: South End Press.

Moraga, Cherrie and Gloria Anzaldua. 1981. *This Bridge Called My Back: Writings by Radical Women of Color*. Watertown, MA: Persephone.

Moreno, Dorinda. 1979. "The Image of the Chicana and the La Raza Woman." *Caracol* 2:14–15.

Mujeres en Marcha. 1983. *Chicanas in the 80s: Unsettled Issues*. Berkeley, CA: Chicano Studies Publication Unit.

Muños, Carlos, Jr. 1974. "The Politics of Protest and Liberation: A Case Study of Repression and Cooptation." *Aztlan* 5:119–41.

Nabokov, Peter. 1969. *Tijerina and the Courthouse Raid*. Albuquerque, NM: University of New Mexico Press.

Navarro, Armando. 1974. "The Evolution of Chicano Politics." *Aztlan* 5:57–84.

Nelson, Eugene. 1966. *Huelga: The First 100 Days*. Delano, CA: Farm Workers Press.

Nieto, Consuelo. 1974. "The Chicana and the Women's Rights Movement." *La Luz* 3(September):10–11, 32.

———. 1975. "Consuelo Nieto on the Women's Movement." *Interracial Books for Children Bulletin* 5:4.

Orozco, Yolanda. 1976. "La Chicana and 'Women's Liberation.' " *Voz Fronteriza* (January 5):6, 12.

Piven, Frances Fox and Richard A. Cloward. 1979. *Poor People's Movements: Why They Succeed, How They Fail*. New York: Vintage.

Portillo, Cristina, Graciela Rios, and Martha Rodriguez. 1976. *Bibliography on Writings on La Mujer*. Berkeley, CA: University of California Chicano Studies Library.

Riddell, Adaljiza Sosa. 1974. "Chicanas en el Movimiento." *Aztlan* 5:155–65.

Rincon, Bernice. 1971. "La Chicana: Her Role in the Past and Her Search for a New Role in the Future." *Regeneracion* 1(10):15–17.

Rowbotham, Sheila. 1974. *Women, Resistance and Revolution: A History of Women and Revolution in the Modern World*. New York: Vintage.

Ruiz, Vicki L. 1987. *Cannery Women, Cannery Lives: Mexican Women, Unionization, and the California Food Processing Industry, 1930–1950*. Albuquerque: University of New Mexico Press.

Segura, Denise. 1986. "Chicanas and Triple Oppression in the Labor Force." Pp. 47–65 in *Chicana Voices: Intersections of Class, Race and Gender*, edited by Teresa Cordova et al. Austin, TX: Center for Mexican American Studies.

Shockley, John. 1974. *Chicano Revolt in a Texas Town*. South Bend, IN: University of Notre Dame Press.

Vidal, Mirta. 1971. "New Voice of La Raza: Chicanas Speak Out." *International Socialist Review* 32:31–33.

White, Frances. 1984. "Listening to the Voices of Black Feminism." *Radical America* 18:7–25.

Wong, Germaine Q. 1980. "Impediments to Asian-Pacific-American Women Organizing." Pp. 89–103 in *The Conference on the Educational and Occupational Needs of Asian Pacific Women*. Washington, DC: National Institute of Education.

Woo, Margaret. 1971. "Women + Man = Political Unity." Pp. 115–16 in *Asian Women,* edited by Editorial Staff. Berkeley, CA: University of California Press.

Zavella, Patricia. 1987. *Women's Work and Chicano Families: Cannery Workers of the Santa Clara Valley.* Ithaca, NY: Cornell University Press.

Zinn, Maxine Baca. 1975a. "Political Familism: Toward Sex Role Equality in Chicano Families." *Aztlan* 6:13–27.

———. 1975b. "Chicanas: Power and Control in the Domestic Sphere." *De Colores* 2/3:19–31.

———. 1982. "Mexican-American Women in the Social Sciences." *Signs: Journal of Women in Culture and Society* 8:259–72.

———. 1984. "Mexican Heritage Women: A Bibliographic Essay." *Sage Race Relations Abstracts* 9:1–12.

The Development of Feminist Consciousness Among Asian American Women

Esther Ngan-Ling Chow

This article examines the social circumstances, both current and past, that have affected the development and transformation of feminist consciousness among Asian American women. Gender, race, class, and culture all influenced the relative lack of participation of Asian American women in the mainstream feminist movement in the United States. It concludes that Asian American women have come to terms with their multiple identities and define feminist issues from multiple dimensions. By incorporating race, class, and cultural issues along with gender concerns, a transcendent feminist consciousness that goes beyond these boundaries may develop.

Like other women of color, Asian American women as a group have neither been included in the predominantly white middle-class feminist movement, nor have they begun collectively to identify with it (Chia 1983; Chow forthcoming; Dill 1983; Loo and Ong 1982; Yamada 1981). Although some Asian American women have participated in social movements within their communities or in the larger society, building ties with white feminists and other women of color is a recent phenomenon for Asian American women. Since Asian American women are a relatively small group in the United States, their invisibility and contribution to the feminist movement in the larger society may seem insignificant.[1] Furthermore, ethnic diversity among Asian American women serves as a barrier to organizing and makes it difficult to these women to identify themselves collectively as a group. Because approximately half of Asian American women are foreign-born, their lack of familiarity with the women's movement in the United States and their preoccupation with economic survival limit their feminist involvement. The use of demographic factors such as size, ethnic diversity, and nativity, without an examination of structural conditions, such as gender, race, class, and culture, will not permit an adequate understanding of the extent of feminist activism of Asian women in the United States.

What are the social conditions that have hindered Asian American women from developing a feminist consciousness, a prerequisite for political activism in the feminist movement? From a historical and structural perspective, this article argues that the feminist consciousness of Asian American women has been limited by their location in society

Chow, Esther Ngan-Ling. 1987. "The Development of Feminist Consciousness Among Asian American Women." *Gender & Society* 1(3): 284–299. Reprinted by permission of Sage Publications, Inc.

and social experiences. A broader perspective is needed to understand the development of feminist consciousness among Asian American women who are subject to cross-group pressures.

The intent of this article is primarily conceptual, describing how gender, race, class, and culture intersect in the lives of Asian American women and how their experiences as women have affected the development of feminist consciousness. The ideas are a synthesis of legal documents, archival materials, and census statistics; participant observation in the civil rights movement, feminist movement, Asian American groups, and Asian American organizations since the mid-1960s; interviews and conversations with Asian American feminists and leaders; and letters, oral histories, ethnic newspapers, organizational newsletters, films, and other creative writings by and about Asian American women.

Gender Consciousness: Precursor of Feminist Consciousness

Gender consciousness is an awareness of one's self as having certain gender characteristics and an identification with others who occupy a similar position in the sex-gender structure. In the case of women, an awareness of femaleness and an identification with other women can lead to an understanding of gender power relations and the institutional pressures and socialization processes that create and maintain these power relations (Weitz 1982). Ultimately, gender consciousness can bring about the development of feminist consciousness and the formation of group solidarity necessary for collective action in the struggle for gender equality (Christiansen-Ruffman 1982; Green 1979; Houston 1982).

Being female, awareness of gender roles, and identification with other women are the major ingredients in building gender consciousness. However, it is necessary to understand the social contexts in which the gender consciousness of Asian American women has developed. Domination by men is a commonly shared oppression for Asian American women. These women have been socialized to accept their devaluation, restricted roles for women, psychological reinforcement of gender stereotypes, and a subordinate position within Asian communities as well as in the society at large (Chow 1985). Within Asian communities, the Asian family (especially the immigrant one) is characterized by a hierarchy of authority based on sex, age, and generation, with young women at the lowest level, subordinate to father-husband-brother-son. The Asian family is also characterized by well-defined family roles, with father as a breadwinner and decision maker and mother as a compliant wife and homemaker. While they are well protected by the family because of their filial piety and obedience, women are socially alienated from their Asian sisters. Such alienation may limit the development of gender and feminist consciousness and render Asian women politically powerless in achieving effective communication and organization, and in building bonds with other women of color and white feminists.

In studying the majority of women activists who participated in various movements for oppressed groups, Blumberg (1982) found that participation in these movements affected the development of gender consciousness among women, which later, because of sexism in the movements, was transformed into a related but distinctive state of awareness—a feminist consciousness. For Asian American women, cross-group allegiances can hinder the development of feminist consciousness or expand it into a more universal view. Women who consider racism and classism to be so pervasive that they cannot embrace feminism at the same level may subordinate women's rights to other social concerns, thus limiting the development of feminist consciousness. Women who are aware of multiple oppressions and who advocate taking collective action to supersede racial, gender, and class differences may develop a feminist consciousness that transcends gender, racial, class, and cultural boundaries.

Awakening Feminist Consciousness

In the wake of the civil rights movement in the early 1960s and the feminist movement in the mid-1960s, Asian American women, following the leads of black and Hispanic women, began to organize (Chow forthcoming; Ling and Mazumdar 1983; Lott and Pian 1979; G. Wong 1980). Initially, some better educated Asian American women formed women's groups to meet personal and family needs and to provide services to their respective organizations and ethnic communities. These groups, few in number and with little institutionalized leadership, were traditional and informal in nature, and usually supported philanthropic concerns (G. Wong 1980). While there had been a few sporadic efforts to organize Asian American women around specific issues and concerns that did not pertain to women (e.g., the unavailability or high cost of basic food, Angel Island, the World War II internment of Japanese Americans), these attempts generally lacked continuity and support, and the organization of Asian American women was limited as a political force. Nevertheless, these activities, as stepping stones for future political activism, allowed Asian American women to cultivate their gender consciousness, to acquire leadership skills, and to increase their political visibility.

In the late 1960s and early 1970s, many Asian American women activists preferred to join forces with Asian American men in the struggle against racism and classism (Fong 1978; G. Wong 1980; Woo 1971). Like black and Hispanic women (Cade 1970; Dill 1983; Fallis 1974; Hepburn et al. 1977; Hooks 1984; Terrelonge 1984), some Asian American women felt that the feminist movement was not attacking racial and class problems of central concern to them. They wanted to work with groups that advocated improved conditions for people of their own racial and ethnic background or people of color, rather than groups oriented toward women's issues (Fong 1978; G. Wong 1980; Woo 1971), even though they may have been aware of their roles and interests and even oppression as women.

As Asian American women became active in their communities, they encountered sexism. Even though many Asian American women realized that they usually occupied subservient positions in the male-dominated organizations within Asian communities, their ethnic pride and loyalty frequently kept them from public revolt (Woo 1971). More recently, some Asian American women have recognized that these organizations have not been particularly responsive to their needs and concerns as women. They also protested that their intense involvement did not and will not result in equal participation as long as the traditional dominance by men and the gendered division of labor remain (G. Wong 1980). Their protests have sensitized some men and have resulted in changes of attitudes and treatment of women, but other Asians, both women and men, perceived them as moving toward separatism.

Asian American women are criticized for the possible consequences of their protests: weakening of the male ego, dilution of effort and resources in Asian American communities, destruction of working relationships between Asian men and women, setbacks for the Asian American cause, cooptation into the larger society, and eventual loss of ethnic identity for Asian Americans as a whole. In short, affiliation with the feminist movement is perceived as a threat to solidarity within their own community. All these forces have restricted the development of feminist consciousness among Asian American women and their active participation in the feminist movement. (For the similar experience of black women, see Hooks 1984.)

Other barriers to political activism are the sexist stereotypes and discriminatory treatment Asian American women encounter outside their own communities. The legacy of the Chinese prostitute and the slave girl from the late nineteenth century still lingers. American involvement in Asian wars continues to perpetuate the image of Asian women as cheap whores and exotic sexpots (e.g., images such as "Suzie Wong" for Chinese women, the "geisha girl" in the Japanese teahouse, the bar girls in Vietnam). The "picture bride" image of Asian women is still very much alive, as U.S. soldiers and business men brought back Asian wives from China, Japan, Korea, and Vietnam with the expectation that they would make perfect wives and homemakers. In the last few years, a systematic importation through advertisements in newspapers and magazines of Asian "mail-order brides" has continued their exploitation as commodities and has been intensively protested by many Asian American communities. Mistreatment, desertion, divorce, and physical abuse of Asian wives or war brides have been major concerns for Asian American women (Kim 1977). The National Committee Concerned with Asian Wives of U.S. Servicemen was specifically organized to deal with these problems.

The result of these cross-pressures is an internal dilemma of choice between racial and sexual identity at the personal level and between liberation for Asian Americans (in the broader sense for all racial and ethnic minority groups) and for women at the societal level. Lee (1971, p. 119) reported interviews with two Asian American feminists who reflected the mixed feelings of many Asian American women. One woman, Sunni said:

> We are *Asian* women. Our identity is *Asian*, and this country recognizes us as such. We cannot afford the luxury of fighting our Asian counterparts. We ought to struggle for Asian liberation first, and I'm afraid that the "feminist" virtues will not be effective weapons. There is no sense in having only women's liberation while we continue to suffer oppression as Asians. (Lee 1971, p. 119)

Another woman, Aurora, took the opposite view:

> History has told us that women's liberation does not automatically come with political revolutions; Asian liberation will not necessarily bring Asian women's liberation. . . . We ought to devote our energies to feminism because a feminist revolution may well be the only revolution that can bring peace among people. (Lee 1971, p. 119)

When Asian American women began to recognize injustice and became aware of their own strengths as women, some developed a feminist consciousness, giving top priority to the fight against sexism and for women's rights. Some sought to establish women's caucuses within existing Asian American organizations (e.g., the Organization of Chinese American Women), while others attempted to organize separately outside of the male-dominated Asian American organizations (e.g., the Organization of Pan American Women and the National Network of Asian and Pacific Women).

343

Asian American women began to organize formally around women's issues in the early 1970s. Yet many of these groups were short-lived because of lack of funding, grass-roots support, membership, credible leadership, or strong networking. Those that endured included women's courses and study groups sponsored by Asian American studies programs on college and university campuses, multilingual and multicultural service programs in women's health or mental health centers (e.g., the Asian Pacific Health Project in Los Angeles and the Asian Pacific Outreach Center in Long Beach, the Pacific Asian Shelter for Battered Women in Los Angeles), and writers' groups (Pacific Asian American Women's Writers West).

A few regional feminist organizations have been formally established and are in the process of expanding their influence and building up their networks from the grass-roots level to the national one. These organizations include the National Organization of Pan Asian Women, the National Network of Asian and Pacific Women, Asian American Women United, the Pilipino Women's League, the Filipino American Women Network, the Vietnamese Women Association, and the Cambodian Women for Progress, Inc.[2] These feminist organizations aim to advance the causes of women and racial and ethnic minorities, to build a strong Asian sisterhood, to maximize the social participation of Asian American women in the larger society, and to effect changes through collective efforts in education, employment, legislation, and information. The active participants in these feminist organizations are mostly middle-class Asian women, college students, professionals, political activists, and a few working-class women (G. Wong 1980).

Racial Cross-Pressures

Joining the white feminist movement is a double-edged sword, for Asian American women experience oppression not only as women in a society dominated by men but also as minorities facing a variety of forms of racism that are not well understood by white feminists (Chia 1983; Chow 1982; Fujitomi and Wong 1976; Kumagai 1978; Loo and Ong 1982). The structural racism of American institutions, which limit access to resources, opportunities, prestige, privileges, and power, affects all the racial and ethnic minority groups of which Asian American women are a part (Chow forthcoming; Dill 1983; Hepburn et al. 1977; LaRue 1976; Loo and Ong 1982; Palmer 1983; Wong et al. 1979).

Legal restrictions, as one form of racism, were used to exploit cheap labor, to control demographic growth, and to discourage family formation by Asians. These restrictions also hindered the development of gender consciousness and political power among Asian American women. Since the mid-1850s, the legal and political receptivity to Asian Americans, men and women, has been low in the United States (Elway 1979; Pian 1980). The U.S. immigration policies generally emphasized imported cheap labor and discouraged the formation of family unity. Some laws specifically targeted Asian American women. As early as the 1850s, the first antiprostitution law was passed in San Francisco, barring traffic of Chinese women and slave girls. The Naturalization Act of 1870 and the Chinese Exclusion Act of 1882 forbade the entry of wives of Chinese laborers. In 1921, a special act directed against Chinese women kept them from marrying American citizens. The Exclusion Act of 1924 did not allow alien-born wives to enter the United States, but their children could come; this act separated many families until the passage of the

Magnuson Act in 1943. The Cable Act of 1932 stipulated that American-born Chinese women marrying foreign-born Asians would lose their U.S. citizenship, although they could regain it through naturalization later. The passage of antimiscegenation laws (e.g., the California Anti-miscegenation Law in 1906), ruled unconstitutional by the U.S. Supreme Court in 1967, barred marriage between whites and "Mongolians" and laborers of Asian origins, making it impossible for Asians to find mates in this country. As a result, bachelor communities mainly consisting of single Asian men became characteristic of many Asian groups, especially the Chinese (Glenn 1983).

In spite of political pressures, repressive immigration laws, and restrictive and discouraging economic hardships, a few Asian women did come to the United States. Chinese women came in the 1850s, followed by Japanese women, who came during the late 1890s, and Filipino and Korean women who migrated in the early part of the twentieth century. These women were "picture brides," merchant wives, domestics, laborers, and prostitutes. In the popular literature, they were generally portrayed as degraded creatures, cheap commodities, and sex objects who took jobs from whites, spread disease and vice, and corrupted the young. Descriptions of their sexist, racist, and economically deprived living conditions reveal a personal and private resistance marked by passive acceptance, suppression of feelings, silent protest, withdrawal, self-sacrifice, and hard work (Aquino 1979; Gee 1971; Jung 1971; Louie 1971; J. Wong 1978; Yung 1986).

The repressive immigration laws were repealed after World War II, and the number of Asian families immigrating to the United States increased. By 1980, the sex ratio was balanced for the first time in the history of this racial and ethnic group. Women now constitute half of the Asian American population (U.S. Bureau of the Census 1981). Although many of the repressive laws that conspired to bar the sociopolitical participation of Asian American men and women have changed, the long-term effect of cultural, socioeconomic, and political exploitation and oppression are still deeply felt, and there are new forms of discrimination and deprivation. The passage of the Immigration Reform and Control Act of 1986, setting restricted immigration quotas for family members of Asian American and Hispanic Americans, recalls earlier repressive legislation. As long as legal circumstances restrict the immigration of the mothers, daughters, and sisters of the Asian American women in the United States, the full development of their gender and feminist consciousness will be hampered.

The long history of racism in the United States has left its mark on feminism. Some Asian American women feel repelled by the racial composition, insensitivity, and lack of receptivity of some white women in the feminist movement (Fong 1978; Yamada 1981). They argue that white feminists do not fully understand or include issues and problems that Asian American women confront. White feminists are not aware of or sympathetic to the differences in the concerns and priorities of Asian American women. Without understanding the history and culture of Asian American women, some white feminists have been impatient with the low level of consciousness among women of color and the slow progress toward feminism of Asian American women.

Although some degree of acceptance of Asian American women and women of color by certain segments of the white feminist movement has occurred, many problems remain (Bogg 1971; Dill 1983; Hepburn et al. 1977; Hooks 1984; Lee 1971). Ideological acceptance does not necessarily lead to full structural receptivity. Conscious and rigorous efforts have not been made by many of those active in white feminist organizations to recruit Asian American women and other women of color openly, to treat them as core groups in the movement, and to incorporate them in the organizational policy and decision-making levels. Palmer (1983) points out that ethnocentrism is a major reason that feminist organizations treat race and class as secondary and are not fully accepting of women of color. Hooks (1984) is critical of a feminist movement based on the white women who live at the center and whose perspectives rarely include knowledge and awareness of the lives of women and men who live at the margin. Dill (1983, p. 131) states, "Political expediency drove white feminists to accept principles that were directly opposed to the survival and well-being of blacks in order to seek to achieve more limited advances for women." the same is true for Asian American women.

Inconsistencies between attitudes and behavior of white women are highly evident in the "token" membership of minority women in some feminist organizations, which indicates simply a superficial invitation to join. For women of color, these frustrations of not being included in the "white women's system" run parallel to those experiences of white women who try to break into the "old boy's network." Consequently, Asian American women feel more comfortable making allies with women of color (e.g., the National Institute for Women of Color) than with their white counterparts. While there are interethnic problems among Asian American women and between them and other women of color, social bonding and group allegiance are much more readily established, and common issues are more easily shared on the basis of race and ethnicity. A separate movement for women of color may be a viable alternative for the personal development of Asian American women and other women of color and for their struggle for liberation and social equality.

Economic Conditions and Class Cleavages

Economic exploitation and class cleavages also account for the limited development of feminist consciousness and political activism among Asian American women. American capitalism demands cheap labor and the economic subordination of certain groups, resulting in a dual or split labor market. Certain minorities, primarily blacks, Mexican Americans, and Asian Americans, are treated as internal colonized groups exploited culturally, politically, and economically (Almquist 1984; Blauner 1972; Bonacich 1972).

Asian American women have lived in racially segregated internal colonies such as Chinatown, Little Tokyo, and Little Saigon. They have experienced social isolation, ghettoization, poverty, and few opportunities for personal growth and emancipation. Limited resources and lack of access to information, transportation, and social services have made them rely on their families for support and protection. They must also work to maintain them financially. The labor force participation of Asian American women is much higher than that of white and black women (U.S. Bureau of the Census 1983), but many of them have worked in the secondary labor market sector, which is characterized by long working hours, low pay, and low prestige. Although their educational levels are relatively high, 70 percent are concentrated in clerical, service, and blue-collar work, and are facing tremendous underemployment (U.S. Bureau of the Census 1983; U.S. Commission on Civil Rights 1978).

Cultural values that emphasize hard work and that place a stigma on idleness prevent Asian American women from not working and going on welfare. Asian American households generally have a greater number of multiple breadwinners per family than the general U.S. population. The financial burdens on many Asian American women pressure them to continue struggling for economic survival for the good of their families, sacrificing their own interests, and suppressing their feelings and frustrations even in the face of gender and racial discrimination. They have little time to examine the implications of their economic situations; they do not fully understand the dynamics of class position; and they are not likely to challenge the existing power structure.

How economic and class conditions hinder feminist consciousness and political activism is evident for Chinese working-class women living in Chinatowns in many cities. Subject to the impact of internal colonization, their work world is an ethnic labor market, offering few good jobs, low pay, long hours, limited job advancement, and relative isolation from the larger society. The film *Sewing Woman* (Dong 1982) vividly describes the ways in which a working-class Chinese woman attempts to balance her family, work, and community responsibilities. Unionization of garment factory workers in Chinatown is only the beginning of a long process of political struggle for these women.[3]

In a study of Chinatown women, Loo and Ong (1982) identify the major reasons for the lack of integration of these working-class women into the feminist movement. First, Chinatown women do not relate comfortably to people outside their ethnic subgroup, which produces social distancing and alienation. Second, Chinatown women face varied problems, so no political movement that addresses only one of these will claim their allegiance. Third, although the women's movement aims to improve conditions for all women, the specific concerns of Chinatown's women are often not those of the women's movement. For instance, health, language, and cultural adjustment are major issues for low-income immigrant women. These are not the foci of the women's movement. Fourth, Loo and Ong demonstrate that the psychological profile of Chinatown women is not that of political activists. Chinatown women lack a sense of personal efficacy or control over outcomes in their lives, do not have a systematic understanding of the structural and cultural elements of a society that produces sexism, and tend to blame themselves for social problems. And finally, Chinatown women perceive themselves as having more in common with Chinatown men that with white middle-class women.

Although class cleavages exist among Asian American women, political allegiance is easily achieved because of racial bonding. Initially, the highly educated and professional, middle-class Asian American woman organized politically and involved themselves in the feminist movement, in some cases organizing Asian American women's groups (G. Wong 1980). Although some of these groups may tend to advance middle-class interests, such as career mobility, there have also been efforts to incorporate the needs of working-class Asian American women. Because race and ethnicity cut across classes and provide a base for political identification, economic barriers are much easier to overcome among Asian American women than between them and white women. Nevertheless, there is still a great need to address issues concerning working-class Asian American women and to mobilize them to join feminist efforts.

Cultural Factors and Barriers

Asiatic and U.S. cultures alike tend to relegate women to subordinate status and to work in a gendered division of labor. Although Asiatic values emphasizing education, achievement, and diligence no doubt have accounted for the high aspirations and achievements of some Asian American women, certain Asiatic values, especially when they are in conflict with American ideas, have discouraged Asian women from actively participating in the feminist movement (Chow 1982, 1985). Adherence to Asiatic values of obedience, familial interest, fatalism, and self-control may foster submissiveness, passivity, pessimism, timidness, inhibition, and adaptiveness, rather than rebelliousness or political activism. Acceptance of the American values of independence, individualism, mastery of one's environment through change, and self-expression may generate self-interest, aggressiveness, initiative, and expressive spontaneity that tend to encourage political activism; but these are, to a large extent, incompatible with the upbringing of Asian American women.

Although the cultural barriers seem to pose a greater problem internally for Asian American women, a lack of knowledge and understanding of the cultural and language problems faced by Asian American women widens the gap between them and white women (Moschkovich 1981). Further effort is needed to enhance cultural awareness and understanding in order for women of all kinds to develop a transcendent consciousness, a more inclusive experience of sisterhood.

Conclusion

Paradoxically, Asian American women (like other women of color) have much to gain from the white feminist movement; yet they have had a low level of participation in feminist organizations. Since feminist consciousness is a result as well as a source of feminist involvement, Asian American women have remained politically invisible and powerless. The development of feminist consciousness for Asian American women cannot be judged or understood through the experience of white women. Conversely, white women's understanding and definition of feminist consciousness needs to be more thoroughly rooted in the experiences of women of color. The same cross-pressures that hinder the political development of women of color could be a transcending political perspective that adds gender to their other consciousness and thus broadens political activism.

Notes

1. According to the 1980 Census, there are 3.5 million Asian Americans in this country, constituting 1.5 percent of the total U.S. population. Women constitute 51 percent of the total Asian American population in the United States.
2. *Pilipino* and *Filipino* are acceptable terms used to describe people from the Philippines and can be used interchangeably. The U.S. Bureau of Census has used the term *Filipino* since 1900. Now *Filipino* is a commonly used term for the group and it also can be found in *Webster's Dictionary*.
3. Personal discussion with the union representative in Local 23–25 of the ILGWU in New York Chinatown.

References

Almquist, Elizabeth M. 1984. "Race and Ethnicity in the Lives of Minority Women." Pp. 423–453 in *Women: A Feminist Perspective,* edited by Jo Freeman. 3rd ed. Palo Alto, CA: Mayfield.

Aquino, Belinda A. 1979. "The History of Philipino Women in Hawaii." *Bridge* 7:17–21.

Blauner, Robert. 1972. *Racial Oppression in America.* New York: Harper and Row.

Blumberg, Rhoda Lois. 1982. "Women as Allies of Other Oppressed Groups: Some Hypothesized Links Between Social Activism, Female Consciousness, and Feminism." Paper presented at the Tenth World Congress of the International Sociological Association, August 16–22, Mexico City.

Bogg, Grace Lee. 1971. "The Future: Politics as End and as Means." Pp. 112–115 in *Asian Women,* edited by Editorial Staff. Berkeley, CA: University of California Press.

Bonacich, Edna. 1972. "A Theory of Ethnic Antagonism: The Split Labor Market." *American Sociological Review* 37:547–559.

Cade, Toni. 1970. *The Black Woman.* New York: Mentor.

Chia, Alice Yun. 1983. "Toward a Holistic Paradigm for Asian American Women's Studies: A Synthesis of Feminist Scholarship and Women of Color's Feminist Politics." Paper presented at the Fifth Annual Conference of the National Women's Studies Association, Columbus, OH.

Chow, Esther Ngan-Ling. 1982. *Acculturation of Asian American Professional Women.* Washington, DC: National Institute of Mental Health, Department of Health and Human Services.

———1985. "Acculturation Experience of Asian American Women." Pp. 238–251 in *Beyond Sex Roles,* edited by Alice G. Sargent. 2nd ed. St. Paul, MN: West.

———Forthcoming. "The Women's Liberation Movement: Where Are All the Asian American Women?" In *Asian American Women,* edited by Judy Yung and Diane Yen-Mei Wong. San Francisco, CA: Asian American Women United.

Christiansen-Ruffman, Linda. 1982. "Women's Political Culture and Feminist Political Culture." Paper presented at the Tenth World Congress of the International Sociological Association, Mexico City.

Dill, Bonnie Thornton. 1983. "Race, Class, and Gender: Prospects for an Inclusive Sisterhood." *Feminist Studies* 9:131–150.

Dong, Arthur. 1982. *Sewing Women.* San Francisco: Deep Focus.

Elway, Rita Fujiki. 1979. "Strategies for Political Participation of Asian/Pacific Women." Pp. 133–139 in *Civil Rights Issues of Asian and Pacific Americans: Myths and Realities.* Washington, DC: U.S. Commission on Civil Rights.

Fallis, Guadalupe Valdes. 1974. "The Liberated Chicana—A Struggle Against Tradition." *Women: A Journal of Liberation* 3:20.

Fong, Katheryn M. 1978. "Feminism Is Fine, But What's It Done for Asian America?" *Bridge* 6:21–22.

Fujitomi, Irene and Dianne Wong. 1976. "The New Asian-American Women." Pp. 236–248 in *Female Psychology: The Emerging Self,* edited by Susan Cox. Chicago, IL: Science Research Association.

Gee, Emma. 1971. "Issei: The First Women." Pp. 8–15 in *Asian Women,* edited by Editorial Staff. Berkeley, CA: University of California Press.

Glenn, Evelyn. 1983. "Split Household, Small Producer and Dual Wage Earner: An Analysis of Chinese-American Family Strategies," *Journal of Marriage and Family* 45:35–46.

Green, Pearl. 1979. "The Feminist Consciousness." *Sociological Quarterly* 20:359–374.

Hepburn, Ruth Ann, Viola Gonzalez, and Cecilia Preciado de Burciaga. 1977. "The Chicana as Feminist." Pp. 266–273 in *Beyond Sex Roles,* edited by Alice Sargent. St. Paul, MN: West.

Hooks, Bell. 1984. *Feminist Theory: From Margin to Center.* Boston, MA: South End Press.

Houston, L. N. 1982. "Black Consciousness Among Female Undergraduates at a Predominantly White College: 1973 and 1979." *Journal of Social Psychology* 118:289–290.

Jung, Betty. 1971. "Chinese Immigrant Women." Pp. 18–20 in *Asian Women*, edited by Editorial Staff. Berkely, CA.: University of California.

Kim, Bok-Lim. 1977. "Asian Wives of U.S. Servicemen: Women in Shadows." *Amerasia Journal* 4:91–115.

Kumagai, Gloria L. 1978. "The Asian Women in America." *Bridge* 6:16–20.

LaRue, Linda. 1976. "The Black Movement and Women's Liberation." Pp. 216–225 in *Female Psychology: The Emerging Self*, edited by Susan Cox. Chicago, IL: Science Research Associates.

Lee, G. M. 1971. "One in Sisterhood." Pp. 119–121 in *Asian Women*, edited by Editorial Staff. Berkeley, CA.: University of California.

Ling, Susie and Sucheta Mazumdar. 1983. "Editorial: Asian American Feminism." *Cross-Currents* 6:3–5.

Loo, Chalsa and Paul Ong. 1982. "Slaying Demons With a Sewing Needle: Feminist Issues for Chinatown Women." *Berkeley Journal of Sociology* 27:77–88.

Lott, Juanita and Canta Pian. 1979. *Beyond Stereotypes and Statistics: Emergence of Asian and Pacific American Women*. Washington, DC: Organization of Pan Asian American Women.

Louie, Gayle. 1971. "Forgotten Women." Pp. 20–23 in *Asian Women*, edited by Editorial Staff. Berkeley, CA.: University of California Press.

Moschkovich, J. 1981. "—But I know You, American Women." Pp. 79–84 in *This Bridge Called My Back: Writings by Radical Women of Color*, edited by C. Moraga and G. Anzaldua. Watertown, MA: Persephone.

Palmer, Phyllis Marynick. 1983. "White Women/Black Women: The Dualism of Female Identity and Experience in the United States." *Feminist Studies* 9:152–170.

Pian, Canta. 1980. "Immigration of Asian Women and the Status of Recent Asian Women Immigrants." Pp. 181–210 in *The Conference on the Educational and Occupational Needs of Asian Pacific American Women*. Washington, DC: National Institute of Education.

Terrelonge, Pauline. 1984. "Feminist Consciousness and Black Women." Pp. 557–567 in *Women: A Feminist Perspective*, edited by Jo Freeman. 3rd ed. Palo Alto, CA.: Mayfield.

U.S. Bureau of the Census. 1981. *1980 Census of Population: Supplementary Reports*. Washington, DC: U.S. Department of Commerce.

U.S. Bureau of the Census. 1983. *1980 Census of Population: Detailed Population Characteristics*. Washington, DC: Department of Commerce.

U.S. Commission on Civil Rights. 1978. *Social Indicators of Equality for Minorities and Women*. Washington, DC: U.S. Commission on Civil Rights.

Weitz, Rose. 1982. "Feminist Consciousness Raising, Self-Concept, and Depression." *Sex Roles* 8:231–241.

Wong, Germaine Q. 1980. "Impediments to Asian-Pacific-American Women Organizing." Pp. 89–103 in *The Conference on the Educational and Occupational Needs of Asian Pacific American Women*. Washington, DC: National Institute of Education.

Wong, Joyce Mende. 1978. "Prostitution: San Francisco Chinatown, Mid and Late Nineteenth Century." *Bridge* 6:23–28.

Wong, Nellie, Merle Woo, and Mitsuye Yamada. 1979. *3 Asian American Writers Speak Out on Feminism*. San Francisco, CA.: SF Radical Women.

Woo, Margaret. 1971. "Women + Man = Political Unity." Pp. 115–116 in *Asian Women*, edited by Editorial Staff. Berkeley, CA.: University of California Press.

Yamada, Mitsuye. 1981. "Asian Pacific American Women and Feminism." Pp. 71–75 in *This Bridge Called My Back: Writings by Radical Women of Color*, edited by C. Moraga and G. Anzaldua. Watertown, MA: Persephone.

Yung, Judy. 1986. *Chinese Women of America: A Pictorial History*. Seattle, WA: University of Washington Press.

Chapter 7—Equality and Liberation, Feminism and Women's Rights in the Nineteenth and Twentieth Centuries

Study Questions

1. How did many white women in the nineteenth century use acceptance of domination in the home as a power base for activism? Do you see this as a viable power base today, regardless of race? Why or why not?

2. What factors contributed to the passage of the Nineteenth Amendment? What lessons can today's feminists learn from the tactics of the suffrage movement?

3. What is the basis for a social change movement? What conditions laid fertile ground for the first and second waves of feminism?

4. How did the Civil Rights movement serve as a catalyst for the second wave of feminism? What is seen as the "heart and soul" of feminism in the 1960s and 1970s? Why?

5. Name and describe briefly the approaches to feminism that emerged during the second wave. How has this multiplicity helped the cause of feminism as a social, political, and economic movement aimed at equality for all people?

6. The women of color feminist movement focuses on the systems of oppression. Name these systems. How can this approach help women recognize, accept, and celebrate difference?

7. What is the basic precept of a radical feminist perspective? According to Hagen, why is it important that this perspective be maintained?

8. The theme of the poem "Crisis of Faith" is about the ebb and flow of feelings toward commitment to an ideology. Discuss in small groups your own thoughts and feelings as they pertain to feminist ideology in general; follow with a large group discussion.

9. In the context of Garcia's article on Chicana feminist discourse, what initially attracted Chicanas to the white feminist movement? What was lacking?

10. Cherríe Moraga talks about the danger of ranking oppressions. What is its impact on women of color feminists?

11. Choose an issue important to women's equality, i.e. pay equity, day care. In small groups, describe the difference in approach by employing each of the feminist theories.

12. According to Chow's article, what two conditions, other than being female, help bring women to a feminist consciousness?

13. After reading both Chow and Garcia, discuss why it is difficult for women of color to break away from nationalist movements? What is the importance of such a move?

WOMEN AND POLITICS

Patricia Schroeder

Introduction

The national political arena, historically the exclusive province of white males, has seen women's increasing participation and visibility. As women make their way past obstacles to their inclusion in politics at a national level, their collective voice becomes a force that shapes bold new feminist agendas. In this chapter, U.S. Representative Patricia Schroeder's discussion of women and politics, reflected in the following questions, illuminates the path women are charting as elected officials advocating women's rights:

- Women's political power is reflected in part by voting patterns. How has the number of women voters compared to men's numbers since 1980?
- What has characterized women's participation in the political system since the 1970s?
- How have public attitudes changed toward elected women officials?
- How does women's political representation at the state level compare to that at the national level?
- What is the significance of a "critical mass" of women in politics?
- What are two of women's key strengths and resources in their efforts to gain political ground?

- In what ways has the Congressional Caucus for Women's Issues increased women's political power and promoted women's concerns?
- How do the Economic Equity Act and the Health Equity Act propose to raise women's economic status and improve women's health?

The Political Climate

We live in a fascinating time. On the one hand there is a growing hostility toward "feminism"; at the same time, support for women's rights grows stronger by the day. How many times do we hear someone say, "I'm not a feminist, but. . . ." You can fill in the blank with any number of denials of equality women face today. The irrational fear of the word *feminism* has not stopped the women's movement. There have always been women and men who understand that the denial of rights to any group weakens society as a whole. Denial of rights blocks the creativity necessary for people to form a truly great nation. The gift of living in a democracy is that, in theory, it allows room for creativity and greatness to flourish.

Women have always played a vital role in designing this country's unique form of democracy. The United States is populated by more women than men. In 1980

Schroeder, Patricia. 1992. "Women and Politics." Printed by permission of the author.

women voters outnumbered men by 5.5 million; since then, more women than men have voted in each national election. In fact, by 1988 ten million more women than men voted. We must understand what our role has been in the past in order to grasp our potential political power for the present and the future.

Democracy in its classical form is based on a sharp distinction between the public and private sides of life. As philosopher Hannah Arendt asserts in her book, *The Human Condition* (1958), the public was the arena of politics. It was where citizens with resources—men— gathered to debate the future of their communities. When our founding fathers got together and decreed that "All men are created equal," it was this classical democracy that they emulated. Of course, we now know that what they meant was that all white male landowners are created equal. In fact, it was only because free women and slaves—both women and men—tended to the necessities of life— food, shelter, and clothing, for example, that these men had the freedom to meet, debate, and design the political system with which we live today.

While slavery has been abolished, most legislators still have wives. Without someone at home to tend to today's hearth, the halls of Congress and most other legislative bodies would be silent. Ninety percent of the U.S. Congress is made up of men with wives who can stay at home and care for the needs of their private lives. In the general public, less than 10 percent of families fit this "Ozzie and Harriet" profile. It is precisely this lack of common experience that begins to explain the inability of Congress to comprehend, both cognitively and emotionally, issues like child care, parental leave, and sex discrimination. Even if they do under-stand these issues intellectually, they still just do not get it.

Gradually, as our country became more prosperous and the provision of basic needs consumed less time, women began to volunteer in the community and form associations to exercise their talent, knowledge, and vision. As a result of their responsibilities at home, women entered the world of organized politics well trained in fields like health care, education, social welfare, and business transactions. These experiences from private lives were quickly becoming official political concerns. The past thirty years have been especially intriguing. In the 1960s we broke through the feminine mystique: women could also be strong, forceful, and assertive. In the 1970s we wanted equality, and downplayed gender differences. Being "equal" often meant being as much like a man as you could be. It meant denying feminine values like empathy, honesty, and sincerity.

Then came the 1980s. We lived through a decade in which Ronald Reagan and nostalgia ruled. There was no "we," only "me," and every attempt was made to re-live the 1950s. One by one, women began to disappear from the federal government. As Susan Faludi notes in her book, *Backlash: The Undeclared War Against American Women*:

> new female judicial appointments fell from 15 percent under Carter to 8 percent. The number of female appointees requiring Senate confirmation plunged, too, making Reagan the first president in more than a decade not to better his predecessor's record. On the White House staff, the number of women appointed dropped from 123 in 1980 to 62 in 1981.

At the start of Reagan's second term . . . the administration immediately discontinued both the Coalition on Women's Appointments and the Working Group on Women. Appointed women's numbers fell even more steeply, and, for the first time since 1977, not one woman ranked high enough to attend the daily senior staff meetings or report to the president. (Faludi 1991, 257)

Typically the women who *did* receive political appointments were from the "New Right." They usually held positions with meaningless, inflated titles but no authority. Or they were in positions of administering the administration's most antifeminist policies.

It was not difficult for the Bush administration to do very little and claim to be progressive. The reality is that the Bush administration did not even come close to raising the influence of women to where it was when Jimmy Carter left office.

If I could step into the future—say, to the end of the twenty-first century—the first thing I would do would be to see what historians said about the 1990s. I believe it will be seen as the decade when women emerged as a formidable force—a force that actually began to chip away at traditional male dominance.

Women As Candidates

The fourth woman to serve in the United States Senate—elected as the widow of an incumbent—spent most of her time knitting and doing crossword puzzles. She did not speak much because she hated to take time away from the boys ("They seem to enjoy it so much!"). Her only piece of legislation dealt with mandatory parachutes on airlines. It never passed.

When I ran for office in 1972, there were still only two ways for women to run for Congress—as the widow of the incumbent or as challenger in a hopeless

race. Scenario number two was how I was chosen to run. It is encouraging to see that the process by which women become candidates has opened up considerably. We even have examples of political parties actively seeking women candidates in races they have a good chance of winning!

Today, growing numbers of women are ready to run. They have higher levels of education and experience in occupations which have traditionally nurtured political candidates—such as lawyers, business leaders, and community activists. According to a 1991 poll conducted by Celinda Lake, a noted Democratic strategist, fewer than one in ten Americans would vote against a candidate simply because she was a woman.

Since I entered Congress two decades ago, the number of women holding office has increased. In 1972, according to the National Women's Political Caucus, 362 women served in state legislatures, or about 1 percent. By 1991 that number had risen to 1,359, or 18 percent. Similarly, in 1972, seven, or 1 percent, of the nation's mayors were women. In 1991 that number had increased to 151, or 17 percent (National Women's Political Caucus 1991).

When we look at national offices, the results are not as impressive. In 1971 there were two women in the U.S. Senate; in 1991 there were still only two. In 1971 there were thirteen women in the House of Representatives. By 1991 it had twenty-nine, an increase from 3 percent to about 6.5 percent. At this rate it will be another 200 years before women in Congress reach parity with men.

One danger in looking at increasing numbers of successful women candidates is to think of this growth as representing significant progress. Six and a half percent of the House of Representatives, elected from a pool that comprises over

50 percent of our population, is not even close to status quo. In her studies of parliaments worldwide, Elise Boulding (1977) determined that when women comprise 25 to 30 percent of political offices at every level, a critical mass is reached. It is at this point that women begin to greatly influence their government's policies as well as change the dynamics of politics. We will have to act fast if we are to reach a critical mass before our great grandchildren are born.

Some say women will gain political ground as candidates because people are anti-incumbent and disillusioned with politics in general. In this climate women represent the quintessential "outsider you can trust." Neil Newhouse, a Republican political strategist, said in a December 1991 *Washington Post* article, "I asked this one fellow what had been most important to him when voting in the recent city election. Was it the issues? Was it the character of the candidates? What exactly motivated your vote? 'I just voted for all the women,' the man replied." This "trustworthy outsider" image may help women gain political ground. However, there is a force much stronger that may prove to be the source of political clout as yet unexperienced by women. That force is anger. Women are angry about the effects that failed public policy has had on their lives. This anger is leading to a growing understanding that we must become the policymakers as well as the driving force which influences them.

The United States Congress and Women

Congress really is an "old boys" club, run on seniority and steeped in tradition. It is overwhelming to enter as a freshman member of Congress and try to imagine that you will ever have a position that al-

lows you to address your agenda. Add to this the fact that you are one of a handful of females and you begin to wonder just what you have gotten yourself into. It took a while, but eventually the women in Congress realized they needed to work together if they were ever going to accomplish anything.

When I arrived in Washington in 1973, the congresswomen were meeting informally over lunch to exchange information and plan legislative strategy. We soon decided to become a formal entity to be seen as a unified body and increase our political clout. In 1977 the Congresswomen's Caucus was formed. Yet we still had trouble being very effective. In the beginning all congresswomen were members, including those who did not want the Congresswomen's Caucus to upset the status quo in any way. Some were afraid that they would be labeled feminists, or that they would be seen as representing "women's issues." The feminists were afraid that they would be muzzled. Agreements were few and far between. The Congresswomen's Caucus in its early form was more an ongoing tea party than a convincing legislative caucus. Nevertheless, we collected data on issues such as alimony, child support, and Small Business Administration loans, which helped identify the problems women faced and the changes that needed to be made. We also worked hard to push the Carter administration to evaluate the role of women at every level of government.

The Congressional Caucus for Women's Issues

Suddenly it was 1981, and in came the Reagan administration. Not only was this administration opposed to the ERA and clearly anti-choice, but it proceeded to slash the budgets of almost every program we cared about. It was time to reorganize. We raised dues to the Caucus from $50 to $2,500, putting us on a par with other legislative service organizations and ensuring a commitment from those members who joined. The congresswomen who had been members in name only dropped out. Soon we opened nonvoting membership to congressmen but retained leadership by creating an executive committee of women members.

Thus, the Congressional Caucus for Women's Issues was born. Membership today stands at about 170, the highest it has ever been. The Caucus's primary purpose is to promote legislation to improve the status of women and eliminate discrimination from federal programs and policies. The Caucus's staff provides weekly and monthly publications to members and has established an informal clearinghouse on issues of importance to women. The Caucus's newsletter, *Update*, is an excellent source of information for anyone interested in women's issues. It comes out ten times a year and can be requested by contacting any Caucus member's office. As public awareness of the Congressional Caucus for Women's Issues has grown, so has the clout with their constituents membership brings for male members.

The Economic Equity Act

In the beginning, the legislative agenda seemed endless. We needed to find a way to address a variety of issues and at the same time work together to get something actually accomplished. This challenge led to what I think was the most significant decision to come out of our reorganization plan. We agreed to introduce in each session an omnibus legislative package which we named the Economic Equity Act (EEA). The EEA is aimed at achieving a measure of economic equity for women. In 1973 women were still earning 59 cents for every dollar earned by a man. Our country was beginning to learn firsthand what was meant by the term "feminization of poverty."

The EEA is designed to improve the economic well-being of American women and families. When the Caucus puts the EEA together we consult not only with members of Congress, their staffs, and House and Senate committee staffs, but also with national women's and civil rights organizations. Individual provisions are introduced separately by Caucus members. The Caucus then uses the omnibus legislative package to educate and inform their colleagues, the press, and the public. As a package, the legislation attracts attention whereas separately the individual bills may come and go without notice.

We often ask for systemic change. It can take years before the changes are understood and the right climate for change has been fostered. Social Security, one of the first projects the Caucus took on, is an excellent example. For a variety of reasons, women often find that as they get older they also get poorer. Under the umbrella of pension reform, the Caucus became concerned about sex discrimination in the Social Security system.

At its inception in 1935, Social Security was based on the premise that there would only be one breadwinner in a family. In 1939 supplemental benefits were added for a worker's dependents—his wife and children. By the 1970s it was clear that Social Security no longer reflected America's diverse families, nor met the needs of most women. It was also clear that Congress would do nothing to change this situation without a push.

Under Social Security, earnings records are maintained for individual workers only. Women who are homemakers move in and out of the work force, work regularly but earn less than their husbands, or get divorced and are punished by this system. For many women the end result is the same as if they had not worked at all. For Social Security purposes, under the Caucus's plan a couple's earnings would be added together rather than accounted separately. That combined figure would appear on each spouse's earnings record. A spouse who left the labor force for homemaking and childrearing would continue to receive earnings credits from the other spouse's income. In the case of divorce, each spouse would be entitled to half the earnings credits accumulated during the marriage. Widows would inherit the total earnings credits accumulated by the couple. Earnings sharing recognizes marriage as an interdependent economic partnership. This is a fundamental change in how policy is set. It will not come easily.

The most recent EEA was introduced on October 8, 1991. It is a package of twenty-four bills organized under four titles: Title I, Employment Opportunities; Title II, Women in Business; Title III, Economic Justice; and, Title IV, Retirement Equity. Under Title IV may be found the "Social Security Modernization Act"—we are *still* trying to change the Social Security system. The 1991 EEA responds to the fact that by the year 2000, two out of three new entrants into the work force will be women. By that same year, 86 percent of all jobs will require postsecondary education or training. Yet the vast majority of working women today—74 percent—continue to be clustered in nonprofessional jobs.

The bills included in the EEA would, among other provisions, expand nontraditional job training; provide educational and professional opportunities in science and mathematics; increase procurement opportunities for women business owners; and establish a commission to investigate ways to break the "glass ceiling," allowing women to advance through the management ranks. The EEA would also expand benefits for part-time workers.

While over the years issues have changed, the need for a package of legislation to address women's economic needs has not. In fact, we must realize that the goals of the EEA are vital if our country is to be a player in today's world. Economic security for women means economic security for the nation.

The Women's Health Equity Act

Caucus members were and are also keenly aware of inequities in women's health care. In December 1989 the Caucus called for a General Accounting Office (GAO) study of the extent to which women have been excluded from research funded by the National Institutes of Health (NIH). We were not at all surprised to find out that women were routinely excluded from most studies.

The explanation for this seemed to be that women were more "difficult" to study. If one were to take a random sample of 100 adult men, or so the argument went, they would all be in a similar metabolic state, whereas in every group of 100 women there would be many variables to consider. They might be at different stages in their menstrual cycle; some might be postmenopausal; some might be pregnant or nursing. As a result, the findings issued by NIH studies might or might not be true for women.

By June 1990, the GAO reported that the NIH had made little progress toward including women in clinical trials. Following this report, the Caucus introduced the Women's Health Equity Act (WHEA).

Like the Economic Equity Act, the WHEA was an omnibus package of legislation, this time with the intent to improve the status of women's health. The WHEA, introduced in February 1991, consists of twenty-two bills which address deficiencies in three crucial areas: research, services, and prevention. As a direct result of all this attention, the NIH has established an Office of Research on Women's Health which will work to ensure that the policy on women's inclusion in clinical trials is implemented.

The Road Ahead

Today, women are making tremendous inroads into the political process; the days of knitting and glorified tea parties are a distant memory. Congresswomen and elected women officials at all levels are making their mark in every arena, and voters are sending a clear message to incumbents that a vote against women—as represented by the 1991 Senate confirmation of Clarence Thomas to the U.S. Supreme Court—will not be tolerated. Politicians are having to reconsider the economic and political structures of a rapidly changing world, and campaign themes run more toward preserving our domestic values than running around the globe engaged in a zero-sum game.

But we must never let political rhetoric fool us. We need to take it at face value, then look beyond into what our candidates and politicians are really saying through their voting records and affiliations. As women, we still have a long road ahead of us toward achieving economic and health equity. We are faced with the formidable struggle of protecting such fundamental rights as freedom of choice. We have yet to convince our country's business communities and elected officials of the changed nature of the American family and the tremendous need today for family and medical leave.

Today, women still constitute a mere 2 percent of the Senate and 5 percent of the House. If we are to win the uphill battle of achieving equity for women, we need to raise these numbers—period. We must elect officials of both genders who are sensitive to issues affecting women and families. Without continuous attention to and work in these and other areas, we may begin to think we have reached the top of where we can go when, in fact, it will be simply another false summit.

References

Arendt, Hannah. 1958. *The human condition*. Chicago: University of Chicago Press.

Astin, Helen S., and Carole Leland. 1991. *Women of influence, women of vision: A cross-generational study of women and change*. San Francisco: Jossey Bass.

Boulding, Elise. 1977. *Women in the twentieth-century world*. Sage Publications, Walsted Press.

Cantor, Dorothy, and Toni Bernay. 1992. *Women of power*. Boston: Houghton Mifflin.

Faludi, Susan. 1991. *Backlash: The undeclared war against American women*. New York: Crown Publishers.

Foulkes, Diane L. 1992. *White political women*. Knoxville: University of Tennessee.

National Women's Political Caucus. 1991. *Fact sheet on women's political progress*. Washington, D.C.

Ries, Paula, and Anne J. Stone, eds. 1992. *The American woman, 1992–93: A status report*. New York: Women's Education and Research Institute, W. W. Norton.

Resources

Center for the American Woman and Politics (CAWP)
Rutgers University
New Brunswick, NJ 08901
(908) 932–9384

National Women's Political Caucus (NWPC)
1275 K Street NW, Suite 750
Washington, DC 20005
(202) 898–1100

EMILY'S List
1112 16th Street NW, Suite 750
Washington, DC 20023
(202) 887–1957

Women's Research and Education Institute (WREI)
1700 18th Street NW, Suite 400
Washington, DC 20009

National Commission on Working Women
2000 P Street NW
Washington, DC 20036
(202) 872–1782

The Personal Is Political: The Intersection of Private Lives and Public Roles Among Women and Men in Elective and Appointive Office

Susan J. Carroll

ABSTRACT. This article investigates similarities and differences in the relationship between "public" and "private" in the lives of women and men who hold elective and appointive office. An analysis of data collected through surveys of federal appointees and state legislators indicates that men's political choices may be more influenced by private sphere considerations than commonly believed, but that private sphere concerns are nevertheless of greater significance to women than to men. Findings provide support for a conceptualization of public and private as an interrelated system of social relations rather than as two largely separate spheres of existence.

A sharp demarcation between public and private life has characterized both Western political thought and the empirical study of politics by political scientists. Jean Bethke Elshtain has argued that the split between public and private life in Western political philosophy dates back to the ancient Greeks and played a critical role in Aristotle's *Politics*. Aristotle drew a clear and sharp distinction between the public world of the *polis* and the nonpublic world of the household (Elshtain, 1974). According to Alison M. Jaggar, the distinction between public and private spheres of existence has been evident not only in the work of Aristotle and the ancient Greeks, but also in "all previous political theory, although it plays a different role in different contexts and is construed differently" (1983, p. 143).

The perceived content of public and private spheres and the boundary between them have shifted over time. For example, economic activity, once considered to occur largely in the private sphere, now is generally considered to be part of the public sphere. Nevertheless, despite historical and cultural variations in the meaning of public and private, conventional political activity, long associated with men, has generally been viewed as

Carroll, Susan J. 1989. "The Personal is Political." *Women & Politics* 9(2): 57–67. Reprinted by permission of the publisher, The Haworth Press, Inc., 10 Alice Street, Binghamton, NY 13904.

part of the public realm.[1] Similarly, Jaggar has noted, "Whenever the distinction has existed, the private realm has always included sexuality and procreation, has always been viewed as more 'natural' and therefore less 'human' than the public realm, and has always been viewed as the realm of women" (1983, pp. 127–128).

Contemporary empirical studies of political actors and political behavior have reflected underlying assumptions about the division of life into public and private spheres and the greater association of men with the public and women with the private realm. With the exception of research on childhood socialization, issues of family influence, household responsibilities, and private sphere activities have been largely ignored in explaining the political behavior of men. In contrast, when women have been the object of research attention, family and household considerations have been assumed to have a major influence on their political behavior and thus have been subject to investigation or emphasized in interpreting women's attitudes and actions (e.g., Campbell et al., 1960, pp. 483–493; Pomper, 1975, pp. 67–89; Lane, 1959, pp. 209–216; Kirkpatrick, 1974; Diamond, 1977; Sapiro, 1983; Stoper, 1977; Lee, 1977; Lynn & Flora, 1977). Despite many differences between traditional political science and the new scholarship on women and politics in their explanations of women's behavior, the two bodies of literature have shared a focus on the importance of private sphere concerns as an influence on women's public sphere activity.

In the process of investigating women's behavior and comparing it to the behavior of men, feminist scholars have discovered that families and private sphere considerations may not be as irrelevant to men's political behavior as political scientists have traditionally assumed them to be. For example, Diane Kincaid Blair and Ann R. Henry found that family considerations played an important role in accounting for voluntary departures from the Arkansas state legislature (1981). Their findings stand in stark contrast to earlier literature on legislative turnover that largely ignored private sphere factors and emphasized instead low salaries as the major cause of voluntary departure. This paper will build on the foundation laid by Blair and Henry by arguing that so-called private sphere considerations are not only important to men's decisions to leave office, but also are often important to their decisions to seek office as well.

However, while suggesting that men's political choices and actions may well be more influenced by private sphere considerations than commonly recognized, I also argue that both the traditional literature and the new feminist scholarship are correct in their assumption that those concerns commonly associated with the "private sphere" are of greater significance to women than to men. The private and the public do appear more closely intertwined in the lives of politically active women than in the lives of politically active men. In fact, the interconnections between the public and private in the lives of politically active women seem sufficiently strong to call into serious question the common practice of conceptualizing contemporary existence as divided into two largely distinct and mutually exclusive spheres.

To examine the relationship between the "public" and "private" in the lives of politically active women and men, this paper relies on data from surveys of women and men serving in elective office and in high-level federal appointive positions during the early 1980s. Despite differences in the pattern of findings for women appointees and for women elected officials, both patterns point to a relationship between private and public that is different from that which exists for male public officials.

Description of the Data Sets

In the spring of 1981 under a grant from the Charles H. Revson Foundation, the Center for the American Woman and Politics (CAWP), a unit of the Eagleton Institute of Politics at Rutgers University, surveyed women and men serving in elective offices at various levels of government as well as women and men who had been appointed to high-level positions in the Carter administration. In the spring of 1984, CAWP replicated its study of Carter appointees by surveying women and men who had served in top appointive positions in the first term of the Reagan administration. The analysis in this paper focuses on federal appointees in both presidential administrations and state legislators throughout the country. State legislative office is considered because it is the highest level of elective office with a significant concentration (15.6% as of 1987) of women officeholders.

For the study of state legislators, questionnaires were mailed in May 1981 to the population of 137 women state senators and 769 women state representatives serving in office across the country. Response rates were 53.3% for women state senators and 58.1% for women state representatives. CAWP systematically sampled the same number of male state senators within each state as there were female state senators for a total of 136 male senators. Similarly, CAWP systematically sampled one-half the number of male state representatives in each state as there were female state representatives for a total of 382. Response rates for the comparison samples of men were 50.0% for state senators and 52.6% for state representatives.

For the studies of presidential appointees, CAWP surveyed the universe of women serving during the first term of both administrations in the following positions: cabinet member, deputy secretary, under secretary, deputy under secretary, assistant secretary, deputy assistant secretary, administrator, deputy administrator, and agency director. To select comparison samples of men, CAWP stratified the population of male appointees by job title and systematically sampled the same number of men as there were women serving in each job title category. Surveys were conducted by phone in May 1981 for Carter appointees and May 1985 for Reagan appointees. Response rates were 78.7% for women in the Carter administration, 73.3% for men in the Carter administration, 56.6% for women in the Reagan administration, and 62.9% for men in the Reagan administration.[2]

"Private Life" Influences on State Legislators' Decisions to Seek Office

The influence of family members on state legislators' decisions to run for legislative seats was assessed through three questions on the CAWP survey. First, legislators were presented with a list of eleven factors that might influence decisions to seek office and asked to rate on a three-point scale the importance of each factor in their decisions. One of these factors pertained to the reactions of the legislator's spouse (Table 1) and another dealt with the age of the legislator's children (Table 2). At a later point on the questionnaire, legislators were directed to select from a list of nine factors the three factors that were most important in influencing their decisions to run for the legislature. One of the factors on the list was "the support of my spouse and/or family" (Table 3).[3]

More than three-fourths of married legislators of both sexes reported that the approval of their spouses played a very important role in their decisions to run for office (Table 1). In fact, spouse approval of the decision to run was rated very important by larger proportions of legislators, both female and male, than were several factors (e.g., money, concern over public policy issues, and political ambition) commonly believed to be important in affecting decisions to seek office.[4] Gender differences in ratings of the importance of spouse approval are insignificant; married men were as likely as married women to report that the approval of their spouses played a critical role in their decisions.

In contrast, gender differences are apparent in state legislators' assessments of the importance of childrearing considerations in affecting the timing of their decisions to run for legislative seats (Table 2). Women state legislators with children were significantly more likely than their male counterparts to report that the age of their children was a very important factor in their decisions to seek office. For women state legislators, childrearing considerations and spouse approval were about equally critical to their decisions to run. For

Table 1. *Gender Differences in Importance of Spouse Approval in Affecting Decisions to Run Among Married State Legislators*

	State Senators		State Representatives	
	Women %	Men %	Women %	Men %
Importance in decision to run of "Approval of my spouse"				
Very important	84.7	78.3	82.6	81.2
Somewhat important	11.9	20.0	13.9	17.0
Not important	3.4	1.7	3.5	1.8
	100.0	100.0	100.0	100.0
N =	(59)	(60)	(339)	(165)
tau_c =	.06		.01	
$p \leq$	.20		.39	

Table 2. *Gender Differences in Importance of Children's Age in Affecting Decisions to Run Among State Legislators with Children*

	State Senators		State Representatives	
	Women %	Men %	Women %	Men %
Importance in decision to run of "My children being old enough for me to feel comfortable not being at home as much"				
Very important	81.7	44.4	73.4	54.6
Somewhat important	15.0	33.3	20.2	33.1
Not important	3.3	22.2	6.4	12.3
	100.0	100.0	100.0	100.0
N =	(60)	(54)	(327)	(130)
tau_c =	.39		.16	
$p \leq$	.0001		.0001	

Table 3. *Gender Differences in Proportions of State Legislators Who Identified Spousal and/or Familial Support as One of the Three Most Important Factors Affecting Their Decisions to Run for Office*

		State Senators		State Representatives	
		Women %	Men %	Women %	Men %
Rated "The support of my spouse and/or family" as one of the three factors most important in influencing the decision to run					
Married Legislators		79.6	60.7	86.1	77.5
	N =	(49)	(56)	(310)	(160)
	tau$_b$ =	.20		.11	
	p ≤	.02		.009	
Legislators with Children		78.5	59.6	81.2	73.1
	N =	(65)	(57)	(357)	(160)
	tau$_b$ =	.20		.09	
	p ≤	.01		.02	
Married Legislators with Children		80.9	60.4	85.8	75.7
	N =	(47)	(53)	(288)	(148)
	tau$_b$ =	.22		.13	
	p ≤	.01		.004	

men in the legislatures, spouse approval was clearly a more significant factor than any concern over responsibilities to their children. Nevertheless, a majority of male state representatives and a near-majority of male state senators with children rated childrearing considerations as a very important influence on their decisions to seek office.

The fact that larger proportions of women than men attach importance to private life concerns in making decisions to run for office is perhaps best illustrated by responses to the question asking legislators to select from a list of nine factors only the three factors that most affected their decisions (Table 3). Among both sexes large majorities of married legislators, legislators with children, and married legislators with children identified "the support of my spouse and/or family" as one of the three most important factors. However, despite the fact that married men were as likely as married women to rate spouse approval as very important to their decision to run (Table 1), smaller proportions of married men than married women identified spousal and family support as uppermost in importance when placed in a context where the importance of such support had to be assessed relative to the importance of other factors (Table 3).

These findings from CAWP's survey of state legislators indicate that so-called private sphere concerns play a major role in decisions to seek public office. Although previous research with predominantly male samples has rarely pointed to family considerations as a major factor in decisions to run for office, findings from this study suggest that most married men who decide to run for legislative seats seriously consider the reactions of their wives in making their decisions. Probably because men generally take less responsibility on a day-to-day basis for the care and supervision of children than do women (Hartmann, 1981), concern about child care responsibilities less often than the approval of their spouses is an important factor affecting men's decisions.

Despite the fact that concerns commonly associated with the "private sphere" seem to influence men's decisions to seek office to a far greater extent than the traditional political science literature would indicate, these concerns loom larger in women's decisions than in men's. Although married women are not significantly more likely than married men to rate spouse approval as critical to their decisions to run for office, women more often than men point to the support of their spouses and families as important relative to other considerations. Moreover, women with children are much more likely than men with children to report that concerns about child care affected the timing of their decisions.

"Private Life" Situations of Female and Male Public Officials

Data regarding the marital status, supportiveness of spouses, and presence and age of children among female and male public officials provide further evidence that concerns traditionally associated with the "private sphere" have a greater influence on women's political choices and actions than on men's. The private life situations of women in elective and appointive office differ substantially from those of their male counterparts. Also, although the private life situations of men in both types of office look much alike, the private life situations of the two groups of women are highly dissimilar.

An examination of the marital status of elective and appointive officeholders provides the most dramatic illustration of these patterns (Table 4). In both elective and appointive office, women were less likely than men to have been married at the time they were surveyed. Moreover, the marital status of men in the state legislatures closely resembles that of men in the two presidential administrations. Almost equal proportions of male elected officials and presidential appointees were married. In contrast, the marital status of women in elective office differs notably from the marital status of women in appointive office. Women appointees were much less likely to be married than were women state legislators. Although women appointees were slightly more likely than women state legislators to be divorced or separated, the major difference is apparent in the "single, never married" category. About one-fourth of women appointees in the Carter administration and almost one-third of women appointees in the Reagan administration had never married, compared with fewer than one-tenth of women state legislators.

Among appointees and state legislators who were married, sex differences are also apparent in officeholders' reports of their spouses's general attitudes toward their political involvement (Table 5).[5] Larger proportions of women than men had spouses who were very supportive of their involvement in politics and government; in fact, overwhelming majorities of women reported fully supportive spouses. While majorities of married men also claimed that their spouses were very supportive, men showed greater variation than women in levels of spousal support for their political activities.

In addition to differences in marital status and spousal support, female and male officeholders differ with respect to childrearing (Table 6). Although women and men in elective office were about equally likely to have children, women state legislators were less likely than their male counterparts to have young children under the age of 12. Female appointees were also less likely than male appointees to have young children, but

Table 4. *Gender Differences in Marital Status Among Officeholders*

	State Senators		State Representatives		Carter Appointees		Reagan Appointees	
	Women %	Men %	Women %	Men %	Women %	Men %	Women %	Men %
Marital Status								
Married	68.1	89.4	72.1	84.0	53.4	86.0	47.6	81.0
Single, never married	2.8	3.0	8.7	9.0	24.1	3.5	31.0	11.9
Divorced/Separated	13.9	7.6	11.0	4.0	18.9	10.6	21.5	7.2
Widowed	15.3	—	8.2	3.0	3.4	—	—	—
	100.0	100.0	100.0	100.0	100.0	100.0	100.0	100.0
N =	(72)	(66)	(437)	(200)	(58)	(57)	(42)	(42)
X^2 =	13.4		15.9		16.5		10.2	
df =	3		3		3		2	
p ≤	.004		.001		.001		.007	

Table 5. *Gender Differences in Spousal Support Among Officeholders*

	State Senators		State Representatives		Carter Appointees		Reagan Appointees	
	Women %	Men %	Women %	Men %	Women %	Men %	Women %	Men %
Spouse's Attitude Toward Political Involvement								
Very supportive	87.8	62.7	82.7	58.2	90.3	71.4	100.0	72.7
Somewhat supportive	8.2	23.7	14.3	27.9	9.7	22.4	—	15.2
Indifferent	2.0	5.1	1.0	5.5	—	—	—	3.0
Somewhat resistant	2.0	8.5	2.0	8.5	—	6.1	—	9.1
	100.0	100.0	100.0	100.0	100.0	100.0	100.0	100.0
N =	(49)	(59)	(307)	(165)	(31)	(49)	(20)	(33)
tau_c =	.25		.23		.19		.26	
p ≤	.002		.001		.02		.006	

the most notable difference between women and men in appointive office is in the proportion who had no children whatsoever. While fewer than one-tenth of male Carter appointees and one-fifth of male Reagan appointees were childless, one-half of the women in both administrations had no children.

As was true for marital status, the childrearing situations of men are similar across both elective and appointive office while the childrearing situations of women in elective and appointive office differ markedly (Table 6). Men in elective and appointive office were very similar in their propensity to have children and in the proportions whose youngest child was 12 or older. In contrast, women appointees were much more likely than women in elective office to be childless and less likely to have a youngest child who was 12 or older.

Table 6. *Gender Differences in Age of Youngest Child Among Officeholders*

	State Senators		State Representatives		Carter Appointees		Reagan Appointees	
	Women %	Men %	Women %	Men %	Women %	Men %	Women %	Men %
Age of Youngest Child								
Under 12 years old	14.1	27.9	11.2	22.8	18.9	36.8	21.4	27.9
12 years old or older	74.6	60.3	72.4	61.7	31.0	54.4	21.4	53.5
No children	11.3	11.8	16.3	15.5	50.0	8.8	57.1	18.6
	100.0	100.0	100.0	100.0	100.0	100.0	100.0	100.0
N =	(70)	(66)	(429)	(193)	(58)	(57)	(42)	(43)
X^2 =	4.3		14.7		23.5		14.6	
df =	2		2		2		2	
$p \leq$	.12		.0007		.0001		.0007	

In combination, these findings regarding family situations suggest that the interconnections between "private" lives and "public" activities are stronger for women than for men. Apparently, married women with spouses who are not fully supportive of their political activity rarely seek and achieve appointment or election to public office. Perhaps married women with spouses who are less than fully supportive chose not to seek office; perhaps they are less often asked to run for or serve in office.[6] By contrast, some married men appear to pursue their political interests with only lukewarm support from, or occasionally against the wishes of, their spouses.

In a similar fashion, women with children tend to wait until their children are grown before pursuing their political aspirations.[7] Men more often pursue public office despite their parental responsibilities.

The fact that women appointees in both presidential administrations were far more likely to be unmarried and childless than their male counterparts suggests that the women far more often than the men had chosen to delay marriage and childrearing, or to bypass marriage and childrearing completely, in order to pursue careers.[8] Most of the men had pursued both family and career simultaneously, suggesting that career decisions were made without a perceived need to choose between career and marriage or children.

It is likely that childrearing responsibilities more often deter women than men from pursuing high-level, federal appointments. However, those responsible for making appointments may also apply a double standard, viewing women who have children as likely to have less time to devote to their jobs while making no such judgments about men who have children. Regardless, it is clear that private lives and political careers are more highly interrelated and interconnected for women than they are for men.

Conclusions and Discussion

The findings presented in this paper have several implications for political scientists. These implications pertain to political scientists' underestimation of the importance of so-called private life concerns for understanding political behavior, the utility of viewing "public" and "private" as separate spheres, and the probability that women have a distinctive perspective that may affect their attitudes and behavior in office.

The first implication of this paper is that "private life" considerations may have a much more important effect on political behavior than the traditional political science literature has recognized and should be routinely investigated as a possible influence on the political attitudes and activities of men as well as women. The findings of this paper suggest that few men make decisions to run for office without some consideration of family responsibilities and reactions. Recent political history also points to this conclusion. For example, several possible contenders in the 1988 presidential race, including Gary Hart, Ted Kennedy, Mario Cuomo, and Bill Clinton, withdrew from the race at some point or declined to run for "personal" reasons. Clearly, the so-called "public/private split" (Elshtain, 1974) in Western political thought is an incomplete one at best when applied to contemporary politics.

While the responses and actions of politically active men cast doubt upon the extent to which "public" and "private" constitute truly separate spheres of existence, the responses and situations of politically active women dramatize even more strongly the limitations of a conceptualization that divides contemporary existence into two distinct and supposedly unrelated spheres. The private world of the family and household has typically been envisioned as a haven from the heartless world of work and politics (Jaggar, 1983, p. 144; Elshtain, 1974, p. 471). However, many feminist theorists have been highly critical of the public/private dichotomy, arguing that, in the words of Rosalind Petchesky, it "distorts reality, that it is every bit as much an ideological construct as are the notions of 'male' and 'female' themselves" (1979, p. 377). Petchesky argues that public and private (or "production" and "reproduction" in the Marxist view) "far from being separate territories like the moon and the sun or the kitchen and the shop, are really intimately related modes that reverberate upon one another and frequently occur in the same social, physical, and even psychic spaces" (1979, p. 376). Feminists have popularized the slogan, "The personal is political." Although the saying has several possible interpretations (Gould, 1983), one meaning is that the personal and the political are inseparable; they are part of the same system of relations and not two distinct, mutually exclusive realms.

Clearly, the findings about the influence of private concerns on women's decisions to run for office and the private life situations of women officeholders would seem a better fit to a model of public and private conceptualized as an interrelated and interconnected system of social relations and activities, rather than as two largely separate and mutually exclusive spheres of existence. For women, personal life choices have affected public careers and public life choices have had an impact on private life situations. Although to a lesser extent this would appear to be true for men as well, the interconnections of public and private are clearer and stronger among politically active women. Men, to a much greater extent than women, have been able to pursue political activities without consequences to their personal lives and to make private life choices without consequences for their political careers. The findings for women officeholders provide empirical support for the alterative conceptualization of public and private offered by Petchesky and other feminist theorists. A dualistic conception of public and private as largely separate and mutually exclusive spheres of existence does not adequately portray the reality of these women's lives; rather, public and private in the lives of women officeholders seem to constitute a holistic system of interrelated social relations where any action taken or choice made has repercussions throughout the system. For women who hold high-level elective and appointive positions in government, Jaggar's conclusion seems most appropriate: "the distinction between the so-called public and private spheres obscures their interpenetration and essential unity" (1983, p. 146).

The final implication of the analysis presented in this paper relates to possible gender differences in the attitudes and behavior of women and men in office and suggests a topic worthy of future research. The fact that women and men have a different relationship to those aspects of existence that traditionally have been considered public and private has generally been viewed as detrimental to women. Zillah R. Eisenstein has explained, "The division of public and private life as one that differentiates the woman (private) from the man (public) is the overarching ideological tool of patriarchy" (1984, p. 16). The view of women as nonpublic beings whose concerns focus on the private sphere has been used to restrict their participation in politics. Moreover, as Elshtain has observed, men are perceived as having two statuses, as public and as private people, and are judged differently in the two domains while women, even when they enter public life, are perceived as having only one status and continue to be viewed as "private" persons (1974).

Although there can be no doubt that the differential association of women and men with "public" and "private" has restricted women's access to politics and the public world, feminist scholars in recent years have stressed the idea that women's differences from men can provide an important supplement or corrective to men's influence on society (e.g., Gilligan, 1982; Eisenstein & Jardine, 1985; Eisenstein, 1983; Ruddick, 1980). Applied to politics, this line of argument would suggest that women may bring a perspective to politics that is presently lacking. The greater integration and interconnections of "public" and "private" in the lives of politically active women might lead them to support, advocate, and initiate different types of public policy proposals from those that men have traditionally supported, advocated, and initiated. The fact that women do not seem to leave the "private" behind when they enter the "public" world suggests that they might show a greater sensitivity and concern than men traditionally have for issues such as child care, consumer protection, care of the elderly, and teen pregnancy. They also might be more likely than men to consider the possible implications for families and family life of policy proposals dealing with work, the economy, military matters, and other so-called public issues. If such a relationship exists between the interconnectedness of public and private in the lives of women officeholders and their views and actions on public policy, we may well witness a more humanistic and holistic politics as increasing numbers of women join the ranks of officeholders. The possible existence of such a relationship would seem to merit attention in future research.

Notes

1. Feminist historians have challenged this common assumption by arguing that many activities historically undertaken by women within the "private" sphere were, in fact, political. See, for example, Kerber, 1980; Ryan, 1979; Freedman, 1979; DuBois et al., 1980.
2. For the Carter study, CAWP surveyed regulatory commissioners as well as the occupants of the other positions listed. Because commissioners were not included in the Reagan study, they are excluded from this analysis. Also excluded from

the analysis because their numbers are so few are the two women members of the Carter cabinet and the one woman and one man in the Reagan cabinet who responded to the survey.

3. The other factors included public officeholding experience, experience working in campaigns, experience working on the staff of an elected official, participation in a candidate training program or workshop, support from occupational organizations, support from women's organizations (asked only of women), support from other types of organizations, and support from a political party.

4. Money was rated very important by 64.4% of female and 55.0% of male legislators. Concern over public policy issues was rated very important by 68.1% of women and 67.5% of men. Political ambition was rated very important by 14.1% of women and 22.8% of men.

5. This measure is a more general one than the measure of spouse approval reported earlier. This measure assesses perceptions of the spouses' general attitude toward the officeholders' overall involvement in politics and government. The earlier measure dealt specifically with perceived spouse approval of the decision to run for the state legislature. While gender differences were not apparent on the measure of spouse approval of the decision to run, they are apparent on the question tapping spousal support for the officeholder's political involvement more generally.

6. The fact that several studies have found that women and men running in comparable electoral circumstances fare about equally well with the voters (e.g., Darcy & Schramm, 1977; Darcy, Welch, & Clark, 1987) suggests that discrimination in voting is not a major reason why few married women with less than fully supportive spouses are present among elective officeholders. Nevertheless, married women with less than fully supportive spouses may anticipate voter prejudice against them, and this may deter them from seeking office.

7. The fact that women often delay running for office until their childrearing responsibilities have diminished has been observed in other studies. See, for example, Johnson & Carroll, 1978, p. 16; Kirkpatrick, 1974, p. 230; Githens, 1977.

8. Women appointees in both administrations were younger than the men. The median age of men in both administrations was 46 while the median age was 40 for women in the Carter administration and 38 for women in the Reagan administration. Although female and male appointees thus were at somewhat different places in their life cycles, none of the women in the Carter administration and only one woman in the Reagan administration were under 30. Although some of the women in their 30s may yet have children, it seems unlikely that differences in the marital and childrearing patterns of female and male appointees are due solely, or even largely, to age differences between the two groups.

References

Blair, D. K., and Henry, A. R. (1981). The family factor in state legislative turnover, *Legislative Studies Quarterly, 6*(February), 55–68.

Campbell, A. et al. (1960). *The American voter.* New York: John Wiley & Sons.

Darcy, R., and Schramm, S. S. (1977). When women run against men. *Public Opinion Quarterly, 41,* 1–12.

Darcy, R., Welch, S., and Clark, J. (1987). *Women, elections, and representation*. New York: Longman.

Diamond, I. (1977). *Sex roles in the State house*. New Haven: Yale University Press.

DuBois, E. et al. (1980). Politics and culture in women's history: A symposium. *Feminist studies*, 1(Spring), 26–64.

Eisenstein, H. (1983). *Contemporary feminist thought*. Boston: G. K. Hall.

Eisenstein, H., and Jardine, A. (1985). *The future of difference*. New Brunswick: Rutgers University Press.

Eisenstein, Z. R. (1984). *Feminism and sexual equality*. New York: Monthly Review Press.

Elshtain, J. B. (1974). Moral woman and immoral man: A consideration of the public-private split and its political ramifications. *Politics and Society, 4*, 453–472.

Freedman, E. (1979). Separation as strategy: Female institution building and American feminism, 1870–1930. *Feminist Studies, 3*(Fall), 512–529.

Gilligan, C. (1982). *In a different voice*. Cambridge: Harvard University Press.

Githens, M. (1977). Spectators, agitators, or lawmakers: Women in state legislatures. In M. Githens and J. L. Prestage (Eds.), *A portrait of marginality*. New York: David McKay.

Gould, C. C. (1983). Private rights and public virtues: Women, the family, and democracy. In C. Gould (Ed.), *Beyond domination: New perspectives on women and philosophy*. Totowa, NJ: Rowman & Allanheld.

Hartmann, H. I. (1981). The family as the locus of gender, class, and political struggle: The example of housework. *Signs, 6*(Spring), 366–394.

Jaggar, A. M. (1983). *Feminist politics and human nature*. Totowa, NJ: Rowman & Allanheld.

Johnson, M., and Carroll, S. (1978). Profile of women holding office. In the Center for the American Woman and Politics (Compiled by) *Women in public office: A biographical directory and statistical analysis* (2nd ed.). Metuchen, NJ: Scarecrow Press.

Kerber, L. (1980). *Women of the Republic*. Chapel Hill: University of North Carolina Press.

Kirkpatrick, J. J. (1974). *Political woman*. New York: Basic Books.

Lane, Robert. (1959). *Political life*. New York: The Free Press.

Lee, M. M. (1977). Toward understanding why few women hold public office: Factors affecting the participation of women in local politics. In M. Githens and J. L. Prestage (Eds.), *A portrait of marginality*. New York: David McKay.

Lynn, N., and Flora, C. B. (1977). Societal punishment and aspects of female political participation: 1972 National Convention Delegates. In M. Githens and J. L. Prestage (Eds.), *A portrait of marginality*. New York: David McKay.

Petchesky, R. (1979). Dissolving the hyphen: A report on Marxist-feminist groups 1–5. In Z. R. Eisenstein (Ed.), *Capitalist patriarchy and the case for socialist feminism*. New York: Monthly Review Press.

Pomper, G. (1975). *Voters' choice*. New York: Harper and Row.

Ruddick, S. (1980). Maternal thinking. *Feminist Studies, 6*(Summer), 342–367.

Ryan, M. P. (1979). The power of women's networks: A case study of female moral reform in antebellum America. *Feminist Studies, 5*(Spring), 66–85.

Sapiro, V. (1983). *The political integration of women*. Urbana: University of Illinois Press.

Stoper, E. (1977). Wife and politician: Role strain among women in public office. In M. Githens and J. L. Prestage (Eds.), *A portrait of marginality*. New York: David McKay.

Eleanor Roosevelt*

ROOSEVELT, Anna Eleanor, Oct. 11, 1884–Nov. 7, 1962. Social reformer.

Anna Eleanor Roosevelt was born in New York City, the first child of Elliott and Anna (Hall) Roosevelt. Descended on both sides from distinguished colonial families active in commerce, banking, and politics, Eleanor seemed destined to enjoy all the benefits of class and privilege. By the time she was ten, both her parents had died, as had a younger brother, leaving Eleanor and her second brother, Hall, as the only survivors.

From that point forward, Eleanor Roosevelt's life was characterized by paradox. A woman of remarkable self-control, she yet reached out to touch the world in profoundly emotional ways. Although committed to the traditional idea of women as primarily responsible to husband and family, she personified the strength of the independent woman. Both by fate and by will, she became the most important public woman of the twentieth century.

Eleanor Roosevelt remembered herself as "a solemn child, without beauty. I seemed like a little old woman entirely lacking in the spontaneous joy and mirth of youth." She experienced emotional rejection early: her mother called her "granny" and, at least in Eleanor's memory, warmly embraced her son while being only "kindly and indifferent" to her little girl. From most of her family young Eleanor received the message that she was "very plain," almost ugly, and certainly "old-fashioned." When her parents died, she went to live with her maternal grandmother, who was equally without warmth. As a cousin later remarked: "It was the grimmest childhood I had ever known. Who did she have? Nobody."

In fact, she had one person—her father. "He was the one great love of my life as a child," she later wrote, "and . . . like many children, I have lived a dream life with him." Described by his friends as "charming, impetuous . . . generous, [and] friendly," Elliott Roosevelt developed with Eleanor an intimacy that seemed almost magical. "As soon as I could talk," she recalled, "I went into his dressing room every morning and chattered to him . . . I even danced with him." She dreamed of the time when she and her father "would have a life of our own together."

But Elliott Roosevelt's capacity for ebullient play and love also contained the seeds of self-destruction. He was never able to provide stability for himself and his family, and his emotional imbalance caused his banishment from the household. He nourished the relationship with Eleanor through letters to "father's own little Nell," writing of "the wonderful long rides" that he wanted them to enjoy together. But when his long-awaited visits occurred, they often ended in disaster, as when he left Eleanor with the doorman at his club, promising to return but going off on a drunken spree. The pain of betrayal was exceeded only by a depth of love for the man who she believed to be "the only person who really cared."

The emotional void caused by her father's death persisted until, at the age of fifteen, she enrolled at Allenswood, a girls' school outside of London presided over by Marie Souvestre. The daughter of the French philosopher and radical Emil Souvestre, she passionately embraced unpopular causes, staunchly defending Dreyfus in France and the cause of the Boers in South Africa. Souvestre provided for Eleanor a deeply needed emotional bond, confiding in her as they toured the continent together, and expressing the affection that made it possible for the younger woman to flower. Roosevelt remembered the years at Allenswood as "the happiest years" of her life: "Whatever I have become since had its seeds in those three years of contact with a liberal mind and strong personality."

Souvestre's imprint was not lost when Eleanor Roosevelt returned to New York City at seventeen to come out in society. In the rush of parties and dances, she kept her eye on the more serious world of ideas and social service. She plunged into settlement house work and at eighteen joined the National Consumers' League, headed by FLORENCE KELLEY. The League was committed to securing health and safety for workers, especially women, and as Roosevelt visited factories and sweatshops, she developed a lifelong commitment to helping the poor. She also joined the Junior League and taught calisthenics and dancing at the Rivington Street Settlement House. Much of Eleanor Roosevelt's subsequent political activism can be traced to this early involvement in social reform.

At the same time, Eleanor Roosevelt was secretly planning to marry her cousin Franklin Roosevelt. Like Elliott Roosevelt, his godfather, Franklin was spontaneous, warm, and gregarious. But Franklin Roosevelt also possessed good sense and singleness of purpose. Eleanor Roosevelt saw in him the spark of life that she remembered from her father; he, in turn, saw in her the discipline that would curb his own instincts toward excess.

After their marriage on March 17, 1905, the young Roosevelts settled in New York City while Franklin finished his law studies at Columbia University. For the next fifteen years Eleanor Roosevelt's public activities gave way to other concerns. Sara Roosevelt, Franklin's mother, objected to her work at the settlement house because she might bring home diseases. The Roosevelts' first child, Anna, was born within a year (1906), James the next year, and two years later Franklin. Eleanor Roosevelt cherished her children, but it was not a happy time. Her mother-in-law dominated the household, and she came to feel that "Franklin's children were more my mother-in-law's children than they were mine." But she did not rebel. She feared hurting her husband and losing his affection, and she experienced a profound sense of inadequacy about her abilities as a wife and mother that continued throughout her life. The death of her third child, seven months after his birth, only reinforced her pain and unhappiness. Three additional children were born in the next six years—Elliott in 1910, Franklin Jr. in 1914, and John in 1916. But motherhood could not be fulfilling in a household ruled by a mother-in-law who told the children they were hers: "Your mother only bore you."

Between 1910 and the beginning of World War I, Eleanor Roosevelt's activities revolved increasingly around her husband's growing political career. Elected as the Democratic assemblyman from Dutchess County, N.Y., in 1910, Franklin Roosevelt rapidly became a leader of insurgent anti-Tammany forces in Albany and Eleanor Roosevelt found herself organizing frequent social-political gatherings. In 1913 he was appointed assistant secretary of the navy and she became expert at hosting multiple social events while managing a large household and moving everyone to Campobelo in New Brunswick during the summer, then to Hyde Park, and back to Washington.

The entry of the United States into World War I in 1917 provided Eleanor Roosevelt, as her biographer Joseph Lash has noted, with "a reason acceptable to her conscience to free herself of the social duties that she hated, to concentrate less on her household, and plunge into work that fitted her aptitude." She rose at 5:00 A.M. to coordinate activities at Washington's Union Station canteen for soldiers on their way to training camps, took charge of Red Cross activities, supervised the knitting rooms at the navy department, and spoke at patriotic rallies. Her interest in social welfare led to her drive to improve conditions at St. Elizabeths Hospital for the mentally ill, while her sensitivity to suffering came forth in the visits she paid to wounded soldiers. "[My son] always loved to see you come in," one mother wrote. "You always brought a ray of sunshine."

After Franklin Roosevelt's unsuccessful campaign for the vice presidency in 1920, the Roosevelts returned to New York where Eleanor became active in the League of Women Voters. At the time of her marriage, she had opposed suffrage, thinking it inconsistent with women's proper role; now she coordinated the League's legislative program, drafted laws providing equal representation for men and women, and worked with Esther Lape and Elizabeth Read on the League's lobbying activities. In 1922 she joined the Women's Trade Union League (WTUL)—then viewed as "left-leaning"—and found there friends as well as political allies. In addition to working for maximum hour and minimum wage laws for women, she helped raise funds for WTUL headquarters in New York City and developed warm ties to its leaders, including ROSE SCHNEIDERMAN and MAUD SWARTZ, both immigrants.

When her husband was paralyzed by polio in 1921, Eleanor Roosevelt's public life expanded still further as she became his personal representative in the political arena. With the aid of Louis Howe, Franklin Roosevelt's political mentor who had become her own close friend, she first mobilized Dutchess County women, then moved on to the state Democratic party, organizing all but five counties by 1924. "Organization," she noted, "is something to which [the men] are always ready to take off their hats." No one did the job better. Leading a delegation to the Democratic National Convention in 1924, she fought for equal pay legislation, the child labor amendment, and other planks endorsed by women reformers.

By 1928, Eleanor Roosevelt had become a political leader in her own right. Once just a political wife, she gradually extended that role into a vehicle for asserting her own personality and goals. She headed up the national women's campaign for the Democratic party in 1928, making sure that the party appealed to independent voters, to minorities, and to women. After Franklin Roosevelt's election as governor of New York, she was instrumental in securing FRANCES PERKINS'S appointment as the state's industrial commissioner. She dictated as many as a hundred letters a day, spoke to countless groups, and acted as an advocate of social reform and women's issues.

Eleanor Roosevelt's talent for combining partisan political activity with devotion to social welfare causes made her the center of an ever-growing female reform network. Her associates included Marion Dickerman and Nancy Cook, former suffragists and Democratic party loyalists; MARY DEWSON, who was president of the New York Consumers' League from 1925 to 1931; and MARY DREIER of the WTUL. She walked on picket lines with Rose

Schneiderman, edited the *Women's Democratic News,* and advised the League of Women Voters on political tactics. Not only did her political sophistication grow, but she also learned to uphold her beliefs even if she caused "disagreement or unpleasant feelings." By standing up for women in politics, she provided a model for others to follow.

During the 1932 campaign which led to her husband's election to the presidency, Eleanor Roosevelt coordinated the activities of the Women's Division of the Democratic National Committee, working with Mary Dewson to mobilize thousands of women precinct workers. After the election, Dewson took over direction of the Women's Division. She corresponded daily with Eleanor Roosevelt both about appointing women to office and about securing action on issues that would appeal to minorities, women, and such professional groups as educators and social workers. Together they brought to Washington an unprecedented number of dynamic women activists, including ELLEN WOODWARD, Hilda Worthington Smith, and Florence Kerr. MARY ANDERSON, director of the Women's Bureau, recalled that women government officials had formerly dined together in a small university club. "Now," she said, "there are so many of them that we need a hall."

Eleanor Roosevelt also provided a national forum for transmitting the views and concerns of these women. At regular press conferences for women reporters, she introduced MARY MCLEOD BETHUNE and other women leaders to talk about their work with the administration. These sessions provided new status and prestige for the female press corps; they also underlined the importance to Eleanor Roosevelt of women's issues and created a community of women reporters and government workers.

Eleanor Roosevelt's own political role was best seen in the 1936 reelection drive when she used the educational approach developed by the Women's Division in 1932 as a primary campaign weapon. More than 60,000 women precinct workers canvassed the electorate and for the first time women received equal representation on the Democratic platform committee, an event described by the *New York Times* as "the biggest coup for women in years."

Eleanor Roosevelt's fear that there would be no active role available to her as first lady had been unfounded. She toured the country repeatedly, surveying conditions in the coal mines, visiting relief projects, and speaking out for the human rights of the disadvantaged. Through her syndicated newspaper column "My Day," which first appeared in January 1936, and through radio programs and lectures, she reached millions and communicated to the country her deep compassion for those who suffered. At the White House, in turn, she acted as advocate of the poor and disenfranchised. "No one who ever saw Eleanor Roosevelt sit down facing her husband, and holding his eyes firmly, say to him 'Franklin, I think you should . . . or, Franklin surely you will not' . . . will ever forget the experience," Rexford Tugwell wrote. She had become, as columnist Raymond Clapper noted, a "Cabinet Minister without portfolio—the most influential woman of our times."

But if Eleanor Roosevelt had achieved an unparalleled measure of political influence, it was in place of, rather than because of, an intimate personal relationship with her husband. Probably at no time after their first few years together did Franklin and Eleanor Roosevelt achieve the degree of intimacy that she once described as caring so much that a look and the sound of a voice would tell all. Not only did Sara Roosevelt remain a dominant presence, but Franklin had embarked on his own interests and enthusiasms, often different from those of his wife. The dissimilarities in their temperaments became a permanent barrier. While he loved to party, she held back, telling her daughter Anna in a letter from Warm Springs, Ga., in 1934, that she "always felt like a spoil-sport and police-man here."

During his years as assistant secretary of the navy, Franklin Roosevelt had often indulged his fun-loving instinct, causing a lasting breach in the marriage. When his wife was away, his frequent companion had been Lucy Mercer, Eleanor's social secretary. Over time, their relationship became intimate. Eleanor Roosevelt learned of the affair in 1918 and offered to divorce him. Although Franklin refused her offer, and Sara Roosevelt engineered an agreement for them to stay together if her son stopped seeing Lucy Mercer, Eleanor Roosevelt's marriage would never again achieve the magical possibility of being "for life, for death."

Some observers have connected Eleanor Roosevelt's reemergence as a public figure with her profound anger at her husband's betrayal. Yet her activism predated her discovery of the Mercer affair, going back to World War I and ultimately to the settlement house years. The Lucy Mercer affair, like Franklin's polio, reinforced her move toward public self-assertion, but did not in itself cause a transformation. What it did cause was a gradual reallocation of emotional energy away from her husband. Throughout the 1920s a warmth of tone and feeling continued in her letters to and about him. Yet gradually their lives became more separate. She might be jealous of his secretary, Missy LeHand, or even of her daughter Anna, for the ease with which they supplied Franklin Roosevelt with fun and enjoyment. But part of her also accepted the idea that others must provide what she could not give. In a poignant piece entitled "On Being Forty-five," written for *Vogue* in 1930, Eleanor Roosevelt wrote that by middle-age a woman must recognize that the romantic dreams of youth are over. The forty-five-year-old woman "must keep an open and speculative mind . . . [to] be ready to go out and try new adventures, create new work for others as well as herself, and strike deep roots in some community where her presence will make a difference to the lives of others."

Taking her own advice, Eleanor Roosevelt transferred her emotional attachments to others. In 1926 she had moved with Nancy Cook and Marion Dickerman into Val-Kill, a newly constructed cottage at Hyde Park. The event accurately symbolized her growing detachment from Franklin and his mother. Although she returned to "the big house" at Hyde Park when her husband was present, it was always with a sense of resentment and regret. She and Dickerman purchased Todhunter, a private school in New York City where Eleanor Roosevelt taught three days a week even after Franklin was elected governor of New York. The three women also jointly managed a furniture crafts factory at Val-Kill. After 1920, she and Louis Howe developed profound bonds of affection and support, each carrying the other loyally through crises with Franklin and the vicissitudes of party politics. Harry Hopkins, director of the WPA, also became an intimate. But her most carefree relationship was probably that with Earl Miller, a former state trooper and subsequently a body-guard for the Roosevelt family who became a close companion. Miller encouraged her to drive her own car, take up horseback riding again, and develop confidence in her personality.

With these and others, Eleanor Roosevelt developed a rich emotional life. Although she frequently appeared cold and distant, she passionately cared for her children and friends. Writing to her daughter Anna on Christmas Eve in 1935, she noted: "It was hard to decorate the tree or get things distributed without you . . . and if anyone says much I shall weep." She expressed similar affection in daily letters to LORENA HICKOK, the former journalist and assistant to Harry Hopkins, who moved to Hyde Park after a falling-out occurred between Eleanor Roosevelt and Marion Dickerman and Nancy Cook in the late 1930s. Most surprising of all, perhaps, she poured out her feelings to distant correspondents, answering the many pleas for help which came to her with either a sensitive letter, an admonition to a federal agency to take action, or even a personal check. The poor wrote to her because they knew she cared, and in caring, she found an outlet for her powerful emotional needs.

The same compassion was manifested in Eleanor Roosevelt's advocacy of the oppressed. Hearing about the struggle of Appalachian farmers to reclaim their land, she became a champion of the Arthurdale (W.Va.) Resettlement Administration project and devoted her lecture fees as well as her influence to help the community. She invited to the White House representatives of poor southern textile workers and northern garment workers, seating them next to the president at dinner so that he might hear of their plight. She and Franklin Roosevelt had worked out a tacit understanding which permitted her to bring the cause of the oppressed to his attention, and allowed him, in turn, to use her activism as a means of building alliances with groups to his left. Although the president frequently refused to act as she wished, the dispossessed at least had an advocate.

Largely because of Eleanor Roosevelt, the issue of civil rights for black Americans received a hearing at the White House. Although like most white Americans she had grown up in an environment suffused with racism and nativism, she was one of the few voices in the administration insisting that racial discrimination had no place in American life. As always, she led by example. At a 1939 Birmingham meeting inaugurating the Southern Conference on Human Welfare, she placed her chair so that it straddled the black and white sides of the aisle, thereby confounding local authorities who insisted on segregation. She resigned in the same year from the Daughters of the American Revolution after they denied the black artist Marian Anderson permission to perform at Constitution Hall. Instead, and in part through Eleanor Roosevelt's intervention, Anderson sang to 75,000 people from the Lincoln Memorial.

Eleanor Roosevelt also acted as behind-the-scenes lobbyist for civil rights legislation. With alacrity she accepted the suggestion of Walter White, executive secretary of the NAACP, that she act as an intermediary with the president in the association's attempt to secure legislation defining lynching as a federal crime. She also agreed to be patron of an NAACP-sponsored exhibit in New York City of paintings and drawings dealing with lynching, and attended the showing. Although she lost out in her campaign for the president's strong endorsement of an antilynching bill, she had communicated to him her anger that "one could get nothing done." Continuing to speak forthrightly for the cause of civil rights, she addressed the NAACP's annual meeting in June 1939 and joined the biracial protest organization a few weeks later. As the threat of war increased, Eleanor Roosevelt joined her Negro friends in arguing vigorously for administration action to eliminate discrimination in the armed services and in defense employment. Although civil rights forces were not satisfied with the administration's response, the positive changes that did occur were due in large part to their alliance with Eleanor Roosevelt.

She brought the same fervor to her identification with young people. Fearing that a whole generation might be lost to democracy because of the depression, she reached out to make contact with them. Despite warnings from White House aides, between 1936 and

1940 Eleanor Roosevelt became deeply involved in the activities of the American Student Union and the American Youth Congress, groups committed to a democratic socialist program of massively expanded social welfare programs. She advanced their point of view in White House circles, and invited them to meet the president. Although she was later betrayed by some of her young allies who followed the Communist party line and denounced the European war as imperialistic after the Nazi-Soviet Non-Aggression Pact of 1939, she continued to believe in the importance of remaining open to dissent. "I have never said anywhere that I would rather see young people sympathetic with communism," Eleanor Roosevelt wrote. "But I have said I would rather see the young people actively at work, even if I considered they were doing things that were a mistake."

With the onset of World War II, Roosevelt persisted in her efforts for the disadvantaged. She insisted that administration officials consult women activists and incorporate roles for women as a major part of their planning for wartime operations, and she intervened repeatedly with war production agencies as well as the military to advocate fairer treatment for black Americans. When it seemed that many New Deal social welfare programs would be threatened by war, Eleanor Roosevelt became their defender. Increasingly she devoted herself to the dream of international cooperation, aware more than most of the revolution rising in Africa and Asia, and of the dangers posed by the threat of postwar conflict.

But her energies in the war were directed primarily to human needs. When Jewish refugees seeking a haven from Nazi persecution received less than an enthusiastic response from the State Department, Eleanor Roosevelt served as their advocate. Families separated by war always found an ally when they sought her help, and wounded veterans in army hospitals far from home received from her visits the cherished message that someone cared.

As the war proceeded, the worlds of Franklin and Eleanor Roosevelt became still more separate. They were frequently adversaries and the president was less able to tolerate her advocacy of unpopular causes. In search of release from the unbearable pressures of the war, he had come to rely on the gaiety and laughter of his daughter Anna, and other women companions, including Lucy Mercer Rutherford, who, unknown to Eleanor, was with Franklin Roosevelt in Warm Springs when he died of a cerebral hemorrhage in April 1945.

With great discipline and dignity, Eleanor Roosevelt bore both the pain of Franklin's death and the circumstances surrounding it. Her first concern was with carrying forward the policies in which they had both believed despite their disagreements. Writing later about their relationship, she commented: "He might have been happier with a wife who had been completely uncritical. That I was never able to be and he had to find it in some other people. Nevertheless, I think that I sometimes acted as a spur . . . I was one of those who served his purposes." What she did not say was that Franklin Roosevelt had served her purposes as well. Though they never retrieved their early intimacy, they had created an unparalleled partnership to respond to the needs of a nation in crisis.

Not long after her husband's death, Eleanor Roosevelt told a reporter: "The story is over." But no one who cared so much for so many causes, and was so effective a leader, could long remain on the sidelines. Over the next decade and a half, she continued to be the most effective woman in American politics. In long letters to President Harry S. Truman, she implored the administration to push forward with civil rights, maintain the Fair

Employment Practices commission, develop a foreign policy able to cope with the needs of other nations, and work toward a world system where atom bombs would cease to be a negotiating chip in international relations.

Appropriately, President Truman nominated Eleanor Roosevelt as a United States delegate to the United Nations. There she argued, debated, and lobbied for the creation of a document on human rights that would embody standards which civilized humankind would accept as sacred and inalienable. Finally on Dec. 10, 1948, the Universal Declaration of Human Rights, fundamentally shaped by her, passed the General Assembly. Delegates rose in a standing ovation to the woman who more than anyone else had come to symbolize the cause of human rights. Even those in the United States who had most opposed her applauded: "I want to say that I take back everything I ever said about her," Michigan Senator Arthur Vandenberg commented, "and believe me, it's been plenty." At times during the New Deal a figure of scorn among some conservatives, Eleanor Roosevelt was fast becoming a national heroine.

The cause of world peace and the desire to help the victims of war quickly became central to Roosevelt's efforts. In moving speeches that vividly portrayed the suffering wrought by war, she sought to educate the United States to its postwar responsibilities. She had traveled through England noting the names of all the young men who had died during the war, she told an audience. "There is a feeling that spreads over the land," she said, "the feel of civilization that of itself might have a hard time coming back." If the United States wished to avoid such a world, it must help those who had suffered, and avoid isolationism.

Although Eleanor Roosevelt disagreed profoundly with some of the military aspects of United States foreign policy, she supported the broad outlines of its response to the Soviet Union in the developing cold war. In debates at the UN she learned quickly that Soviet delegates could be hypocritical, and on more than one occasion she responded to their charges of injustice in America by proposing that each country submit to investigation of its social conditions—a suggestion the Soviets refused. She refused in 1947 to support the newly formed Progressive party with its platform of accommodation toward the Soviet Union, and instead spearheaded the drive to build Americans for Democratic Action, a group which espoused social reforms at home and support of Truman's foreign policy.

Throughout the 1950s Eleanor Roosevelt remained a singular public figure, able to galvanize the attention of millions by her statements. She became one of the staunchest advocates of Israel, argued vigorously for civil rights, and spoke forcefully against the witch hunts of McCarthyism. When Dwight D. Eisenhower became president in 1953 she resigned her UN post, but she continued to work tirelessly through the American Association for the United Nations to mobilize public support for international cooperation. She also gave unstintingly of her time to the election campaigns in 1952 and 1956 of her dear friend Adlai Stevenson, who brought to politics a wit and sophistication that she admired.

The private sphere, however, remained most precious. "The people I love," Eleanor Roosevelt wrote her friend and physician David Gurewitsch, "mean more to me than all the public things. I only do the public things because there are a few close people whom I love dearly and who matter to me above everything else." The Roosevelt children remained as much a trial as a comfort. After Franklin Roosevelt's death, she lived at Val-Kill with her secretary, Malvina Thompson (1893–1953), and her son Elliott and his family. More often than not, family gatherings degenerated into bitter arguments. But her grandchildren brought joy as did friends, old and new.

As she entered her seventies, Eleanor Roosevelt had become the first lady of the world. Traveling to India, Japan, and the Soviet Union, she spoke for the best that was in America. Although she did not initially approve of John F. Kennedy and would have much preferred to see Adlai Stevenson nominated again in 1960, she lived to see the spirit of impatience and reform return to Washington. In 1962 she sponsored hearings in Washington, D.C., where young civil rights workers testified about the judicial and police harassment of black protesters in the south.

It was fitting that Eleanor Roosevelt's last major official position was to chair President Kennedy's Commission on the Status of Women, to which she was appointed in December 1961. More than anyone else of her generation she had exemplified the political independence and personal autonomy that were abiding themes of the women's movement. Eleanor Roosevelt had not been a militant feminist and, like most social reformers, she had opposed the Equal Rights Amendment (ERA) until the mid-1940s, believing that it would jeopardize protective labor legislation for women. During the depression she accepted the popular view that, at least temporarily, some married women should leave the labor force to improve the chances of the unemployed. On occasion, she also adopted male-oriented definitions of fulfillment. "You are successful," she wrote in a 1931 article, "when your husband feels that he has been a success and that life has been worthwhile."

But on the issue of women's equality as in so many other areas, Roosevelt most often affirmed the inalienable right of the human spirit to grow and seek fulfillment. Brought up amidst anti-Semitic and anti-Negro attitudes, she had transcended her past to become one of the strongest champions of minority rights. Once opposed to suffrage, she had grown to exemplify women's aspirations for a full life in politics.

Eleanor Roosevelt participated in the activities of the Women's Commission until August 1962, testifying on behalf of equal pay laws at a congressional hearing in April of that year. She died at her home in New York City in November from a rare form of tuberculosis. Twenty years earlier she had written: "You can never really live anyone else's life, not even your child's. The influence you exert is through your own life and what you've become yourself."

Despite disappointment and tragedy, Eleanor Roosevelt had followed her own advice. "What other single human being," Adlai Stevenson asked at her memorial service, "has touched and transformed the existence of so many? . . . She walked in the slums . . . of the world, not on a tour of inspection . . . but as one who could not feel contentment when others were hungry." Because of her life, millions of others may have experienced a new sense of possibility. She would have wished for nothing more.

[The Eleanor Roosevelt Papers at the Franklin Delano Roosevelt Library, Hyde Park, N.Y., represent the most comprehensive collection of material available. Of particular interest are her correspondence with Walter White of the NAACP, material about her family, especially her father, and drafts of articles and lectures. Other relevant collections at Hyde Park are the papers of Mary Dewson, Hilda Worthington Smith, and Lorena Hickok; the papers of the Women's Div. of the Democratic Nat. Committee; and those of Anna Roosevelt Halsted. Several manuscript collections at the Schlesinger Library, Radcliffe College, bear directly on Eleanor Roosevelt's life: see especially the papers of Mary

Anderson, Mary Dewson, Mary Dreier, and Ellen Woodward. Of Eleanor Roosevelt's own writings the most valuable are *This I Remember* (1949); *This Is My Story* (1937); *Auto-biography* (1961); and *It's Up To the Women* (1933). She also wrote a monthly column, "If You Ask Me," for the *Ladies' Home Jour.* from June 1941 to spring 1949 and in *McCall's* after 1949. The best place to begin reading about her is Joseph Lash's excellent two-volume biography, *Eleanor and Franklin* (1971) and *Eleanor: the Years Alone* (1972). Other books that cast light upon the Roosevelt family include James Roosevelt, *My Parents: A Differing View* (1976), and Elliott Roosevelt, *An Untold Story* (1973), both of which offer personal views by the Roosevelt children. Another useful biography is Tamara Hareven, *Eleanor Roosevelt: An American Conscience* (1968.)

Towards a New Strategy for the ERA: Some Lessons from the American Woman Suffrage Movement

Suzanne M. Marilley

ABSTRACT. This article compares the 1970s ERA movement with the American woman suffrage movement in order to identify a potentially more successful strategy for a future movement. The similarities and differences in the nature of the opposition, the issues articulated, and the alliances formed by both movements are examined. It is argued that the leaders of a future ERA movement must celebrate women's differences, challenge more effectively the notion that women need men's protection, select issues that concern most women, and form firmer alliances.

The defeat of the equal rights amendment in June 1982 closed the most recent chapter of organized conflict about women's political status. Analysts of the struggle subsequently identified the main reasons for failure: a lack of state organizations for the ratification campaign, unpreparedness for Phyllis Schlafly's targeted challenge in traditionally-oriented states, the growth of fear that the ERA would change women's roles in the home, the unexpected legal benefits that the Supreme Court gave women during the 1970s without the ERA, and opponents' effective linkage, however false it was, of ERA to legal abortion (Boles, 1979, 1982a, 1982b, 1986; Deutchman & Prince-Embury, 1982; McGlen & O'Connor, 1983, 1988; Steiner, 1985; Berry, 1986; Carroll, 1986; Dehart-Mathews & Mathews, 1986; Mayo & Frye, 1986; Mansbridge, 1986; Pleck, 1986). To pass an ERA in the future, reform leaders must be better prepared organizationally and ideologically to cope with these obstacles.

One resource future ERA leaders can use for guidance in redesigning their arguments and strategies is the experience of American woman suffrage reformers. Woman suffragists suffered numerous defeats: out of 480 state campaigns in the movement's first 40 years, only 17 referenda reached the ballot; victories were won in only two states, Colorado and Idaho (Catt, 1923, pp. 109–110). Many men and women in the 19th and

Marilley, Suzanne M. 1989. "Towards a New Strategy for the ERA: Some Lessons from the American Woman Suffrage Movement." *Women & Politics* 7(4): 23–42. Reprinted by permission of the publisher, The Haworth Press, Inc., 10 Alice Street, Binghamton, NY 13904.

early-20th centuries perceived female enfranchisement as a harbinger of erosion in women's roles. It took woman suffrage leaders almost 50 years to cultivate enough elite and grass-roots support to pass and ratify the 19th Amendment.

Both woman suffragists and ERA reformers faced two fundamental challenges. First, they had to adapt goals for social change to the reform options available in the American political system. Second, the leaders had to put the reforms in appealing packages. Both steps require compromises that break down long-run goals for social change into achievable intermediate goals such as the vote and prohibitions against sex discrimination. Reform leaders dedicated to social role change often resist these compromises, especially initially. But the achievement of political reform requires shrewd manipulation of the political system as it is. According to John Kingdon (1984), the survival test of a public policy reform in the American political system is its "technical feasibility, value and a reasonable chance for receptivity among elected decision makers . . ." (p. 138).

The 1970s ERA campaign failed because it did not meet the criteria of anticipated public acquiescence, and it was not accepted by enough state legislators. Although sizable majorities approved of ERA throughout the ratification process, these majorities shrunk during the decade as the organized opposition led by Phyllis Schlafly cast doubt on the reform, particularly upon the gender role changes it would foster (Mansbridge, 1986). These doubts became powerful enough to leave the reformers three states shy of a constitutional amendment. By contrast, woman suffrage campaigns succeeded only after they had met Kingdon's criteria plus one other: the reform leaders' acceptance of suffrage as an intermediate goal, not a rule requiring the transformation of men's and women's social roles (Kraditor, 1965).

Comparative historical analysis of the similarities and differences between suffrage and ERA reform strategies, the nature of the opposition, and the various blends of social and political initiatives in the two movements can show how to satisfy Kingdon's criteria in a future campaign. Comparisons between the suffrage and 1970s ERA movements can locate both the mistaken and the successful strategies for overcoming resistance in public opinion and the political system. For example, comparisons distinguish individual leaders' errors and defeats from the obstacles posed by more permanent underlying structures of bias and political institutions. If the suffrage and the ERA movements are seen as different stages in a connected process that is self-informing—the transformation of women from a politically excluded to an included, equal, powerful group—then these comparisons will unify American women's political history and strengthen future reform leaders.

Key Issues in the Defeat of the 1970s ERA

The basic lack of preparation for both ratification campaigns in the states and Schlafly's opposition caused initial acceptance for ERA in the public as well as in state legislatures to erode. In *Why We Lost the ERA*, Jane Mansbridge (1986) explains how the ERA's early acceptance and rapid progress towards ratification could not be sustained. Because she presents her findings as both a political scientist and activist, they serve as case study materials for comparison with past or future initiatives. After summarizing Mansbridge's critical analysis of the ERA leaders' ideology, organization, and strategy, I compare them with those of the American suffrage leaders.

According to Mansbridge (1986), the ratification slowdown can be partially attributed to confusion among reform leaders, activists, and opponents of larger goals for social change—drafting women and guaranteeing abortion rights—with the amendment's actual limited legal capacity (see also, Berry, 1986). These mistaken conceptual associations generated skepticism among voters and legislators about the ERA's impact (Boles, 1986). Many analysts agree with Mansbridge that the opposition successfully shifted "debate away from equal rights" and focused sharply "on the possibility that the ERA might bring substantive changes in women's roles and behavior" (Mansbridge, 1986, p. 20; see also, Boles, 1982a; McGlen & O'Connor, 1983). Gender role changes were feared enough to halt ratification in certain states even though survey data confirm there was a majority of support for ERA throughout the ratification process, including pluralities even in the nonratified states in 1982 (Daniels, Darcy, & Westphal, 1982, pp. 578–584; see also, Deutchman & Prince-Embury, 1982; McGlen & O'Connor, 1988). Mansbridge (1986) explains this contradiction by demonstrating that along with high levels of support for the ERA there were high levels of resistance to change in gender roles (pp. 20–28).

Second, the reform leadership was far more diffuse and disorganized than the opposition's. The National Organization for Women (NOW) and ERA America each had separate executive structures that designed and implemented strategies for change. Beyond this, the national and state reformers sometimes were sharply separated. The Stop ERA forces, in contrast, were much more unified. While there were important tactical disputes in the opposition's camp, Schlafly remained their leader (Mansbridge, 1986, pp. 165–177).

Third, the entry of fundamentalist ministers into the opposition's leadership ranks in the late 1970s—a process that Mansbridge says was largely unperceived by the ERA leaders and the media—added to the strength of the anti-ERA forces (Mansbridge, 1986, pp. 174–176). The New Right gained considerable mass support during this period: by tying Stop ERA directly to the major goals of their program, these fundamentalists and traditional populist reformers damaged the amendment's chances. ERA opponents' more formidable organization and their vigorous consensus were the resources used to block ERA's passage. Kingdon cites blocking activity as the most successful initiative used by organized interests in the American political system: blocking legislation is much easier than getting it passed (1984, pp. 73, 158–9).

Given the public climate of distrust of the ERA at the time of its defeat and the likelihood that the amendment would today be defeated in the Senate, Mansbridge (1986) calls for a moratorium on a national campaign. She argues that reformers can overcome "institutional deafness," an "inability to hear or understand what others are saying," by making careful, critical analysis of their decisions (pp. 3, 191). In reviewing the 1970s campaign and preparing for the next, she adds, reformers should accept the limits of the Constitution and the need for compromise despite their ideological differences (pp. 90–148, 191).

In *Why ERA Failed*, Mary F. Berry (1986) concurs with Mansbridge's assessment and urges the reformers to study past constitutional amendment campaigns, particularly the successful ones, to discover useful strategies and tactics. According to Berry, the most important steps towards a new campaign are timing, the creation of a consensus state by state, and allaying the fears about "doing harm to their lives and the lives of other females and males" (Berry, 1986, p. 120). In light of Berry's and Mansbridge's views, the following analysis of suffrage leadership and strategy identifies some means future ERA leaders could use to satisfy Kingdon's requirements of technical feasibility, public acqui-escence, and acceptance by elected representatives.

The suffrage movement differed considerably from the ERA campaigns: it was waged without television, the federal government was much weaker, the amendment passed Congress only after many states had suffrage laws and strong suffrage organizations, and women were visibly barred from voting. Still, there are profound similarities be-tween the two efforts. First, the strongest resistance suffragists faced was the ideological opposition to change in gender roles and traditional relations between males and fe-males. Second, the reformers had difficulty defining the "tangible benefits" that the right to vote would produce; exaggerated claims were often made. Third, there were conflicts between organizations: unified national leadership and strong local and state networks developed slowly.

The American Woman Suffrage Movement: A Brief Summary

The American woman suffrage movement grew out of the American antislavery and woman's rights movements. The latter began at the Seneca Falls Convention of 1848, where the pioneer equal rights reformers asserted in their *Declaration of Sentiments* that women were men's political equals (Stanton, Anthony, & Gage, 1889, pp. 70–73). After the Civil War, when they realized that women would neither be enfranchised nor granted equal political rights as black men were by the 14th and 15th Amendments, the vote became their overriding goal. The struggle for the vote endured for 50 years after the first campaign in Kansas in 1867; most of the time was spent recruiting supporters for state constitutional amendments that, in turn, became stepping stones to the passage of the Nineteenth Amendment in 1920 (Flexner, 1975; Sinclair, 1965; Grimes, 1967; Kradi-tor, 1971; O'Neill, 1971; Morgan, 1972; Scott & Scott, 1982).

American woman suffragists' ultimate success is owed to the strategy they fashioned to overcome institutional obstacles and ideological resistance. There were three compo-nents of the suffragists' strategy: ideology, alliances, and organization. Developing a con-vincing ideology to win over legislators, male voters, and traditional women was the most challenging part of the movement. Suffragists faced similar opponents to those ERA reformers encountered in the 1970s: religious fundamentalists and women who wanted to protect their perceived privileges as second-class citizens. They overcame the opposi-tion of both by testing and revising arguments for woman's rights based upon both women's similarities to and differences from men (Cott, 1987, pp. 19–20). For example, leaders such as Susan B. Anthony (1876) and Elizabeth Cady Stanton (1988) stressed women's similarities with men and called for legal consistency while Frances Willard (1890) and Jane Addams (1910, [1965]) invoked women's differences from men—moral authority and housekeeping skills—as sorely needed political resources that qualified women to vote. Carrie Chapman Catt (1923), the victorious leader, used both.

Suffragists formed alliances by defining the relationship between suffrage and other women's issues. After two decades of ideological and tactical disputes, the reformers agreed to disagree about all issues besides suffrage: they made the vote their single issue. In doing so, however, leaders such as Anthony and Catt did not isolate the vote from temperance and other women's issues. Instead, they defined suffrage as a prerequisite for other reforms. Packaging suffrage as an end essential for other women's political goals engendered bargaining among ideologically diverse groups that, in turn, expanded support for the vote. For example the alliance forged between Colorado suffragists and temperance reformers in the late 1880s became largely responsible for the passage of woman suffrage in 1893 (Marilley, 1985).

The organizational capacity of the movement grew as leaders led campaigns at the national level and in the states from the early 1870s. Because before 1930 the focus of power for civil rights reforms rested in state governments, the suffragists focused from the early 1870s on winning victories in the states. Some state organizations were more than 40 years old by the time the Nineteenth Amendment passed Congress: the means of coordination between state and national leaders had had ample time to develop. The 1970s ERA reformers' comparatively rapid success in Congress left them with little time to build autonomous organizations in the states.

Woman Suffragists' Ideology and Recruitment of Support

The American woman suffrage reformers' toughest opponents were those who defended women's political exclusion as appropriate because women's differences from men—biological, social, and work-related—disqualified them. Day after day and decade after decade, woman suffragists faced arguments that women should accept dependence on male protection, the same assertions Schlafly made (Kraditor, 1968). Suffrage opponents graphically warned that enfranchised women would destroy the family. Similarly, the hardest lesson for 1970s ERA supporters to accept was the gradual shift among legislator and the public at large from strong support to equally strong skepticism and even some outright opposition based on fears of the social change ERA might generate. The chief reason Mansbridge (1986) cited for opposition to the ERA was deep resistance to change in traditional male and female sex roles that nonactivist amendment supporters expressed (pp. 20–28; see also, Mayo & Frye, 1986).

The suffragists' most formidable opponents were ministers. In July 1837, Massachusetts clergy issued the tract, "A Pastoral Letter of the General Association of Massachusetts to the Congregational Churches Under Their Care," condemning Angelina and Sarah Grimke for speaking against slavery in public because they violated scriptural teachings about women's place (Gurko, 1976). Ministers who held similar views denounced woman's rights reformers' initiatives at several annual conventions during the 1850s; Anthony joined the suffrage movement during this decade because such ministers refused to accommodate women leaders in the early temperance movement (Marilley, 1985, pp. 130–133, 155–163). One of the most vocal opponents of the Colorado woman suffrage campaigns in 1876–77 was Roman Catholic Bishop J. Machebeuf (Jensen, 1959, p. 45). Many clergy supported the reform by 1910; however, Catholic priests leaned towards the opposition even late in the struggle (Flexner, 1975, p. 309).

During the early 1850s woman's rights reformers could not dispel fundamentalist interpretations of women's roles (Marilley, 1985). They decided instead that when clerical opposition could not be avoided, to insist that democratic principles were more appropriate than the traditional Biblical limits on women's sphere. Stone and William Lloyd Garrison justified woman's rights and change in women's roles by appealing to democratic principles in the Declaration of Independence and the Constitution (Marilley, 1985). Garrison bluntly asserted that regardless of what any book might teach, the "rights of any human being are equal, absolute, essential, and inalienable in the person of every member of the human family, without regard to sex, race, or clime" (Stanton, Anthony, & Gage, 1969, p. 383). Stanton did not stop challenging the clerical arguments. She sequentially published *The Woman's Bible,* her own translation of the Bible with commentary on the most controversial passages regarding women (Stanton, 1895; Stanton et al., 1989; see also, Flexner, 1975, p. 226).

The organized opposition of some women, such as Phyllis Schlafly, to demands for equal rights has distinguished woman's rights movements from those of other politically excused groups in western democracies (Harrison, 1978). Both the ERA and woman suffrage reformers had to cope with resistance and condemnation from members of their own sex: this opposition generates intra-group conflict that has been absent among ethnic and racial minority groups in their equal rights struggles. Except for those who perceived ERA as a threat to protectionist legislation from the late 1920s to the mid-1960s, the female defenders of women's privileges over women's rights in both movements have been disproportionately wealthy (Flexner, 1975, pp. 305–307).

Coping with female opponents is much more complex and difficult than fending off ministers because women advocate continuing special protections that the wealthy among them have enjoyed for centuries. Those women who celebrate and defend women's lack of rights force reformers to prove that their vision of less protected, more financially independent women would really be better for all women. Even though most women do not enjoy the leisure attributed to those who are wealthy and non-working, the ERA reformers were unable to displace the notion that women's primary responsibilities were motherhood and taking care of the home (Mansbridge, 1986). The suffragists challenged wealthy opponents by recruiting wealthy members of their own, such as Mrs. O. H. P. Belmont, to promote the vote (Flexner, p. 250).

ERA's opponents capitalized on the fears of gender role change; woman suffragists faced similar opposition (Flexner, 1975; Marilley, 1985). These fears can be displaced by hope and a determination for women and men to share roles and responsibilities. Some suffragists, notably Frances Willard (1890) and Jane Addams (1910, [1965]), dispelled fears of gender role change by arguing that women's special identity and unique resources could be more fully shared with the vote. For example, Willard (1890) argued that to fulfill their divinely ordained role as moral authorities and to protect themselves and their children from male abuses of physical power, women had to win the vote and make laws. She conceived of the vote as a means for women to obtain political power rather than simply legal equality; with this appeal, she recruited many more women than the suffrage leaders did between 1876 and 1895 (Bordin, 1986, pp. 97–128). Introduced in 1910, Addams' famous portrait of women as much needed "housekeepers" for government rallied suffrage support from men as well as women (Addams, 1910, [1965], pp. 144–151; see also, Flexner, 1975; Buenker, 1973; and Scott & Scott, 1982).

Appeals for the ERA that imitate those Willard and Addams made for the vote could diminish the intensity of the threat to public goods that McGlen and O'Connor (1988) identify as ERA opponents' major resource. Future ERA reformers should take their lessons from Willard and Addams as well as from Stanton, Anthony, and Stone. They must show not only why women deserve equal rights; they must focus on the public's need for women's resources and women's need for equal political power. ERA reformers should take a more offensive strategy: directly challenge their opponents to prove why women should not have equal rights. Such challenges would put the opposition in the awkward position of devaluing women, a posture unlikely to generate support.

The Problems of Related Issues and Forming Alliances

Another useful lesson that the American woman suffrage movement has to teach ERA reformers is that strong links must be made between the amendment and traditional women's issues and roles. The resounding defeat suffrage reformers incurred in Kansas in 1867 demonstrated that there was little support for woman's rights outside the educated, northeastern men and women in Garrison's antislavery organization (Flexner, 1975; DuBois, 1978; Marilley, 1985). The strong link that Frances Willard, a midwesterner and president of the WCTU, forged between temperance and votes for women broke through class, cultural, and ideological barriers that Anthony, Stone, and Stanton failed to penetrate (Bordin, 1981; Scott & Scott, 1982). Only after woman suffragists followed Willard's example and assumed leadership in the Colorado temperance movement, did they tap the resources and support of many women who had not yet given serious consideration to votes for women (Marilley, 1985).

The 1970s ERA reform leaders were also educated, urban, and white elites. These leaders failed to make firm ties to traditionally-minded women supporters at the outset; as a result, some state ERA organizations lacked firm foundations (Boles, 1979). The reform leaders' later adoption of women in the military and abortion as related issues reinforced the barriers between themselves and traditional women. Although most ERA leaders tried to avoid the abortion issue, the pronounced overlap between abortion supporters and ERA activists alienated members of the public and legislators alike (Mansbridge, 1986).

It is perhaps easier in theory than in practice to call for a much sharper division between future ERA and abortion rights reformers. To break the barrier between traditionally-minded women and the ERA, however, such a demarcation would be necessary (McGlen & O'Connor, 1983). Again, current reformers can look to the suffragists for strategic advice. The suffrage and temperance reformers not only maintained separate organizations; they insured that leaders who held office in both were not in highly visible executive positions during key campaigns, a feat much more difficult to achieve in the face of contemporary mass media (Marilley, 1985).

Most importantly, the suffragists vigilantly held to a single-issue strategy; they proclaimed the vote as their only goal, and leaders who wanted a forum for another issue had to go elsewhere (Marilley, 1985, pp. 373–377). The advantage of this strategy was the formation of a coalition that included prohibitionists, racists, anti-child labor reformers, Republicans, and Democrats but left the suffragists in control. The obvious disadvantage of this technique for future ERA leaders is the suffragists' contradiction of egalitarian principles—principles that suffrage leaders eschewed more than they practiced—by including racists (Flexner, 1975). The 19th Amendment probably would not have been ratified by 1920 without the support of racist states such as Texas, Arkansas, and Tennessee—states that passed woman suffrage before 1920. ERA reformers would be ill-advised to imitate the suffragists' bigotry; however, they must be prepared to keep the ERA related to, but not synonymous with, any other single issue.

To pass an ERA, future reformers must win support from those who value the strengths associated with traditional women. For example, the chances of the ERA's success would be greatly improved if the leaders would qualify their support of abortion rights with the acknowledgement that complex ethical issues arise with most abortion decisions. A critical mass of abortion critics whose members do not share the ideologically reactionary views of the right-to-life movement has been growing slowly. These critics can be found among ethicists in philosophy and theology as well as in progressive religious congregations and social justice organizations. For instance, in her article, "Ethical Problems of Abortion," Sissela Bok (1981), a supporter of the right to abortion, argues that the legalization of abortion does not provide moral justification for every abortion (pp. 45, 68). In addition, Margaret Farley (1987), Beverly Harrison (1987) and Ginny Earnest Soley (1986) each offer insightful criticisms of arguments defending abortion laws that future ERA reformers could profit from. A new ERA movement whose leaders sought the participation and advice of such scholars and activists would help them to shed reputations as unreflective pro-abortionists, a label that many in the public audience associated with the movement after Schlafly's campaign (Steiner, 1985; Gallup & Castelli, 1987).

While distance from abortion would benefit reformers, there are some issues appealing to traditional women that could be more visibly linked to the ERA. For example, the League of Women Voters has called for legislation to reduce the damage acid rain causes (Stanfield, 1986). Women's traditional concern to protect the health of their families could be articulated with this issue: the conflict could pit men from the coal and utility industries against mothers, thus showing clearly that while women are politically included, they still play a marginal role in making public policy. Another traditional women's group that the new coalition would benefit from is Mothers Against Drunk Driving (MADD). MADD vigorously opposes recent federal legislation that allows states to raise the speed limit. The ERA leaders could use this issue to show that mothers' views are not taken seriously enough by the lawmakers.

A focus on economic issues and concerted efforts to expand cross-class and inter-racial alliances among women would also be useful in a future ERA campaign. Fair wages and improved working conditions became rallying cries for suffragists in the late 19th and early 20th centuries. Despite the close ties that women and blacks formed during the civil rights movement and sustained within the labor-led coalition in the Democratic Party, these ties have become frayed. After the passage of the Voting Rights Act of 1965, women turned their attention away from strengthening cooperative initiatives between blacks and whites and the powerful and the poor and towards winning rights for themselves (Palley, 1982). The struggle for the ERA focused mainly on issues that concerned middle-class, white women—affirmative action for high paying jobs, entry into formerly all-male post-graduate education, and the like. According to Paula Giddings (1984) the leaders of the ERA campaigns have been almost all white; as a result, they lost an opportunity to build a coalition with black women (pp. 340–348). A coalition of black and white reformers demanding equal rights could have kept economic issues well ahead of abortion rights and the combat issue, the two controversies that most damaged the ERA.

Both current and future leaders should do as much as possible to include black and other minority women. Black women would strengthen ties between ERA supporters and the black community: the concerns of most women—for day care, fair wages and salaries, and family services—would not be subordinated to those of elite white women.

The ERA would become an authentic civil rights movement to make all women politically included.

The Importance of State Organizations

Another critical step for ERA reformers to improve their chances is to develop unified state organizations to lobby legislatures to pass state constitutional amendments and thereby ease the federal ratification process. Lucy Stone and Henry Blackwell's failure to win majority support for votes for women in the Kansas suffrage referenda in 1867 convinced them that the primary task of a national suffrage organization was to build grass-roots support through state suffrage campaigns (Flexner, 1975, pp. 149–150, 154–8). Blackwell and Stone's preference for state efforts was one reason for their split in 1869 with Anthony and Stanton, who put priority on passing suffrage at the national level. Anthony and Stanton's National Woman Suffrage Association (NWSA) and Stone and Blackwell's American Woman Suffrage Association (AWSA) united as the National American Woman Suffrage Association (NAWSA) in 1890 largely because Anthony and Stanton had accepted that the state campaigns were as important as the national one (Flexner, 1975, p. 226). NAWSA's eventual power as a national organization derived from the expansion of Stone and Blackwell's decentralized infrastructure and state victories. Janet Boles (1982) describes a striking contrast between strides made by the ERA and suffrage movements in the states at the beginning of the federal ratification process:

> Even though the general trend of state and federal policy and court decisions in the area of sex discrimination was consistent with the ERA, only five states had ERA's in their state constitutions before 1972. In contrast, by 1919 fifteen states had granted full voting rights to women and eleven others had extended presidential suffrage to women. (p. 16)

The success of Carrie C. Catt's "Winning Plan" for national suffrage owes much to the unified, well-seasoned state organizations she expertly coordinated (Flexner, 1975, pp. 290–92). By contrast, in her case study of the Illinois ratification effort, Mansbridge (1986) argues that the two separate organizations, the National Organization of Women (NOW) and ERA Illinois, often had contrasting leaders and strategies that inhibited coordination (pp. 165–177). Multiple leadership initiatives hindered crafty meshing of public and private reform tactics. The NOW reformers—mostly young, recent residents of Illinois—preferred to pressure legislators by using open, often loud, media politics and demonstrations. In contrast, the ERA Illinois reformers most of whom were older, locally-rooted women well-seasoned in electoral politics opted for quiet moral suasion and deal-making. The larger, more dedicated membership of the NOW organization made it predominate over ERA Illinois; however, Mansbridge's analysis suggests that organizational unity would have produced a more appropriate mix of ERA Illinois's subtle strategies and NOW's overt tactics (Mansbridge, 1986).

A quick review of the organizational evolution during the woman suffrage movement reinforces Mansbridge's argument. The infrastructure that executed state and federal constitutional campaigns for suffrage developed slowly and painfully. Despite the NWSA's concentration on winning gains in Congress and the AWSA's focus in the states between 1870 and 1890, the competition and varied strategies among leaders impeded progress. Only after the reunification of the two wings in 1890 and the coordination of the national with the state campaigns, did the suffragists win state amendment campaigns where a voter referendum was required for ratification (Marilley, 1985). The powerful grass-roots state organizations that led the ratification drive in 1919 and 1920 emerged from these campaigns.

The suffragists' victory in Colorado in 1893 was their first in a state requiring a voter referendum for a constitutional amendment. The AWSA leaders had directed an earlier effort in 1876 and 1877 that failed. Among the many changes between the late 1870s and 1893 was that of infrastructural coordination between state and national leaders. Not only did the newly unified NAWSA offer coherent guidance from the East, but also and more importantly, the 1892–93 campaign was initiated and directed by Colorado women (Marilley, 1985). In fact, the national elders strongly resisted the first requests that Coloradan Ellis Meredith and her co-leaders made for financial support (Marilley, 1985; see also, Stanton, Anthony & Gage, 1969; Wheeler, 1981). The assumption of responsibility by women with strong ties to local party leaders, the press and other influential figures gave the movement momentum and vigor that the earlier effort had lacked (Marilley, 1985).

Catt participated in the Colorado victory as a novice reformer. She learned from Anthony that success derived from continuous dialogue between state and national leaders, a process evidenced in the correspondence between Anthony and Meredith (Marilley, 1985, pp. 368–81). Catt did not design her famous plan until 1916, after 11 successful state amendment campaigns, enough to make women influential in presidential elections. Without the experienced state leaders and tightly connected network formed during previous state amendment campaigns, Catt could not have executed her plan (Flexner, 1975, pp. 286–292, 319–337).

Mansbridge neither criticizes the lack of communication between NOW and ERA Illinois nor advocates specific organizational reforms to promote cooperation in a future effort. This brief comparison of the state organizational problems she describes with the suffragists' organizational strength in one of their first state victories suggests that a more unified effort directed by the ERA Illinois leaders would probably be much more successful. The immense territory of the United States and the federal political structure provide more leverage to people who are already tied into the local and state power structure than to newcomers. Mansbridge states that she was one of the few new local residents to attend ERA Illinois meetings. Future reformers would be well-advised to follow her example: always consider and sometimes follow the strategic judgments of those who have struggled against a particular geopolitical status quo (Mansbridge, 1986). Again, the assumption of a single-issue identity for ERA would facilitate such a sharing of power: as long as there was a consensus that ERA was the highest priority, and that it was independent of other issues, state and local leaders would be free to build coalitions they considered appropriate.

Towards a New Era: A New Constituency and the Problem of Timing

There are two major reasons for passage of an ERA: (1) to reinforce the rights women have gained through legislation and litigation, and (2) to create a powerful sanction against the treatment of women as inferior to men. The proposal by Steiner (1985) that the Court "establish sex as a suspect classification" (pp. 109–10) would fall short of these goals. Judicial opinions favoring women can be reversed much more easily without an ERA than with it. Despite the profound opposition to the idea of change in gender roles, much change has proceeded during the past ten years: for instance, increasing numbers of married women work, including mothers of young children. An ERA would give needed psychological support to men and women ordaining new divisions of labor in the home and workplace.

Yet, as impatient as the recent ERA reformers may be to launch another national reform campaign there are good reasons to wait for more accommodating conditions. Even though the ERA was defeated narrowly, the loss is perceived as a sore failure. To say as Molly Yard (1988) did in a recent solicitation of funds for a new campaign, "people who wait for 'the right time' may do nothing but wait," (p. 2) is to ignore the history of similar constitutional amendment campaigns, especially woman suffrage. In 1987 NOW President Ellie Smeal introduced this same appeal (p. 2). Bringing the ERA before Congress now, before new supporters are recruited and especially given the conservative composition of the Senate, can only undermine the chances for building the kind of majority coalition that could insure ratification.

The adoption of a long range perspective for the success of an ERA—accepting that this sort of reform will not be achieved quickly—would be a prudent first step. The suffragists struggled for almost 50 years before the Nineteenth Amendment passed. The leaders need more time to reconsider the reasons for the ERA's failure, modify strategy, and rebuild a support base so that they can cultivate a consensus for ERA in the state legislatures as well as in Congress and among the public. State ERA campaigns could be launched: state suffrage laws and consitutional amendments created the foundation for winning the vote at the national level. The election of women into state legislatures and Congress would produce more ready-made allies for an ERA campaign.

Besides putting more women into elective office, ERA leaders must cultivate a different constituency. In her article, "Women at the Polls," Carol Matlack (1987) asserts that most women are concerned about family and child-care issues, issues that NOW leaders have not identified as highest priorities. Neglecting these issues is a mistake if these leaders want to keep the ERA visible and build a firmer base of support than they had in the 1970s.

New issues, arguments, and allies would recruit middle-of-the-road supporters for the kinds of goals the ERA originally symbolized. Support from such constituencies is essential if the ERA is to be seen as necessary. The amendment's leaders must be able to depict opponents such as Phyllis Schlafly as ideological extremists and to avoid this label themselves. Only after woman suffragists elucidated their aim as political inclusion, not changes in women or society, did they garner the support necessary for victory. ERA supporters should imitate the suffragists' conversion of many would-be opponents by compromising on the issues that damaged them most.

References

Addams, J. (1910, [1965]). Why women should vote. In C. Lasch (Ed.), *The social thought of Jane Addams* (pp. 143–151). Indianapolis: Bobbs-Merrill. Reprinted from: *Ladies Home Journal*, January 1910, 27, pp. 21–22.

Berry, M. F. (1986). *Why ERA failed*. Bloomington: University of Indiana Press.

Bok, S. (1981). *Ethical problems of abortion*. In T. A. Shannon (Ed.), *Bioethics* (pp. 19–45). Ramsey, NJ: The Paulist Press.

Boles, J. K. (1979). *The politics of the Equal Rights Amendment*. New York: Longman.

Boles, J. K. (1982a). Systemic factors underlying legislative responses to woman suffrage and the Equal Rights Amendment. *Women & Politics*. (1–2), pp. 5–22.

Boles, J. K. (1982b). Building support for the ERA: A case of "too much, too late." *PS, 15* (4), pp. 572–577.

Boles, J. K. (1986). The Equal Rights Movement as a non-zero-sum game. In J. Hoff-Wilson (Ed.), *Rights of passage* (pp. 54–62). Bloomington: Indiana University Press.

Bordin, R. (1981). *Woman and temperance*. Philadelphia: Temple University Press.

Bordin, R. (1986). *Frances Willard*. Chapel Hill: University of North Carolina Press.

Buenker, J. D. (1973). *Urban liberalism and progressive reform*. New York: Norton, chap. 4.

Carroll, B. (1986). Direct action and constitutional rights: The case of the ERA. In J. Hoff-Wilson (Ed.), *Rights of passage* (pp. 63–75). Bloomington: Indiana University Press.

Catt, C. C. (1923). *Woman suffrage and politics*. New York: Charles Scribner's Sons.

Cott, N. (1987). *The grounding of modern feminism*. New Haven: Yale University Press.

Daniels, M. R., Darcy, R., and Westphal, J. W. (1982). The ERA won—at least in the opinion polls. *PS, 15* (4), pp. 578–584.

Dehart-Mathews, J. and Mathews, D., (1986). The cultural politics of the ERA's defeat. In J. Hoff-Wilson, (Ed.), *Rights of passage* (pp. 44–53). Bloomington: Indiana University Press.

Deutchman, I. E., and Prince-Embury, S. (1982). Political ideology of pro-and-anti-ERA women. *Women & Politics, 2* (1/2), pp. 39–55.

Dubois, E. (1978). *Feminism and suffrage: The emergence of an independent women's movement in America, 1848–1869*. Ithaca, New York: Cornell Univ. Press.

Farley, M. (1987). Liberation, abortion and responsibility. In S. E. Lammers and A. Verhey (Eds.), *On moral medicine* (pp. 434–438). Grand Rapids, MI: William B. Eerdmans.

Flexner, E. (1975). *Century of struggle: The woman's rights movement in the United States* (rev. Ed.), Cambridge, MA: Harvard University Press.

Gallup, G. Jr., and Castelli, J. (1987). *The American Catholic people: Their beliefs, practices, and values*. New York: Doubleday.

Giddings, P. (1984). *When and where I enter*. New York: William Morrow.

Grimes, A. (1967). *The puritan ethic and woman suffrage*. New York: Oxford University Press.

Gurko, M. (1976). *The ladies of Seneca Falls*. New York: Schocken Books.

Harrison, B. W. (1987). Theology and morality of procreative choice. In S. E. Lammers and A. Verhey (Eds.), *On moral medicine* (pp. 422–33). Grand Rapids, MI: William B. Eerdmans.

Harrison, B. (1978). *Separate spheres*. London: Billing and Sons, Ltd.

Jensen, B. B. (1959). The woman suffrage movement in Colorado. Unpublished Master's thesis, University of Colorado at Boulder.

Kingdon, J. W. (1984). *Agendas, alternatives, and public policies*. Boston: Little, Brown.

Kraditor, A. S. (1971). *The ideas of the woman suffrage movement*. New York: Quadrangle Books.

Kraditor, A. S. (1968). *Up from the pedestal*. New York: Quadrangle.

McGlen, N. E., and O'Connor, K. (1983). *Women's rights*. New York: Praeger.

McGlen, N. E., and O'Connor, K. (1988). Towards a theoretical model of counter-movements and constitutional change: A case study of the ERA. *Women and Politics, 8* (3/4).

Mansbridge, J. (1986). *Why we lost the ERA*. Chicago: University of Chicago Press.

Marilley, S. M. (1985). *Why the vote? Woman suffrage and the politics of democratic development, 1820–1893*. (PhD diss., Harvard University) also: (Ann Arbor: University Microfilms International, 1986).

Matlack, C. (1987, December 19). Women at the polls. *National Journal*, pp. 3208–3215.

Mayo, E., and Frye, J. K. (1986). The ERA: Postmortem of a failure in political communication. In J. Hoff-Wilson (Ed.), *Rights of passage* (pp. 76–89). Bloomington: Indiana University Press.

Morgan, D., (1972). *Suffragists and Democrats*. East Lansing, MI: Michigan State Univ. Press.

O'Neill, W. (1971). *Everyone was brave*. Garden City, New York: Quadrangle.

Palley, M. L. (1982). Beyond the deadline. *PS, 15* (4), pp. 588–91.

Pleck, E. (1986). Failed strategies: Renewed hope. In J. Hoff-Wilson (Ed.), *Rights of passage* (pp. 106–120). Bloomington: Indiana University Press.

Scott, A. F., and Scott, A. (1982). *One half the people: The fight for woman suffrage*. Urbana: The University of Illinois Press.

Sinclair, A., (1965). *The emancipation of the American woman*. New York: Harper and Row.

Smeal, E. (1987). Citizen petition letter for the ERA. National Organization for Women. Wednesday, March.

Soley, G. E. (1986, October). To preserve and protect life. *Sojourners* magazine, pp. 34–37.

Stanfield, R. L. (1986, June 14). The acid rainmakers. *National Journal*, pp. 1500–1503.

Stanton, E. C. (1895). *The woman's Bible, Part 1*. New York: European Publishing Company.

Stanton, E. C. et al. The revising committee. (1898). *The woman's Bible, Part 2*. New York: European Publishing Company.

Stanton, E. C., Anthony, S. B., and Gage, M. J. (1889). *History of woman suffrage, Vol. I*. Rochester, New York: Charles Mann.

Stanton, E. C., Anthony, S. B., and Gage, M. J. (1969). *History of woman suffrage, Vols. II and IV*. New York: Arno and the New York Times.

Steiner, G. Y. (1985). *Constitutional inequality*. Washington, DC: The Brookings Institution.

Wheeler, L. (1981). *Loving warriors: A revealing portrait of an unprecedented marriage*. New York: The Dial Press.

Willard, F. (1890). Frances Willard: Extracts from her 4th of July speech. *The Woman's Journal*, 24 January 1890, Boston, MA, p. 30.

Yard, M. (1988). I want ERA written into the Constitution. National Organization for Women, Wednesday, September.

The Complete Text of the Equal Rights Amendment

Section 1.
Equality of rights under the law shall not be denied or abridged by the United States or by any State on account of sex.
Section 2.
The Congress shall have the power to enforce, by appropriate legislation, the provisions of this Article.
Section 3.
This Amendment shall take effect two years after the date of ratification.

Chapter 8—Women and Politics
Study Questions

1. According to the U.S. Census Bureau, there are more women than men in this country. Why aren't more women in office? Are numbers and outcome related? Why or why not?

2. "While slavery has been abolished, most legislators still have wives." Why is this a public wake-up call?

3. What important issues still lie ahead concerning economic and health equity for women? What has the Women's Health Equity Act set in motion? Do you believe universal health care is important? Why or why not?

4. The life of Eleanor Roosevelt points up the importance of relationships. In small groups, discuss how relationships hinder us. How do they help. Also, discuss the effect of the role models in your life. Who are they? How did they affect you?

5. In Carroll's article, what is meant by "the personal is political"? What concerns in your life fit this definition? Is there a separation of the two spheres in a woman's life? Why or why not?

6. In "Toward a New Strategy for the ERA . . . ," Marilley asserts feminists have much to learn from the suffrage movement. Do you agree with her "single issue" strategy? Why or why not?

7. Write a short (1–2 page) essay on why you feel the ERA has failed to become a reality. Use supporting evidence from Marilley's article. Do you think it will ever pass? Why or why not?

8. Discuss the following questions in the large group:

   a) What factors do you feel keep women from demanding changes in the workplace?
   b) Do you believe women's point of view differs to a degree that could change the shape of politics? Why?

WOMEN AND THE LAW

Jacqueline St. Joan

If Ours is "A Government of Laws, and Not Men," Then Who Are All These Lawyers at the Courthouse in Dark Suits and Ties?

Today, when I enter my courtroom and take my seat behind the bench, everyone who is able to do so stands, and remains standing, until I am seated and invite them to do likewise.

My first entry into the world of the law was very different. It occurred on a cold and gloomy day in January 1961. I accompanied my high school friend, Sue Anderson, to her father's big law office overlooking Pennsylvania Avenue in downtown Washington, D.C. Within the dark paneled walls, by the big warm desks near the tall windows, we watched the inaugural parade of John F. Kennedy. In these staunch mahogany surroundings, with forest green lights and burgundy leatherbound books, I knew that I did not belong there. I was fifteen and I was female.

A few years later, when I was a student at Georgetown University, I entered the legal profession as a part-time secretary, a position I obtained through the student placement office. The employer wanted a trustworthy Catholic girl who could type, had good manners, and could speak a little French. After class I caught the city bus headed for downtown Washington to meet with my new employer. The bus was already crowded, its air conditioning broken. I stood in the crowded aisle, my books on my hip, my dress wrinkling, my sprayed hairdo falling. At Fourteenth and K streets I emerged into the heavy downtown air, traffic fumes, and bright diffused light. Within two minutes I entered a revolving door into the relieving cold and quiet blessing of an office building. I worked at minimum wage for several months for this lawyer, and was glad to have the job.

Two thousand miles, nine years, one marriage, two children, one divorce, and one college degree later, I entered a Denver storefront office to answer an employment ad, and was hired as a legal secretary. I think I earned just above minimum wage. It was enough to disqualify me from welfare, but with two children, I still qualified for food stamps, even though I worked full time. Within a few months I discovered firsthand just what lawyers do, and realized that I certainly could do it and make three times the money as well. Within two years I was enrolled in law school, within five years I had a law degree, within nine years I had my own small firm, and within fifteen years I had become a judge.

I review this story because it is the private outline behind the public role I play today as a judge, and in itself it can show both the ways in which my story belongs to the *general* story of women of my generation and also the ways in which it is a story that is *particular* to me. As I will try to explain later, this mixing of the general with the particular in the context of the stories of real women's lives is one of the methods of approaching law from a specifically feminist perspective. Furthermore, my story is not just a typical American individualist version of "rags to riches." I want to emphasize an approach to human development which acknowledges the substantial influence that social factors have on whether or not any particular individual succeeds.

This is not to say that stories of individuals overcoming difficult circumstances are not inspirational or of worth, but only that they do not account for all or even most of the story. For example, in my own case, I think of some of the following factors: What if I had lived only a mile from where my home was located in racially segregated northern Virginia in the 1950s and were of African instead of Italian-Irish descent? What if my parents has been unable to afford a parochial school education for me? What if I had been paralyzed in a car accident at an early age? What if the U.S. economy had been in recession during my college years so that scholarships, loans, and jobs were not available? What if, after my divorce, the eligibility requirements for Aid to Families with Dependent Children (AFDC) had been higher and my children and I could not have qualified for assistance? What if just a year or two before I applied to law schools, those schools had not begun admitting women in much larger numbers than previously? These questions touched on the privileges and barriers I have experienced in my life, the kind that one usually takes for granted. To increase one's consciousness means to become aware of these social factors and specifically how they operate. Surely all of these (and many others) influenced the paths in my life quite apart from my own personal intentions, resources, and grit.

In this essay I want to raise questions about the role of the law in our lives and particularly in the lives of women. There is not an aspect of our lives that is not affected, regulated, or somehow controlled by law. From the moment we awaken in the morning and turn on the light (the utility rates for which are regulated by law) until the time we place our heads back down on our pillows (whose tags remind us not to remove them under penalty of law—the contents of pillows are regulated by law), in this society we operate within a system based on the belief that good laws properly control the lives of citizens, and that without laws, people would not conduct themselves in an orderly and socially acceptable way.

Law is even further glorified because, as the saying goes, ours is a "government of laws, and not men," meaning that as citizens we are protected against tyranny because it is The Law, and not individuals, that controls our lives through government.

- Do you agree with this statement? Disagree?
- How can we view the history of U.S. law from a perspective that considers its varied impact on women?
- How and why have women been excluded from lawmaking and from the legal profession until only recently?
- How has the entry of women into the profession affected the law and vice versa?
- How do feminists both agree and disagree on the use of law as a means of social change?

• What is jurisprudence? What is feminist jurisprudence? How may it affect the law in the future?

These are some of the questions addressed in this essay and in the readings which follow.

The Erasure of Women From United States Legal History

One reason we study history is to broaden our perspectives on today's issues. A historical viewpoint reveals how the law has been based on white male norms and serves male interests as a group. In 1971, for the very first time, a law was declared unconstitutional based on gender. (*Reed v. Reed* 1971). The law in question was an Idaho statute which preferred men automatically over women as executors of the estate of deceased persons. The court ruled that where men and women are equally qualified, a man may not be appointed executor solely on the basis of sex.

Women were not allowed to vote in many states until seventy years ago. This means that my grandmother, who was required to follow the law and to pay taxes, had no right to vote for or against those legislators who made the laws and collected her taxes. It also took a very long time (about forty-five years) for the woman suffrage amendment to be passed from the date of its introduction into the U.S. Congress. This means that if the suffrage effort had begun in 1920 instead of in 1875, and had proceeded at the same pace, women could still be prohibited today from voting in political elections. The Equal Rights Amendment (ERA) to the U.S. Constitution was first introduced in Congress in 1923. Almost seventy years later it still is not a part of the Constitution, although it is included in sixteen state constitutions (Lefcourt 1990).

From the very beginning of United States history the law has not reflected women's perspectives on the issues of citizenship and political rights. Common law is the body of English law which was adopted by the new states, except Louisiana, which based its law on the French Napoleonic code. Common law was developed by judges through the process of individual decision making. It continues today in the form of written decisions interpreting the law in the context of the facts of particular cases. Under common law, married women had no legal existence except through their husbands, which, according to the doctrine of coverture, meant that the wife and the husband were one—and that *one* was the husband. Thus, for example, any wages earned by a married women belonged to her husband; she could neither own her own property nor enter into contracts. Similarly, African Americans, as slaves, had no legal existence except as chattel (a term derived from the word cattle, meaning property that can be moved from place to place, unlike real estate, for example). Because slave women were property, legally, they could not be raped since as chattel they had no legal ability to give or to withhold consent. The new Constitution included political rights (such as voting) only for a certain elite—white men who owned property—that is, the white male merchants, farmers, and professional and upper classes. Thus the vast majority of people living in this country in 1776 were excluded from participation in this new "democracy."

The fundamental hypocrisy of the history of United States law is that the republic which claims to create the common good by protecting the rights of the individual from the tyranny of the state has, at the same time, excluded from those protections the majority of the population whose labor and energy has been exploited by the enfranchised. Examples of exploitation are abundant: the theft of labor through slavery, the theft of resources through the extermination of Native Americans, the theft of sexual and domestic services through the confinement of most women to childbearing and housework. This schism between the democratic ideal and its reality took violent form in the Civil War and continued through Reconstruction, the struggle for women's right to vote, the history of the American labor movement, and the civil rights and women's movements of the 1950s, 1960s, and 1970s. In a real sense these groups on the margins of privileged white male society constitute a majority of the American people, and they have tried to redefine through the law, the political lives of all of us—that is, how we govern ourselves as a people.

After the American Revolution, married elite women made few demands for inclusion or legal protection in the new republic, due in large part to their acceptance of moral leadership in the private sphere—the home. Men in greater part abandoned private life for the role of controlling all public life. One famous complaint on women's behalf, however, has been recorded in Abigail Adams's request to the revolutionaries who were creating a new government. She asked that they take into consideration the condition of women. Her husband, John Adams, replied:

> As to your extraordinary Code of laws, I cannot but laugh. We have been told that our Struggle has loosened the bands of Government everywhere. That Children and Apprentices were disobedient, that schools and Colleges were grown turbulent, that Indians slighted their Guardians and Negroes grew insolent to their Masters. But

your Letter was the first intimation that another Tribe more numerous and powerful than all the rest were grown discontented. We know better than to repeal our masculine System. (Hoff 1991, 60)

Indeed, in the 1800s women's economic power declined under the laws of the new republic. Fewer women were granted the right to be executors of their husbands' estates, and a smaller percentage of an estate was assigned to a widow. Both of these changes occurred in the courts by judges defining the common law. State legislative grants of property rights to widows was an important measure of power because generally the paternalistic law had recognized a wife's dependent status and, if she were widowed, provided a kind of guaranteed percentage of family wealth to her as inheritance, called dower. However, this wealth and the control of it was often challenged by sons; and, under interpretations of law that increasingly favored men's economic activity, women's dower rights also were weakened (Hoff 1991).

Married women in most states were subject to the doctrine of coverture; thus, they could not own or sell property, nor could they contract without their husband's consent. Widows had few rights against creditors' claims on their husband's lands, nor could they even write wills or have access to their husbands' personal estates without permission. Women could not obtain custody of their children in the event of divorce. During the middle and late 1800s various states began to pass married women's property acts, and eventually the concept of coverture disappeared. Yet, by 1900 only 39 percent of the states allowed women to keep separately their own wages and only 70 percent of the states allowed a woman to write a will without her husband's consent (Hoff 1991).

Women reformers took an active part in community life in the early 1800s on the issues of both temperance (anti-alcohol and wife abuse) and abolition (antislavery). Those who work today in their communities to combat substance abuse, battery, and racism continue the legacy begun by these foremothers. By the mid-1800s, these reformers began to take collective action on women's rights, as well as on their abolitionist beliefs and commitment. The Declaration of Sentiments, passed in 1848 at a conference in Seneca Falls, New York, while having no legal authority, was a new public statement on behalf of women. It decried the detriment to women of their being restricted by the institutions of both marriage and religion, the harm caused by wife beating and the dual standards of morality, and other dangers inherent in marriage (Boller and Story 1988).

According to Hoff (1991), both Elizabeth Cady Stanton and Susan B. Anthony "and other radical feminists of their time reasserted for the remainder of the century that 'marital bondage' was 'woman's chief discontent'":

> We are not dreamers or fanatics; and we know that the ballot when we get it, will achieve for woman no more than it has achieved for man . . . The ballot is not even half the loaf; it is only a crust, a crumb . . . But woman's chief discontent is not with her political, but with her social and particularly, her marital bondage. The solemn and profound question of marriage . . . is of more vital consequence to women's welfare, reaches down to a deeper depth in women's heart and more thoroughly constitutes the core of the woman's movement, than any such superficial and fragmentary question as woman's suffrage. (Hoff 1991, 139–40)

By affirming that their freedom was connected to the freedom of all women, these first feminists took a collective rather than an individual approach to the liberation of white women as well as to the liberation of slaves. The advent of the Civil War marked a decline of interest and activity in white women's rights, and in its aftermath feminists were unsuccessful in getting Republican leadership in Washington to include women in the Reconstruction Amendments (Thirteenth, Fourteenth, and Fifteenth), which guaranteed equal protection of the laws and the right to vote to black men. Although the amendments do not expressly exclude women, judges have most often interpreted them in that way (*Bradwell v. Illinois* 1873). After the Civil War, the Supreme Court's decisions interpreting the Reconstruction Amendments limited their protections to distinctions based solely on race (*Slaughterhouse Cases* 1873). Yet women began to bring their challenges to discriminatory laws and oppressive conditions into the courts in the arena of public life (for example, rights of citizenship, voting, practicing law, and employment)—especially in state legislatures (Hoff 1991)—and in the arena of private life (*Bradwell v. Illinois* 1873; *Minor v. Happersett* 1875; and In re *Lockwood* 1894).

In *Minor v. Happersett* (1875), for example, because a married woman had no legal existence and was thus prevented from suing, Virginia Minor, an active suffragist, had to file suit through her husband. They challenged the refusal of Missouri officials to even allow her to register to vote, asserting that as a woman she was a citizen and thus should be allowed to vote, since voting is a hallmark of citizenship in a democracy. A unanimous Supreme Court disagreed and held that although women are persons and citizens within the meaning of the

Constitution, the original framers of that document never intended that all citizens also be voters (recall the words of John Adams to Abigail Adams) and that women were in that class of persons not to be considered voters. Thus, the only way women would be able to obtain the right to vote would be by constitutional amendment, and the struggle for such an amendment was reignited because of the necessity borne of this case, drawn directly from the original exclusionary notions of the framers of the Constitution. It was not until 1920 when the Nineteenth Amendment was ratified that women in the United States were granted the most basic right of citizenship in a democracy—the right to vote (Flexner 1959).

Women's paths through United States history are very different from what one usually studies in school. Here is where feminists agree and the historically male dominated fields of law and history diverge. One could easily understand that there have been many kinds of histories going on simultaneously since 1776. The dominant history, "the official story," is the one generally found in history books. Furthermore, traditional American history and theory have created ways of thinking about law and of practicing law which are dominant and which make more difficult original thought and action outside of the law's usual theoretical boundaries. Women's experience has also been influenced by the dominant male social constructs, but to the extent that women's rights have been suppressed, so too have their voices been erased from the official version of the nation's history.

Women Hold Up Half the Sky (and Move Mountains As Well): Women in the Legal Profession

In July 1869 Arabella Babb Mansfield became the first woman to be permitted to practice law in the United States. Her entry was challenged and her admission to the bar upheld by the Iowa Supreme Court (Hoff 1991). Major impediments restricted women's access to the legal profession, and those few who had been allowed to practice usually had to obtain a special act of the state legislature. The doctrine of coverture had a critical impact on a woman's ability to practice law. How could a lawyer effectively represent others when she could not even contract or have any legal existence apart from her husband? Since being single was disapproved, women who married and practiced law usually practiced with their husbands—and were more often clerical than professional employees.

By 1920 all states permitted women's admission to state bars, but real participation in the profession remained at token levels until the 1970s (Morello 1986). Today about 20 percent of all lawyers are women; in 1970 women made up only 3 percent of the profession. Today some law schools have student populations of 50 percent or more women. In the nation's largest firms only 8 percent of the partners (i.e., the owners of the business) are women. Similarly, women nationwide are only 10 percent of federal and state court judges (Colorado Women's Bar Association 1991).

What is the meaning of this exclusion of women from the practice of law? What does this mean for the future? Historian Joan Hoff, citing the theories of historian Mary Beard, argues that in the United States men have refused to concede rights and privileges to women until those rights and privileges were no longer of great value to men (Hoff 1991). In many ways women's recent entry into the legal profession amounts to a measure of men's discarding or sharing certain parts of the field of law which hold little interest or profit—for example, mid-level government positions, legal aid, public defense, prosecution, small and solo firms, family and social service agencies, lower courts, and non tenure track positions in law schools. At the same time, men in the profession have maintained a strong grip on other parts of the field of law—tenured professorships and partnerships in firms primarily representing moneyed commercial clients.

The post-1970s generation of female lawyers is breaking new ground in both theoretical and practical ways. Many are responsible for the legal challenges to women's rights both in the workplace and at home, in the schools, and to their rights within the criminal justice system. Women law professors and practitioners are forging a new feminist jurisprudence, a new way of thinking about women and the law that could form the basis for future legal action. At the same time, many women are more dissatisfied with their work in the profession (44 percent) than are men (29 percent) (Colorado Women's Bar Association 1991). The reasons for women's dissatisfaction, varying with the individual, may reflect the overall disparity in pay, but most often they relate directly or indirectly to gender issues—for example, the lack of promotional opportunities, the expectation that women should act and behave as men, the exclusion from socially connected "boys' clubs," the expectation that women will soothe male egos and cover their mistakes, and the excessive demands on employee time to the detriment of personal and family time.

Underlying these difficulties is the raw fact that the profession has been dominated by white Western males since the origin of our common law in Britain in the thirteenth century. Thus law as an institution is a patriarchal tool which has been used as an instrument of oppression.

Its rulings have justified blatant exploitation. The legal profession is facing the challenge of transformation by recognition that so-called female traits are valuable assets to the profession as well. The resistance both inside and outside of the profession to this transformation of the law and the unwillingness to demystify its exalted status is a problem many women attorneys confront. Generally speaking, the field of law is behind other fields in its self-examination and detachment from traditional thinking. Law will most likely follow, and not lead, challenges to patriarchal power. Much change must occur in the operation of the profession itself before great progress will be made by the field as a whole. This is so because a challenge to law as an institution is a challenge to one of patriarchy's most powerful tools, the legal profession.

One of the ways in which feminists have tried to use the legal system to benefit women has been through the challenges in the area of women and employment—for example, through issues of pay equity, "protective legislation," and sexual harassment.

Pay Equity and Comparable Worth: What's a Dollar to You is Still Only 59 Cents to Me

The primary federal laws dealing with sex-based wage discrimination are the Equal Pay Act of 1963 and Title VII of the Civil Rights Act of 1964. The Equal Pay Act applies only to women working in jobs "substantially equal to jobs held by men." Title VII broadly prohibits employment practices that discriminate "because of race, color, religion, sex or national origin." Cases brought using these two laws generally arise from individuals filing complaints about treatment by their employers that adversely affects the individual who is a member of one of the "protected classes" within the statute. Exactly what amounts to "discrimination" has been left up to the courts to decide. Some cases have turned on whether or not the employer's practice is discriminatory because it treats people in the class differently from people not in the class, or because overall the practice creates a disparate impact upon the class of protected persons. For example, the U.S. Supreme Court case *Griggs v. Duke Power Company* (1971) was one in which the employers required certain diploma and testing requirements for all applicants for certain jobs, the overall effect of which resulted in a disproportionate number of African Americans being excluded from hiring. In a case such as this, the employer may claim that the questionable practice (in this case, requiring diplomas) is necessary to the job; but even if the defendant claims this, the plaintiff has the chance to show that a "less discriminatory alternative" exists than the challenged policy.

In looking at sex discrimination in the paid labor force, we know that generally speaking the market is sex-segregated; that is, there are certain fields which remain dominated by either men or by women—for example, heavy equipment operators vs. secretaries. In recognition of this reality, feminist lawyers created the concept of discrimination based, not on equal pay for equal work, but on equal pay for comparable work. In many fields there is no way to compare, for example, the pay of male secretaries to female secretaries because this kind of analysis does not address the underlying issue of job categories being *de facto* segregated according to sex, with the less favorable wages being paid equally to those (few) men and women who work in the female sex-segregated occupations.

In *County of Washington v. Gunther* (1981), the U.S. Supreme Court held that sex-based wage discrimination claims under Title VII need not necessarily be based on the idea of "equal pay for equal work." The court did not address what kinds of claims could be brought, but allowed courts in Title VII cases to have jurisdiction to consider other legal theories than just equal pay for equal work. Unfortunately, few courts are doing so even though they can.

In a case from the state of Washington, *American Federation of State, County, and Municipal Employees (AFSCME) v. State of Washington* (1983), a suit was brought under Title VII by 15,000 state employees in traditionally female job categories claiming pay disparities between their pay and the pay of those employees in male job categories. They claimed, based on a study conducted by the state of Washington, that certain jobs, while not identical, were comparable in terms of their worth to the employer. The study had documented by means of a point system the comparable value between different kinds of occupation. This idea is like saying that a nurse (a "female" occupation) should be paid equally to a person in a profession of comparable societal value, for example, a tree surgeon (a "male" occupation), when historically in this hypothetical example, tree surgeons had been paid 20 to 30 percent more. The trial court acknowledged comparable worth as a valid legal theory under Title VII, and found that the evidence as a whole supported an inference of intentional discrimination and ruled in favor of the plaintiffs. The court held that the structure of the state compensation system had a disparate impact on those employed in female jobs and thus was illegal.

However, the plaintiffs lost the case on appeal when the Ninth Circuit basically said in 1985 that using standard market distinctions in pay for certain job categories, regardless of the statistical data, was not sufficient evidence of intentional sex discrimination to allow the plaintiffs to prevail. In other words, there can be no challenge to the market itself. If the market is unfair, there may not be legal redress.

"Protective" Legislation and False Paternalism: Or, Why Can't a Woman Be More Like a Man?

From the turn of the century to the recent past, the U.S. Supreme Court has upheld the idea of protective legislation for women. Protective legislation, or false paternalism, was based on the dominant idea of women solely as childbearers, and it had the economic effect of limiting women's access to certain occupations, thus limiting their ability to compete with men. In 1908, in *Muller v. Oregon*, the court stated:

That woman's physical structure and the performance of maternal functions place her at a disadvantage in the struggle for subsistence is obvious. This is especially true when the burdens of motherhood are upon her. Even when they are not, by abundant testimony of the medical fraternity, continuance for a long time on her feet at work, repeating this from day to day, tends to injurious effects upon the body, and, as healthy mothers are essential to vigorous offspring, the physical well-being of women becomes an object of public interest and care in order to preserve the strength and vigor of the race.

This kind of thinking justified the restrictions of women from certain occupations (mining and bartending) or limited night work, or set a certain maximum number of hours, or granted women benefits men did not have, for example, minimum wage, and rest breaks. The acceptance of these practices continued for over fifty years.

Discrimination against pregnant women in the workplace is still widespread and is a central area of struggle because the assumptions for the discrimination are based squarely on the reproductive capacities of women and the historical assignment of women to the private sphere of family life segregated from the public life of the workplace. Thus these ideas were used to justify excluding women from promotions ("She might become pregnant and leave the job after we've invested all this training in her") and mandatory maternity leaves ("It's not appropriate for our customers to see women in advanced stages of pregnancy").

These kinds of practices were challenged in the courts after the passage of Title VII. In 1971 the Supreme Court invalidated a company policy which refused employment to women with school-age children, but which would hire men with school-age children (*Phillips v. Martin-Marietta Corporation* 1971). However, five years later in *General Electric v. Gilbert* (1976), the Supreme Court refused to strike down an employer's exclusion of pregnancy from their employees' health and disability benefits. The court reasoned that since only women and not men could become pregnant, the employer was not denying a benefit to women that men had, but that in fact if the employer had provided female employees with coverage for pregnancy it would have provided them with a benefit unavailable to male employees! After widespread criticism, Congress passed the Pregnancy Discrimination Act of 1978 (PDA) which was intended to reverse the effects of the *Gilbert* decision. It required employers to give pregnant women *at least* the benefits already provided other workers—that is, that employers treat pregnancy as any other physical condition for purposes of fringe benefits.

Some states have passed laws expanding the rights of pregnant workers. A California law mandates employers to provide up to four months unpaid pregnancy disability leave, with the right to return to the same or similar job. Employers challenged this law in *California Federal Savings & Loan Association v. Guerra* (1987) and the Supreme Court held that the PDA does not prohibit different treatment of pregnancy so long as it increases employment opportunities for women and removes barriers to their employment.

In all these cases involving legislation that claims to be protective of women due to their reproductive capacities, the complementary questions of equal treatment will arise: Should not the same limitations on work hours be applied to male workers who also tire after a long day's work? Should not the pregnancy leave protections be extended to male workers with temporary disabilities?

This is America: Sexual Harassment as Discrimination

In 1991 President George Bush nominated a federal appeals court judge, Clarence Thomas, to fill the U.S. Supreme Court seat left vacant by the retirement of Justice Thurgood Marshall. Confirmation hearings were held by the Senate Judiciary Committee, which was prepared to refer the nominee to the entire Senate, when a news reporter revealed the FBI report, a confidential part of the Senate investigation, had evidence that Judge Thomas had sexually harassed a former employee, Anita Hill, a tenured law professor at the University of Oklahoma.

Faced with the dilemma of the public exposure of its failure to investigate the allegations in the FBI report, the Senate committee met privately to consider what to do. Most senators wanted the Thomas confirmation rushed to a vote the next day, believing that they had sufficient votes to confirm his appointment. At the same time, a group of congresswomen, led by Patricia Schroeder, chair of the Congressional Caucus for Women's Issues, and Barbara Boxer, Democrat of California, marched to the Senate meeting room to demand that the senators delay the confirmation vote until after a full inquiry into the allegations of sexual harassment.

For the next three days, hearings were held and nationally televised. The issue of sexual harassment in the workplace became a common topic of conversation around the country because of the willingness of Anita Hill to give voice to the nature and extent of her injury. Other women as well, both supporters and opponents of Judge Thomas's nomination, testified about their own experiences with sexual harassment. Generally, the Senate committee, composed entirely of wealthy white men, seemed confused, ignorant, patronizing, hostile, and generally incompetent to deal with the reality being put before them. The hearings called into question not only the character of Judge Thomas and the ineffectiveness of our representational system of government, but also the capacity of men to understand and to recognize the meaning of sexual harassment.

The Equal Employment Opportunity Commission (EEOC) guidelines, 2g CFR Sec. 1604.11 (1980), define sexual harassment as follows:

Harassment on the basis of sex is a violation of Sec. 703 of Title VII. Unwelcome sexual advances, requests for sexual favors, and other verbal or physical conduct of a sexual nature constitute sexual harassment when (1) submission to such conduct is made either explicitly or implicitly a term or condition of an individual's employment, (2) submission to or rejections of such conduct by an individual is used as the basis for employment decisions affecting such individual, or (3) such conduct has the purpose or effect of unreasonably interfering with an individual's work performance or creating an intimidating, hostile, or offensive working environment.

Thus sexual harassment can include unwelcome flirtations and graphic comments that make a woman uncomfortable and impede her work performance or interfere with her employment opportunities. In addition sexual harassment may include a hostile work environment with public display of offensive images of women, on-going sexist jokes, leering, intrusive personal questions, or any condition which causes a woman to feel humiliated on account of her sex.

It has been said that sexual harassment is the first offense ever defined and created by women (Littleton 1989). The EEOC guidelines and definitions reflect women's experience of sexual harassment; they were written from a women's point of view. They prohibit "unwelcome conduct" (the woman's perspective) regardless of what the accused may have "intended" (the male's perspective). Often when courts try to discern the meaning of conduct, they will use the standard of what "a reasonable man" would consider the meaning to be. More recently, courts are beginning to adopt a "reasonable woman" standard specifically for sexual harassment issues, recog-

nizing that women often feel victimized by statements that men claim are harmless.

The issue of sexual harassment reveals the tension between a woman worker's right to be a sexual being and her right to be free from the unwanted sexual language and conduct of males in the workplace. It was not until 1975 that the term came into use to describe the abusive conduct which had harmed women's employment opportunities throughout their working lives. Sexual harassment is a continual reminder to a woman that she is seen primarily sexually and only secondarily as a valuable employee. It is a way of letting women in the workplace know that they do not really belong. It imposes on women the secondary burden of having to handle their sexuality carefully on the job while men are required to carry no such additional burden of employment.

While it seems that sexual harassment is employment discrimination (in other words, that men harass women in the workplace *because* they are women, that is, because of the social meaning of female sexuality), it has only been very recently that the courts have *recognized* it as employment discrimination (Littleton 1989). In 1986 the Supreme Court held that sexual harassment creating a hostile work environment may be the basis of a lawsuit even where the plaintiff can show no negative employment consequences (that is, that the employee was not fired or demoted) (*Meritor Savings Bank v. Vinson* 1986). Sexual harassment claims may be brought against employers directly where the offending party is a supervisor. Claims may be brought against employers because of the behavior of co-workers and even customers, because the theory behind Title VII as a whole is that employers shall bear the responsibility for eliminating job discrimination.

Because litigation based on sexual harassment, while dating back some twenty years, has only recently been sanctioned by the Supreme Court, much of the development of legal standards for claims and defenses is being developed in the lower courts. Judges in the lower courts have some difficulty in drawing lines between what is proper and what is not proper conduct for men in the workplace. The attitude appears to be somewhat like the earlier attitudes towards judicial determinations in rape cases. Not so long ago it was a requirement in a rape case, for example, that the victim have a corroborating witness or the case could be dismissed. It was also standard practice for the jury in a rape case to be instructed by a judge that the law requires that they examine the testimony of the female person named in the information with caution. Through massive organizing efforts and consciousness-raising, these impediments to prosecution of rape cases have been eliminated.

The voice and vision of Anita Hill in the Clarence Thomas hearings have opened the eyes and ears of some men and women to the implications and meaning of sexual harassment to women. Still, more organizing and consciousness-raising will be necessary to educate and pressure the judiciary to see these offenses through the eyes of and in the voices of women.

Been Down So Long: The Arrival of a Feminist Jurisprudence

In light of women's relatively recent access to the legal profession, it is remarkable that a growing, energetic, and promising body of work is now being produced which may affect not only the future of women's rights but also the future of how we think about law entirely.

This is the field known as feminist jurisprudence. It has developed from a confluence of ideas generated in the second wave of feminism among radical feminists and critical legal studies scholars, among French feminists and other philosophers, and as interpreted largely by law professors, lawyers, theoreticians, and activists. It is some of the most creative and interesting legal thought to occur in American history.

What do we mean by feminist legal thinking? Recognizing that there is no one theory that unifies and explains all, there are some recognizable aspects described by Deborah Stone. First, feminist jurisprudence includes a commitment to deriving knowledge from experience, rather than just from abstract ideas, and to including the experiences of people who have been excluded historically from mainstream thinking (Stone 1989). This idea also includes the willingness to expose the privileged assumptions of dominant legal theories, including the historical benefits to white middle- and upper-class males from notions of legal liberalism and rampant individualism. The criminal courts, under pressure from victims' rights groups, have begun to take into consideration, for sentencing purposes, the statements by victims of the impact on them of the crime that was committed. The U.S. criminal justice system has focused most attention on the rights of the accused because of the specific protection of those rights set forth in the Constitution (for example, right to counsel, right to trial by jury, right to cross-examine accusers, and presumption of innocence). In many cases the victims of crimes are most notable in criminal cases by their absence. In the vast majority of everyday crimes, victims may not be notified of court dates, may be too traumatized to want to participate, may be penalized by employers for leaving work to come to court, or may just not be allowed to speak in criminal cases. This invisibility of the victim is beginning to be addressed, to ensure that victims as well as defendants receive fair treatment and are not made powerless or revictimized by the criminal justice system.

Second, feminist jurisprudence is a commitment to recognizing the relational existence of individuals and using that relatedness as the starting point of our analysis (Stone 1989). This idea assumes that our very essence and how we perceive and think are created in relation to others. Its opposite concept is the idea that the "individual adult is an autonomous entity whose autonomy in decisionmaking is the most fundamental value to be protected by the legal and political system" (Stone 1989, 2). An essential challenge of feminism is to preserve a commitment to the individual while recognizing the overwhelming power and importance of the collective in creating reality.

This is the point I was attempting to illustrate in describing part of my personal career track at the beginning of this essay. I attribute its progress not merely to my own choices, but more importantly, to the social facts and influences that interacted with my personal will. The law has recognized the importance of collective life in various standards and remedies it has devised—many of which are now under public attack. Equal opportunity and affirmative action, for example, are derived from a theoretical recognition that from society's point of view few individuals can advance either quickly enough or at all where there have existed historical barriers to their advancement because they are white women or people of color. Thus, the law recognizes that a socially constructed problem requires a socially constructed solution. In the commercial

arena, the law has always recognized how certain historical realities must be addressed by socially constructed remedies. For example, during the late 1800s in the period of American industrial expansion and labor abuses, the Supreme Court determined that a corporation was a "person" within the meaning of the Constitution and this was entitled to certain constitutional protections of due process (Hoff 1991). The rationale for this decision included the recognition that as industry expands, it needs entities apart from the owners of the business that can shield the owner's enormous resources from suits against the business. Otherwise, the courts reasoned, capitalists would be unwilling to risk their fortunes by investing in new businesses and thus the economy would collapse because it could no longer expand. Similarly, the law recognized insurance as a means of socially distributing the expense of personal and property losses within society, when in fact the distribution does not include certain kinds of protection for those unable to afford any insurance.

Finally, feminist jurisprudence makes a commitment to interaction rather than hierarchy as a mode of social control. This includes making and enforcing laws that allow for new ways of seeing, of knowing, or of being open to new information (Stone 1989). Revealing previously suppressed points of view and exposing the effects of gender, race, and class are considered part of the growing methodology of feminist legal thinking.

An example of this kind of commitment to allowing new ways of looking at old problems and exposing the effects of gender is in making public women's private lives. One of the central themes of feminist jurisprudence is the analysis of how power in our society is distributed between men and women and how free women are, or are not, to have power over themselves. Historically the roots of United States law were in republican soil, planted by men who followed the philosophies of Locke, Rousseau, and other leaders of the Enlightenment, including the sacred "founding fathers," the drafters of the Declaration of Independence, the American heroes whose lives were filled with moral and logical contradictions. For example, Thomas Jefferson was a slave owner yet wrote that "all men are created equal," an obvious hypocrisy. Another hypocrisy among revolutionary republican ideas was that private virtue was expected of women but not of men. Originally, the theories of the Enlightenment included the undivided notion that it was virtuous to subordinate one's own self-interest to the common good. This idea included a kind of private morality combined with public service. Yet in colonial times virtue was redefined by assigning the role of public service to men and the role of private service to women (Hoff 1991). In post-revolutionary America, as men focused on the accumulation of personal wealth, women were abandoned by men to be confined as bearers of personal morality and to the tasks of rearing and of educating future generations to civic responsibility.

This separation between the personal and the political is at the heart of feminist criticism. The law created the idea of a private sphere (a man's home) as a zone of noninterference by the law. Yet it is in this very sphere that women have lived expressly without the protections of the law. Women have arguably both benefitted and been oppressed by this division. For example, in colonial days, the law would not interfere with a man's right to beat his wife so long as the rod was no thicker than his thumb. (This is the sexist origin of the term "the rule of thumb").

Thus women could seek no legal redress through the criminal courts for daily physical abuse because what a man did in his own home was not the community's business. On the other hand, two hundred years later, it was the creation by the courts of a constitutional right of privacy which prohibited states from enacting laws that would forbid the sale of contraceptives. That right was later extended to include a woman's constitutional right to choose to have an abortion under court-defined circumstances (*Roe v. Wade* 1973).

Some agree that divorce reform in many ways is the most radical and productive reform occurring for women in society today because it strikes at the heart of women's subordination in both the public and private spheres. When divorce is seen as a process of redistributing the power within the marital relationship (both custodial power over children and control over income and assets), it becomes clearer that men and women are silently at war and each divorce on some level is a battle that may be negotiated or fought. A groundbreaking, though controversial, work by Lenore Weitzman has demonstrated a new way of looking at divorce—from a women's point of view. In summary, her work shows how women, as a class, are financially devastated by divorce settlements and court decisions—even when these may appear to be fair on a case-by-case analysis. Her conclusions are that within one year of divorce the average ex-wife's standard of living has decreased 73 percent while the average ex-husband's has increased 42 percent (Weitzman 1988). In addition, the divorce courts are hearing testimony from women who are speaking courageously of abuse, rape, and various forms of deprivation they may have suffered during the marriage, as well as speaking about what may have been suffered by their children. It is no wonder, then, that feminist divorce attorneys report that often their clients' husbands have urged them not to seek independent legal advice, suggesting, for example, that they do their own divorce or share the same lawyer to save money (which may prevent the wife from discovering her true legal rights). Some husbands continue throughout the divorce process to try to disempower their wives by emotional manipulation and ongoing sabotage of their self-esteem. One of the effects of women entering the profession has been to voice the suppressed oppression, rights, and needs of women and their children.

What do we have to look forward to in feminist legal theory? Whereas masculinist jurisprudence claims neutrality and universality, feminist jurisprudence claims a voice for the silenced, mislabeled women whose life experiences have been lived through all of the male-referenced definitions: victims, mothers, wives, daughters, employees. As Deborah Stone puts it, "If there is anything defining about feminism, it is the empirical commitment to studying gender per se and to empowering women so that gender will no longer matter for the distribution of important privileges, opportunities, resources, and burdens" (Stone 1989, 3). Furthermore, it may be that women essentially have a relational approach to morality, as Carol Gilligan suggests, and that this sense of justice is based on a valuing of life as a web of interdependence and connection—rather than as single threads of autonomy and separation and alienation (Gilligan 1982). This perspective of interdependence may prove to be the most necessary element in the human psyche today, and the human spirit, for the survival of the environment, the political world, and the human race, not to mention the very world we all inhabit.

References

American Federation of State, County, and Municipal Employees (AFSCME) v. State of Washington, 578 F. Supp. 846 (W.D. Wash. 1983, 770 F. 2d. 1401 (9th Cir. 1985).

Boller, Paul F., and Ronald Story. 1987. A more perfect union: Documents in U.S. history. Vol. 1. Boston: Houghton Mifflin.

Bradwell v. Illinois, 83 U.S. 130 (1873).

California Savings and Loan Association v. Guerra, 1Q7 S. Ct. 683, 93 L.Ed. 2d 613 (1987).

Colorado Women's Bar Association. October 1991. The Advocate 13:2 quoting statistics from the second annual Colorado Minority Women Lawyers' Conference.

County of Washington v. Gunther, 452 U.S. 161, 101 S. Ct. 2242, 68 L. Ed. 2d 751 (1981).

General Electric v. Gilbert, 429 U.S. 125 (1976).

Gilligan, Carol. 1982. In a different voice. Cambridge, Mass.: Harvard University Press.

Griggs v. Duke Power Company, 401 U.S. 424 (1971).

Griswold v. Connecticut, 381 U.S. 479 (1965).

Hoff, Joan. 1991. Law, gender, and injustice. New York: New York University Press.

Lefcourt, Carol, ed. 1990. Women and the law. New York: Clark Boardman Co., Ltd.

Littleton, Christine. 1989. Feminist jurisprudence: The difference method makes. Stanford Law Review 41:751.

Meritor Savings Bank v. Vinson, 477 U.S. 57 (1986).

Minor v. Happersett, 88 U.S. 162 (1875).

Morello, Karen Berger. 1986. *The invisible bar: The woman lawyer in America, 1638 to the present.* Boston: Beacon Press.

Muller v. Oregon, 208 U.S. 412 (1908).

Phillips v. Martin Marietta Corporation, 400 U.S. 542 (1971).

Roe v. Wade, 410 U.S. 113 (1973).

Slaughterhouse cases, 16 Wall 36 (1873).

Stone, Deborah. 1989. Feminism, law, and social policy. Syllabus obtained from Feminist Curricular Resources Clearinghouse.

Weitzman, Lenore J. 1988. Women and children last: The social and economic consequences of divorce law reforms. In Sanford M. Dornbusch and Myrah Strober, eds. *Feminism, children, and the new families.* New York: Guilford Press.

Midnight Train to US

Ann C. Scales

You're catching me at a funny, introspective time, between projects, so to speak. Just last week I signed off, as they say in the law review biz, on a manuscript entitled *Militarism, Male Dominance, and Law: Feminist Jurisprudence as Oxymoron?*[1] It was about how law and militarism are intimately related, how militarism and male dominance are intimately related, and how feminism is inconsistent with all of them. The legal work and the analysis and the making of my argument are done. What you're hearing today is the residue in my brain, the *swimmy* thoughts I've been left with, a commentary on participating in the enterprise of feminist legal theory. I want to speak today from the heart, as Nixon used to say. I want to talk about the possibility of being happy as a lawyer. The pathology I describe is my own. But because I suspect that law school is the domain of the self-hater, maybe there is something here you can use.

I was impatient for the world to change, as I was forged in the sixties. It was an ambivalent time to choose to become a lawyer. Vietnam changed the way we think about law and undermined any residual faith in the constitutional *qua* constitution. It exposed the *Realpolitik* of our structure of government: the executive branch runs everything; the Congress manages public opinion by farting away its energy; the judiciary primarily sits back and says, "Hey, this is all legitimate, this is what makes the U.S.A. great." Those of us who made the choice to become lawyers then had to have known we were devoting our lives to a largely cynical enterprise, but I thought I was ready for it.[2]

Politically, the lesson of law school was this: government is important, law is important, you therefore have a really important job. The hierarchy, harshness, and slow movement of the law are all *necessary and fair*. So go to it, and accept the big bucks as just compensation for the frustration you will encounter.

I was in a serious downward spiral, ending up on Wall Street. I've indulged for years in the standard rationalizations about that. Some of them may have some validity in some cases. But while I still have your attention, let me take the opportunity to urge you not to go to work for a big firm. There are three reasons not to, as listed by the wise and, I think, happy lawyer Anne Simon:[3] (1) you get used to the money; (2) you're helping

Scales, Ann C. 1990. Excerpts from "Midnight Train to US." *Cornell Law Review* 75(3): 710–726. © Copyright 1990 by Cornell Univeristy. All rights rserved. Reprinted by permission of the author and publisher.

1. Ann C. Scales, *Militarism, Male Dominance, and Law: Feminists Jurisprudence as Oxymoron?* 12 Harv. Women's L.J. 25 (1989).

2. Coming from the sixties, I have recently realized, had a personally disabling effect on me. One of the lessons of the sixties for teenagers, from the slaughter of Vietnam to the killing of Bobby Kennedy, was "only the good die young." The negative implication of this lesson was if you didn't die, you were not good, or tender-hearted, or really idealistic, or committed, or at least not sufficiently so. The best you could hope for was to make the world safe for the good.

3. I am grateful to Anne Simon for talking about this with my Feminist Legal Theory class at Boston College Law School in the Fall of 1988. The text here is an application and elaboration of her insight.

them; (3) you learn bad habits. I wasn't around big firm practice long enough to get used to the money. But I did help them. I was part of the crackerjack kamikaze associate troops who got the Ford Motor Company out of a real scrape in the Pinto cases. I can't say I'm proud of that.

And I learned lots of bad habits. I learned how to do things the most expensive way possible. As an associate, pursuing to death a little piece of someone else's case, I learned very little about very little. I learned that legal judgments are the end of the matter, the end of the relationship with clients and their aspirations. I learned that lawyers are free to walk away from someone else's time and money, badly invested. And I learned that it has to be that way—that practicing law is necessarily an expensive and exhaustive accumulation of details and delays, which may or may not get anywhere or mean anything.[4] I've worked hard to unlearn my big firm bad habits and to recover from the experience. I would say I'm very lucky, but my witch friends say to give myself and the goddess a little credit. My spirit survived.

Teaching more or less happened to me. It was incredibly good news for me that contemporary feminists jurisprudence also happened. I fell into a new field, into its construction from the ground up. It is wildly exciting to be able to have this community, to know these distinguished women, to participate in something that at least seems to be living. The bad news is that, as a law teacher, I am still helping them. I'm a good teacher. I can clearly and efficiently train people to do lawyerly evil clearly and efficiently. And even when my students avoid those pitfalls, I wonder how many fine young minds am I helping to send off to be wasted as lawyers.

When we do act, our political actions must be trivialized by external means. I gave some examples of this last night.[5] It *always* happens to women, and it always happens to all people who speak out against war: they, after all, stand in the shoes of women. To call conscientious objectors effeminate is the best way to silence them and minimize their

---

4. Contrary to some feminists criticisms of law and legal education, I don't think that law school taught me to be a cut-throat adversarial person. Law school may do that to some people, but I think I already *was* that way. I was impatient for the world to change, and prepared to *force them to be free*. Law is, after all, about social policy backed by force. Insofar as there is a meaningful division between nonviolent activism and armed struggle, I suspect lawyers like me tend more toward the armed struggle camp. We are soldiers of a sort, only very inefficient ones.

5. The first example is the case that led to the development of the problematic "battered women's syndrome" defense. In State v. Wanrow, 88 Wash. 2d 221, 559 P.2d 548 (1977), a woman killed a man who had threatened some children and molested one of them. The Washington Supreme Court reversed her murder conviction on the ground, *inter alia*, that the equal protection clause requires that the jury be allowed to consider her subjective impressions of the situation, and her unequal physical strength. *Id.* at 558–59. This can be seen as subjectivization and trivialization of women's perception of oppression,because "[t]he Wanrow court did not take the next step; to consider whether the objective self-defense standard embodies a male standpoint." Catharine MacKinnon, *Toward Feminist Jurisprudence*, 34 Stan. L. Rev. 703, 725 n.96 (1982) (emphasis deleted).

The Washington court clarified its view of women in a later case. A woman was not allowed even to try to prove sexual abuse by her father on the ground that the harm was too subjective, therefore unverifiable, despite expert psychiatric testimony. Tyson v. Tyson, 107 Wash. 2d 72, 727 P.2d 226 (1986) (refusal to apply "discovery rule" to toll statute of limitations).

The last example is Greenham Women Against Cruise Missiles v. Reagan, 591 F. Supp. 1332 (S.D.N.Y. 1984), *aff'd*, 755 F2d 34 (2d Cir. 1985). When the Greenham women came to this country to demonstrate the illegality of the deployment of Cruise missiles in England, they were thrown out of court pursuant to the political question doctrine. United States Attorney Rudolph Giuliani argued that they had vastly oversimplified defense matters (girls are dumb), and that their real problem was that they didn't know how to cope in a necessarily dangerous world (girls are fluffy).

numbers. The same thing happens with civil disobedience prosecutions. The Thoreauian formula says civilly disobedient citizens have to suffer the punishment. It means that they must pay for divergent subjectivity; it means they weren't objective, they were silly and arrogant and wrong.

We can't cave in to that. I love the Greenham women because, though working with two strikes against their credibility (as women and as peace activists), they never caved in to *anything*. They wouldn't obey court orders to leave, they forced arresting police to talk about what their wives thought of them, they refused to pay fines, they put the police and judges and the military on trial in the courtroom, they sang and chanted through their own trials, they subverted the other jail inmates, they broke into the jails and danced on *those* roofs, and upon release they were all right back out there.

It was surely an important lesson for me, to be forced to see the narrowness of my lawyerly view of the world. But there came to be a downside to that lesson. I began to wonder, does it always have to be that hard to be part of history? The peace-activist women I met seemed to me to be so serious, so single-minded, so intent upon a consistent feminist politics and process. And I didn't think they approved of me. I hadn't lived in the mud for eight years, and, being a lawyer, I was pretty clearly from the other side, an emissary from the belly of the beast. In working on that project since 1987, I sometimes felt like a plaintiff's malpractice lawyer at a convention of the College of Obstetricians and Gynecologists. I felt that I had to work harder at it, so I did. I was living and breathing nuclear war, and its connections to absolutely everything. I found myself thoroughly redefining "fun." I questioned all of my judgments. I couldn't listen to Gladys Knight sing "Midnight Train to Georgia," because it was sentimental and politically incorrect for *her to rather live in his world than be without him in hers.*[6] I seriously considered giving up teaching and law and becoming a peace pilgrim.

Achieving this healthy relationship among self, others, and world is a very tough mission. There is strife in personal relationships. As Adrienne Rich says, two people together is a miracle[7] There are immense difficulties that arise among people of different cultures. In my state of New Mexico, the coexistence of Indian and Hispanic and Anglo peoples is a miracle. The authorities tell us that there is inevitable conflict among different sovereigns. That the world still exists is, indeed, a miracle.

Feminist theory discloses a particularly poignant struggle with the tension between individual and community. I have found it to be best explained in Robin West's wonderful article, *Jurisprudence and Gender.*[8] The "official" story about women's lives is that told by "cultural feminists": for women, connection is existential and morally *prior* to individual autonomy. The official harm women face, therefore, is the harm of separation. The downside, or unofficial version, of this is that told by radical feminists: women's connectedness is the source of women's oppression. Intimacy becomes intrusion. The unofficial harm women face, therefore, is the threat of the dissolution of our individual boundaries. In Robin's words, we "secretly wish that everyone would get the hell out of our lives so that we could pursue our own projects."[9] This desire is not for mere solitude

---

6. Jim Weatherly, *Midnight Train to Georgia,* © Eric Records 1971.

7. Adrienne Rich, *Love Poem No. XVIII,* in The Dream of a Common Language 34 (1978).

8. Robin West, *Jurisprudence and Gender,* 55 U. Chi. L. Rev. 1 (1988).

9. *Id.* at 36.

or individual achievement. Rather it is the residue of a long history of women's invisibility. I don't fear that my selfness will be silenced; rather that I will never have a self. I fear that I can never heal from my internalized non-personhood.[10]

As an example of this struggle, consider the fortunes within the feminist community of Carol Gilligan's book, *In a Different Voice*.[11] You will recall that Gilligan's book described her findings that little boys tended to address moral problems in a hierarchical, rights-based, formalistic way. Little girls tended to address the same problems in a contextualized, relationship preserving, equitable way. When this book was published in 1982, we fell over ourselves to embrace it. Very soon after that wave of acceptance, there was an equally large wave of suspicion, some outright rejection.[12]

But in spite of this critical storm, Gilligan's work has shown amazing staying power. It just hit too close to home. As Robin West says, "I don't know of any woman who hasn't recognized herself somewhere in this book."[13] So the task is to use Gilligan's insights without being demoralized by criticisms. Yes, it is dangerous to institutionalize a "women's point of view," without due diligence to thwart those who would exploit these findings. Yes, it is cultural imperialism to discuss a women's point of view without regard to race and class. Yes, it is possible that the nurturing, relationship-boundedness that women express is a result of violent inculturation into the system of dominance and submission. And, yes, women have learned to use nurturing as a means of manipulation. But that doesn't make the values expressed by women in Gilligan's book bad or unimportant or unnecessary to the survival of the planet. It just makes them heretofore unchosen. We need to choose them now. As Robin West—she certainly no fluffy

---

10. West distinguishes this from a more familiar, masculine version of the tension between individual and community expressed in the legal system. From the male point of view, the official value of law, represented by traditional legal liberalism, is autonomy. The official harm threatened by existence in society is annihilation of the self. What West calls the "unofficial story" is that told by critical legal studies. The individual values autonomy, but has a perpetual longing for connectedness. The harm he fears is alienation, loneliness, and isolation. *Id.* at 7–12.

The stories for men and for women are not just mirror images of each other. The subjectivity craved by spokesmen for the unofficial male story is not the same subjectivity depicted by cultural feminists. They value intimacy because it helps them overcome their separateness—intimacy is hard for them. For us it is "ridiculously easy." Likewise, liberals fear annihilation from without. Women's is a fear of annihilation from within; a fear of having my emerging self overcome, not ended. *Id.* at 40–41.

11. Carol Gilligan, *In a Different Voice*. (1982).

12. The criticisms were of different types. Feminists in the social science community criticized Gilligan's methodology, though in fairness to her, she admitted the limitations of her small samples and disclaimed any intention to make any generalizations. Some liberal feminists thought her work gave away our hard-fought gains in the area of equality. I argued that the book was dangerous because it *was* so popular, and its findings so easily generalized and co-opted. I see this in various law school curricula: a few pages of *In a Different Voice* get assigned sometime in the first year, usually as a way of opening the subject of alternative dispute resolution. So we leap to suggest that somehow women's voices can be incorporated into a thoroughly incompatible male scheme, without fully discussing the pathology of that scheme. So Gilligan's observations get lost. As Gilligan observed, when little Jake and little Amy speak at the same time, Amy's voice gets drowned out.

Other radical feminists argued that the ethic of care described by Gilligan tended to reify women's powerlessness, to glorify women's lack of self-esteem in the moral realm the same way that we have been taught to eroticize submission in the sexual realm. Or as MacKinnon put it with characteristic pithiness, we're not talking about a brave new world in a different voice, we're talking about the same old oppression in a higher register. *See* Ellen C. DuBois, Mary C. Dunlap, Carol J. Gilligan, Catharine A. MacKinnon, Carrie J. Menkel-Meadow, *Feminist Discourse, Moral Values, and the Law—A Conversation*, 34 Buffalo L. Rev. 11, 25 (1985).

13. West, *supra* note 19, at 20.

sentimentalist—says, "I can't imagine any project more crucial, right now, to the survival of this species than the clear articulation of the importance of love to a well-led public life. . . . [14]

The development of a feminist political theory must be very high on our agenda. There are so many important questions here: whether we believe in the very idea of a state;[15] whether we must have a theory of human nature; how to deal with the actual inequality in distribution of resources; what a feminist understanding of community is; whether there should be rules at all; how rules should work; whether feminist processes we use among ourselves can serve in international relations; and whether sovereignty is a concept that makes sense anymore. We need to get to these questions, but in the meantime we have to deal with the state as constituted in other than a schizophrenic way.

I don't think this has to be so hard. I think we make it hard by internalizing the logic of the fathers that says we have to be consistent in their linear terms, and that we have to believe in the state in order to use it. To throw an all or nothing choice at us is to say we can't tell the difference between oppression and liberation. We can. We can resist the pressure to idealize the state, and rights, and law. The issue is knowing the difference in a particular case. The issue is knowing that we can *trust ourselves* to do that.[16]

This corresponds to what I would say is the third option in our relationship to law and the state. It is based on the process of recovering from an addiction. It is a matter of critical disengagement that allows for careful attending to the important things that are going on, with our abilities and sanity intact. You are probably tired of hearing about addiction.[17] Indulge the addiction model one more time, for I think it does help to explain how we become undermined, ineffectual, and unhappy.

---

14. *Id.* at 65. I am not suggesting that we have to choose the values of connectedness and caring and survival over our individual freedom or well-being or moral agency. To posit that either set of values must be relinquished in favor of the other is simply to buy right back into the same destructive dichotomy between self and world.

15. The state as constituted and understood just doesn't have very much to do with us. As Robin West points out, the creation of a state is a very male response to a male idea of the state of nature. In that male state of nature, all people, meaning all men, are created equally. They thereby have equal separate personhood, and equal physical force with which to protect that personhood. Implicit in this realm is the threat of mutual assured destruction, should they have to resort to physical force to protect their space. The response to that vulnerability is the creation of a state that required respect for that equal freedom and potential force. As West points out, if it makes any sense to postulate a state of nature at all, females would not likely presume equality. We're not equal in physical strength of the kind assumed by the male model, and our experience of life is of unequal vulnerabilities and strengths. If our response to this natural inequality were to create a superstructure, it would by definition not be neutral or abstract. West, *supra* note 19, at 63.

16. People of color have articulated this in their critique of the critique of rights. Beginning with the centrality to liberalism of "rights," critical legal theory portrayed rights as powerful tools of legitimation for an unprincipled capitalist regime. Rights, in that critique, are otherwise indeterminate and meaningless. I understand part of the "minority critique of the critique of rights" this way: hey, don't talk to us about how rights are worthless when you've never needed any. Reliance on rights (hence, on the state) has been a powerful focal point of the civil rights struggle. We know rights can be used to oppress; but they can also be used to liberate. To say that it has to be one or the other is to say to us that we can't tell the difference. *See, e.g.,* Kimberlé W. Crenshaw, *Race, Reform, and Retrenchment: Transformation and Legitimation in Anti-Discrimination Law,* 101 Harv. L. Rev. 1331 (1988); Patricia S. Williams, *Alchemical Notes: Reconstructing Ideals from Deconstructed Rights,* 22 Harv. C. R.–C. L. L. Rev. 401 (1987).

17. I understand there are now over 2000 twelve-step meetings per week in Los Angeles alone, and I have heard the criticism that twelve-stepping is just another trendy, quasi-religious self-improvement hoax. I don't know whether the program has really become trendy. I do know that, for substance abusers a step away from dying, it works. I also know that it has nothing to do with religion, and teaches that there are no prepackaged easy answers.

Anne Wilson Schaef, sort of the Grace Slick of the co-dependence movement, has written a book entitled *When Society Becomes an Addict*.[18] Her thesis is that the violent, lying, cheating state of the world and the widespread malaise among the citizenry constitutes an addictive system. She defines addiction as anything in our lives over which we are powerless. Now power is the most addictive thing ever invented. The government, business, and other agents of "civilization as we know it" are very strung out on power. These entities can't get around to doing anything they might usefully do because they are too busy consolidating their own power. Ordinary people are co-dependent with respect to the power addiction of government, where co-dependence is defined as an addiction to another entity and its problems. We feel, and largely are, powerless with respect to the big guys' power addiction. So we tolerate it, and cover for it, and live as if it weren't there. In the parlance, we enable it.

The manifestations of addictive behavior on both sides are dishonesty, denial, self-centeredness, the need for control, and crisis orientation. Let's just consider these briefly to illustrate.

Dishonesty: It is everywhere—it's our way of life. The prominence of "spin-doctors" in the presidential campaign leaps to mind. My favorite example comes from corporate America. Pepperidge Farm Cookies, itself owned by Campbell's—the world's largest soup company—has opened a product line called the "American Collection." You can get Nantucket Cookies and Santa Fe Cookies and so on. The package of each of these states that Pepperidge Farm has made "classically American cookies," and "that meant making each cookie one of a kind, with an individual personality all its own. So [we] gave them rugged, irregular shapes, just as if someone had lovingly shaped each cookie by hand."[19] Dig it. No one made them by hand. Pepperidge Farm spent millions of dollars earned from us to design and build a machine that can regularly make the cookies irregular. It's a hoax. And they are bragging about it. And we are eating cookies and loving it. And "classically American"? You bet. Multi-layered lies are as American as homemade cookies.

Denial: Denial is the engine of nuclearization. Consider the concept of "limited nuclear war" (or, as defense strategists call it, "sub-holocaust engagement"). Consider nuclear weapons production. From Hanford to the Savannah River to Rocky Flats, the truth is that we have been poisoning ourselves for national security. And the defense industry is admitting and denying in the same breath. "Ethics in Government" stuff is about denial. Why was it even imagined that John Tower could be Secretary of Defense? Not because of alcoholism or "womanizing," but because of his intimacy with defense contractors. And we, the people, in the name of "realism," enable this, allow the government to get away with it.

Self-Centeredness: Everything that happens in the world is either for or against the United States, from the Persian Gulf to Nicaragua. When tragedy strikes, the sole focus for the evening news is how many "American lives" were lost. During Grand Slam tennis tournaments, the commentators obsess about how many Americans are left to compete. (Notice how Martina Navratilova almost never fits this bill. But that's another sad story.)

---

18. Anne Wilson Schaef, *When Society Becomes an Addict* (1987).

19. This example is discussed in Joel Achenbach, *Creeping Surrealism: Does Anybody Really Know What's Real Anymore?* reprinted in Utne Reader Nov.–Dec. 1988, at 112.

The need for control: This is the meaning of contemporary life, and we call it INS, IRS, State Department, abortion, sexual preference. The legal expression for the pathological need to control, and the "justification" we co-dependents enable, is "the slippery slope." If I'm allowed to make love with a consenting adult woman, anything goes, and incest has to be accepted. As if it weren't already. If pornography is recognized as a violation of civil rights, then instant total censorship will kick in and *Bingo*—it's a police state. And on and on.

Crisis orientation: In the lives of addicts, to portray whatever happens as a crisis is to give the illusion of being alive. In the life of a government, to portray the president's cold as newsworthy, to make events out of non-events is an argument that the government is doing something, and diverts attention from what the government is really doing or allowing.[20]

If you accept or will entertain the addiction model, the next process is recovery. And the first step to recovery is detachment. Recovery requires radical detachment in the case of chemical dependencies, but a more complex kind of detachment in the cases of other addictions. That is to say, when it comes to lots of what are called co-dependent systems, we don't reject the addictive thing. Food addicts can't give up food, sex addicts don't give up sex, law/state addicts shouldn't give them up either. Instead, we have to detach in a way that is radically *re-evaluative* of the relationship between ourselves and the addictive thing, person, or process.

Such a detachment allows us to recognize our role as lawyers. The law is not wonderful, does not itself make a better world. Mainly, the law oppresses people. What we do as lawyers is stand between the law and the people it is hurting. We arrange *breathing room* for people who are being smothered. Once in a while, we assist those engaged in other political activities; we keep the law off their backs so they can make a better world. This is the rub in the abortion battles.[21] The authors of the brief are argle-bargling about how to portray the right to privacy as constitutionally sound. I say, fine, guys, if it works. But the issue in this case is not constitutional integrity. The issue is women's survival. Calling abortion illegal doesn't stop abortions. But that's exactly what the Supreme Court can't understand: that what they say makes no difference in what people will do. The law can't decide what practices there will be. The law can only make it easier or harder, can either provide a little breathing room or tie plastic bags around women's heads.

Compare what I said earlier about walking away from clients and their bad investments when the decision comes down. The law of the fathers *wants* us to think that what it has to say is the end of the matter. But it is only one stage of the real proceedings, often only the beginning. A different kind of lawyering must be a matter of four principles: (1) *don't do work you hate,* in law school or in practice;[22] (2) don't represent clients who are doing bad things; (3) try to engage in a critical and constructive relationship

---

20. The war on drugs is the best example of this. Lump together all illegal drugs, whether life-threatening or not, ignore the most pervasive killers, tobacco and alcohol, turn it into a full time crusade for individual will power, and don't worry about homelessness and poverty and the deficit and nuclear war.

21. *See, e.g.,* Webster v. Reproductive Health Servs., 109 S. Ct. 3040 (1989).

22. Mari Matsuda said this at a conference at Harvard in 1987. It has stuck with me.

with your clients and their cause, their aspirations, their vision; (4) take every lawyering job as an opportunity to be in a critical relationship *with yourself*, and to *learn something*.[23]

When you have clients with whom you can do that it is a wonderful experience. It is powerful medicine for solipisim or for any feelings of lonesomeness or ineffectuality. It is as close as people ordinarily come to the dream of actually sharing or exchanging experience, being karmically connected. And it will represent a major therapeutic reconstruction of law.

When I use words like "faith" and "miracle," I'm not advocating passivity. I advocate active surrender, and it is only an apparent paradox. Just as alcoholics must first admit powerlessness in order to achieve some agency in their lives, we must detach from law in order to achieve peace with ourselves and clarity in our projects. There is a mystery in it, something difficult to explain or even understand. And that is something central to the revolutionary method of feminism. MacKinnon put it this way:

> Feminism affirms women's point of view by revealing, criticizing, and explaining its impossibility. This is not a dialectical paradox. It is a methodological expression of women's situation, in which the struggle for consciousness is a struggle for world; for a sexuality, a history, a culture, a community, a form of power, *an experience of the sacred*.[24]

Nor do I advocate religion. We mustn't confuse spirituality with religion. To do so, I think, is a peculiar disease of white people (as Grace Paley calls us, especially appropriate here, people of colorlessness[25]). Rather, I am responding to another false dichotomy, that between rationality and irrationality. It's a split we see even among feminists— between "cultural feminists" and some other kind of feminists, I suppose the rational, political kind. It is false, because to say that only so-called rational knowledge counts is not to make the so-called irrational go away, it is only to devalue it. That is exactly what patriarchy has done to women's traditional ways. And the feminist critique of patriarchy adds up, I believe, to an allegation that what counts as "rational" knowledge is simply male subjectivity, hence male belief, hence male faith—elevated to the status of objective reality.

How can we possibly account for the pervasiveness and staying power of patriarchy except by seeing the ideological significance of ritual?[26] Ritual is patterned action—the way culture enacts and confirms its values. Look at the available rituals, how pervasive, and how *incredibly effective*. Look at the rituals of sex-role differentiation, wherein, for women, the values enacted and confirmed are that we are fodder for the cannon, here to be consumed ultimately irrelevant to history. Look at the rituals of education. These, it must be said, become high church in law school: the importance of authority, our own

---

23. This is another wise comment from Anne Simon, in her talk to my Feminist Legal Theory seminar.

24. MacKinnon, *supra* note 28, at 637 (emphasis added).

25. Grace Paley, quoted in personal conversation between me and Gwyn Kirk.

26. For example, in 1984, the Department of Energy considered an amazing proposal to deal with high-level nuclear waste, which has a minimum half-life of 10,000 years. The idea was to train and lay the groundwork for perpetuation of what the Department of Energy called "an atomic priesthood"—persons who by myth and parable and instilling faith could get across the necessity of staying away from dump sites, and who could still do the job—due to the power of ritual—even if languages disappear and other social structures become extinct, even if the world as we know it comes to an end. *The Albuquerque Tribune*, Nov. 12, 1984, at A–7, col. 1.

inadequacy, the competition for grades, law review, jobs in the "good firms." (What makes them good firms? Do they do any good?) Look at the empty and expensive rituals of electoral politics.

Now, ritual went wrong somewhere in here. The values enacted and consolidated by patriarchal ritual are that the self and others are to be feared, the self and the universe must be rigidly controlled, and value is given only in exchange for obedience where we are isolated in silence.[27] But ritual doesn't have to be that way. Ritual can be an opening to the great forces in life. Greenham is an ongoing ritual,[28] enacting and affirming an unmediated experience. We need to reclaim ritual—to create ritual. There has to be a way for us to say to ourselves and our students and our clients, it is okay for us to be alive, we belong here, this land *is* our land, regardless of the allegations of the government or the corporations or the military. Here we are today, talking about all the things we are talking about: sharing hope, passion, communion, a new kind of ritual. It's a miracle.

Given the world as it is, how is it possible that we can even get out of bed every morning? If you're a corporate CEO or a Congressman or a law professor, it can be titles, money, power over others, false glory. For the rest of us it is faith and other inexplicable phenomena: spirit, eros, immanence, being here now, laughter, enchantment, pleasure, believing that there can be healing. It is an Experience of Love, and an Experience of Grace.

---

27. Starhawk, *Truth or Dare: Encounters with Power, Authority, and Mystery* 66 (1987).
28. *Id.* at 149.

Toward a Feminist Jurisprudence and History

Joan Hoff

Although radical feminists tended to dominate both theoretical and organizational concepts of the Second Women's movement in its early years, from roughly 1967 to 1972, they were overshadowed by assimilationist feminists during the 1970s and could not often be distinguished from the pluralist feminists in the 1980s and at the beginning of the 1990s. Only recently have they once again emerged as a major voice of U.S. feminism. One of these radical feminist attorneys has urged a legal standard "that would ask simply whether laws challenged as sex-discriminatory empower women and enable them to participate as full members of the society."[1]

Thus, the revolution in the legal status of women in the United States remains not only unfinished and bourgeois but also one that is stalemated at the moment—with assimilationists and pluralists talking past one another, for the most part, and the Mugwumps talking only to one another. Although a number of Critical Legal Studies and radical feminist lawyers have talked about breaking this current political and legal stalemate by constructing a model for feminist jurisprudence, only a few of them have proceeded very far theoretically. The formulation I find most plausible has been offered by Robin West. However, Catharine MacKinnon and Rhonda Copelon have also contributed to my thinking on this topic. MacKinnon, for example, has for a number of years been the leading spokesperson for the brand of radical legal feminism that most separates itself from liberal and Marxist legalism. She insists that in the "zero-sum" game that the adversarial system of justice in the United States represents, women always lose because they are the ultimate victims of male legitimization of power and sexuality because the law functions to rationalize only the liberal or Marxist versions of reality as constructed by men. Somehow, and MacKinnon never quite makes this clear, women must begin to come together and assert their critical consciousness by analyzing their own privatization and substituting experience in the face of the ahistorical and false reality that characterizes the current legal system. To engage in the "practice of politics of all women in the face of its theoretical impossibility" seems to pose an almost hopeless agenda. Yet MacKinnon insists that words like *hope* and *despair* are outside of her analysis because she seems to think that reorientation of theory alone will begin to ameliorate the

Hoff, Joan. 1991. "Toward a feminist jurisprudence and history." In *Law, Gender and Injustice: A legal history of U.S. women.* New York University Press. Reprinted by permission of the publisher.

1. Sylvia A. Law, "Rethinking Sex and the Constitution," *University of Pennsylvania Law Review* 132 (1984): 968 (paraphrasing MacKinnon); Robin L. West, "Jurisprudence and Gender," *University of Chicago Law Review* 55, no. 1 (Winter 1988); 37.

powerlessness of women in contemporary society. And, indeed, her 1979 theoretical work on the sexual harassment of women has had practical, legal results in the courts.[2]

Rhonda Copelon, on the other hand, deals more optimistically and specifically with constitutional ideas about equality and suggests specific legal strategies for exposing historical and legal fictions that have blamed the victims of patriarchal political economies, rather than demystifying and transforming those systems through what she calls "constitutionalization." Much of her argument for the liberation of women is for them to refuse any longer to subscribe to the separation between the public and private spheres of human existence in order to begin to bring about this new constitutionalism. She argues, for example, that the much-touted "right of privacy" as currently interpreted by the courts, especially in the struggle for abortion rights, does not represent women's best interests. Hence, women's (and men's) personal lives must be authenticated differently by the legal system and public policy in order for the state to take responsibility for the disadvantaged groups or individuals in society, rather than continuing to blame them for their lack of self-sufficiency. Both MacKinnon and Copelon, like other radical feminist legal theorists, are concerned with providing some kind of meaningful legal and socioeconomic autonomy for women that their past and present socioeconomic conditioning does not instill in them. Thus they argue that male legal doctrines about autonomy and privacy, as those in abortion case law, are not as positive or self-empowering for women as a feminist jurisprudence or constitutionalism would have made them.[3]

The search for collective female empowerment is central both to feminist jurisprudence and to feminist history, and each requires a moral as well as a political vision. The greatest weakness of both MacKinnon's and Copelon's approaches to it is that neither proceeds very far, if at all, for suggesting solutions for women's past and present inequality *outside* of the law. They seem to be saying that since the law is the problem, the law must also be the solution. Robin West's analytical approach to a feminist jurisprudence contains some of the elements of both MacKinnon's and Copelon's writings, but her search for female autonomy and authenticity sometimes takes her outside the letter and the institution of the law. Likewise, poststructural relativism is threatening to either discredit or destroy the type of feminist history devoted to analyzing and combating the oppression of women.

After analyzing what it means to be a *human being* from the point of view of four intellectual groupings—liberal legalism, critical legal theory, cultural feminism, and radical feminism—West ultimately concludes that "the subjectivity of human existence told

---

2. Catharine A. MacKinnon, *Feminism Unmodified: Discourses on Life and Law* (Cambridge, Mass.: Harvard University Press, 1987), 1–17, 32–62, 103–16, 215–28; Kenneth Karst, "Woman's Constitution," *Duke Law Journal* 1984, no. 3 (June 1984): 448, 455, 473–77.

3. Rhonda Copelon, "Beyond the Liberal Idea of Privacy: Toward a Positive Right of Autonomy," in Michael W. McCann and Gerald L. Houseman, eds., *Judging the Constitution: Critical Essays in Judicial Lawmaking* (Glenview, Ill.: Scott, Foresman, 1989), 291–320; and Sarah Slavin, "Authenticity and Fiction in Law: Contemporary Case Studies Exploring Radical Feminism," *Journal of Women's History* 1, no. 3 (February 1990): 123–31.

	Cultural Feminism	Radical feminism
Value (or Longing):	Intimacy	Individuation; Integrity
Harm (or Dread):	Separation	Invasion Intrusion

	The Official Story (Liberal legalism and cultural feminism)		The Unofficial Story (Critical legalism and radical feminism)	
	Value	Harm	Longing	Dread
Legal Theory (human beings)	Autonomy	Annihilation; Frustration	Attachment; Connection	Alienation
Feminist Theory (women)	Intimacy	Separation	Individuation	Invasion; Intrusion

Source: Robin West, "Jurisprudence and Gender," University of Chicago Law Review 55, no. 1 (Winter 1980), p. 37.

by feminist theory and legal theory contrast at every point. There is no overlap."[4] She arrives at this conclusion by using four-celled topologies to differentiate legal theory and feminist theory. She describes the liberal and critical legal theorists' ideas about separateness and contrasts them with the cultural and radical feminists' ideas about difference. Then she categorizes these respective theories in terms of what she considers to be their most relevant overt and covert meanings: VALUE (or longing) and HARM (or dread). After that she creates an eight-celled typology by combining what she finds common or underlying in the "official stories" and "unofficial stories" about value and harm on the part of her original four subject groupings. She does this, however, by collapsing liberal legalism and critical legalism into one category and doing the same thing with cultural

---

4. In her own words in "Jurisprudence and Gender," this is how West describes the concepts in the charts on 410.

First, and most obviously, the "official" descriptions of human beings' subjectivity and women's subjectivity contrast rather than compare. According to liberal theory, human beings respond aggressively to their natural state of relative physical equality. In response to the great dangers posed by their natural aggression, they abide by a sharply anti-naturalist morality of autonomy, rights, and individual spheres of freedom, which is intended to and to some extent does curb their natural aggression. They respect a civil state that enforces those rights against the most egregious breaches. The description of women's subjectivity told by cultural feminism is much the opposite. According to cultural feminism, women inhabit a realm of natural *inequality*. They are physically stronger than the fetus and the infant. Women respond to their natural inequality over the fetus and infant not with aggression, but with nurturance and care. That natural and nurturant response evolves into a naturalist moral ethic of care which is consistent with women's natural response. The substantive moralities consequent to these two stories, then, unsurprisingly, are also diametrically opposed. The autonomy that human beings value and the rights they need as a restriction on their natural hostility to the equal and separate other are in sharp contrast to the intimacy that women value, and the ethic of care that represents not a limitation upon, but an extension of, women's natural nurturant response to the dependent, connected other.

The subterranean descriptions of subjectivity that emerge from the unofficial stories of radical feminism and critical legalism also contrast rather than compare. According to the critical legalists, human beings respond to their natural state of physical separateness not with aggression, fear and mutual suspicion, as liberalism holds, but with longing. Men suffer from a perpetual dread of isolation and alienation and a fear of rejection, and harbor a craving for community, connection, and association. Women, by contrast, according to radical feminism, respond to their natural state of material connection to the other with a craving for individuation and a loathing for invasion. Just as clearly, the subterranean dread men have of alienation (according to critical legalism) contrasts sharply with the subterranean dread that women have of invasion and intrusion (according to radical feminism) (pp. 38–39).

424

and radical feminism. By cross-tabulating these unofficial and official stories, she is then able to show contradictions in both legal and feminist theory at the unofficial, or "subterranean," level of existence but also shows how more alike critical legalism and radical feminism are to each other at the official, or "conscious," level of existence. Conversely, she demonstrates in what areas liberalism and cultural feminism also are alike and yet different. Therefore, the following charts allow West to indicate where she believes all four groupings fail to provide a sound basis for a feminist jurisprudence and to offer her own.

West begins to construct a feminist jurisprudence by noting that the "official" and "unofficial" responses of individual women and men, as described by these four groups, contrast in terms of substance if not structure. All deny the "subterranean desires that permeate their lives" *out of fear* that if they are expressed, they "will be met by either violence or rejection by the dominant culture." Thus, according to West, "men deny their need for attachment and women deny their need for individuation." Although both Critical Legal Studies and radical feminists appear to have similar descriptions of subjectivity, in fact they do not. Critical Legal Studies theorists depict individuals wanting connection and fearing alienation, while radical feminists claim that women want intimacy and fear separation. All they share is their "outsider's status," from the point of view of mainstream liberals (both legal and cultural) whose rhetoric reflects the status quo.[5]

Borrowing from Roberto Unger and Duncan Kennedy (but primarily the latter), West goes on to assert that the human being who, according to liberal legalism, "values autonomy and fears annihilation" "precludes the women described by feminism [and necessary] for the development of feminist jurisprudence." West notes that the "fundamental contradiction" that explains these diametrically opposed interpretations is an *experiential*, not a logical, one. To create a feminist jurisprudence capable of going beyond the liberal legalism of those advocating special rights versus equal rights, radical feminists must begin systematically to expose this experiential contradiction—namely, the "women's (and men's) existential and material circumstance . . . is itself one of contradiction."[6] According to West:

> The potentiality for physical connection with others that uniquely characterizes women's lives has within it seeds of *both* intimacy and invasion, and therefore women rightly value the former while we dread and fear the latter, just as the necessity of physical separation, for men, carries within it the seeds of *both* intimacy and alienation, and men rightly value the former and dread the latter. If this is right, then *all four* accounts of human experience—liberal legalism, critical legalism, cultural feminism and radical feminism—are saying something true about human experience. Liberal legalism and critical legalism both describe something true about male experience, and cultural feminism and radical feminism both describe something true about female experience. If Kennedy is right, then men simply live with an experiential contradiction. In a parallel fashion, cultural feminism and radical feminism may both be *true* although contradictory. The contradiction between them may be experiential rather than logical. Women may both value intimacy and dread the intrusion and invasion which intimacy implies; and women may both fear separation and long for the individualization which separation would bring.[7]

---

5. Ibid., p. 42.

6. Ibid., pp. 43, 53 (quotations).

7. Ibid., p. 53

From this premise, West then suggested the following way to create a "reconstructive feminist jurisprudence" that would finally make "feminist reform rational."[8] By "rational" West does not mean "male," as most assimilationists and even some moderate pluralists do, but "rational" from a radical feminist point of view. If different groups of women do legitimately "fear" men, the law must be redesigned to alleviate these fears without resorting to male legal rationales or by deconstructing these fears into illusions. Thus, West believes that neither equality through more (male) choice, as advocated by the assimilationists, nor equality through obtaining (male) power, as advocated by some radical pluralists, may reflect or result in achieving the subjective well-being of women because they are outwardly rather than inwardly directed. West goes so far as to claim that the goals of both liberal legalism and pluralist legalism "have the potential to backfire—badly—against women's true interests," which she insists remain largely ignored or silenced in their subjective, hedonic lives. "My substantive claim is that woman's happiness or pleasure—as opposed to women's freedom or equality—should be the ideal toward which female legal criticism and reform should be pressed," concludes West, "and that women's misery, suffering and pain—as opposed to women's oppression or subordination—is the evil we should resist."[9]

While West has taken the "fundamental-contradiction" theories of Unger and Kennedy further than any other radical legal theorist by trying to construct a feminist jurisprudence that does not automatically assume, as both assimilationists and pluralists do, that an improvement in objective conditions will improve the subjective reality of most women's lives, she does not connect her own and their analysis of this contradiction with the interconnection between the passing of the modern era and the incoherency of liberal individualism. It is not simply that liberalism with all its inconsistencies was suited to the modern era of individualization, promoted first by commercial and then by capitalistic development with its emphasis on male equality, rationality, and superiority in the family and state. It is also that liberalism has not been able to offer an alternative to the "nature of persons [or, to use West's term, "human beings"] that is better suited to a global, linked world system."[10] The "fundamental contradiction" *is* liberalism itself, now that the era of globalization—especially with respect to the relation of persons to community and culture—is emerging.

In these great historic sea changes from premodernism to modernism and now to postmodernism, the social construction of women probably was (and is) more in tune with first and third societal transformations rather than our own modern time. This is because both pre- and postmodernism stress that persons (human beings) are members of communities first and not simply isolated individuals who operate as sovereign agents.[11] It is for this reason that relational feminist jurisprudence cannot build upon the

---

8. Ibid., pp. 68–70.

9. Robin West, "The Difference in Women's Hedonic Lives: A Phenomenological Critique of Feminist Legal Theory," *Wisconsin Women's Law Journal* 3 (1987): 87–90 (quotations at 89–90).

10. Edward E. Sampson, "Globalization and Psychology's Theory of the Person," *American Psychologist* 44 (June 1989): 914–15, 917 (quotation).

11. Ibid., pp. 918–19 (quotations). Sampson goes on to note that the "personal being" who is "clearly constituted within the social world" learns this through psychological symbiosis. The best example can be found in the way "mothers do not talk *about* the child's wishes and emotions; they *supply* the wishes, needs, intentions, wants and the like, and interact with the child as if it had them" (Sampson quoting R. Harre, *Personal Being* [Cambridge: Harvard University Press, 1986], pp. 105, 720).

increasingly obvious contractions of past and present liberal legalism, but it can begin to ride the crest (and needs) of the future of postmodern globalism. Already, psychologists are suggesting that feminist perspectives of women today probably will form the basis for the human psychology of the postmodern future. Why should any less be true of feminist jurisprudence, since it also rests on the inter- and intraconnected constitutive persons that women have been socialized to be?

Individual rights only make sense in a Lockean society based on the belief that "persons are understood to be an antecedent to any kind of constitutive community," rather than the other way around. If persons of the future are to be those "whose very identities are constituted by social locations," then women already possess many of the constitutive perspectives necessary for developing this new postmodern human self protected by human rights. In a globally relational setting, feminist jurisprudence would appear both more rational and necessary than it does now, at the end of the postmodern era with its excesses of individualization. The fundamental contradiction of the liberal individualist view of human nature—whether in its female or male versions—is not the basis upon which to build a feminist jurisprudence, as West maintains. Instead, even the contradictions about human nature projected by radical feminism must be rejected in the name of community identity based on fairness and equity. Otherwise, remnants of liberal individualism and liberal legalism will continue to confound indefinitely women's civil rights and sexuality.

Nonetheless, analyses like West's offer the hope that the 1980s and 1990s will not become the 1920s and 1930s for female activism if a feminist jurisprudence becomes reality and if a common woman's langauge can once again be identified and utilized by reformers rather than reactionaries. While these tasks will be difficult to accomplish (unlike the interwar years in which the First Women's movement drowned in the sea of largely unreflective fragmentation accompanied by the illusory adoption of male language to achieve female goals),[12] at least the correct questions are now being asked and a few tentative and provocative answers are being suggested.

Perhaps before the end of this century, women in the United States will reunite behind a more relational approach to improving their status and society; but by the beginning of the 1990s, there was every indication that the equal rights approach of liberal legalism will remain intact for the rest of the century. To the degree that radical feminists anticipate and transform the future of the U.S. political economy rather than continue to react to its ever-changing contemporary manifestations, they will ultimately be judged as the true visionaries. My own resolution to the problem of how to move from liberation to emancipation is through radical feminism. However, the liberal historical and legal barriers have kept most women in the United States of the past and present from endorsing practicing this brand of feminism, let alone constructing a feminist jurisprudence.[13] As Catharine MacKinnon has said: "justice [for women] will require change, not [simply more] reflection . . . [but] new jurisprudence, a new relation between life and law."[14]

---

12. Carroll Smith-Rosenberg, *Disorderly Conduct: Visions of Gender in Victorian America* (New York: Knopf, 1985), pp. 252–305, 358, n. 127; and idem, "Discourses of Sexuality and Subjectivity: The New Woman, 1870–1936," in Martin B. Duberman et al., eds., *Hidden from History: Reclaiming the Gay and Lesbian Past* (New York: NAL, 1989), pp. 277–94.

13. West, "Jurisprudence and Gender," pp. 68–70.

14. Catharine A. MacKinnon, "Feminism, Marxism, Method, and the State: Toward Feminist Jurisprudence," in Sandra Harding, ed., *Feminism and Methodology* (Bloomington: Indiana University Press, 1987), p. 149.

1989 Declaration of Interdependence

Joan Hoff

When in the Course of Human Events, it becomes necessary to create a new bond among the peoples of the earth, connecting each to the other, undertaking equal responsibilities under the laws of nature, a decent respect for the welfare of humankind and all life on earth requires us to Declare our Interdependence.

We recognize that humankind has not woven the web of life; we are but one thread within it. Whatever we do to the web, we do to ourselves. Whatever befalls the earth befalls also the family of the earth.

We are concerned about the wounds and bleeding sores on the naked body of the earth: the famine; the poverty; the children born into hunger and disease; the destruction of forests and fertile lands; the chemical and nuclear accidents; the wars and deaths in so many parts of the world.

It is our belief that man's dominion over nature parallels the subjugation of women in many societies, denying them sovereignty over their lives and bodies. Until all societies truly value women and the environment, their joint degradation will continue.

Women's views on economic justice, human rights, reproduction and the achievement of peace must be heard at local, national, and international forums, wherever policies are made that could affect the future of life on earth. Partnership among all peoples is essential for the survival of the planet.

If we are to have a common future, we must commit ourselves to preserve the natural wealth of our earth for future generations.

As women we accept our responsibility and declare our intention to:

- Link with others—young and old, women and men, people of all races, religions, cultures and political beliefs—in a common concern for global survival;
- Be aware in our private, public and working lives of actions we can take to safeguard our food, fresh water, clean air and quality of life;
- Make women's collective experiences and value judgments equal to the experiences and value judgments of men when policies are made that affect our future and future generations;

Hoff, Joan. 1991. "Declaration of Interdependence." In *Law, Gender, and Injustice: A legal history of U.S. women.* New York University Press. Reprinted by permission of the publisher.

Drawn from the words and philosophies of: The drafters of the U.S. Declaration of Independence (July 4, 1776); Chief Seattle to President Franklin Pierce (1855); Wangari Maathai, founder, Green Belt Movement, and Chair, National Council of Women of Kenya (1988); The UN Population Fund (1988); Women's Foreign Policy Council; The World Commission on Environment and Development (1987); Spiritual and Parliamentary Leaders Global Survival Conference, Oxford (April 1988).

- Expose the connections between environmental degradation, greed, uncontrolled militarism and technology devoid of human values. Insist that human and ecological values take absolute precedence when decisions are made in national affairs;
- Change government, economic and social policies to protect the well-being of the most vulnerable among us and to end poverty and inequality;
- Work to dismantle nuclear and conventional weapons, build trust among peoples and nations, and use all available international institutions and networks to achieve common security for the family of earth.

We also declare that, whenever and wherever people meet to decide the fate of the planet, it is our intention to participate on an equal footing, with full and fair representation, equivalent to our number and kind on earth.

Why Some People Be Mad at Me Sometimes

Lucille Clifton

they ask me to remember
but they want me to remember
their memories
and i keep on remembering
mine.

The American Way of Death—á Erik

Claribel Alegría

Si arañas día y noche la montaña
y acechas detrás de los arbustos
(la mochila-fracaso va creciendo,
abre grietas la sed en la garganta
y la fiebre del cambio
te devora)
si eliges la guerrilla,
ten cuidado,
te matan.

Si combates tu caos
con la paz,
la no violencia,
el amor fraternal,
las largas marchas sin fusiles
con mujeres y niños
recibiendo escupidas en la cara,
ten cuidado,
te matan.

Si tu piel es morena
y vas descalzo
y te roen por dentro los lombrices,
el hambre,
la malaria:
lentamenta te matan.

Si eres negro de Harlem
y te ofrecen canchas de fútbol
con el suelo de asfalto,
un televisior en la cocina
y hojas de marihuana:
poco a poco te matan.

Si padeces de asma,
si te exaspera un sueño
—ya sea en Buenos Aires
o en Atlanta—
que te impulsa de Montgomery
hasta Memphis
o a cruzar a pie la cordillera,
ten cuidado:
te volverás obseso
y sonámbulo
y poeta.

Si naces en el ghetto
o la favela
y tu escuela es la cloaca
o es la esquina,
hay que comer primero,
luego pagar la renta
y con el tiempo que te sobra
sentarte en el andén
y ver pasar los coches.

Pero un día te llega la noticia,
corre la voz,
te la da tu vecino
porque tú no sabes leer
o no tienes un cinco
para comprar el diario
o el televisor se te ha jodido.
De cualquier modo
te llega la noticia:
lo han matado,
sí,
te lo han matado.

"The American Way of Death" from *Woman of the River*, by Claribel Algería, translated by D. J. Flakoll. Reprinted by permission of the University of Pittsburgh Press. © 1989 by Claribel Algería.

The American Way of Death—to Erik

Claribel Alegría

If you claw the mountain day and
night
and lie in ambush behind the
shrubs
(the backpack of failure growing
heavier,
thirst opening cracks in your throat
and the fever for change
devouring you)
if you choose the guerrilla path,
be careful,
they'll kill you.

If you combat your chaos
through peace,
nonviolence,
brotherly love,
long marches without guns,
with women and children
being spat at in the face,
be careful,
they'll kill you.

If your skin is dark
and you go barefoot
and your insides are gnawed by worms,
hunger,
malaria:
slowly they'll kill you.

If you are a black from Harlem
and they offer you football fields
paved with asphalt,
a television in the kitchen
and joints of marijuana:
little by little they'll kill you.

If you suffer from asthma,
if a dream exasperates you
—whether in Buenos Aires
or Atlanta—
that takes you from Montgomery
to Memphis
or across the Andes on foot,
be careful:
you'll become obsessed,
a sleepwalker
a poet.

If you are born in the ghetto
or shantytown
and your school is the gutter
or the street corner,
first of all you must eat,
then pay the rent
and in the time left over
sit on the curb
and watch the cars go by.

But one day the news reaches you,
the word spreads,
your neighbor tells you
because you can't read
or don't have a dime
to buy the newspaper
or the television is screwed up.
Whichever way,
you learn the news:
they've killed him,
yes,
they've killed another one.

431

[Untitled]

Jennifer Locke

The personal is the political . . .

I got up to clear the dishes from the table. I felt distant from the women's conversation around me, talk of babies' achievements and great adventures with the kitchen appliances and who's sleeping with whom. I glanced over at the knot of men that always formed on the porch after the holiday meals: my three brothers ringed around my father, absorbed in intense conversation. I had tried at various times to join their circle but couldn't understand any of the "legalese," the stories of subpoenas and interrogatories and plea bargains. I envied their bonds, their intimacy, the obvious importance of their mysterious conversation as I scraped dried gravy off the plates.

The men in my family all became lawyers. All four of them. My father used his profession as a great escape from the incessant demands of my mother. Far into the evenings he had clients to see and trials to prepare for. Meanwhile my mother waged war with alcoholism and mental illness. I remember after one of her trips to a mental hospital, when the effect of the shock treatments began to wear off, she discovered that my father had signed away her "power of attorney" and had taken another mortgage on the house. At age eight, listening to her rage, I knew this was a terrible power indeed and that she no longer had it. My younger sister followed my mother into housewifery and married a young and very sweet millionaire, only to discover that all his inherited wealth was locked in trust funds that were designed so that the wives could never touch the money. It was clear who had the power, and it wasn't the women.

After several tries at various careers, including wanderer and cook, I decided to become a social worker. I discovered that when my clients had trouble with welfare, slumlords, or the police, a phone call from a lawyer instantly produced far more effective results than one from a social worker. All of my clients were poor and uneducated and powerless in the face of these institutions. They needed more than what a social worker could give. It was clear who had the power, and it wasn't the poor people.

I struggled with the decision to go to law school. Whereas my brothers had never doubted that they would be lawyers and had attended law school directly from college, I searched my soul to see if this was what I really wanted, if I really felt capable of it. I had spent my early life listening to the message that the boys should be lawyers and the girls should be secretaries until they find a lawyer to marry. Although I had always fought that message, the damage to my core self-confidence had been profound, and I did not trust my own abilities. I decided to go to law school, but to make it my own experience. I refused to take any tuition money from my father. My mother, bitterly divorced after twenty-seven years with my father, felt I was betraying the women in the family and "selling out." My sister felt abandoned, now faced with being the only non-lawyer among the siblings, and furious that I had not chosen a domestic route so that our babies could be kissing cousins. I was afraid of the webs of relationships that bound these women, afraid ever to be so utterly dependent on a man. I knew who had the power, and it wasn't the wives and mothers.

I came into law school trailing my own strands of relationships. I was an excellent friend to many people, never forgetting a birthday or an anniversary of a traumatic event. I was tied to the matriarchy of my mother's family, had spent thousands of hours sitting around kitchen tables gossiping. I was an aunt to three kids and felt it my duty to take them to the circus. I had a lover, a stormy but fascinating relationship that consumed tons of energy. "Physicists used to believe that the world was made up of particles. But recently they had found out they'd been wrong: The world, unsuspectedly, was made up of little tiny strings."[1] I had always known this, and both loved and resented my own strings. I was ready to work hard, extra hard to make up for my lack of self-confidence, but I was not prepared for what hit me the first week of law school. I felt as if a Mack truck had backed up and dumped its load on me. I couldn't keep up with the volumes of reading. I couldn't understand any of the cases, and I fell into a puddle of insecurity reminiscent of seventh grade.

I had read Carol Gilligan and knew that in many ways I was a classic "Amy."[2] I, too, defined responsibility as responding to the needs of others,[3] and suddenly I was no longer able to do it in my usual conscientious way. I simply did not have the time to attend every birthday party. The women in my family did not understand, and they let me know that they felt ignored and abandoned. I felt guilty and selfish. The insidiousness of the adversarial system crept into my own life: I began to see my strings to other people as chains of obligation; I began to resent my own sense of caring for my friends and family outside of law school. I began to battle my Amy-ness.

Classes rolled on. During the second week I sat in Property and jumped when I heard my name called. Sweat began pouring from my armpits; I turned scarlet. The professor was asking about a detail in one of those incomprehensible cases, something about where the court had gotten the law it was applying. I remembered babysitting a week earlier with the two young children of this same professor, all three of us fantasizing about our ideal dream house. Our imaginations had warmed to the task, and we had created something together that none of us could have dreamed up alone. I remembered the occasional wonderful class I had attended in college where learning had been an experiential, dynamic adventure undertaken by teacher and students together. I wrenched myself back to the class and stared hard at the book. I knew that my brain was about to be exposed to the class and that if my answer was stupid I could be turned down by the myriad of study groups that had been sprouting. I had no idea where the court had

---

1. Lorrie Moore, *Strings Too Short to Use*, in *Anagrams* 25 (1986).

2. Carol J. Gilligan, *In a Different Voice* 25–39 (1982).

3. *Feminist Discourse, Moral Values, and the Law—A Conversation*, 34 Buffalo L. Rev. 11, 44 (1985) (Carol Gilligan speaking). The article is an edited transcript of a conversation amongst Isabel Marcus, Paul J. Spiegelman, Ellen C. DuBois, Mary C. Dunlap, Carol J. Gilligan, Catharine A. MacKinnon, and Carrie J. Menkel-Meadow. [hereinafter *Feminist Discourse*]

gotten the law; in fact, I figured it had just made it up. Through this sweaty experience I was being indoctrinated into the so-called "Socratic method" of teaching. Aside from establishing the professor as the authority in the classroom,[4] the "Socratic method," which I view as a game of "guess what I'm thinking,"[5] alienates students.[6] The message came across clearly in the first week: students know nothing, our past experience is irrelevant,[7] and we should not think critically. We are here to learn the rules and to "think like a lawyer." We are not supposed to react emotionally to a case, for emotions do not belong in this world of legal reasoning.[8] Emotions are a sign of weakness and will isolate a student.[9]

I knew that I had come into law school well-groomed in the Amy way of thinking. I slowly realized how disadvantaged I was compared to how well-prepared the Jakes of the world were for this type of training. I knew that my brothers had not fought law school so hard, whereas I felt like it was a personal assault on my life, my time, and my values.

Many of the Jakes in my class formed what I called "the boy's club," taking up several rows in the back, talking sports, never allowing a woman to sit next to them. They seemed to take right to the school, able to sling around the policy arguments that made no sense to me. (Overcrowding of judicial dockets? Preserve stability in business transactions? These things had no meaning in my life.) They saw the world as governed by rules, principles, hierarchy; they viewed people as isolated individuals competing with each other. They believed the function of the law is to assure that this competition is conducted fairly.[10]

Although I was not too surprised at the Jakes, I was really perplexed by many of the young women in my class. They were confident, articulate, perfectly shaped and groomed, and frighteningly conservative. They didn't seem to be struggling with the disparate loyalties that I was, or to notice that the material was sexist. They didn't seem to fit either the Amy or the Jake stereotype, but had characteristics of both. They could argue abstract principles like Jake but appeared to be hungry for approval and voiced no opinions on anything. They were apolitical, and seemed to believe that they could walk right into the large law firms and would not encounter harassment or discrimination. I guess they believed that things really have changed. I overheard one woman in the cafeteria, talking to a group of young men, say, "Well, I'm not one of those feminists." Feminism in Reagan-Bush-era law school had become a dirty word.

---

4. *See* Carrie J. Menkel-Meadow, *Feminist Legal Theory, Critical Legal Studies, and Legal Education or "The Fem-Crits Go to Law School,"* 32 J. Legal Educ., 61, 67 (1982). *See also* Karl E. Klare, *The Law-School Curriculum in the 1980's: What's Left?* 32 J. Legal Educ. 336, 342 (1982).

5. *Cf.* Duncan Kennedy, *Legal Education as Training for Hierarchy,* in The Politics of Law: A Progressive Critique 40, 42 (David Kairys ed. 1982). "[O]ne struggles desperately, in front of a large audience, to read a mind determined to elude you." *Id.*

6. Menkel-Meadow, *supra* note 4, at 67.

7. *See* Paul J. Spiegelman, *Integrating Doctrine, Theory and Practice in the Law School Curriculum: The Logic of Jake's Ladder in the Context of Amy's Web,* 32 J. Legal Educ. 243, 253 (1982). "[T]he first-year curriculum's sharply restricted focus on logical analysis gives students the message that their feelings and experience are inapplicable and inappropriate. Its skepticism about ideas, language, and authority undermines students' sense of order, reality, and values." *Id.*

8. *See* Kennedy, *supra* note 5, at 42.

9. *See id.*

10. *Cf.* Spiegelman, *supra* note 7, at 247–48.

I struggled to learn this thing they called "legal reasoning." It seemed to elude me at every turn. I kept wanting to discuss what a particular case meant in an historical or political context, but the professors were totally unwilling to stray from the casebooks. I didn't understand why we didn't analyze the underlying assumptions of each judicial opinion. The Amy in me was hungry for the context of each case.[11] We performed our analyses on the level of identifying the rule and several competing policy considerations, ignoring the personal level of how the actual parties were affected by the litigation and the level of social theory, philosophy, and politics.[12] The appellate court cases seemed to dangle in the air, representing principles unto themselves. I didn't know that "legal reasoning is an array of highly stylized modes of justificatory rhetoric."[13]

I'm embarrassed to say that in the first semester I was too overwhelmed with the work load and the strangeness of the language to begin to protest the material that was taught. Torts was an exercise in hierarchy. The "Socratic method" in this class was purely an instrument of humiliation. Once the professor honed in on a student, it was only a matter of time before the hypotheticals became so ridiculous that the student was lost, unable to answer the questions, and made to look like a fool. If a student answered several questions successfully, the professor grew more aggressive. It appeared as personal effrontery that we might actually understand the material. Ultimately the class ended up silent, few people volunteering to answer questions, most of us trying to hide.

There was another unspoken tension within the classroom as the professor obviously struggled not to appear sexist. He tried to change pronouns occasionally, creating hypotheticals with male cheerleaders or nurses. He intimated that he had been in trouble before with women students because of sexist remarks. Yet, he clearly had no idea how not to be sexist. He didn't understand that the casebook itself was sexist,[14] nor did he know how to give us historical information about tort law and how it affects women and minorities. And I didn't know enough to try to explore the issues of consent, the use of "reasonable force" in self-defense for women, or the problems involved in pursuing a claim of sexual abuse when the abuse is remembered only years later.

I finished my last exam on December 23, and on December 24 my brother's lover, who had grown to be a loving part of our family over the past five years, was killed by a drunk driver. I stumbled back into law school at the beginning of the second semester weighted down with grief and anger and no place to put it. I couldn't see the sense of trying to learn contracts, of sweating over consideration. I tried to tell several classmates about the tragedy, but they were obsessed with school. Death could not interrupt one's studies. The strands of my webs were in disarray, but I had to prepare for final exams in February. I put my tears on hold and crammed. I found some escape in this prioritizing

---

11. *CF.* Spiegelman, *supra* note 7, at 248. Like Amy, I was frustrated by the fixed hypothetical in which the dilemma was locked. I was similarly frustrated in trying to get to know other students, feeling I was only supposed to relate to them around the school experience without knowing the context of their lives. The greatest evils to Amy are detachment from others and failing to respond to their needs. In law school, no one seemed to have any needs.

12. *See* Menkel-Meadow, *supra* note 4, at 68.

13. Klare, *supra* note 4, at 340.

14. *See* Carl Tobias, *Gender Issues and the Prosser, Wade, and Schwartz Torts Casebook,* 18 Golden Gate U. L. Rev. 495, 498 (1988).

of duties, using Jake's ladder to climb out of my sorrow. I followed the examples of the men in my family and silenced my inner voice.

It was when my Introduction to Lawyering and Professional Responsibility [ILPR] instructor came out with a passionate and critical opinion of the material we were supposed to learn, and suggested that we read Duncan Kennedy's article,[15] that my voice began to return. I felt the burden of an imposed silence begin to lift. I seized onto Kennedy's article, having seen the hierarchy established in the first semester. I began to protest the material, the methods of teaching, and most of all, what it was doing to me. I re-read Gilligan and wanted to again speak out in my Amy-voice.

I found myself choking on the purely capitalist values in contracts and how they were not even acknowledged, never mind questioned.[16] In Contracts we learned to pull arguments out of a grab bag, magical phrases such as "encouraging the free market," "protecting the freedom to contract," "upholding the sanctity of the writing," "never undermining the security of transactions" or "clogging the judicial dockets." But I said very little in class, because I was scared of the professor.[17] I hid my deep sense of disappointment, having hoped this woman professor would be a mentor, would teach in a different style.[18] Instead she was a drill sergeant, not unkindly but relentlessly questioning students until we got the doctrine down pat. Always uncertain of the material, I never even dared ask a question. Yet I was shocked when we failed even to mention a phrase in an opinion where the judge analogized the difference between assent and non-assent to a contract to the difference between seduction and rape. Both were only matters of degree.

But in Property I felt more brave. I overheard classmates refer to the tenants who were fighting for the right to minimum housing standards as "scumbags" and "freeloaders." I was afraid of being judged, yet on several occasions I erupted anyway. Although I received positive feedback when I defended the tenants, the class attitude was hostile when I spoke about a decision that completely undermined the Married Women's Act in England. The judge in that case refrained from making a ruling to provide the husband an opportunity to "convince" his wife to support his decision to sell the family home. The husband had made this decision without consulting his wife. The "convincing" resulted in "a little slapping," and the police and a doctor had to be called. The wife still refused to agree, so the judge ruled in such a way that the husband went bankrupt and the wife became destitute. I was furious and I expressed it. Many of my classmates slammed their

---

15. Kennedy, *supra* note 5, at 40.

16. *Cf.* Klare, *supra* note 4, at 339. Klare goes on to say:

[S]tudents learn from the emotional content of the law curriculum that they ought to distrust their own deepest moral sensibilities; that they ought to avoid global and political inquiry (because it is dangerous, simplistic and unlawyer-like); that they ought to revere hierarchy; and that manipulating vulnerable people is an acceptable form of professional behavior.

Id. at 341.

17. Compare Stephanie M. Wildman, *The Question of Silence: Techniques to Ensure Full Class Participation.* 32 J. Legal Educ. 147, 150 (1982), who remarks that the most damaging part of silence is that it interferes with the ability to learn the substantive material. This was true for me, as I found myself "tuning out" when an underlying assumption offended me.

18. See generally Menkel-Meadow, *supra* note 4, at 77, for a discussion of women professors who follow traditional legal education patterns in their teaching; see also Kennedy, *supra* note 5, at 56, who comments that most female and black law teachers appear to assimilate thoroughly the style of white male teachers, or appear insecure and unhappy.

notebooks shut and packed up to leave, not listening to all (this was not exam material). I had broken a rule in law school and was marginalized as a result: I had become an hysterical female.[19] I also raised the issue which I felt the book tiptoed around, that women had always been considered property and that women in today's society still participate in this principle by trying to attach themselves to the "right man" to gain esteem, money, security. Again I was met with hostility. The professor responded by throwing his hands in the air, saying, "What could we do, isolate two continents and put all the women on one and all the men on another?" Through his response he gave the class permission to ignore or ridicule my comments.

When we read the Gilligan excerpt in the ILPR course materials, I felt the stirrings of another conflict. Although I will readily admit my own Amy-ness, I had never really liked Amy much. Several women students told me that they were quite excited by the article, identified right away with Amy, and felt empowered because their way of thinking was finally being acknowledged.[20] Although the professor touched upon it, we did not really have time to examine why there are Jakes and Amys, and why they frequently correspond to gender differences.

I have an image of Jake's ladder, the rungs consisting of lofty principles such as predictability, right and wrong, property rights, justice. Yet the top of the ladder is suspended in mid-air, leading nowhere. A Jake can make a compelling argument for the administration of impartial justice, but end up standing on principle alone, disconnected from flesh and blood and human hearts. Yet I always envisioned Jake's ladder with its feet tangled in an Amy-web. The men who cling the most desperately to the rungs of the ladder are those who had to flee passionately the webs of their mothers, who wove the strands too tightly, probably because mothering was their sole purpose in life. The aching wound left when the little boy wrenches away from mother and begins to imitate father is soothed by the satisfactions of autonomy, competition, and the achievements of independence. Depersonalization becomes a self-protection from that threatening world of sticky relationships.

I envision Amy, on the other hand, to be mired in her web of relationships, lacking a sense of identity separate from her relationships. Although Amy certainly has some extraordinary skills and a unique vision of the interdependence of things, to discuss her without discussing the forces that created her felt incomplete to me. I see Amy as essentially a political creature with a highly refined sense of connections because a woman's rights traditionally have depended on her connection to a man.[21] Although we did talk about what can happen to the voice of Amy in the legal system, in typical law school

---

19. *See* Kennedy, *supra* note 5, at 57, for comments on how outrage is considered naive, irrelevant, and probably wrong. Kennedy goes on to examine how the showing of emotions will isolate and incapacitate the student. *Id.* at 44.

20. *See* Spiegelman, *supra* note 7, at 253. He discusses how simply telling the story of Amy and Jake has an amazing effect on the classroom and empowers the students.

21. *See generally* Nancy S. Erickson, *Sex Bias in Law School Courses: Some Common Issues*, 32 J. Legal Educ. 101, 111 (1982): "Women have always been conditioned to be very sensitive to men's words, acts, body langauge, and nuances of expression, in order to please men so that they will protect us, support us and our children, and especially so that they will not beat, rape, or otherwise hurt us. Men have not been similarly conditioned to be sensitive to women's words and feelings." See also *Feminist Discourse* (Carrie Menkel-Meadow speaking), *supra* note 4, at 57, for a comment on women's dependence on men.

fashion we skirted why Amy and Jake are the dominant stereotypes in our society. We also did not discuss the violence that such rigid roles wreak on individual personalities.[22] Again, I chose to remain silent. The struggle within me to balance my Amy-ness with some Jake-ness felt too raw to be exposed to what felt like a basically competitive, judgmental group of young law students.

I was amazed when my ILPR professor gave us permission to write about ourselves, our thoughts, our process through this year in law school. I had resigned myself outwardly to accepting that the professors possessed all the knowledge and that we students had none worth mentioning. Somehow I have managed to crawl through this year with most of my relationship strands intact, in spite of having missed two or three baby showers and a birthday here and there. I have learned enough "legalese" to understand that the conversations between the men in my family are exercises in maintenance of the hierarchy, with my brothers competing for my father's approval. What I had thought was intimacy is really depersonalization.

I am angry at what I have been taught this year and concerned about what I have not been taught. The things that are relevant to me, such as poverty law, discrimination law, family law, and feminist jurisprudence are considered "fringe" courses and are taught only sporadically. The marginalizing of these subjects—and the denigrating comments made about them by some of the professors—ultimately has the effect of denigrating the content.[23]

I am afraid that law school is a small taste of the larger legal world. I am afraid of what Kennedy prophesies: "You will come to expect that as a lawyer you will live in a world in which essential parts of you are not represented, or are misrepresented, and in which things you don't like will be accepted to the point that it doesn't occur to people that they are even controversial."[24] I am afraid that my financial situation will be so frightening by the end of my third year that I will beg for the chance to join a large, hierarchical law firm as a junior associate and claw my way up the ladder. I am afraid of losing the voice that I have struggled over my lifetime to develop and express. I am grateful for the opportunities I have had to identify the struggles, the anger, and the fears. I intend to keep this knowledge at the forefront over the next couple of years and not fail to protest when that essential part of me is ignored. I owe this responsibility to myself.

22. *See generally* Erickson, *supra* note 21, at 111. "The notion that men, in a society that silences women, live in a state of contentment, security, and psychological well-being is absurd."

23. *See* Erickson, *supra* note 21, at 103.

24. Kennedy, *supra* note 5, at 57.

Chapter 9—Women and the Law
Study Questions

1. St. Joan's personal account of her life could be construed as "if women only work hard enough" or "some women are just lucky." What are the traps in this type of analysis?

2. What does St. Joan see as the fundamental hypocrisy of the law? What is its impact?

3. During the first wave of feminism, women took a collective approach. What does this mean? How can it inform feminism today?

4. What important issue concerning the view of sexual harassment in the law emerged during the Clarence Thomas hearings? What impact have the hearings had on women? Did (do) you believe Anita Hill? Why or why not?

5. The courts have only recently recognized sexual harassment as discrimination. Why? What cultural change is necessary for sexual harassment to be seen as a viable legal issue?

6. Why is it difficult for women to bring charges of sexual harassment?

7. Why has the legal system, historically, been unresponsive to women concerning domestic abuse situations or other matters of the family?

8. How has "protective" legislation created a double bind for women? What, according to feminist theory, is the underlying cause of this double bind?

9. In "Midnight Train to US," Scales talks about cultural feminists versus political/radical feminists. On what is her distinction based? What negative consequences does she see in this split?

10. After reading Hoff's "Toward a Feminist Jurisprudence and History," do you think feminist jurisprudence is an oxymoron? Why or why not? Is either/or thinking the basis for change? Why or why not? Incorporate issues from St. Joan's description of the emergence of feminist jurisprudence.

11. Jennifer Locke's law school experience illustrates the importance of how we learn being part of what we learn. What are the insights you gained from this article?

12. How does the legal system promote victimization of women?

13. Over a period of time, follow a current legal case involving a woman as plaintiff or defendant. Critique its approach in view of the law as a political system. Does such a system take into account the personal issues of a woman's life? Should it? Why or why not?

PART FOUR

IMAGINATION, CREATION, AND EXPRESSION

WOMEN AND SPIRITUALITY

Alice Reich

A group of women gathers for dinner in a home in the San Francisco Bay area in 1989. They include a composer, a filmmaker, a psychotherapist, writers, teachers, and political activists. They are black, white, Asian, and Native American. Their conversation ranges over such topics as the environment, archaeology, travel, giving birth, and raising children. At the center of their conversation, at the center of the gathering itself, and at the center of these women's lives is the subject of contemporary feminist spirituality.

Indeed, these women, Jean Shinoda Bolen, Carol Christ, Charlene Spretnak, Starhawk, Merlin Stone, Mary Tallmountain, Luisah Teish, Kim Chernin, Susan Griffin, Elena Featherston, and Shekinah Mountainwater are among the authors of landmark works on that spirituality. This chapter raises such questions as

- Why is it essential that women define spirituality for themselves?
- In what ways do women re-create and celebrate spiritual identity?
- What is gained by reclaiming the history of goddess worship?
- How is female power defined in relation to spirituality?
- What is spiritually significant about women's bodies and bodily functions?
- Why are women perceived as being spiritually connected to "nature"?

- Of what significance are African American and Native American traditions to the practice of women's spirituality?

As women's voices are being heard in every other facet of late twentieth century life, so they are being heard in the realm of the spiritual, redefining symbols, rituals, and roles. Women interested in spirituality are creating exciting art, doing extensive research, writing books, and building a community. Women are reinvigorating the traditions of Native Americans and Africans. They are studying archaeology, mythology, history, and psychology. They are seeking images, symbols, and rituals to enspirit and empower them *as women* in ways that women are rarely empowered in patriarchal religions.

Spirituality is that which connects people to something beyond themselves and gives a deeper meaning to life. Spirituality goes beyond the ordinary world to another realm. It creates an awareness of being part of an entire web of life, enables people to communicate with their ancestors or animals or the spirits of natural beings and objects. Spirituality infuses otherwise ordinary experience with intensified meaning and makes scientifically unexplainable events possible. It cannot be defined by a particular mood: it may bring peace, joy, tears, or ecstasy.

But it tells people that something goes beyond the seen world of the individual, connecting humans with each other, living and dead; with nature, animate and inanimate; and with cycles of recurring time and eras of passing time. Spirituality tells people that they are part of something greater than themselves and their immediate conditions.

Every human society has devised and codified, or ritualized, certain beliefs and behavior that address spiritual needs. Anthropologists say that religion is a human universal. This does not mean that every person is religious, but that every culture has developed a system of beliefs and practices that address universal problems. Human beings everywhere suffer loss, experience confusion in their attempts to make meaning of their experience, and struggle with the apparent inability of good to triumph over evil. People everywhere have constructed views of the cosmos which help them live with these difficulties (Geertz 1973). Women experience further levels of difficulty, including the troubles that beset them when they turn to patriarchal institutions to fulfill their humanity. Women are told in churches that they may not sit with the men, speak with the men, stand with the men, or serve with the men. Women's spirits go hungry rather than being nourished.

Spirituality is central to most religions, but it is often distorted by issues of power and hierarchy. Religion is at once a set of embodied beliefs which seek to understand the ultimate meaning of existence *and* a social institution. As a social institution it fits with other institutions in maintaining social order. If a society is patriarchal, religion will both mirror and recreate that patriarchy, giving men power over women, valuing men and their experiences over women and their experiences. In patriarchal religions, not only can women not find images and stories that empower them, but, as we saw in Chapter 2, these images and women may themselves actually be denigrated and deemed inferior. When women turn to sacred writings or figures of wisdom they find stories of men who are heroes, who have struggled and won, and who have lost and survived; and, too frequently, women who cause evil or who suffer in silence.

The need felt by women raised in patriarchal traditions to create an authentic women's spirituality is not a new phenomenon. Feminists in the nineteenth and early twentieth centuries, for example, were also concerned with finding a spirituality that empowered women, or at least with critiquing the religions that did not. Among her many writings, Elizabeth Cady Stanton published *The Woman's Bible* (1898), commenting on the passages in both the Old and New Testaments that pertained to women. Charlotte Perkins Gilman better known for her fiction and writing on economics, criticized patriarchal religion as death-centered and otherworldly and, hence, not helpful to life on earth (1923).

As scholars, activists, and practitioners, women have created an impressive amount of new writing, art, symbolism, and ritual. To achieve an authentic spiritual existence, some women have gone to their own roots, whether these be in Africa, in Native American traditions, in Western Europe, or elsewhere; some women have gone to other traditions, particularly Native American, African, or Buddhist; other women have struggled within and against their churches; and many women have created whole new ways of expressing their spirituality. Women's spirituality counters the devaluing of women and women's experiences with symbols, images and rituals that celebrate the female as sacred and the sacred as female. Nonpatriarchal traditions, including many of the Native American and African religions, have provided a richness of symbolism (Allen 1986 and 1991; Teish 1985). Other symbols and rituals arise through a struggle within patriarchal churches, where women find the subversive spaces within which their voices can be heard, rework translations of the Bible, rewrite prayers and services, and find new roles for women (Ruether 1983). Women also have constructed new traditions through recovering and remaking symbols from history and prehistory and fusing them with imagination, as quilters take pieces of fabric and stitch them together into a new creation (Starhawk 1989).

Rediscovering symbols and rituals, stories, and the images that speak to women from the Judeo-Christian tradition has required digging deep into the roots of Western civilization. For women in other traditions, Native American and African, for example, it has been more a matter of getting the [white] "man off your eyeball," as Alice Walker says (1982, 168). Sometimes this has required looking beneath a layer of imposed religion for indigenous traditions; sometimes it has meant recovering a fading language to hear the stories that have nearly been lost.

Women of different cultural traditions have different experiences, different resources, and different needs with regard to their spirituality. Native American women have struggled more to keep their traditions alive while many Protestant and Catholic women have struggled against the patriarchal histories of their traditions. African American women have lived with a Christianity that they and their brothers made very much their own, that both inspired the oppressed and gave them strength to fight their oppres-

sion. Women of all traditions have inherited complex and contradictory stories and symbols, some of which honor and empower them, others of which silence and degrade them. What women's spirituality means is that women become the active creators, questioners, preservers, and shapers of their own spiritual lives. In contemporary women's spirituality several common threads cut across, or weave through, differing cultural backgrounds.

Women's spirituality is characterized, first of all, by a sense of the connectedness of the whole of life. This connection not only crosses apparent boundaries between human and other species, it includes "inanimate" nature as well. It also connects people through time, tying them together with generations past and generations yet unborn. Secondly, women's spirituality conceives of the divine as immanent, that is, within humans, rather than transcendent, or outside them. The poet Ntozake Shange spoke for many women when she said, "I found god in myself and . . . I loved her fiercely" (1977, 63). Individuals and their immediate conditions are as important as that greater life force to which all are connected; it is not a matter of the superiority of that which is within over that which is around one, for they are ultimately one and the same. This conception of immanence listens for and honors the spirit within, rather than focusing on some distant and ineffable power.

Consistent with these two sets of ideas, women's spirituality is also characterized by a radical egalitarianism which replaces traditional hierarchical organization. This egalitarianism says that not only are all humans on the same plane, but humans, nature, and the divine are on the same plane. This equality does not imply similarity. In fact, it honors diversity by refusing to create hierarchies of difference. It means that communication can be direct rather than mediated through religious specialists such as priests, and that a multitude of voices speak. Another hierarchy which is eliminated in women's spirituality is that which places the spirit, or the mind, as separate from and superior to the body. The body is valued, its changes and processes celebrated rather than ignored or feared. The body is sacred as nature is sacred; the cycles of both provide a framework for ritual activity. Finally, women's spirituality seeks expression in female and nature imagery, including images of female wisdom, divinity, and the sacred.

Female Divinity

In Alice Walker's novel *The Color Purple*, Shug asks Celie to describe the God she sees in her mind's eye. Celie describes the patriarch of the Old Testament, with flowing white hair and ice-blue eyes. Shug explains to Celie that she will never find the love and comfort available to her with that conception of God (Walker 1982). The male God of Judaism and Christianity has dominated Western religion for centuries, and many women from these traditions have found the need to look beyond this fatherly image to recover female divinity. They have discovered that this god is not only a relative newcomer in the history of the human species, but he is, as a sole male deity, unusual in the religions of the world. Of the hundreds of religions in which there are named deities, only Judaism, Christianity, and Islam have no female deity.

Much has been written on the cultures that preceded the Judeo-Christian tradition in the West. Merlin Stone (1976) wrote one of the first and clearest books demonstrating both the depth and breadth of the worship of goddesses and their destruction in the ancient Near East.

Marija Gimbutas (1982, 1989, 1991) has published volumes on her analysis of archaeological findings of goddess worship in Europe. Judith Ochshorn (1981) has chronicled the transition from polytheism to male monotheism during the time of the Old Testament. In the early 1980s, finding books on goddess worship in the West was difficult; now it is nearly impossible to keep up with the literature. Feminist scholars, for example, Carol Christ and Judith Plaskow (1979), Mary Daly (1973), and Rosemary Reuther (1983) have done this work in part as a piece of the scholarship in women's studies, but they have done it also in answer to a voice inside that questioned the nature of divinity.

What this scholarship has shown is that worship of goddesses dates back many thousands of years all over the face of the earth. Throughout the area that Westerners ethnocentrically refer to as "the cradle of civilization" goddess worship was spread both deep and wide. There were great goddesses, such as Isis, or Inanna/Astarte/Asherah, and many minor female deities. Images of the goddesses remain in art, myth, and poetry. Their worship and worshipers were long-standing and widespread, and they were systematically destroyed as the hegemony of the single male god was installed.

Much of the archaeological data remains open to various interpretations. Knowing exactly what the small female figurines carved by the Upper Paleolithic peoples of Europe some 25,000 years ago meant to them is difficult. Though more recent findings include more confirming evidence of the worship of goddesses, questions remain. Still, the work of feminist scholars has demonstrated beyond doubt that earlier androcentric interpretations of prehistory are also only speculative and need to be challenged with a diversity of views.

Women interested in female divinity have also looked to other religions, including world religions, such as Hinduism or Buddhism, and local religions, including the indigenous religions of Africa and the Americas. In hundreds of religions, goddesses are creators or embodiments of the earth, moon, or sun. Goddesses of agriculture, music, health, and learning reign, as do Goddesses of the sea, the mountains, the forest, and of childbirth, nurturing, time, and death (Monaghan 1990).

Native American traditions provide a wealth of images and stories of goddesses. Some of this knowledge has been layered over through colonialism and the often distorted writings of white travelers and scholars. Paula Gunn Allen (1986, 1991) is one Native American scholar who is reclaiming and publishing this knowledge and telling the stories of Spider Woman, Changing Woman, and White Shell Woman. Telling the stories not only helps to keep them alive, it helps Native Americans in their claims to their own identity within the larger culture. The stories do not simply represent what is sacred in Native American life; they recreate and strengthen the sacred. Allen includes stories from Central and South America as well as North America in her collection. She tells of Tonantzin, the Aztec mother goddess, who survives, as many indigenous goddesses do, through a process known as syncretism. Many peoples whose own traditions were overpowered by Christianity have been able to keep their own deities in the form of saints and have been able to incorporate their own meanings and symbols into their versions of Christianity. The Virgin of Guadalupe, the patron saint of Mexico, for example, appeared at the site of a much earlier temple of Tonantzin and carries many of the associations and tra-

ditions of the earlier Aztec goddess. The virgin of Guadalupe stands upon a crescent moon; Tonantzin was also associated with the moon. As worshipers had made pilgrimages to the shrine of Tonantzin, so they continued to visit the shrine of the Virgin of Guadalupe. And early priests worried that the worshipers did not know the difference between the two figures, calling them both our Lady or Our Mother (Wolf 1979). Goddesses survive, but often in disguise.

Africans became Christians in large part as, against their will, they entered the Western Hemisphere. Their own deities, however, survived in the form of saints, in stories, and in the new religions of Voudou and Candomble (Teish 1985). The "Aunt Nancy" tales have kept alive the spirit of Anansi, the Spider. Anansi is a trickster figure whose stories are told in Ghana and throughout West Africa (though the spider may have different names in different cultures). Teish relates the New World charm known as the Seven African Powers to the Yoruba deities Elegba, Obatala, Yemaya, Oshun, Chango, and Ogun; and in a creative move appropriate to feminist spirituality, she substitutes the goddess Oya for the seventh deity, the god Orula (1985).

The Buddhist deity known as Kwannon, Kwan yin, Tara, or simply the Green Goddess, represents compassion. She has spoken to many women, from those who were attracted to her image on their travels and brought home a statue for their mantelpiece, to those who have pursued her more deeply in a spiritual quest (Galland 1990).

The discovery of the range and variety of images of female divinity has been empowering for women's spirits and has stimulated artists, musicians, and writers. It has expanded women's views of the sacred and of themselves. This emphasis on goddesses is not, however, without controversy. Academics voice concern such as those mentioned regarding archaeology. Is this interpretation of female images correct? How is it possible to know what a goddess meant to people long dead and with no written tradition to explain themselves? This question of meaning also applies to living cultures. Is it possible, for example, for one who is not Navaho, has not lived the life of the Navaho in the land of the Navaho, to understand Changing Woman's true meaning? This question is related to another serious ethical question. When whites turn to Native American spirituality (whether or not they make money from this turn, though they often do), are they not exercising yet another form of colonization and exploitation?

A final concern might be called a theological one: Is this emphasis on goddesses not simply replacing one external (male) authority with another (female) one? Sonia Johnson, a radical feminist who has written of her journey away from the Church of Jesus Christ of Latter-day Saints, the Mormons, (1981), says of the goddess traditions:

> I had no desire to go back to ancient Goddess religion. I rapidly rejected the notion of putting a skirt on God, calling him "the Goddess," and worshipping essentially the same sort of being, entrapped in dogma and hierarchical trappings. God in drag is still God. (1987, 6)

Margot Adler (1986) argues that the danger lies not in female images of divinity *per se* but in collapsing all of the female attributes into a Great Goddess. This monotheism destroys the potential of the myriad goddesses to support and give spirit to diversity, to mirror women in a great variety of ways. For both Johnson

and Adler, and for other women, a primary concern is that divinity be seen *within* humans, not outside of them, defining and judging them.

Immanence vs. Transcendence

In the conversation between Alice Walker's characters Shug and Celie cited previously, Shug goes on to explain to Celie that God is inside her: "God is inside you and inside everybody else. You come into the world with God. But only them that search for it inside find it" (Walker 1982, 166). Zora Neale Hurston's Janey describes "the jewel down inside herself" (1978, 138). This notion of the divine within characterizes much of women's spirituality, whatever the tradition. It honors what is best in everyone, and what connects all of us with one another. The notion of God speaking from within, of an inner voice which gives each person her own authority, is not unique to women, and it is not new, even in Christianity. Her belief in and preaching of this concept of God caused Anne Hutchinson's excommunication from her congregation in Puritan Massachusetts and her banishment from the country in 1638 (Evans 1989). She was excommunicated because the god of whom she spoke undermined the authority of the family, the community, and the church. The patriarch's punishment of Anne Hutchinson, however, did not still that inner voice, nor dim its "inner light" as that light guided South Carolina Quakers Sarah and Angelina Grimké in their fight to abolish slavery just as it pointed the way for the largely Quaker organizers of the 1848 Seneca Falls, New York Women's rights meeting (Lerner 1971; Rossi 1988) The concept of the sacred as immanent creates a powerful spiritual equality of us all, one that undermines the clerical authority of the few and is often seen as heresy within institutionalized religion and within institutionalized social, political, and economic arrangements.

The sacred within is even more integrated in many Native American traditions, where the concept of self is far less individualized and separate than in Western thought. Who one is, is defined in terms of kinship, lineage, clan, and people that includes a world of spirits. A Hopi woman not only has an image of a female creator, Spider Woman, at the heart of her universe, but is a member of a clan which stretches back to the creation of that universe. She identifies with the earth as mother and the corn that grows from that earth. Whenever she looks up into her world, she looks in one of the four sacred directions; when she sees clouds, she sees the spirits of her ancestors. Her life, work, and social world are all embedded in and infused with the sacred (Ferrero 1986).

This integration is one of the things that makes tribal cultures so appealing to members of modernized societies, but it cannot be borrowed (or even stolen) in weekend workshops, in symbols and stories that are taken back to the museums, or penthouse coffee tables in the city. To try to capture Native American spirituality by taking its stories and rituals into a different world is like cutting a piece from a quilt in order to appreciate the quilt itself. The cultures of Native Americans are very attractive to whites. But it must seem to Native Americans that having taken every material thing they had, whites are now stealing even their spiritual traditions. This theft does not mean one people cannot learn from another, because of course they can. But doing so requires sensitivity, humility, and a degree of grace that most people from dominant cultures do not exhibit. How is it possible to get along, to share, and to learn from one another? This is an extremely difficult question and one that must be handled with great thoughtfulness and care. One lesson from feminism is useful here: Always let people speak for themselves in their own voices. It is crucial that whites approach this intercultural conversation with understanding and great tenderness for the complexity and fragility of the web of historical and social relationships that have laid the groundwork and are part of the present.

Earth, Nature, Redemption, and Connection

The parallel between woman and the earth, each as givers of life, has created a symbolic connection between earth and female in cultures all over the world. While there are exceptions, the notion of the earth as mother, as that which gives life, is widespread. This association of the earth as female, as mother, as giver of life, and as goddess speaks to women in a great many spiritual traditions. Where the earth and nature are revered rather than dominated, this parallel can be a powerful recognition of the sacred in women, but it is increasingly an equally powerful reminder to those in cultures that do not treasure the earth, or women, that something is wrong (Sanday 1981).

In some conceptions of patriarchal religions, a god associated with the sky and with the spirit has gained dominion over the earth, the female, and the body. The creation story told in the Book of Genesis provides a basis for just such a hierarchical dichotomy between male and female, mind and matter, and humans and nature. Many women see a relation between the male domination of women and children and the ecological devastation facing us all at the end of the twentieth century.

Authors ranging from the archaeological (Eisler 1987) to the artistic (Oda 1988) include in their discussion of women's spirituality a note of crisis concerning our environment and its depredation and a hope that a return to a vision of the female/earth as sacred can save us from destruction.

Many spiritual traditions concern themselves with some form of redemption. In women's spirituality, the focus is on redemption of the world in which we live. While much of the writing is concerned with the individual gaining power through the discovery of what is divine within, a nearly universal sense of urgency regarding the threats of warfare and environmental destruction exists in tandem. Leslie Marmon Silko (1977; 1991) created incredibly powerful images of the relationship between external devastation and internal healing and the importance of spiritual traditions to counter the evil that is afoot in the world. Women's spirituality looks to earth-based and life-loving symbols, metaphors, and rituals with a sense of both hope and urgency for the future of humanity and for the planet. The desirability of reconnecting ourselves with the earth, our bodies with our spirits, our hearts with our minds, and our social institutions with our human needs, provides not only a thoughtful content, but also a series of programs for action for women of spirit.

Some feminists have worried that a spiritual focus will keep women from the political work they must do in order to achieve a just and peaceful world; that spirituality, in itself, is too close to the "opiate of the masses" that Marx saw in religion, or that it is too concerned with individual well-being to energize social change. In fact, women's spirituality provides a genuine theoretical basis for activism as it defines each person's well-being in terms of the well-being of the entire planet. An authentic spirituality teaches that the means and the ends, or in more spiritual terms, the goal and the path, are one: We create peace by living peace; the world we live in is the only one we have; and we must care for it every day. The writings of Charlene Spretnak (1982) and Starhawk (1982) attest eloquently to the synergy between spiritual and political modes.

The sense of being at one with the universe lies at the heart of mystical traditions throughout the world. Whether it is "the peace that passeth understanding" or nirvana, a sense of oneness with the universe shapes both the goal and the experience of the religious practitioner. This awareness of connectedness has led women in many different directions. For some, the emphasis is on connection with nature which may result in a deep commitment to ecology and environmental activism. Certainly not all spiritual women are involved in animal rights or are vegetarians, but either or both of these may be a response to a growing awareness of being connected with all life. Many women find themselves more deeply engaged with peace movements and nonviolent philosophies as they find themselves feeling the hurt inflicted upon others in war and other forms of violence. The music of the Washington, D.C.-based group Sweet Honey in the Rock gives voice not only to African and African American musical traditions, but to the plight of women, blacks, and workers everywhere.

One powerful form of connectedness that cuts across many spiritual traditions is that of connection to the ancestors, whether they be one's immediate family, the people of one's tribe or nation, or all women who have ever lived. Luisah Teish devotes a significant portion of her book on African American spiritual practices to one's relationship with one's ancestors and includes a ritual for unknown ancestors (1985). Sonia Johnson describes in riveting detail the help that she garnered from ancestral Mormon women in her struggle with the priesthood of the Church of Jesus Christ of Latter-day Saints (1981). And Anderson and Hopkins tell about Leah Novick, a woman rabbi in California who has begun calling the names of women who have been forgotten or who had no descendants to pray for them on High Holy Days (1991). Many women say that the women who have come before provide the necessary support and courage for the struggle to become whole; the generations to come after provide the motivation.

Practices and Cycles

Spirituality is embodied in practices many of which, though not all, can be called rituals. Rituals are patterned actions that both express and evoke the awareness of connectedness. They create connections with larger communities of belief, including past and future generations, as all perform the same actions. They create connections with cycles of nature or annual calendars, as the same rituals are performed with each reoccurrence; they create connections between everyday life and the sacred, as meaning is infused into objects and action. While many institutionalized rituals require hierarchy and authority for their performance, women's spirituality emphasizes the ability of each person to create and participate in ritual. Some of these rituals may celebrate the passing of seasons or phases of the moon (Budapest 1989; Iglehart 1983; Starhawk 1989; Walker 1990). Others celebrate the stages of the life of an individual or community. Coming-of-

age rituals which celebrate the passage from girlhood to womanhood are found in many cultures. Lincoln provides an interesting discussion of traditional women's initiation rites, including the Navaho Kinaalda (1981). The Kinaalda not only celebrates a girl's first menstruation, it transforms her into a woman, able to bear children and take her place as an adult among the Navajo (Lincoln 1981). Carol Christ describes a lovely coming-of-age ritual which she and a friend created for the friend's daughter's entrance into womanhood (1987). Yet another emphasis of ritual practice is on seeing the sacred embodied in the ordinary activities of women (Ochs 1983).

This focus on cycles, the cycles of individual lives and transitions and the cycles of nature, is common to feminist and female spiritual traditions. One of the most ancient images of a female figure is the Venus of Laussel. Carved into a cave wall in France, this abundant nude holds aloft a crescent with thirteen hatch marks. Alexander Marshak sees this as an association of the female with the moon, and thus with a very early calendar (1972). Just as the menstruating female goes through thirteen 28-day cycles in a calendar year, so does the moon. This association of the female with the moon is found in religions all over the world. Likewise, the passage of the individual through life—from young woman to mother to ancient, is found in images of a triple goddess, particularly in northern Europe (Graves, 1966). These goddess images celebrate the female body in all of its changes, again creating a mirror of diversity rather than a model of perfection.

Cycles of nature, as the wheel of the year turns through the seasons, are celebrated in ritual. Peoples all over the world mark the periods of lengthening and shortening days, the end of winter, and the time for the ground to lie fallow. Starhawk writes of the celebration points of the pagan calendar, many of which are found in the modern calendar under different names (1989). For example, winter solstice celebrates the return of the light; many December rituals involve lights, including Christmas and Hanukkah. Spring equinox marks a return to fertility of the earth and animals; both the egg and the rabbit associated with Easter have this association with fertility as well. One of the great pagan holidays is October 31, when "the veil is thin that divides the worlds," and ghosts and humans walk side by side (Starhawk 1989, 193). This is the time of Halloween and the Day of the Dead in modern calendars.

Practices in women's spirituality may be largely celebratory, but they may also be pragmatic. Healing as a spiritual practice calls upon the wholeness that is at the heart of spirituality. The curanderas, the women healers, of Latino communities derive their ability to heal from their knowledge of the unity of mind and body, of individual and community. Santeria, calling upon the old deities in the guise of saints for healing, is found at the conjunction of African and Catholic traditions and is practiced extensively by women.

These practices, based on the connections between humans and nature, and between the seen and the unseen, have often been referred to as magic. Magic, for those who believe in it, is a particularly intense way of paying attention to and focusing one's energy and awareness, of finding and becoming attuned to different rhythms in the cosmos. For those who do not believe in it, magic may be seen as anything from nonsense to evil. Some women who currently practice magic identify themselves as witches. They argue that women unfairly perse-

cuted as witches during the Renaissance were not evil but were punished for their independence, a real threat to the dominant patriarchal religion (Ehrenreich and English 1973; Starhawk 1982).

The Creative Spirit

Spirituality is not first and foremost a matter of the intellect. It is about the heart, the soul, and the spirit. It must address the senses at a level that goes beyond everyday life. Spirituality does this through art, music, and ritual. As we shall see in Chapter 11, the flowering of women's art expresses the flowering of women's spirit as the end of the century approaches. Women are creating wonderful art that expresses their new-found spirit of celebration of the female and the sacred. Goddess traditions have stimulated painting, sculpture, ceramic arts, jewelry, and fabric arts (Gadon 1989; Lippard 1983). Mayumi Oda (1988) tells of her paintings of goddesses:

> I began to feel in touch with my own power as a woman. It was as if a sun inside me had finally broken through the clouds . . . Goddesses are a projection of myself, my desire and my dreams. They help me to see who I am and who I want to be. Through my creative process, I have been creating myself (58, 66).

Women's music ranges from the rediscovery of the medieval work of Hildegard of Bingen to the powerful amalgam of spirituality and politics found in the African American group Sweet Honey in the Rock.

Certainly one of the best places to find the expression of women's spirituality is in literature, whether it be the poetry of Joy Harjo (1990), Luci Tapahonso (1987), Judy Grahn (1982), or Marge Piercy (1988); the novels of Alice Walker (1982) or Margaret Atwood (1972); the work of Paula Gunn Allen (1991) or Linda Hogan (1990); or the journals and autobiographical writings of Maya Angelou (1970) or Etty Hillesum (1983). In novels, poetry, and autobiography, women's voices convey their journeys of spiritual growth, their connection to the earth, and the sacredness of everyday life.

A somewhat less permanent expression of the creative spirit is in women's rituals and ritual spaces. Rituals, as discussed above, are a set of patterned, symbolic activities. Women involved in ritual use color, scent, music, and other objects and activities to create symbolic expressions of time, connection, and transition. Most of these rituals are not recorded in any public way, though some authors mentioned above discuss ritual structure (Budapest 1989; Iglehart 1983; Starhawk 1989; Walker 1990). Central to the construction of ritual is the creation of sacred space and sacred time. While spirituality may infuse the everyday activities of women, the reminder of the connection to that which goes beyond the particular experience is what gives it its sacred quality. In Native American traditions, which arise from and are connected to a particular geography, sacred space may be marked by particular mountains or other landmarks which are also symbolic and carry meaning beyond their immediate existence. One mountain may represent a direction that may be associated with a color, time of year, stage of the life cycle, precious stone, and segment of the sacred story of the people. When people are not so connected to a specific geography, they remake sacred spaces through orienting a building (literally, making it face the East) or simply drawing a circle within which space is sacred.

The altar is a sacred space found throughout the world. It holds the mem-ory of events, as in Christianity where the altar in the church recreates the table at which Jesus offered the Last Supper. The altar holds the memory of particular beings, human, or spirit. It marks a particular space as sacred, different from the space around it. Many women make altars in their homes, some consciously and some unconsciously. Some altars are deliberately religious in their expression, such as shrines to the Virgin Mary or to a patron saint. Others might be more accurately called domestic shrines, with family photographs and objects. Turner (1982) has studied the home altars of Latina women as a unique form of folk art, combining religious, aesthetic, and domestic functions. A home altar might contain statues of the Virgin and saints, candles and flowers, family photographs, natural objects such as shells or stones, pictures or statues of political figures (particularly John and Robert Kennedy), and ordinary household objects such as buttons or teacups. Both the creative spirit and the spirit of creativity are essential to women's spirituality. Women's creations both express their spirits and result in new symbolic forms for the practice of their spirituality.

Conclusion

Spirituality is about wholeness; it is about healing the rifts between the human and the divine, the mind and the body, and humans and nature. It is about eliminating artificial categories of separation and replacing them with the celebration of both connection and diversity. For women who have often hidden or silenced their spirits in order to survive, spirituality is about reclaiming their own wholeness. Women who live in patriarchal society often hide within themselves in order to be desirable, acceptable, and literally, in order to survive. Edna Pontellier, the heroine of Kate Chopin's novel, *The Awakening*, feels this "dual life—that outward existence which conforms, the inward life which questions" (1976, 15). And Janey, in Zora Neale Hurston's novel *Their Eyes Were Watching God*, "had an inside and an outside now and suddenly she knew how not to mix them" (1978, 112–13). The inside may become so buried that a woman forgets it is there. A crucial aspect of a woman's spiritual journey is the recovery and healing of this buried, splintered self, the discovery and use of her authentic voice.

Thus, spirituality brings one to a different kind of consciousness. As women in patriarchy lose awareness of their true selves, so people in modern industrial society lose consciousness of the connectedness of all of life. A spiritual awakening brings consciousness of the world around as well as of the world within. This consciousness means paying attention to where the things one requires for survival come from and what happens to the waste; paying attention to one's action, the action of others, and their consequences; and paying attention to seen and unseen connections in the world of humans and the world of nature.

This consciousness also means an awareness of and responsibility for our role in shaping the society we live in. All social institutions, whether they address our material or our spiritual needs, must be continually reshaped and reinvigorated to reflect the actual lived reality of those they are meant to serve. All of our social practices require continual scrutiny and attention to what ends are being served and whose needs are being met. All of us as human beings must be aware of ourselves not just as creatures, but as creators of our lives. Women who take active responsibility for their own spirituality will not only "find god in [themselves] and love her fiercely" (Shange 1977, 63), they will assure a living changing spirituality that is responsive to and as vibrant as women themselves.

References

Adler, Margot. 1986. *Drawing down the moon*. Boston: Beacon Press.

Allen, Paula Gunn. 1986. *The sacred hoop: Recovering the feminine in native American Indian tradition*. Boston: Beacon Press.

———. 1991. *Grandmothers of the light*. Boston: Beacon Press.

Anderson, Sherry Ruth, and Patricia Hopkins. 1991. *The feminine face of God*. New York: Bantam Books.

Angelou, Maya. 1970. *I know why the caged bird sings*. New York: Random House.

Atwood, Margaret. 1972. *Surfacing*. New York: Simon and Schuster.

Budapest, Zsuzsanna E. 1989. *The grandmother of time: A women's book of celebrations, spells, and sacred objects for every month of the year*. San Francisco: Harper Collins.

Christ, Carol. 1987. *Laughter of Aphrodite: Reflections on a journey to the goddess*. San Francisco: Harper and Row.

Chopin, Kate. 1976. *The awakening*. Norton critical ed. New York: W. W. Norton and Co.

Ehrenreich, Barbara, and Deirdre English. 1973. *Witches, midwives, and nurses: A history of women healers*. Old Westbury, N.Y.: The Feminist Press.

Eisler, Riane. 1987. *The chalice and the blade: Our history, our future*. San Francisco: Harper and Row.

Evans, Sara M. 1989. *Born for liberty: A history of women in America*. New York: The Free Press.

Ferrero, Pat. 1986. *Hopi: Songs of the fourth world.* New Day Filmstrip.

Gadon, Elinor W. 1989. *The once and future goddess.* San Francisco: Harper and Row.

Galland, China. 1990. *Longing for darkness: Tara and the Black Madonna, a ten-year journey.* New York: Viking.

Geertz, Clifford. 1973. Religion as a cultural system. In *The interpretation of cultures.* New York: Basic Books.

Gilman, Charlotte Perkins. 1976. *His religion or hers?: A study of the faith of our fathers and the work of our mothers.* Westport, Conn.: Hyperion Press.

Gimbutas, Marija. 1982. *The goddesses and gods of old Europe: Myths and cult images.* Berkeley: University of California Press.

———. 1989. *The language of the goddess.* San Francisco: Harper and Row.

———. 1991. *The civilization of the goddess: The world of old Europe.* San Francisco: Harper Collins.

Grahn, Judy. 1982. *The queen of wands: Poetry.* Trumansburg, N.Y.: Crossing Press.

Graves, Robert. 1966. *The white goddess.* New York: Farrar, Straus and Giroux.

Harjo, Joy. 1990. *In mad love and war.* Middlebury, Conn.: Wesleyan University Press.

Hillesum, Etty. 1983. *An interrupted life: The diaries of Etty Hillesum, 1941–1943.* New York: Pantheon Books.

Hogan, Linda. 1990. *Mean spirit.* New York: Athaneum.

Hurston, Zora Neale. 1978. *Their eyes were watching God.* Urbana: University of Illinois Press.

Iglehart, Hallie. 1983. *Womanspirit: A guide to women's wisdom.* San Francisco: Harper and Row.

Johnson, Sonia. 1981. *From housewife to heretic.* Garden City, N.Y.: Doubleday.

———. 1987. *Going out of our minds: The metaphysics of liberation.* Freedom, Calif.: The Crossing Press.

Lincoln, Bruce. 1981. *Emerging from the chrysalis: Studies in rituals of women's initiation.* Cambridge: Harvard University Press.

Lippard, Lucy. 1983. *Overlay: Contemporary art and the art of prehistory.* New York: Pantheon Books.

Marshak, Alexander. 1972. *The roots of civilization.* New York: McGraw Hill.

Monaghan, Patricia. 1990. *The book of goddesses and heroines.* St. Paul, Minn.: Llewellyn Publications.

Ochs, Carol. 1983. *Women and spirituality.* Totowa, N.J.: Rowman and Allanheld.

Ochschorn, Judith. 1981. *The female experience and the nature of the divine.* Bloomington: Indiana University Press.

Oda, Mayumi. 1988. *Goddesses.* Volcano, Calif.: Volcano Press.

Patai, Rafael. 1990. *The Hebrew goddess.* Detroit: Wayne State University Press.

Piercy, Marge. 1988. *Available light.* New York: Alfred A. Knopf.

Ruether, Rosemary Radford. 1983. *Sexism and god-talk: Toward a feminist theology.* Boston: Beacon Press.

Sanday, Peggy Reeves. 1981. *Female power and male dominance: On the origins of sexual inequality.* Cambridge: Cambridge University Press.

Shange, Ntozake. 1977. *for colored girls who have considered suicide when the rainbow is enuf: a choreopoem.* New York: Macmillan.

Silko, Leslie Marmon. 1977. *Ceremony.* New York: Viking.

———. 1991. *Almanac of the dead.* New York: Simon and Schuster.

Spretnak, Charlene. 1982. *The politics of women's spirituality: Essays on the rise of spiritual power within the feminist movement.* Garden City, N.Y.: Anchor/Doubleday.

Stanton, Elizabeth Cady. [1898] 1974. *The woman's Bible.* Seattle: Seattle Coalition Task Force on Women and Religion.

Starhawk. 1982. *Dreaming the dark: Magic, sex, and politics.* Boston: Beacon Press.

———. 1989. *The spiral dance: A rebirth of the ancient religion of the great goddess.* San Francisco: Harper and Row.

Stone, Merlin. 1976. *When God was a woman.* New York: Harcourt, Brace, Jovanovich.

Tapahonso, Luci. 1987. *A breeze swept through.* Albuquerque: West End Press.

Teish, Luisah. 1985. *Jambayala: The natural woman's book of personal charms and practical rituals.* San Francisco: Harper and Row.

Turner, Kay. 1982. Mexican American home altars: Towards their interpretation. *Aztlan* 13:309–26.

Walker, Alice. 1982. *The color purple.* New York: Harcourt, Brace, Jovanovich.

Walker, Barbara. 1990. *Women's rituals: A sourcebook.* San Francisco: Harper and Row.

Wolf, Eric. 1979. The virgin of Guadalupe: A Mexican national symbol. In *Reader in comparative religion: An anthropological approach.* 4th ed. Edited by William A. Lessa and Evon Z. Vogt. New York: Harper and Row.

Wynne, Patrice. 1988. *The womanspirit sourcebook.* San Francisco: Harper and Row.

Witchcraft and Women's Culture

Starhawk

The unhewn stones are newly risen. Within their circle, an old woman raises a flint knife and points it toward the bright full moon. She cries out, a wail echoed by her clan folk as they begin the dance. They circle wildly around the central fire, feeling the power rise within them until they unite in ecstatic frenzy. The priestess cries again, and all drop to the earth, exhausted but filled with a deep sense of peace. A cup of ale is poured into the fire, and the flames leap up high. "Blessed be the mother of all life," the priestess says, "May She be generous to Her children."

The birth is a difficult one, but the midwife has brought many women through worse. Still, she is worried. She has herbs to open the womb and stop the blood, herbs to bring sleep, and others to bring forgetfulness of pain. But now her baskets are almost empty. This year she could not go gathering at the proper times of the moon and sun. The new priest and his spies are everywhere—if she were to be caught digging simples in the moonlight it would be sure proof of witchcraft, not just against herself but against her daughters and sisters and her daughter's daughters. As she pours out the last of her broth for the laboring woman, the midwife sighs. "Blessed Tana, Mother of mothers," she breathes softly, "when will the old ways return?"

The child is in a state of shock. Her memories of the last three days are veiled in a haze of smoke and noise that seem to swirl toward this climax of acrid smells and hoarse shouting. The priest's grip is clawlike as he forces her to watch the cruel drama in the center of the square. The girl's eyes are open, but her mind has flown far away, and what she sees is not the scene before her: her mother, the stake, the flames. She is running through the open field behind their cottage, smelling only clean wind, seeing only clear sky. The priest looks down at her blank face and crosses himself in fear. "Devil's spawn!" he spits on the ground. "If I had my way, we'd hold to custom and burn you too!"

It is the night of the full moon. Nine women stand in a circle, on a rocky hill above the city. The western sky is rosy with the setting sun; in the east the moon's face begins to peer above the horizon. Below, electric lights wink on the ground like fallen stars. A young woman raises a steel knife and cries out, a wail echoed by the others as they begin the dance. They circle wildly around a cauldron of smoldering herbs, feeling the power rise within them until they unite in ecstasy. The priestess cries again, and all drop to the earth, exhausted, but filled with an overwhelming sense of peace. The woman pours out a cup of wine onto the earth, refills it and raises it high. "Hail, Tana, Mother of mothers!" she cries. "Awaken from your long sleep, and return to your children again!"

From earliest times,[1] women have been witches, *wicce*, "wise ones"—priestesses, diviners, midwives, poets, healers, and singers of songs of power. Woman-centered culture, based on the worship of the Great Goddess, underlies the beginnings of all civilization. Mother Goddess was carved on the walls of paleolithic caves, and painted in the shrines of the earliest cities, those of the Anatolian plateau. For her were raised the giant stone circles, the henges of the British Isles, the dolmens and cromlechs of the later Celtic countries, and for her the great passage graves of Ireland were dug. In her honor, sacred dancers leaped the bulls in Crete and composed lyric hymns within the colleges of the holy isles of the Mediterranean. Her mysteries were celebrated in secret rites at Eleusis, and her initiates included some of the finest minds of Greece. Her priestesses discovered and tested the healing herbs and learned the secrets of the human mind and body that allowed them to ease the pain of childbirth, to heal wounds and cure diseases, and to explore the realm of dreams and the unconscious. Their knowledge of nature enabled them to tame sheep and cattle, to breed wheat and corn from grasses and weeds, to forge ceramics from mud and metal from rock, and to track the movements of moon, stars, and sun.

Witchcraft, "the craft of the wise," is the last remnant in the west of the time of women's strength and power. Through the dark ages of persecution, the covens of Europe preserved what is left of the mythology, rituals, and knowledge of the ancient matricentric (mother-centered) times. The great centers of worship in Anatolia, Malta, Iberia, Brittany, and Sumeria are now only silent stones and works of art we can but dimly understand. Of the mysteries of Eleusis, we have literary hints; the poems of Sappho survive only in fragments. The great collections of early literature and science were destroyed by patriarchal forces—the library of Alexandria burnt by Caesar, Charlemagne's collection of lore burnt by his son Louis "the Pious," who was offended at its "paganism." But the craft remains, in spite of all efforts to stamp it out, as a living tradition of Goddess-centered worship that traces its roots back to the time before the triumph of patriarchy.

The old religion of witchcraft before the advent of Christianity, was an earth-centered, nature-oriented worship that venerated the Goddess, the source of life, as well as her son-lover-consort, who was seen as the Horned God of the hunt and animal life. Earth, air, water, fire, streams, seas, wells, beasts, trees, grain, the planets, sun, and most of all, the moon, were seen as aspects of deity. On the great seasonal festivals—the solstices and equinoxes, and the eves of May, August, November, and February,—all the countryside would gather to light huge bonfires, feast, dance, sing, and perform the rituals that assured abundance throughout the year.

When Christianity first began to spread, the country people held to the old ways, and for hundreds of years the two faiths coexisted quite peacefully. Many people followed both religions, and country priests in the twelfth and thirteenth centuries were frequently upbraided by church authorities for dressing in skins and leading the dance at the pagan festivals.

But in the thirteenth and fourteenth centuries, the church began persecution of witches, as well as Jews and "heretical" thinkers. Pope Innocent the VIII, with his Bull of 1484, intensified a campaign of torture and death that would take the lives of a estimated 9 million people, perhaps 80 percent of whom were women.

The vast majority of victims were not coven members or even necessarily witches. They were old widows whose property was coveted by someone else, young children with "witch blood," midwives who furnished the major competition to the male-dominated medical profession, free-thinkers who asked the wrong questions.

An enormous campaign of propaganda accompanied the witch trials as well. Witches were said to have sold their souls to the devil, to practice obscene and disgusting rites, to blight crops and murder children. In many areas, the witches did worship a Horned God as the spirit of the hunt, of animal life and vitality, a concept far from the power of evil that was the Christian devil. Witches were free and open about sexuality—but their rites were "obscene" only to those who viewed the human body itself as filthy and evil. Questioning or disbelieving any of the slander was itself considered proof of witchcraft or heresy, and the falsehoods that for hundreds of years could not be openly challenged had their effect. Even today, the word *witch* is often automatically associated with "evil."

With the age of reason in the eighteenth century, belief in witches, as in all things psychic and supernatural, began to fade. The craft as a religion was forgotten; all that remained were the wild stories of broomstick flights, magic potions, and the summoning of spectral beings.

Memory of the true craft faded everywhere except within the hidden covens. With it, went the memory of women's heritage and history, of our ancient roles as leaders, teachers, healers, seers. Lost, also, was the conception of the Great Spirit, as manifest in nature, in life, in woman. Mother Goddess slept, leaving the world to the less than gentle rule of the God-Father.

The Goddess has at last stirred from sleep, and women are reawakening to our ancient power. The feminist movement, which began as a political, economic, and social struggle, is opening to a spiritual dimension. In the process, many women are discovering the old religion, reclaiming the word *witch* and, with it, some of our lost culture.

Witchcraft, today, is a kaleidoscope of diverse traditions, rituals, theologies, and structures. But underneath the varying forms is a basic orientation common to all the craft. The outer forms of religion—the particular words said, the signs made, the names used—are less important to us than the inner forms, which cannot be defined or described but must be felt and intuited.

The craft is earth religion, and our basic orientation is to the earth, to life, to nature. There is no dichotomy between spirit and flesh, no split between Godhead and the world. The Goddess is manifest in the world; she brings life into being, *is* nature, *is* flesh. Union is not sought outside the world in some heavenly sphere or through dissolution of the self into the void beyond the senses. Spiritual union is found in life, within nature, passion, sensuality—through being fully human, fully one's self.

Our great symbol for the Goddess is the moon, whose three aspects reflect the three stages in women's lives and whose cycles of waxing and waning coincide with women's menstrual cycles. As the new moon or crescent, she is the Maiden, the Virgin—not chaste, but belonging to herself alone, not bound to any man. She is the wild child, lady of the woods, the huntress, free and untamed—Artemis, Kore, Aradia, Nimue. White is her color. As the full moon, she is the mature woman, the sexual being, the mother and nurturer, giver of life, fertility, grain, offspring, potency, joy—Tana, Demeter, Diana, Ceres, Mari. Her colors are the red of blood and the green of growth. As waning or dark moon, she is the old woman, past menopause, the hag or crone that is ripe with wisdom, patroness of secrets, prophecy, divination, inspiration, power—Hecate, Ceridwen, Kali, Anna. Her color is the black of night.

The Goddess is also earth—Mother Earth, who sustains all growing things, who is the body, our bones and cells. She is air—the winds that move in the trees and over the waves, breath. She is the fire of the hearth, of the blazing bonfire and the fuming volcano; the power of transformation and change. And she is water—the sea, original source of life; the rivers, streams, lakes and wells; the blood that flows in the rivers of our veins. She is mare, cow, cat, owl, crane, flower, tree, apple, seed, lion, sow, stone, woman. She is found in the world around us, in the cycles and seasons of nature, and in mind, body, spirit, and emotions within each of us. Thou art Goddess. I am Goddess. All that lives (and all that is, lives), all that serves life, is Goddess.

Because witches are oriented to earth and to life, we value spiritual qualities that I feel are especially important to women, who have for so long been conditioned to be passive, submissive and weak. The craft values independence, personal strength, *self*—not petty selfishness but that deep core of strength within that makes us each a unique child of the Goddess. The craft has no dogma to stifle thought, no set of doctrines that have to be believed. Where authority exists, within covens, it is always coupled with the freedom every covener has, to leave at any time. When self is valued—in ourselves—we can see that self is everywhere.

Passion and emotion—that give depth and color and meaning to human life—are also valued. Witches strive to be in touch with feelings, even if they are sometimes painful, because the joy and pleasure and ecstasy available to a fully alive person make it worth occasional suffering. So-called negative emotion—anger—is valued as well, as a sign that something is wrong and that action needs to be taken. Witches prefer to handle anger by taking action and making changes rather than by detaching ourselves from our feelings in order to reach some nebulous, "higher" state.

Most of all, the craft values love. The Goddess' only law is "Love unto all beings." But the love we value is not the airy flower power of the hippies or the formless, abstracted *agape* of the early Christians. It is passionate, sensual, personal love, *eros*, falling in love, mother-child love, the love of one unique human being for other individuals, with all their personal traits and idiosyncrasies. Love is not something that can be radiated out in solitary meditation—it manifests itself in relationships and interractions with other people. It is often said "You cannot be a witch alone"—because to be a witch is to be a lover, a lover of the Goddess, and a lover of other human beings.

The coven is still the basic structure of the craft, and generally covens meet at the times of full moons and the major festivals, although some meet also on new moons and a few meet once a week. A coven is a small group, at most of thirteen members—for the thirteen full moons of the year. Its small size is important. Within the coven, a union, a merging of selves in a close bond of love and trust, takes place. A coven becomes an energy pool each member can draw on. But, because the group remains small, there is never the loss of identity and individuality that can happen in a mass. In a coven, each person's individuality is extremely important. Each personality colors and helps create the group identity, and each member's energy is vital to the working of the group.

Covens are separate and autonomous, and no one outside the coven has any authority over its functioning. Some covens may be linked in the same tradition—meaning they share the same rituals and symbology—but there is no hierarchy of rule. Elder witches can and do give advice, but only those within the coven may actually make decisions.

Covens are extremely diverse. There are covens of hereditary witches who have practiced rites unchanged for hundreds of years, and covens who prefer to make up their own rituals and may never do the same thing twice. There are covens of "perfect couples"—an even number of women and men permanently paired, and covens of lesbian feminists or of women who simply prefer to explore women's spirituality in a space removed from men. There are covens of gay men and covens that just don't worry about sexual polarities. A few covens are authoritarian—with a high priestess or high priest who makes most of the decisions. (Coveners, of course, always have the option of leaving.) Most are democratic, if not anarchic, but usually older or more experienced members—"elders"—assume leadership and responsibility. Actual roles in rituals are often rotated among qualified coveners.

Rituals also vary widely. A craft ritual might involve wild shouting and frenzied dancing, or silent meditation, or both. A carefully rehearsed drama might be enacted, or a spontaneous poetic chant carried on for an hour. Everyone may enter a deep trance and scry in a crystal ball—or they may pass around a bottle of wine and laugh uproariously at awful puns. The best rituals combine moments of intense ecstasy and spiritual union, with moments of raucous humor and occasional silliness. The craft is serious without being dry or solemn.

Whether formal or informal, every craft ritual takes place within a circle—a space considered to be "between the worlds," the human world and the realm of the Goddess. A circle can be cast, or created, in any physical space, from a moonlit hillside to the living room of a modern apartment. It may be outlined in stones, drawn in chalk or paint, or drawn invisibly with the point of a sword or ceremonial wand. It may be consecrated with incense, salt water, and a formal invocation to each of the four quarters of the universe, or created simply by having everyone join hands. The casting of the circle begins the ritual and serves as a transition into an expanded state of consciousness. The power raised by the ritual is contained within the circle so that it can reach a higher peak instead of dissipating.

The Goddess, and if desired, the Horned God (not all traditions of the craft relate to the male force) can be invoked once the circle is cast. An invocation may be set beforehand, written out and memorized, but in our coven we find the most effective invocations are those that come to us spontaneously, out of the inspiration of the season, the phase of the moon, and the particular mood and energy of the moment. Often we invoke the Goddess by chanting together a line or phrase repeated over and over: "Moon mother bright light of all earth sky, we call you" is an example. As we chant, we find rhythms, notes, melodies, and words seem to flow through us and burst out in complex and beautiful patterns.

Chanting, dancing, breathing, and concentrated will, all contribute to the raising of power, which is the essential part of a craft ritual. Witches conceive of psychic energy as having form and substance that can be perceived and directed by those with a trained awareness. The power generated within the circle is built into a cone form, and at its peak is released—to the Goddess, to reenergize the members of the coven, or to do a specific work such as a healing.

When the cone is released, any scattered energy that is left is grounded, put back into the earth, by falling to the ground, breathing deeply, and relaxing. High-energy states cannot be maintained indefinitely without becoming a physical and emotional drain—

any more than you could stay high on methedrine forever without destroying your body. After the peak of the cone, it is vital to let go of the power and return to a calm, relaxed state. Silent meditation, trance, or psychic work are often done in this part of the ritual.

Energy is also shared in tangible form—wine, cakes, fruit, cheesecake, brownies, or whatever people enjoy eating. The Goddess is invited to share with everyone, and a libation is poured to her first. This part of the ritual is relaxed and informally social, devoted to laughing, talking, sharing of news any business that must be done.

At the end, the Goddess is thanked and bid farewell, and the circle is formally opened. Ending serves as a transition back into ordinary space and time. Rituals finish with a kiss and a greeting of "Merry meet, merry part, and merry meet again."

The underlying forms of craft rituals evolved out of thousands of years of experience and understanding of human needs and the potentials of human consciousness. That understanding, which is part of women's lost heritage, is invaluable, not just in the context of rituals and spiritual growth, but also for those working toward political and social change, because human needs and human energies behave the same in any context.

Witches understand that energy, whether it is psychic, emotional, or physical, always flows in cycles. It rises and falls, peaks and drops, and neither end of the cycle can be sustained indefinitely, any more than you could run forever without stopping. Intense levels of energy must be released and then brought down and grounded; otherwise the energy dissipates or even turns destructive. If, in a ritual, you tried to maintain a peak of frenzy for hours and hours, you would find that after a while the energy loses its joyful quality, and instead of feeling union and ecstasy, you begin to feel irritated and exhausted. Political groups that try to maintain an unremitting level of anger—a high-energy state—also run out of steam in precisely the same way. Releasing the energy and grounding out allows the power itself to work freely. It clears channels and allows you to rest and recharge and become ready for the next swing into an up cycle. Releasing energy does not mean losing momentum; rather, real movement, real change, happens in a rhythmic pattern of many beats, not in one unbroken blast of static.

Craft rituals also add an element of drama and fantasy to one's life. They allow us to act out myths and directly experience archetypes of symbolic transformation. They allow us, as adults, to recapture the joy of childhood make-believe, of dressing up, of pretending, of play. Magic, by Dion Fortune's definition, "the art of changing consciousness at will," is not so far removed from the creative fantasy states we enter so easily as children, when our dolls become alive, our bicycles become wild horses, ourselves arctic explorers or queens. Allowing ourselves, as adults, to play and fantasize with others, puts us in touch with the creative child within, with a deep and rich source of inspiration.

The craft also helps us open our intuitive and psychic abilities. Although witchcraft is commonly associated with magic and the use of extrasensory powers, not all covens put a great deal of stress on psychic training. Worship is more often the main focus of activity. However, any craft ritual involves some level of psychic awareness just in sensing the energy that is raised.

Ordinarily, the way into the craft is through initiation into an already established coven. However, because covens are limited in size and depend on some degree of harmony between personalities, it is often difficult to find one that is open to new members and that fits your preferences. In San Francisco, Los Angeles, and New York, covens often run open study groups and can be found through publications and open universities. In other areas of the country, it may be difficult to locate a practicing coven at all.

However, there is nothing to stop you from starting a coven or a *circle*—a term I use for a group whose members meet for rituals but are not formally initiated—on your own. Women, especially, are more and more joining together to explore a Goddess-oriented spirituality and to create rituals and symbols that are meaningful to us today. Starting your own circle requires imagination, creativity, and experimentation, but it is a tremendously exciting process. You will miss formal psychic training—but you may discover on your own more than anyone else could teach you. Much of what is written on the craft is biased in one way or another, so weed out what is useful to you and ignore the rest.

I see the next few years as being crucial in the transformation of our culture away from the patriarchal death cults and toward the love of life, of nature, of the female principle. The craft is only one path among the many opening up for women, and many of us will blaze new trails as we explore the uncharted country of our own interiors. The heritage, the culture, the knowledge of the ancient priestesses, healers, poets, singers, and seers were nearly lost, but a seed survived the flames that will blossom in a new age into thousands of flowers. The long sleep of Mother Goddess is ended. May She awaken in each of our hearts—Merry meet, merry part, and blessed be.

Note

1. This article is limited to the history of traditions that come from northern Europe. Southern and eastern Europe, Asia, India, Africa, and the Americas all have rich traditions of Goddess religions and matricentric cultures, but to even touch on them all would be impossible in a short essay. The history presented here is the "inner" or "mythic" history that provides a touchstone for modern witches. Like the histories of all peoples, its truth is intuited in the meaning it gives to life, even though it may be recognized that scholars might dispute some facets of the story.

Spiraling into the Nineties

Mary Daly

As we move into the final decade of this millennium, how can women work to exorcize the evils that overwhelm us and at the same time Realize our capacity for ecstasy? Since there is no point in settling for anything less, this is the question I will attempt to address.

Uh, oh! I am hearing voices. "Who does she think she is, with her impossible questions and grandiose schemes? Why doesn't she just do re-search in academentia and leave the scheming to us?" Luckily I recognize those voices. They're coming from the old brotherhood of doubt demons who are always trying to undermine women's Self-confidence, and their cohorts the blah demons with their energy-draining "blah, blah, blah." The Time has come to switch them off. Now—That's better. To continue:

We have just come through a decade of escalating violence against women and all of the oppressed, and against earth, air, fire, water—the elements that sustain and constitute all Life. On the foreground level—the level of man-made horrors—this has been and continues to be a time not only of genocide and gynocide, but also of biocide—the devastation of all forms of Life. This level is very real.

Yet there are also Other levels, Other dimensions. I often refer to these simply as "the Background," meaning the Realm of Wild Reality, the Homeland of women's Selves and of all other Others—the Time/Space where auras of plants, planets, stars, animals, and all Other animate beings connect. As a philosopher, I would say that the Background *is* whenever/wherever we actively participate in Be-ing, the Verb of Verbs. In other words, it *is* when/where we are really Alive.

Re-membering my own Voyage as a Radical Feminist philosopher, I am intensely aware of the struggle to stay on my True Course, despite undermining by demons of distraction and fragmentation that have always attempted to pull me off course. These I gradually Dis-covered and learned to Name as agents and institutions of patriarchy, whose intent is to keep me—and indeed all living beings—within the strangle-hold of the foreground, that is, fatherland. My True Course was and is Outercourse—moving beyond the imprisoning mental, physical, emotional, spiritual walls of the state of possession. Insofar as I am focused on Outercoursing, naturally I am surrounded and aided by the benevolent forces of the Background.

This Voyage could also be called *Innercourse*, since it involves delving deeply into the process of communication with the Self and with Others—a process that demands profound and complex Passion, Re-membering, Understanding. It could also be called *Countercourse*, since it requires Amazonian Acts of Courageous Battling. However, its primary/primal configuration is accurately Named *Outercourse*, for this is a Voyage of

Spiraling Paths, Moving Out from the State of bondage. It is continual expansion of thinking, imagining, acting, be-ing.

I think I just heard someone say "That's fine for her, but I'm not a philosopher. I'm just . . ." Time to switch off the doubt demons again, dear reader. After all, a philosopher is really a lover of wisdom—a seeker—one who is on a Quest. If someone thinks she/he *has* wisdom, *owns* it, then she/he is not a philosopher. If you are a seeker, I am talking to you.

The Moments of Outercourse

The Spiraling Paths of Outercourse move from Moment to Moment. Unlike mere instants, Moments are Momentous. And they have Momentum. They have the Power to hurl us on an Intergalactic Voyage. Moments are Acts of Hope, Faith, and Biophilic Bounding. They are ontologically and politically significant, because they occur when a woman speaks and acts Courageously. Such speaking (Be-Speaking) and acting elicits responses from the world around her, to which she, in turn, is challenged to respond. She is challenged to move beyond foreground limitations.

Because the Moments of Outercourse are active in nature, I call them Moments/Movements of be-ing. For they propel Journeyers into ever more A-mazing Acts of Courage and Imagination. They are Metamorphic points of contact with one's Genius, one's Muse. They are similar to Virginia Woolf's "moments of being" in that they are revelatory; that is, they can be seen as windows or doors to the Background. But they are also something else, something E-motional. They are Acts of Qualitative Leaping *through* these portals further and further into the Background. I think that whenever a woman Leaps in this way she brings others with her—by example, by inspiration. Her Courage is contagious. Hence Moments/Movements of Outercourse are Political/Metapolitical.

The Politics/Metapolitics of Outercourse: Piracy

Having been a Pirate for many years, I am speaking from a Piratic perspective. I have Righteously Plundered treasures of knowledge that have been stolen and hidden from women and I've struggled to Smuggle these back in such a way that they can be seen as distinct from their mindbinding trappings. After Voyaging for awhile, I began Reclaiming this stuff by Naming it in New ways, in order to render its liberating potential accessible to women. For example, many light years ago I Plundered the christian idea of "the Second Coming" and transformed it to mean "the Second Coming of women." Since then, I have moved on to far more Daring and Disreputable Deeds.

There are many Other Sister Pirates Out there/here, with a great Diversity of Plundering and Smuggling skills. Take healing, for example. Pirates who are healers must range far and wide in order to Righteously rip off women's own healing tradition, which has been stolen, scattered, and partially destroyed. Then they have to sort it out from the poisonous distorting context in which it has been hidden and Smuggle it back to us.

This brings me to the subject of the Pirate's Craft. My Time Traveling adventures and my life as a Pirate have been possible because of my Craft. The word *craft* means, among other things, skill and cunning. Wild women sometimes refer to our strength, force, skill, and occupations as Witchcraft. My own particular Craft involves writing and the forging of philosophical theories.

Craft is etymologically related to the verb *crave*. Voyaging women Spiral with our Craft/Crafts because we crave something, because we have a strong longing for something. That "something" is the free unfolding and expansion of our be-ing. Propelled by Wonderlust, by Wanderlust, our Quest *is* the expansion of our be-ing.

Taking charge of our Crafts is a primary/primal task of women as Pirates, who are overcoming the "woman as vessel" motif that prevails in Stag-nation. Women under phallocratic rule are confined to the role of vessels/carriers, directed and controlled by men. Since that role is the basic base reversal of the very be-ing of Voyaging/Spiraling women, when we direct our own Crafts/Vessels we become reversers of that deadly reversal. In this process we become Crafty.

Crafty Pirates dare to sail across the vast Realm which I Now Name the Subliminal Sea. This contains deep Background knowledge, together with countless contaminants—the man-made subliminal and overt messages disseminated through the media and other patriarchal means for the purpose of mind manipulation. The heat generated by the Movement of our Crafts causes droplets from the Subliminal Sea to rise around us, forming a mist. Spiraling into the mist, we confront the contaminants and Dis-cover our buried Memories and tradition. This process is both exorcism and ecstasy. Indeed, it is Be-Dazzling, that is, eclipsing the foreground world by the brilliance of be-ing. In the Light of Be-Dazzling we are enabled to Dis-cover the hidden connections that make Sense of our Lives.

Time Traveling Now

Voyagers gifted with the Terrible Vision that rips through the mist of man-made mysteries/mystifications can Spiral full speed backward, around, and ahead with our Craft of the Fourth Dimension, which is the Craft of Time Travel. Having seen through the fabricated past, we can Envision our true Past. As the Past changes, the Present and the Future change.

For Now there is available a personal/political/historical context in which earlier Moments can be Re-membered. Hence the Present Moment can be Seen in a Be-Dazzling Light. Women who accept the Invitation to Outercourse accept the challenge to Spin and Weave the broken connections in our knowing, sensing, and feeling, becoming Alive again in our relationships to ourSelves and to each Other.

As I see our situation in the early Nineties, what is required is a Spiraling series of Victories over the fragmenters of women's Present and of our Memories, including our Memories of the Future. Such a series of Victories, that is, Moments of Spinning Integrity, cannot be viewed as mere linear progression. When a Voyager Spirals into Outercourse she experiences Overlapping of the Moments of her earlier Travels—a conversation Now with those Moments. The repetitious aspect of Spiraling enriches her experience of Movement. There is an accumulation of Acts of Momentous Re-membering and thus she gathers Momentum for whirling ahead. Yet the most crucial Moments are always Now, and that is why Now is always the special target of the fragmenters of our lives.

Fragmentation often takes the form of enforced distracted busy-ness (a type of sloth imposed especially upon women), which is associated with psychic numbing. The encroachment of fragmentation, which manifests itself now in seemingly endless divisions within and among women, involves also the breakdown of nature by phallotechnocrats and the splitting of women from nature.

In this Age of Fragmentation, Sisterhood can seem like a lost and impossible dream. Much of the knowledge and many of the memories that were reclaimed in the so-called "second wave" of feminism have re-turned to a subliminal level in women's psyches. At this Time it is essential to Re-call our knowledge that all of our Spiraling Paths are interconnected. Herein lies the hope for resolving miscommunications arising from "generation gaps" and time warps, as well as from ethnic, cultural, and class differences. When Pirates Realize the interconnectedness among all our Spiraling Moments, it begins to become possible to possible to respect and celebrate our Great Diversity. Secure in our understanding of our Common Quest, we can Dis-cover these rich variations as a Tremendous Treasure Trove, and as sources of fuel for the Voyage.

In Other words, I see hope that we can travel in Intergalactic Concordance!

At this High Moment of writing I am hearing voices again. "What 'concordance' is she talking about? There's nothing but discordance around here," they whine. "That Daffy Daly with her incurable absurd optimism, slashing and dashing all over the space—a lyrical lunatic, a Capitalizing crackpot!"

It's the tiresome crowd of spaced-out party poopers, trying to take the Wind out of my sails. Yep—Here come the doubt demons, still trying to keep up with my Craft, clinging to their colleagues the blah demons, attempting to give me the blahs.

Must I explain once again that I am indeed *proud* to be a member of the Lunatic Fringe? This I define as "Crackpot Crones in tune with the moon, propelled by Pure Lust, who dare to Spin Wildly, always." Indeed, from my Positively Peculiar Perspective, the Lunatic Fringe is the truly moving center of the women's movement, comprising those who choose always to Survive/Thrive on the Boundaries, refusing compromise

The Invitation to Outercourse naturally implies a summons to Spiral into this Moving Center.

Entering the Age of Cronehood

The Impossible/Possible Dream of Radical Feminism has never died. It is true that for many, especially in the course of the decade of decadence we have just Survived, it seemed to fade. What happened, in fact, is that it receded, somewhat, into the depths of the Subliminal Sea. But Sister Pirates, who are also divers, have worked to retrieve it. Moveover, it is Surfacing again, seemingly of its own accord. I think that our Time is coming round again, as we enter the Nineties.

However, this re-surging of the Dream is no mere passive event, no spectator sport. It must be Realized. This is a Tremendous Challenge. I think that as Voyagers we now face the Challenge of entering the Age of Cronehood of Radical Feminism. It is probably the case that the so-called "first wave" of feminism, in the nineteenth century, did not surge into the Age of Cronehood, even though there lived individual Crones, such as Sojourner Truth and Matilda Joslyn Gage. For as a collective Movement, feminism became "stuck," and there was not the possibility then of fully seeing the multiracial, multiclass, and indeed planetary dimensions of the women's movement. Nor was it possible to know that our Sister Earth is in mortal danger.

In the "second wave," although there has been a dreary expenditure of energy reinventing the wheel, we are moving toward understanding that a Qualitative Leap into Cronehood is necessary for Survival.

It is a desperate time, but desperation, too, is a gift. Desperation combined with Furious Focus can hurl a significant New Cognitive Minority of women into the Age of Cronehood, the Time of Realizing the Fourth Dimension. While feminists have always been a minority under phallocratic rule, the New Cognitive Minority includes women who constitute a memory-bearing group—Crones who have "been around" and can Recall earlier Moments, and who can *bear* the memories, learn from them, and open the way for change.

There is, of course, imminent danger of succumbing to psychic numbing. We could continue to drift as vessels driven by men in power. But we have the Power to Choose. We *can* seize the decade by taking charge of our Crafts. We *can* Move.

I recommend that we hasten to acquire New Virtues in order to Spiral into the Nineties. First, there is the Virtue of Rage. A Metamorphosing Sage rides her Rage. Rage is a transformative focusing force that awakens transcendent E-motion. When unleashed, it enables women as Furies to breathe Fire and fly into freedom.

The New Virtue of Courage takes many forms. Central to all of these is the Courage to Be through and beyond the state of negation, participating in the Unfolding of Be-ing, continuing on the Journey always. Such Courage is Outrageous. It transforms women into Positively Revolting Hags who reverse the reigning reversals, becoming ever more Offensive, more Tasteless.

Tasteless Travelers acquire the Courage to Leave hopeless institutions and other foreground fixations. We gain Courage to See—to become dis-illusioned. And all of this amounts to the Courage to Sin. I am not alluding here to the petty sort of sinning that is forbidden and therefore incited by the "major religions" of phallocracy. I am talking about Sinning Big. For a woman, to Sin is to Be. To Sin Big is to Be the Verb which is her Self-centering Self.

I suggest that women in the Age of Feminism's Cronehood need also to develop the Virtue of Disgust—the habit of feeling and expressing our profound revulsion at the conglomerates of toms, dicks, and harrys—and their henchwomen—who are hell-bent on destroying all Life.

Hand in hand with Disgust comes the Virtue of Laughing Out Loud. This is the Lusty habit of boisterous Be-Laughing women. It is our habit of cracking the hypocritical hierarchs' houses of mirrors, defusing their power of deluding Others.

The cackling of Crones together cracks the man-made universe. It creates a crack through which Cacklers can slip into Realms of the Wild. Laughing Out Loud is the Virtue of Crackpot Crones who know we have only Nothing to lose. We are the Nothing-losers.

"But it's so dangerous," whisper the doubt demons. "And so inappropriate," sniff the blah demons. Oh, those party poopers again.

"Get lost!" I say. And they do. Whew! It feels so fine to lose Nothing. Daring Intergalactic Sailors/Sisters, our Time has come—Time to find our own Space Out Here with the Sun.

Whoops—I Sense that my Craft is about to take off again, Spiraling farther Out. I wish you lots of Nothing-losing. It's an erratic, ecstatic experience—this hurling our Lives as far as we can go, Now, in the Be-Dazzling Nineties!∞

"Eyes: A Poem of Ireland and Answer to a Question."

Kathleen Cain

One of my old mothers
came upon a red deer
late one evening
near the Paps of Anu.

They startled one another
but both stood still.
And when she saw
the pools of eyes
that doe swam in

my ancient mother never forgot them—
sent the memory staring
through her blood.

Cain, Kathleen. 1981. "Eyes: A Poem of Ireland and Answer to a Question." Printed by permission of the author.

Part Four—Imagination, Creation, and Expression
Chapter 10—Women and Spirituality
Study Questions

1. Define *immanence*. What is your view of this concept?

2. Why do many feminists feel it is important, in our culture, for women to define their own spirituality? Why is organized religion often oppressive to women? Can a woman survive spiritually while being part of an organized religion? If yes, how? If not, why not?

3. What are the characteristics of women's spirituality? How is difference celebrated?

4. Why do feminists believe it is important to "always let people speak in their own voices"? Do you agree? Why or why not? What can be learned by honoring others' voices, and your own?

5. What does women's spirituality teach to underscore the importance of both spiritual and political activism?

6. Women's spirituality celebrates the world and everything in it. Explain. Why is this important for not only women, but all living things?

7. In "Witchcraft and Women's Culture," Starhawk describes how witchcraft has survived. How was this survival possible? What is its import?

8. In Daly's philosophy regarding our future what is meant by *Outercourse*? What basis does she use as a starting point? Why?

9. How does Daly reclaim what she "smuggles" and rework it so it is accessible to women?

10. Daly says ". . . we have the Power to Choose. We *can* seize the decade by taking charge of our Crafts." To Daly, what is "craft"? How can women gain power by taking charge of "our crafts"?

11. Daly talks about entering the "Age of Cronehood." What issues, in her opinion, need to be addressed that go beyond the work of the first wave of feminism? Why is this important?

12. Discuss in small groups your creative outlets. These may include but need not be limited to the "arts."

WOMEN IN THE ARTS: PERSPECTIVES ON GENDER AND CREATIVITY

Margo Linn Espenlaub

Introduction

With the emergence of the contemporary women's movement, feminists began to address the inequities faced by women within academies of the arts and in the professional world of artistic production. Educational opportunities for training in the visual, literary, and performing arts, not open to women until the late nineteenth century, continued to reflect gender bias and discrimination. Historical texts excluded artistic works by women but legitimized the representation of the female image as an object of study by men. Domestic art produced by women was assigned a lesser status than were objects of "fine" art. If women's works were acknowledged in the artistic mainstream, they were identified as exceptions. Many feminists pointed out that women involved in artistic production existed in an isolation that was largely framed by cultural definitions of femininity.

The recognition and valuation of women's work in the arts has been the task of feminist scholars and critics for the past several decades. Art created by women has been expressed in many forms: architecture, ceramics, dance, design, drama, drawing, film, music, painting, performance, photography, poetry, printmaking, prose, sculpture, and textiles. Understanding the diversity of artistic forms and of the women who create them underscores the need to challenge traditional assumptions which have assigned women a marginal status in the arts.

This chapter will broadly address issues and questions that have been raised by feminist scholars with regard to women and creative expression in the visual, literary, and performing arts.

- How has the exclusion of women artists from art history texts reinforced gender roles and stereotypes?
- Why have women been denied access to formal education in the arts?
- What has been the standard for assessing the value and worth of women's artistic works?
- Why have notable women in the arts been seen as exceptions?
- Why have crafts been demeaned as lesser art?
- Is there an essential difference between women's and men's art?

- How has the women's movement helped women artists?
- What advocacy issues still need to be addressed by women in the arts?

History of the Arts Revised

Art history texts of the twentieth century have systematically left women out of the historical record (Parker and Pollock 1981) and relegated their work to a secondary status. On the basis of gender alone much of the literary work produced by women over the last two centuries has been trivialized (Showalter 1985) and the contributions to culture and society ignored. Women musicians have been praised throughout history for their performance skills, but prior to the twentieth century, composition was seen as unfeminine and inappropriate as a profession for women (Jezic 1988). Women painters and sculptors have often worked in isolation unable to rely upon a larger community of artists and gallery affiliations to take their work seriously (Lippard 1976; Chadwick 1990). The history, economics, and politics of art still perpetuate an ideology which is androcentric and exclusive (Chadwick 1990).

Exclusionary history does not reveal the activity of women in the visual arts, literature, and the performing arts, nor does it reveal the various concerns of women who engage in the process of creative expression. Initially, the first task of feminist art critics and researchers in the 1970s was to reclaim women artists who had been forgotten, ignored, or marginalized by a tradition that honored only the achievements of men (Parker and Pollock 1981). A revised historical record now reveals that women have been working for centuries in the various mediums of artistic expression.

During the Middle Ages, women who chose to live in convents gained high levels of literacy and artistic skills as expressed in the form of manuscript illumination (illustrated texts). Hildegard of Bingen, a twelfth-century German abbess, writer, and composer of music, represents this tradition (Jezic 1988; Chadwick 1990). French author Christine de Pisan supported herself and her children by writing professionally. Her 1405 work, *La Cité des Dames (The City of Ladies)*, describes a utopian place in which accomplished women throughout history come together to celebrate their many achievements. An early feminist writer, Christine de Pisan advocated equal rights and historical recognition for women (Gilbert and Gubar 1985; Chadwick 1990). In fifteenth-century Spain, the poems or "old songs *(canciones)*" of Florencia Pinar "may be considered among the earliest feminist poems in Spanish" (Flores and Flores 1986, xiv).

During the sixteenth and seventeenth centuries, women painters such as Sofonisba Anguissola and Artemisia Gentileschi in Italy, Judith Leyster and Rachel Ruysch in Holland, and Angelica Kauffmann in England were examples of the many European women artists producing notable work (Chadwick 1990). In New Spain (Mexico) feminist author and poet Sor Juana Inés de la Cruz in her 1693 work, *Repuesta a Sor Filotea (Reply to Sor Filotea)*, challenged the oppression of patriarchal church authority in its silencing of women (Flores and Flores 1986; Candelaria 1990). Women writers in the seventeenth century, such as the English poet and playwright Aphra Behn began publishing their works (Gilbert and Gubar 1985). This tradition continued to grow and develop into the next century as in the publications of Anne Finch, Fanny Burney, and the feminist Mary Wollstonecraft in

England as well as Phillis Wheatley, American poet and freed slave (Gilbert and Gubar 1985).

The novel, a developing genre of literature in the eighteenth century, became, by the nineteenth, a popular and successful form for women writers (Gilbert and Gubar 1985). In the United States, many novelists such as Susan Warner, Harriet Beecher Stowe, Rebecca Harding Davis, and Louisa May Alcott enjoyed commercial success (Coultrap-McQuin 1990). Despite these advances, women writers still experienced discrimination, achieving only limited careers provided they adhered to the normal definitions of the female voice and role in society (Coultrap-McQuin 1990).

In spite of educational restrictions in the nineteenth century, women composers began to emerge in Europe and America (Jezic 1988): in France, Louise Farrenc and Lili Boulanger, and in the United States Amy Beach, whose works were performed internationally (Jezic 1988). Similarly, the notable artist Rosa Bonheur enjoyed international success from her paintings of animals, a subject that she studied in the slaughterhouses and cattle markets of Paris (Harris and Nochlin 1976). Lilly Martin Spencer, an American artist born in England, popularized depictions of domestic scenes in her paintings. She supported her family from the sale of her art while her husband managed the domestic work of children and home (Harris and Nochlin 1976; Rubinstein 1982). Harriet Hosmer, Edmonia Lewis, and Anne Whitney are representative of several American women sculptors who studied in Rome and received public commissions for works produced in the United States (Rubinstein 1982; Chadwick 1990).

Training in the Arts

No creator is born fully developed artistically. There must be a transfer of knowledge and skills so that creativity can flourish. Historically, women have been excluded from the means of gaining education that would have enabled them to create in the artistic idiom of their time. Few women in painting, sculpture, and music have had access to mentors and apprenticeships in the arts unless they came from families who supported their daughters' endeavors (Nochlin 1973 and 1988; Jezic 1988; Chadwick 1990).

Prior to the late nineteenth century, women in the visual arts were denied admittance to academies, studios, and workshops where drawing from a nude male figure was considered a fundamental skill in preparation for painting and sculpture (Nochlin 1973; Chadwick 1990). Even though women were allowed limited admittance into art academies beginning in the mid-nineteenth century, they were barred from life drawing classes. At the Pennsylvania Academy, women art students were assigned specific times in segregated classes to draw from plaster casts of the nude (Rubinstein 1982). The protection of feminine delicacy and the prescribed roles of white middle class women in Europe and America were embodied in this Victorian attitude toward women's education.

Many of the "great" male writers in literary history often had the support of a sister, such as Dorothy Wordsworth, or a wife, such as Sonya Tolstoy, to recopy and edit their texts (Spender 1989). The supportive role of wife also included caring for household and business affairs while their husbands pursued professional writing careers (Olson 1977). Literary accomplishment was often only possible for women if they wrote under a male pseudonym. This was especially true in England in the mid-nineteenth century when Charlotte Brontë published under the pseudonym of Currer Bell and Mary Anne Evans was known professionally as George Eliot. In the United States women authors chose female pseudonyms in order to maintain a respectable distance from the fame and popularity gained from their published novels and short stories. Sara Payson Parton wrote under the pseudonym of Fanny Fern and Sara Jane Lippincott wrote as Grace Greenwood (Coultrap-McQuin 1990). Women writers have not always deferred to male identity in order to align with male "greatness," but most certainly the canon of great writing has not included and valued women's literature as original and important (Showalter 1977; Gilbert and Gubar 1984). As British novelist and essayist Virginia Woolf affirmed in *A Room of One's Own*, "it is the masculine values that prevail" (Woolf 1929).

The recognition of women's literature has been due to the influence of the women's movement and the development of feminist literary criticism, which in turn has been applied to feminist critiques of the visual and performing arts. This criticism, based on an interdisciplinary model, views women's artistic achievement as connected to the cultural, historical, and political contexts in which they live and work (Showalter 1977). Feminist literary criticism challenges the canon, the traditional hierarchy of male-centered and male-defined categories which judge and value works of art. These categories have systematically marginalized or ignored women as producers of art, but have placed emphasis on images of the female as either passive sexual objects, or as dangerous, evil, and manipulative. Feminist criticism thus seeks to reinstate women's self definition as subject, rather than object, of study through the affirming voice of the first person "I" in the literary text (Gilbert and Gubar 1984).

For the past twenty years feminist scholars have been reclaiming women artists from centuries of neglect. The results of this ongoing research are most often found in publications dealing exclusively with women's art while the percentage of representative women artists in "general" art history books still remains small. In the 1970s, feminists exposed the exclusionary practices of museums and galleries in not exhibiting art by women. Several women's organizations were formed to address these issues: Women Artists in Revolution (WAR) and Women in the Arts (WIA) in New York; Womanspace and the Los Angeles Women's Building in California (Gouma-Peterson and Mathews 1987); and the Women's Art Registry of Minnesota (WARM) (Maksymowicz 1990). Early publications in women's art, such as the *Feminist Art Journal*, are no longer in print but serve as good historical reference to the issues and perspectives addressed by feminists in the early years of the women's movement. Current publications include: *Heresies, Women's Art Journal, Women Artists News* (formerly *Women Artists Newsletter*), and *Women of Power*. These reflect the growing body of literature representing women artists and their work (Gouma-Peterson and Mathews 1987). The fact that women have always been creating works of art (Parker and Pollock 1981) can no longer be denied given their very existence in history. But being involved in the process of making art does not necessarily allow women access to the profession, let alone provide them value and recognition for their work. Rather, they, and what they create, are more likely relegated to obscurity—even anonimity.

The Measure of Greatness

The Western art tradition which assigns the terms "great" or "master" to white males only has criticized women who create art for not measuring up to its established categories (Greene and Kahn 1985). Many feminists assert that women writers of diverse ethnic and racial heritages have also not been included in the canons of literature created by men. Throughout art, literary, and musical history these canons, as structures and categories, have imposed standards, or norms, against which women's creative work has been judged.

In her essay, "Why Have There Been No Great Women Artists?" Linda Nochlin (1973) challenges the belief that great art can only be produced by men. She addresses the assumption that creative genius is a male birthright, a "mysterious essence," identified and reinforced by unrestricted access to education and training (Nochlin 1973, 7). Nochlin notes that the monograph, a treatise on the life and work of an individual artist, has traditionally been written about men, and adds that while women were allowed access to education in the 1800s, they were denied full privileges and opportunities because of cultural attitudes that reinforced the proper roles of women in the domestic sphere. When women sought to publish or to exhibit their creative work professionally, they were criticized and their work was judged as amateurish, unprofessional, and certainly not the product of individual creative genius (Nochlin 1973).

The difference between men's and women's status in the arts is based upon biological determinism and male privilege. This cultural bias also determines which sex will receive public recognition for artistic work (Chadwick 1990). Implied is the assumption that women are naturally inferior to men and are therefore not destined to become "great" artists. If women are assigned the status of greatness, they are most often seen as exceptions to the male artistic tradition or valued as muses serving as inspiration for male creativity and genius (Chadwick 1990).

Art and Craft

Alongside the individual achievements of women artists there has been a long history of women working both individually and collectively to create functional objects for everyday use. That collaborative creators of such objects, often referred to as ordinary women, have rarely been credited gives the impression that the basket, ceramic piece, or quilt was a lesser creation "crafted" by many hands rather than created by individual genius. The assumption that art should be pure, nonfunctional, and untainted by the complexity of life experience places its definition in the hands of a powerful hierarchy which can own it, manipulate its value, and discriminate against its creators. "It is precisely the specific history of women and their art work that is effaced when art historical discourse categorizes this kind of art practice as decorative, dexterous, industrious, geometric" (Parker and Pollock 1981, 78).

For centuries Native American women have been making functional objects to gather and store food and water, and to clothe and provide shelter for the people of their tribal nations. These women gathered fibers for making baskets, clay for making ceramic vessels, and wool for weaving blankets. They processed leather for creating storage bags and clothing. Contemporary professionals in museums and galleries have praised the art of Native Americans for its geometric design elements (Rubinstein 1982). This valuation has consequently elevated a "functional" art form to a higher status while at the same time reinforcing the anonymity of women who have traditionally produced these objects.

Immigrant women from England and Europe used their experience and skills in making functional objects for use in a newly formed American culture. Knowledge of their craft in needlework, quilt-ing, and weaving was passed on to new generations of women. American quilting bees developed as social events in which communities of women came together and collaborated on the design and execution of appliquéd and pieced quilts (Parker and Pollock 1981; Rubinstein 1982). Many designs symbolized cultural rituals such as migration, marriage, and the settling of communities (Parker and Pollock 1981). Quilts produced in the nineteenth century were often political

Figure 11.1. "Medallion." 1987. Pieced by Arbie Williams. Restructured and quilted by Willia Ette Graham. In *Who'd A Thought It: Improvisation in African-American Quiltmaking,* by Eli Leon. San Francisco Craft and Folk Art Museum. Photo by Geoffry Johnson. Reprinted by permission of the publisher, San Francisco Craft and Folk Art Museum.

statements drawing on the abolition, social reform, and suffrage movements (Chadwick 1990).

African American women quilters have also displayed a connection to cultural history and geography through their pieced quilts, which can be seen as rhythmically connected to music and dance. Innovative in pattern and color, and representative of African identity, these designs are distinctly unique from those found in European American quilts. The tradition of quilting, continued by contemporary African American women, creates visual narratives of cultural heritage, spirituality, and independence (Lyon 1987; Thompson 1987; Ferrero, 1987).

During the late 1800s, women began working as professional designers of ceramics and textiles. The Society of Decorative Art of New York City was organized by U.S. designer Candace Wheeler in 1877 to promote the sale of women's domestic crafts (Chadwick 1990). Wheeler advocated educational and professional opportunities for women who were involved in the decorative arts (Waller 1991). During this period, the Arts and Crafts movement emerged in the United States and in England. China painting became a professional opportunity for women to apply their skills in the art of ceramics. Mary Louise McLaughlin and Maria Longworth Nichols individually experimented with techniques in glazing that influenced future professional art potters in America (Chadwick 1990).

Architect Sophia Hayden was awarded the commission to design the Women's Building as part of the World's Columbian Exposition held in Chicago in 1893. It was here that women artists displayed the range of their artistic production. Represented in this exposition were functional objects and textiles produced by Native American, Asian, and African women. Other displays included prints by women engravers from the European Renaissance through the nineteenth century as well as two large murals created by American artists Mary Cassatt and Mary McMonnies. Sculpture by Vinnie Ream Hoxie and Edmonia Lewis was exhibited (Chadwick 1990; Waller 1991). And composer Amy Beach wrote *Festival "Jubilate"* opus 17 (1892), an orchestral work commissioned for the Women's Building (Jezic 1988).

Women's art in the nineteenth century came to be recognized as an expression of middle class domestic life, valued for its "feminine" qualities and isolated from the professional world of public exhibitions (Chadwick 1990). Creativity, when applied to the domestic setting, could be part of a woman's life as a decorative or functional skill. In this setting, as well as in female seminaries, skills in the decorative arts were passed on to succeeding generations of women who would similarly inhabit and domesticate their homes.

Gender arrangements based upon private/public dichotomies are rooted in social, political, and economic systems that continue to limit visibility and recognition of women's creativity. When museums and galleries agree to show certain artistic works, those works become valuable commodities in the art market. Supposedly the artist is seen as separated from her or his work in order to evaluate it according to "objective" criteria. This might appear to be fair and just, but it is not. So-called objective criteria are those based upon an exclusionary history of greatness, of claims to formal knowledge of art, the celebration of individual male genius, and a tradition in which women have been denied participation (Chadwick 1990).

Essentialism in Art

During the 1970s feminist scholars began to reclaim the historical representation of women artists and writers from the Middle Ages to the twentieth century. They sought to define the ideology of gender difference as socially constructed rather than biologically determined and inevitable (Greene and Kahn 1985; Chadwick 1990). Androcentric bias assigns women's alleged lack of genius or creative ability to her biological inferiority and her unpredictable female nature. This deterministic view separates and differentiates males and females and supports the roles of "masculine" and "feminine" as naturally given. Feminists have stressed the inequality and injustice of an androcentric tradition that defines female as a lesser being and, therefore, her creative products as lesser art (Gouma-Peterson and Mathews 1987). The different and opposing positions of women and men reinforce these distinctly unequal relations within the process of creativity and professionalism in the arts (Parker and Pollock 1981).

For some feminists, the notion of an essentially unique female identification and experience—essentialism—can be applied to the analysis of creative works produced by women. From this perspective, an essential "female nature" (Humm 1990, 64), derived biologically, renders female qualities as positive, self-affirming, creative, and valuable for society (Nielsen 1990). Essentialism in art identifies the creative process as a gender-specific activity connecting all women throughout history. It asserts that women's art cannot be compared to men's art because categories for judgment have been determined by male-identified definitions.

During the 1980s, many feminists challenged the concept of essentialism in art

since the evaluation of creative works based upon gender difference perpetuates the stereotype of a "masculine" form and style identified as "masterful." Teresa De Lauretis, in *Technologies of Gender*, adds that "the notion of gender as sexual difference and its derivative notions—women's culture, mothering, feminine writing, femininity, etc.—have now become a limitation, something of a liability to feminist thought" (De Lauretis 1987, 1).

Essentialism continues to be debated among feminists in the arts. Do women create paintings, sculpture, architecture, literature, or music that is universally "feminine" by nature? How can audiences and critics of artistic works perceive this essence? Other feminists believe that identifying differences *among* women is imperative. This view underscores the idea that women's art is shaped by gender, race, ethnicity, age, and sexual identity, therefore representing diverse cultural and historical contexts (De Lauretis 1987; Lippard 1990).

The Image of the Female

Feminists have identified images that depict women as sexual objects in the visual arts and media as created by men, and intended for a "male gaze" (Mulvey 1975; Kaplan 1983; Betterton 1987). The gaze of the spectator is that of a voyeur who occupies a privileged position and who is allowed to look at and act upon the female image (Kaplan 1983). Similarly, in literary texts images of the female are "created" and controlled by male writers who objectify and sexualize the female in masculine terms (Gilbert and Gubar 1984). In music, traditional feminine stereotypes have been assigned to the female voice which in turn are performed as gender-defined roles in musical compositions. As

Susan McClary states in *Feminine Endings: Music, Gender, and Sexuality*, "musical representations of masculine bravura or feminine seductiveness in Indiana Jones movies resemble in many respects those in Cavalli's seventeenth-century operas" (1991, 8). This action not only demands the image of female to be on male terms, but also denies the woman writer, musician, or visual artist any possibility of creating her own self-image, on her own terms, and from her own perspective.

The depiction of women as sexual beings and the application of feminine stereotypes such as weakness, vulnerability, dependence, and seductiveness, underscores the patriarchal need to idealize women as objects and property (De Lauretis 1987) to be sold, traded, consumed, controlled, and discarded. Such images are not only found in visual, literary, and musical arts, but also permeate U.S. culture through television and advertising. The female image represents an idealized version of women fantasized through masculine interpretation (Gilbert and Gubar 1985). The male gaze imposes an imperative upon women to conform to and imitate such sexualized images.

Sexual objectification of the female body is also explicit in pornographic materials. Pornography can be understood as an expression of heterosexism and misogyny supported by cultural attitudes that sanction masculine control over women's lives and women's bodies (Dworkin 1989). Feminists have formed arguments on both sides of this issue. One view holds that a legal definition of pornography would interfere with individual artistic expression and offend the First Amendment right of free speech. It is feared by many artists that their creative works would become subject to the scrutiny of censorship and funding sources in the arts would diminish.

Other feminists argue that pornography is the ultimate expression of misogyny and gynophobia which has so permeated the fabric of American culture that it is often not recognized as harmful to women. Proponents of this view emphasize the connections between harmful acts perpetrated against women in the forms of rape, domestic violence, and sexual abuse with pornographic images of women being subjected to physical violation and torture. Such images, seen frequently in films, videos, and advertising, condone, even encourage, violent hostility and aggression towards women (MacKinnon 1987).

Feminist critiques of language, or discourse, between viewer and object challenge misogynist frameworks within the visual arts (Chadwick 1990) and film. Here feminists have addressed the ways in which patriarchal language silences women (Mulvey 1975; Kaplan 1983; De Lauretis 1984; Betterton 1987). In films where the male imperative is hostile to an image of female autonomy and strength, the female voice speaks from a vulnerable location confined by the camera's frame of reference. What is outside this frame and not seen by the audience can be understood as threatening, suspicious, dangerous, and certainly holds a position of power over the female (Kaplan 1983). An example of this male imperative in films produced over the last several decades is given in a feminist analysis of *The Stepford Wives* where "men create robot duplicates of their wives which have no will and become men's sexual slaves" (Boruszkowski 1986, 16).

Many feminist critics and historians have expressed concern with a cultural ideology that assumes the interaction, or discourse, between the observer and the observed to be entirely based upon male power and exploitation of the female image. In *Looking On: Images of Femininity in the Visual Arts and Media*, Rosemary Betterton stresses the importance of investigating "how *women* [author's italics] look at images of women" (1987, 217). If viewers assume there is only one monolithic female image, than all women remain bound together by ideological sameness. In this way, women's personal identities are not revealed and there is denial of the unique differences among them (Tichner 1988).

Many women artists have presented the female image in ways that challenge masculine perspectives. In the early decades of the twentieth century Suzanne Valadon in France and Paula Modershon-Becker in Germany worked from nude female models in nontraditional contexts. Each artist, often using herself as subject, depicted the nude in ways that redefined notions of female sexuality and motherhood (Betterton 1987; Chadwick 1990). Valadon, for example, "combined roles of model and artist and by doing so disrupted the normative relationships of masculine creativity and feminine passivity" (Betterton 1987, 226). Interested in the ideal of "womanhood," Modersohn-Becker presented her nurturing female subjects as connected to nature (Chadwick 1990, 217).

In the 1940s, self-portraits by Mexican artist Frida Kahlo reveal a personal struggle for female identity linked to "political, social, and emotional structures" (Lowe 1991, 57). During the 1970s, American painter Sylvia Sleigh challenged the exclusive tradition in Western art of male artists working from female nudes. In her work, Sleigh depicts male nude models as subjects of study by the female artist (Rubinstein 1982; Chadwick 1990).

Figure 11.2. "Virginia Woolf." Copyright © 1979 by Judy Chicago. Ceramic plate from place setting from *The Dinner Party*. Photo by Donald Woodman. Reprinted by permission of Judy Chicago and Donald Woodman.

Other contemporary American women artists have aligned their work with themes in nature, the cycle of seasons, or goddess mythology. The sculpture of Michelle Stuart, Alice Aycock, Mary Miss, and Nancy Holt reflect such concerns (Chadwick 1990). Miriam Schapiro, Faith Ringgold, and Joyce Kozloff incorporated elements of domestic art and textile design in their patterned paintings. Performance artists such as Laurie Anderson, Faith Wilding, and Rachel Rosenthal have produced art as social commentary (Rubinstein 1982). During the 1970s and 1980s, women folk musicians such as Linda Allen, Hazel Dickens, Holly Near, and Bernice Johnson Reagon popularized the narratives of women's lives and work, cultural diversity, social injustice, and themes of peace and war (Wenner and Freilicher 1991). Female power and self-identity have been addressed by rock musician and performer Madonna. Her multiple visual images combined with music "engage . . . provocatively with ongoing cultural conversations about gender, power, and pleasure" (McClary 1991, 150).

Women writers also address the tyranny of the white male text in confining women to stereotypical images of sexuality and servitude. Paula Gunn Allen, Lorna Dee Cervantes, Sandra Cisneros, Michelle Cliff, Maxine Hong Kingston, Audre Lorde, Tillie Olson, Adrienne Rich, Muriel Rukeyser, Leslie Marmon Silko, Alice Walker, Mitsuye Yamada, and many other twentieth century authors make visible the diversity and intensity of the female voice. These writers struggle against conventions that oppress their individual racial and ethnic heritages, their sexual identities, and their value as literary women (Anzaldúa 1990; Gilbert and Gubar 1985). The lack of dominant culture privilege is a concrete measure of the intensity of their struggle.

Art and Politics

The politics of feminist art reflect many of the issues addressed by the contemporary women's movement. Feminist artists such as Judy Chicago and Miriam Schapiro, along with feminist art critics, such as Lucy Lippard and Linda Nochlin (Rubinstein 1982), began revising historical accounts to include women and the diversity of their artistic expression. This process continues today as cultural and political inequities still exist for women in the arts.

Judy Chicago's *The Dinner Party* exemplifies the feminist position of reclaiming women's identities in a visual art statement. Chicago's work honors 39 women throughout history with individual place settings consisting of a ceramic plate and needlework runner placed upon a triangular table with equal sides measuring 48 feet in length. The names of 999 additional women are scripted into the tile platform which supports the table. Designed and orchestrated by Chicago in the 1970s, this collaborative project included the expertise of designers, needlework artists, and china painters. When the exhibit first opened in 1979 at the San Francisco Museum of Modern Art, thousands of people attended (Chicago 1982). Despite favorable response, critical reaction dismissed the project as not having been created by a singular individual. Criticism also arose over Chicago's choice of vaginal imagery for the ceramic plates (Chadwick 1990).

Controversy over *The Dinner Party* continues into the 1990s. Initially accepted as a gift by the University of the District of Columbia (UDC), Chicago's work was to be a permanent exhibit as part of a proposed "multicultural art center" (Lippard 1991, 39). However, conflicting reports, incorrect media accounts, and "attacks against art on 'moral' grounds" (Lippard 1991, 39) created a

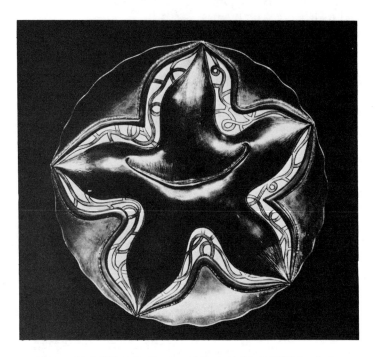

Figure 11.3. "Natalie Barney." Copyright © 1979 by Judy Chicago. Ceramic plate from place setting from *The Dinner Party*. Photo by Donald Woodman. Reprinted by permission of Judy Chicago and Donald Woodman.

climate in which conservative members of Congress initiated and passed an amendment undercutting the operating budget of UDC. With future maintenance and care of *The Dinner Party* undermined, Chicago withdrew her gift. Quoted in an interview with feminist art critic Lucy Lippard, Chicago stated that *The Dinner Party* "was assaulted, . . . exactly at the moment it was going to enter history" (Lippard 1991, 49). This action, taken against permanent visibility of Chicago's artwork, once again represents patriarchal control that can silence artistic expression and censor representation of the female image from a women-centered perspective.

Social and political consciousness-raising is also found in performance art.

Suzanne Lacy, in collaboration with Leslie Labowitz, organized *In Mourning and in Rage* performed in Los Angeles in 1978 as a public protest against rape. Lacy's art expressed the politicized statement that women would no longer be silent nor accept the increasing violence perpetrated against them. Performed by ten women, nine dressed in black and one in red to express rage, this piece demonstrated how "each mourner broke her imposing silence to condemn a form of sexual violence: rape, incest, woman battering, mutilation murders, and sex-violent advertising and entertainment" (Lacy 1981, 14).

Public art by women has addressed issues of peace and war. Ceramic artist Barbara Donachy designed and collaborated

Figure 11.4. "The Nuclear Arsenal Project." 1983. Barbara Donachy. Exhibit, Boston Science Museum, 1986. Photo by George J. Riley. Reprinted by permission of Barbara Donachy and George Riley.

with over seventy volunteers to produce her *Nuclear Arsenal Project: Amber Waves of Grain*. This work, a miniature replica of the 35,000 nuclear warheads, missiles, submarines, and bombers in the United States nuclear arsenal, is composed of thousands of hand-cast clay cones comprising a "landscape" for political aware-

ness. Donachy, a Colorado artist, first exhibited her project in New York City in 1983. It has subsequently been viewed throughout the United States and Germany where audience response has ranged from appreciation to anger (Clegg 1984).

Figure 11.5. "The Great Wall of Los Angeles." Copyright © Judy Baca, begun 1976. Dust bowl Refugees (detail). Reprinted by permission of Judy Baca.

Figure 11.6. "The Great Wall of Los Angeles." Copyright © Judy Baca. detail, 1980 section. 1940s: Japanese being forcibly taken to internment camps during World War II. Reprinted by permission of Judy Baca.

Collaboration has been the basis for Judith Baca's *The Great Wall of Los Angeles* which began in 1976 under her direction and supervision (Rubinstein 1982). This mural, over 2,000 feet in length, depicts the social, cultural, and political history of people in southern California along with their struggles and triumphs (Pohl 1990). Baca's art, like that of other contemporary muralists, such as the "Mujeras Muralistas" in San Francisco, brings public visibility to diverse ethnic origins and cultural identities (Rubinstein 1982; Chadwick 1990). Such forms of public art draw viewers into the struggle, the oppression, and the reality of people's lives. In a society which practices exclusion through racism and sexism, art as social commentary not only expands awareness of cultural traditions and ritual imagery but also challenges the categories and assumptions of a Western European art history tradition. Lucy Lippard, in *Mixed Blessings: New Art in a Multicultural America,* expresses the importance of multicultural awareness in the visual arts. "Both women and artists of color are struggling to be perceived as subject rather than object, independent participants rather than socially constructed pawns" (Lippard 1990, 11).

Native American women artists, working in both contemporary and traditional mediums, often recreate their lives as visual and cultural narratives. Artists Jaune Quick-to-See Smith and Harmony Hammond organized and curated the exhibition, *Women of Sweetgrass, Cedar, and Sage,* which opened in New York City in 1985 at the Gallery of the American Indian Community House (Chadwick 1990). This exhibit of art by thirty contemporary Native American women documents, for example, beadwork by Imogene Goodshot, basketry by Mary Adams and Florence Benedict, ceramic sculpture by Otellie

Loloma, and paintings by several artists including Sylvia Lark, Dorthea Romero, and Jaune Quick-to-See Smith (Smith 1987; Chadwick 1990).

During the 1980s feminist art critics and historians further investigated the issues of context and subjectivity as frameworks for understanding the historical circumstances and social influences that shape the artistic work of women. Artists such as Barbara Kruger and Jenny Holzer deconstructed the hierarchy of categories still present in the arts. Using photographs accompanied with text, Kruger "emphasizes the way in which language manipulates" as she successfully "undermines the assumption of masculine control over language and viewing" (Chadwick 1990, 356). Also interested in cultural interpretations of language, Holzer's large public posters and signs carry messages in the form of "Truisms" or "Inflammatory Essays" (Chadwick 1990, 356). Exploring words as systems of visual symbols encoded with multiple meanings, these artists challenge the ideology of "pure" objectivity within patriarchal language.

Since 1985, the politics of feminist art have been expressed through the work of an anonymous group of women artists calling themselves the Guerrilla Girls. Their posters, designed to include statistical information "exposing patterns of sexism, racism, and censorship in the art world" (*MS.* 1990, 63), have become familiar additions to buildings in New York City (Chadwick 1990). The Guerrilla Girls, when speaking on television and on college campuses, protect their anonymity by wearing gorilla masks, a creative act intended to raise public awareness of the inequity and invisibility faced by women artists (*Ms.* 1990).

Creative contributions are evident in the productions of women choreographers, composers, and artistic directors. Performance artist Rachel Rosenthal, active in the 1970s Women's Art Movement in Los Angeles, explores environmental issues and global consciousness as in her 1990 work, *Pangaean Dreams,* performed in Berkeley, California (Hanson 1991). Choreographers Cleo Parker Robinson and Judith Jamison head professional dance companies that tour nationally and internationally. Based in Denver, The Cleo Parker Robinson Dance Ensemble and Theatre offers opportunities for artists to display their creativity through multicultural, multimedia productions (Robinson). Jamison, director of the Alvin Ailey American Dance Theater in New York, conducts performances and workshops that give recognition and visibility to the legacy of African American dance (Gladstone 1991).

Women musicians and composers contribute their talents in a diversity of styles and expressions. Musicians including Tracy Chapman, Alberta Hunter, Miriam Makeba, Bonnie Raitt, Phranc, and performance artist Laurie Anderson address social issues of sexism, racism, and homophobia through their jazz, blues, rock, country, and folk music. Composer Ellen Taaffe Zwilich, whose works have been performed internationally, won the Pulitzer Prize in music for her 1982 work, *Symphony No. 1* (Findlen 1991). A conductor of international reputation, JoAnn Falletta is also music director of The Women's Philharmonic (Women's Philharmonic). This all-women orchestra,

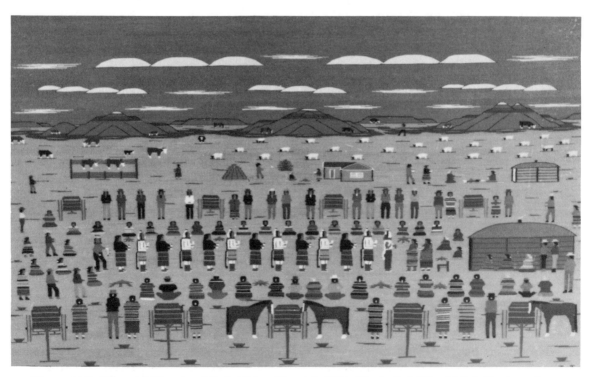

Figure 11.7. "Pictorial Weaving." Isabel John (Navajo). 1984. Wool, 61 1/2" × 99." Collection of Fredrick and Jan Mayer. Photo by James O. Milmoe, 1985. Reprinted by permission of Ann S. Daley and James O. Milmoe.

conducted by Falletta, performed the works of women composers at the 1992 celebration of the National Organization for Women's twenty-fifth anniversary in Washington, D.C. (Ireland 1992).

Conclusion

Throughout history, women have produced works of art leaving a rich artistic legacy for women of today. While some artists gained recognition according to traditional male defined standards, many others found forms of expression based upon their material world. Embracing various mediums and genres of expression, women in the arts are diverse. They include women with disabilities as well as differences such as race, ethnicity, class, age, and sexual identity.

Although feminist artistic expression can be dated to the fifteenth century, it was not until the 1970s and the 1980s that the women's liberation movement informed the world of art. The development of feminist scholarship and profes-

sionalism are eroding institutional obstacles to women's participation in the arts. Women-owned galleries, bookstores, and recording and publishing companies, provide the means for women's creations to be seen, read, and heard. These woman-centered institutions promote public recognition and exposure needed for legitimacy.

Systematic exclusion from and attitudinal barriers against women's participation in the arts have not been able to defeat female creativity. Dialogue about the content and form of artistic expression and changing perceptions about women's works of art continue to challenge established male defined standards of achievement. Women artists, despite the persistence of oppression and discrimination against them, continue to create words and images that reveal truths and transmit symbols of cultures which are vital to an inclusive understanding of the history of artistic expression.

References

Anzaldúa, Gloria, ed. 1990. *Making face, making soul haciendo caras: Creative and critical perspectives by women of color.* San Francisco: Aunt Lute Foundation Books.

Betterton, Rosemary. 1987. *Looking on: Images of femininity in the visual arts and media.* London: Pandora.

Boruszkowski, Lilly Ann. 1986. The Stepford wives: The re-created women. *Jump Cut* 32:16–19.

Broude, Norma, and Mary D. Garrard. 1982. *Feminism and art history: Questioning the litany.* New York: Harper and Row.

Candelaria, Cordelia Chávez. 1990. Reviews. *Frontiers: A Journal of Women's Studies* 11(1): 85–86.

Chadwick, Whitney. 1990. *Women, art, and society.* London: Thames and Hudson.

Chicago, Judy. 1979. *The Dinner Party: A symbol of our heritage.* Garden City, N.Y.: Anchor Books.

————. 1980. *Embroidering our heritage: The Dinner Party needlework.* Garden City, N.Y.: Anchor Books.

————. 1982. *Through the flower: My struggle as a woman artist.* Garden City, N.Y.: Anchor Books.

Clegg, Nancy. 1984. Forever amber: Missiles toe the line: What price fame? *Westword*, September.

Coultrap-McQuin. 1990. *Doing literary business: American women writers in the nineteenth century.* Chapel Hill: The University of North Carolina Press.

De Lauretis, Teresa. 1984. *Alice doesn't: Feminism, semiotics, cinema.* Bloomington: Indiana University Press.

———. 1987. *Technologies of gender: Essays on theory, film, and fiction.* Bloomington: Indiana University Press.

Dworkin, Andrea. 1989. Pornography is a civil rights issue. *Women of Power* 13:48–53.

Ferrero, Pat, producer/director. 1987. *Hearts and hands.* San Francisco: Ferrero Films (video cassette).

Findlen, Barbara. 1991. Landmark albums of the last 20 years. *Ms.* 1(4):68–69.

Flores, Angel, and Kate Flores. 1986. *The defiant muse: Hispanic feminist poems from the Middle Ages to the present.* New York: The Feminist Press.

Fuss, Diana J. 1989. Essentially speaking: Luce Irigary's language of essence. *Hypatia* 3(3):62–80.

Gladstone, Valerie. 1991. Arts: Judith Jamison leaps forward. *Ms.* 11(3):80–81.

Gilbert, Sandra M., and Susan Gubar. 1984. *The madwoman in the attic: The woman writer and the nineteenth-century imagination.* New Haven: Yale University Press.

———. 1985. *The Norton anthology of literature by women.* New York: W. W. Norton and Co.

Gouma-Peterson, Thalia, and Patricia Mathews. 1987. The feminist critique of art history. *Art Bulletin* 69:326–57.

Greene, Gayle, and Coppelia Kahn. 1985. *Making a difference: Feminist literary criticism.* London: Methuen.

Hanson, Jo. 1991. Rachel Rosenthal: Pangaean dreams. *Women Artist News* 15(4):16–17.

Harris, Ann Sutherland, and Linda Nochlin. 1989. *Women artists: 1550–1950.* 2nd ed. New York: Los Angeles County Museum of Art and Alfred A. Knopf.

Heller, Nancy G. 1987. *Women artists: An illustrated history.* New York: Abbeville Press.

Hess, Thomas B., and Elizabeth C. Baker, eds. 1973. *Art and sexual politics: Women's liberation, women artists, and art history.* New York: Art News Associates, Macmillan Publishing Co.

Humm, Maggie. 1990. *The dictionary of feminist theory.* Columbus: Ohio State University Press.

Ireland, Patricia. 1992. A Vision for the Future. *National NOW Times* 24(3):6.

Jezic, Diane Peacock. 1988. *Women composers: The lost tradition found.* New York: The Feminist Press.

Kaplan, E. Ann. 1983. *Women and film: Both sides of the camera.* New York: Metheun.

Kelly, Joan. 1984. *Women, history, and theory.* Chicago: The University of Chicago Press.

Kelley, Mary. 1984. *Private woman, public stage: Literary domesticity in nineteenth-century America.* New York: Oxford University Press.

La Duke, Betty. 1985. *Compañeras: women, art, and social change in Latin America.* San Francisco: City Lights Books.

Lacy, Suzanne. 1981. Learning to look: The relationship between art and popular culture images. *Exposure.* 19(3):8–15.

Lauter, Estella. 1990. Re-enfranchising art: Feminist interventions in the theory of art. *Hypatia* 5(2):91–106.

Leon, Eli, ed. 1987. *Who'd a thought it: Improvisation in African-American quiltmaking.* San Francisco: San Francisco Craft and Folk Art Museum.

Lim, Shirley Geok-lin. 1989. *The forbidden stitch: An Asian American women's anthology.* Corvalis, Ore.: Calyx Books.

Lippard, Lucy R. 1976. *From the center: Feminist essays on women's art.* New York: E. P. Dutton.

———. 1990. *Mixed blessings: New art in a multicultural America.* New York: Pantheon Books.

———. 1991. Uninvited guests: How Washington lost *The Dinner Party. Art In America* (December):39–49.

Lowe, Sarah M. 1991. *Frida Kahlo.* New York: Universe Publishing.

MacKinnon, Catharine A. 1987. *Feminism unmodified: Discourses on life and law.* Cambridge, Mass.: Harvard University Press.

Maksymowicz, Virginia. 1990. WARM—Women's art registry of Minnesota. *Women's Artists News* 15(30):28–30.

McClary, Susan. 1991. *Feminine endings: Music, gender, and sexuality.* Minneapolis: University of Minnesota Press.

Moers, Ellen. 1963. *Literary women: The great writers.* New York: Oxford University Press.

Ms. 1990. The guerrilla girls. 1(2):60–63.

Mulvey, Laura. 1975. Visual pleasure and narrative cinema. *Screen* 16(3):6–18.

Nielsen, Joyce McCarl. 1990. *Sex and gender in society: Perspectives on stratification.* 2nd ed. Prospect Heights, Ill.: Waveland Press.

Nochlin, Linda. 1973. Why have there been no great women artists? In *Art and sexual politics: Women's liberation, women artists, and art history.* Edited by Thomas B. Hess and Elizabeth Baker. New York: Macmillan Publishing

———. 1988. *Women, art, and power and other essays.* New York: Harper and Row.

Norwood, Vera, and Janice Monk, eds. 1987. *The desert is no lady: Southwestern landscapes in women's writing and art.* New Haven: Yale University Press.

Olsen, Tillie. 1977. One out of twelve women who are writers in our century. In *Working it out: Twenty-three women writers, artists, scientists, and scholars talk about their lives and work.* Edited by Sara Ruddick and Pamela Daniels. New York: Pantheon Books.

Parker, Rozsika, and Griselda Pollock. 1981. *Old mistresses: Women, art, and ideology.* New York: Pantheon Books.

Placksin, Sally, 1982. *American women in jazz, 1900 to the present: Their words, lives, and music.* New York: Seaview Books.

Pohl, Frances K. 1990. The world wall: A vision of the future without fear: An interview with Judith F. Baca. *Frontiers* 9(1):33–43.

Pollock, Griselda. 1988. *Vision and difference: Femininity, feminism, and the histories of art.* London: Routledge.

Rich, Adrienne. 1986. *Blood, bread, and poetry: Selected prose, 1979–1985.* New York: W. W. Norton and Co.

Robinson, Cleo Parker. Promotional material, Cleo Parker Robinson Dance Theatre, 119 Park Avenue West. Denver, Colorado, 80205.

Robinson, Hilary, ed. 1987. *Visibly female: Feminism and art today.* New York: Universe Press.

Rosenblum, Naomi. 1986. Women in photography: An historical overview. *Exposure* 24(4):6–26.

Rubinstein, Charlotte Streifer. 1982. *American women artists: From early Indian times to the present.* Boston: G. K. Hall and Co.

Schor, Naomi. 1987. *Reading in detail: Aesthetics and the feminine.* New York: Methuen.

Showalter, Elaine, ed. 1985. *The new feminist criticism: Essays on women, literature, and theory.* New York: Pantheon Books.

———. 1977. *A literature of their own: British women novelists from Brontë to Lessing.* New Jersey: Princeton University Press.

Sobek, María Herrera, and Helena María Viramontes, eds. 1988. *Chicana creativity and criticism: Charting new frontiers in American literature.* Houston: Arte Publico Press.

Smith, Jane Quick-to-See. 1987. Women of sweetgrass, cedar, and sage. *Women's Studies Quarterly* 15(1&2):35–41.

Spender, Dale. 1989. *The writing or the sex? Or why you don't have to read women's writing to know it's no good.* New York: Pergamon Press.

Thompson, Robert Farris. 1987. From the first to the final thunder: African-American quilts, monuments of cultural assertion. *In Who'd a thought it: Improvisation in African-American quiltmaking.* Edited by Eli Leon. San Francisco: Craft and Folk Art Museum.

Tilchen, Maida. 1984. Lesbians and women's music. In *Women-identified women.* Edited by Trudy Darty and Sandee Potter. Palo Alto, Calif.: Mayfield Publishing Company.

Tichner, Lisa. 1988. Feminism, art history, and sexual difference. *Genders.* 3:93–128.

Waller, Susan. 1991. *Women artists in the modern era: A documentary history.* Metuchen, N.J.: The Scarecrow Press, Inc.

Wenner, Hilda E., and Elizabeth Freilicher. 1991. *Here's to the women: One hundred songs for and about American women.* New York: The Feminist Press.

Women's Philharmonic. Promotional material. 330 Townsend Street, San Francisco, California, 94107.

Woolf, Virginia. 1929. *A room of one's own.* New York: Harcourt Brace Jovanovich.

Zaimont, Judith Lang, Catherine Overhauser, and Jane Gottleib, eds. 1987. *The musical woman: An international perspective, 1984–1985.* Vol. 2. Westport, Conn.: Greenwood Press, Inc.

The Living Legacy of Chicana Performers: Preserving History through Oral Testimony

Yolanda Broyles-González

Virtually nothing is known about the participation of Chicanas in the 200-year history of theater in what is today the southwestern United States.[1] Secular and of course ritual performance forms—storytelling, song, theater, healing practices, prayer, hymns, and blessings—have existed for the past two centuries and much longer, but the role of women in these performances has become a lost legacy. As in other realms of history, women in performance have been erased. And the erasures and distortions born of gender discrimination are intensified in the case of Chicanas, where race and class discrimination have made their reality appear triply insignificant to mainstream keepers of the historical record, in this case theater historians. Chicana performance for the most part belongs to working-class women's history; Chicana performers have typically come from the working class and have rarely left it.

In researching and reconstructing Chicana performance history, therefore, I have found my richest and almost exclusive source of information to be women performers themselves. It is through oral histories—hours and hours of audiotape interviews—that I have begun to develop an understanding of the life, work, and struggles of Chicana performers. I began interviewing Chicanas almost ten years ago. None of these women had ever delivered an oral history before; despite the prominence of oral history in the 1970s and 1980s, it has not been fully exploited in research on Chicanos. The oral history collection I have assembled constitutes the most extensive testimonial archive on Chicana performers in the United States.[2] What I offer below—a segment from one oral history with performer Diane Rodríguez, a veteran of El Teatro Campesino—is a brief fragment demonstrating only some of the research directions that this collection supports. Yet it illustrates the treasure house of insight that is oral history, and its relevance to Chicana performance history.

Oral histories, for instance, allow us to begin to reconstruct the role of women in the popular tradition of itinerant tent shows in the southwest. Chicanas were often the dominant forces or leaders in those acting ensembles. Only one of these women has been even briefly documented: La Chata Noloesca, who headed an international touring company

Broyles-Gonzáles, Yolanda. 1990. "The Living Legacy of Chicana Performers: Preserving History through Oral Testimony." *Frontiers* 11(1): 46–52. Reprinted by permission of the publisher.

and reached the big time of Spanish-speaking New York vaudeville. There is much yet to be uncovered about such women. In my interviews with the legendary Chicana singer Lydia Mendoza, for example, I began to reconstruct the performance history of her mother, Leonor Zamarripa Mendoza, who headed the Mendoza family touring variety show. Leonor Zamarripa Mendoza functioned as artistic director, arranged the musical numbers, helped improvise the comic sketches, and for many years sewed all the costumes—not to mention the fact that she taught Lydia Mendoza how to play the guitar.

One of the collection's principal emphases is the history of El Teatro Campesino, founded in 1965 as a vehicle of Chicano political activism. In its beginnings El Teatro Campesino performed mainly *actos* (highly improvisational skits) that gave bold, humorous expression to the labor problems of farmworkers. In addition to regular performances in support of the United Farm Workers Union—often on the backs of flatbed trucks—the group also played college campuses and repeatedly toured Europe.

In the course of the 1970s El Teatro Campesino changed from a farmworkers' group to a predominantly student group. As the group's thematics broadened to include a variety of Chicano issues—educational, cultural, spiritual—Teatro Campesino plays became longer and more intricate. Yet the vivacious performance style established in the early years remained a constant throughout El Teatro Campesino's development, even after its dissociation from the union in 1967. It was a style deeply rooted in the oral performance tradition of Mexican popular theater and indigenous (Aztec and Mayan) wisdom. Among the popular traditional genres adopted by El Teatro Campesino were the seasonal sacred pageants performed in Chicano/Mexican communities for hundreds of years, the dramatized *corrido* (traditional narrative ballad), and the *mito* (myth). Plays using combinations of these forms were also performed, all of them based in the Theater of the Sphere performance school developed by the company.[3]

A great deal has been said and written about El Teatro Campesino, and much of that commentary has of course relied to some extent directly on the company's performances. But it has relied equally—particularly in the years immediately following El Teatro's founding, and again in very recent years—on statements made by Luis Valdez. One voice has represented the company to the outside world; one vision has become the official one. When I began writing about the Teatro from a woman's perspective, a whole new history emerged. I cannot here enumerate the contributions of the individual women of El Teatro Campesino; let me say simply that they were in the forefront of the company's creative achievement, as I have shown elsewhere.

In addition to reconstructing women's role in traditional Chicano/Mexicano performance arts, oral history can also provide a minority perspective on the contemporary white mainstream performance arts and on the barriers that women of color encounter in commercial theater. The experiences of Chicana/Mexicana women who have successfully mainstreamed and of those who have not have never been studied and documented. Diane Rodríguez, in the following oral history, gives us insight into that experience as well as other dimensions of her life as a performer.

Diane Rodríguez came to El Teatro Campesino in 1970 at the age of 18 and became a full-time member in 1973 after completing her B.A. at the University of California at Santa Barbara. The segments of oral history presented here are from the year 1983, when she was positioned between a desire to continue within a dissolving Teatro Campesino ensemble and concomitant efforts to find work within the world of commercial theater. This document speaks to a range of experiences anchored in the dailiness of a performer's work, but it also highlights the 1980s trend from artistic collectivity to individuality, a trend furthered both by the withdrawal of public funding for alternative organizations and projects under Reaganomics and by the decrease in political militancy as compared to earlier decades. In 1983, after the Teatro Campesino playhouse in San Juan Bautista "went dark," most former ensemble members moved away to work elsewhere. Diane Rodríguez is active in theatrical work, has acted in various feature films, and can currently be seen performing in the comedy act "Latins Anonymous" out of Los Angeles. She has also done costume design for various shows and teaches acting classes for youth at Plaza de la Raza in Los Angeles.

BROYLES-GONZÁLEZ: Could you describe what you have done outside your work with El Teatro Campesino? What is a Chicana up against in the world of "commercial theater," or theater that is not alternative, as the Teatro Campesino used to be? Do you regard your experiences as representative?

RODRIGUEZ: The last performance I did here in San Juan Bautista was in January of 1982, and I didn't perform again until this fall. So it was over a year and a half, almost two years, that I didn't perform here. I think my experiences are pretty representative. That's on my mind a lot right now: how and why I've only reached a certain point . . . in commercial theater. One of the reasons is because I've been doing Teatro Campesino, and that's been my choice, my career.

Barely two years ago I decided to venture out to see how I fared. And then there were many realizations. . . . But one of the big things was that I went to San Diego to the Old Globe Theatre, and there I saw my old ex-roommate. . . . We first met in 1972, and I loved her, I loved her. I've never loved a woman like that. I mean I wanted to talk forever. I wanted to sit up until five in the morning, all night, just talking about whatever. It was usually she that would say, "We should go to bed, we have a class in the morning." . . . That was in college, when I was in Santa Barbara. And she was an inspiration. . . . She was an actress. And I was an actress. Of course, she's Irish so she looks very "American," very classic. She can pass for Irish or Greek or Jewish; she's got a wonderful "universal" look. And of course I look very Latin, very Indian, very dark.

In school I got cast in roles that were mostly comical and were definitely not me, and very far and few between. My friend Chris and I were at the same level. I didn't look up to her; it was a fair exchange, and I always felt good about that. Well, ten years have passed. . . . In the meantime I've done the Teatro Campesino, and I've been very proud of what I've done and the way that the group has gone. I saw Chris and we were reunited after all this time. Here she was in the commercial theater and doing leads. And I was called by the Old Globe Theatre in San Diego to do an educational tour in which there are four people that they hire, and they have to fill certain slots. I filled the "woman" slot and the "ethnic" slot. (Actors Equity—the actors' union—demands that the theater fill certain slots.) I was then offered a small role in their year subscription season. I did that and made a lot of money and was able to do Shakespeare, though for a children's tour, and was able to work with some good people in a small ensemble piece, although I had a small role. And here was Chris a year older than I was, and I felt of equal talent. . . . But I had certainly another look, and it's far easier for her to get roles. It is, and that's the reality. There are no roles for us, for me, for any of the women that have worked with El Teatro Campesino; there are so few roles. And in the film industry, there are certain slots that you do fill but they are so menial that money-wise it may be good, but image-wise it's senseless. I've also been trying to make a dent in regional theaters. I have been writing notes, sending resumes, calling people, because I want to work. I don't want to just be cast because of a slot. I know that the Actor's Union is trying to have theaters hire what they call "ethnics"—I hate that term, but that's what we're all under: "ethnics." But I want them to hire me because of what I can give you in a show, not just to fill that slot.

I wrote to the casting director at the Old Globe Theatre in San Diego and I said, "David, let me know if there's anything this season. But *please,* I don't want to do educational tours. I've paid those dues for you. Two shows, two tours. And it's hard performing for kids, high school, junior high, or grammar school. It's the bottom of your list, you know. That show is the bottom, that tour is on the bottom scale of your whole theater operation." And I don't want that. I'd rather not do it, not work, even though it pays. It paid well for me because I did double jobs, I had to work double hard. And that's the other thing: I have to work harder than anybody. . . .

BROYLES-GONZÁLES: What theater houses have you auditioned for?

RODRIGUEZ: I've auditioned for the Berkeley Repertory Theater. ACT is closed; they have their own company and they don't audition outside. I've auditioned for the Berkeley Rep, and the San Jose Repertory Theater came to see me in the *Pastorela.* . . . Those were the two biggest ones besides ACT in the Bay area. And then I've worked at the Old Globe, which is the other big regional theater. The other one in California is the Mark Taper Forum, and the South Coast Rep, which is in Irvine. I've auditioned for the majority of them. . . . In case something doesn't happen here in San Juan Bautista, I've got to make a living somewhere. . . .

BROYLES-GONZÁLEZ: So you're prepared to work somewhere else, in Denver, for a few months?

RODRIGUEZ: Usually the engagement lasts eight weeks, two months . . . not too bad. It's like a three-week rehearsal, or a two-week rehearsal, and a six-week or five-week run. All that involves is memorizing your lines and talking. I mean, it doesn't involve creating a new piece, like we've always done in the Teatro. It's much different from what we've done in San Juan Bautista. . . .

You know, recently I got a Christmas card from a friend that I met through Peter Brook. Her name is Helen Mirren. She's a very big actress in London. . . . I seem to have these friends that are very white and are doing very well. And I always wonder if I had been white, where I would be. You always wonder. . . . I do, at least, in this business. Of course, everyone could say, . . . "If I had had a different mouth, I wonder where I would be?"

BROYLES-GONZÁLEZ: But it happens to too many Chicanas. There's a pattern. I mean, look at Socorro Valdez, for example. She runs on pure talent, but she has none of the looks that sell.

RODRIGUEZ: Her looks are not marketable outside El Teatro Campesino. She'll always get the role of maid or campesina. I'm real negative, you know, about that. I don't think it's changed in the last ten or fifteen years. I think it's real hard in commercial acting. I think people are racist; there's still a lot of racism. People have kind of just shifted and hid it under the table a little bit, but I think it's just as strong as it has ever been. I really do. People would be much more comfortable if you never mentioned what ethnicity you are, if you never made yourself a little different. . . . If you're going to start saying, "You know, I'm a Chicana. And hey, there's a saying in Spanish. . . ." Well, I've been teased constantly about that. And teased in a patronizing way. They don't know how to deal with you. And when you're an actor, and you work in those big theaters, you work with people from Ohio, not just Californians. Ohio or Missouri or any other place. The only Mexicans they knew—and they call you Mexican—are the farm workers that pass through. So for you to be acting with them is very foreign to them. . . . The chances for Chicanas in their profession are very limited. And the profession is based on looks; 99 percent of the job is based on looks. Certainly if you're what the standard beauty is, it's easier. If you have a really gorgeous look to you, then you've got it easier.

BROYLES-GONZÁLEZ: What startled me was the realization that this was also happening in the Luis Valdez production *Corridos;* . . . casting decisions were based primarily on good looks and secondarily on talent.

RODRIGUEZ: You know, you're right; it's unfortunate because the show could have been better with performers that are more developed. . . . Socorro was a real knockout in terms of the women; and she stood out *so much* because the others didn't reach out. It really needs to be evened out, because otherwise it's going to be a little off balance. It's great for her, but in terms of the whole ensemble, it's not going to quite work.

Socorro Valdez has lived through the experience of El Teatro Campesino. The other *Corridos* cast members have not. With the Teatro Campesino women . . . you're preforming to be an actor, you're preforming because there is a reason, there's something you want to communicate, there's something you want to show; it's important and you want audiences to see it. . . . It's urgent. It's in your very being, that urgency to be on stage. There is a general energy or movement that . . . all have . . . developed . . . through osmosis in working with each other and watching each other. There's a style that we all have when we act. I've trained so that I can act in another style: more subtly, and more realistic, more naturalistic. I've had to train outside Teatro Campesino for that; and I'm confident when I do that kind of acting as well. But the Teatro Campesino style is not what a lot of people can do, either: the movement, the body . . . making the spine come alive . . . so that it's moving the body, so that the bones and everything are moving with you. Working with the *calavera* [skeleton costume], that's an amazing thing, because when you're not being *calavera* you're still aware of every movement. And the sense of comedy. Not that every piece was funny, but Teatro was humorous. We have a sense of comedy and of what is funny, what is joyful, what is play, and that's important, too. . . .

BROYLES-GONZÁLEZ: It seems that the plays since *Fin del mundo* [1980] are very different from the ones before in terms of the sense of "urgency" you referred to, as well as in terms of acting style. You don't have the old Teatro Campesino ensemble acting in the productions since *Fin del mundo*. The temporary hired actors do not possess the sense of urgency you mentioned. El Teatro Campesino is no longer an ensemble but rather a production company. Where is it headed?

RODRIGUEZ: I think we're really searching. . . . This year there's *Corridos*. . . . We're going to do the *Virgen del Tepeyac* next year . . . but anything else we're not sure of. We don't know what kind of material to do; we don't know at this point what we're doing. We're all committed to make it work, but we don't know how it's going to work yet. Are we all going to come back as we did before? That is a real possibility. I could see us making a complete turn. We [the ensemble members] have been dispersed, but perhaps a year down the line we'll all be together again . . . myself, Luis Oropeza, Joe, Andres, Socorro, Olivia, Smiley, Roberta. . . .

We have to figure out how we're going to do new plays so that we develop people to write our material. Not our material, but material that other people can do as well, other pieces that can be performed not just in California but all over the country. . . . There's so little material that we can perform like that. The black population, you know, surpasses the Hispanic population in this country, and they do have more of a body of theatrical work. There are more plays that can be performed by black performers. We don't even have that . . . and when you take most of Luis Valdez's plays, or . . . something like *Fin del mundo* and script it, it doesn't make sense. Because the piece that we performed in 1980 was a visual piece, and to explain that in a script and to have another theater company do it—well, they just couldn't. So the search is to find someone who can write a play that can be produced by other people, a play that doesn't take a Teatro Campesino to do it.

BROYLES-GONZÁLES: Everywhere I go, Chicanos are saying, "We have no theater pieces." Certainly we don't have a strong theater tradition of that kind. We have a tremendously strong popular theater, a theater tradition based on improvisation and nonverbal theatrics—like everything that the Teatro Campesino was doing. The Teatro Campesino did not invent that style, but rather reproduced it because the members of the Teatro had grown up in that tradition. Almost every character of the Teatro had already existed in some form in Mexican popular theater. . . . It's an oral tradition, not a print culture or "script" tradition. If some Chicanos have now surrendered the tradition of improvisational theatrical creation, then they naturally will find themselves floundering without plays, because ready-made plays are a phenomenon of print culture. Even within the Teatro Campesino it wasn't until 1980, as far as I can tell, that something was scripted before you started working on it.
RODRIGUEZ: Yeah, '79, I guess. . . . Scenes were created and then more scenes were added, all based on our improvisations. We've basically not written things down. . . . Is it now that we're going to change that? That . . . for these next hundred years, or fifty years, we're going to try to change or evolve that tradition so that we can then have play scripts that can be produced by others? . . . It's not change, but evolve.

BROYLES-GONZÁLEZ: I find that things usually change of their own accord as one's economic class changes. Certain types of cultural practices thrive within certain kinds of material conditions, and not in others. Print culture has traditionally been an artistic domain of the bourgeoisie. I think that wanting now to have scripts after having made *Zoot Suit* is not accidental. A different class consciousness began to emerge. It's like changing classes. Suddenly individual playwriting is the thing and the oral performance tradition is no longer valued; it appears deficient to some.
RODRIGUEZ: It's a class thing. Definitely. And I know that I want a better standard of life. In some ways I'm satisfied with this standard of life. We don't always get a paycheck every month, but we manage. We don't have a family. . . . If we did we'd have to

do better than what we do now. And grass-roots means not having much money. . . . That's what it meant all the years we were doing it. . . . I personally don't want to live that way any more.

As I said the other day, if it came to us having a project and a life and death situation with the Teatro Campesino, I'd work for very little to keep it going. But I have to be assured that down the line I'd get something; that I would be taken care of. I think Olivia and I both agreed: if next January we're going to come work for menial because it's going to help improve our entire situation here with this company, then I'd do it. . . . But I've got to know that there's a payoff. For example, I might rehearse for free but then tour and then draw a salary. . . .

BROYLES-GONZÁLEZ: I don't know, maybe the old troupe could get into show business, but it doesn't seem like show business is into that kind of group act.
RODRIGUEZ: We just have to get the right steps here; we have to develop material here and then take it out. . . . We still have to sit down and decide: who's going to do it? When are we going to do it? What are we going to write about? Those questions take planning and time and we have not actually answered them. We've sat down many a time to talk; but money had dictated other things. We really need to sit down and reorganize. . . . The present organizational chart of the company was developed for a grant that we got from the NEA, the institutional advancement grant. Then because federal funding was cut, we probably only got half of the grant, if even that. And here we're left with this huge overbuilt organizational chart which does not function for us, and we're still working under that chart.

BROYLES-GONZÁLEZ: A chart which includes groupings such as the "Core Group" and "The Board of Directors," etc.?
RODRIGUEZ: Yes, all that stuff. It was created in an effort to make us bigger, to support a larger company. And it's not working. We haven't figured out our financial base yet. . . . Those kinds of things need really to be looked at this next year before we can even plan a show or plan artistically what we're doing. We certainly had things that we wanted to do this year, but just because of . . . our finances, that's just not possible. We're going to have to say no to certain projects. . . . The NEA budget was cut and money was not allotted any more.

I have no sense of how it would all change. It's very complicated. We're all sort of sticking it through and seeing where it's going to all go. It's just a struggle. We had a meeting the other night, you know. We have come to a point of asking: where are we going now? It was a good meeting, and we all felt very committed to staying and seeing it out: making sure that we followed our course, whatever it's going to be, that we be here to do it, and I'm committed to that. It's important, and we can't let it go. . . . And all of us have got to take an active part. . . . We have to be more active than we have ever been.

BROYLES-GONZÁLEZ: How can you be active here with El Teatro Campesino when you are having to look for work elsewhere? How can a company be sustained when people come and go as the occasion arises?
RODRIGUEZ: Well, when I was gone I wasn't as active as I am now. You just take time off and trust that everyone else will keep it going while you're gone and then come back

and plug in when there's work for you. Luis Oropeza, for example, has been gone a long time. He comes to all our meetings, but he hasn't been here in ages. And he is definitely willing to come back. But he's got to come back for a solid thing.

BROYLES-GONZÁLEZ: How have you gone about trying to establish yourself as an actress outside El Teatro Campesino? Have you had to retrain into another style of acting?
RODRIGUEZ: I think you have to think of yourself as a business, as a product . . . so as to be prepared. You always have to think basic things. You have to think . . . is my hairdo versatile? Is my hair too short and too spiked? . . . If your mouth is too big and if your teeth are too big, you're only going to play certain roles. Hardcore reality; face the facts. . . . This is what you want to do in the outside commercial world. Here in San Juan Bautista with El Teatro Campesino, I've been able to do more than that because I'm not as stereotyped as I am out there.

You have to really be in check and realistic. Are you a lead? a character actress? . . . And then you have to market yourself that way. If you're weak in certain aspects, you've got to be realistic. If you're not too good in the subtle acting of the naturalistic style, if you've done Chicano teatro for ten years and you're real good at the movement and the big characters and the comedy, but you can't fine tune it, you've got to go into training of a different kind. Luis Oropeza, because he was in San Francisco, was instrumental in getting me familiar with what was happening there and I went to a wonderful acting school called the Jean Shelton Acting School. . . . I studied there for two years off and on. . . . And then I would take dance wherever I was. . . . In San Diego, I found a dance school which is my favorite and I went and studied there for nine months. . . . And whenever I could I took voice, mostly singing. . . . You have to go out and compete, and there's so many kids in this country that are going to professional acting training schools. . . . There are training programs in many universities. Approximately seven of them are real good. So you have to be up to par.

BROYLES-GONZÁLEZ: The training in the Teatro Campesino, if I understand it correctly, is not quite transferable to the outside world. There is that division in styles.
RODRIGUEZ: There is the division in styles. But there's always something special about you as a Teatro person. . . . People say that there's a presence. You're always noticed in a show, always. You know, it's just a special energy that comes from being with the Teatro. And to me, that's worth it all. . . .

BROYLES-GONZÁLEZ: What you mentioned about the self having to become a business and having to package yourself in a certain way, does that then stereotype you in your own eyes?
RODRIGUEZ: No, . . . I know I'm very versatile. I know I can play youth; you know, I have a sense of youth and I have a sense of age and I can play a lot in between. I can play very feminine or very masculine. I can play very high drama or I can play low farce. . . . As far as being stereotyped: they're going to stereotype you in commercial theater; you don't have to do anything. And I'm not saying that commercial theater is what you should go after, either. That's why I want the Teatro Campesino to work out for us. I would rather really not have to deal with the business. If I get called and I go in for a reading and I get cast, that's fine. But I'm not gonna be down in Los Angeles waiting around. I'm just not the type. I've got to be doing something here. And that's why

this is here. . . . We haven't quite figured out all the angles yet, but I'm confident we will. And we'll come back again with something different and new and exciting.

BROYLES-GONZÁLEZ: Why don't the former ensemble members all get together and do something? Does it have to go through the office? Sometimes I get the impression that the new Teatro Campesino organization—the top-heavy administrative body—effectively stifles creativity and creative initiative.

RODRIGUEZ: But I don't think we want to do that. We've already done that. . . . I like having organization and I like being paid. And I like having my standard of living higher, and I like being in a professional theater company versus what is known as an alternative theater company. I like that more now at age 32. Alternative theater companies—like the Teatro Campesino until now—don't pay as well, or pay anything, or pay very little, and you live collectively. Teatro de la Esperanza, for example: they pay and they share responsibilities and the whole thing. I'm not there. I don't want to do that any more. . . . But I still have not left behind the cause of why I'm doing theater. I just want it to be different. . . . I want it to be on another level.

BROYLES-GONZÁLEZ: What is the piece you have enjoyed the most with the Teatro? Is there anything that stands out particularly in that spectrum of experiences?

RODRIGUEZ: Roles? Very few; there have been very few roles in Teatro Campesino that I have thoroughly enjoyed. Because of what they're saying and who they are. I've played María Rasquachi, the wife in *La gran carpa de la familia Rasquachi*. . . . She was strong, but she wasn't my favorite. I just wouldn't want to be in her situation . . . a victim of economics and machismo. . . . The two roles that I have enjoyed the most have been Satanás [Satan] and La Muerte [Death]. They've been basically androgynous roles. I haven't enjoyed the women roles at all. . . . I've played the mother, the girl friend . . . the standards—the role of Chata in *Fin del mundo* (1980), who I never liked and I never did well because I couldn't like her. I couldn't. It's too bad, because I didn't think I could do justice to the role—if there was any justice to that role. . . . What has been fun is the opportunity to play that male/female role like Satanás . . . oh, it's wonderful, it's freedom. Like Santanás or La Muerte in *La Carpa*. It was a wonderful, wonderful piece. And the roles of Satanás or Muerte are wonderful because you can do everything. . . . As far as the women and as far as the repertory goes, that has been a strong point. The women have also managed to play men or males very well. The men played women's roles in the early days, but I don't think the men played women with credibility; I think it was more like a joke. The female roles have been weak. The nonfemale roles I've played have not been weak. These nonfemale roles—well, they stand out.

BROYLES-GONZÁLEZ: What is your sense nowadays of school kids; when you perform in schools, when you talk with them?

RODRIGUEZ: I go into some of the schools and they vaguely know what a Chicano is but they really don't. Even in colleges, they just don't know. They don't know what the Teatro Campesino was or what the sixties or seventies meant and what we were striving for. They don't know. They're very individually oriented, just toward themselves. There's not a social sense to them.

You know, I can't have just the responsibility to myself; I feel a sense of responsibility to more. When I was in San Diego, I spoke to classes at the university. And whenever

I'm asked, I say that my generation had to keep pushing to get through. I try to let everyone know that there's something still to be gained and we haven't gotten it yet. We still have to fight a little bit more.

BROYLES-GONZÁLEZ: One of the things I have observed is the sense of loyalty that Teatro Campesino members to some extent share. Where do you stand emotionally with the Teatro? And is it hard to share that emotion? How has that evolved?

RODRIGUEZ: We are in love with the Teatro Campesino. . . . It's difficult to talk about El Teatro Campesino to outside people because it's like a marriage. You know, you just don't really talk about what's going on inside. . . . I also see everyone having more . . . belief in themselves and what they can do. We used to have a general, collective sense of what we could all do, but we were almost faceless. We were in the Teatro Campesino . . . and who knew who Olivia was? Who knew who Diane was? And now it's better for us now, at our age, that we are known as who we are as individuals and what we each have to contribute. . . . Most of us are thirty or plus now. . . . It's good for us to be able to express how the struggle has been for us. . . . It's a joyful struggle; you do it because there's hope and there's progress and it's joyful; but it is a struggle. And to be under someone's wing or many people's wings, to be in the shadows for many years and to believe that one day you'll come out, you must have a strong sense of yourself. That's what's happened to a lot of us. When Felix and Lilly came, they were a very strong force in the company, very strong, very, very influential. When they left, a light happened, a shadow had been lifted, and all of us started blossoming, growing. That was in 1976. It was wonderful. I was as if this darkness had been lifted from us, and that started off an evolution that continued into 1979. Luis was in New York with *Zoot Suit* and Joe [José Delgado] was here and there was not enough money to pay for us, to pay our salaries . . . and Joe said, "I've got to lay everyone off." We had never been laid off. So in 1979 there was another point where we had to begin fending for ourselves and trying to make a living on our own, while still staying close. It's been a struggle, and all of us are here because we want to be here and because we believe in it. And that makes me feel good— to look around at everybody and know that they all want to be here. It's not that someone is dictating to us that we must be here and must believe what they are saying. Rather, we all have our own input and we all want to be here because we can contribute.

BROYLES-GONZÁLEZ: It's interesting that there was what you call this faceless bunch of people. Yet there was one person [Luis Valdez] that was not faceless. His name was made known; and in this society that means that he would be viewed as the one with the monopoly on talent. He would come to be regarded as the great individual.

RODRIGUEZ: Nobody knows how to deal with a group. America is not equipped for that. They don't know how to deal with a group. They deal with individuals. They understand individuals; the business understands individuals. Show business is set up on individual status, you know. . . . I've been able to work so many years and not have to get another job because I've had a group. Of all my actor friends, I think I've been the one who has been the most employed throughout most of these last ten to twelve years, because I belong to a group. . . . I wish more people had an opportunity to belong to a group. Because you can really do a lot more. You can really be more of a theater artist, and not just one specialized thing. You can do many things and develop them all equally. . . . You know my friend Chris, she's a wonderful actress, but I also can do costume design. There was a need in El Teatro Campesino and I had to fill it. That came from doing group work. Costume design was my other focus. I'm continually working on that and can make a living on it. . . . Of course I need training, I'm not by any means fully trained for it. But I can definitely get it together and do a show. . . . Eventually, I'm sure it will blossom into designing for other theater companies, but I'm not really going after that at this point. I have a knack for it, and an interest, and a love for it. . . . I like fitting people, and I like putting them into a costume. Costuming is a work dimension that allows me to be more of a total artist in the theater. Or more spherical. I've thoroughly appreciated that opportunity. . . . I started doing it in '75. A long time ago. . . .

Another [thing] I developed is that *si se puede* attitude that I remember chanting forever when we were on marches. It sticks with me. Isn't that amazing? When those things are said, . . . generally . . . people don't take them individually to heart. But here it sunk in. . . . I thought, "O wow, I can do this." And acting—if you're not a natural, there's so much to learn. You can be talented and not be a natural. A natural is someone who just doesn't need training. They don't need voice training, for example; they can just do it. They've got all the instrument ready when they're young. But for someone like me: you have talent, but you just have to carve it out. It's all there, it's a diamond, but it's got to be polished. . . . In order to have been a part of this company, you have to have incredible strength. You also have to have your ego very much in check, because no one lets you get away with anything that you don't deserve to get away with. Do you know what I mean? You'll be teased if it's real phony. Almost like a family. They help mold you. Those of us who have survived all the changes have a strength.

BROYLES-GONZÁLEZ: Why do you do theater?

RODRIGUEZ: Just in terms of my own essence and spirit, I do theater because I'm crazy and need an outlet. . . . It helps me be crazy and live calmly. . . For me personally, it's . . . the way I can live and expend my energy, because I have tons of it and don't know what to do with it normally. That's one reason. The other is because what we do here is important. I'm concerned about all my other Chicano brothers and sisters. I want to do material that relates to us. I want to do material that we can share, that's not just solely for a Chicano audience: material that can bring others in and can give a view of how we look, how we think, how we feel. And sometimes the pieces don't totally accomplish that. But they accomplish one part of it, and that's good. We have to strive to make it better in the next piece. To express values, new values, express ways of living here, express what it is to be an American of my color, in my color . . . that's why I like doing it. It's expressive.

Notes

1. Among the pioneers in the reconstruction of Chicana performance history are Thomás Ybarra-Frausto, "La Chata Noloesca," and Yvonne Yarbro-Bejarano, "Teatro poesía by Chicanas in the Bay Area: Tongues of Fire," both published in *Mexican American Theatre: Then and Now*, edited by Nicolas Kanellos (*Revista Chicano-Riqueña*, 11, no. 1 [1983]). Also pertinent are other incisive essays by Yarbro-Bejarano, such as "The Role of Women in Chicano Theater-Organizations," *Revista Literaria de El Tecolote* 2, no. 3 (1981): 4, and "The Image of the

Chicana in Teatro," in *Gathering Ground: New Writing and Art by Northwest Women of Color,* edited by Jo Cochran, J. T. Stewart, and Mayumi Tsutakawa (Seattle, Wash.: Seal Press, 1984), 90–96. On Chicana performers of El Teatro Campesino see Yolanda Broyles-González, "Women in El Teatro Campesino: '¿Apoco estaba molacha La Virgen de Guadalupe?' " in *Chicano Voices: Intersections of Class, Race and Gender,* edited by Teresa Cordova et al. (Austin: Center for Mexican American Studies, University of Texas, 1986), 162–87, and "Toward a Re-Vision of Chicano Theatre History: The Women of El Teatro Campesino," in *Making A Spectacle: Feminist Essays on Contemporary Women's Theatre,* edited by Lynda Hart (Ann Arbor: University of Michigan Press, 1989), 209–38. On the construction of the female subject in Chicano theater see Yvonne Yarbro-Bejarano, "The Female Subject in Chicano Theatre: Sexuality, 'Race,' and Class," *Theatre Journal* (December 1986), 389–407.

2. I have interviewed various women numerous times during the past ten years. All my interviews are an ongoing process. The ongoing interview allows documentation of different stages of development in a performer's life. Such interviews are more complete and accurate than something recollected from the distant past, and they go into much greater depth than one-shot interviews—not to mention that a person being interviewed takes a one-shot interview and interviewer far less seriously than an interviewer who has established a long-term relationship with the interviewee. The oral history segment presented here was collected December 28, 1983, in San Juan Bautista, California, at the home of Diane Rodríguez. This segment will be published in its entirety, along with various other oral histories, in the forthcoming book *El Teatro Campesino: An Oral HIstory.*

3. One chapter of my forthcoming book *El Teatro Campesino: Four Cardinal Points* treats the Theater of the Sphere performance philosophy.

The Politics of Women's Music: A Conversation with Linda Tillery and Mary Watkins

Mary S. Pollock

"Women's music" came into being in the early seventies, in response to a women's political movement that needed artistic expression. The political movement gave women musicians both an understanding of the ways in which they were shut out of the male-dominated music industry and the collective consciousness to organize. The results are women's recording and distribution companies, women's concert production companies, a women's music circuit whose audience is mainly women, and, to a certain extent, a distinctive "women's music" sound, characterized by accessibility, intimacy within musical groupings, woman-identified lyrical themes, musical eclecticism, and the musical integrity that comes from not trying to reach mass audiences.

Linda Tillery and Mary Watkins have been part of the women's music circuit almost since its "official" beginning, the foundation of Olivia Record Company in 1973 in Washington, D.C. Both Tillery and Watkins have performed a variety of roles in the women's music industry, with Olivia based in Oakland, California, with Redwood Records (founded by Holly Near), and on their own labels. They have produced records for other musicians, provided musical support on the albums of other artists, and released solo albums featuring their own music. Both of them seem to be constantly on the road, and both of them continue to grow and change musically as they collaborate, not only with each other, but with different configurations of musicians whose styles and traditions confront and influence one another.

The peculiar eclecticism of women's music results from the intensity and variety of possibilities for collaboration. From the very beginning almost all the musicians in the circuit have been classically trained. In addition, each of them brings to the blend another tradition. For example, such artists as Meg Christian have worked in the folk tradition; Cris Williamson and June Millington have brought in pop/rock influences; Izquierda and Holly Near have drawn on Latin rhythms. Watkins and Tillery are largely responsible for the strong strain in women's music of various black musical idioms—jazz, rhythm and blues, gospel.

I spoke with Tillery and Watkins the day after their featured performance at a women's music festival in Austin, Texas. The festival had been a perfect illustration of the eclecticism of women's music. All the performers except these two were local, and all were women, but they represented many different musical traditions. The circumstances of the interview seemed to steer the conversation toward the topics of originality versus tradition, the dynamics between the musician and the audience, and women in music. And because I believe that we owe it to ourselves and our artists to understand the processes of their art, I asked some theoretical questions about how songs are written, how arrangements are established, how it feels to collaborate with other musicians, and what is involved in the recording process.

POLLOCK: Linda, how much of your music is traditional, and how much is your own creation?

TILLERY: I aspire to carry on the musical traditions I grew up with. My parents had a lot of records, mostly blues, rhythm and blues, and big-band jazz—Count Basie, Duke Ellington, singers like Sarah Vaughan and Dinah Washington. My musical background and training also come from the Baptist Church and gospel music. That music is still "home" to me. I also have a little bit of classical training, but I don't consider that my own. That's another form of music I've taken in along the way. As a woman-identified woman, a womanist, I'm trying to carry on that tradition and speak with the voice that will be most understandable. I don't know that I'm doing anything new. I'd have to say I'm more a traditionalist than an original: I'm a black American woman, carrying on a rich, full musical tradition that has supported me and a lot of other people for several hundred years—black American music. Last night, when I said that "folk music" varies according to where your folks are from, I was trying to explain something about my own music.

WATKINS: I'm both original, I think, and traditional. Most of what I perform is my own music, but it partly originates from tradition. How original it is, I don't know—I just do what I feel. While I was growing up in Colorado, I heard pop tunes and country and western music. I didn't hear much big-band music or jazz until I was older. I started to notice rhythm and blues when I was about twelve, and I was exposed to classical music from the time I was about twelve. Really, I feel that all kinds of music belong to me, if that makes sense. I love all kinds of music, and I'm just going to let that lead me where it leads me.

POLLOCK: Has your classical training influenced the way you do jazz?

WATKINS: The classical training has probably influenced my approach to jazz in bad ways and good ways. I used to think of a recital as a death sentence, and it's taken me a while to relax about performing. That has to do with an attitude classical performers and teachers have about correctness, I think. And even when I was a classical piano student, I tended to want to do things *my* way, and I always wanted to go for the emotions. I always wondered, "Why do I have to follow the letter of the law here? Why can't I just go for the spirit?" All that is a jazz attitude. I've talked to other jazz musicians who initially were classical artists. They say that they had the same problem I've had in getting rid of that concern with correctness, learning to abandon themselves to the music and *go*. To make a complete musical statement in jazz, you have to fly and live dangerously. Anyway, classical training did influence my attitude: I had a hard time letting go when I played.

And then, there's the question of technique: I've had to relearn some things because classical and jazz techniques are different. I have to get around the piano a new way. For example, I've abandoned some of the fingerings used in classical music. Now I use my little fingers and thumbs on the black keys all the time. But as long as I tried to use that classical training for jazz, I was hung up all the time.

On the other hand, I never had a problem making the transition from classical rhythms and harmonies to jazz. That ease probably came from my lack of discipline: I preferred improvising to practicing. Looking back on it, I see that I never could have been a concert pianist. I'd get started on whatever piece in the standard repertoire, get a few bars into it, and think, "Gee, what if he'd done it *this* way?" Then I'd be "off to the races," and I'd end up having to cram all of my real practicing into the hour before my lesson. It's just natural for that kind of musician to move into jazz.

Of course, the classical training has been a positive help in some ways. I was always interested in composition, and the symphony always inspired me, thrilled me. The first time I heard a big orchestra, I was just a kid, but I thought, "Gee, *I* could do that." When I got into junior college, nobody talked about composition. The attitude was, "We already have enough composers. Why do we need any more?" But then when I moved to Howard University, where they *did* offer composition, I just came alive. My favorite teacher there was a composer who was very supportive of me. I hadn't been interested in school until I could study composition. Then I was happy and didn't have to be pushed at all. I still don't have to be pushed because I'm allowed to do the work that I love to do. I initiate contacts with groups wanting music; for example, I contacted the symphony orchestra in my home town, Pueblo, Colorado, and asked if they wanted some of my music. They did.[1]

POLLOCK: What else came from your classical training?

WATKINS: Well, classical music always made sense to me. When I sat in rehearsals at school, listening to the conductor as he worked with different sections of the band, I noticed the way the instruments sounded together and just never forgot it. Composers have to know that kind of thing in order to be able to express colors, feelings. At the time, I didn't know I would be writing orchestral music, but I filed the information away. In the same way, I learned from piano lessons. They reinforced what I learned from the hymn book at church. Everything about basic harmony is in the hymns, and classical harmony always made perfect sense to me. Even contemporary music is based on those classical harmonies—it's more dissonant, of course, but the principles are the same. It's funny how I learned all those lessons without being aware of what I was learning.

POLLOCK: I'm really interested in what goes into the process of arranging, as well as the process of composition, because it seems to me it's in working out arrangements that you might be most aware of other musicians, and even most aware of your listeners. And, too, that's the point at which you're thinking about the music in terms of the whole, in terms of melody, harmony, words, *and* timbre or instrumentation. There never seems to be anything arbitrary about arrangement for either of you. How conscious *is* this process?

TILLERY: For some reason, the first word that comes to my mind is "commercialism." We've all been affected by commercial music; and I don't think that's all bad. When I put together an arrangement, I always ask myself, "Will people be able to relate to this?" Accessibility is one thing I mean when I say "commercial." If a melody is too complex, often listeners *can't* digest it. At the same time, if the musician is capable of performing complex music, anything too simple won't be interesting to perform. You certainly don't want to put yourself to sleep. So the music has to be interesting for the performer and accessible for the audience.

Personally, I like lyrics that come right at me, that aren't too introspective, especially if the music is polyrhythmic or polytonal. In that case you can bet saturated with the music too quickly if the words are also complicated. And I usually know within the first four or five bars of a song or an arrangement whether I'm going to like it or not.

POLLOCK: I imagine part of your concern with accessibility goes along with being a good performer. But does your concern for the audience ever inhibit your ability to improvise, or does the audience ever energize you, so that you improvise in more interesting ways?

TILLERY: Well, improvising is an art, a skill that you learn, and certainly, the audience affects you in your ability to do that, just as they can affect you in a lot of other ways.

I'm getting better at improvisation. Behind the music Mary and I do, there's a basic three-chord, twelve-bar blues. A musician can extend the blues, make substitutions and changes so it will be more interesting and hip. That's what happened with be-bop tunes, which a lot of people think are too complicated. But I like that sort of complication. A simple blues in C has just three chord changes, and after you go over something like that again and again, you run out of ideas. But if you make some substitutions in the pattern to begin with, there are more ways you can improvise on top of the basic line.

Improvisation, as Mary has been saying, is basic in her work, and it's what I'm learning to do better. Improvisation means making a statement, then later on taking off from there, deviating from it and elaborating on it. A few years back, I studied with a vocalist in San Francisco, a master improvisor. (We used to call it "scat," but my teacher won't use that word.) And I've learned a lot just from listening to singers like Ella Fitzgerald. She's got a great tone. For the last forty or fifty years, this woman has been singing like a bird! I'm beginning to find I can free myself from the words the way she can and then get into the music *itself*. When I do that, I'm very much aware of my voice as in instrument, which functions like an alto sax, a horn, doing little rhythmic or harmonic patterns. I used to have to think about that more, but now sometimes, I'll hear something like a horn sound coming out of my mouth, something that isn't lyrical at all. I'm starting to think in notes, and it's really exciting.

When you're doing this, the musicians working with you are extremely important. I can listen to a keyboard player, pick up her suggestions, and reproduce them or take them further. That's good interplay.

POLLOCK: We've been talking about arrangement and about composition in very general terms. How do songs get written? Tell me about the stages.

WATKINS: Well, it can be pretty complicated. "Womanly Way," for instance—that's a song Linda, Diane Lindsay, and I wrote—has an interesting story.[2] Linda came up with the lyrics and melody, so it basically expresses her, and it's mostly her song. But at first it didn't have a harmonic structure. Why don't you talk about it, Linda?

TILLERY: I really wanted to write some of the music on my first album, the one on the Olivia label. I was beating my brains out until somebody suggested that if I'd just relax, whatever was in my head could come out. One night when I was on the way to a movie, this little song started going through my head, and I really liked it. I kept singing it over so I'd remember it, wrote it down on a paper bag I picked up from the sidewalk, and got to the theatre just as the first verse was completed. Whenever there was a scene in the movie with a lot of light, I'd get out the brown paper bag and sing the verse over so I wouldn't forget it. A few days later, I sang it to Diane Lindsay, who's a bass player, to establish the rhythm. The song needed a bridge, so Mary helped me with that. Once we got all the chords, we were able to arrange it and establish the groove beneath the melody. I don't play the piano or the guitar, so when I think of a melody and some lyrics, It's important for me to get somebody else to help me with the harmonic structure. Sometimes it *is* painful to have to depend on somebody else for that. Anyway, the song was completed in several stages. The melody and the chords in many songs are so interdependent that it's hard for me to think about writing a song unless I can work out all the parts. Sometimes a melody suggests a harmonic structure, but just as often, a series of chords can suggest a melody.

WATKINS: I don't think you ought to underestimate yourself as a songwriter. You wrote the chords to "Wonderful." You wrote that whole thing. You do have a guitar, and you know how to play it. The first time you did that song for me, it was complete.

TILLERY: But that's a simple song. Actually, I do like it. It came from personal experience. The melody came into my head one day when I was just sitting around strumming. (The melody usually does come first for me.) Then the words started coming, and it turned into a song. I was excited because that was the first song I had ever completed all by myself.

POLLOCK: When did you first start making up songs?

TILLERY: Well, I've dabbled for a long time, but I haven't written a lot. People tell me my ideas are good, so I probably should write more than I do. But I have a block about trusting my ideas, and sometimes that really gets in the way. Often I'll throw out a song before I've really gotten started on it. Another problem is that I spend too much time worrying about the fact that I don't write more music, that I don't trust my instincts enough. I know that I must be willing to try with songwriting, to have the same kind of confidence with it that I have in my singing.

Of course, the problem is not just my insecurity. I usually hear things in more complicated forms than I'm able to put down on paper. I like the challenge of jazz, the harmonic and rhythmic tensions. There's nothing obvious about jazz, nothing simple. It's wonderful to perform, but very difficult to write.

POLLOCK; Mary, does Linda's way of composing sound anything like yours?

WATKINS: Sometimes when I'm doing a piano solo, I will just improvise it from the ground up. When I'm focused and centered, I'll get a musical idea or a little theme, like Linda was saying, and I'll harmonize it. First I might have dissonant chords under the melody, so it sounds like what I'm playing is just chords. Then maybe I'll play the same theme in a major tonality. Doing that is exciting, especially when I can stay centered. Melody and harmony usually come to me simultaneously.

"A Chording to the People" I wrote for my manager, who plays the recorder and wanted a simple little melody.[3] I started playing the melody on the piano, and it sounded so simple, like a little Gregorian chant, that I couldn't help wondering what kind of song it would make if I added some interesting rhythms. So in that case, I expanded a simple melody into a larger piece. Pieces get written in different ways. Some simply, others in more complex ways. Sometimes the whole thing, words and notes, comes at once. I feel when that happens I *have* to write it down, even though ordinarily I don't write things down, because I'm not a prolific lyricist.

POLLOCK: Do you have a musical shorthand?

WATKINS: No, I've just had to get fast. I use a tape recorder more now than I've ever done before, but I notice that as I rely more on it, my ear doesn't seem quite as sharp. Anyway, I try to get a concept down as completely as possible, as fast as I can, because it's so easy to lose it. It's especially easy to lose a piece that's not in a pop or commercial vein. I can always correct my mistakes later on if I have written the song down. Actually, songs are *never* permanently fixed. I can change them, or another performer can change or rephrase anything I might have come up with.

POLLOCK: Do you revise much?

WATKINS: I don't like to, but I'm more willing to do it than I used to be because I've accumulated so many things that could be pretty good if I'd take the time to refine them. Often I like things more later than I do right after I've written them down, so I've learned not to throw anything out.

TILLERY: That's true. One time I went over to Mary's house, hoping she could give me a ballad or a soul song. As I described what I wanted, she said, "Oh, I have this old thing I wrote, you know, a long time ago. I'm not sure what it is, or if I can find it." But she went over to this stack of sheet music—I like to tell this story about how Mary files things away—and she rustled through two thousand pages until she found this song, "You and Me." I just loved the melody and the chord structure. It was my kind of song!

I like to work with Mary for several reasons. Consistency and style are important. It's important for me to become familiar with other people's styles so I know who I can play off in the best way. I need the right kind of drummer, the right kind of bass player, and, particularly, the right kind of keyboard support. That's where my ideas come from—the dialogue with the other players. If I work with a piano player who plays only basic triads, I don't get many ideas to take off from, whereas if I play with someone who works in a lot of different variations, anything can happen!

POLLOCK: Does Mary surprise you sometimes while you're performing?

TILLERY: Yes, she does! She surprised me last night, as a matter of fact—on her solo in "Summertime." I assume she plays real well. I expect that, but sometimes she extends herself a little further and plays exceptionally well. That's a real get-off. I love that spontaneity and surprise.

POLLOCK: When that happens, do you have a hard time getting back on track?

TILLERY: Sometimes. But lately, I've had the experience of surprising myself. Sometimes when I can actually reproduce a very complex idea I hear in my head, I go into another plane for a minute. It's so satisfying to pull that off that sometimes I lose my concentration, step back and glow for a minute before I can get back into it. But then, there's the opposite problem of mistakes. It's hard for me to separate myself from the other performers, so if one of them makes a mistake, it can throw me off. I have to remind myself, though, that there are people watching, so I *don't* turn around and say "You're rushing," or "You're dragging."

WATKINS: The bass line to me is really important. When I'm soloing, if the bass starts to go in a direction where I don't happen to be moving, what I'm trying to say is affected. It's really bad if that happens at a moment when I'm just about to peak. Then, if the other person goes somewhere else, the whole experience can just flatten. I mean, it's kind of like a climax that didn't quite happen. In a way, I'd like to get past being so affected by what goes on around me. If I could, my concentration would be better. Sometimes I tend, not so much now as I used to, to think like a producer while trying to perform. That gets in the way of total abandon.

POLLOCK: Well, you *are* a producer, so I suppose that is only natural. As a producer, you must be very much aware of the differences between live performances and recording sessions. For example, I wonder if knowing you can go over a piece of music many times ever affects how you improvise.

WATKINS: There are two ways of looking at it. I like recordings of live performances. I did a live recording with Maiden Voyage Big Band and an extra twenty-piece string section one time that really worked out well. And I've recorded under controlled studio conditions, too. In a live performance, you can't go over it or put it off until a day when you're in the mood. And sometimes, a recording in that situation turns out to be really good. Sometimes I think live performances are better because you only have that one chance, and you know you can't stop and start over. You just have to *do* it, and sometimes I think the less you repeat it, the better.

I do sometimes like to do studio albums *because* the conditions are controlled: you can get a kind of quality in the studio that you can't get from a live performance. And yet I think I'd *always* want to record solos from live performances. You know, when you just go for it. The fresher the music, the more it just seems to have a life of its own.

TILLERY: There are a lot of toys in a studio, and often if people aren't in awe of it, they want to play with all of it at once, not realizing how much skill is involved. And then there's the lack of spontaneity that Mary was getting at. I like performing in front of people because I like the emotional response they give. In a studio, you have only your own ears and those of the producer, who's *supposed* to be an ideal audience. But when you perform live and in front of people, there is an exchange of energy and emotion that you cannot get when you're singing to a microphone and four walls. I very much believe in music as a source of healing and power, a unifying source. And you need people to have that interaction. Often I can just feel that warmth from the audience, and that is real important to me, so I feel like giving more. And the more I give, the more there is. So I have a constant flow of energy and ideas. That's hard to get in an overdub. Like Mary said, if you can cut it live, you have the actual exchange and interplay of energy. That's the best.

POLLOCK: Mary, do you feel the same way about the audience?

WATKINS: Yeah. Of course, there are different kinds of audiences. For instance, I played in June Millington's rock band on a concert tour one time, but I also did a solo piano opening act.[4] I really don't like playing solo piano for people who are there to hear rock, but sometimes they're receptive. That's my stuff, I guess. Sometimes my head starts doing these numbers: "Well, let's see," I'll say to myself, "this is a rock crowd tonight, so I'd better play something raunchy." I prefer to set the mood myself, see, and not have to go with the mood set by another performer. That way, I can stretch out and do things with classical elements, or I can do spiritual or jazz music. Sometimes I get in a mood just to let the music flow out, and I can't do that in a nightclub.

POLLOCK: Because you feel the audience isn't really there for *your* music?

WATKINS: That's in *my* head; that's a little trick my head plays on me sometimes, when the audience might be perfectly receptive to whatever I want to do. There's some basis for that attitude, of course. When I opened for June on the tour, in both D.C. and

Indianapolis I expected the audiences to be inattentive because both times were in bars. But, although the Washington audience was as rude and noisy as I expected, the Indianapolis audience turned out to be attentive and appreciative. They had come to hear rock, but they had come to hear me, too.

POLLOCK: I have a question that is nasty but needs to be asked. I've heard people say that rock and jazz aren't good musical idioms for women, and they see the relative scarcity of women rock and jazz musicians as evidence for their beliefs. Even some feminists have referred to rock, especially as a male musical idiom, which politically correct women musicians should avoid. What would you say to those people?

TILLERY: Well, I have a nasty response. I get extremely angry when people tell me that rock—really what they're talking about is rhythm-based music—is not a good way for a woman to go. The music that I grew up with and that I understand most is music created by my ancestors, my family. Blues, rhythm and blues, and jazz are part of our tradition, and I resent the fact that anyone would say these are not good idioms for women. That's telling me that I shouldn't express my own culture, that some other tradition would be me appropriate for me. And that, to me, is racist.

POLLOCK: What advice would you give a white woman doing rock and jazz, who was having to cope with that sort of remark?

TILLERY: To grow up. You have to express yourself in whatever way is right for you.

POLLOCK: Things are changing very fast right now, but until recently it was very hard for a woman to make it in rock and jazz. Holiday and Joplin, for instance, were casualties of the system. Why do you think women have had such a tough time?

TILLERY: It's been difficult for women in popular music in general, especially for women who are not vocalists. It's actually been hard for women in the music industry all the way around because the music industry is male dominated. The only way that will change is for us to persevere.

Performers experience a lot of different pressures, not all of which have to do with the music itself. A lot of the pressure comes from the tension between what you internalize from the outside and who you really are inside. I've decided that if being a musician ever makes me lose a sense of my own identity, I'll stop doing it. You see, rock—and we're using the term loosely—has become a white American teenage panacea. Rock stars are the cultural heroes for teenagers, performers who stand on a stage and represent a lot of what kids want to be in their fantasies. This attitude has very little to do with music, and it's dangerous. If the musician ever starts to take on that identity created by the music business or by the audience, she or he can lose the real identity. I would never want to alter myself to please an audience. I want to be what is most natural for me, and people who enjoy me in that way I want to come to my performances. People who don't enjoy me as I am had better stay away because I obviously don't have what they want.

Afterword

All art is political. Literature, painting, and music do not originate and exist in a realm apart from life, contrary to what we may have been told by the voices of patriarchal culture—referred to wryly in Honor Moore's "Polemic #1" as "the Art Delivery Machine."[5] Rather, the production of art is profoundly affected by the artist's cultural and political environment, and art directly or indirectly expresses the forces at work in that environment. Gender and race are cultural and political constructs and, partly *as* cultural and political constructs, determine the way an artist's work is presented and the way it is perceived. Gender and race determine, too, both the artist's modes of expression and the ideas that take shape in tones, words, colors, movement.

Contemporary feminist artists, constantly accused of "politicizing art," have through alternative production and distribution organizations laid bare the politics of traditional art production and delivery. And, more of less subtly, they have brought to the surface the political content inherent in all art. In *The Pornography of Representation*, Suzanne Kappeler points out that art, as well as other kinds of representation, has political ramifications because "Representation is . . . one of the most fundamental structures of conceptualization."[6] In other words, we know ourselves in part through the way we are represented. To be empowered, women must understand that their images of themselves have been created by a politically empowered patriarchy, in whose best interest is the suppression of all women and of all persons of color. One of the most significant accomplishments of the women's movement in recent years has been the creation of women's galleries, presses, journals, record and music distribution networks, and record companies. These ventures have of course given the women involved some economic power, but more important, women now have a different kind of cultural and political environment in which to produce art—in which to create the images through which we know and understand ourselves.

As I talked with Mary Watkins and Linda Tillery, I realized that their awareness of race and gender politics influences their decisions about the public life of their music, as well as the artistic decisions they make within the music itself. When Linda Tillery speaks of herself as a black American she is pointing out that art is political expression. This association of art and politics also underlies, I think, her response to my question about critics of women in rock. The theory is that rock, as well as other rhythm-based music, is incapable of expressing any but a male point of view. Tillery points out that this criticism is racist: such a restriction would prohibit her from creating within her own cultural idiom. Mary Watkins's studied eclecticism makes an equally important though different political statement. She says that all music "belongs to me," and, like many other contemporary women musicians, finds freedom of expression by mixing genres and idioms in unexpected, "incorrect" ways. Watkins's heterogeneous pieces are exercises in cultural pluralism.

Tillery speaks of struggling to set her own voice free—as a singer through training in improvisation and through learning to relate to audience, as a composer through working to overcome the inernalized censors that inhibit women artists, I suspect, far more profoundly than they do men. Watkins speaks similarly of the struggle to find a setting in which her voice as composer could be nurtured and heard. For Tillery, the struggle to hear herself and to be heard has meant not only deliberate training within the black musical tradition but also recording and distributing her albums through women's record companies and working with women's production companies. Watkins, too, has worked with these women's companies. Her compositions are most often performed by women. She herself frequently contributes to the public life of other women musicians by producing their records.

Both these artists are intensely aware of the dynamics between the musician and her music, between the music and the media of its production and distribution, between the media and the audience. Talking with them reminded me that the "art delivery machine" must be acknowledged and evaded in every separate link of the fragile chain that connects these musicians with their audience. I hope this chain can be strengthened. Our culture and our world are in need of the positive representations we hear in the music of these women.

Notes

1. "Potomac Park," performed in 1976 by the Pueblo Civic Symphony, Pueblo, Colorado.
2. On *Linda Tillery*, as is "Wonderful." Diane Lindsay is a songwriter, performer, and producer with Olivia Records.
3. On Mary Watkins, *Something Moving.*
4. June Millington was formerly with rock band Fanny, and is now a performer, songwriter, and producer with women's record companies, most recently involved in a project on Third World women's music.
5. Honor Moore, "Polemic 1," *in The New Women's Survival Sourcebook,* Kirsten Grimstad and Susan Rennie, eds. (New York: Alfred E. Knopf, 1975), 105.
6. Suzanne Kappeler, *The Pornography of Representation* (Minneapolis: University of Minnesota Press, 1986), 3.

Discography

Tillery, Linda. *Linda Tillery.* Olivia BLF 917. 1977.

———. *Secrets.* 411 Records BLF 736. 1986. (Distributed by Redwood Records.)

Watkins, Mary. *Something Moving.* Olivia BLF 919. 1978.

———. *Spiritsong.* Redwood Records RR 8506. 1985.

———. *Winds of Change.* Palo Alto Records 8030. 1982.

For an Asian Woman Who Says My Poetry Gives Her a Stomachache

Nellie Wong

You would rather scream out your anger in a workshop
and then you would find peace
and you ask if I find peace
by becoming more angry in my poetry

You turn to my sister-poet and say she's found peace
because her style is soft
and mine shouts

I jokingly say that I do find peace
when I sleep for at least 6 hours
but I give you my one true answer:

Peace does not exist
not while a woman is being raped
a child is being abused
a lesbian is being beaten
a man is denied work because of his race

and if I could document my life in snapshots
I would take hours to describe the pains
of being a girl and a young woman
who thought beauty
was being white
        useless
        a mother
        a wife

seen only in the eyes of the racist beholder
wrapped in the arms of the capitalist media
starved in the binds of patriarchal culture

and how I screamed in silence for years
beating myself down, delirious in my victimization
preferring the cotton-spun candy I thought was life

and now in my hours of awakening
as my hair turns white
my anger moves, a storm into the sunlight
where women and men fight alongside each other
in the battles against degradation, poverty, manipulation, fear
where anger is pure as the love I have for freedom
where desire is the catalyst for action
where the possibilities are rice and flowers and children
growing strong everywhere

Not Just Because My Husband Said

Ana Castillo

if i had no poems left
i would be classified *working class intelligentsia*
my husband said
having to resort to teaching or research
grow cobwebs between my ears
if i had no poems left

if i did not sing in the morning
or before i went to bed, i'd be as good as dead
my husband said
struck dumb with morose silence or apathy
my children would distrust me
if i did not sing in the morning

if i could not place on the table
fresh fruit, vegetables tender and green
we would soon grow ill and lean
my husband said
we'd grow weak and mean and useless to our neighbors
if i could not place fresh fruit on the table.

Chapter 11—Women in the Arts:
Perspectives on Gender and Creativity
Study Questions

1. How does "gender arrangement" affect the status of women's art? What are the criteria for art's intrinsic value? What systems have served to support this dichotomy?

2. What is feminist essentialism in art? On what assertion is it based? Does this notion effectively answer the gender arrangement dichotomy? Why or why not?

3. Explain, through your own experience, the "male gaze" as it affects your perceptions of yourself.

4. In small groups followed by the large group, discuss whether you think pornography contributes to the sexual objectification of women to the extent that it should be censored.

5. How does art as social commentary expand the awareness of our current political context?

6. Do female artists need a separate voice to be heard? Why or why not?

7. According to Broyles-Gonzalez, what are the threats to Chicana performance history in Western (patriarchal) society? Do these issues affect all marginalized groups?

8. How did the 1980s affect Teatro Campesino's impact in regard to connectedness and issues of oppression?

9. Referencing both "The Living Legacy . . ." and "The Politics of Women's Music . . .," discuss what important issues are brought to light through the art of marginalized groups? What are the barriers these artists must face?

10. Nellie Wong's poem is about her emerging consciousness. What lessons does she share? As an Asian woman, does her awareness also describe a feminist consciousness? How?

11. In small groups discuss what Ana Castillo is expressing about her relationship to art as opposed to how the patriarchy views women's art. Is women's art an emblem of women's worth or simply a frill? Discuss in the context of Castillo's poem.

CONCLUSION

The Future of Feminism: The Struggle to Work Together

Tara Tull

Introduction

As we move toward the twenty-first century, the feminist movement will continue the historical struggle to create a society where men and women live as equals. This section focuses on a key strategy for creating such a society—coalition politics. The history of feminism in the United States and, in particular, the history of the past twenty years of the contemporary feminist movement, points to the necessity for building coalitions in order to achieve goals which include diverse women's needs and perspectives.

The readings in this section focus on various aspects of coalition politics, including both barriers to and strategies for building coalitions. Some questions the readings suggest include:

- What is the feminist agenda for the future?
- What strategies would be most effective for achieving feminist goals and objectives?
- What is the relationship between coalition politics and feminism?
- What is the difference between "coalition" and "alliance"?
- What are some of the barriers that block alliances both between and within different groups?
- What are possible strategies for overcoming those barriers?
- How are global alliances formed?

Redefining Women's Role in History: From Victim to Agent

The move toward coalition politics takes place within the context of a feminist re-examination and redefinition of women's role in history. Gerda Lerner writes in *The Creation of Patriarchy*, "Women are and have been central, not marginal, to the making of society and to the building of civilization" (Lerner 1986, 4). Lerner's work, based on earlier research done by Mary Ritter Beard, provides a critical shift in feminist historical analysis from the definition of women as the passive "victims" of history to a definition of women as historical agents. An understanding of women's participation in history is important for feminist theory, the feminist movement, and the future of feminism because "it is the relationship of women to history which explains the nature of female subordination, the causes for women's cooperation in the process of their subordination, the conditions for their opposition to it, the rise of feminist consciousness" (Lerner 1986, vii).

Early efforts to examine the relationship of women to history resulted in defining women as an oppressed "class."

The work of such feminists as Shulamith Firestone, Kate Millet, Susan Brownmiller, and Gloria Steinem pointed out the systematic patterns of oppression and victimization operating in women's lives. Violence against women, the sexual objectification of women in the media, and the lack of economic power held by women are three of the factors that sparked an analysis of women as victims in a patriarchal society.

Work uncovering and explaining the system of oppression based on gender is a necessary and ongoing element of feminism. Progressive political movements must first define, describe, and analyze the nature of the oppression that the movement seeks to end. In other words, a system of oppression must be understood as such prior to any social action to eradicate that system. Nonetheless, if in our analysis of sexism feminists define women only as the passive victims of history, we deny the role women play in history, absolve women from responsibility for the state of the world, and create a bleak picture of political reality with little hope for change.

The feminist movement is changing its understanding of women's relationship to history from women as passive victims of history to women as active participants in history, thereby creating the potential for women to construct a very different society than the existing one. This shift in how we, as feminists, understand women is important for the future of feminism because it points to the necessity for women to take responsibility for our own lives and history. It is a move away from the focus on victimization which dominated early contemporary feminism and toward a closer examination of how to use the power women have to end that victimization. Understanding the past and women's participation in that past is necessary in order to facilitate change in the future.

Unity and Diversity: From Identity Politics to Coalition Politics

One critical element in developing a social change movement after a system of oppression has been recognized and articulated is to develop pride in identities that have been despised or ignored by mainstream society. Audre Lorde, an African American lesbian feminist poet, emphasizes the necessity of reclaiming socially unacceptable identities:

> It is learning how to stand alone, unpopular and sometimes reviled, and how to make common cause with those others identified as outside the structures in order to define and seek a world in which we can all flourish. It is learning how to take our differences and make them strengths. (Lorde 1984, 112)

For Lorde, difference is a source not only of strength but also of identification with others who are "outside the structures." Difference, then, becomes the basis for articulating a politics of identity.

Identity politics, a politics based on identification with a specific group that has historically lacked economic, social, and political power, has been and still is a necessary and dynamic force within the feminist movement. "Oppressed groups need to have separate spaces in which to gain their self-respect, name themselves, and discover their own history" (Alperin 1990, 31). An acceptance of and pride in one's own cultural heritage, gender, sexual identity, and class background provides the self-esteem and group identity necessary to develop a social change movement.

An important first step for the development of the feminist movement was the reclamation and redefinition of "woman." In patriarchal culture, "woman" had been defined not only as different from, but also as less than, "man." Thus, in the late 60s and early 70s, feminist activism and scholarship began, by necessity, with an effort to reclaim the identity "woman." This effort led to criticism of liberal white feminists for using the word "woman" to refer only to white, middle-class, able-bodied, heterosexual women. The experiences, needs, and histories of poor women, lesbians, Jewish women, women of color, women with disabilities, and older women were often not recognized and thus not addressed by the mainstream white feminist movement even as late as the early 1980s.

A critique of mainstream feminism by women of color, lesbians, and working-class women has pushed diverse feminist theorists and activists to incorporate the specifics of the various systems of oppression into their political analysis. Over the past twenty years, feminist theory and practice have been moving from an exclusive focus on the commonalities between women to an understanding of the importance of the differences (Cole 1986). As Caryn McTighe Musil states, "If the seventies were dominated by the exhilaration of discovering and naming ourselves as women, bound together in sisterhood, the eighties have been dominated by the discovery and definition of our differences as women" (Musil 1990, vi).

Recent feminist scholarship has added complexity to the concept of identity. Feminists have recognized that "woman" is not a single homogeneous identity. Gender is no longer reified as the sole or most significant factor to affect an individual's identity. Race, class, and ethnicity are recognized as among the critical elements which combine with personal experience and cultural history to create multifaceted identities for women.

Another analytical shift is the understanding that the definition of particular identities changes over time. In an article titled "Black Feminism: The Politics of Articulation," Pratibha Parmar writes, "The social and psychological construction of identities is an ongoing process which defies any notion of essential or static determinants. Identities are never fixed but complex, differentiated and are constantly repositioned" (Parmar 1990, 116). Her point is that identities are the result of complex and fluid historical and personal processes. Therefore, any given identity exists in the context of a particular historical moment and is subject to the forces of cultural and personal change.

These shifts in the feminist analysis of identity and how it functions in human lives construct a vastly more complex political framework from within which to design strategies for change. This complexity necessitates new political strategies which honor both our unity as women and our diversity as human beings. Identity politics, though a vital aspect of radical political activity, are not enough to eradicate systemic oppression.

Though it is critical for people with similar identities to take pride in their identity and to seek support from one another, one limitation of identity politics is the potential for political fragmentation into increasingly more specific identity groups and thereby the loss of collective strength. Oppressive systems thrive on the division of people into competing groups. In order for identities to be useful, a move must be made from recognizing oppression to resisting it (Adams 1989). Bell hooks, an African American feminist theorist, challenges us to engage in "strategies of politicization that enlarge our conception of who we are, that intensify our sense of intersubjectivity, our relation to a collective reality" (hooks 1989, 107). Mary Louise Adams, a Canadian lesbian feminist and co-editor of *Resources for Feminist Research*, believes that "identity politics is not an end in itself; it is a precursor to further, more broad based and hence more effective, activity" (Adams 1989, 26). A politics based on identity is a precondition to political agency that is most useful when it functions as a springboard for the development of coalitions with other oppressed peoples. Barbara Smith, a black lesbian feminist, states that "there is no way that one oppressed group is going to topple a system by itself. Forming principled coalitions around specific issues is very important" (Smith and Smith 1980, 126).

Coalition Politics: A Definition

The *American Association of University Women's Tool Catalog* explains that "a coalition is an alliance of individuals and/or organizations working together to achieve agreed-upon goals." Coalitions pull diverse groups of people with similar objectives together in order to achieve specific mutual goals. Coalitions are sometimes temporary. For example, diverse groups could come together to support a specific candidate or issue during an election and thereafter disband. On the other hand, the National Domestic Violence Coalition is an example of a coalition founded to act as an ongoing umbrella organization for agencies that focus on domestic violence. Either way, coalition work has the potential to build ties between both individuals and organizations. The long-term effect of coalition politics can be lasting alliances between people.

Building Alliances

Coalition work is a political strategy for achieving limited specific goals. Building long-term alliances between people, on the other hand, can achieve broad-based political change. The editors of *Bridges of Power: Women's Multicultural Al-* *liances* clarify this distinction: "Out of our vision of alliance formation we see allies as people who struggle together on a number of progressive fronts, not just on a single issue that might emerge in a short-term coalition. We see coalitions as short-term solutions and alliance formation as ongoing, long-term arrangements for more far-reaching structural change" (Albrecht and Brewer 1990, 4). "Alliance formation," in these terms, is a means to achieve a feminist agenda for the future.

In an article entitled "Alliances between Women: Overcoming Internalized Oppression and Internalized Domination," Gail Pheterson develops a six-point conceptual framework with a useful definition of alliance:

> **Alliance** is knowledge of, respect for, and commitment between persons who are in essential ways different but whose interests are in essential ways akin. For dominant groups, alliance is a process of sharing power and resources with others in society in order to create structures equally responsive to the needs and interests of all people. This process requires giving up one's drive to superiority, giving up one's prejudices against others, and embracing a more flexible relation to oneself, to others, and to society as a whole. For oppressed groups, alliance is a readiness to struggle with dominant groups for one's right to an equal share of power and resources. This readiness necessitates recognition of and indignation against oppression and it generates the collective confidence and strength to bring about change. Furthermore, readiness necessitates recognition and acceptance of, never gratitude for, true alliance. (Pheterson 1986, 149)

Pheterson's definition outlines some of the practical steps that need to be taken in the work to create alliances between people, such as sharing resources, developing flexibility, and considering the needs and interests of diverse populations.

Coalitions and Alliances: The Struggle to Work Together

Bernice Johnson Reagon, in a speech titled "Coalition Politics: Turning the Century," provides sage advice on how coalitions function. "Coalition work is not work done in your home. Coalition work has to be done in the streets" (Reagon 1983, 301). In other words, coalition work requires individuals to leave their places of safety and comfort, Reagon's "home," in order to reach out to each other. Coalition work is often painful because the participants are directly confronted with human difference. This pain has caused some feminists to back away from coalition work with the sense that they are doing something wrong. However, discomfort does not signify the failure of coalition to Reagon, but rather the difficult reality of the dynamics of diverse people working together. The difficulty and discomfort means that the participants in coalition work are, in fact, confronting difference at the level where change happens.

Defining, studying, and understanding the painful barriers between and within groups of people is a step towards creating coalitions. The historical result of racism, sexism, homophobia, anti-semitism, and classism is vast economic, social, and political power imbalances based on race, gender, sexual identity, religious affiliation, and class in our society. One of the barriers created by these cultural power imbalances is privilege. In an article entitled "White Privilege and Male Privilege: A Personal Account of Coming to See Correspondences through Work in Women's Studies," Peggy McIntosh draws parallels between male, white, and heterosexual privilege (1988). McIntosh defines privilege as advantages and "unearned assets" that people in positions of power have, but often fail to recognize. Privilege is the result of systems of oppression which benefit one group of people over others. The denial of the existence of privilege and a sense of entitlement to privilege by people in power creates a barrier between those with privilege and those without. In order to remove this obstacle, the existence of privilege must be recognized and acknowledged. Once privilege is acknowledged and examined, it becomes necessary for those with power to work to dismantle the very system which gives them power in order to facilitate the creation of coalitions. Sandra Harding posits an important question for those in positions of privilege to consider: "What should we be doing in order to be desirable allies from *their* perspectives?" (Harding 1990, 17). Harding's question provides a perspective from which to analyze and undermine privilege.

One of the effects of privilege which further divides people is guilt. Audre Lorde strongly believes that "guilt and defensiveness are bricks in a wall against which we all flounder; they serve none of our futures" (Lorde 1984, 124). Guilt is an emotion that does not motivate people to work for change, but rather causes defensiveness and separates people from each other. The guilt of people in positions of privilege, i.e. white, rich, or heterosexual, is therefore detrimental to coalition work. Anger is a more appropriate and motivating response to oppression and injustice. Lorde believes that anger has the potential to fuel the fires of change. In order to build strong coalitions, feminists need to learn to face each other's anger with honesty and to use our own anger in a creative and useful manner.

Another stumbling block for coalition work which political activists often face is the tendency, in the process of examining the parallels and intersections between the various forms of oppression, to rank one form of oppression as more important than another. Cherríe Moraga, a Chicana lesbian feminist, writes, "The danger lies in ranking the oppressions. The danger lies in failing to acknowledge the specificity of the oppression" (Moraga 1981, 29). This tendency to consider one particular form of oppression as more critical than others alienates potential allies. In order to form "principled coalitions," feminists cannot trivialize or tolerate any form of oppression. Political activists, including feminists, cannot afford to isolate themselves by declaring their own political agenda as the most important. The ultimate goal of feminism is to eradicate all oppression, not just sexism, and to create a more humane, diverse, and culturally rich world in which to live.

Global Feminism: Global Alliances

In this textbook, the authors have focused on the issues, concerns, and experiences of women in the United States. Learning about this country and the cultures within it is a starting place from which to develop a feminist analysis and an agenda for the future with a global vision. As feminists, we cannot stop our understanding of oppression and vision for freedom at our national borders. "As a people seeking change, we must move beyond the concept of nation-state, which is another expression of patriarchy whereby groups battle for domination over each other on the basis of geographical territory. Instead, we must be global, recognizing that the oppression of women in one part of the world is often affected by what happens in another, and that no woman is free until the conditions of oppression are eliminated everywhere" (Bunch 1987, 301). Feminism, as defined by Charlotte Bunch, has the power to be a transformational politics which reaches far beyond those issues that have been traditionally considered women's concerns.

As citizens of the United States, we must be especially aware of the enormous impact that our government and corporations have on the peoples of the world. Our politics must incorporate an understanding of apartheid in South Africa and the role of U.S. corporations in that country, the prostitution industry in Thailand and the Philippines that was the result of the U.S. military presence during the Vietnam war, and the struggles of women in Latin America under dictatorships politically and economically supported by the U.S. government. With this knowledge comes responsibility for the economic and political decisions made in the United States which affect women, men, and children all over the globe.

The globalization of our political analysis provides a source of strength for feminism. Women throughout the world are and have been fighting for their rights within their own cultures. Just as we can learn from the history of feminism in the United States, we can learn from the struggles of women worldwide and find inspiration and hope from their example. The Mothers of the Plaza in Argentina have won international recognition for their work to find their loved ones who were "disappeared" by the government. In 1980, Iceland elected a feminist president and by 1990 members of the Women's Alliance, a feminist political party, held six seats in the parliament. These acts of courage and political strength can motivate and inform the activities of the feminist movement in this country and around the world.

A successful example of feminist coalition building resulted from a United Nations declaration which designated 1975 through 1985 as the Decade for Women. Three international women's conferences were organized to honor the decade. These conferences brought women together from all parts of the globe to discuss their issues and propose strategies for political change. The participants of the 1985 Nairobi Women's Conference envisioned feminism as a truly transformational and global politics:

> As feminists, we are striving for a fundamental restructuring of the social and economic order, one that does not reproduce the hierarchies under which we presently live. To accomplish this, we need to develop more concrete and powerful strategies at the local, regional, and global levels; to strengthen our links and networks; to be supportive and aware of each others' struggles; and to be in positions to ensure that the implementation of our visions have a longer-lasting impact (Cagatay, Grown and Santiago 1986, 471).

In order for feminism to transform current political and social structures, the feminist agenda for the future must incorporate issues as diverse as reproductive rights, racism, environmental ethics, violence, and poverty because each of these issues affects women directly. We are each responsible for shaping our own individual lives and ultimately, shaping our society. The direction that the feminist movement takes in the future will be the result of the decisions, actions, and visions of women and men today.

References

Asian American Women United of California, eds. 1989. *Making waves: An anthology by and about Asian American women*. Boston: Beacon Press.

Adams, Mary Louise. 1989. There's no place like home: On the place of identity in feminist politics. *Feminist Review* 31:22–33.

Albrecht, Lisa, and Rose M. Brewer, eds. 1990. *Bridges of power: Women's multicultural alliances*. Philadelphia: New Society Publishers.

———. 1990. Bridges of power: Women's multicultural alliances for social change. In *Bridges of power: Women's multicultural alliances*. Edited by Lisa Albrecht and Rose M. Brewer. Philadelphia: New Society Publishers.

Alperin, Davida. 1990. Social diversity and the necessity of alliances: A developing feminist perspective. In *Bridges of power: Women's multicultural alliances*. Edited by Lisa Albrecht and Rose M. Brewer. Philadelphia: New Society Publishers.

Anzaldúa, Gloria, and Cherríe Moraga, eds. 1981. *This bridge called my back: Writings by radical women of color*. New York: Kitchen Table: Women of Color Press.

Anzaldúa, Gloria, ed. 1990. *Making face making soul haciendo caras: Creative and critical perspectives by women of color*. San Francisco: Aunt Lute Foundation Books.

Browne, Susan E., Debra Connors, and Nanci Stern, eds. 1985. *With the power of each breath: A disabled women's anthology*. Pittsburgh: Cleis Press.

Bulkin, Elly, Minnie Bruce Pratt, and Barbara Smith. 1988. *Yours in struggle: Three feminist perspectives on anti-Semitism and racism*. Ithaca, N.Y.: Firebrand Books.

Bunch, Charlotte. 1982. Copenhagen and beyond: Prospects for global feminism. *Quest* 5(4):25–33.

———. 1987. *Passionate politics: Feminist theory in action*. New York: St. Martin's Press.

Çağatay, Nilüfer, Caren Grown, and Aida Santiago. 1986. The Nairobi Women's Conference: Toward a global feminism? *Feminist Studies* 12(2):401–12.

Caraway, Nancie E. 1991. The challenge and theory of feminist identity politics: Working on racism. *Frontiers* 12(2):109–29.

Chai, Alice Yun, and Ho'oipo De Cambra. 1989. Evolution of global feminism through Hawaiian feminist politics. *Women's Studies International Forum* 12(11):59-64.

Cochran, Jo Whitehorse, Donna Langston, Carolyn Woodward, eds. 1988. *Changing our power: An introduction to women's studies.* Dubuque: Kendall/Hunt.

Cole, Johnetta. 1986. *All American women: Lines that divide, ties that bind.* New York: The Free Press.

Davis, Angela. 1981. *Women, race, and class.* New York: Vintage Books.

———. 1990. *Women, culture, and politics.* New York: Vintage Books.

Dill, Bonnie Thorton. 1983. Race, class, and gender: Prospects for an all-inclusive sisterhood. *Feminist Studies* 9(1):131–50.

Giddings, Paula. 1984. *Where and when I enter: The impact of black women on race and sex in America.* New York: Bantam Books.

Harding, Sandra. 1990. The permanent revolution. *Women's Review of Books* 7(5):17.

hooks, bell. 1981. *Ain't I a woman: Black women and feminism.* Boston: South End Press.

———. 1984. *Feminist theory: From margin to center.* Boston: South End Press.

———. 1989. *Talking back: Thinking feminist, thinking black.* Boston: South End Press.

Howe, Florence, and Marsha Saxton, eds. 1987. *With wings: An anthology of literature by and about women with disabilities.* New York: Feminist Press at the City University of New York.

Hull, Gloria, Patricia Bell Scott, and Barbara Smith, eds. 1982. *All the women are white, all the blacks are men, but some of us are brave: Black women's studies.* New York: The Feminist Press.

Jordan, June. 1985. *On call: Political essays.* Boston: South End Press.

Kaye/Kantrowitz, Melanie. 1990. The next step. *NWSA Journal* 2(2):236–44.

Lerner, Gerda. 1986. *The creation of patriarchy.* New York: Oxford University Press.

Lorde, Audre. 1984. *Sister outsider.* Freedom, Calif.: The Crossing Press.

Lugones, Maria. 1987. Playfulness, "world"-travelling, and loving perception. *Hypatia* 2(2):3–19.

Macdonald, Barbara, and Cynthia Rich. 1983. *Look me in the eye: Old women, aging and ageism.* San Francisco: Spinsters/Aunt Lute.

McIntosh, Peggy. 1988. *White privilege and male privilege: A personal account of coming to see correspondences through work in women's studies.* Wellesley, Mass.: Wellesley College, Center for Research on Women, Working Paper #189.

Molina, Papusa. 1990. Recognizing, accepting, and celebrating our differences. In *Making face making soul haciendo caras: Creative and critical perspectives by women of color.* Edited by Gloria Anzaldúa. San Francisco: Aunt Lute Foundation Books.

Moraga, Cherríe. 1981. La Guera. In *This bridge called my back: Writings by radical women of color.* Edited by Gloria Anzaldúa and Cherríe Moraga. New York: Kitchen Table: Women of Color Press.

Morgan, Robin. 1984. *Sisterhood is global: The international women's movement anthology.* New York: Anchor Books.

Musil, Caryn McTighe. 1990. Foreword. In *Bridges of power: Women's multicultural alliances.* Edited by Lisa Albrecht and Rose M. Brewer. Philadelphia: New Society Publishers.

Parmar, Pratibha. 1990. Black feminism: The politics of articulation. In *Identity, community, culture, difference.* Edited by Jonathan Rutherford. London: Lawrence and Wishart.

Peace and Freedom: The Magazine of the Women's International League for Peace and Freedom. 1991. Special Edition: Lesbians: We Are Your Sisters. 51(3).

Pheterson, Gail. 1986. Alliances between women: Overcoming internalized oppression and internalized domination. *Signs* 12(1):146–60.

Reagon, Bernice Johnson. 1983. Coalition politics: Turning the century. In *Home girls: A black feminist anthology*. Edited by Barbara Smith. New York: Kitchen Table: Women of Color Press.

Sherover-Marcuse, Ricky. 1981. Toward a perspective on unlearning racism: Twelve working assumptions. *Issues in Cooperation and Power* (7):14–15.

Smith, Barbara, ed. 1983. *Home girls: A black feminist anthology*. New York: Kitchen Table: Women of Color Press.

Smith, Barbara, and Beverly. 1981. Across the kitchen table: A sister-to-sister dialogue. In *This bridge called my back: Writings by radical women of color*. Edited by Gloria Anzaldúa and Cherríe Moraga. New York: Kitchen Table: Women of Color Press.

Taylor, Verta. 1989. The future of feminism: A social movement analysis. In *Feminist frontiers II* 2nd ed. Edited by Laurel Richardson and Verta Taylor. New York: McGraw-Hill, Inc.

Zinn, Maxine Baca, Lynn Weber Cannon, Elizabeth Higginbotham, and Bonnie Thornton Dill. 1986. The costs of exclusionary practices in women's studies. *Signs* 11(2):290–303.

There Is No Hierarchy of Oppressions

Audre Lorde

I was born Black and a woman. I am trying to become the strongest person I can become to live the life I have been given and to help effect change toward a livable future for this earth and for my children. As a Black, lesbian, feminist, socialist, poet, mother of two including one boy and a member of an interracial couple, I usually find myself part of some group in which the majority defines me as deviant, difficult, inferior or just plain "wrong."

From my membership in all of these groups I have learned that oppression and the intolerance of difference come in all shapes and sizes and colors and sexualities; and that among those of us who share the goals of liberation and a workable future for our children, there can be no hierarchies of oppression. I have learned that sexism (a belief in the inherent superiority of one sex over all others and thereby its right to dominance) and heterosexism (a belief in the inherent superiority of one pattern of loving over all others and thereby its right to dominance) both arise from the same source as racism—a belief in the inherent superiority of one race over all others and thereby its right to dominance.

"Oh, says a voice from the Black community, but being Black is NORMAL!" Well, I and many Black people of my age can remember grimly the days when it didn't used to be. I simply do not believe that one aspect of myself can possibly profit from the oppression of any group which seeks the right to peaceful existence. Rather, we diminish ourselves by denying to others what we have shed blood to obtain for our children. And those children need to learn that they do not have to become like each other in order to work together for a future they all will share.

The increasing attacks upon lesbians and gay men are only an introduction to the increasing attacks upon all Black people, for wherever oppression manifests itself in this country, Black people are potential victims. And it is a standard of right-wing cynicism to encourage members of oppressed groups to act against each other and so long as we are divided because of our particular identities, we cannot join together in effective political action.

Within the lesbian community I am Black and within the Black community I am a lesbian. Any attack against Black people is a lesbian and gay issue, because I and thousands of other Black women are part of the lesbian community. Any attack against lesbians and gays is a Black issue because thousands of lesbians and gay men are Black. There is no hierarchy of oppressions.

Lorde, Audre. 1983. "There is no hierarchy of oppressions." *The Bulletin of the Council on Interracial Books for Children.* Reprinted by permission of the author.

It is not accidental that the Family Protection Act, which is virtually anti-woman and anti-Black, is also anti-gay. As a Black person, I know who my enemies are and when the Ku Klux Klan goes to court in Detroit to try and force the Board of Education to remove the books the Klan believes "hint at homosexuality," then I know I cannot afford the luxury of fighting one form of oppression only. I cannot afford to believe that freedom from intolerance is the right of only one particular group. And I cannot afford to choose between the fronts upon which I must battle these forces of discrimination wherever they appear to destroy me. And when they appear to destroy me, it will not be long before they appear to destroy you.

Making Common Cause:
Diversity and Coalitions

Charlotte Bunch

I want to begin by questioning the title of this panel, "Common Causes: Uncommon Coalitions—Sex, Race, Class, and Age." In my twenty years of political organizing, I have been part of numerous coalitions. Some were successful, others disastrous, and most fell somewhere in between. I am not sure that any were really uncommon. For coalitions are one of the most common strategies for creating social change, and the problems that accompany them are recurring themes in all movements. Discourse about when, where, and how to build coalitions is particularly important when we seek to make change that is inclusive of diverse perspectives. For feminists, the ability to create a movement that includes and responds to the diversity of women's lives is crucial.

What feminists need to explore is why coalition efforts have not been more common in our movement, and what is required to build effective coalitions? We must ask why, instead of coalescing more, women have to continually separate into distinct groups in order to be heard? Whether on the basis of race, class, age, ethnic identity, sexual preference, or physical abilities, each group has had to find a separate space and identity in order to create conditions where their perspectives would be seen by others. Why do we have such difficulty responding to diversity, and how can we move beyond the necessity of separatism to building inclusive coalitions? In short, I want to talk about how to make coalitions more common, less frightening, more comprehensive, and more successful.

I assume that if coalitions are to work, there must be a common cause. The reason to go through the process, which is often painful and difficult, is because we have some shared goal, broadly or narrowly defined, that motivates us to work across diverse lines. As diverse groups unite around some common goal, there is greater possibility of learning about and incorporating diversity at a deeper level. The particulars of each coalition vary, of course. But assuming that one goal of feminism is struggling against domination in all its forms, then a critical issue for all our coalitions is how to approach diversity and domination.

Diversity and Domination

Patriarchy has systematically utilized diversity as a tool of domination in which groups are taught that certain powers and privileges are the natural prerogatives of some people. We learn in childhood that such things as sex and race bring differences in power and privilege, and that these are acceptable. This idea that difference justifies domination is deeply embedded in society and defended as natural. Take, for example, the refrain: "there will always be poor people" used to perpetuate class privileges. But as women who have challenged the so-called naturalness of male supremacy, feminists must also question it in other areas of domination.

When power hierarchies are accepted as inevitable, people can be manipulated to fear that those who are different are a threat to their position and perhaps even to their survival. We are taught to be afraid that "they" will hurt us—either because they are more powerful or because they want our privileges. While that fear takes multiple forms depending on where we fit in the various scales of domination, all of us are taught to distrust those who are different. Some aspects of this fear may be necessary to survival—whites *do* lynch blacks, men *will* rape women—and we must watch out for such dangers. But fear and distrust of differences are most often used to keep us in line. When we challenge the idea that differences must be threatening, we are also challenging the patriarchal assignment of power and privilege as birthrights.

Opposing the ways that differences are used to dominate does not mean that we seek to end diversity. Feminist visions are not about creating homogenized people who all look like a bland middle-class television ad. Many aspects of diversity can be celebrated as variety, creativity, and options in life-styles and world views. We must distinguish between creative differences that are not intrinsically tied to domination and the assignment of power and privilege based on the distinctive characteristics of some. Diversity, when separated from power to control others, provides valuable opportunities for learning and living that can be missed if one is embedded in an ethnocentric way of seeing reality.

Diversity among feminists today can be a resource for gaining a broader understanding of the world. We see more clearly and our ability to create effective strategies is enhanced if we move beyond the boundaries of our assigned patriarchal slot. Quite specifically, in 1985, white women can look to the growing women of color movement in the West and to feminism in the Third World as sources of both insight and information. But too often, we fail to respond to each other's potential for enriching our lives and the movement because of unconscious fears of race, class, or national differences. It is not just a matter of learning about race and class—although that is important—but also of understanding women's lives and the world as viewed by others.

Learning from a wider diversity of women and making coalitions does not mean watering down feminist politics as some fear. Rather, it requires engaging in a wider debate about those politics and shaping their expressions to respond to more women's realities. I see this process as reclaiming the radical spirit of feminism that calls for going to the roots of oppression. In the United States, for example, this wave of feminism began in the 1960s in close connection to the black civil rights movement and its demand for recognition of the rights of racially diverse groups. Yet, racism is all too often reflected in the lack of acknowledgment of those origins and the invisibility of women of color who were a part of feminism's resurgence. As Gloria T. Hull and Barbara Smith note in *But Some of Us Are Brave* (Old Westbury, N.Y.: The Feminist Press, 1982, p. xx), "Black women were a part of that early women's movement as were working-class women of all races." This included famous speakers such as Florence Kennedy as well as women like the welfare rights mothers that worked in the late '60s in coalition with Washington, D.C., Women's Liberation to achieve improvements in the city's health services for women. In the 1970s, efforts to develop diverse coalitions and a broader-based agenda were often eclipsed by many factors including intense movement controversies and the media's emphasis on the pursuit of equality within the system. By focusing again on the diversity and depth of women's perspectives and needs in the 1980s, I see feminists reasserting the radical impulse for justice for all and thus strengthening the movement as a force for fundamental change.

There is commonality in the fact that all women are subordinated, but when we examine our diversity, we see that the forms that takes are shaped by many factors. Female oppression is not one universal block experienced the same way by all women, to which other forms of exploitation are then added as separate pieces. Rather, various oppressions interact to shape the particulars of each woman's life. For example, an aging black lesbian who is poor does not experience oppression as separate packages—one sexism, one poverty, one homophobia, one racism, and one ageism. She experiences these as interacting and shaping each other. Seeing this interaction is vital for coalitions around issues.

Too often analysis of women's oppression isolates single factors such as class or sexual preference in a simplistic manner, trying to show the effects of each separately. But this fails to take account of their interrelatedness. Further, it often winds up in battles over a hierarchy of seriousness of forms of oppression or over how one really is the cause of the other. But a feminist method suggests the necessity of looking at their interaction—at how race, class, sex, and age oppression shape each other. For example, race and class affect an older woman's problems—whether it means being abandoned in her house, trapped in an abusive nursing home, or entirely homeless. Or in looking at the exploitation of women's work, we can see the effect of factors such as race, homophobia, or physical disability, as well as class.

Strategies that fail to examine how female exploitation is shaped in different forms often set some women up against others. The interactive approach—taking into account female diversity—is thus essential for effective coalitions. However, it is often difficult to look at all the features of oppression because they are complex and demand continuous reevaluation of our assumptions. Further, attitudes and emotions around diversity are deeply rooted and often volatile. Systems such as racism, anti-Semitism, classism, nationalism, and homophobia are so much a part of the culture that surrounds us from birth that we often have biases and blind spots that affect our attitudes, behavior, strategies, and values in ways that we do not perceive until challenged by others.

Many problems that arise in coalitions stem from resistance to being challenged about oppressive attitudes and reactions. These need to be approached matter-of-factly, not as moral judgments on one's personhood, but as negative results of growing up in patriarchal culture. We must change such attitudes and behavior because they oppress others and interfere with our own humanity as well as impede the process of creating feminist strategies and coalitions. For example, white middle-class North Americans are often unaware that the perspectives of that culture—which usually coincide with the media's portrayal of reality—are not the only way of seeing the world. Since these ethnocentric biases are reinforced constantly, we must make an extra effort to see other points of view. This does not mean that nothing of this culture is of value. It simply means that we must go beyond its limits to see what can be taken as useful and not oppressive, and what must be challenged.

In looking at diversity among women, we see one of the weaknesses of the feminist concept that the personal is political. It is valid that each woman begins from her personal experiences, and it is important to see how these are political. But we must also recognize that our personal experiences are shaped by the culture with its prejudices—against people of color, lesbians and gay men, the aged, and so on. We cannot, therefore, depend on our perceptions alone as the basis for political analysis and action—much less for coalition. Feminists must stretch beyond, challenging the limits of our own personal experiences by learning from the diversity of women's lives.

Divisive Reactions to Diversity

In the 1980s, various groups, such as the women of color movement, are expanding the definitions of, and possibilities for, feminism. But many women's reactions to diversity interfere with learning from others and making successful cross-cultural, multiracial coalitions. I call these divisive reactions because, bringing up racism or class or homophobia is not itself divisive to the movement. Rather, what is divisive is ignoring such issues or being unable to respond to them constructively. I want to outline some reactions that I have seen interfere with efforts at coalition-building and suggest ways of getting beyond them.

The most obviously divisive reaction is *becoming defensive* when challenged around an issue of diversity. If one is busy making explanations about how some action or comment was not really what you meant, it is hard to listen and understand criticism and why it is being made. This does not mean passively accepting every critical comment—for in dealing with such emotional topics, there will be exaggerations, inaccuracies, or injustices that must be worked out. But these problems do not excuse anyone from struggling with the issues. If one remains open, while retaining a sense of your own authenticity, it is usually possible to deal with these by listening and responding constructively. If a critique does not make sense to you, ask about it, or try to figure out what led to it—even if it seems unfair. It is not always easy to listen to criticism first and then sort through what it means, but it is the job of feminists to do just that. To listen carefully, to consider what other views mean for our work, and to respond through incorporating new understandings where appropriate—this is a feminist necessity if we are to make coalitions among diverse women.

Often defensiveness is related to another unhelpful reaction—*guilt*. It may be appropriate to experience shame over the actions of one's ancestors or at how one has participated in another's oppression. But personal guilt is usually immobilizing, particularly if one sits with it for long. Successful coalitions are not built on feeling sorry for others or being apologetic about one's existence. Coalitions are built around shared outrage over injustice and common visions of how society can be changed. Few of us had control over our origins, and the point is not to feel guilt about the attitudes or privileges that we inherited. The question is what are we going to do about them now—how are we going to change ourselves and work to end domination in the world? For example, white women feeling sorry about something like racism is not as useful to women of color as working to eliminate it in society as well as in one's personal life.

Often women are sidetracked by *overpersonalization* when dealing with diversity. The issues raised are personal and do require individual change, but it is important not to get stuck there. Sometimes feminists become so involved in trying to be pure and personally free of any oppressive behavior that they become paralyzed and fear taking any political action because it might not be correct. Yet, it is through concrete efforts to challenge domination—no matter how small—that we learn and can become more effective and more inclusive in our political work. For example, if a man tells me that he is becoming totally antisexist but is not in some way challenging the structures of patriarchal power that continue to oppress women, then his personal changes—if I believe him at all—are of minimal value to me. The same is true for women of color who see some whites talking about racism but not taking action against it in the world.

Another aspect of overpersonalization is *withdrawal.* Sometimes feminists have become so personally hurt by criticism or feel so left out when a group is creating its own space, that they withdraw from political engagement. For example, some heterosexuals during the height of lesbian feminist challenges in the 1970s withdrew into their feelings of being attacked or left out rather than working on how they could fight homophobia while still being with men personally. This only reinforced the separation between us. I see similar behavior among some white women today. The hurt is often understandable because there is pain in confrontations around difficult issues, and feminists sometimes spend more energy criticizing women's oppressive behavior than taking on the systems of oppression. Still, reacting to this by withdrawing prevents learning from what has happened. This is sometimes like children who want to be center stage and pout when not in the forefront. Instead, we need to see that at any given moment one group may be the creative edge of the movement, but that will enrich all of us in the long run.

One of the more infuriating reactions is *acting weary and resentful* when someone brings up "that issue" again. No one is more tired of homophobia and having to bring it up again than a lesbian like myself. Probably women of color feel the same way about racism, Jewish women about anti-Semitism, the elderly about ageism, and so on. But the problems still exist and someone must address them. Until feminists learn to include the concerns and perspectives of those women whose oppression we do not directly experience, then the "others" will have to keep bringing up those issues. We must strive to become "one-woman coalitions"—capable of understanding and raising all issues of oppression and seeing our relationship to them—whites speaking about racism, heterosexuals about homophobia, the able-bodied about disabilities, and so on. Only as we do this will we be able to build lasting coalitions.

The last divisive reaction that I want to include here is *limiting outspoken "minority women" to "their issues."* When someone speaks out strongly about her group's specific oppression, she often becomes a token whose leadership in other areas is restricted. For example, I have felt pressure either to work only on lesbian issues, or to downplay them if I am involved in other areas of feminist activity. Yet, while I am out of the closet and concerned about homophobia, there are many other topics that I want to address besides lesbianism, just as women of color have much to say about many issues in addition to racism. To counter this tendency, I decided in the late '70s that I would not write any more only about lesbianism, but instead I would address other subjects and incorporate my lesbian feminist analysis within them. Women of all races, classes, ages, and nations have much to say on a whole variety of topics from their particular perspectives. If we limit each to one identity and approach feminism as a string of separate unrelated issues, we narrow the possibilities for insight, growth, and leadership throughout the movement.

Our chances of building successful coalitions are greater if we can avoid divisive reactions such as these and see diversity as a strength. As we struggle to learn from our differences rather than to fear or deny them, we can find our common ground. In this process, we also build the atmosphere of good faith and respect necessary for strong coalitions. For while we do not need to love one another or agree on everything, we do need to be able to challenge each other from the assumption that change is possible. Another requirement when diverse groups coalesce is that each be clear about its bottom line. We must each know what we need in order to survive in a coalition and how to communicate that to others.

Coalitions that are successful must also be aimed at taking meaningful action in the world. Coalition is not abstract. It functions when groups or individuals are working together around something that each cares about and sees as advancing its goals or vision, or at least protecting the space necessary to develop that. When a coalition has some effect, then it is worth going through the trouble and strife of making it work. It is in the process itself that we often discover the common causes that make it possible to create common coalitions of women in all our diversity working toward both common and varied feminist visions.

The Uses of Anger: Women Responding to Racism

Audre Lorde

Racism. The belief in the inherent superiority of one race over all others and thereby the right to dominance, manifest and implied.

Women respond to racism. My response to racism is anger. I have lived with that anger, ignoring it, feeding upon it, learning to use it before it laid my visions to waste, for most of my life. Once I did it in silence, afraid of the weight. My fear of anger taught me nothing. Your fear of that anger will teach you nothing, also.

Women responding to racism means women responding to anger; the anger of exclusion, of unquestioned privilege, of racial distortions, of silence, ill-use, stereotyping, defensiveness, misnaming, betrayal, and co-optation.

My anger is a response to racist attitudes and to the actions and presumptions that arise out of those attitudes. If your dealings with other women reflect those attitudes, then my anger and your attendant fears are spotlights that can be used for growth in the same way I have used learning to express anger for my growth. But for corrective surgery, not guilt. Guilt and defensiveness are bricks in a wall against which we all flounder; they serve none of our futures.

Because I do not want this to become a theoretical discussion, I am going to give a few examples of interchanges between women that illustrate these points. In the interest of time, I am going to cut them short. I want you to know there were many more.

For example:

- I speak out of direct and particular anger at an academic conference, and a white woman says, "Tell me how you feel but don't say it too harshly or I cannot hear you." But is it my manner that keeps her from hearing, or the threat of a message that her life may change?

- The Women's Studies Program of a southern university invites a Black woman to read following a week-long forum on Black and white women. "What has this week given to you?" I ask. The most vocal white woman says, "I think I've gotten a lot. I feel Black women really understand me a lot better now; they have a better idea of where I'm coming from." As if understanding her lay at the core of the racist problem.

- After fifteen years of a women's movement which professes to address the life concerns and possible futures of all women, I still hear, on campus after campus,

"How can we address the issues of racism? No women of Color attended." Or, the other side of that statement, "We have no one in our department equipped to teach their work." In other words, racism is a Black women's problem, a problem of women of Color, and only we can discuss it.

- After I read from my work entitled "Poems for Women in Rage,"* a white woman asks me: "Are you going to do anything with how we can deal directly with *our* anger? I feel it's so important." I ask, "How do you use *your* rage?" and then I have to turn away from the blank look in her eyes, before she can invite me to participate in her own annihilation. I do not exist to feel her anger for her.

- White women are beginning to examine their relationships to Black women, yet often I hear them wanting only to deal with little colored children across the roads of childhood, the beloved nursemaid, the occasional second-grade classmate—those tender memories of what was once mysterious and intriguing or neutral. You avoid the childhood assumptions formed by the raucous laugher at Rastus and Alfalfa, the acute message of your mommy's handkerchief spread upon the park bench because I had just been sitting there, the indelible and dehumanizing portraits of Amos 'n Andy and your daddy's humorous bedtime stories.

- I wheel my two-year-old daughter in a shopping cart through a supermarket in Eastchester in 1967, and a little white girl riding past in her mother's cart calls out excitedly, "Oh look, Mommy, a baby maid!" And your mother shushes you, but she does not correct you. And so fifteen years later, at a conference on racism, you can still find that story humorous. But I hear your laughter is full of terror and dis-ease.

- A white academic welcomes the appearance of a collection by non-Black women of Color.** "It allows me to deal with racism without dealing with the harshness of Black women," she says to me.

- At an international cultural gathering of women, a well-known white American woman poet interrupts the reading of the work of women of Color to read her own poem, and then dashes off to an "important panel."

If women in the academy truly want a dialogue about racism, it will require recognizing the needs and the living contexts of other women. When an academic woman says, "I can't afford it," she may mean she is making a choice about how to spend her available money. But when a woman on welfare says, "I can't afford it," she means she is surviving on an amount of money that was barely subsistence in 1972, and she often does not have enough to eat. Yet the National Women's Studies Association here in 1981 holds a conference in which it commits itself to responding to racism, yet refuses to waive the registration fee for poor women and women of Color who wished to present and conduct workshops. This has made it impossible for many women of Color—for instance, Wilmette Brown, of Black Women for Wages for Housework—to participate in this conference. Is this to be merely another case of the academy discussing life within the closed circuits of the academy?

---

*One poem from this series is included in *Chosen Poems: Old and New* (W. W. Norton and Company, New York, 1978), pp. 105–108.

**This Bridge Called My Back: Writings by Radical Women of Color* edited by Cherríe Moraga and Gloria Anzaldúa (Kitchen Table: Women of Color Press, New York, 1983), first published in 1981.

To the white women present who recognize these attitudes as familiar, but most of all, to all my sisters of Color who live and survive thousands of such encounters—to my sisters of Color who like me still tremble their rage under harness, or who sometimes question the expression of our rage as useless and disruptive (the two most popular accusations)—I want to speak about anger, my anger, and what I have learned from my travels through its dominions.

*Everything can be used/ except what is wasteful/ (you will need/to remember this when you are accused of destruction.)**

Every woman has a well-stocked arsenal of anger potentially useful against those oppressions, personal and institutional, which brought that anger into being. Focused with precision it can become a powerful source of energy serving progress and change. And when I speak of change, I do not mean a simple switch of positions or a temporary lessening of tensions, nor the ability to smile or feel good. I am speaking of a basic and radical alteration in those assumptions underlining our lives.

I have seen situations where white women hear a racist remark, resent what has been said, become filled with fury, and remain silent because they are afraid. That unexpressed anger lies within them like an undetonated device, usually to be hurled at the first woman of Color who talks about racism.

But anger expressed and translated into action in the service of our vision and our future is a liberating and strengthening act of clarification, for it is in the painful process of this translation that we identify who are our allies with whom we have grave differences, and who are our genuine enemies.

Anger is loaded with information and energy. When I speak of women of Color, I do not only mean Black women. The woman of Color who is not Black and who charges me with rendering her invisible by assuming that her struggles with racism are identical with my own has something to tell me that I had better learn from, lest we both waste ourselves fighting the truths between us. If I participate, knowingly or otherwise, in my sister's oppression and she calls me on it, to answer her anger with my own only blankets the substance of our exchange with reaction. It wastes energy. And yes, it is very difficult to stand still and to listen to another woman's voice delineate an agony I do not share, or one to which I myself have contributed.

In this place we speak removed from the more blatant reminders of our embattlement as women. This need not blind us to the size and complexities of the forces mounting against us and all that is most human within our environment. We are not here as women examining racism in a political and social vacuum. We operate in the teeth of a system for which racism and sexism are primary, established, and necessary props of profit. Women responding to racism is a topic so dangerous that when the local media attempt to discredit this conference they choose to focus upon the provision of lesbian housing as a diversionary device—as if the Hartford *Courant* dare not mention the topic chosen for discussion here, racism, lest it become apparent that women are in fact attempting to examine and to alter all the repressive conditions of our lives.

---

*From "For Each of You," first published in *From A Land Where Other People Live* (Broadside Press, Detroit, 1973), and collected in *Chosen Poems: Old and New* (W. W. Norton and Company, New York, 1982), p. 42.

Mainstream communication does not want women, particularly white women, responding to racism. It wants racism to be accepted as an immutable given in the fabric of your existence, like eveningtime or the common cold.

So we are working in a context of opposition and threat, the cause of which is certainly not the angers which lie between us, but rather that virulent hatred leveled against all women, people of Color, lesbians and gay men, poor people—against all of us who are seeking to examine the particulars of our lives as we resist our oppressions, moving toward coalition and effective action.

Any discussion among women about racism must include the recognition and the use of anger. This discussion must be direct and creative because it is crucial. We cannot allow our fear of anger to deflect us nor seduce us into settling for anything less than the hard work of excavating honesty; we must be quite serious about the choice of this topic and the angers entwined within it because, rest assured, our opponents are quite serious about their hatred of us and of what we are trying to do here.

And while we scrutinize the often painful face of each other's anger, please remember that it is not our anger which makes me caution you to lock your doors at night and not to wander the streets of Hartford alone. It is the hatred which lurks in those streets, that urge to destroy us all if we truly work for change rather than merely indulge in academic rhetoric.

This hatred and our anger are very different. Hatred is the fury of those who do not share our goals, and its object is death and destruction. Anger is a grief of distortions between peers, and its object is change. But our time is getting shorter. We have been raised to view any difference other than sex as a reason for destruction, and for Black women and white women to face each other's angers without denial or immobility or silence or guilt is in itself a heretical and generative idea. It implies peers meeting upon a common basis to examine difference, and to alter those distortions which history has created around our difference. For it is those distortions which separate us. And we must ask ourselves: Who profits from all this?

Women of Color in America have grown up within a symphony of anger, at being silenced, at being unchosen, at knowing that when we survive, it is in spite of a world that takes for granted our lack of humanness, and which hates our very existence outside of its service. And I say *symphony* rather than *cacophony* because we have had to learn to orchestrate those furies so that they do not tear us apart. We have had to learn to move through them and use them for strength and force and insight within our daily lives. Those of us who did not learn this difficult lesson did not survive. And part of my anger is always libation for my fallen sisters.

Anger is an appropriate reaction to racist attitudes, as is fury when the actions arising from those attitudes do not change. To those women here who fear the anger of women of Color more than their own unscrutinized racist attitudes, I ask: Is the anger of women of Color more threatening than the woman-hatred that tinges all aspects of our lives?

It is not the anger of other women that will destroy us but our refusals to stand still, to listen to its rhythms, to learn within it, to move beyond the manner of presentation to the substance, to tap that anger as an important source of empowerment.

I cannot hide my anger to spare you guilt, nor hurt feelings, nor answering anger; for to do so insults and trivializes all our efforts. Guilt is not a response to anger; it is a response to one's own actions or lack of action. If it leads to change then it can be useful, since it is then no longer guilt but the beginning of knowledge. Yet all too often, guilt is just another name for impotence, for defensiveness destructive of communication; it becomes a device to protect ignorance and the continuation of things the way they are, the ultimate protection for changelessness.

Most women have not developed tools for facing anger constructively. CR groups in the past, largely white, dealt with how to express anger, usually at the world of men. And these groups were made up of white women who shared the terms of their oppressions. There was usually little attempt to articulate the genuine differences between women, such as those of race, color, age, class, and sexual identity. There was no apparent need at that time to examine the contradictions of self, woman as oppressor. There was work on expressing anger, but very little on anger directed against each other. No tools were developed to deal with other women's anger except to avoid it, deflect it, or flee from it under a blanket of guilt.

I have no creative use for guilt, yours or my own. Guilt is only another way of avoiding informed action, of buying time out of the pressing need to make clear choices, out of the approaching storm that can feed the earth as well as bend the trees. If I speak to you in anger, at least I have spoken to you: I have not put a gun to your head and shot you down in the street; I have not looked at your bleeding sister's body and asked, "What did she do to deserve it?" This was the reaction of two white women to Mary Church Terrell's telling of the lynching of a pregnant Black woman whose baby was then torn from her body. That was in 1921, and Alice Paul had just refused to publicly endorse the enforcement of the Nineteenth Amendment for all women—by refusing to endorse the inclusion of women of Color, although we had worked to help bring about that amendment.

The angers between women will not kill us if we can articulate them with precision, if we listen to the content of what is said with at least as much intensity as we defend ourselves against the manner of saying. When we turn from anger we turn from insight, saying we will accept only the designs already known, deadly and safely familiar. I have tried to learn my anger's usefulness to me, as well as its limitations.

For women raised to fear, too often anger threatens annihilation. In the male construct of brute force, we were taught that our lives depended upon the good will of patriarchal power. The anger of others was to be avoided at all costs because there was nothing to be learned from it but pain, a judgment that we had been bad girls, come up lacking, not done what we were supposed to do. And if we accept our powerlessness, then of course any anger can destroy us.

But the strength of women lies in recognizing differences between us as creative, and in standing to those distortions which we inherited without blame, but which are now ours to alter. The angers of women can transform difference through insight into power. For anger between peers births change, not destruction, and the discomfort and sense of loss it often causes is not fatal, but a sign of growth.

My response to racism is anger. That anger has eaten clefts into my living only when it remained unspoken, useless to anyone. It has also served me in classrooms without light or learning, where the work and history of Black women was less than a vapor. It has served me as fire in the ice zone of uncomprehending eyes of white women who see in my experience and the experience of my people only new reasons for fear or guilt.

And my anger is no excuse for not dealing with your blindness, no reason to withdraw from the results of your own actions.

When women of Color speak out of the anger that laces so many of our contacts with white women, we are often told that we are "creating a mood of hopelessness," "preventing white women from getting past guilt," or "standing in the way of trusting communication and action." All these quotes come directly from letters to me from members of this organization within the last two years. One woman wrote, "Because you are Black and Lesbian, you seem to speak with the moral authority of suffering." Yes, I am Black and Lesbian, and what you hear in my voice is fury, not suffering. Anger, not moral authority. There is a difference.

To turn aside from the anger of Black women with excuses or the pretexts of intimidation is to award no one power—it is merely another way of preserving racial blindness, the power of unaddressed privilege, unbreached, intact. Guilt is only another form of objectification. Oppressed peoples are always being asked to stretch a little more, to bridge the gap between blindness and humanity. Black women are expected to use our anger only in the service of other people's salvation or learning. But that time is over. My anger has meant pain to me but it has also meant survival, and before I give it up I'm going to be sure that there is something at least as powerful to replace it on the road to clarity.

What woman here is so enamored of her own oppression that she cannot see her heelprint upon another woman's face? What woman's terms of oppression have become precious and necessary to her as a ticket into the fold of the righteous, away from the cold winds of self-scrutiny?

I am a lesbian woman of Color whose children eat regularly because I work in a university. If their full bellies make me fail to recognize my commonality with a woman of Color whose children do not eat because she cannot find work, or who has no children because her insides are rotted from home abortions and sterilization; if I fail to recognize the lesbian who chooses not to have children, the woman who remains closeted because her homophobic community is her only life support, the woman who chooses silence instead of another death, the woman who is terrified lest my anger trigger the explosion of hers; if I fail to recognize them as other faces of myself, then I am contributing not only to each of their oppressions but also to my own, and the anger which stands between us then must be used for clarity and mutual empowerment, not for evasion by guilt or for further separation. I am not free while any woman is unfree, even when her shackles are very different from my own. And I am not free as long as one person of Color remains chained. Nor is any one of you.

I speak here as a woman of Color who is not bent upon destruction, but upon survival. No woman is responsible for altering the psyche of her oppressor, even when that psyche is embodied in another woman. I have suckled the wolf's lip of anger and I have used it for illumination, laughter, protection, fire in places where there was no light, no food, no sisters, no quarter. We are not goddesses or matriarchs or edifices of divine forgiveness; we are not fiery fingers of judgment or instruments of flagellation; we are women forced back always upon our woman's power. We have learned to use anger as we have learned to use the dead flesh of animals, and bruised, battered, and changing, we have survived and grown and, in Angela Wilson's words, we *are* moving on. With or without uncolored women. We use whatever strengths we have fought for, including anger, to help define and fashion a world where all our sisters can grow, where our children can love, and where the power of touching and meeting another woman's difference and wonder will eventually transcend the need for destruction.

For it is not the anger of Black women which is dripping down over this globe like a diseased liquid. It is not my anger that launches rockets, spends over sixty thousand dollars a second on missiles and other agents of war and death, slaughters children in cities, stockpiles nerve gas and chemical bombs, sodomizes our daughters and our earth. It is not the anger of Black women which corrodes into blind, dehumanizing power, bent upon the annihilation of us all unless we meet it with what we have, our power to examine and to redefine the terms upon which we will live and work; our power to envision and to reconstruct, anger by painful anger, stone upon heavy stone, a future of pollinating difference and the earth to support our choices.

We welcome all women who can meet us, face to face, beyond objectification and beyond guilt.

We Colorado Women Have a Vision . . .
It Is the Year 2001, and . . .

We have created a peaceful world, decentralized, creative, humanized with proud ethnic diversity. . .

We have made a difference because we voted, ran for office, lobbied for the Women's Budget, empowered ourselves and others and believed that human needs come first. . .

We have replaced the military model of security with one based on international cooperation and interdependence. . .

We have learned the politics of inclusion, how to deal with differences without being mutually destructive. . .

We have achieved a 50% cut in the military budget and are working on reallocating the next 50% as well to meet our human needs: housing, childcare, health, nutrition, education. . .

We have established here in Colorado an Institute for Economic Conversion (from military to civilian production), and have created a state cabinet position on Human Priorities.

We have established a multi-lingual (including Spanish, Hmong, ASL, TTY among others . . .) clearinghouse on Civil Rights in Colorado. . .

We have ratified the Copenhagen Convention outlawing all forms of discrimination. . .

We have come to value women's work, upgrading civil and political occupations, providing training where needed and equalizing salaries, titles, benefits. . .

We have empowered and validated those who were systematically driven out of the political process. . .

We have safe houses and sanctuaries for any persecuted or abused persons. . .

We have no longer, a Third World. . .

We have many different modes of communication through art, literature, music. . .

We have determined that all bills passed must have a human impact statement. . .

We have achieved solidarity among ourselves and allow for diversity and mutual support through networking. . .

We have women serving as Secretary General of the United Nations and U.S. Secretary of State. . .

We have international networking among women's organizations as well, with agenda sharing on local, national and international levels through computers and other communication modes. . .

We have reconstituted the U.S. Commission on Women. . .

Colorado Women's Agenda. 1986. "We Colorado Women Have a Vision . . . It Is the Year 2001, and . . ." Reprinted by permission of the authors.

We have built politically relevant coalitions, thought out and articulated clearly what we want, deepened our understanding of our interdependence, and reassessed our own competence to bring about change. . .

In this year 2001, THERE ARE NO NUCLEAR WEAPONS ANYWHERE ON THE EARTH

Conclusion: The Future of Feminism: The Struggle to Work Together
Study Questions

1. Distinguish between power and "empowerment" as it relates to women. What is the source of each? Why is each useful in the struggle for equality?

2. As feminist theory began to emerge, what issues of identity led scholars to redefine what constitutes "woman"? What is the importance of identifying differences among women?

3. Why is it important that we know about women's active participation in history?

4. What is a significant barrier created by cultural power imbalances? How can this barrier be removed? What are the ramifications if barriers are not recognized?

5. What does Audre Lorde mean by "the hierarchy of oppressions"? What is its effect on the building of alliances? When we recognize and deconstruct hierarchy, what can we begin to recognize in ourselves and in our relationship to others?

6. In small groups, describe yourself in the context of identity politics. Who are you, politically? Which issues are the same, which different, from others in your group? Are there people at hand with whom you could build an alliance? Why or why not?

7. In reference to "Making Common Cause . . . ," how does the patriarchal system use difference to divide? Why is recognizing, accepting, and celebrating difference valuable for building alliances and coalitions?

8. Bunch carries the idea of "the personal is political" further than others have. What is her approach and how does it fit the effective building of coalitions and alliances?

9. What, according to Bunch, are women's reactions to diversity that divide them? What is her solution for each?

10. Is the anger Lorde talks about in her essay a dichotomy of white women versus women of color? Why or why not?

11. "I am not free while any woman is unfree, even when her shackles are different from my own." Explain this quote in the context of Lorde's explanation of how women affect each other's lives.

12. Coalition building must be multifaceted. What are the core issues that need to be recognized and dealt with? Why is this groundwork so important?

13. Discuss in small groups how you were socialized to deal with and express anger. What happens if anger is unexpressed? What are the barriers to women expressing anger across race, class, and gender lines?

CONTRIBUTORS

MARYLEA BENWARE CARR, who authored the study questions at the end of each chapter, teaches women's studies at Metropolitan State College of Denver and Front Range Community College in Westminster, Colorado. She has published papers concerning raising the self esteem of women in nursing homes and is currently working on designing a curriculum focusing on women and the mass media. Formerly, Carr spent several years in Illinois as a newspaper writer and editor and in hospital public relations before earning her M.S. in Women's Studies from Mankato State University in Minnesota. Her B.S. in Communications is from the University of Illinois.

MARGO LINN ESPENLAUB teaches women's studies at Metropolitan State College of Denver. A doctoral candidate in women's studies in literature at the Union Institute Graduate School, she is currently researching autobiographical narratives of contemporary women. Espenlaub holds a master of humanities from the University of Colorado at Denver and previously worked for over twenty years as a visual artist.

MONYS A. HAGEN, assistant professor of history and women's studies at Metropolitan State College of Denver, is a specialist in women's and business history. Hagen received her B.A. from the University of Minnesota and her M.A. and Ph.D. in women's history from the University of Wisconsin. She completed a postdoctoral fellowship in business history at The Ohio State University.

ALETTE OLIN HILL is associate professor of technical communications, specializing in international communications, at Metropolitan State College of Denver. She is the author of *Mother Tongue, Father Time: A Decade of Linguistic Revolt* (Bloomington: Indiana University Press, 1986). She received her Ph.D. in Indo-European linguistics from the University of North Carolina, Chapel Hill.

GERALDINE R. MADRID, a Metropolitan State College of Denver alumna with a double major in anthropology and multicultural women's studies, is a program coordinator at the Latin American Research and Service Agency (LARASA) in Denver. Her honors and achievements as an undergraduate include the Outstanding Woman Award and the League of Women Voters Women to Watch Award. A Chicana feminist interested in research on women of color and student development, her future plans include an M.A. in women's studies and a Ph.D. in a related discipline.

ANNETTE BENNINGTON McELHINEY is associate professor of English and women's studies at Metropolitan State College of Denver. She has published papers on pioneer women's diaries, Tillie Olsen's fiction, mentoring, and multicultural women writers, and is currently compiling and editing an anthology on violence against women in contemporary American short fiction. Formerly, McElhiney was a registered nurse in Missouri and Kansas, and later secured her B.A. and M.A. in English and American literature from the University of Missouri at Columbia and her Ph.D. in English from the University of Denver.

PATRICIA McVEY-RITSICK, a 1992 graduate of Metropolitan State College of Denver with an English education major, is a reentry student. A member of Sigma Tau Delta English Honorary, she is interested in teaching multicultural literature. Her plans include graduate school.

JANET MICKISH, executive director of the Colorado Domestic Violence Coalition, has worked in the area of domestic violence for the past seventeen years in both grass-roots and academic programs. She has worked with a wide range of criminal justice and social service organizations concerning violence against women and has produced numerous popular press and professional publications in this area. Mickish also teaches women's studies courses at Metropolitan State College of Denver. She received her Ph.D. in sociology from Southern Illinois University at Carbondale.

LINDA BENNINGTON NOLAN attended the University of Missouri at Columbia. She is a single mother with a sixteen-year-old daughter. Employed as an office manager for an allergist, she encourages women of all ages to avoid—and to get out of—abusive relationships.

ALICE REICH is professor of anthropology at Regis University in Denver. Her research on goddesses and spirituality began with a slide show which she has been presenting and revising since 1979. She holds a doctorate in anthropology from the University of Colorado at Boulder.

PATRICIA SCHROEDER serves Colorado's First Congressional District in the United States House of Representatives. She holds a baccalaureate degree from the University of Minnesota and a law degree from Harvard University. As a leader, she is one of this country's strongest advocates for women and is a founder of the Congressional Caucus for Women's Issues.

JACQUELINE ST. JOAN is a county judge in Denver, currently presiding in the Protective Orders Court. She writes poetry and has published essays in a variety of feminist publications and anthologies. She holds the J.D. from the University of Denver.

SHARON SILVAS, president and chief executive officer for Front Range Woman, Inc., and publisher of *Colorado Woman News*, has been published by *McCalls, Mother Root Journal, The Denver Magazine,* and *Colorado Business Magazine,* among others. She is a member of the Women's Institute for Freedom of the Press and the Denver Women's Press Club, and has received the Matrix Byliner and Vanguard awards from Women in Communications. She holds a B.A. in communications and theater from the University of Colorado at Denver.

TARA TULL is coordinator of Women's Services at Metropolitan State College of Denver. She teaches lesbian studies and is interested in women's activism and coalitions. She holds an M.S. in women's studies from Mankato State University in Minnesota.

JOAN M. VAN BECELAERE is administrative coordinator for the Office of International Education at the University of Colorado at Denver. She is currently engaged in graduate study in applied philosophy at the University of Colorado, Boulder, and is nearing completion of a Ph.D. in educational policy in the Graduate School of Public Affairs at the University of Colorado at Denver. Van Becelaere holds a master of divinity degree from the Iliff School of Theology in Denver.

JODI WETZEL, with twenty years experience in administering academically based women's programs, is professor of history and director of the Institute for Women's Studies and Services at Metropolitan State College of Denver. Formerly she represented the Rocky Mountain/Southwest on the coordinating council of the National Women's Studies Association. Wetzel holds a Ph.D. in American studies from the University of Minnesota.

CARMEN BRAUN WILLIAMS is associate professor of psychology and women's studies at Metropolitan State College of Denver. She teaches courses in psychology of women and has written and presented numerous papers in African American women's psychology. Her Ph.D. in clinical psychology is from The Pennsylvania State University.

INDEX

Minority women. *See* Women of color
Minneapolis Domestic Partner Act, 177
Misogyny, 16, 21, 92
Mora, Pat, 192, 287
Moraga, Cherríe, 330, 331, 522
Morrison, Toni, 312
Mother Teresa, 63
Motherhood, 32, 40, 160, 161, 177–88
    Afrocentric ideologies of, 178–80, 181, 182, 184–85, 187, 188
    compulsory, 178
    Eurocentric views on, 178–79
    and idea of "othermothers," 161, 181, 183, 184, 185, 186, 187
    nurturing imperative of, 33, 206
    and social learning theory, 184
Mothers Against Drunk Driving (MADD), 390
Mothers of East Los Angeles (MELA), 161
Mothers of the Plaza, 522
Mott, Lucretia, 298, 299n
Mount Holyoke, 69
Movies, status of women in, 82–83
Ms., 249
Mujeres Activas en Letras y Cambio Social (MALCS), 335
Mujeres en Marcha, 335
Muller v. Oregon (1908), 117, 405
Multicultural, 1, 11, 21–22
Murray, Judith Sargent, 68, 296
Murray, Pauli, 311
Music, 85
Musil, Caryn McTighe, 519

N

Nairobi Women's Conference, 523
Naming, the importance of, 90
National American Women Suffrage Association (NAWSA), 303–6, 305, 307, 391, 392
National Association for the Advancement of Colored People (NAACP), 378, 381
National Association of Afro-American Women, 303

National Association for Chicano Studies (NACS), 335–36
National Association of Colored Women (NACW), 303
National Commission on Working Women, 360
National Committee Concerned with Asian Wives of U.S. Servicemen, 343
National Consumers League, 302n, 307
National Domestic Violence Coalition, 520
National League of Women Voters, 307, 375, 376, 390
    peace efforts of, 306
National Network of Asian and Pacific Women, 343
National Organization of Pan Asian Women, 344
National Organization of Women (NOW), 309, 385, 391, 392, 393
    early exclusionary policies of, 312
    and lesbians, 313
National War Labor Board, 251
National Woman Suffrage Association (NWSA), 300, 391
National Woman's Party (NWP), 304
    advocates Equal Rights Amendment, 307–8
    disavows work of black suffragists, 305
    opposes social feminism in battle for ERA, 307
    peace efforts of, 306
    radicalism of, during WWI, 305
National Women's Political Caucus (NWPC), 311, 355, 360
National Women's Studies Association, 5, 535
National Women's Trade Union League, 307
Native American, 108, 443–45, 447–49, 453
    Kinaalda (Navajo), 451
    kinship networks, 162
Native American women, 36, 169
    artists, 475–76, 485

    Plains Indians, 162
    roles of, 162, 167
Natural rights doctrine, 296
    and women, 296–97
Navratilova, Martina, 418
New Right, 264, 355, 385
    effect on women's movement, 314–15
New York Times, 80
Nineteenth Amendment, 306, 323, 384, 386, 387, 389, 393, 399–402, 538 *See also* Suffrage
Nixon administration, and affirmative action, 256
North American Indian Women's Association, 312
Northeastern Federation of Colored Women's Clubs, 305
Norton, Eleanor Holmes, 252

O

Oberlin College, 69
Occupational segregation. *See* Employment
Office of Research on Women's Health, 359
Oppression, 518–22, 530, 538, 539
    patriarchal, 172
    and idealization of oppressor, 37
Older Woman's League, 206
Olivia Record Company, 503
Oral contraceptives, 112
Organization of Chinese American Women, 343
Organization of Pan American Women, 343
Orbach, Susie, 28, 32, 37

P

Pacific Asian American Women's Writers West, 344
Pacific Asian Shelter for Battered Women, 344
Paid labor force. *See* Employment
Paley, Grace, 420
Palmer, Judith, 9–10
Park, Maude Wood, 307
Parmar, Pratibha, 519
Parenthood, single, 172. *See also* Families